THE PHILIPPINE WAR
1899–1902

THE PHILIPPINE WAR
1899–1902

Brian McAllister Linn

University Press of Kansas

Unless indicated otherwise, photographs are reprinted courtesy of
the U.S. Army Military Institute.

Published by the University Press of Kansas (Lawrence, Kansas
66049), which was organized by the Kansas Board of Regents and is
operated and funded by Emporia State University, Fort Hays State
University, Kansas State University, Pittsburg State University, the
University of Kansas, and Wichita State University

Library of Congress Cataloging-in-Publication Data

Linn, Brian McAllister.
The Philippine War, 1899–1902 / Brian McAllister Linn.
p.   cm. — (Modern war studies)
Includes bibliographical references and index.
ISBN 0-7006-0990-3 (cloth : alk. paper)
ISBN 0-7006-1225-4 (pbk : alk. paper)
1. Philippines—History—Philippine American War, 1899–1902.
I. Title. II. Series.
DS679.L57   2000
959.9'031—dc21   99-33549

British Library Cataloguing in Publication Data is available.

Printed in the United States of America

10 9 8 7

The paper used in this publication meets the minimum requirements
of the American National Standard for Permanence of Paper for
Printed Library Materials Z39.48–1984

CONTENTS

ILLUSTRATIONS

PREFACE

This book is intended to provide a history of the military operations in the Philippine archipelago between 4 February 1899 and 4 July 1902. On the face of it, a military history of a war nearly 100 years old may seem superfluous at best. Nowadays textbooks and popular histories summarize the Philippine War in a few clichés—the water cure, civilize 'em with a Krag, kill everyone over ten, reconcentration camps—all of which convey an overall impression of a conflict characterized by brutality and atrocities. Any reader who questions the proposition that in barely three years an expeditionary force averaging some 25,000 combat troops terrorized over 7 million people into subjugation—an argument grossly insulting to Americans and Filipinos alike—is currently at a loss. The centennial of the Philippine War seems a particularly good time to reexamine the conflict and apply some much needed correction to the popular view.

To write a narrative history of military operations in the Philippine War poses unique problems. As recent scholarship by both American and Filipino scholars has conclusively proved, the war varied greatly from island to island, town to town, even village to village. Even the relatively brief conventional war of 1899 was restricted to the area around Manila and central Luzon. In some areas there was long and bitter armed struggle marked by atrocities and widespread destruction, but in other areas—roughly half the archipelago's provinces—there was little or no fighting. There were considerable variations in the nature and tempo of military operations, in the strategic goals of both sides, and in the conduct of the war.

Because of these considerations, this book is organized somewhat differently than previous histories. The first half, with the exception of a chapter on the Visayas, covers the conventional operations on Luzon in 1899. The second half studies the guerrilla warfare and pacification campaigns waged in the different regions of the archipelago. Much to my regret, I have found it impossible to accord each area or campaign equal space. In some cases, I have dealt only briefly with significant individuals or major campaigns because they have been extensively covered in other works, including my own. In contrast, I have emphasized campaigns that have been largely overlooked, such as Negros, or those about which a great deal of poor history has been written, such as Samar.

Some readers may wonder at the terminology in this book. Other authors have referred to the Philippine Insurrection, the Philippine-American War, the Filipino-American War, or the Fil-American War. To my mind, Philippine War is the most neutral and has the added advantage of being used by both contemporary and current authors. It avoids both the diminution of Filipino resistance as "insurrection" and the implication that the conflict was a conventional war between nation-states. Moreover, it accurately conveys the book's focus on the United States military effort, much in the spirit that a Philippine scholar recently termed the conflict "the American war." I have used the terms "resistance," "revolutionaries," "*insurrectos,*" "rebels," and "insurgents" to refer to those Filipinos who supported an independent Philippine nation and offered armed resistance to United States authority. None of these terms are intended as pejorative or in any way implying a lack of respect. Neither should they be taken to mean a unified, archipelago-wide political movement, or even to imply obedience to the authority of Emilio Aguinaldo or the Philippine Republic.

Because the focus of this book is on American military operations, I have relied largely on sources found in the United States. As the bibliography and notes indicate, there has been some use of Philippine secondary literature as well as the captured documents titled the Philippine Insurgent Records in the National Archives. I initially hoped to write a book that covered both sides equally. However, a visit to several archival collections in the Philippines, as well as long conversations with specialists in the Islands, convinced me that the Filipino side must await another scholar. The theft of thousands of revolutionary documents from the Philippine National Archives only increases the difficulty of this project.

Specialists may question my choice of personal names and place-names. For personal names I have followed the Filipino practice of dropping the accent mark on Hispanicized names (i.e., Trias, not Trías; Samareno, not Samareño). For most place-names I have used the modern Filipinized spelling (i.e., Marikina, not Mariquina). As a caveat, it should be noted that throughout the war soldiers operated in unmapped areas and fought in jungles, swamps, and thickets devoid of geographic landmarks. Events were often placed in terms the reader understood—"some six miles up the trail" or "near the barrio west of town" or "after a four-hour march"—but which are incomprehensible to the modern scholar. Officers obtained the names of towns, rivers, and mountains from the inhabitants and communicated through interpreters, in Spanish, or in pidgin or "bamboo." Not surprisingly, a particular village may appear on different reports by the name its villagers called it, by the name its municipality gave it, by the name the Spanish government accorded it, or by the name given by people in another municipality. Even a large town such as San Pedro Makati might be alternately San Pedro, Makati, or Macati. That there might be three or four other towns with similar names in the immediate vicinity makes errors inevitable.

Finally, over the past two decades at conferences in the United States and the Philippines, I have run into a surprising number of academics who assume that anyone who studies the American military and the Philippine War must be, at best, an unreconstructed imperialist. I doubt that any disclaimer of mine would weaken such a misconception. Nevertheless, I would like to emphasize that in seeking to explain the United States' military success in the Philippines, I am by no means supporting or even condoning the annexation of the Islands.

ACKNOWLEDGMENTS

I first began research in the Philippine War for a master's thesis over twenty years ago. As can be imagined, in the years following I have accumulated a fair number of debts. My mentor at The Ohio State University, Allan R. Millett, deserves much of the credit for sparking my interest in the war and urging me to pursue it. When I was an unknown graduate student, John Gates, Edward M. Coffman, Pete Maslowski, and David F. Trask graciously provided advice and support, and they have continued to do so ever since. Mike Briggs at the University Press of Kansas encouraged me to keep writing even when I did not want to.

This work could not have been completed without great assistance from a number of institutions. Texas A&M University has been generous in awarding funds and time. I did most of the final research while on a Faculty Development Leave in 1995–96 and with the support of a Scholarly and Creative Activities Grant in 1997. My colleagues have been very supportive, especially R. J. Q. Adams, Joseph Dawson, and James Bradford. Walter Buenger read the manuscript and made a number of helpful suggestions. The U.S. Army Center of Military History first encouraged this project with a dissertation year fellowship, and then with a Visiting Professorship in 1995–96. For several years I have been privileged to lead a seminar on the war at the U.S. Marine Corps School of Advanced Warfighting. I owe a great debt to Joe Crookston, Rex Estilow, and the SAWS students. Their intelligence, enthusiasm, and ability to speak from experience have often challenged my own perceptions and required me to revise many of my ideas.

No historian has been better assisted by archivists than I have. I would like to single out the following for special praise: Tim Nenninger, Mitch Yockelson, and Richard Pueser at the National Archives; Louise Arnold, David Keough, John Slonaker, and Richard Sommers at the U.S. Army Military History Institute; and John Mountcastle, Andrew Birtle, Graham Cosmas, and Edgar Raines from the U.S. Army Center of Military History. Thanks to the staff at the Huntington Library; the Manuscripts Division of the Library of Congress; the Massachusetts Historical Society; the Minnesota Historical Society; the Special Collections of the U.S. Army Military

Academy Library; the Manuscripts and University Archives Division, Allen Library, University of Washington; the Washington Historical Society. A special thanks to the Vinton Trust for letting me read the diary of Francis Henry French.

I would like to thank the Naval Institute Press for allowing me to use material from my articles: "We Will Go Heavily Armed: The Marines' Small War on Samar, 1901–1902," in *New Interpretations in Naval History: Selected Papers from the Ninth Naval History Symposium,* ed. William R. Roberts and Jack Sweetman; and "The Struggle for Samar," in *Crucible of Empire: The Spanish-American War and Its Aftermath,* ed. James C. Bradford. Also much gratitude to the Academia Puertorriqueña de la Historia for permission to use material that first appeared in "Taking Up the White Man's Burden," in *1898: Enfoques y Perspectivas,* ed. Luis E. Gonzales-Vales.

Many of the ideas for this book were put forth at two excellent conferences in 1996, the International Conference on the Centennial of the 1896 Philippine Revolution in Manila and the Simposio Internacional de Historiodores en torno el 1898 in Puerto Rico. I owe much to the respective organizers—Dr. Bernadita Reyes Churchill and Dr. Luis E. Gonzales-Vales, as well as to the comments I received from Norman Owen, Luis Agrait, Ricardo Jose, and Jose S. Arcilla. A very special thank-you to Malcolm and Bernadita Churchill for acting as tour guides in the Philippines.

I would also like to thank Pat Morgan, George and Jamie Sinks, Ray Stokes and family, and Richard Hall. Much aloha to my Hawaii "ohana" of Robert and Shirley Kamins and to Bob, Tessa, and Tom Dye. My two sisters, Susan and Andrea, and my mother and her MacAdam clan are the best family one could have. Thanks also to my wife, Diane, who has had to live with the Philippine War for twenty years and put up with several extended absences, both when I was doing research and when I was writing. There are numerous people I have stayed with on research trips, or sent drafts to, or corresponded with by letter and e-mail. I know that I am forgetting to thank most of them, and hope they will forgive me with the same good spirit they have shown me in the past. There is one person, however, whose contribution deserves far more acknowledgment than my modest skills as a writer allow, as he is well aware. As a partial repayment, this book is dedicated to my good friend, editor, and father, James R. Linn.

PART ONE
Conventional Operations
1899

ONE

THE AMERICANS
ARRIVE

On 3 May 1898, Maj. Gen. Nelson A. Miles recommended to Secretary of War Russell A. Alger that a small 5,000-man expedition be sent from San Francisco "to occupy the Philippines."[1] Miles was responding to a request from President William McKinley, who was eager to take advantage of Commodore George Dewey's victory over the Spanish squadron at Manila Bay two days earlier. Because Dewey had cut the transoceanic cable, the president had little idea of the magnitude of Dewey's accomplishment and even less of the situation in the Philippines. Moreover, the nation had gone to war with Spain barely a week earlier for the ostensible purpose of liberating Cuba, something that in no way required the dispatch of forces halfway across the globe to Asia. But McKinley was a consummate politician who believed in seizing opportunity. Fully cognizant that war's good fortune could change overnight, he sought to reinforce success but avoid an irrevocable commitment. He thus directed that an expedition be sent, but why, and for what eventual purpose, is still unclear.[2]

The underlying reasons for the United States' involvement in the Philippines is one of the most hotly debated subjects in the history of both nations. Much of this debate stems from the putative influence of such factors as imperialism, social Darwinism, the quest for Asian markets, the "Yellow Press," and domestic concerns. Unfortunately, it is very difficult to trace the effect of any or all of these either on McKinley or on the formation of national policy. In part this is due to the president's unwillingness to confide his opinions or plans either to paper or to his advisers. He was a master of listening patiently and giving visitors the impression of complete agreement with their views; but he kept his own counsel and rarely could be pinned down. That McKinley was in contact with imperialists, that he listened to their arguments, that he was concerned with both domestic business and Asian trade—of these there is no doubt. But efforts to prove that the president was guided by an imperial master plan have lacked the documentation sufficient to raise them above speculation.

3

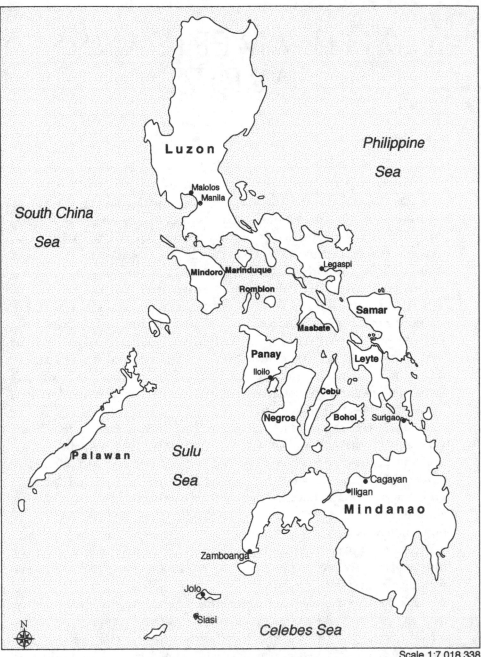

Luzon

Philippine

Sea

South China

Sea

Malolos
Manila

Mindoro Marinduque

Legaspi

Romblon

Samar

Masbate

Panay

Leyte

Iloilo

Cebu

Negros

Bohol

Surigao

Palawan

Sulu

Sea

Cagayan

Iligan

Mindanao

Zamboanga

Jolo

Siasi

Celebes Sea

N

Scale 1:7,018,338

The Philippines

Moreover, there is an equally plausible, and far better documented, argument that American involvement in the Philippines was accidental and incremental. Under this view, neither the president nor his key advisers sought an empire. Essentially pragmatic and opportunistic, they viewed Manila as a bargaining chip with Spain for Cuba or for securing trade interests in Asia. As the consequences of their actions unfolded, they expanded their horizons from Manila to Luzon, and then the entire archipelago, but each time they were following less a premeditated course than seeking to deal with an immediate crisis. Each decision, in turn, committed them further. Ultimately, a series of plausible misunderstandings—the belief that the Filipinos were incapable of self-government, the illusion that the archipelago was economically valuable, the fear of setting off a war among the Great Powers, and, perhaps most important, the belief that popular opinion demanded it—all led McKinley to decide that the annexation of the Philippines was the only rational course. He was aware that this decision might provoke war with Filipino nationalists, but he sincerely, if naively, believed it could be avoided.[3] The president proved quite prescient in his observation that "while the result of a conflict with our troops could not for a minute be in doubt, yet if such a conflict should break out it would engender jealousy and hatred on the part of the natives which could not be overcome for many years."[4]

McKinley's initial uncertainty, his hesitation to commit himself, or the nation, to a policy in the Philippines would place an enormous burden on his military subordinates. The first to bear this cross was Maj. Gen. Wesley Merritt, who was designated as overall commander of the Philippine expedition. Merritt, who met with McKinley for several hours on 12 May, wired the president the next day that he still did not know "whether it is your desire to subdue and hold all of the Spanish territory in the islands, or merely to seize and hold the capital."[5] A week later, the president responded. Sidestepping Merritt's question of the islands' ultimate fate, he noted only that the defeat of the Spanish fleet and the need to secure peace with Spain "rendered it necessary . . . to send an army of occupation to the Philippines for the twofold purpose of completing the reduction of Spanish power . . . and of giving order and security to the islands while in the possession of the United States."[6]

The president's ambiguous instructions increased the confusion among the officers charged with the execution of military policy. What did McKinley mean by stating that the archipelago was "in the possession of the United States"? Dewey initially believed all the president planned was the occupation of the naval base at Cavite and perhaps Manila. Persisting in the delusion that he controlled not only the waters of Manila Bay but also the city and its surrounding territory, Dewey maintained that 5,000 troops would suffice as a garrison for Manila. The army's commanding general, Miles, was even more confused. In a two-week period he outlined no fewer than three different missions: on 3 May the expedition's purpose was "to occupy the Philippine Islands"; by the sixteenth it expanded to "possession" of the "Philippine Islands"; but two days later it was only "to command the harbor of Manila," and was "not expected to carry on a war to conquer an extensive territory."[7] Unfortunately, such confusion and misunderstanding would continue to plague relations between civilian and military leaders and between Washington and soldiers in the Philippines.

However evasive on the army's military goals in the Philippines, McKinley was far more articulate about how Merritt was to establish a military government. With breathtaking complacency, he assumed that Dewey's victory had rendered Spanish authority in the islands null and void. He thus gave top priority to "the severance of former political relations of the inhabitants and the establishment of a new political power." Upon arrival, Merritt was to issue a proclamation declaring that the United States came to protect the inhabitants and their property and to guarantee their individual rights. The general was to follow local laws and procedures as much as possible, and, at his discretion, those civic officials who accepted American authority would continue in office. The army was to open ports and assist the resumption of trade, and was prohibited from appropriating private property except where needed. Nevertheless, the military governor's authority was to be "absolute and supreme and immediately operate upon the political condition of the inhabitants."[8]

Given the uncertainty and conflicting interpretations of the Philippine expedition's mission, it is not surprising that there soon emerged a vigorous debate over its size and composition. The War Department's prewar decision to concentrate virtually all the Regular units for operations against Cuba meant that only the 14th Infantry Regiment, recently arrived from Alaska, was ready for immediate deployment. The bulk of the expedition would have to come from state militia units. In his initial estimate of 3 May, Miles proposed that the expeditionary force consist of a rather large brigade, some 5,000 troops, drawn from the national guards of the western states.[9] Merritt immediately demanded more troops, especially Regulars. In part, this dispute was due to Miles's selfishness; he invariably thought that other commanders could do with far less than he. In part, it was due to Merritt's petulance at being passed over for command of the more prestigious Cuban campaign. But the fundamental difference lay in their justifiable confusion over the expedition's mission. Miles foresaw a limited role for the expedition and believed it would face little opposition. Merritt, more prescient, argued that Spanish power was far from broken and, more important, that millions of Filipinos "will regard us with the intense hatred born of race and religion."[10] On 11 May the War Department compromised by increasing the expedition to 12,000 men, but it denied Merritt's request that the majority of the troops be Regulars. Instead, Merritt's force, later designated the 8th Corps, would be made up primarily of state militia.[11]

Accordingly, even as the United States stood on the threshold of a great leap toward Pacific empire, no one knew what the agents of empire were supposed to be doing. Not the soldiers speeding toward San Francisco, not the harried staff officers at the port, not Brig. Gen. Thomas M. Anderson, appointed to command the first expeditionary brigade, not the 8th Corps commander, Merritt, not the commanding general, Miles, not even the commander in chief. With the benefit of a century's hindsight, their confusion and lack of direction are almost inconceivable. But it was part and parcel of the disordered leap toward empire in 1898. And nowhere was that disorder so apparent as in the mobilization of the nation's armed forces.

By 1898, the U.S. Navy had benefited from over a decade of intellectual ferment and warship construction. In his books and essays, Capt. Alfred Thayer Mahan had provided a carefully integrated argument for a modern fleet by linking economic prosperity and national greatness with sea power. Although he emphasized the decisive fleet action, Mahan also stressed the long-term effects of sea power—particularly the capture of enemy colonies and the slow strangulation of a naval blockade. A series of competent secretaries of the navy steered legislation through Congress to retire the relics of the Civil War and replace them with modern steel warships. That this construction benefited the nascent steel industry only increased its political appeal. At the start of the war with Spain the nation had seven modern warships, including four battleships, which would prove more than sufficient to overcome Spain's poorly maintained squadrons.[12]

The U.S. Navy also boasted a veteran and cohesive officer corps. Most of the senior officers were, like Dewey, veterans of the Civil War, who had begun their service on wooden sailing ships. The junior officers tended to be Annapolis graduates, technically competent and well versed in the intricacies of steam power and iron ships. Navy officers were expected to perform a variety of missions ranging from negotiating treaties to suppressing pirates. Their wide experience tended to make them quick to take action and obtain Washington's approval later.

In the Pacific the navy had maintained a tiny flotilla of warships and gunboats, charged with protecting commercial and religious activities in Asia. As tensions with Spain increased in the 1890s, naval strategists developed a contingency plan for a strike at the Spanish squadron stationed in Manila Bay and for possibly capturing Manila. The planners did not consider annexation. As with similar thrusts at Puerto Rico and the Canary Islands, this was to be a supporting operation designed to weaken Spain's ability to defend the main focus of operations, Cuba.[13] Accordingly, on 25 April 1898, Dewey had received orders to take his Asiatic Squadron immediately to the Philippines, find the enemy warships, and destroy them. Running the batteries guarding Manila Bay on the night of 30 April, Dewey located the Spanish off the naval base of Cavite. The commodore's six warships far surpassed the defenders' vessels in speed, armor, firepower, and the respective skill of their crews. The battle on 1 May was little more than a massacre. Three Spanish ships were sunk, six others scuttled, and there were 371 casualties, including 161 killed in action; the Americans had 9 men wounded. The victory had numerous and momentous results, but the most immediate was that it left Dewey in a difficult position. He cabled to his superiors that his warships' guns could secure the surrender of Manila at any time. But should he do so, he would immediately become responsible for its inhabitants—an obligation he could not possibly fulfill. Ground forces alone had the ability to occupy territory. Much to his annoyance, Dewey had to wait in Manila Bay for a sister, and rival, service to secure the fruits of his victory.[14]

Unlike the navy, the U.S. Army had not planned for a war of conquest in the Philippines and was ill prepared to shoulder the burden of empire. The army was administered by the War Department and subordinated to civilian control; the president was the army's commander in chief, and his deputy, the secretary of war, directed the War Department. Usually inexperienced, the secretary was dependent on the powerful heads of the staff departments, the bureaucrats who handled the army's administrative and supply services. The army's emphasis on its managerial functions was also manifest outside of Washington. The professional standing force—what was called the Regular Army—was not organized into tactical commands but divided among geographic departments and districts. The government assigned generals and colonels to administrative duties, and company officers served as Indian agents, engineers, and teachers.

The Regular Army's combat strength was composed of hard, tough, experienced soldiers led by an officer corps whose upper ranks were dominated by Civil War veterans and whose junior officers—a misleading term as many lieutenants were in their forties—were usually West Pointers. These men had benefited from technological and tactical reforms in the last decade of the century. The field artillery, organized into four- or six-gun batteries, was built around the 1884 heavy 3.2-inch steel breech-loading cannon. With a range of 6,600 yards, it could fire canister, solid shot, or shells, but it lacked a re-coil system. For operations against mobile enemies, the artillery used the 1.65-inch Hotchkiss mountain gun, which weighed only 117 pounds and could be disassembled and carried on three mules. After decades of wrangling, the War Department had replaced the dangerously obsolescent single-shot black powder .45–70 Springfield with the smokeless-powder .30 caliber Krag-Jorgensen five-shot magazine rifle. New extended or open order tactics were issued in 1891: as some squads provided supporting fire, others advanced in a series of short rushes, took cover, and then supported their comrades, re-peating the process until they closed with the enemy and used their bayo-nets. The artillery was to provide suppressing fire, pushing forward as close as possible and firing directly at the enemy. Although senior officers still exerted a great deal of authority, these tactics imposed far more initiative on the junior and noncommissioned officers and required far more intelligent, highly motivated, and self-disciplined soldiers. Ironically, the new weapons and tactics would prove themselves not against modern European armies but in the jungles and paddies of the Philippines.[15]

From its experiences in the Civil War and the Indian campaigns, the Regu-lar Army had derived an informal but widely accepted pacification doctrine that balanced conciliation and repression. Officers sought to separate the noncombatants from armed opponents, to restore order, and to make such reforms as to ensure against further outbreaks. Those who continued to re-sist were dealt the hard hand of war: their crops and homes were destroyed and their persons subject to imprisonment, expulsion, and death. This infor-mal doctrine had a legal justification in General Orders (G.O.) 100, or "In-structions for the Government of Armies of the United States in the Field," which imposed strict limits on the occupying army. Issued during the Civil War and widely recognized in Europe, G.O. 100 emphasized the occupier's obligation to restore order, protect property, and treat civilians with justice and humanity. But such restraint on the occupier's part must be met by re-ciprocal restraint in the subject population. Continued resistance—through guerrilla warfare or assisting the enemy—was a crime and was subject to immediate retaliation. Guerrillas and those who supported them could suf-fer the confiscation or destruction of their property, imprisonment, and even, under certain circumstances, summary execution. Armed with G.O. 100, efficient small-unit tactics and weapons, managerial experience, and a long tradition of frontier fighting, the U.S. Army brought impressive, if unrecog-nized, strengths to the problem of irregular war.[16]

Limited by Congress to 28,000 soldiers, the Regular Army was a peace-time organization. For its wartime manpower the United States relied on volunteer citizen soldiers. In theory, all male citizens between sixteen and forty-five were liable for military service in the state militia and could be called into federal service to repel invasion and suppress insurrection. In practice, by the 1890s the term "militia" applied to an estimated 115,000 volunteers in the various state guards. There was a wide divergence in the state units, ranging from well-equipped and drilled military organizations to fraternal societies to strikebreakers. Like the Regulars, by 1898 the militia was uncertain of its mission in the next century. Disliking riot duty, the National Guard Association sought recognition as the federal reserve, but only if units kept their state identities and officers. As war with Spain approached, state militiamen descended on their congressmen and governors, demanding a part in the glorious struggle against the hated "Dons."[17]

Political constraints, and its own obtuseness, frustrated the War Department's mobilization efforts against Spain. Given the small size of the army and the navy's early primacy in operations involving Cuba, the Regulars resigned themselves to a supporting role. Congressional regulations and the conservatism of bureau officers hampered any stockpiling of weapons and supplies, but far more pernicious was the consensus that 50,000 to 100,000 Regulars would be sufficient for any contingency. But to the War Department's shock, its proposal was rejected by Congress, in large measure because it contained no role for the militia. After consultation with the militia lobby, a compromise was speedily hammered out and passed by Congress on 22 April 1898. This act created a Volunteer Army organization to serve alongside the Regular Army, the soldiers to enlist for one year or the duration of the war with Spain. Together with the 1899 Army Act, it ensured that the Philippine War would be one more American conflict fought with two distinct organizations, Regulars and Volunteers.[18]

In the weeks following, President McKinley made a number of decisions on manpower mobilization. The War Department, aware that the Regulars had barely enough equipment and facilities to handle their newly authorized strength of 67,000, wanted a slow and controlled mobilization of the Volunteer Army. It planned for a Volunteer force of 60,000 that would be thoroughly trained and equipped before it was deployed. But this was politically unacceptable, for it was only half the estimated strength of the National Guard. No sensible governor wanted the responsibility of deciding which units would have a chance for glory and which would stay at home. Nor were the state units willing to make this choice. Some voted that if any one of their units was not mustered in, none would go. McKinley did not wish to confront the state governors or turn away eager soldiers. On 23 April, the president announced that instead of 60,000, he would ask for 125,000 Volunteers.

This call was politically sound, but for the War Department, already stretched by the demands of concentrating the Regulars, McKinley's decision destroyed the slim hope of an orderly, efficient mobilization.[19]

The declaration of war with Spain on 25 April and the subsequent call-up of Volunteers was greeted in most communities with an enthusiasm that appears almost unbelievable a century later. A decade of economic convulsion and social turmoil had left many eager for any noble cause that would take the nation's mind off its internal problems. The Yellow Press portrayed Spain as fanatical, merciless, wicked, and corrupt, and it reinforced American views of their nation's role as the great liberator, destined to bring freedom and civilization to the oppressed peoples of the world. "We go to the far away islands of the Pacific," thundered Lt. Col. Edward C. Little of the Philippines-bound 20th Kansas Volunteer Infantry Regiment, "to plant the Stars and Stripes on the ramparts where long enough has waved the cruel and merciless banner of Spain."[20] For others, the war offered a chance to heal the wounds of sectional conflict. Nationalists took pride in the fact that both Northerners and Southerners rushed to serve against the common foe. McKinley's appointment of a few hoary Confederate officers, however questionable as a military experiment, shrewdly played on this theme of reconciliation. So, too, did a flood of sentimental doggerel in which figured the theme of two volunteers, one a son of the blue and the other a son of the gray, mingling their dying blood under Old Glory. Indeed, the Civil War was a powerful inspiration for young Americans determined to prove they had the courage and manliness of their fathers. Politicians, clergymen, teachers, and relatives bombarded recruits with exhortations to match the exploits of the heroes of Gettysburg and Shiloh, and veterans lined the march route, tearfully calling, "God bless you boys."[21]

McKinley's call for 125,000 volunteers threatened to expose the hollowness of the National Guards' claim that it was the nation's reserve. In order to avoid any legal challenge to militiamen fighting overseas, the War Department hit upon the expedient of requiring them to take a new oath of enlistment. Governors would call out the militia, which would assemble in camps where they could be sworn into federal service as individuals for the duration of the war: if a sufficient number from a Guard regiment took this dual oath, they would be reconstituted in federal service and keep their state identity. Although it sidestepped the constitutional question, and threw the burden of mobilizing the Guard on the states, this expedient created a number of problems. The War Department wanted a balanced force, but the overwhelming number of state companies were inexpensive infantry; as a result, most cavalry, artillery, and staff units had to come from other sources. The department's demand that infantry regiments be organized along wartime lines—some 1,212 officers and men in three battalions of four companies each—rendered a number of militia officers superfluous, required others to accept lower rank, and placed soldiers from one company under "outsiders" from another town. Internal factions and feuds fragmented regiments, politicians lobbied for commissions for their friends and allies, and soldiers and officers refused to serve under their new superiors.[22] Determined to make their quotas and ensure they would qualify for service, state militias adopted an elastic definition of Guard membership. As the 1st Wyoming's scattered companies moved toward the state capital, their officers had the trains stop at every station so they could sign up eager volunteers until the regiment was filled. When Company B, 13th Minnesota, mustered 112 officers and men into service on 7 March, all but 12 of its enlisted men were new volunteers. Thus despite their Guard affiliation, the majority of the Volunteers who served in 1898—and especially in the Philippines—were inexperienced and untrained recruits who signed up in a burst of martial spirit.[23]

The troops destined for the Philippines quickly discovered that enthusiasm carried armies only so far. They were assigned to San Francisco's chilly, damp Camp Merritt, a place that one soldier summed up: "Of all the bum campgrounds this takes the pie."[24] Located near Golden Gate Park, the former racetrack was one mile from the coast and constantly swept by cold winds, rain, and fogs so dense that soldiers could not see or hear their officers. Facilities were rudimentary. Sand clogged the toilets and water supply and sifted into tents, weapons, clothes, and food. The soldiers' miseries were compounded by an absence of tents, shoes, mess kits, canteens, and other necessities. Clothing scarcely warranted the name uniform: soldiers dressed in an assortment of blue wool, brown canvas, and white linen. A regimen of hard training further added to their complaints. Recognizing the inexperience of their troops, officers drilled their men relentlessly. Packed with 14,000 soldiers, many of who were physically unprepared for army life, Camp Merritt soon came to resemble a pesthole. In late July Company G, 1st Tennessee, had 59 out of its 106 soldiers on sick call or in the hospital.[25]

The few Regular Army officers in San Francisco worked mightily to overcome the myriad problems, but they were hampered by the lack of supplies, competition from the Cuban theater, and the tremendous pressure to get troops onto transports as rapidly as possible. The navy had bought up most of the available shipping, and army officers had to secure contracts with the owners of the few remaining oceangoing vessels. The absence of transports meant that the 8th Corps would have to be broken into smaller commands and dispatched weeks apart. Compounding their problems was the complete lack of information. The War Department's small intelligence office, the Office of Military Information, was already overextended, and it took several months to compile and distribute its valuable source book *Military Notes on the Philippines*. In the meantime, Washington provided what data it could: on one occasion, Merritt's aide received a highly confidential War Department dispatch consisting of an encyclopedia article on the Philippine Islands.[26]

Because Merritt was occupied in arrangements with Washington and did not arrive in San Francisco until after the first expedition sailed, most of the work was done by his highly competent subordinate, Maj. Gen. Elwell S. Otis. Born in 1838, Otis was a graduate of Harvard Law School who, as an officer in the 140th New York Infantry, had helped close the gap in the Union line at Little Round Top during the Battle of Gettysburg. His exceptional combat record, intelligence, and obvious ability won him a commission in the Regular Army. In the next three decades, Otis published several articles on military law, wrote a highly regarded work on Native Americans, supervised the new infantry and cavalry schools, chaired the board that selected the excellent Krag-Jorgensen rifle, and revamped the army's recruiting service. In San Francisco his superb skills as an administrator were obvious. He supervised training, secured supplies, and imposed discipline on the troops. The timely dispatch of troops to the Philippines—when contrasted with Maj. Gen. William B. Shafter's chaotic Cuban expedition—owed more to him than to any other officer. Unfortunately for his reputation, Otis carried out his duties with a brusque efficiency that did little to endear him to either the soldiers or the press.[27]

The commander of the first expedition, Brig. Gen. Thomas M. Anderson, was a courtly, patient, and courageous officer. In the Civil War he had participated in most of the great battles of the eastern theater and later had fought the Kiowa and Cheyenne. Like Otis, he was a skilled lawyer and an advocate of army reform, and duty in the South during Reconstruction and in the West putting down race riots had given him ample experience in civil affairs. To their credit, both McKinley and Secretary of War Alger recognized that Anderson must "be governed by events and circumstances of which we can have no knowledge," and they gave him the "fullest discretion."[28] Anderson later summarized these instructions as "Do the best you can."[29]

On 25 May, Anderson led the 1st California and 2nd Oregon regiments and a battalion of his old regiment, the 14th Infantry—a total 115 officers and 2,386 enlisted men—through a "mob of howling, struggling, cheering friends" to the San Francisco docks.[30] One soldier was almost blinded when a well-wisher, moved by patriotic spirit, rolled up the flag he was waving and hurled it into the marching columns. As the troop transports steamed out of the harbor, hundreds of boats sounded their horns and an assortment of bands played patriotic airs.[31]

No sooner had the shoreline disappeared than Anderson's men learned that war was not all parades and cheering. The three transports were ocean packets that had been hastily converted into troopships. The officers' quarters were comfortable staterooms, and their dining facilities were excellent. In these pleasant surroundings, Col. James F. Smith of the 1st California held classes for his officers and senior sergeants on discipline, regulations, posts and guides, sanitary duties, patrolling, and hygiene. In contrast, his 980 enlisted men and their supplies were crammed into a space 10 feet high, 425 feet long, and 60 feet wide. Their bunks stacked four high, some men had to crawl over a half dozen bodies to get to their sweat-soaked, moldy straw mattresses. The transports heaved and pitched, there were too few toilets, and soon the lower decks were almost awash in vomit. The fresh meat spoiled within a week, and thereafter the men received little but fatty canned bacon, potatoes, coffee, and hardtack bread, wretchedly prepared and served so inefficiently that by the time a soldier had made it through the chow line the food had congealed to a cold, slimy, gray mass known as "slum." The citizen soldiers chafed in poorly fitting uniforms, made all the more uncomfortable when their shoddy underclothes disintegrated after a few washings. During their brief two-hour turn on the upper decks, the troops worked off some of their considerable anger with calisthenics and boxing matches. Discipline was poor. Unable or, in their soldiers' eyes, unwilling to alleviate the miserable conditions of the enlisted men, the officers kept to themselves. By the end of the voyage most of the soldiers had been transformed into malcontent "cranks and growlers" who wished they had never enlisted.[32]

On 30 June, after more than a month at sea, the expedition finally arrived at Manila Bay, still guarded by Dewey's small but proud squadron, and anchored off Cavite. The troops clamored for a chance to show the "Jack Tars" what they could do, but instead of leading them against Manila, Anderson put them to work as stevedores. They had to unload 440,000 rations, roughly 1,000 tons of food, and hundreds of boxes of ammunition, commissary stores, camp equipage, and cooking supplies. Since Cavite's docks could not accommodate the transports, everything had to be loaded onto *cascos*—large, narrow, flat-bottomed barges of 50 to 125 tons capacity—towed by steam launches to the docks, and then dragged through the mud from the dock into decrepit warehouses. The troops toiled in monsoons and sweltering heat; when their work details were over, they collapsed in their tiny shelter tents, sleeping with their heads and feet out in the rain. Poor diet and exhaustion took their toll: just three days after arriving, over 100 men in the

2nd Oregon had fever and diarrhea; within the week roughly a third of the regiment was on sick report. Morale, severely damaged by the long voyage, sank even further.[33]

While Anderson's men were undergoing this ordeal, the military authorities in San Francisco were pressing forward. On 15 June the second expedition sailed, consisting of 158 officers and 3,404 soldiers under Brig. Gen. Francis V. Greene, a prominent New York Republican. This expedition suffered from the same horrible shipboard conditions as its predecessor with the added excitement of a fire in the coal hold, which caused one transport to list so heavily that on one side passengers could see nothing but sky and on the other nothing but sea. Even more dangerous was the quantity of highly explosive gas the fire generated. Only on arrival in Manila Bay on 17 July was the fire extinguished. Twelve days after Greene's departure, a third expedition of 198 officers and 4,642 men under Brig. Gen. Arthur MacArthur, accompanied by Merritt, set forth, arriving on 25 July. These three expeditions, a total of 10,946 officers and men, were all that arrived before the First Battle of Manila.[34]

The Philippine archipelago comprises over 7,000 islands, which cover an area of 500,000 square miles. Three major island groups stretch north to south: Luzon, which at 44,235 square miles is the largest and most populous island and the site of the capital city of Manila; the 25,302 square miles of the Visayas Islands, which include Cebu, Leyte, Negros, Panay, and Samar; and Mindanao Island and the Sulu archipelago, a string of small islands that extends to Borneo. Within individual islands, mountains, swamps, jungles, and bodies of water further separate the inhabitants: on Luzon alone the Ilocanos, Pampangans, Pangasinans, Tagalogs, and Bicols all speak different languages. As geographers have noted, the term "Filipino" is no more accurate in describing a people of one race and culture than is the term "American."[35] Relations among the tribal groups are often strained; the Muslim, or Moro, population of Mindanao and Sulu continues to resist incorporation into the Christian Filipino polity, often by force of arms.

With the exception of the Moro areas, the Philippines were colonized and Christianized by Spain in the sixteenth century. In many respects, the Filipinos became Hispanicized: educated people learned Spanish; the population became devout, if somewhat syncretic, Catholics; and the forms of Spanish administration were copied. But although Spain dominated, it did not replace the indigenous local cultures. Indeed, until the mid–nineteenth century, its rule remained concentrated in Manila, with policies focused on trade with Mexico and China. In the countryside, the poor and undermanned imperial government ruled by confirming the authority of local chieftains. Together with landowners and prominent businessmen, these evolved into the *principales,* which effectively controlled local politics. Although American witnesses were appalled at the exploitation of the peasantry and the almost absolute authority of the *principales,* the patron-client relationship could benefit both parties. Generations of *taos* (peasants) relied on their patrons for land and seed, for protection against both the state and the lawless, and for numerous essentials such as religious fees and support after a bad harvest. In return, the rural elite extracted not only a portion of the crops and the performance of numerous small chores, but also public homage and respect. This deference was reinforced by folk religion, wherein the powerful were imbued with supernatural powers or *anting-anting* (talismans), which secured divine protection. More prosaic powers derived from closely restricting access to political power. Under the Spanish a municipality might have several thousand inhabitants in the main town and even more in the surrounding villages and barrios, but less than a dozen qualified to vote. Accordingly, civic office—be it barrio head, town councilor, or *presidente/alcalde* (mayor)—was limited to the *principale* class. Even so, elections were bitterly contested. Then, as now, "Philippine politics [were] plagued by electoral bribery, violence, intimidation, and dynastic rivalries."[36]

In the nineteenth century, competition from other European powers in Asia and the loss of much of their American empire led to increased efforts by Spain to make the Philippines profitable. The imperial authorities sought to impose more control on the provinces, a goal that threatened the *principales.* Commercial agriculture and internal trade were promoted: land values increased; new areas were opened to cultivation; and traditional agriculture, based on custom and personal relations between patron and client, no longer proved as profitable. In some areas, landlords concentrated their holdings, forcing their workers into debt peonage. The displaced often became *ladrones* (brigands) or joined militant religious sects. In some provinces, such as Batangas, new alliances cemented by fictive kinship, school ties, and business connections consolidated power among a very few. In other areas, turf wars over land, trade, or political rank pitted family against family, clergy against laity, town against town. In the midst of this socioeconomic turmoil, the islands were struck by a series of natural and epidemic disasters: drought, floods, and insects devastated crops; malaria, smallpox, cholera, and typhoid ravaged humans; rinderpest debilitated livestock. By the 1890s much of the Philippines was in severe distress, plagued by social tension, disease, hunger, banditry, and rebellion.[37]

The late nineteenth century also witnessed the emergence of a Filipino national consciousness. The writings of Jose Rizal publicized abuses in the imperial system and advocated the inclusion of talented Filipinos in the government and clergy. He was especially critical of the Catholic Church and the friar orders, which controlled enormous estates and also acted as government agents. Rizal and his supporters sought modest change, not revolution, but his writings articulated a collective sense of grievance among educated Filipinos, or *ilustrados*. It is still not clear whether this movement represented an emergent Filipino nationalism or merely ethnic identity, class consciousness, an estrangement from Spain, and a desire for local autonomy. But, when combined with the deterioration in living conditions, it represented a potent threat to Spanish rule.

Bankrupt, torn by faction, and embroiled in an expensive and bloody war in Cuba, the imperial government was ill prepared to deal with the unrest in the archipelago. Unwilling to grant reforms, in part because to do so would antagonize powerful economic interests and force a confrontation with the Church, Spain also lacked the capacity for effective repression. Its army numbered only some 18,000 regulars, including 2,000 Spaniards, and was already overextended pacifying Moros and bandits.[38]

In late summer 1896 the Manila authorities uncovered a conspiracy by a small and obscure nationalist organization, the Katipunan. As they began arresting its members, its leader, Andres Bonifacio, issued a call to arms. Initially the Spanish military response was characterized more by indiscriminate violence than effectiveness, and the Katipuneros were able to seize control of most of the Tagalog area south of Manila. But the Katipuneros could not consolidate their gains; personal and regional animosities were so great that participants drew knives and revolvers at councils of war. At a conference on 22 March 1897, a faction from Cavite province replaced Bonifacio with one of their own, Emilio Aguinaldo y Famy. The deposed supremo was quickly arrested, tried, and executed by Aguinaldo's supporters; Aguinaldo's personal responsibility for the killing is still controversial.[39] Having frittered away their temporary success on internal squabbles, the Katipuneros were ill prepared to meet the counteroffensive. By February 1897 the Spanish, assisted by thousands of Filipino volunteers, had recaptured every rebel-held town. Much of Cavite was devastated: using the notoriously unreliable Spanish figures, one correspondent concluded the province's population had dropped from 135,000 to 97,000.[40] Many Katipuneros scattered and returned to their civilian occupations; others began guerrilla warfare in the hills. Aguinaldo trekked into the mountains of Bulacan province and established a stronghold at Biak na bato, 125 miles from Manila. His forces numbered some 600 soldiers and perhaps 1,400 civilians, far more than the area could support, and they soon suffered from malnutrition and disease.

Emilio Aguinaldo

By now, what had begun as an insurrection by a secret society had evolved into a revolution. Aguinaldo now called for reforms that all Filipinos— or at least the elite—could agree on: the expulsion of the friars; representation in the Spanish Cortes; and an end to discriminatory laws. Escalating the political stakes, on 5 November, Aguinaldo declared the Philippines independent, assumed the title of president, and called upon all Filipinos to rise against Spain. That same month, he ordered the abandonment of position warfare and the adoption of a strategy of protracted war. From now on municipal councils would serve as the de facto government in each town, appointing military and civil officials, raising militias, and establishing ties to other town councils. The militia would live in or near the town, gathering to raid isolated Spanish detachments, root out spies and traitors, and collect taxes.[41]

Although sometimes cited as the birth of a sovereign Philippine nation, Aguinaldo's grandiose pronouncements were in stark contrast to the realities of his situation, driven from his province, besieged in the mountains, and supported only by ragtag guerrillas ravaged by disease and hunger. Nevertheless, the Spanish were too weak to destroy him. Some of their units had lost 40 percent of their strength; the rest were exhausted, and the prospect of forcing the remaining revolutionary diehards out of their mountainous stronghold promised only further casualties. The government recognized no help could be expected from Spain, where attention was increasingly focused beyond the Cuban imbroglio to the far more ominous specter of a war with the United States. As a result, both Aguinaldo and the authorities were receptive when Pedro de Paterno, an ambitious Manila attorney, offered to negotiate a truce. The ensuing pact of 14 December 1897 is still controversial. Aguinaldo claimed that he secured a Spanish promise for extensive political and social reforms, an amnesty, reparations, and a large payment (which could buy weapons when he resumed the struggle). A less charitable explanation is that the imperial government bribed him—and that he did not stay bought. Certainly it is difficult to reconcile this capitulation with his proclamation of an independent republic barely a month earlier. Whatever the deal, Aguinaldo and several key followers soon left for Hong Kong.[42]

By the time of his departure, Aguinaldo had emerged as the most important leader of Luzon's nationalist movement, and, for better or worse, he would continue to shape the course of the anticolonial resistance. His admirers depict him as a gallant, steadfast patriot whose primary failing was believing that others, particularly the Americans and his *ilustrado* advisers, were as honorable as he.[43] To his critics he was an opportunistic warlord, a treacherous and prevaricating military incompetent who was "little more than a tool in the hands of active and more or less reliable advisors."[44] The "real" Aguinaldo is difficult to discover, for like his opponent McKinley, he seldom revealed his thoughts. Conscious of his limited education, he wrote little, and much that is attributed to him, including his three somewhat contradictory autobiographical publications, was largely the work of others.[45]

Aguinaldo was born into a relatively modest *principale* family in Kawit (Cavite Viejo), Cavite, in 1869. His father, who died when the boy was nine, held a number of civic offices and owned several farms and a sugar factory. Aguinaldo quit school in his early teens to further the family interests and engage in interisland trade, and by the 1890s had become involved in Kawit politics, served in several civic offices, and formed close connections with other Cavite politicians. Among his civic responsibilities was leading local militia against bandits, which gave him quasi-military experience with weapons and small-unit tactics. By 1896 he was a man of influence in his province, chafing under a government that refused to grant him the political and economic power he felt he deserved, and he made common cause with other rural elites against the Spanish. When he joined the Katipunan is still uncertain, but in 1896 he rallied Kawit behind the rebels. Aguinaldo soon proved a poor general—both as a field commander and as a strategist—but a consummate coalition builder. By the end of the year he had emerged as the only person who could hold together the alliance of *ilustrados,* warlords, and local politicians that made up the nationalist leadership.[46]

Once having left for Hong Kong, Aguinaldo found himself increasingly cut off from events in the Philippines. By taking his most loyal military leaders into exile, he had lost much of his personal influence over the resistance in the archipelago. Those who remained, such as Francisco Macabulos in Luzon, or the clandestine revolutionary councils that sprang up on the islands of Panay and Negros, had little connection, and even less loyalty, to Aguinaldo. Indeed, many outside of the Tagalog region espoused a federalist form of nationalism wherein each island and tribal group had virtual autonomy. For their part, the exiles engaged in mutual recriminations, culminating in a lawsuit against Aguinaldo for back wages. To avoid litigation, in April he departed for Europe, a move that, as his critics note, displayed a complete lack of understanding of the imminent Spanish-American conflict. It was not until he arrived in Singapore on 21 April, the date on which Spain and the United States broke off relations, that he became aware of the situation, and then only when Howard H. Bray, an English fortune hunter, introduced him to the American consul, E. Spencer Pratt.

The exact nature of the discussions between Pratt and the exiled president are still controversial. Aguinaldo later claimed Pratt promised the United States "would at least recognize the independence of the Philippine Islands, under a naval protectorate."[47] Pratt maintained that all he had done was urge Aguinaldo to return to Hong Kong and meet with Dewey, whose squadron was about to undertake operations against the Spanish in the archipelago. Bray, who served as interpreter, corroborated Aguinaldo's explanation, but since Aguinaldo paid him $5,000 and promised him a lucrative government appointment, he is a questionable source. A charitable interpretation is that Pratt's use of words such as "liberty" and "freedom," intended to refer to American traditions of civil and property rights, were mistranslated to indicate United States support for Filipino independence. Whatever the precise nature of the agreement, Aguinaldo had everything to gain and nothing to lose by accepting assistance.[48] His colleagues in Hong Kong concurred. As Jose Alejandrino wrote to a sympathizer, "Even without our help the Yankees could take over the country . . . and the only manner to counteract their intentions is that we be sufficiently armed. It is with this idea that we help them."[49] It was only much later, after the Spanish had been defeated and the United States had announced its plans to annex the archipelago, that charges of promised independence and betrayal arose.

Aguinaldo, who missed Dewey's departure, was transported to Cavite by an American steamer, disembarking on 19 May. He met with Dewey immediately, but again the conversations become a source of much debate. Aguinaldo later claimed that Dewey confirmed Pratt's assurance of independence. Dewey insisted he made no such pledge and that, far from seeking to free the Philippines, Aguinaldo's first request was to be sent to Japan. And indeed, Aguinaldo's repeated success in securing verbal commitments—coupled with his inability to support any of them with documentary evidence—must render his veracity, if not his intelligence, suspect to any but the most uncritical supporter. For his part, Dewey was an irascible man of limited political skills who regarded the Filipino revolutionaries as annoyances and Aguinaldo as no more than "the rebel chief."[50] If Dewey was using Aguinaldo, he was being used in return, and the evidence indicates that Aguinaldo got the better of the bargain. In addition to transport and prestige, Dewey turned over about 100 rifles, and the United States consul in Hong Kong purchased another 2,000—more than enough for Aguinaldo to reassert his claims to leadership of Luzon's independence movement.[51]

Once in Cavite, Aguinaldo moved quickly to consolidate his power. On 23 May he declared himself dictator for the duration of the crisis. On 12 June he proclaimed the independence of the Philippines, and on 23 June he announced the formation of the Revolutionary Government complete with an executive, congress, and courts.[52] His constitutional adviser, Apolonario Mabini, developed a plan for local government, which Aguinaldo promulgated on 18 June. Recognizing that with the collapse of Spanish authority, power had devolved upon municipalities, the decree required all local governments to hold elections and elect a *presidente*, town council, and barrio chiefs. This new government, having taken an oath to the newly independent Philippine state, would then elect a provincial assembly, which in turn, would elect a governor. The provincial government would then select two or three delegates to attend a constitutional convention in preparation for the implementation of a republican government. Extensive property qualifications limited the electorate, effectively putting, or keeping, political power in the hands of those "most characterized by their education, their social position, and their honorable conduct."[53] Aguinaldo's revolution was political, not social. He and his followers were determined to secure power for the *principales;* they had no intention of sharing it with the peasantry.

Aguinaldo also sought to assert his control over the scattered military forces that were harrying the Spanish. On 20 June he promulgated a two-tier military organization, the regular troops (later the Army of Liberation) and the Revolutionary Militia, which consisted of all who wished to assist in the fight for liberation. To assure order in the areas freed from Spanish rule, he ordered that each province be divided into zones, each under a commanding officer, who, in turn, would be subordinate to the provincial *jefe superior politico-militar.*[54] In practice, where local military chiefs already wielded power, he conferred rank and titles on them, but he also sent loyal officers, often with a cadre of experienced soldiers, to represent his interests or appointed trusted supporters to the top political and military positions. Despite these efforts, the revolution spread beyond Aguinaldo's control. On the Visayan island of Panay, local revolutionaries under Martin Delgado orchestrated a revolt among the militia and drove the Spanish into Iloilo City. On Mindanao, rebels, Spanish, and Moros engaged in a vicious three-sided civil war.[55]

Aguinaldo was much helped by his Spanish opponents, who bungled their slim chance of uniting the Filipino population against either the Americans or the rebels. The imperial authorities could either concentrate in Manila against the 8th Corps' attack and risk losing the provinces, or trust in Manila's fortifications and keep most of their troops on internal security duties outside the city. They chose the latter, with the result that the isolated and unsupported garrisons were soon besieged by Filipino irregulars. The government made another mistake by establishing a militia and placing former Katipuneros in command positions. The militia did little to oppose either Aguinaldo or the Americans, but it provided weapons and rudimentary training to those most committed to Spain's overthrow.[56]

As local forces were mopping up Spanish resistance in the provinces, Aguinaldo's relations with the Americans underwent a profound transformation. He had enjoyed (he claimed) good relations with Dewey, in part because there was no reason for the two men to have much intercourse. But with the disembarkation of Anderson's expedition at Cavite on 30 June, two days after the proclamation of the republic, a new factor was thrust into the equation. On his first visit Aguinaldo inquired into America's intentions; Anderson responded that he was a soldier with no authority to make policy or recognize Aguinaldo's government, but that he hoped both sides would cooperate to fight the Spanish. Anderson added somewhat elliptically that the United States had no colonies, and Aguinaldo declared himself satisfied. But the interview left both men suspicious—a feeling that intensified in the following weeks. Anderson reported not only that Aguinaldo was passively resisting his efforts to obtain transport and supplies but also that the rebels had increased their efforts to capture Manila before the rest of the expeditionary force arrived.[57]

By the time Merritt landed on 25 July, the situation had developed into what one scholar has termed a "curious triangular contest" among the Spanish, Americans, and Filipino revolutionaries.[58] The Spanish condition was desperate. There were 70,000 people in Manila, most of them crammed into the old walled city (Intramuros). Food was in short supply, and the ever-present fear of either insurgent attack or uprising, both of which were assumed to be the prelude to a general massacre, terrified the defenders.[59] Aguinaldo also faced severe problems. Although his forces had invested the city, they proved unable to break through the Spanish line of blockhouses. Both sides were of roughly equal strength—some 13,000 soldiers—and the fighting consisted largely of Spaniards and Filipinos skirmishing from their trenches. In view of this protracted stalemate, it is interesting to speculate on whether Aguinaldo could have concentrated his forces and assaulted the city in late June when the Spanish were demoralized and their defenses weak. Had he done so and captured the city, or even occupied the suburbs up to the Walled City, he might well have thwarted American efforts to exclude his forces from occupation. But, in what in retrospect appears a serious military mistake, Aguinaldo sent many of his best military commanders and most dedicated soldiers to expand his control over the provinces.

The 8th Corps' problem was essentially to take Manila in such a way that the revolutionary forces were excluded. This would be very difficult, for the rebels stood between the Americans and the Spanish lines. Through adroit diplomacy, Greene convinced Gen. Mariano Noriel to move his soldiers aside, so that on 29 July the Americans took up a narrow front facing north, their left flank anchored on Manila Bay and their right on a swamp. Conditions were appalling: rain alternated with baking heat; the trenches filled with water and mud; shoes and clothes rotted; snipers made any exposure dangerous; and Spanish raids killed fifteen and wounded fifty-three. Equally disheartening, a daring reconnaissance by the 8th Corps' intelligence officer, Maj. J. Franklin Bell, revealed no easy way to overcome the city's defenses.[60] Sandwiched on a narrow front between Manila Bay and Noriel's forces, Merritt had little choice but a frontal assault north against the strongpoints of Fort San Antonio Abad and Blockhouse 14. Complicating matters was Dewey, for contrary to his earlier claims that he could take the city by himself, he now professed to lack sufficient firepower even to support the assault.[61]

By now it was clear that the shared interest of the Spanish and Americans in keeping Aguinaldo's forces at bay had become a stronger concern than whether Merritt's soldiers could take the city at all. Through the good offices of the Belgian consul, Dewey and the Spanish governor struck a deal that if the city's waterfront batteries did not fire, the navy would not shell the city.[62] The admiral believed the agreement ensured that the Spanish would resist only enough to satisfy honor—and avoid court-martial. Merritt took the more literal view that the agreement was limited to the enemy batteries facing seaward and did not inform his subordinates that the Spanish intended to surrender.[63]

What might be called the First Battle of Manila on 13 August resulted in more than enough casualties to satisfy honor. Merritt's soldiers moved up through a blinding rain into the muddy trenches shortly after six in the morning. Despite the miserable conditions, morale was high. At 9:35 A.M., the navy cruisers and gunboats and the 3.2-inch guns of the Utah Battery began to shell the enemy trenches and Fort San Antonio Abad. Other warships took up stations menacing the city's seaward batteries. At 10:25, Greene's brigade began its attack, the troops advancing out of their trenches, then lying down while the navy fired its big guns into the Spanish positions. After a short bombardment, the troops moved forward along Manila Bay, approaching within 100 yards of the enemy trenches and then awaiting another bombardment. An eight-inch shell tore into the rear of the fort, and the defenders retreated up the road to Intramuros. Greene's brigade followed them through the suburb of Malate, crossed the Pasig River, and swept north and west around Intramuros, seizing the suburb of Binondo. To Greene's right, MacArthur's brigade had a tougher time, running into sharp resistance at Blockhouse 14 and losing five killed and thirty-eight wounded before it reached the Walled City and discovered the Spanish commander had already raised the white flag. The weary soldiers, lashed by a tropical rainstorm, immediately turned their attention to disarming their recent enemies and keeping Aguinaldo's furious soldiers out of the city.[64]

To some observers, the entire affair was a "sham battle" in which, in correspondent John F. Bass's words, "the gloves were padded."[65] Indeed, it seemed as if almost as much fire was exchanged between the army and the navy as between the Americans and the Spanish. Correspondents watching from his flagship accepted Dewey's claim that he had succeeded in negotiating the surrender of the whole city and that the army's attack was both inefficient and unnecessary. One newsman wrote the navy had all but taken the city, "but the ill-considered haste of the army in advancing cost the lives of a score of men."[66] Another opined that the soldiers "were of use simply to police the city after it was reduced to submission by our gallant fleet."[67]

Perhaps in response, Anderson published an account that claimed the army took Manila by storm, with no help at all from the navy.[68]

Predictably, the First Battle of Manila created a crisis in Fil-American relations. On the evening before the attack, Merritt had informed Aguinaldo that his forces were forbidden to enter Manila. American commanders were instructed to first overcome the Spanish, then shift to block Filipino incursions: "Forcible encounters with the insurgents in carrying out these orders will be very carefully guarded against, but pillage, rapine, or violence by the native inhabitants or disorderly insurgents must be prevented at any cost."[69] The unexpected Spanish resistance prevented the split-second timing required by such a complicated plan, and thousands of armed insurgents entered the suburbs, where they were confronted by soldiers demanding that they leave. In several places angry Filipino and American soldiers almost came to blows, and Anderson recalled that for several hours "conditions were critical," but the Filipinos "maintained good discipline."[70] Late in the afternoon Merritt, who had observed the battle from afloat, almost provoked a battle when he ordered the suburbs cleared. Anderson convinced him this was impossible; all the Americans could do was keep armed insurgents out of the city proper, bring up artillery for support, and request that Aguinaldo recall his troops. Tensions remained high the next day. A 1st Colorado outpost was fired on by some 300 insurgents. Rushing up reinforcements with fixed bayonets, the Colorado's colonel confiscated the Filipinos' weapons. Fortunately, negotiations defused the situation and secured a temporary arrangement: the 8th Corps controlled the Walled City, and Aguinaldo's soldiers remained in the suburbs. For the time being, both sides were content to await developments.[71]

In retrospect, Aguinaldo may have made a crucial mistake on 13 August. Some Filipino officers, most notably Antonio Luna, believed that he should have joined Merritt's attack. Had he been able to coordinate his forces so that all participated, they might have broken into the Walled City. Even if they were stopped, they would almost certainly have prompted stiffer Spanish resistance and thus kept the Americans out. Given that the peace protocol between Spain and the United States had already been signed, a delay of even a few days might have had enormous consequences for McKinley's efforts to claim the islands. A Filipino attack would almost certainly have provoked a war with the United States, but it would have been war on conditions far more favorable than those that existed five months later. Aguinaldo, however, apparently never considered such action. Instead, believing the Americans planned to capture him, he remained in Bacoor and took no part in the battle. As was to happen again and again, at critical times Aguinaldo hesitated, allowing events to overtake him rather than seizing the moment.

TWO

A DIFFICULT
SITUATION

On the day the Stars and Stripes was raised over Manila, Merritt and Dewey sent a telegram to Washington. Aguinaldo's forces were "pressing" for joint occupation of the city, and the situation was "difficult." They requested immediate clarification of how far they were to be allowed to proceed in "forcing obedience," bluntly asking whether the government was "willing to use all means to make the natives submit to the authority of the United States."[1] On 17 August the War Department replied that the 8th Corps' mission was to protect the property and persons of all people within the limits of Manila and its environs. Not only would there be no joint occupation, but the "insurgents and all others must recognize the military occupation and authority of the United States."[2] In microcosm, this exchange highlighted the different perceptions of officials in Washington and Manila—differences that would continue throughout the Philippine War. Surrounded by Aguinaldo's army, the military command's main concern was the permissible limits to action for immediate self-defense. In contrast, McKinley and his advisers downplayed the threat of war and perceived the 8th Corps' mission as securing the city and, increasingly, paving the way for United States sovereignty.

Washington's passivity was frustrating to officers dealing with a growing crisis in Manila. As one Idaho major noted, conditions in the city were "conducive to demoralization of the army."[3] One soldier commented, "A more filthy place I never saw. . . . The stench is something awful."[4] The heat, constant rain, and humidity were exhausting and gave some Volunteers an ever-present feeling of suffocation, as if they were breathing thin water instead of air. Aguinaldo had cut off the water supply and refused to restore it until Merritt made concessions. Typhus, malaria, dengue, and a dozen other diseases flourished in fouled sewers, stagnant backwashes, and public wells. Manila's social services were virtually nonexistent; Spanish officials had suspended all productive labor, but they continued to obstruct the conqueror's efforts. Aguinaldo's troops freely entered the city: some to visit their families, others to rob, and still others to establish revolutionary cells. Outside, in the suburbs, they threw up new field fortifications and exchanged insults with the 8th Corps' outposts. Tensions were high; within three days of the battle a soldier was shot to death by a Filipino sentry.

Merritt worked to defuse tensions, both within and without the city. On 14 August he proclaimed a government of military occupation, assuring the Manileros that the United States would "protect them in their homes, in their employments, and in their personal and religious rights."[5] He had earlier issued a general order to the 8th Corps, reminding his soldiers they were representatives of "a strong, free Government whose purposes are beneficent and which has declared itself in this war the champion of those oppressed by Spanish misrule."[6] Merritt sent deputies to negotiate the restoration of the water supply and prevent the Filipinos from building field fortifications "which would give the appearance that our troops were hemmed in by a besieging force."[7] After some discussion, Aguinaldo agreed to open the water-works and to withdraw his troops from the city limits. In return, Merritt allowed access to all unarmed Filipinos and to officers with sidearms. The inequality of the respective concessions may stem from Aguinaldo's awareness that the peace treaty between the United States and Spain would decide possession of the archipelago. As a result, he devoted his efforts to eliciting a promise that in the event the United States returned the islands to Spain, his troops could reoccupy the areas they had vacated. Merritt initially appears to have been willing to grant this, but he later backed down, offering instead the paltry assurance that Aguinaldo could depend on the "good will" of the army and the "beneficence" of the government.[8] In any event, despite Aguinaldo's promise, his troops continued to construct field fortifications and to harass outposts; as one officer observed, a "state of siege" existed.[9]

Although he deserves credit for averting an immediate outbreak of hostilities and for establishing the broad outlines of military government, Merritt was ill suited as proconsul. In his midsixties and in poor health, he was frustrated by McKinley's refusal to provide clear guidelines and by Miles's unceasing efforts to restrict the size, composition, and duties of the 8th Corps. The miserable conditions in Manila further increased his desire to return home. On 25 August he requested to be relieved; a day later, he received the welcome orders to advise the peace delegation in Paris. His departure touched off a "hegira" of officers applying for transfer back to the United States.[10]

Elwell S. Otis, who assumed command on 29 August, was to become one of the most unpopular, maligned, and controversial commanders in the islands. Bearing an oft-remarked resemblance to a beagle with muttonchop sideburns, he was the target of considerable scorn: Arthur MacArthur sneered that Otis was "a locomotive bottom side up on the track, with its wheels revolving at full speed," and Dewey described him as "a pincushion of an

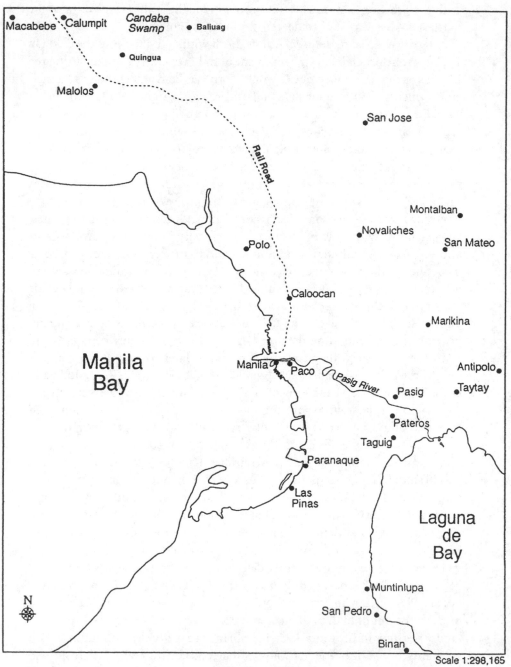

Macabebe • •Calumpit *Candaba Swamp* • Baliuag

• Quingua

Malolos•

•San Jose

Montalban•

•Novaliches

San Mateo•

Rail Road

•Polo

•Caloocan

•Marikina

Manila
Bay

Manila• •Paco

Pasig River

•Pasig

Antipolo•
•Taytay

•Pateros

Taguig•

•Paranaque

Laguna
de
Bay

•Las
Pinas

N

•Muntinlupa

San Pedro•

Binan•

Scale 1:298,165

Manila region

28

old woman."[11] Even now, authors have delighted in taking potshots: Leon Wolff dismissed Otis as a "tedious old lawyer in khaki," and H. W. Brands skewered him as "the Philippine war's answer to George McClellan, without the latter's good looks."[12] The general's most strident critic, Stuart Miller, perversely terms Otis "a man of limited ability and understanding," and yet accuses him of cleverly masterminding the outbreak of war.[13]

Otis was neither physically impressive nor particularly likable. In constant pain from his war wounds, overworked, and harassed by ambitious subordinates, he could be sarcastic, meddlesome, overbearing, and mulish. Extreme shifts in mood—ranging from sanguine overoptimism to almost frantic alarmism—made him singularly unfitted to serve as McKinley's key source of information on the Philippine situation. Perhaps most seriously, he consistently underestimated his opponents. His connections with Manila's elite convinced him that respectable propertied Filipinos desired annexation and that Aguinaldo and his followers sought to create a Tagalog dictatorship and plunder the islands. As a general Otis suffered from a number of shortcomings, but none was greater than his compulsion to cut corners and get by on the bare minimum. Time and again he denied his commanders the resources to perform their missions and deprived his soldiers of such essentials as modern rifles, cavalry mounts, transportation, food, clothing, and medical facilities. Unable to delegate authority, he too often became a prisoner of his paperwork and immersed himself in detail, losing perspective on the war and his army. As one unfriendly witness noted, Otis "lived in a valley and works with a microscope, while his proper place is on a hilltop, with a spy-glass."[14]

Yet the 8th Corps' commander was both more interesting and more capable than the caricature "Granny" Otis created by his detractors. From the beginning, he recognized the importance of civil as well as military priorities and the necessity of conciliating the Filipino population. Tasked with creating a viable foundation for colonial government, he possessed a formidable intellect, legal training, reforming interests, and managerial experience. Nor should his considerable skills as a strategist be overlooked: his forces were never defeated, every one of his campaigns was successful, and, judged by conventional standards of military victory, Otis won the war. If he did not achieve all the results he or his subordinates hoped for, this was hardly Otis's fault alone.

Otis's first priority was to protect his military position. He entertained no doubt that if armed Filipino troops were allowed into Manila the result would be a bloodbath. Nor, given the widespread mistreatment and killing of soldiers, priests, and noncombatants that occurred in parts of the archipelago, is it easy to challenge this conviction. That being the case, Otis had to establish a clear line of demarcation between the 8th Corps and Aguinaldo's army. Unfortunately, his manner was both hasty and undiplomatic: on 8 September he peremptorily ordered Aguinaldo to withdraw all military forces from Manila's suburbs within a week or face "forcible action."[15] There followed some tense negotiations as Aguinaldo, aware that his unruly army might refuse such a humiliating concession, sought to mitigate these demands. The situation was ominous; one South Dakota private reported his unit was on alert for days and fully expected war to break out.[16] Otis eventually modified his tone, and Aguinaldo's forces withdrew amid much ill feeling on 16 September. Unaware that he had narrowly averted a crisis (largely self-created), Otis wired Washington that conditions had improved and even claimed that he had sufficient troops to accomplish his task.[17] But soon, using Spanish maps, Otis decided the revolutionary forces were still within Manila's limits and insisted they withdraw. Aguinaldo rejected these new demands, arguing that the areas Otis claimed as suburbs were independent villages. Both sides sent troops into the contested zones, creating a number of incidents.

On 21 December Otis received McKinley's long-overdue instructions outlining the government's policies toward the Philippines. Once again, the president ignored military issues for civil ones. He made a number of disingenuous claims, among them that the destruction of the Spanish fleet and the capture of Manila had "practically effected the conquest of the Philippine Islands." His assertion that "the future control, disposition, and government of the Philippine Islands are ceded to the United States" rested on the recent treaty with Spain, which the Senate might well reject. Building on these shaky grounds, McKinley declared that "the actual occupation and administration of the entire group of the Philippine Islands becomes immediately necessary" and ordered that military government "be extended with all possible dispatch to the whole of the ceded territory." The army was to "win the confidence, respect, and affection of the inhabitants" both by its own good conduct and by demonstrating that "the mission of the United States is one of benevolent assimilation, substituting the mild sway of justice and right for arbitrary rule."[18]

Although the butt of many a sardonic comment, McKinley's "benevolent assimilation" policy was of vital importance. First, it clearly outlined the United States' claim to the entire archipelago and ruled out any hope of either national or, perhaps equally important, regional independence. Second, it made the army the instrument not only of enforcing this "lawful rule" upon recalcitrant rebels but also of protecting Filipino lives, property, and civil rights. McKinley's decision to assign this dual mission was to prove of immense significance. In order to follow it, army officers would have to devote at least as much attention to civic projects, public works, government, and education as they would to military operations. In pursuit of the enemy, they must never lose sight of their responsibilities as representatives of American values or of their obligations to support and protect those who had submitted to the nation's authority. Whether intentionally or not, McKinley had established conciliation as the cornerstone of military policy in the Philippines. Convinced that the Filipinos "will come to see our benevolent purpose," McKinley maintained that "time given the insurgents can not hurt us and must weaken and discourage them."[19]

Unfortunately, Otis could not devote all his efforts to winning the hearts and minds of the Filipino people, for the daily task of cleaning up the city and keeping the 8th Corps healthy kept him working long into the night. The reports of officers charged with inspecting the Volunteer units are filled with references to infected quarters, "revolting" latrines, rotting equipment, bad food, disease, and so forth.[20] The 1st Nebraska was quartered in a dank warehouse on the Manila docks, where the men slept on wet stone floors, with no place to eat except the street or bunks, no washing facilities, and inadequate sanitation. By mid-October six Nebraskans had died and seventy-eight were so sick they were recommended for early discharge—and this regiment's disease rate was among the lowest in its brigade.[21]

Otis set to work on the mutually compatible goals of improving the health of the 8th Corps and making Manila a symbol of the benefits of American rule. The appointment of his friend Brig. Gen. Robert P. Hughes as provost marshal on 3 September brought in a highly competent and energetic officer with years of experience in the inspector general's office. Complaining that "the only way to get my wishes carried out would be to divide into fifteen hundred people and attend to the work alone," Hughes threw himself into his task.[22] Under his direction inspectors ranged the streets, poking into slaughter-houses, marketplaces, dispensaries, and hospitals, and clearing up garbage and filth. He reestablished a police force, backed up by a provost guard of three regiments. Father W. D. McKinnon, in charge of establishing a secular public education system, soon quintupled the number of open schools. The army also began an ambitious program of public works, revising the city's lighting and water systems, rebuilding roads and bridges, and hiring dozens of refuse collectors. Many Volunteers found themselves practicing their civilian occupations as accountants, clerks, schoolteachers, and so forth.[23]

Otis also devoted much of his time to turning his disparate command into a coherent, disciplined army. Thrown together in the rush to get troops to

Manila, the 8th Corps contained everything from hardened Regulars to Volunteers who had barely learned how to march before being shipped overseas. Troops were always coming or going: in November, for example, Otis received the final reinforcements to arrive before the outbreak of war, 233 officers and 6,258 men. But that same month the War Department ordered that each infantry company was to be reduced to 80 men through the discharge of all the sick, then its parent regiment was to be brought up to 1,200 men by adding 30 soldiers to each company. In some regiments a quarter of the soldiers were sent home, their places filled by new recruits. The resulting turmoil in the ranks, as veterans left and new recruits arrived, can hardly be imagined.[24] Losses were especially high among senior officers and noncoms, who often proved too old and out of shape for active service in the tropics; they made a long, painful progression from sick quarters to hospital to transport. Dozens of others were removed from command in order to staff Manila's social services and administration.

The presence of thousands of soldiers, exceptionally well paid by Asian standards, acted like a magnet for prostitutes, gamblers, and liquor merchants. Charges that the army was licensing streetwalkers and sponsoring brothels arose at once and eventually prompted an investigation. To compound the problem, the soldiers' duties were physically exhausting but provided little satisfaction: when not working, they had little to do but lie around their cramped and malodorous quarters. Away from the restraining influence of home, some responded by going on prodigious debauches. A private in the 14th Infantry writing on payday noted his barracks was in an uproar: people were screaming and crying, fistfights were breaking out everywhere, a private had almost been choked to death by a captain—and this after forty-two soldiers had already been locked up in the guardhouse.[25] A soldier in the 1st California complained: "I am thoroughly disgusted with the crowd I am in. . . . Their only idea of pleasure seems to be in doing the town and coming back beastly drunk. We were paid off the first of the week, and the barracks has seemed like a home for inebriates ever since."[26]

An overwhelming problem for Otis was that roughly three-quarters of the 8th Corps were State Volunteers who had enlisted to free Cuba, and now that the war with Spain was over they demanded prompt discharge. Yet there was little hope of their immediate relief: the Regular Army had been devastated by disease in Cuba—some units had lost two-thirds of their strength—and would require months to cure its sick, weed out the physically unfit, and recruit new soldiers.

As they demonstrated later on numerous battlefields, the Volunteers had an abundance of spirit and élan, but they were hostile to the slavish subordination they associated with the Regular Army. They expected their officers to treat them as fellow citizens; those who acted as petty tyrants, abused their rank, or put on airs were sure to find themselves the targets of scorn and derision, if not worse. When a highly unpopular inspector approached one outpost, the sentry greeted him with a mock fit of knee-shaking panic, much to the amusement of his comrades.[27] The men were not hesitant to write home to complain of perceived abuses. Colonel John M. Stotsenburg, a Regular who assumed command of the 1st Nebraska, was so strongly denounced by veterans and their relatives that the state legislature petitioned the War Department to investigate his misconduct. Guardsmen and miners in the 1st Idaho's Company F continued their prewar hostilities; the captain, a "scab militia man," court-martialed members of the Miners Union at the slightest excuse.[28] The 1st California was split between partisans of Col. James F. Smith and Lt. Col. Victor Duboce. The enlisted men's quarters were wretched; one compared them to "dogs" in a "kennel" upon whom the officer "hogs" in their "airy sty" looked down in "grunting disapproval."[29] Adding to their unhappiness was the conviction that Smith had kept them in the Philippines in order to gain promotion to general, prompting the guardhouse wits, who took to singing "Twinkle, Twinkle, Little Star" every time he walked by.[30] In September the Californians' collective resentment sparked an ugly incident at an amateur review. When the officers entered, they were greeted with an icy silence; but as sketch after sketch reminded the soldiers of their superiors' petty tyrannies, they became more and more angry, and soon "a shower of gallery invectives" poured down on the officers. Only the presence of soldiers from other regiments prevented a riot.[31]

Otis was singularly inept in his handling of the Volunteers. Although he had proved an exceptional commander of citizen soldiers in the Civil War, he never achieved a rapport with the "Boys of '98." Even before he arrived in the Philippines, he had alienated many of them both by his aloofness and by his insistence on drill and discipline at Camp Merritt. During a ten-day stop at Honolulu, he forbade his soldiers more than six hours' leave ashore, a decision that one soldier concluded was due to Otis's wish "to impress us with the facts that we were slaves and that our welfare was of minor consideration."[32] In the Philippines, he soon infuriated the 8th Corps by imposing numerous restrictions on the soldiers' free time and closing the saloons on Sunday. Private William Cuffe spoke for many Volunteers when he said of Otis, "I wish His Satanic Majesty had a Holt [*sic*] of the Old Viper that he is."[33]

As Otis struggled to master the myriad responsibilities of office, Aguinaldo was also consolidating his position. Eager to establish a government that could secure recognition at home and abroad, in June he had called for elections for a constitutional convention. The assembly that opened on 15 September at the town of Malolos, some twenty miles north of Manila, was hardly representative. The franchise was so restricted as to make a mockery of any claim to popular mandate: in Batangas City, a municipality of 33,000 inhabitants, only 78 people were even eligible to vote. Entire islands were excluded: in one particularly unfair example, all four delegates appointed to represent the Visayan island of Cebu were Tagalogs from Luzon. However fiery their rhetoric about the revolution and nationhood, the Malolos delegates were, like the military chiefs, almost entirely landowners, professionals, and merchants; they had no intention of sharing either political or economic power with the peasantry, who composed over nine-tenths of the Filipino population.[34] But despite their common background and self-interest, they were already sharply divided. A few had become convinced that an independent Philippines was an impossibility and that the best course was to secure favorable terms from the United States. Others, perhaps even the majority, were moderates. Their experience with Spanish authoritarianism and their local connections impelled them toward a system where power was shared by federal and provincial governments. Finally, there were what might be termed the authoritarians, led by Apolinario Mabini, who believed that only a strong, centralized national government backed by a strong army could secure independence. Aguinaldo, increasingly influenced by Mabini, rejected a moderate constitution and filled his cabinet with hard-liners. With his government divided internally, unrecognized abroad, and with little control outside of Luzon, Aguinaldo's declaration of the Philippine Republic on 23 January 1899 was essentially a hollow gesture.[35]

As Maj. J. Franklin Bell, the 8th Corps' intelligence officer, had reported on 29 August, Aguinaldo was "experiencing considerable difficulty in maintaining control over his loosely organized forces" and was "powerless" to discipline corrupt, insubordinate, or brutal officers because that would end their allegiance.[36] One general, for example, whose forces had taken control of three provinces, was reported to have said Aguinaldo would have to conquer them before he acknowledged his authority. In some areas the depredations of armed gangs claiming to represent the revolutionary government had already sparked resistance and rebellion. Aguinaldo countered by sending trusted veterans of the 1896 revolt with contingents of soldiers to serve as political-military governors in the provinces. The combination of political legitimacy, backed by comparatively well-armed and well-disciplined troops, was usually enough to secure vocal obedience, if not compliance. Nevertheless, the inability of Aguinaldo or anyone else to impose discipline on the factious and insubordinate officer corps was a serious, perhaps even fatal, weakness.[37]

As part of his efforts to consolidate power, Aguinaldo attempted to create a unified European-style army out of the disparate military forces around Manila. Formally called the Army of Liberation of the Philippines, it was given the nomenclature and organization of a modern conventional force: units were divided into line and light infantry or cavalry and artillery, grouped into battalions and divisions, and assigned staff and field officers. But with the exception of a few units composed of veterans of the Spanish army, the revolutionary forces remained a "loose federation of municipal militia, each town having its own band of volunteers who served under their own leaders."[38]

As with many peasant armies, the Army of Liberation's strength was its infantry. Physically tough, inured to hardship, able to move rapidly in difficult terrain, requiring neither extensive logistical lines nor sophisticated equipment, it had been sufficient to roll up the demoralized Spanish garrisons in the countryside. The army's critical weaknesses were its lack of training, its weaponry, and its officers. Some soldiers received rudimentary instruction from European manuals, but Aguinaldo never instituted a systematic training program or attempted large-unit maneuvers. His soldiers would fight with courage, especially when sheltered by field fortifications, but they were incapable of maneuvering in formation or of performing any but the most simple tactical movements; nor could they fight together as a coherent entity. The insufficiency of modern firearms was even more critical. The U.S. Navy and its intelligence service did an excellent job of intercepting arms shipments; therefore, the Filipino forces had to rely chiefly on captured rifles and ammunition. Lacking the facilities to manufacture either smokeless powder or high-quality cartridges, their arsenals could only produce, with great time and labor, homemade black powder and casings, with consequent inferiority of accuracy and rate of fire.[39]

Perhaps the most glaring weakness in the Army of Liberation was its officer corps. Aguinaldo and his subordinates handed out promotions and commissions with abandon: by September 1898 the Army of Liberation boasted eighteen generals and innumerable colonels and *commandantes* (majors). Even more officers were commissioned by the independent revolutionary councils in the Visayas or by provincial governors. Many of these officers tended to view the military chain of command as essentially personal: they might obey the direct orders of a friend or a social superior but not necessarily those of his deputy. A U.S. Navy officer dispatched to ensure the rebels respected foreign property wrote after an interview with one of Aguinaldo's deputies that the man was quite willing to do this, "but he practically admitted that he might not be able to control his men, and this seems to be the case everywhere."[40] The problems at the top were replicated in the lower levels. With the exception of some highly competent engineers, the entire officer corps was unprofessional and amateurish. Often their family and political connections allowed them to disobey orders with relative impunity, and their petty tyrannies and exactions alienated the people they were supposed to protect. General Jose Alejandrino recalled his fellow officers as patriotic and brave young men, but he made no mention of them studying tactics, drilling their troops, or otherwise mastering the profession of arms.[41]

Aguinaldo's efforts to turn the Army of Liberation into a conventional force brought to the fore Antonio Luna. A distinguished pharmacologist and sometime editor, Luna is one of the war's most controversial characters. Both before and after his appointment as General in Chief of Operations in February 1899, Luna sought to put his wide reading in European military manuals to practical use with the Army of Liberation. The effort would prove unsuccessful, in part due to Luna's own personal shortcomings: incapable of disciplining himself, he was prone to violent, almost psychotic, rages. Luna's problems were exacerbated by Aguinaldo. The president recognized that military strength was the ultimate arbiter of power—as his execution of Bonifacio proved—and he was determined that he alone would control the army.[42]

Given such leaders, placed in such circumstances, the negotiations between Otis and Aguinaldo that began in January 1899 were probably doomed from the start. Malolos's directions to its delegation—that the United States must first recognize the Philippine Republic as an independent and sovereign nation—left little room for compromise.[43] Hughes, one of the American delegates, complained, "The trouble is to get a secure basis to talk upon. These people use our phrases and terms in quite a difference sense from the way we use them, and so don't understand us any better then we do them."[44] On 4 February, the very date that fighting broke out, he predicted, "The men on both sides seem to have become weary of the tension, and all wish for a collision. It is coming, and no one can forecast a day ahead."[45]

Soldiers on both sides, acutely aware of the accelerating war preparations, added their own personal antipathy to the growing estrangement. Correspondent John F. Bass commented that while relations had initially been good between Americans and Filipinos, "race differences have made themselves felt, which antagonize the native and exasperate our men."[46] A Nebraskan spoke for many soldiers when he wrote home, "If they would turn the boys loose there wouldint [sic] be a nigger left in Manila twelve hours after. . . . The niggers will find out after [a] while they are not fooling with the Spaniards."[47] Both sides engaged in intimidation: soldiers would walk two abreast on Manila's narrow streets and yell "Gangway!" to warn people to move aside or be pushed. Filipino soldiers soon took up this practice, shouting "Gangway Americano!"[48] Scuffles were common. One, a relatively minor affair, was described by a soldier in the 14th Infantry: "An armed [Filipino] officer tried to stop one of our boys from taking firewood, [the soldier] stopped long enough to knock his face in and then carried his wood."[49]

Far more dangerous were the outbreaks of firing between outposts, any one of which had the potential to escalate to full-scale war. Major William A. Kobbé remarked that random firing on the lines was so common that when the war began he did not summon his troops until he heard cannons.[50] On 21 December fighting almost broke out when Filipino soldiers, objecting to a sentry stationed on Paco Bridge, announced they would fire on him if he was not removed. Anderson assembled some 4,000 troops in preparation for a battle, but after a conference he removed the sentry. On 1 January, Otis notified McKinley of the "excited condition of affairs"; three days later he reported a threatened uprising within Manila to coincide with an attack.[51] Rumors abounded: assassins had targeted American officers; clandestine arsenals were filled with weapons and incendiaries; secret societies had infiltrated the city. On 12 January every unit in the southern lines and the three regiments of the provost guard were turned out in full readiness for an expected attack. Hughes estimated that as many as 50,000 Filipinos had fled the city, many of them openly admitting they were going to serve with Aguinaldo. Once again both sides tottered toward war, only somehow to pull back.[52]

In the meantime, to the south another crisis loomed. After the fall of Manila, the Spanish general Diego de los Rios had assumed supreme political and military authority and made his headquarters at the important commercial port of Iloilo City, situated on the southern tip of the island of Panay in the Visayas.[53] Rios encouraged the formation of militia units captained by local *principales* throughout Iloilo Province and learned too late that many Ilongo militia officers were committed to Panay's independence. On 28 October the companies of Martin Delgado at Santa Barbara and Quintin Salas at Dumangas revolted. Joining with other militia officers, landowners, and merchants, they formed the Revolutionary Central Committee of the Visayas. Besieged in Iloilo City and believing his own Filipino troops unreliable, Rios asked Madrid's permission to turn the city over to the United States.[54]

In the face of this windfall, the Americans temporized. Only on 13 December, after receiving an urgent petition for immediate occupation from Iloilo's business community, did Otis request authorization from the War

Department. Both McKinley and the secretary of war were absent, and for a week Washington dithered before giving its consent. Finally granted clear direction, on 24 December Otis placed Brig. Gen. Marcus P. Miller in command of the 1st Separate Brigade, consisting of the 18th and 51st Iowa Infantry and a battery of the 6th Artillery, and ordered him to occupy Iloilo City. Sure that the expedition would be peaceful, Otis gave Miller extensive instructions for setting up a military government. As a goodwill gesture, he repatriated the Visayans who had been captured in Manila serving with the Spanish army.[55]

Miller's brigade did not leave Manila until 26 December, and by then the situation had drastically altered. After weeks of delay, Madrid authorized Rios to withdraw to the port of Zamboanga on Mindanao but did not inform him that the peace treaty gave the United States sovereignty over the archipelago. Rios, concerned lest he be attacked while embarking, summoned Iloilo's municipal officials and announced he planned to depart on 24 December. The officials just as promptly contacted Delgado and arranged for him to occupy the city on 26 December. A day later, as Miller's transports lay off the island of Mindoro, Lt. Col. Charles L. Potter, who had been conducting a reconnaissance of the Visayas, informed Miller that insurgent troops had peacefully entered Panay's capital and proclaimed the Federal State of the Visayas. Potter did not think there would be any violence if the Americans landed, but he warned that the recent arrival of Aguinaldo's delegates had inspired the Visayans and was making them increasingly hostile.[56] Potter's report was accurate but incomplete. The newly created Federal State was a junta of Iloilo Province's military leaders, local dignitaries, and the city council. Like the Malolos government, it was far from representative: the other Visayan islands were represented by Ilongos. As John Schumacher notes, "It professed allegiance to the Malolos government, at least in a general way," but it often pursued quite independent policies.[57] Thus, for example, when Aguinaldo sent a trusted Tagalog subordinate, Gen. Ananias Diocno, to take command, the local troops continued to obey Delgado.

The military forces on Panay, estimated at some 4,000 *tiradors* (riflemen) and 14,000 *macheteros* (bolomen), were divided into a number of conflicting groups under Delgado's nominal leadership. The largest contingent were the Ilongos, organized into provincial "brigades" throughout Iloilo Province; Capiz and Antique Provinces both had their own local forces. In addition, there were between 1,000 and 1,500 soldiers from Luzon. The first of these contingents had arrived in December under Diocno; two other contingents under Leandro Fullon and Angel Salazar were smuggled in over the next few months. The Luzon contingents were a mixed blessing. Comparatively well armed and disciplined, they maintained strong unit cohesion. But their leaders had little interest in cooperating with the Visayans and feuded with Delgado. As the Americans were soon to learn, the insurgent military organization was even more diffuse and decentralized in the Visayas than it was in Luzon.[58]

When the 1st Brigade and the cruiser *Baltimore* arrived in Iloilo Bay on the morning of the 28th, they found a complicated and volatile situation. Miller dispatched three aides to meet with the revolutionary council. The general's accompanying letter proclaimed the transfer of governmental authority to the United States, which "succeeds, by virtue of conquest, supplemented by treaty stipulation, in all the rights heretofore exercised by Spain in these Islands."[59] The council asked if Miller had brought any instructions from Malolos, without which they could not surrender. The American envoys returned, and both sides prepared for a landing the next day. What followed next is unclear. According to one account, Miller began lowering his troops into boats when a committee of merchants arrived begging him not to land lest Delgado fire the town. Then the captain of the *Baltimore* refused either to blockade the harbor or to shell an old Spanish fort that the insurgents were repairing. In exasperation, Miller notified Otis that he planned to mount Gatling guns on his landing boats and assault the fort, "inviting the Captain of the Baltimore to help defend us by attacking the enemy."[60] At this point, Potter returned from Manila with new and vague instructions from Otis, which enjoined Miller both to be conciliatory and to make an armed landing. Clearly Otis was torn between the twin poles of McKinley's orders to demonstrate United States sovereignty and at the same time to avoid provoking war.

Cast into limbo, Miller tried negotiating. On 30 December he met with delegates from the revolutionary committee, who again refused to turn over control of the city without permission from Malolos, for should they do so, "their lives and property would be in danger."[61] Deadlocked, Miller informed Otis he could take the city, but only at the cost of high casualties and widespread property destruction. Both Otis and Washington quickly ordered Miller to delay, urging him to publish McKinley's "benevolent assimilation" proclamation and assure the residents the expedition's purpose "is to give them a good government and security in their personal rights."[62] Miller had no patience with this approach, wiring Otis, "Let no one convince you that peaceful measures can settle the difficulty here, unless you first settle matters peacefully in Manila and Luzon Island. . . . I think the longer we wait before the attack the harder it will be to put down the insurrection."[63] Nonetheless, he distributed McKinley's proclamation, but in its original form, including several patronizing phrases that Otis had deleted. The Ilongos promptly forwarded the original text to Malolos, which reveled in this fresh evidence of American duplicity.[64]

Regardless of his own feelings, Miller abided by his orders and once again turned his attention to winning the Ilongos over by reason. Like both Otis and McKinley, Miller attributed resistance to Filipino ignorance, and his letter emphasized that the army did "not come among you as invaders and conquerors, but as friends to establish and maintain a government which will accord to the people what is the heritage of all free peoples, the full measure of individual rights and liberty."[65] This prompted a request for negotiations, and on 11 January his aide Acting Surgeon Henry Du R. Phelan was ably debated by attorney Raymundo Melliza. Phelan began by asserting United States sovereignty over the archipelago and emphasized the benefits that Filipinos could expect under its rule. Melliza responded: "We have fought for our independence and feel that we have the power of governing, and need no assistance; we are showing it now." Since the surrender of Iloilo "involved the integrity of the entire Republic," it could not be considered without discussions with Malolos. Phelan replied that without American aid the Filipinos would still be under Spanish domination and that no Philippine government had any status in international law, whereas all nations accepted that the Treaty of Paris placed the islands under United States sovereignty. Moreover, he pointedly remarked that only when the Americans arrived had the Ilongos raised the issue of Malolos's authority. He warned that the expedition could destroy Iloilo at "any time, but we did not want to commit a hostile act but wanted to land as friends." Melliza was up to this challenge, replying that Miller was free to raze Iloilo, since all the property in it belonged to the foreigners, but should he land, "We will withdraw to the mountains and repeat the North American Indian warfare."[66] Like the negotiations at Manila, the sole outcome of these talks appears to have been to make clear the unbridgeable gap between the two sides.

In the meantime, the soldiers on the transports went through an ordeal much like their comrades at Manila. They drilled and practiced landing exercises but most of the time had little to do but lie around the deck, trade rumors, endure insults, and watch the daily improvement of Iloilo's defenses. By now the expedition was running short of food and water, and the troops were thoroughly sick of the unvaried diet of bacon, beans, and hardtack. As in Manila, a number of incidents—including a vicious knifing of two sentries by boatmen—kept tensions high.[67] The waiting was hardest on the 51st Iowa, which had been stuck on the transport *Pennsylvania* for almost three months. The men's sweat-soaked mattresses were so infected with vermin they had to be destroyed, and the men themselves were lice-ridden. On 5 January, Miller tried to give the ship-weary regiment some shore time on an island across from the town, but as the first two boatloads reached the shore they were met by over 100 armed Filipinos and the men ordered back to the hated transport. The soldiers were eager to "get a wack [*sic*]" at their enemies and were "smiling every day to think how nice it will be to blow them old guns from the Rebels in the air with ours."[68] But the heat, humidity, and tedium of shipboard life gradually demoralized the 51st; factions and personal feuds culminated in a near riot, the men "hooting and howling" at their officers.[69] The next day, Miller ordered the 51st back to Manila: the troops finally disembarked on 2 February after ninety-four days at sea.

Although the stalemate at Iloilo City frustrated Miller, embarrassed the Americans, and made the occupation of the city more difficult, Otis had sound reasons for delay. In Malolos, the war party hoped the United States would make an armed landing, rallying the moderates, and the population, behind the Philippine Republic. Lacking such an incident, Otis believed their government would collapse. Already the American policy of benevolence was winning converts among the more influential citizens.[70] Moreover, both Otis and Miller recognized that without more troops the 1st Brigade could do little but occupy the city, where it would soon be hemmed in by insurgent trenches, thus replicating the situation in Manila.

THREE

THE BATTLE
OF MANILA

Finally, after almost half a year of negotiations, minor incidents, shootings, alarms, and unremitting tension, the impasse at Manila erupted into open hostilities on the night of 4 February 1899. But the circumstances surrounding the outbreak are still matters of strong dispute. The actual events are still unclear, as is the much larger issue of who, if anyone, was responsible for starting the war. In addition to the obvious tendency of each side to blame the other for firing the first shots, there is the confusion of night combat and the fact that much of the fighting was uncoordinated, even leaderless. To complicate matters even further, not only do the participants often contradict each other—and sometimes themselves—but some writers later added details, too often with scant regard for historical veracity.

In the five months since the fall of Manila, the Army of Liberation, whose numbers have been estimated at anywhere from 15,000 to 40,000, had maintained a loose envelope around the American positions. They had improved and extended their already impressive fieldworks, emplaced artillery, and created a number of strongpoints. Aguinaldo's agents had smuggled in arms and organized militia in many of Manila's neighborhoods; on 9 January, in preparation for the outbreak of fighting, he issued directions for these militia, together with the city's inhabitants, including women and children, to assist the Army of Liberation in its attack.[1]

At the beginning of February the U.S. Army forces in the Philippines numbered some 800 officers and 20,000 men, of whom 77 officers and 2,338 men were in Cavite or in transports off Iloilo, another 8,000 were on duty within Manila, and the rest, about 11,000, were in a pentagonal defensive line shaped like home plate, which extended some sixteen miles around the city. Across the Pasig River and facing north were the two brigades of Maj. Gen. Arthur MacArthur's 2nd Division. Brigadier General Harrison G. Otis (no relation to Elwell S. Otis) commanded the 1st Brigade: the 20th Kansas, whose left flank rested on Manila Bay; the 3rd U.S. Artillery (assigned as infantry); the 1st Montana; and the 10th Pennsylvania. Brigadier General Irving Hale's 2nd Brigade linked up with Otis's brigade and extended far-

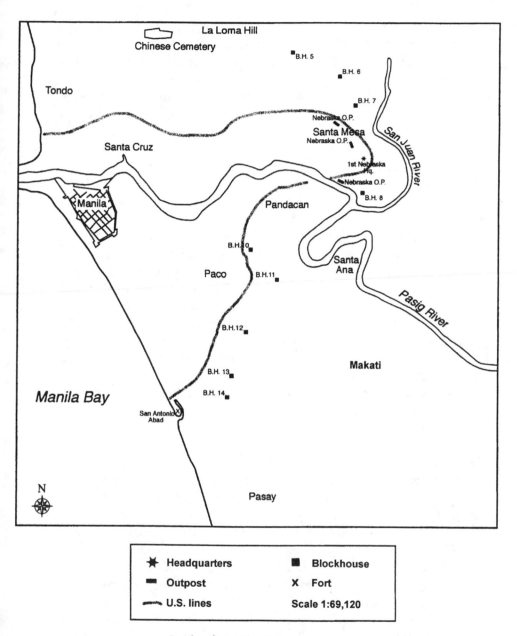

La Loma Hill
Chinese Cemetery

Tondo

B.H. 5

B.H. 6

B.H. 7

Nebraska O.P.
Santa Mesa
Nebraska O.P.

Santa Cruz

1st Nebraska Hq.
Nebraska O.P.
B.H. 8

Manila

Pandacan

Santa Ana

B.H. 10

Paco

B.H.11

B.H.12

Makati

B.H. 13

B.H. 14

Manila Bay

San Antonio Abad

N

Pasay

San Juan River

Pasig River

★ Headquarters	■ Blockhouse
▬ Outpost	X Fort
〜 U.S. lines	Scale 1:69,120

Battle of Manila, February 1899

43

ther southeast: the 1st South Dakota at San Miguel; the 1st Colorado at Sampaloc; and, at the narrow, or catcher's, end of home plate, the 1st Nebraska's station at Santa Mesa. Across the Pasig began the left wing of Maj. Gen. Anderson's 3,850-man 1st Division. Facing east and south along the banks of Concordia Creek (or estuary) and running from the Pasig River to Blockhouse 12 was Brig. Gen. Charles King's 1st Brigade: the 1st Idaho; the 1st Washington; and the 1st California. From the blockhouse to Fort Malate on Manila Bay was Brig. Gen. Samuel Ovenshine's 2nd Brigade of ten companies of the 14th U.S. Infantry, the 1st North Dakota, and six troops of the 4th Cavalry.[2]

Despite frequent references to "lines," the 8th Corps' defensive system was a series of semiautonomous regimental commands stationed to guard the most obvious avenues of attack. Units were separated by islands and mudflats, creeks, bamboo and scrub thickets, villages, rice fields, and swamps. Each regiment kept the bulk of its troops back several hundred yards in prepared positions, relying on outposts and patrols to warn of attack. A network of telegraph lines and prearranged rocket signals kept the commanders in contact with brigade and division. Although the only tactical disposition possible given the 8th Corps' limited manpower, it formed a very porous front. Some outposts of the opposing forces were hundreds of yards apart, separated by swamps, water, or bamboo groves. In other areas, particularly at bridges, villages, and roads, the sentries stood almost face-to-face and could, as their temperaments suited, trade insults or cigars. Patrols were continually moving into disputed zones, and if not challenged might soon be followed by outposts and then a permanent garrison behind field fortifications. Thus soldiers, especially sentries, knew they could be easily surrounded and cut off, a recognition that encouraged a great deal of shooting at shadows and noises. Officers, aware that their units might face a major attack without immediate support, jealously guarded any position that might prove crucial in a fight and were quick to react to what they viewed as encroachments.

The most precarious position was at the extreme northeast of the line in the Santa Mesa district. At this point, the San Juan River loops back on itself, creating a small pocket open only at the north. The Filipino troops held the high ground along the river loop and also Blockhouses 6 and 7 at the north. A pipeline carrying water from the Marikina waterworks crossed the road leading over the river. This exposed position had been held since late December by the Nebraskans backed up by two 3.2-inch field guns from the Utah Battery. They were exposed to fire on three sides, but to the north, the only direction not blocked by water, there was no barrier to a direct attack, just a small sluggish stream that could be easily crossed. Accordingly,

Col. John M. Stotsenburg stationed his regiment several hundred yards behind the front lines, where they were sheltered by earthworks. His outer perimeter was held by two lines of pickets, the first of which were three outposts consisting of a platoon of between twenty-five and thirty men. Perhaps a hundred yards beyond each outpost were squad, or "cossack," posts of six to ten soldiers under a noncom. One or two officers were detailed to walk the outposts and ensure that the guards were awake and alert.

Both the extreme vulnerability of the Nebraskans' position and the absence of a physical barrier made relations between the two sides exceptionally tense. Stotsenburg, who believed Col. Luciano San Miguel's soldiers were continually pressuring his outposts and trespassing on his territory, worried that these incidents and provocations might escalate. On 2 February he ordered that in the event of attack the men were to hold their positions and prohibited them from taking the offensive, or even shooting until fired upon—and then only at the command of their officers. Later critics to the contrary, these orders hardly indicate a secret plan to provoke a war.[3]

Unfortunately, events soon moved beyond Stotsenburg's control. On the night of 1–2 February, Filipino patrols crossed into what the Americans viewed as the neutral zone and occupied Santol, a small village—perhaps half a dozen shacks—located at a split in the road between Manila and the pumping station at Marikina. Stotsenburg's division commander, MacArthur, sent a note to San Miguel emphasizing that in view of the current tension it was absolutely necessary that the line of demarcation be observed by both sides, and drawing attention to the occupation of the village by a garrison "very active in exhibiting hostile intentions."[4] San Miguel replied that he knew nothing about this encroachment and would give orders that the troops be withdrawn. But when Stotsenburg protested to the officer at Santol, the man responded by drawing a line in the dirt and daring him to cross it. Stotsenburg restrained himself and ordered his subordinate on the scene, "Do not make any trouble with armed Filipinos in the village. They have *no right* there however. Our line is the line of *Blockhouses*. Let matters rest until further orders."[5] On 4 February, Stotsenburg, after consulting with Hale, sent a squad into the disputed village with orders "to hold that village and under no circumstances to give it up to the insurgents."[6] The patrol found the village deserted, but sentries reported a force of 500 Filipinos in the area. Aware that the occupation was likely to provoke a response, Stotsenburg cautioned his outpost commander, "Be sure to be ready for any emergency and take all precautions to prevent attack, especially at night."[7]

That evening, Lt. Bert D. Whedon took command of the outposts near the disputed village and the San Juan Bridge. He visited an eight-man post stationed at the intersection of three roads, ordering them not to allow armed Filipinos to enter the village or its vicinity. If challenged, the soldiers were to arrest the encroachers, but if this was impossible they were to fire on them. In order to prevent anyone slipping by, they were to send small patrols a short distance along the roads toward the blockhouses every half hour. Accordingly, at about 8:00 P.M., three soldiers began walking from Santol toward Blockhouse 7. By then it would have been quite dark, and it is likely their path was bordered by heavy brush, further obscuring the view. After proceeding roughly 100 yards, the patrol waited a few minutes. What happened next is still unclear. According to one Filipino account, the patrol suddenly and without warning fired on Cpl. Anastacio Felix and two companions, who were peaceably standing in the doorway of Blockhouse 7.[8] According to most American participants, Pvt. William Grayson was a short distance in front when suddenly three (or four) armed men appeared five yards ahead of him. He immediately called "Halt," as did another soldier. Instead, the Filipinos continued to advance and cocked their weapons, provoking Grayson to call "Halt" again and then fire, as did his companions. The three soldiers then fell back, perhaps sprinting, to Santol, where Whedon met them. By this time they could, or thought they could, hear enemy forces approaching from Blockhouse 7. Whedon sent a soldier back to warn the Nebraska camp that an attack was imminent. When the first Filipinos appeared, both sides fired, and Whedon fell back to a water pipeline that provided cover. For about five minutes both sides blazed away, then the firing tapered off.[9]

Initially, some soldiers dismissed this shooting as the actions of nervous sentries, but the firing soon spread along the northern lines until most of Hale's brigade was engaged. Filipino soldiers infiltrated the Nebraskan positions, and much of the regiment was soon shooting at shadowy figures. After some desperate fighting, they drove the insurgents back from their camp and into the brush.[10] An hour after Grayson's first shots, the 1st Colorado's outposts came under attack. Lieutenant Colonel Cassius Moses brought up eight companies to support them, and there was sporadic gunfire until shortly before daybreak, when a general firefight began. Colonel A. S. Frost's 1st South Dakota was also attacked and two soldiers killed. Colonel A. L. Hawkins' 10th Pennsylvania pushed back three probes on their advanced positions and withstood heavy but inaccurate fire all night.[11] To the south, across the Pasig River from the Nebraskans, the soldiers in King's brigade were called to arms and for half an hour stood in their trenches waiting for an attack. They were then dismissed and sent back to quarters, only to be called out an hour later. Shortly before 3:00 A.M. firing increased, and by morning it extended all along the 1st Brigade's front.[12]

For most Manileros, the battles on the outskirts were a gala event, and thousands swarmed to the waterfront or the suburbs to catch the view. But for the respective commanders of the provost guard and the Filipino revolutionary cells, the gunfire on the outskirts signaled the start of a confrontation within the city. It was one which the Americans won handily. The outbreak of fighting took Aguinaldo's organization in Manila completely by surprise; there was no coordinated revolt, but rather a number of random acts of arson and sniping by people who, in Hughes's words, "had more fighting pluck than wisdom."[13] But Hughes sent his Provost Guard of three regiments of infantry out in the streets immediately, sealing off thoroughfares, dispersing large gatherings, and keeping a close watch on suspected neighborhoods. Dozens, perhaps hundreds, of suspects were arrested; those who resisted were treated harshly, for the soldiers believed they were facing an insurrection. Hughes laconically noted of some arsonists that "when the police company got through with them the undertaker had enough business for the day."[14] The suppression of the Manila disturbances was a crucial, if often overlooked, part of the battle of 4–5 February. The Guard's prompt action secured the city and prevented the terrifying prospect of the 8th Corps facing attack in all directions.

U.S. firing line during the Battle of Manila, February 1899

Along the northern line, MacArthur had developed a relatively simple contingency plan: in the event of enemy attack, the entire 2nd Division would launch an all-out offensive on the main enemy line along Santa Mesa Ridge, which dominated the northern front. After capturing the blockhouses, it would seize the fortified strongpoints at the Chinese hospital and cemetery and La Loma Church, which were clustered along the ridge. Simple in concept, the plan was difficult in execution. The 2nd Division would have to assault across open rice fields and bamboo thickets, then uphill over broken ground against enemy troops protected by earthworks, barbed wire, and cemetery headstones.

Sunday morning, 5 February, dawned bright and clear, and with it the offensive began. The gunners from the Utah Battery fired their two 3.2-inch field guns at enemy blockhouses and trenches. The cruiser *Charleston* sent its huge eight-inch shells into strongpoints in the interior as the *Callao* raked the enemy positions along Manila Bay with artillery and machine guns. Under the cover of the gun smoke, the troops moved forward over the open rice fields, advancing in rushes, firing by platoons, and took the blockhouses with little resistance. The second part of the assault was more difficult. On the extreme left of the line along Manila Bay, the 20th Kansas had to attack across rice paddies and small clusters of nipa huts. With their diminutive colonel, "Fighting Fred" Funston in the lead, the Kansans charged far past their objectives, capturing earthworks and trenches almost to the town of Caloocan before MacArthur recalled them. To the 20th's right, Maj. William A. Kobbé's 3rd Artillery had less success. The Regulars moved into a narrow corridor, blocked by dikes to their front and swamps on their flanks. Under a withering cross fire, five soldiers died and another nineteen were wounded before the 3rd finally broke through to open ground. Re-forming, they charged uphill and captured the Chinese church at 2:30. Meanwhile, the Pennsylvania and Montana regiments fought house by house through the suburb of Tondo, then picked their way through thick brush, only to be hit by gunfire from the redoubts on La Loma Church and flank fire from the Chinese cemetery. There the advance stalled while Frost's South Dakota regiment worked around the Filipino left and fought its way through the barbed wire and headstones at La Loma Church. By 4:30 Santa Mesa Ridge was in American hands.[15]

To the right, the assault by Hale's 2nd Brigade proceeded smoothly. Supported by accurate fire from the Utah Battery and by navy gunboats, the brigade moved forward shortly after 8:00 A.M. The Nebraskans cleared the defenses along the San Juan River and then joined the Colorado and Tennessee regiments pressing up San Juan del Norte hill. Hale and his staff kept control of the brigade along its three-mile front, calling in artillery and reinforcements when needed. They even shifted the South Dakotans over to launch a flank attack on La Loma. The regiments advanced in short, limited attacks, the troops firing in volleys and then rushing forward from trench line to trench line. It was almost a textbook operation, demonstrating both the Volunteers' high morale and the soundness of the U.S. Army's tactics.[16]

Thus by the end of the day, MacArthur's division had broken through the main Army of Liberation line of defense and captured the high ridgeline north of Manila. Although some units, particularly the 3rd Artillery, sustained comparatively heavy casualties, the troops were in good spirits. Their discipline, marksmanship, and aggressiveness had surprised their officers and the enemy, and they eagerly awaited the next day.

Along the southern lines, Anderson, believing he faced imminent attack, requested Otis's permission to send the entire 1st Division in a preemptive strike at first light. He had been well briefed by a thorough reconnaissance by Capt. William G. Haan, which showed that the Army of Liberation positions on his left hinged on strongpoints in the suburbs of Santa Ana and Pandacan, a small islet in the Pasig River. Anderson wanted to send King's brigade to attack the enemy positions in echelon, sweeping south to north from the Manila–Laguna de Bay road and trapping them against the Pasig. Ovenshine's 2nd Brigade would move into the suburb of Malate, driving the enemy back, and then wheel left and sweep down the front to King's brigade, turning the entire flank. Four 3.2-inch guns and a four-company battalion of the 1st California under Col. James F. Smith were dispatched to Battery Knoll on King's right flank; a battalion of Wyoming Volunteers was sent to the juncture of the two brigades, where it could reinforce either one. The troops moved through the dark to their preassigned positions on the firing line.

Shortly before 8:00 A.M., satisfied that the northern lines would hold and that Manila was calm, Otis gave permission for Anderson to attack. As artillery shells blasted the Filipino positions, King's brigade of Washington, California, and Idaho regiments crossed Concordia Creek with cheers and volley fire. Their general rode with them, resplendent in a full-dress uniform and smoking a cigar. The Filipinos' return fire revealed their positions to the American artillery, while their tendency to fire high encouraged the attackers by making it safer in the front than at the rear. On the far left along the Pasig, soldiers took cover behind stone walls, cemetery stones, and paddy dikes until stopped by heavy fire from the huge earthworks at the estuary at Pandacan. Supported by enfilading volleys from the Californians, the Idaho regiment launched a headlong assault up the earthworks, driving the defenders back. The commanding officer, Brig. Gen. Pio de Pilar, had been so confident that he had not bothered to plan a retreat route. Now his troops paid for his arrogance. They fled down the banks into the Pasig River, where dozens were drowned or shot.[17]

To the right, as Smith wheeled his 1st California to assault the strongpoint at Santa Ana, he was attacked on his right flank. The Californians should have been covered by a battalion of the 1st Wyoming, but it had been delayed, and for a short time the situation was critical. Showing commendable coolness—and also the discipline of his citizen soldiers—Smith shifted a company to meet the attack; aided by Haan's engineers, they held on until the Wyoming troops arrived. Smith then resumed the assault on the insurgent redoubts at Santa Ana. Their opponents fought desperately and "fell where they fought, filling the trenches with an unbroken line of killed and wounded," but the Volunteers would not be stopped; they swarmed over the fortifications and swept into Santa Ana.[18] The Wyoming troops somewhat redeemed their tardy arrival by pushing the Filipinos out of their fallback position at San Pedro Makati.

At the extreme south of King's brigade, Lt. Col. Victor Duboce and four companies of the 1st California deployed to support the 1st Washington's attack on Blockhouse 11. They immediately encountered heavy sniper fire from Paco, inciting King to order all buildings suspected of sheltering Filipino riflemen put to the torch—an order interpreted to mean virtually every house in the vicinity. The Filipinos defended with great tenacity and often had to be rooted out house by house. For two hours a fight raged at close range, soldiers blasting away at each other before closing with knives and bayonets. Riflemen swept the streets with accurate musketry from the tower and stone walls of Paco Church, even after artillery set it on fire. Only after the attackers torched the entire building did the defenders withdraw.[19]

So far King's attack had worked almost to perfection, but now things unraveled: his victorious regiments, charging after their retreating enemy, began to lose all cohesion. Companies and battalions broke apart, separated by burning houses and rice fields, or because junior officers persisted in attacking wherever they encountered resistance. The battle became a series of small and increasingly disconnected actions. Smith's Californians pursued their fleeing enemies up the Pasig River; for hours no one knew where they were. By noon, King's brigade was scattered, disorganized, and dangerously exposed; fortunately, its opponents were incapable of counterattack.[20]

Anderson's plan had called for Ovenshine's 2nd Brigade to wait for King's attack, then to advance along its entire front and, after driving the Army of Liberation forces back, to turn left and sweep down the front, pinching the

Filipinos between the two brigades. After an artillery barrage from the 6th Artillery and the heavy ten-inch guns of the *Monadnock* had softened up the defenders, the advance would be led by the 1st North Dakota under Lt. Col. William C. Treumann, supported by nine companies of the 14 Infantry under Maj. Carrol H. Potter and three dismounted troops of the 4th Cavalry.

At 7:00 A.M., the 14th advanced 1,000 yards and occupied the old Spanish defense line. For the next three hours, the brigade remained in its trenches, trading shots with Filipino marksmen and watching the heavy shells from the warships' guns throw up geysers of smoke and dirt. Shortly after 10:00 the North Dakotans launched a brief foray that swept away many of the snipers and drove them off. Captain John Murphy, with two companies, attacked over the marshy ground against an enemy blockhouse as Potter's battalion supported it on the right. The Filipinos met the charge with a fierce barrage of riflery. Leading a desperate attack, Lt. Perry L. Miles and six soldiers managed to fight their way into the flaming blockhouse and drive the defenders out. The charge on the blockhouse cost the 14th Infantry eight killed and eighteen wounded.[21] The Regulars pushed on into a morass broken by dense thickets of scrub wood and bamboo as enemy marksmen raked them from entrenchments and treetops on their left flank. Captain Fred Wheeler's nine-company task force should have cleared this area; but, stopped fifty yards short of the enemy trenches, Wheeler inexplicably ordered the men back. The North Dakotans waited for orders to move forward in support—orders that never arrived.

The confusion on the right wing was due to a variety of factors, most of which stemmed from the 8th Corps' poor communications and staff work. Although Anderson later claimed to have sent numerous telegrams and couriers urging Ovenshine to advance, his actual orders were ambiguous: "Use your own judgment, the div. comdr. [Anderson] can only advise."[22] For his part, Ovenshine was a passive spectator: he claimed that Lt. Col. Enoch Crowder, a high-ranking member of Otis's staff, had directed him to delay his attack until the 14th was clear of the brush. Believing himself under Otis's direct command, he disregarded Anderson's instructions to move forward. Only when Crowder finally reappeared and clarified the situation did Ovenshine begin his attack. In the meantime, the Regulars had been subjected to a long and costly cross fire.

By 1:30 P.M., matters had finally been sorted out both at Ovenshine's headquarters and at the front. Major Louis H. Rucker arrived and relieved the shaken Wheeler, then sent the command forward to clear the left flank. At the same time, the 1st North Dakota charged the Filipinos on the right.

These two attacks allowed the exhausted 14th Infantry to break through the thickets and drive the enemy back, occupy the village of Pasay, and then turn left. A battalion of the 1st Tennessee arrived just as the North Dakotans broke through and opened up on the fleeing insurgents. With his front cleared, Ovenshine linked up with King's brigade near San Pedro Makati.[23]

The battle of 5 February was the biggest of the entire Philippine War. Fought along a sixteen-mile front, it involved all or part of thirteen regiments and thousands of Filipinos. It was also the bloodiest battle of the war: American casualties totaled 238, of whom 44 were killed in action or died of wounds; almost half these fatalities were in the two Regular regiments, the 14th Infantry and 3rd Artillery. The more impetuous Volunteers had far fewer casualties. Filipino losses can only be estimated. Anderson claimed his division buried 238 in trenches and took 306 prisoners. The army's official report listed total Army of Liberation casualties as 4,000, of whom 700 were killed, but this is guesswork.[24]

When news of the fighting reached the United States, anti-imperialists immediately charged that the 8th Corps had attacked the Filipinos in a blatant effort to force Congress to pass the treaty with Spain and confirm Philippine annexation. Aguinaldo ordered a full investigation, which concluded the Americans had deliberately provoked the battle.[25] At congressional hear-

Insurgent entrenchments, 1899

ings in 1902, Senator Thomas Patterson grilled MacArthur relentlessly, trying to force an admission that his troops had initiated hostilities without just cause. MacArthur, who was as vain as he was politically obtuse, provided some support to such conjecture by boasting that the entire battle followed his "prearranged plans."[26] Later critics have also hinted strongly at conspiracy. Filipino historian Carlos Quirino maintains, "Obviously the Americans . . . started the war."[27] Stuart Miller goes even further, claiming through a tortuous circumstantial argument that "a series of orders and maneuvers by Otis during the final three weeks of peace . . . indicate that he may have planned and provoked the war."[28]

In turn, Secretary of War Elihu Root spoke for both Washington and the army when he declared, "Our forces were attacked by the Tagalogs, who attempted to capture the city."[29] The officers on the scene were also insistent that their opponents had made the first move. Dewey noted in his diary on 5 February that "the insurgents made a general attack on the Army last night."[30] Otis absolved Aguinaldo of a premeditated attack but stoutly insisted that "war with the insurgents of the Philippines was forced on us and was unavoidable."[31] Taking a page from the anti-imperialists' book, the partisan *Army and Navy Journal* accused the Filipinos of starting the war to "influence the Senate against a treaty which drew upon us the responsibility for preserving order in a country which they could show to be in a state of disturbance."[32] Some Filipino sources support this: Juan Luna, brother of Antonio Luna, stated that many in Aguinaldo's cabinet believed it better to go to war immediately before American reinforcements arrived, and Benito Legarda, a prominent Filipino statesman, wrote Aguinaldo blaming the "war element" in Malolos.[33]

Despite a great deal of heat and conjecture, there is no strong evidence that the initiation of fighting was the result of a conspiracy or even premeditation on either side, and much to indicate the contrary. Aguinaldo certainly did not want the war to begin on 4 February. If so, he would scarcely have left to attend a ball in Malolos or allowed so many of his officers to be absent for the weekend. Moreover, his plan for liberating Manila hinged on his ability to launch an attack on the 8th Corps' positions simultaneously with an uprising by his partisans in the city; and he had not yet infiltrated sufficient troops or weapons. Aguinaldo can, however, be faulted for failing to control his overly bellicose subordinates, for not ensuring they recognized the importance of coordinating their attacks with the insurgents within the city, and for making no effort to stop the fighting until his forces had been badly mauled. Apolinario Mabini, who headed Aguinaldo's cabinet, later criticized him for concentrating all military decision-making power in his hands, and then ignoring the army. As a result, the Army of Liberation was unprepared for battle, and its command system broke down almost immediately. Although individual Filipino soldiers fought with impressive courage— standing their ground until their trenches were clogged with dead—the Army of Liberation functioned not as an army but as a collection of discrete, uncoordinated, and unsupported units.[34]

On the American side, there is equally little evidence of a conspiracy. On a practical level, there were excellent reasons for Otis to avoid initiating a battle, not least that he was expecting 4,000 reinforcements—a 40 percent increase in his combat strength—within a few weeks. All indications are that the firefight of 4 February was unplanned, a random occurrence. Had Grayson's small patrol gone out a few minutes earlier or later, it may have well avoided running into the Filipino patrol altogether. Stotsenburg's reaction clearly shows that far from provoking a battle, he believed he was being attacked and stood on the defensive. A similar belief guided the other colonels along the northern front, who moved up troops to protect their outposts but did not cross the lines. MacArthur's claim that, on hearing of Grayson's skirmish, "I simply wired all commanders to carry out prearranged plans and the whole division was placed on the line" is self-serving hyperbole.[35] Rather, the 2nd Division's regimental and company commanders operated virtually independently, with neither instructions nor support from MacArthur. Indeed, it appears that the 8th Corps' high command was completely unprepared. Otis and Hughes were playing billiards, MacArthur and his staff were playing cards, and most senior officers were absent from their commands. A similar state of unpreparedness existed throughout the 2nd Division: when the fighting broke out, the officers of the 1st Colorado were in their dress whites playing whist.[36]

War was emphatically not desired in Washington. The news, which did not arrive until after the battle was over, stunned the administration, which believed that the situation in Manila was cooling and that the Philippine Republic would avoid conflict until the Filipinos could negotiate with the presidential commission, which was soon to arrive in the islands. The argument that the army, perhaps at McKinley's instigation, began the war to ensure the passage of the Treaty of Paris does not stand up to examination. There is no indication that the outbreak of fighting encouraged the Senate to approve annexation; indeed, the *New York Times* believed that it had led some to vote against acquiring the islands.[37]

Thus the worst charge against the Americans is that they accepted too readily the idea that the confused skirmishing on the night of 4–5 February was the long-anticipated Filipino assault, and moved onto the offensive prematurely. Even accepting this argument, there is little indication that had Grayson's patrol missed the Filipino detachment, or had Otis not attacked the next day, the Philippine War could somehow have been averted. As Hughes's diary shows, the Fil-American negotiations were going nowhere; the two sides were simply too far apart to make any meaningful concessions. Confrontations had been becoming more common and more serious; as the experience of Grayson's patrol shows, it took only one incident to initiate fighting. Finally, it is likely that had war somehow been averted on 4 February, the outcome would have been not peace but an even bloodier conflict. Aguinaldo's plan called for both an attack and an uprising in the city, and what casualties might have resulted from such all-out warfare—with soldiers fighting not only an enemy in front but also thousands of armed civilians in their rear—can only be guessed at.

The offensive of 5 February had taken Anderson's two brigades far beyond their ability to support each other. Ovenshine's brigade was roughly where it should have been at San Pedro Makati, but King's was spread over a seven-mile front to the left and still pushing farther away; on 9 February an expedition by Smith and his 1st California accepted the surrender of the towns of Pasig and Pateros, placing troops fully ten miles southeast of Manila, almost to Laguna de Bay. Despite the absence of organized resistance, the southern front was porous and unstable: Filipino soldiers, to whom Anderson contemptuously referred as "bushwhackers," routinely slipped through and made the area behind the lines no safer than at the front.[38] Otis decided to cut his losses and withdraw: the northern push to Malolos desperately needed troops, and captured orders showed Aguinaldo was planning an uprising in Manila.

On 16 February the three regiments in King's brigade began pulling back. Encouraged by what they took to be a retreat, the Filipinos began firing from brush, ravines, and across the river. Then whole companies and squads appeared, drawn up in parade formation, each man with a uniform, officers on horseback, buglers blowing, and flags flying. They marched forward in good order into oblivion: the Volunteers let them approach and then shredded their lines with Springfield fire. King, who appears to have missed the whole point of the withdrawal, kept Duboce with four companies of the 1st California and two of the 1st Idaho for two full days at Guadalupe under constant sniping and threats of attack before finally recalling them. On the way out they burned the church to prevent its use by the enemy.[39] The Filipinos followed, still convinced that what they were observing was the flight of a defeated army. On the nineteenth there were sharp fights at Pasig town and San Pedro Makati that lasted all morning. The 1st California and 1st

Washington, firing from behind their trenches, inflicted terrible casualties, assisted by the gunboat *Laguna de Bay*, its four Gatling guns "wreaking havoc" on enemy forces on both sides of river.[40] Although now manning a defensive line running from Fort Malate through San Pedro Makati to Santa Ana, the 1st Division continued to launch expeditions out from its lines to clear out snipers and break up enemy concentrations. The southern front was stable, but far from inactive, and Anderson continually pushed for more troops to go on the offensive again.[41]

On the northern front the Americans achieved a signal success on 6 February with the capture of the waterworks at Marikina. This operation appears to have been largely the initiative of Stotsenburg, who recognized the importance of securing Manila's water supply, and guessed that the Army of Liberation would soon fortify the hills around the waterworks. On 5 February he was denied two companies to assist an attack, but he obtained a promise from Otis's chief of staff to send two battalions the next day. However, on 6 February the battalions failed to arrive. Stotsenburg waited and fumed while Army of Liberation forces moved forward, dug in, and began firing on his exposed Nebraskans. At 10:00 A.M., after receiving a note informing him that the reinforcements would not be coming, Stotsenburg took it upon himself to attack, arranging for support from the 1st Colorado. Covering fire was provided by the Utah Battery's two reliable 3.2-inch cannon and two captured Nordenfelt mountain guns, the artillerymen firing a few rounds, then dragging their guns up the road. The Colorado and Tennessee troops joined in the assault, which now stretched out for almost four miles. Sweeping forward in a series of rushes, the Volunteers took hill after hill, trench after trench. The Filipinos fought bravely but could not deal with the accurate riflery from their front and flanks. Seizing a hill overlooking the waterworks, the Americans took cover behind a water pipe and called down artillery on the enemy positions. Charging into the pumping station, they found the machinery dismantled, but a quick search located the missing parts hidden in a coal pile. The pumps were soon put into order and running smoothly; Manila now had a secure supply of water, and the army could continue using the capital as a showpiece for benevolent assimilation. The failure of the defenders to destroy this vital installation was a serious blunder.[42]

Pushed out of its strong position on the Santa Mesa Ridge line, the Army of Liberation re-formed at Caloocan. Twelve miles from Manila, on the extreme left of the American line, this important railroad center also barred the way to Malolos. MacArthur wished an immediate attack, swinging his 2nd Division in a giant right hook. Otis approved the plan but urged MacArthur to delay a few days, not only to permit him to shift reinforcements from the south but also to allow the Filipinos enough time to concentrate their forces into the Caloocan pocket. MacArthur's offensive would then serve the dual purpose of taking Caloocan and trapping the Army of Liberation against Manila Bay. But the continued fighting in the south and the threat of uprising in Manila limited Otis's options, and he could reinforce MacArthur with only the 1st Wyoming and three companies of the 4th Cavalry.

On 10 February MacArthur went on the offensive. Dewey provided naval gun support in the form of the cruiser *Charleston* and the monitor *Monadnock*. Their heavy guns were joined those of the Utah Battery and the 6th Artillery. For almost three hours they blasted the Filipino redoubts. Then at 4:00 P.M. Harrison G. Otis's 1st Brigade charged forward. The 20th Kansas moved along the Manila Bay coast through the woods in front of Caloocan as the 3rd Artillery and 1st Montana made a flanking attack from the right. The black powder from the cannons and Springfield rifles covered the area with smoke. The soldiers became more and more enthusiastic as they realized they were taking few losses: the defenders were firing high, and it was actually safer to advance. No longer worrying about covering fire, the troops began rushing forward, stopping to fire a few rounds, then sprinting again toward the trenches. As the 20th Kansas approached from the front, the flank attack by the 3rd Artillery and 1st Montana closed in as well. The final blow was delivered by Maj. J. Franklin Bell and a company of the 1st Montana, which slipped into town from the east and opened fire on the enemy rear. Convinced they were trapped, the insurgents panicked, many of them dropping their weapons in their anxiety to escape. The Kansans poured over the corpse-filled trenches and charged into the burning town. The defenders made a last stand at the church, where there was a short, vicious fight, before they broke and fled. Caught up in the excitement, an officer yelled "On to Malolos!" and the soldiers raced after the fleeing enemy until furious staff officers managed to head them back.[43]

The capture of Caloocan gave the 8th Corps control of the southern terminus of the Manila-Dagupan Railroad and also secured five engines, fifty passenger coaches, and a hundred freight cars. It dealt another devastating blow to the Army of Liberation, which once again had failed to hold field fortifications against troops attacking over open ground. Yet the 8th Corps did not deliver the coup de grace; the Army of Liberation survived to fight another day.

The abortive defense of Caloocan marked the end of a week of repeated and punishing Filipino defeats. Aguinaldo's response indicates his confusion both over the causes and over the necessary countermeasures to avoid them in the future. Perhaps influenced by Luna, now placed in charge of the Army of Liberation, the president made yet another effort to reorganize it along European lines.[44] But he also mandated that throughout the archipelago all males aged sixteen to fifty-nine must join the militia and equip themselves with bolos. Equally important, Aguinaldo established a guerrilla organization based on the towns and villages. Each municipal government would serve as a committee of defense, and civic officials were now given the duties of military chiefs.[45] These two decrees show the hybrid nature of Aguinaldo's military thought: at the same time he sought to centralize power in a conventional army, he established a decentralized guerrilla organization in the provinces.

With the American lines now between three and six miles from Manila's center, Hughes and the Manila Provost Guard—the 2nd Oregon, 13th Minnesota, 23rd Infantry, and a small artillery battery—were torn between twin responsibilities. Anderson and MacArthur continually attempted to co-opt them for field operations, and their primary task, to maintain order in the capital, was becoming more difficult. Conditions in Manila had so deteriorated since 5 February that troops found the city and its suburbs almost as hazardous as the front lines. Sentries and individual soldiers were attacked by knife-wielding assailants, snipers fired into troops moving about the city, buildings were torched, and standing orders confined soldiers to their bar-

Street fighting in Manila, February 1899

racks. A growing body of evidence pointed to an insurrection within the city that would coincide with an offensive by the Army of Liberation.[46]

On 9 February American suspicions were confirmed by a captured document attributed to Antonio Luna, dated two days earlier, which called for the city's militia to rise and wage "war without quarter." Upon word of the correct date, they would seize control of the outlying suburbs and join the Army of Liberation's attack. Servants were to burn their employers' houses, and all non-Filipinos would be "exterminated." The liberation of Manila would show "foreign countries that America is not capable of maintaining order or defending any of the interests which she has undertaken to defend."[47] If Luna sincerely believed this irresponsible invitation to arson and slaughter would further the cause of independence, he was woefully mistaken. The McKinley administration gave the proclamation wide publicity as evidence of the Filipinos' savagery and inability to govern themselves.

By late February a crisis atmosphere gripped Manila. Learning that a revolt was planned on the evening of the fifteenth, Hughes sent the Provost Guard into the streets to arrest over 100 prominent revolutionary sympathizers. On the twentieth much of the suburb of Paco was burned, apparently because a clandestine gunpowder factory exploded. The flames were brought under control, only to reignite. Hughes soon discovered that this second fire had been set by soldiers: "I am very much ashamed to be a part of this mob of ours but as we are missionaries it is all right. Nothing but fire and sword will make any impression on these people."[48] Such comments indicate both the chagrin that experienced soldiers felt at the callousness and destructiveness of their comrades and their growing frustration at the stubbornness of Filipino resistance.

At 9:00 P.M. on 22 February a fire broke out in a brothel in the Santa Cruz district. The local firefighters either sympathized with the arsonists or feared retaliation, and only the arrival of the city's European volunteer units prevented a conflagration. Even so, the Provost Guard had to use some force to stop rioters from cutting the hoses. The fire at Santa Cruz was no sooner brought under control than a new one broke out in the northern suburb of Tondo next to Manila Bay. Firefighters were confronted by 500 insurgents, who had infiltrated from the north and barricaded the streets and houses, thus putting themselves between the city and MacArthur's division. The sole provost detachments in the Tondo suburb, two 13th Minnesota companies, came under heavy attack until relieved by two companies each of the 2nd Oregon and 23rd Infantry. As the troops lined up on the road separating Manila from Tondo, thousands of panic-stricken refugees rushed past them, while in front the nipa palm roofs flared into towers of flame and bamboo timbers exploded with a noise uncannily like rifle shots. To compound the chaos, shortly after midnight arsonists fired the market in the Chinese suburb of Binondo, less than 100 yards away, setting off a new rush of refugees and more sniping. By now Manila's firemen had either fled or their equipment was too damaged for use. To an observer watching from MacArthur's headquarters, it looked as if the entire city was in flames.[49] But the fire confined itself to a few districts, and by morning most of it had burned out.

Luna's plan had called for the outbreak to coincide with the Army of Liberation's attack on MacArthur's lines at Caloocan so as to join the Manila militia in the city. But for reasons that are still unexplained, beyond some desultory skirmishing there was little fighting in the north. What makes the episode even more curious is Luna's claim that his troops fought their way into Manila but then had to retreat because a battalion from Aguinaldo's home province of Cavite refused to advance.[50] If this implausible story was true—that a general offensive was stopped simply because four companies failed to participate—it speaks volumes for both Luna's generalship and the disorganization in his army. For whatever reason, the passivity of the Army of Liberation is another of the mysteries of the war, and yet another opportunity squandered by the nationalist leaders.

Early in the morning of 23 February, the Provost Guard began to mop up resistance in Manila. Their chief problem was Tondo, where some 150 soldiers and militia had constructed a stone breastwork in front of the bridge. With swamp on both sides and snipers concealed in the surrounding huts, both the barrier and the bridge were formidable obstacles. The Americans could not use artillery for fear of shooting into MacArthur's 2nd Division to the north. Hughes gave Maj. Greenleaf A. Goodale three companies each of the 13th Minnesota and 2nd Oregon, and two each of the 23rd and 4th Cavalry to clear out the Tondo pocket. The mood of the troops may be imagined; they had been up all night fighting fires and snipers, expecting at any minute to find themselves under attack by the entire population. Goodale sent sharpshooters forward, who soon were engaged in a heavy firefight, forcing him to order the houses that sheltered the snipers burned. Forming his troops into three columns, he directed the 2nd Oregon to take the stone barricade. A desperate firefight ensued, both sides blasting away at each other at close range, until the sharpshooters worked their way to the flanks and poured in an enfilading fire. The defenders fell back, and Goodale's column leapfrogged its way over the bridge. Resistance collapsed, many of the enemy fleeing down the burned-out streets to the coastal road, where the gunboat *Callao* sprayed them with machine-gun fire. Goodale later estimated that as many as half the defenders were killed. Perhaps even more would have been shot down, but the pursuers were impeded by hundreds of panic-stricken civilians who grabbed them, begging for mercy.[51]

In retrospect, Hughes's preparations, the efficiency and courage of the Provost Guard, and the skills of some of the firemen made the danger appear much less than it was. But the insurrection of 22–23 February had been a very near thing. By 1:00 A.M. there was virtually no fire-fighting equipment left; had the fires spread, the entire city might have burned down. The Guard had been virtually unaided; indeed, Hughes criticized MacArthur's failure not only to guard his lines against infiltration but even to clear out the enemy forces in his rear.[52]

For Aguinaldo and the Philippine Republic, the Manila revolt was another botched opportunity. The uprising resulted in the destruction of thousands of homes and the deaths of several dozen Filipino soldiers, and perhaps even more civilians, but it accomplished nothing. In spite of Luna's boast that "all the Filipinos in Manila will second us. May the blood of the traitors run in torrents," the general population did not join the insurrection.[53] There was a great deal of looting and some gratuitous arson, but by and large the city's residents were terrified by the flames and shooting and fled into the American-controlled sectors. Although the case cannot be demonstrated, it is very likely that the ease with which Hughes smashed the remaining revolutionary organizations in the city—as well as the relative quiet that followed—was due to the distaste of Manileros for further involvement in revolutionary schemes.

The uprising also marked the end of what might be termed the Second Battle of Manila, which began on the evening of 4 February in a confused clash between two small patrols and ended on 23 February with a vicious street fight and the destruction of much of the city's northern suburbs. The two-week battle had momentous consequences. Never again would Aguinaldo and the Army of Liberation have such an opportunity to inflict a decisive defeat upon the invaders, or to do so at such an opportune time. Had the 8th Corps been driven out of Manila, or even besieged in Intramuros, both the military and political results would have been incalculable. It is quite possible that such a defeat would have been followed by a face-saving peace and withdrawal. Had the 8th Corps taken severe casualties and its troops been demoralized, the ultimate result may well have been the same. But instead, it was the Filipinos who were defeated and demoralized.

The completeness of the U.S. Army's victory has led historians to dismiss it as an unequal, almost unfair, encounter. But so it appears only in retrospect. At the start of the battle Aguinaldo and his supporters stood at the peak of their powers. Almost all officers and many of the soldiers in the Army of Liberation were veterans of months, if not years, of fighting against the Spanish; now they were strengthened by a number of former Spanish soldiers. Troop morale, after the string of victories and the failure of the 8th Corps to respond, was very high. They even had a slight weapons superiority—their captured Mausers outranged the Volunteers' Springfields. Finally, the insurgents could easily infiltrate troops to reinforce their sizable contingent of supporters in Manila and strike the Americans from the front and rear. With almost half a year to prepare for a showdown with the 8th Corps, to develop defensive positions, to train troops, to devise a coherent defense, to implement effective tactics, the Army of Liberation should have performed much better than it did. Indeed, it should have been able to deliver a salutary defeat upon the inexperienced 8th Corps, or at least inflict enough casualties to cripple it for further offensive operations.

The Army of Liberation's defeat was the result of a variety of factors. Their leadership, where there was any, surrendered the initiative at the beginning and failed to capitalize on the numerous American mistakes. Poor planning and logistics led to storing irreplaceable rifles, cannon, ammunition, and supplies close to the lines, where they were quickly captured. These losses, particularly on the southern front, crippled many units and prevented a counterattack, thus allowing the 8th Corps time to consolidate its gains. The army consistently proved incapable of maneuvering; units failed to support each other or to counterattack. Time and time again the Americans charged across open ground against prepared defenses and captured them— tactics that should have been suicidal. Part of this was due to appalling marksmanship, to a lack of weapons, and to defective ammunition. But the disparity of armament does not explain the scope of the defeat. There was no lack of courage and determination in the Army of Liberation. Its soldiers fought with conspicuous bravery and fortitude, as the gory pictures of corpse-strewn trenches attest. But it suffered from a lack of trust and coherence. Too often the sight of one unit giving way led to the others' withdrawal, and this made them especially vulnerable to flank attacks.

The battle had profound effects on Filipino morale. The enemy's marksmanship, mobility, "impetuous charges," and "flanking movements were new to them and filled them with terror."[54] Meeting Luna on 5 February, Col. Jose Alejandrino was astonished to see how "morally and physically crestfallen" he was. Luna bluntly told him, "Our enemies are too strong and superior in means"; if another such attack was launched, the entire army would run away and disband.[55] In a pathetic admission of the depths of the problem, Aguinaldo's 14 February "Instructions for Generals" began, "As our soldiers frequently retreat while in action . . ."[56] He later told MacArthur that at the outset of fighting the soldiers of the Army of Liberation were confident and kept up a heavy fire as their enemies drew close, but "the American lines continued to advance and no men fell. Our men became alarmed at the fact that the American troops seemed to be invincible." MacArthur himself concluded that the Filipino soldiers "never entirely recovered" from this experience.[57] The battle left a deep legacy of mistrust and antipathy among the high command. Luna reportedly threatened to resign over the misbehavior of the troops, and Mabini claimed Aguinaldo's "policy of softness" had contributed greatly to indiscipline: "a military dictatorship is very necessary, . . . in order to repress the abuses of the army, which can only be done by the chief."[58]

In contrast, the battle demonstrated that the 8th Corps was a tough, aggressive, and capable force. Much to the surprise of Regular officers, the Volunteers proved themselves courageous and efficient fighters. Anderson commented that inexperienced troops were usually shaken by flank fire, but despite receiving fire from all directions, the Volunteers displayed "coolness, energy, bravery and élan."[59] Indeed, based on the high casualties taken by the 3rd Artillery and 14th Infantry in confused attacks into the brush, a good case can be made that the Volunteers were the more effective. Their ability to move through swamps, shrub, grassland, and rice paddies, to take redoubt and trenches, to operate in terrain pocked with thorns, bamboo, and mud holes—all impressed both correspondents and the Filipino forces. Their marksmanship was deadly: the much-despised Springfield did fearsome execution at close range; the "ghastly holes" it inflicted further demoralized their opponents.[60] The artillery also performed well, though severely hampered by a lack of transport; the Utah Battery had to drag its guns by hand. Their performance, and the ease of victory, filled the 8th Corps with complete, even foolish, confidence. Morale, always high—some soldiers even checked out of the hospital in order to participate in the battle—soared even higher. In the words of one Wyoming Volunteer: "I would not have missed the fight we had on the 5th of Feb for a thousand dollars it was grate [sic] to see the natives run."[61]

The 8th Corps' problems were largely related to command and discipline. At the top, Otis deserves much credit for developing a workable operational plan. Even the usually hostile correspondent John Bass conceded the general had shown considerable military ability and had mastered the situation.[62] But his division and brigade commanders had great difficulty restraining their eager subordinates, and in some cases themselves. Aggressive to the point of foolishness, American officers repeatedly sent their men in frontal assaults against entrenched opponents. Had their enemies' skill matched their courage, the results would have been catastrophic.

A more ominous development was clear evidence of troop misconduct, brutality, criminal activity, and atrocities. Some incidents could be justified as military necessity—as when Paco Church was burned to clear out snipers and open up fields of fire. But soldiers were so quick to apply the torch that even a hardened veteran like Hughes commented, "It is not our usual way of making war."[63] He was also shocked at "the amount of robbery and looting done by these rowdy troops. . . . They would steal the sandals of a native who had died of small pox."[64] Even more disturbing were reports that soldiers were firing indiscriminately and killing civilians and prisoners. This insinuation surfaced a few days after the battle in the *Manila American*. Although veterans indignantly denied the charge and Anderson demanded an investigation, it was a harbinger of later, stronger accusations.[65] Even as they disparaged the press reports, soldiers eagerly repeated grisly tales with scant regard for veracity, or even plausibility: thus a private of the 51st Iowa wrote that in one day the 14th Infantry had killed 1,200 Filipinos, more than the entire U.S. Army claimed.[66] Such fantastic stories aside, it is clear that soldiers were less than ready to accept surrenders and shot some prisoners. For their part, the Americans accused their opponents of shooting at ambulances, litter bearers, Red Cross workers, and the wounded; of continuing to fire after raising a white flag; and of torturing a wounded doctor to death. According to one eyewitness, after finding the doctor's body, the troops moved on, "feeling that we would have no pity for the savages who finished off our wounded in this barbarous way."[67]

The Second Battle of Manila was thus both a decisive victory and a harbinger of things to come. The 8th Corps was clearly superior on the battlefield, and the Army of Liberation's efforts to meet it there had been disastrous. The obvious question—of primary concern in both Manila and Washington—was whether Aguinaldo and his generals would continue to pursue this ruinous strategy. At the very same time he forwarded news of the great victory of 5 February, a reporter commented: "War Department officials say that the only cause for apprehension is the fear that the Filipinos may take to the interior of the country, practically impassable for American troops in the approaching rainy season, and that a prolonged Indian-fighting style of campaign may follow."[68] Such fears would prove all too well founded in the coming months.

FOUR

THE VISAYAS

As the U.S. Army and the Army of Liberation battled for control of Manila, the war expanded to engulf the south. Fixated on Luzon, later historians have overlooked these Visayan conflicts. But to the American officers who served in the boondocks, the war in the provinces was crucial. Convinced they faced unpopular and imported revolutionary movements, they saw the southern Philippines as a theater where the army could, with relatively little commitment of forces, demonstrate to millions the benefits of United States rule.[1]

The outbreak of war in Manila ended the long and hostile stalemate between Miller's brigade and the revolutionary government in Iloilo City. Tempers had been increasingly frayed, and provocations occurred almost daily. Within the city, relations among the insurgents were almost as tense. From Malolos, Aguinaldo and Mabini demanded that the Panay revolutionaries reorganize according to the 18 June 1898 directive, which would not only bring it under the Philippine Republic's political control but, even more important, require the collection and transmission of the taxes formerly collected by the Spanish. Although proclaiming their loyalty to the Republic, Panay's Federal State of the Visayas steadfastly refused to reorganize, or to accept the authority of Aguinaldo's appointee, Ananias Diocno.[2] They would keep their own government, their own taxes, and their own general, Martin Delgado.

Beyond their unwillingness to subordinate their interests to the Republic, there was little consensus among the Ilongo rebels. Delgado recognized that Iloilo City was indefensible and advocated an immediate withdrawal across the Iloilo River to the nearby towns of Jaro and Molo. But some of his officers wanted to remain and fight, and others wanted to burn the city at the first sign of a landing. For their part, many townspeople, including several members of the revolutionary government, urged that there be no resistance at all. Unable to agree on tactics, the revolutionaries continued both to build fortifications and to store hemp, pine oil, and other combustibles throughout the town.[3]

Watching these preparations, and aware of the contention, Miller urged he be allowed to attack before it was too late: "Delay only increases their determination to resist the United States by force. . . . the quicker the battle

Elwell S. Otis, ca. 1890

comes here, the better it will be."[4] Once he had smashed the revolutionary forces, the situation in the Visayas would be quickly resolved: "I am well satisfied that a great proportion of the inhabitants of Panay, Negros, and Cebu are favorable to our occupation at once."[5] All he required was more troops: the unhappy 51st Iowa had returned to Manila, leaving him only the two battalions of Col. David A. Van Valzeh's 18th Infantry and the Provisional Machine Gun Battery.

On 8 February Miller heard the "good news from Manila": war had broken out and he was to occupy Iloilo as soon as Col. Gracey Childers's 1st Tennessee regiment arrived.[6] Dewey had assured the full cooperation of the small naval squadron under Capt. Frank F. Wilde. Two days later, Miller notified the Federal State of his intention to occupy Iloilo the next day and requested it to order all noncombatants out of the city. The Americans would allow boats to go freely in and out of the port throughout 11 February, but by sunset all armed forces must surrender. Miller concluded with a warning that any effort to close the Iloilo River, improve the defenses, or resist the landing would provoke immediate naval bombardment. Privately, he notified the foreign consuls that he would not land until the twelfth. The general's preparations suggest a sincere effort to ensure an uncontested landing, in keeping with Otis's orders to avoid unnecessary bloodshed and destruction.[7]

On Saturday morning, 11 February, the soldiers prepared to land on the following day. Most were hard at work coaling the transports' bunkers and moving supplies when, a little after 8:30, they heard the boom of artillery across the water. Commander Charles F. Cornwell on the *Petrel* had spotted men working on the earthworks and opened fire. By 9:30 the *Petrel* was firing into Iloilo City, joined by the heavy six- and eight-inch guns of the cruiser *Boston*. Squadron commander Wilde signaled Miller to begin landing, and shortly afterward, on his own initiative, sent seventy-six sailors and marines ashore. By this time much of the town was already on fire, and the flames were spreading rapidly.[8]

Wilde's preemptive action frustrated Miller's plan for an orderly landing, and the Americans went ashore in uncoordinated waves. The first of these, Wilde's small force, landed shortly after 11:00 A.M., entered a deserted fort at the peninsula's tip, and raised the Stars and Stripes. Some of the landing party remained in the fort, while the rest patrolled the waterfront. The army landings did not go as smoothly. The transport that held the 18th Infantry was coaling up, and Van Valzeh insisted on finishing the job before he disembarked his regiment. As a result, ninety minutes elapsed before the Tennessee Volunteers and a battalion of the 18th splashed ashore. Operating in an unknown city, subject to incessant sniper fire from across the river, and battling smoke and flames, the troops struggled through the streets. Four companies of the 1st Tennessee under Lt. Col. Benjamin F. Cheatham managed to work their way to the Jaro Bridge and close off the main landward entrance to the city. Another Tennessee battalion broke through an enemy trench line and took the estuary bridge to Molo. Other soldiers turned to fighting fires and clearing out nests of snipers. By nightfall, Iloilo City was a blackened ruin, but a ruin in American hands.[9]

Accusations flew, at the time and later, that the navy's bombardment set fire to Iloilo and that soldiers continued the burning. However, both the army and the navy claimed the city was fired by the defenders, who had been storing combustibles for weeks. There is support for both views. Army field reports refer to the invaders burning shacks to clear out snipers, but one soldier commented, "Those Gun boats of ours did most of this, and I must say they are the most cruel things in existence."[10] It is also true that the defenders torched oil-drenched refuse piles and houses throughout the city, leading Miller to assert that the navy's premature landing had "made no difference regarding the destruction of property."[11] As part of this confusion, the revolutionary council accused the Americans of wantonly destroying the city but also boasted that the inhabitants had burned their own homes as a patriotic gesture.[12] On balance, the conclusion must be that Iloilo City was destroyed by a combination of arson, naval bombardment, and street fighting, with no one either solely to blame or completely innocent.

The Iloilo landing provoked a vigorous debate between the services as well. Miller's initial report stated only that the town had been captured by forces under his command. But two ship's officers, acting as amateur correspondents, wrote widely circulated accounts that claimed the navy had captured Iloilo, and accused the army of being dilatory and unprepared.[13] When Miller was promoted, Wilde protested that he had been rewarded for an action that should be credited to the navy. Dewey seconded Wilde, declaring unequivocally: "Naval forces captured, occupied and held the fort and city of Iloilo, and drove the Filipinos out, with absolutely no assistance from the Army."[14] Within the navy the story became so distorted that one admiral reported Wilde and "78 jacks" had "held the town" for two hours and that only after the soldiers landed was it fired.[15] The army took its own potshots. Miller commented that he had heretofore avoided criticizing Wilde's "hasty action" and scoffed at the navy's claims: his own troops had captured five-sixths of the city, the main square, and all the important bridges and trenches.[16] Otis was even more furious. He had taken great pains to assure that the occupation would occur without loss of life or destruction of property; the navy's premature attack was absolutely contrary to McKinley's conciliatory policy and might cost the United States millions of dollars in damages.[17]

In retrospect, the entire incident indicates the rivalry that plagued early joint operations in the Philippines. The army's mistakes stemmed from its slow reaction to the navy's surprise attack, Van Valzeh's bumbling, and Miller's disingenuous report. Wilde's behavior was simply irresponsible. He was, or was supposed to be, serving in a supportive role in a cooperative venture, but he acted as if he had a completely free hand. Dewey not only countenanced Wilde's behavior but escalated the disagreement. Finally, the rush by naval officers to issue distorted and accusatory reports in the public press, with the full support of their superiors, indicates that the navy viewed itself as more in competition than cooperation with the army.

While this paper battle raged, Miller faced far more serious and immediate challenges. His problems replicated those of Otis after the capture of Manila. He occupied a burned-out and deserted town, surrounded on three sides by enemy forces. He had to rebuild all public services—water, sanitation, trade, government—and also deal with a substantial military threat. Like Otis, Miller lacked sufficient troops to force his opponents into a decisive battle, much less to conquer and hold all of the island. Like subsequent commanders in the provinces, Miller had to develop policies that conformed both to the directives he received from Manila—specifically the army's mandate to serve as an agent of benevolent assimilation—and to local realities. This required him to combine civil projects with military operations, to find a proper balance of conciliation and coercion. Through enlightened government he tried to revive Iloilo's commercial prosperity and thus show the islanders the benefits of United States rule. At the same time, he sought to create a buffer zone around Iloilo and disrupt the Federal State's forces by spoiling attacks.

Miller's first step was to issue a proclamation that established a military government and promised to respect private property and religion, maintain officials in their posts barring evidence of misconduct, and open the port of Iloilo for trade.[18] On 21 February his second proclamation declared that the Americans "have not come to the Island of Panay as conquerors or invaders, but as friends to protect all Filipinos in their homes, in their employments and in their personal and religious rights." He reiterated his "earnest wish that our two peoples unite as one people in suppressing crime and all lawlessness in the Island." Those who had remained at peace would not be molested, and those who surrendered their weapons and took an oath of allegiance would be paroled and sent home.[19] Another open letter assured Ilongos, and especially the elite, that the Americans recognized the real enemies were the Tagalogs: "All this lawlessness and resistance is by people not belonging to this island and their object is simply to plunder the people of this island."[20] A general order warned the occupying forces of Miller's intention "to pursue a conciliatory policy towards the natives of Panay, and this object will be defeated unless the most stringent efforts on the part of all officers and soldiers are exerted to gain their confidence."[21] Both his messages and his actions were attractive to some: the president, vice president, and several prominent members of the Federal State acknowledged United States rule and remained in Iloilo City.

By early March, Miller had carved out a thin five-mile perimeter running from the harbor across the Iloilo River up toward the town of Jaro and along the peninsula, but he believed the situation to be deteriorating. Insurgents and bandits roamed the countryside, extorting money, kidnapping women, and terrorizing the inhabitants. His troops were under continual sniper fire and rarely could move through the countryside without a skirmish: "The work and duty and fighting so much is wearing out my men and destroying their nerve and I must have another regiment before it is too late."[22] With just a few battalions he could launch an offensive that would "follow these beggars and drive them until they were ready to give in."[23] He pressured Otis for reinforcements: on Panay "the Americans have many friends who are held down by the military element, many are friendly and are anxious to have us attack and destroy the Insurgent army at once." But should this opportunity be lost, then the revolutionary forces would take heart, regroup, and go on the offensive. Already they had turned Delgado's hometown of Santa Barbara into a fortress, and barely out of rifle shot of Iloilo they were building entrenchments "at which work they are rapid and expert."[24]

Miller's gloomy predictions were soon realized. By late March, the 1st Separate Brigade's perimeter was menaced by large Filipino contingents at Jaro and Molo. Iloilo was itself a source of demoralization. There was virtually nothing to do in the dreary, burned-out town; as one soldier commented, "Even the most prosaic brute on earth would become depressed in this place."[25] The strain also told on Miller, whose belief in conciliation gave way to a conviction that "all measures of a bitter war should be used."[26]

Aware of the Americans' weakness, on 16 March Delgado launched 1,000 soldiers in an assault on the small garrison at Jaro. Miller reacted quickly: Maj. Charles Keller's 18th Infantry battalion, supported by a mixed machine-gun and artillery contingent, crossed the Jaro River and attacked the enemy trenches. Four companies of Tennessee Volunteers under Childers crossed the river to the north. Forming into a long skirmish line, they took the insurgents in the flank as Keller's troops broke through the insurgent line. Caught in a withering cross fire, Delgado's troops retreated in disorder to Pavia. It was a crushing defeat: one American was killed and 14 wounded, but at least 50 Ilongos, and perhaps as many as 200, died. Filipino officers had told their men that the invaders would run at the sight of bolos. Confident in this knowledge, the bolomen, who constituted almost three-quarters of the force, charged with élan but were cut down in rows.[27] Delgado fell back to Santa Barbara; many of his soldiers quietly returned to their villages and limited their military activity to service in the local militia. Although they would show considerable tenacity on defense, their defeat at the Jaro River stripped the province's revolutionary forces of their offensive capacity. They might harass and snipe, raid and attack outposts, but they would never again try a concerted push to drive the invaders off the island.

The defeat exacerbated the deep divisions within Panay's revolutionary movement. Military discipline, never good, deteriorated so much that one general wrote, "The army . . . is much divided. . . . every military commander acts according to his own volition."[28] What one of Diocno's officers termed the "profound antagonism between the Visayan and the Tagalog" caused frequent arguments, and occasional bloodshed.[29] Frustrated by its continued refusal either to reorganize or to forward taxes, Aguinaldo declared the Federal State dissolved on 27 April, but the Iloilo council, or what remained of it, continued to meet. That same month, believing that Delgado's Visayans would soon disarm them, most of the Tagalogs in Diocno's expeditionary force withdrew over the mountains north to Capiz Province. Another of Aguinaldo's appointees, Leandro Fullon, put forth the claim that as "General Commanding Visayas" he outranked everyone. Delgado ignored him, and Fullon marched off to Capiz as well, where he duly fell to quarreling with that province's political chief. Unable to surmount their personal\and ethnic rivalries, Panay's revolutionaries remained on the defensive and awaited the next onslaught.[30]

On the American side as well, the battle intensified frustration. Miller continued to press Otis for reinforcements: with a few more regiments he could smash Delgado's army and cut the roads leading over the mountains to Antique and Capiz Provinces. This would disperse the Filipino forces, drive them out of Iloilo Province, and force them to rely on coastal vessels for movement, leaving them easy targets for the navy's patrolling gunboats. But Otis was in no better position to reinforce Miller than he had been a month earlier. As his chief of staff blandly assured another Visayan commander, it was "imperative to throw all our available strength upon the Insurgents of Luzon," since "with the downfall of Insurgent power in Luzon resistance to United States authority in the southern islands will doubtless depart."[31] Miller was sent home, after reaching compulsory retirement age, and Otis restructured the 1st Separate Brigade as the Visayan Military District, comprising Panay and two independent subdistricts on the neighboring islands of Negros and Cebu. He intended to add the Visayan islands of Leyte, Samar, and Bohol to the district once they were occupied. In the meantime, Otis was determined not to become overly involved in what he perceived as a minor theater.

Miller's replacement by Brig. Gen. Robert P. Hughes on 5 May brought to the Visayas the officer who more than any other would shape the American pacification campaign in the central Philippines. Possessed of an exemplary battlefield record—having risen from private to lieutenant colonel by the end of the Civil War—and respected as a leading intellectual, Hughes was a close and loyal friend of Otis. He arrived with the conviction, shared by Otis, that the Visayans were friendly to the United States and that all he had to do was defeat the Tagalogs. However, he rapidly changed his mind and concluded that, at least on Panay, the Visayans were committed to independence. Contemptuous of the Filipino "barefoots," and of most of his colleagues as well, he became more and more frustrated, and more and more willing to sanction repressive measures.[32]

Foreshadowing a key element of his eventual strategy throughout the Visayas, Hughes sought to deprive the enemy military forces of all means of sustenance. As provost marshal in Manila he had already overseen the interdiction of food supplies from the city to the country. On Panay conditions were even more favorable. In 1898 the revolutionaries had recruited thousands of agricultural laborers for military duty and had slaughtered draft animals for rations, creating near famine in some areas. In February 1899, Delgado belatedly sought to reverse this disastrous course by ordering all civilian males back to the fields. Nevertheless, in March the Federal State warned of an agricultural crisis caused by crop failures, scarce labor, and the collapse of trade.[33] Hughes imposed a strict interdiction on foodstuffs flowing out of the island's major port: food could be brought into Iloilo City but none could leave, and workers who lived outside the city were allowed only a daily ration for their families. Delgado denounced the Americans' effort to reduce Panay "to a state of starvation," but his response was to impose his own blockade of all trade to and from Iloilo City.[34] This tactic backfired: by mid-August the population in the American zone had doubled. Although pleased by evidence that his plan was working, Hughes believed that most of the refugees "would be enemies if a favorable opportunity should occur."[35]

Hughes recognized that Panay was an unpromising theater for military operations. His 2,000 soldiers, many of them Volunteers scheduled for return, were stretched in a thin line of outposts from the outskirts of Molo around Jaro and down the Jaro River to the sea. Their sweeps into the countryside accomplished little, because they could not force Delgado into battle. Moreover, the monsoon was about to break, flooding the countryside and preventing a sustained campaign. Impatient with Panay, Hughes sought to achieve results on the far more promising island of Negros, where he believed "it is not evident that we have any occasion to make a fight. The possibilities become better from day to day for a reconciliation with these misdirected people without killing any number of them, and that should be looked after."[36] He confined his forces to their lines around Iloilo City and waited for hunger to wear down the enemy. Although this probably was the only course open to him, Hughes's passivity allowed Delgado to revitalize the resistance in Iloilo Province.

The island that attracted Hughes's attention lay thirty-five miles east of Iloilo; its 4,954 square miles were divided by a mountain chain into the two provinces of Negros Oriental and Negros Occidental. In 1899, Negros had a population of approximately 320,000. The extensive sugar plantations in the north and east made it one of the richest islands in the archipelago—and among the most vulnerable to any disruption of trade. Since it lacked a deepwater port, virtually all the sugar and rice trade went through Iloilo City, and there were close social and economic connections between the Ilongo and Negrense elites. As in most sugar plantation economies, the island's social structure was highly stratified. Many of the richest planters were natives of Panay who had carved out plantations and forced Negrense peasants into debt peonage. During the harvest season, the planters lived on the haciendas; otherwise they resided in beautiful homes in Bacolod, the capital of Negros Occidental. Those Negrenses unwilling to accept servitude fled to the mountains, where many became members of the Babylan sect of Papa Isio (Dionisio Sigobela).

The revolution against Spanish rule on Negros had come quite late and was primarily a local affair, accomplished without violence or much popular participation. Following a brief demonstration by Juan Araneta and several hundred volunteers in Negros Occidental, the Spanish evacuated Bacolod on 6 November 1898. They were replaced by a provisional government—with Aniceto Lacson as president and Araneta as war minister—consisting of some forty-five professionals, planters, and merchants. However, the revolutionaries in Negros Oriental did not accept its authority, and when the Spanish evacuated the provincial capital of Dumaguete on 22 November, they formed their own congress. To complicate matters further, both the Philippine Republic and the Federal State of the Visayas claimed Negros, even to the fiction of appointing representatives for it. But on 27 November the

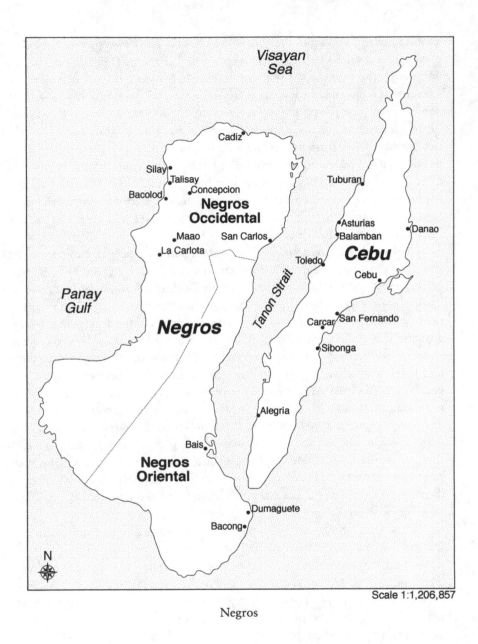

Visayan
Sea

Cadiz

Silay
Talisay
Bacolod Concepcion

**Negros
Occidental**

Tuburan

Asturias
Balamban

Danao

Maao San Carlos
La Carlota

Cebu

Toledo

Cebu

Panay
Gulf

Negros

Carcar San Fernando

Sibonga

Alegria

Bais

**Negros
Oriental**

Dumaguete
Bacong

N

Scale 1:1,206,857

Negros

Bacolod government proclaimed itself the Gobierno Republicano Federal de Canton de Ysla de Negros. Shortly afterward, the Dumaguete government declared it was now the Republica Federal Filipina Canton de Ysla de Negros Oriental. Both assemblies chose the term "canton" to demonstrate their conviction that any Philippine government should be based on a decentralized Swiss system of virtually autonomous provincial assemblies.[37]

Philippine nationalists have harshly criticized the Bacolod government's independent course as "the Negrense betrayal of the revolution."[38] This attitude reflects today's political susceptibilities: now that the Philippines are an independent republic—and the Malolos government is credited as the predecessor—those who failed to support it are reviled as opportunists at best, traitors at worst. But in the fall of 1898 the situation was far less tidy. There was no guarantee that the United States would annex the archipelago, the peace treaty was still unsigned, and there were persistent rumors that Spain would retain the Visayas. Nor was it clear that patriotism was best served by submission to Aguinaldo's government. For all its claims to represent the Filipino people, Malolos tended to regard the Visayas as satrapies to be milked of taxes and recruits. In the Philippine Republic's assembly, Negros's five representatives were all residents of Luzon. In proclaiming a contrary vision that allowed every island (or tribe) the optimum of self-rule, the Negrenses were asserting a far more "Filipino" system than the centralized authoritarian state envisioned by Aguinaldo and Mabini. Indeed, in May 1899, moderates in Aguinaldo's government would draw up a constitution for a similar decentralized federation in which districts corresponding to ethnic divisions would have virtually autonomous powers.[39] For the Negrense elite, the revolution essentially finished with the overthrow of the Spanish and the establishment of a provincial government that guaranteed their property rights. Under these circumstances, their most important priority was to secure the fruits of the revolution, and at this the United States was far better able and willing than was the Philippine Republic.

Recognizing that their proclamation of independence rendered them open to retaliation, and desperate to restore trade, the peace party in the Bacolod assembly determined to find powerful allies. On 12 November it sent a petition to Capt. Henry Glass, whose *Charleston* was blockading Iloilo, requesting that the United States make Negros a protectorate.[40] Glass failed to recognize this opportunity and declined, but the Negrenses did not abandon their efforts. Following Miller's occupation of Iloilo City, President Lacson unfurled the Stars and Stripes over Bacolod and sent a delegation to the general, who sent it on to Otis. The Negrenses—all rich, cultured men—confirmed Otis's deeply held view that only Tagalogs and brigands opposed

United States rule. The general should have been far more suspicious of wealthy merchants who claimed to speak for the inhabitants, and even more wary of promises that just a few companies would guarantee peace and security. But in fairness to Otis, McKinley's instructions that the army provide government and protection throughout the archipelago left him little leeway. On 1 March, Otis appointed Brig. Gen. James F. Smith the military governor of the Sub-District of Negros, part of the newly created Visayan Military District. Indicative of Otis's belief that only a small constabulary was needed "for protection against Luzon insurgents," Smith's entire military force was a 400-man battalion of the 1st California under Maj. Hugh T. Sime.[41]

Smith appeared to be the ideal military governor to help Negros become a showcase for American rule in the provinces. A Catholic, a lawyer, and an experienced politico, he had been one of Otis's chief advisers in structuring the military government. He was firmly committed to benevolent assimilation and took its responsibilities seriously. His diplomatic and administrative abilities were widely recognized and would later lead to his appointment as governor of the archipelago. Both Smith's humanitarianism and his interest in political issues, as opposed to strictly military matters, occasionally placed him in conflict with Hughes.[42]

Arriving at Bacolod on 4 March to a huge ovation, Smith set to work immediately to make Negros a model of self-government. He intended to keep a low profile: as military governor he would control customs and trade, communications, and the police, but the day-to-day business of local government would be in the hands of the locals, or at least wealthy pro-American Negrenses. But he soon found the Bacolod government far different from the enthusiastic and cooperative body its delegates had touted to Otis. When Smith set the assembly the task of drawing up a constitution for the island, it exploded in factional battles. Feuds and rivalries were also common in the countryside, where local officials persecuted their opponents. Frustrated, Smith reorganized the government on 22 July, retaining an advisory council but placing most power in his own hands as military governor. He hoped that elections in October would leave him with a civil government amenable to both peaceful coexistence and hard work.[43]

Unique among the occupied areas, Negros was to have its own 200-man constabulary, a rigorously selected and trained paramilitary force that would implement the law throughout the island. On 11 March, Smith began recruiting this force, and thereafter he constantly sought to improve its pay, rations, medicine, uniforms, and weaponry. Originally assigned to Bacolod, the constabulary were increasingly used as guides for army expeditions. In August they were renamed the Battalion of Native Reserve and placed under Sime's immediate command for field service against brigands and Babylanes. The battalion was to prove among the most successful scout-police forces the U.S. Army raised, without a single deserter or lost rifle in its entire existence.[44]

Smith and Sime also insisted that the 1st California do nothing to disturb harmonious relations with the public. The soldiers were there by invitation of the people, and "every courtesy must be shown" to their hosts. Although there were strict prohibitions on vino and other liquors and on foraging, the troops were otherwise to be "given every liberty."[45] Smith established a list of prices for goods and services—a dozen eggs for a quarter, twenty cigarettes for a nickel—which removed a common source of animosity between soldiers and merchants. His claim that "all the towns occupied by troops and all the places where they have had an opportunity of fraternizing with the people have remained our steadfast friends" was both a boast and an acknowledgment of the importance of good conduct in securing popular support for the occupation.[46]

Despite his good intentions, Smith soon learned—as his colleagues were to discover throughout the archipelago—that benevolent government was possible only when supported by military strength. In Smith's case, until the police could be organized he had only Sime's four companies, a sufficient number had the island been as peaceful and pro-American as the Negrense delegation had promised Otis. But Sime's battalion quickly came under great pressure from guerrillas, bandits, and Babylanes, who raided the coast and countryside, burning, kidnapping, and killing. Smith soon had to send troops to the interior towns of La Carlota and Maao to protect sugar haciendas. In March the occupation of Dumaguete and other towns in Negros Occidental required a second battalion of the 1st California. Even this was not enough. Stretched out over eighty miles, the Americans could not protect the interior from raids nor the coast from incursions from Panay. By late May the situation had become so serious that Negros, which was supposed to require only one battalion, was garrisoned by an entire regiment, and its governor was calling for still more troops.[47]

Compared with that of other islands, the resistance in Negros seldom rose above large-scale brigandage. But to Americans who had assumed the island to be entirely peaceful, the continued disorder was both unexpected and disturbing. Moreover, on Negros the army gained its first experience of phenomena it would later find on other islands: a mélange of opponents, guerrilla warfare, officials who collaborated with both sides, and so on. It was also the first place the army established municipal government, police, and other institutions that would become characteristic of American pacification in the Philippines.

The resistance on Negros was among the most distinct in the Philippine War. On Luzon or Panay the revolutionaries could claim, with some legitimacy, to be fighting to establish a government. They maintained the forms of an alternative system of political administration and fielded military organizations that corresponded to conventional European armies. But on Negros those who fought against United States occupation never established an alternative political entity, and their military forces remained little more than poorly armed rural gangs. For the most part, the class that led the resistance on other islands—the commercial and agricultural elite—here avoided direct participation. The Panay revolutionaries' decision to avoid fighting on Negros provided moral sanction for the Negrense elite's passivity.[48] The local magnates who had risen to prominence in the struggle against the Spanish did not serve as a core of leadership around which guerrilla forces could form. Aguinaldo's military appointee, Juan Araneta, cooperated with Smith and led local forces against brigands. Diego de la Vina, who led the Negros Oriental revolt, left the island after the Americans arrived and never fought against them. Most of the other military commanders in the short-lived independent Negrense governments returned to their haciendas and businesses and did not oppose the occupation.

Because the wealthy and powerful stayed out of the war, leadership devolved on outsiders and those on the margins of society. The most effective guerrilla band, the self-proclaimed "Liberators," was formed by nineteen policemen who deserted on 29 April 1899. Led by Luis Ginete, they provided the core of a larger band that raided plantations and villages, murdering several people and kidnapping women. In late May they boarded a British ship and butchered the crew, including an army officer, thereby graduating from a minor nuisance to a major concern.[49]

A far greater threat were Negros's indigenous Babylanes. Papa Isio, the sect's *baylan* (shaman), had fused socioeconomic grievances, Catholicism, and traditional Visayan folk religion into a heady religious mixture that inspired its followers to fanatical courage, and to devastating attacks on haciendas and merchants. Isio and the Babylanes had a tenuous connection to the independence movement. In 1898 Araneta had given Isio a commission to fight against the Spanish. When Araneta and the Bacolod government went over to the Americans, Isio proclaimed himself Commander of War of the Superior Federal Republic of the Philippines and declared it was "now high time to inundate this Island with blood."[50] He wrote Aguinaldo requesting recognition of his rank, boasting he led a military organization with four generals and a host of minor officers. Aguinaldo did not respond.[51] Isio may not have cared, for he served a higher authority: in a letter to two civil officials, Isio transmitted orders from "our Lord Jesus Christ received in these Military Headquarters."[52]

The Babylanes were especially strong in the Maao, La Castellana, and La Carlota districts of Negros Occidental. Their prophecy of a day of judgment in which the sugar estates would be broken up and the land returned to rice cultivation was a source of inspiration to tenant farmers. The devotees were joined by brigands, some claiming to follow the orders of Aguinaldo or the Panay junta. In April, Babylan arsonists ravaged the area; workers at fifty haciendas burned the fields and buildings and joined the roving bands. Both Smith and Hughes recognized that much of the Babylanes' appeal was directed less against the Americans than the rich, for "the haciendas of Europeans, friends and relatives of insurgent leaders, and friends and relatives of Americanistas suffered alike."[53] Hughes later told a Senate committee that he knew of no case where a hacienda whose owner had paid his workers a decent wage had been burned.[54]

The Babylan-inspired violence in the La Carlota district came at a time when the American military position on Negros was exceptionally weak. The 1st California was scheduled to be replaced on 15 July by ten companies of Col. Charles W. Miner's 6th Infantry. The withdrawal consumed the energy of most officers, for under the army's archaic bookkeeping system they were required to account for all property. Moreover, both the 1st California's tactical commander, the erratic Lt. Col. Victor Duboce, and Capt. John A. Miller at La Carlota were oblivious to the seriousness of the situation. Indeed, Smith first heard about the burning and violence from the mayors of the afflicted towns, not his military commanders. In late June, he ordered Duboce to establish a garrison in one town, only to learn a week later that no troops had been sent and that seven plantations in the area had since burned. Such "flagrant negligence on the part of those charged with the protection of that district" infuriated Smith.[55] He chastised Miller: "Your entire district has been practically burned out and you seem to have no information of what is going on in your vicinity."[56]

Fortunately for the Americans, the uprising, even as it appeared to be growing strongest, was rapidly disintegrating. Their numbers swollen by refugees and opportunists, the rebel bands became larger, less mobile, and more dependent on plunder and looting. The Babylanes' own pillaging forced them to travel farther and farther from their mountain hideouts to find new sources of food. They attacked those who had given them contributions and radicalized the plantation workers with such slogans as "No machinery" and "Equal distribution of lands."[57] Such a clear threat to their own interests provoked a strong reaction among the Negrense elite, especially when contrasted with Smith's efforts to protect property. For self-preservation, they were increasingly drawn into the war.

With the arrival of Capt. Bernard A. Byrne and Companies H and K of the 6th Infantry, the Babylanes now faced fresh troops and a tough, aggressive officer. His spies located two large camps at the mountain villages of Bobong and Salupitan, some fifteen miles from La Carlota. The rebels had surrounded their strongholds with high stockades and blockhouses; towers scanned the countryside, and escape routes provided easy retreat. To overcome these defenses, Byrne decided on a cross-country night march. The expedition was kept a secret from everyone, the spies segregated from all contact and the 105 soldiers given no word until the evening of 18 July, when they were told to fall in with rifles, one day's rations, and a poncho. Leaving shortly after nightfall, the soldiers struggled over muddy rice paddies and dikes, forded streams up to their armpits, pushed through head-high canebrakes, and then, already exhausted, climbed up rugged mountain trails. The darkness was absolute and the rain relentless, forcing each soldier to keep his place by holding onto the belt of the man in front of him. Halting his worn-out command at 3:00 A.M., Byrne waited for daylight as the men ate a breakfast of bacon and cold coffee. An hour later, they started up the mountain that led to Bobong, pulling themselves up by roots and bushes. It took the command over two hours to drag its way up the almost perpendicular slope. By now the troops were scattered over the mountainside, and many were unable to go on. Byrne and six soldiers crawled forward to the summit and saw a few sentries some twenty yards away. Rushing, or perhaps staggering, forward, they killed seven and drove off the rest. As his exhausted men trickled up to the summit, Byrne directed the soldiers on the ridgeline to open fire.

The Babylanes, after a brief period of confusion, retreated to their blockhouses, where they were virtually invulnerable, and began a heavy return fire. Although they controlled the high ground on both sides of the village, Byrne knew his exhausted soldiers—only fifty-five were in any shape to fight—were running low on ammunition. He had to get into the village and drive the rebels out of their defenses, but the sole approach was over a deep chasm spanned by a small footbridge. The captain ordered each of the flanking units to send him fifteen men and scrambled down the slope to the footbridge, his bugler blowing the assembly to guide the detachments. As he started to cross the bridge, Byrne was suddenly confronted by a dozen panic-stricken soldiers. On their own initiative, the flank commanders had each sent sharpshooters to infiltrate the village. Instead of remaining hidden, these men had bunched up, presenting a clear target to dozens of bolomen who poured out of the barracks, slashing and hacking at the stunned Americans. Two soldiers stood their ground, holding back the flood with rifle butt and bayonet; the rest fled toward the bridge. By the time Byrne found them they were in a complete panic, too demoralized to get into line or obey orders. Bolstered by a few other soldiers who followed the bugler's calls, Byrne formed a ragged skirmish line, had the "charge" sounded, and advanced into the village. This impetuous, almost suicidal, action turned the tide. The pursuing bolomen, their leaders cut down by accurate Krag fire, broke and ran, many of them shot down by the flanking parties. The Babylanes lost over 150 men; Byrne suffered one soldier killed and another wounded.[58]

Byrne's victory marked the beginning of a string of American successes that continued for the rest of the summer and into the fall. Harried by columns that crisscrossed Negros, the sectarians disappeared into the mountains or made their way back to the plantations. In dozens of skirmishes and a few large engagements, soldiers and Negrense auxiliaries drove their opponents ruthlessly. On 19 August an escaped prisoner led a ninety-man expedition to a brigand camp in the mountains. Approaching in a drenching monsoon to a few hundred yards from the entrenchments, the troops achieved complete surprise, routing the enemy, killing nineteen, and, most important, capturing eight rifles. On 31 August, after a long march followed by a charge up a steep mountainside, Byrne destroyed a large brigand stronghold, killing twenty-one and capturing an arsenal. A concerted campaign culminated on 2 October with a pitched battle in which a notorious guerrilla, Santillana, and twenty of his followers were killed. Exhausted and thoroughly sick of the war, Luis Ginete and the Liberators surrendered later that month.[59]

Some of the American success was due to tactical adaptations. Smith and his subordinates recognized that sending columns out to hunt down guerrillas was "worse than useless as they immediately retreat to the forests and mountains and nothing is accomplished."[60] Instead, they sought to locate guerrilla strongholds and then launch a quick, decisive strike and ruthlessly pursue the survivors. Operational planning became more sophisticated, integrating mobile forces, Negrense auxiliaries, coastal vessels, base camps, spies, and local militia. In the final campaign against Ginete, the Americans landed detachments at several places to make a wide net that slowly closed on the brigands. Smith also encouraged the formation of a mounted unit, which provided at least a portion of the occupation forces with mobility to match that of their opponents.[61]

The close alliance between army officers and planters, town officials, and local paramilitary forces further contributed to success. The planters who had carved out huge sugar estates and cowed the Negrense peasantry were ruthless and aggressive. Once they perceived a threat to their interests—revolutionaries, brigands, or Babylanes—they were quick to retaliate: one of Smith's best informants was the son of a former revolutionary officer who had been decapitated by Santillana. But it is important to note that collaboration was not restricted to the planter class: in order to protect their villages, local police guided troops through the jungles and hills and even fought the Babylanes and bandits themselves.[62] Such participation led to a conviction, expressed most strongly by Smith, that resistance to United States occupation was due to outsiders or brigands and prevented soldiers from developing an "us-against-them" mentality such as appeared in Samar and Batangas.

Both officers and soldiers recognized that counterinsurgency on Negros had elements of class warfare. One California Volunteer believed the only people who really supported the Americans were the wealthy planters and merchants: "We were respected by the proletariat only because of our numbers."[63] Hughes made this clear at the end of the summer campaign when he wrote Otis that with "fair dealing on the part of the planters with their employees, matters ought to settle down to a working basis. The planters are exceedingly anxious to get back to their sugar fields, and the troops are sending the laborers back with the fear of God and guns in their heads."[64] The army allowed planters and officials a great deal of discretionary power. Araneta, the former head of the revolutionary forces, reported to Smith that he had executed a spy and an arsonist and had given orders that "by means of public executions and other *requisitos legales* the law be carried out and the guilty receive the punishment his crime deserves."[65] One officer reported he had turned Babylan suspects over to local officials with the provision that "it would be better to have these executions done at times when there would be no connection with the fact that American soldiers were present."[66]

Negros was perceived as an ideal place to demonstrate that Filipinos who accepted United States sovereignty would be trusted with a large measure of self-government. In a 13 August proclamation, Smith promised the elections would establish a government where all citizens would receive "the full measure of human liberty which they may be capable of enjoying." It would be one in which both rich and poor would be equal before the law and in which "no person, no official is too high to be punished if he does wrong and no citizen is too humble to secure justice if injured."[67] Behind such rhetoric, Smith moved "to take precautions that would set up good men for office," insisting on such substantial property qualifications that only 5,248 of the island's 320,000 residents were eligible to vote.[68]

In addressing the elected officials at their inauguration on 6 November, Smith gave a clear exposition of the meaning of benevolent assimilation. His first emphasis was on public order: "men who live by the bolo" must be suppressed; civil officials must cease their "petty extortions and illegal exactions" on the "poor and ignorant," and instead provide honest and efficient government, trim bloated bureaucracies, and collect taxes equitably. Turning to happier subjects, Smith emphasized the need for free secular education for all children aged six to fourteen, and a system of public health that would teach elementary sanitation and prevent epidemics. Finally, appealing to commercial interests, he dwelt on the benefits that would come from the army's establishing telegraph communication throughout the island, and on the need for new roads.[69] Such practical goals—public order, efficient local government, education, public health, and communications—were the hallmarks of U.S. Army civic reform during the Philippine War. Humanitarian officers such as Smith sought pragmatic, sensible objectives that provided immediate benefits; but they left untouched the deep social problems of the archipelago.

With the election of a provincial government and the meeting of the assembly, Negros appeared all but pacified. The revolutionaries, never strong, had been unable to mount a sustained challenge. The other sources of resistance—Babylanes and brigands—were only tangentially tied to the nationalist movement and had been badly mauled during the summer and driven back to the mountains. The island required comparatively few troops, a native police force was already in existence, and Smith appeared to be making great strides toward creating a viable and loyal provincial government. To all intents and purposes, by the end of 1899 the U.S. Army had won its first major regional pacification campaign.

In both Iloilo and Negros, the Americans could argue that they were there by invitation. This was not the case on Cebu, a densely populated—over 500,000 in 1902—and elongated island of some 1,700 square miles overall. Like Negros, Cebu had undergone a relatively peaceful transition from Spanish to Filipino rule. Luis Flores headed a provisional revolutionary government, which took over much of the island and isolated the Spanish in Cebu City. On 24 December 1898, the Spanish withdrew and turned control over to a junta of city leaders headed by Pablo Mejia. Two days later, Mejia and Flores combined to form a council for the island, the Junta Popular, and notified Malolos of their actions. The Philippine Republic recognized the Junta but, as was its pattern, ordered it to reorganize along the lines of Aguinaldo's 18 June 1898 directive and, in the meantime, to continue to collect and forward the taxes previously paid Spain. For their part, the Cebuanos acknowledged the Philippine Republic as the national government but followed only those orders they approved of and refused to send it taxes. As in Panay, there were deep divisions within the revolutionary ranks: one anonymous correspondent wrote Aguinaldo denouncing the provincial government for granting military titles to men who were little better than robbers and tyrants.[70]

Cebu's brief effort at self-government ended on 21 February 1899, when, on Dewey's orders, Captain Cornwell of the *Petrel* steamed into Cebu City's harbor. What followed is controversial. Cornwell claimed the city surrendered the next day after he threatened to bombard it. Cebuanos maintained that they agreed only to the occupation of the customs house and that Cornwell promised no interference in the government. Whatever version is true, Cornwell's actions jeopardized interservice relations already badly strained by the Iloilo imbroglio. Otis was furious that the navy's unilateral behavior forced him to divert precious manpower from the critical Luzon theater. As in Negros, he hoped to avoid a large commitment of troops and sent only a four-company battalion of the 23rd Infantry under Maj. Greenleaf A. Goodale. On 14 March, he made Cebu a separate subdistrict of the Visayan Military District and appointed Lt. Col. Thomas R. Hamer of the 1st Idaho as its military governor.[71]

Otis's division of civil and military authority was a mistake. Goodale took a narrow, and probably correct, interpretation of his mission: he kept his soldiers close to the harbor, forbidding them to leave the city, allowing only a few each day out of the barracks. In contrast, within three days after his arrival on 3 April, Hamer telegraphed: "Now is the time to effect our peaceful occupation of the island. . . . [I] am convinced this can be accomplished now without the loss of a man and any considerable delay may cost us a battle."[72] He requested another two battalions of infantry, a light draft steam launch for amphibious operations, and the authority to occupy all the main coastal towns. These requests were rejected: neither Miller in Iloilo not Otis in Manila intended to commit scant resources to a sideshow.

Lacking sufficient military power to occupy the island, Hamer tried diplomacy. He believed that "the better class of natives here, especially the landed proprietors, are seemingly with us, but the lower classes, in common with their brothers throughout the Philippines, are very susceptible to [revolutionary] leadership."[73] In early May he arranged for a prominent Cebuano leader, Julio Llorente, to visit Manila and discuss the extension of American government throughout the island. Llorente told Otis that Cebu's civil and military authorities acknowledged the futility of fighting and were willing to accept United States rule if they were promised autonomy in local affairs and protection from retaliation.[74] Otis, however, would not accept autonomy.

He lacked the manpower to garrison Cebu until he had secured Luzon. When that was done—soon, he believed—resistance would collapse throughout the archipelago. Moreover, both his own personality and his lawyer's background made him uncomfortable with the implications of the Cebuano proposal. He was working at a killing pace to establish a government suitable for the entire archipelago, but first Negros and now Cebu were pressing for their own constitutions. Would his legacy be a dozen balkanized local governments? He directed Hamer not to encourage a constitution for Cebu: "Let the people manage their internal affairs for the present as quietly as possible until some definite policy with regard to all the Islands can be announced."[75]

Hamer was left out on a limb: his authority extended no farther than the suburbs of Cebu City, the provincial government refused to swear allegiance, he lacked troops to force compliance, and diplomacy had not worked. To his credit, he did what he could: after a series of robberies in April, he encouraged Goodale to form joint patrols with the Cebu City police, which soon ventured out of the city to reconnoiter, map the area, and contact village leaders.[76] Perhaps his strongest effort was reserved for the naval blockade, a policy he viewed as destructive to Cebuano interests. The vast majority of Cebu's maritime traders owned small sailing vessels and traded along the coast and among the neighboring islands. Since most of their trade was with "closed" ports and might include contraband items such as meat, rice, matches, and so forth, Hamer was technically supposed to forbid them to sail. Instead, he allowed small vessels to clear Cebu City for all ports except two he believed under revolutionary control. He petitioned Manila to allow such exceptions; otherwise the blockade "means the demoralization of the shipping trade of this port during its enforcement; the throwing of any number of local sea-faring men out of employment and the attendant dangers of having a number of unemployed on our hands here."[77] Hamer's efforts had some success: one insurgent commander complained that the army's "policy of attraction" and its "irreproachable conduct" had won over most of the elite in Cebu City, including the revolutionary provincial government.[78]

The American efforts were greatly assisted by the disarray in Cebu's revolutionary movement. The Junta Popular continued to meet and even occasionally to acknowledge its ties to the Philippine Republic, but most of its members lived in Cebu City and carried out their offices as United States servants. Mejia even gave the money raised to pay the insurgent forces to Hamer.[79] A disgruntled Junta member, Arcadio Maxilom, secured Malolos's confirmation of his self-appointed title as Military Chief of Cebu in March, and in August declared the Junta dissolved and himself Cebu's political and military leader.[80] Most of the local militia who acknowledged his authority remained in their towns to provide protection from bandits and to collect taxes and supplies, but a number of them concentrated at El Pardo, a strongpoint four miles outside Cebu City. They were aided by agents from Luzon who told the credulous villagers "that Americans are black, eat children and live on babies" and that, like the Spanish, they would soon flee, and woe betide those traitors who had collaborated.[81] Hamer found it painful to admit that "the policy followed by us on this island up to date lends some little color to [such stories] from the native point of view."[82]

On 11 June the mayor of Cebu City was assassinated at the front door of his house. This murder of a prominent collaborator in the middle of an occupied town was a major triumph for the revolutionaries. Word quickly spread that he was only the first on a list of sixty, panicking the *americanistas* and prompting the entire city council to threaten resignation. Hughes, who had just taken over the Visayan Military District, responded quickly: on the fourteenth, four companies of the 1st Tennessee and a detachment from the 6th Artillery arrived in the city. Despite these reinforcements, Hamer demanded more troops in order to garrison the island's important towns. By now Hughes was thoroughly sick of Hamer, who, he complained, "seems to need a military mentor."[83] A brief tour of the island had convinced Hughes there was "no active opposition" and that the "people of Cebu are not inclined to fight us."[84] A concerted and well-planned campaign, "brushing away the lawless bands," would soon end any resistance.[85] Hughes heaped advice on Hamer and even initiated his own military operations, sending two companies to the west coast of the island to investigate a reported food shortage and to "familiarize the population with our peaceable intentions and to let them understand that they have nothing to fear from our troops as long as they attend to their own affairs."[86] Given the lack of accord between the two top commanders, it is not surprising that the pacification of Cebu stalled.

On 24 August four soldiers of the 23rd Infantry were "cut to pieces" in an ambush, leading Hughes to write, "This opens the war in Cebu."[87] Taking advantage of the arrival of Col. Simon Snyder's 19th Infantry, Hughes concentrated two companies of the 6th Infantry, a battalion of the 23rd, and the 1st Tennessee on Cebu. The troops were to destroy Maxilom's headquarters, but the campaign proved a fiasco. An exhausting march through the mountains in grueling heat caused eighty soldiers to drop out and killed the artillery's draft animals. Arriving at the strongpoint, the troops struggled up the hill and took two heavily fortified trenches but failed to close with the enemy. The Cebuanos slipped away, and the troops lacked both the supplies and the energy to do anything but return.[88]

With the collapse of the August campaign, Hughes shifted his attention to the more promising theaters of Panay and Negros. He removed Snyder from Hamer's direct command, provoking Hamer to request reassignment on 9 October. Snyder's infantry scoured the hills and the west coast of the island, engaged in a few skirmishes, but achieved little. Secure in the hills and isolated coastal towns, brigands and guerrillas raided with relative impunity. Conditions in the countryside grew so unsettled that troops on Cebu were prohibited from going even a mile from camp in parties smaller than eight.[89] Clearly the situation was deteriorating, and Hughes wanted to shift troops back, but equally strong demands in Panay or Negros prevented his doing so. In October an exasperated Hughes declared "the situation of the [Visayas] command is far from satisfactory and I fore[see] the impossibility of it lasting."[90]

In some respects, the U.S. Army had done quite well in the Visayas. It held the major ports of Iloilo and Cebu and had decisively beaten the armed forces of Panay's insurgent government. On Negros it had suppressed the Babylanes, defeated the guerrillas, and established a civil government. This success is all the more impressive in view of the army's small commitment of resources—barely three regiments—and Otis's focus on the Luzon theater. But to the officers who served there, results were disappointing. Operating on the assumption that only Tagalogs and brigands opposed United States rule, they were both confused and frustrated by the strength of local resistance. With few exceptions, the insurgents avoided battle, preferring to withdraw to the countryside and, by their very presence, check the American efforts to establish local governments and win over the population through benevolent assimilation. The war in the Visayas indicated that resistance would continue even should Aguinaldo be overthrown and his conventional forces destroyed. On Panay and Cebu, political and military leaders with only a slight connection to the Luzon revolutionaries had raised forces to contest the invaders. Even with the cooperation of the Negros elite, the Americans had been forced to fight a tough campaign against brigands and Babylanes. Clearly the army's experience in the Visayas had ominous implications for the course of benevolent assimilation in the rest of the archipelago.

FIVE

THE SPRING CAMPAIGN

Surveying the situation after his victory at Manila, Otis recognized the primacy of the northern Luzon theater and the relative unimportance of the south. In conventional military thinking, the north held the enemy's centers of gravity: its government, its commander in chief, its capital city, and its army. The destruction of all—or, in Otis's optimistic mind—any of these could end the war quickly and painlessly. The north was the more important theater for other reasons as well. The Manila-Dagupan railway was the only transportation route on Luzon that could supply a large field force on prolonged operations. Finally, the north offered more possibilities for Otis to carry out the absolutely essential strategic task of convincing the Filipino people of the benefits of American rule. Despite much evidence to the contrary, he continued to believe that resistance to United States sovereignty was led by Aguinaldo and the Tagalogs; the majority of the Filipino people would aid the army once they were protected sufficiently to witness the benefits of colonial rule. The southern Tagalog provinces of Cavite, Batangas, Laguna, and Tayabas offered barren ground for benevolent assimilation. But in the north, the Americans could break into the provinces dominated by Pampangans, Pangasinans, and Ilocanos—peoples whom Otis believed were eagerly awaiting liberation from Tagalog despotism. Therefore, he decided to limit his objectives to the south. He would extend his lines along the Pasig River to Laguna de Bay, cut the Army of Liberation's north-south logistical lines, and, if necessary, launch preemptive strikes to suppress enemy activity. In the north, he would seek a battle of annihilation, a campaign that would encircle Aguinaldo and his military forces and smash them decisively.

As an astute correspondent noted, although everyone recognized the need to keep up the pressure on the Army of Liberation, "after the first days of active fighting General Otis was brought face to face with the fact that we did not have enough men to carry the war into the interior and still protect Manila and its suburbs."[1] When the war broke out, the 8th Corps had totaled 883 officers and 20,032 men, of whom 11,000 were actually available for service in the line. By mid-April it numbered 967 officers and 25,000 men, but its obligations had grown disproportionately—5,000 soldiers were lost to combat through provost or staff duties, or through confinement in hospitals or prisons; another 5,000 were committed to the Cavite naval base or the Visayas; another 1,000 were needed to relieve the Spanish garrisons in the southern Philippines—leaving only 16,000 available for field operations on Luzon. With every success on the battlefield, the 8th Corps moved farther from Manila and required more soldiers to guard supply lines, garrison towns, and protect communications.[2]

Much of this problem was Otis's fault, for his parsimony led him consistently to underestimate the number of troops he would need. In November 1898 he had maintained that no more than 25,000 were required, and in spite of escalating tensions he did not budge from this figure. After fighting broke out, he raised his estimate to a mere 30,000. Only in late June did he declare that the 30,000 figure referred to "effective troops," meaning a total force of 60,000.[3] Such vague and misleading information enraged his subordinates—who were repeatedly told to make do with far too little—and rendered it impossible for Washington to plan realistically for recruitment.

Further complicating the problem was the fact that over half the 8th Corps was composed of State Volunteers whose military obligation ended with the ratification of the peace treaty with Spain on 11 April. Their retention in the archipelago had provoked a torrent of popular and congressional protest, which both McKinley and the War Department sought in vain to allay. As early as 20 March Otis was told that the citizen soldiers must be "sent home the moment you feel any can be spared."[4] But Otis could not spare them, for not until late May would Regular manpower approach that of the Volunteers, and, as one harried officer noted, when Regulars relieved the state regiments, "in every case more men are taken away than are sent to replace them."[5]

The Regulars were inferior in both quantity and quality to the "boys of '98." The expansion of 1898 had filled the Regulars with wartime service recruits, most of whom had since left, and Cuban fevers and combat had ravaged the older and more experienced soldiers. In December 1898, of the 7,411 Regulars designated for service in the Philippines 1,819 were sick or missing. In the 9th Infantry, of the 1,200 soldiers who arrived in Manila in April, all but 300 were recruits. The 20th Infantry retained barely 200 of its original members when it transferred to the Philippines; a Minnesota volunteer dismissed it as "the greenest lot of rookies I ever laid my eyes on."[6] As late as August 1899, one general commented that the majority of his four Regular regiments were "raw recruits."[7] To compound the Regulars' problems, headquarters in Manila snapped up good officers for staff and govern-

ment duty, leaving young and inexperienced or old and incompetent commanders with the soldiers. Recognizing their limitations, Otis assigned them
to defending the Manila lines, inciting one outraged Iowan to write home:
"You speak of the Regulars helping us; well, they are nearly all in the City.
The volunteers are doing the fighting and the Regs. are resting."[8]

Although temporarily shorthanded, Otis knew that if he could hold on
until the fall the situation would change. On 2 March Congress passed an
army bill with three important provisions: those State Volunteers needed "for
absolutely necessary service" would remain in the archipelago; the Regular
Army would be increased to 65,000; and a separate 35,000-man United States
Volunteer organization would be recruited specifically for service in the Philippines.[9] Allowing six months for recruiting and training, Otis could have an
army of 70,000 Regulars and Volunteers by the fall of 1899. In the meantime, the only reinforcements he could count on were driblets of badly trained
Regulars.

Next to manpower, Otis's greatest problems lay in the physical difficulties of campaigning in the archipelago. Theodore Roosevelt, like many observers in the United States, saw the problem only in military terms: to them
the solution was to "assume aggressive operations and . . . harass and smash
the insurgents in every way until they are literally beaten into peace; entertaining no proposition from them save that of unconditional surrender."[10]
But limited though the fighting had been, the 8th Corps had already learned
that nature was sometimes a more formidable opponent than any armed foe.
Here a day's "hike" might start in choking dust and end in torrential rain
and glutinous mud; en route it might require climbing hills or mountains,
fording streams, estuaries, and rivers, wading through rice paddies and
swamps, and cutting through scrub brush, bamboo, razor-sharp grasses, and
jungle. Sustained campaigning resulted in "breaking down," first of individuals and then of entire regiments, so that when MacArthur's 2nd Division finished one twenty-day campaign, which included several long rests, 2,600 of
its 4,800 soldiers were on sick report. Army doctors agreed that serious diseases such as typhoid, cholera, and chronic dysentery warranted immediate
hospitalization, but more insidious were a multitude of minor ailments such
as sore or rotting feet, low-grade fever, diarrhea, parasites, headaches, chills,
fainting, chronic fatigue, skin diseases, tropical ulcers, and psychological
depression. By May some companies in the 1st Idaho had only 20 soldiers fit
for duty, and the entire regiment could muster barely 300 of its 670 men.
Worse, most soldiers never fully recovered. Sent back to their units, they soon
broke down again. Of the 1,022 members of the 1st Colorado who remained
when the regiment mustered out, the notoriously picayune army surgeons
concluded 196 suffered from a permanent medical disability.[11]

Logistical problems contributed greatly to the soldiers' miseries. Even stripped of all but food and ammunition, an infantry company of seventy-five men required a ton of supplies every five days. This load could not be carried by the soldiers, already burdened with a nine-pound rifle, an equal weight of ammunition, a canteen, a few hardtack and tins of food, and a poncho. In 1899 the War Department sent 2,200 horses and 1,000 mules, but for most operations the army had to rely on carabao carts and porters: the former could go five miles a day in good weather and roads; the latter could carry no more than forty pounds. The result was that usually after the first day of an offensive the lead columns had left their supply wagons miles behind and were living on reduced rations of fatty bacon, coffee, and dry bread, and drinking from polluted wells and streams. Within three days they would run out of food entirely. Unlike Sherman, Otis could not allow his men to live off the land without slowing them down even further, subjecting them to disease and malnutrition, and robbing the very civilians they were supposed to be conciliating.[12]

In addition to purely military problems, Otis also had to deal with the Philippine Commission. A product of both McKinley's good intentions and Otis's overoptimistic reports, it had been sent out in January to resolve Fil-American disagreements and study colonial government. By the time Professor Jacob G. Schurman and his fellow commissioners arrived, war had broken out. Although a member, Otis seldom attended the commission's meetings or sought its advice. A Harvard-trained lawyer with decades of administrative experience, he considered himself—with some reason—far more qualified to establish local governments than Schurman. Moreover, Otis was convinced that as long as the Army of Liberation contested United States sovereignty, he must have a free hand. The commission, somewhat miffed at Otis's indifference, wrote a lengthy report on Philippine conditions, published a manifesto to convince the Filipinos to lay down their arms, and occasionally met with peace commissioners from Malolos. Although largely a nuisance, the Philippine Commission served as a distinct reminder to the army that Washington retained the right to impose its own solution on the islands.[13]

If the Americans faced problems, those of the Army of Liberation were much worse. The Second Battle of Manila had split it almost in two; its only north-south link was a narrow corridor running through the towns of Pasig, Pateros, Taguig, and Muntinlupa between the American lines and Laguna de Bay. In response, Aguinaldo appointed his comrade Mariano Trias commander of the southern section, and thereby lost direct control over the most revolutionary provinces—Batangas, Laguna, and Cavite—as well as over his southern forces.[14]

The northern front offered no such easy solution, for there Aguinaldo was increasingly estranged from his commander, Antonio Luna. After the shocking defeats in February, Aguinaldo had turned to Luna because he seemed the only one able to create a disciplined and effective national army. In many respects, it was a good choice. Luna improved the existing defenses in front of Malolos and on the Pampanga River into strong defensive positions. He raised special battalions of veterans of the Spanish army, sought to cashier incompetent or cowardly commanders, and attempted to force the Army of Liberation into a coherent entity able to perform complex maneuvers on the battlefield. But Luna's laudable measures were designed for a dubious strategy—to fight a conventional war against the far better armed and disciplined 8th Corps. Worse, they were implemented with arrogance, ruthlessness, and outright cruelty. Luna's orders threatened summary execution so often that his troops, punning on his name, referred to him as "General Articulo Uno." He preached discipline and subordination, but often acted as if his personal honor were more important than serving the nation. He openly criticized the government and regularly threatened to resign; on one occasion, he left his army and set out to fight a duel with a rival general; on another occasion, furious that soldiers' families were on a military train, he began whipping them. Even Mabini, who had earlier supported Luna's efforts, was appalled at his cruelty and insubordination, and believed he should be replaced. Luna survived, but his mandate was contingent on battlefield success; without this, his position was fragile indeed.[15]

After the fall of Caloocan, the 8th Corps' next target was obviously the Philippine Republic's capital at Malolos; but Otis delayed for almost a month, in hopes the Army of Liberation would be deployed in its defense. To capture Malolos, the 8th Corps would have to advance against a natural defensive position dotted with villages, scrub thicket, bamboo, marshes, and rice paddies; it would cross six major rivers, several without bridges, as well as innumerable creeks, gullies, and estuaries. Such an expedition first required both the strengthening of the Manila lines and extensive logistical preparations. Thus for over a month the 8th Corps dug trenches, hauled supplies, improved roads, and repaired the battered railroad stock it had found at Caloocan. With the ingenuity and practical skills that characterized the citizen soldiers, they converted an engine and several cars into an armored train. Protected by heavy steel plates and mounting a six-pounder cannon, a Hotchkiss revolving cannon, and two or three machine guns, it served as a supply train and as MacArthur's headquarters. Breaking the monotony were repeated raids and skirmishes all along the ten-mile front. In some areas the fighting was continuous—around the Marikina waterworks alone there were eight engagements in twenty-three days. But by mid-March the 8th Corps had established a formidable defensive line around Manila, thus freeing thousands of troops for offensive operations.[16]

In a move that would have considerable significance later, Otis aimed to deprive Filipino armed forces of food and war supplies. In doing so, he instituted a land equivalent of the effective U.S. Navy blockade, to be discussed in a later chapter. Initially, the Americans had permitted free trade from the city across Manila Bay and Laguna de Bay. But the growing effectiveness of the intelligence service in Manila—particularly the Provost Guard and municipal police—led to the realization that revolutionary agents in the city were collecting or extorting taxes and sending food, matches, oil, clothes, and other war supplies into the enemy lines. One officer witnessed several women leaving the city on a ferry, each of whom would empty a small bundle into a gunnysack—a raid on the boat yielded eight large sacks of rice. As a result, more and more regulations were imposed on trade. On 15 February, less than two weeks after the outbreak of hostilities, males were prohibited from taking rice from the city. This was followed by restricting exit from the city to nine checkpoints, limiting rice exports to two pounds per woman or child, and establishing an extensive and thorough pass system. The Manila garrison's early and escalating efforts at food restriction would make it much easier for officers outside the city to impose far more draconian policies of food deprivation and destruction.[17]

Before striking at Malolos, Otis determined to send an expedition east along the Marikina, Taguig, and Pasig Rivers to Laguna de Bay. By removing the enemy bands that constantly harassed his southern and eastern flanks, it would provide access to a rich agricultural area and ensure the supply of Manila, and it would cut the Filipino army into northern and southern halves and force them to make the long hard journey around the lake's eastern shore. To head this expedition, Otis appointed Brig. Gen. Loyd Wheaton, a hyperactive sixty-two-year-old field officer and "a magnificent, Jove-like swearer" who awed even hardened Regulars.[18] Wheaton had earned a stellar Civil War record followed by decades in which he had done little but supervise a sixty-man infantry company. Otis, who commanded Wheaton's regiment, had noted that his subordinate was highly efficient but unpopular. In the Philippines, however, he soon became a favorite of his soldiers, who appreciated his willingness to share their hardships and risks. He was also popular with correspondents, allowing them to roam about freely, hosting them at his mess, and providing a steady stream of pungent observations.[19]

Otis gave his former captain a provisional brigade—the newly arrived and inexperienced 20th and 22nd Regulars, two battalions each of the 2nd

Oregon and 1st Washington Volunteers, three troops of the 4th Cavalry, a light battery of the 6th Artillery, and the gunboat *Laguna de Bay*. The campaign began on 12 March with a dawn assault on the Filipino position, centered on Guadalupe Church. The Americans advanced in three long lines that stretched two miles across; the 20th and 22nd were to sweep in a wide pivot to take the Filipino position from the south. The artillery blasted away at the church and the trenches, the *Laguna de Bay* cruised along the Pasig River, firing its cannon and Gatling guns into the enemy flank. The defenders fought until 10:00 A.M. and then, as the Regulars began to close in on their southern flank, they pulled back. The brigade crossed the small Taguig River and moved two miles farther forward, where it encountered another large enemy force north of the river at Pasig and yet another to the south at Pateros. The soldiers were now far ahead of their artillery, so they engaged in a long-range firefight for about three hours until the *Laguna* arrived and drove off the defenders with its artillery and machine guns.

In the following days, the brigade fought its way through Pasig, Pateros, and Taguig. The Filipinos fought with skill and determination. They held strong positions, often entrenching in thickets, and did not retreat until they were threatened with envelopment. On two occasions they badly mauled American detachments. On the seventeenth, Wheaton massed his forces and sent them south. With the lake and the *Laguna de Bay* on its left flank and a line of foothills to its right, the brigade advanced fifteen miles to San Pedro Tunasan. That done, Wheaton pulled back, leaving the 1st Washington to hold Pateros, Taguig, and Pasig. The Americans now controlled the Pasig River from Manila to Laguna de Bay, and soon gunboats were patrolling the lake. The southern forces of the Army of Liberation had been given a sharp check, from which it would not recover for weeks.[20]

Wheaton's brief campaign had important strategic effects, but it also gave further proof that the Philippine War would be an extremely destructive one. Wheaton had served under Sherman, and his tactics bore more than a little resemblance to those of his mentor. One correspondent noted that the once-fertile countryside was now desolate—crops trampled, farms and houses burned, towns blackened and depopulated.[21] Street fighting in Pasig destroyed much of a town that had once numbered 8,000 people, and Taguig and Pateros were badly damaged as well. An eyewitness stated that after the attack on Taguig, Wheaton ordered the houses burned for four or five miles along the lake road.[22] Historian William T. Sexton later raised that number to fifteen miles, and Stuart Miller claims that everything in a twelve-mile radius was "burned to the ground"—no mean feat considering that some two-thirds of this area would have been under water.[23] Wheaton, however, maintained, in somewhat elliptical terms, that "the towns from where [the enemy] brought over troops or in which he resisted us [were] burned or destroyed. He burned them himself."[24] This was disingenuous. Fighting in Pasig and Taguig might explain the destruction of those towns, but much of the burning was deliberate: one veteran recalled that as the Americans pulled back "a long black column of smoke sprang up . . . cascoes were dragged up to the fires and burned and the entire district so destroyed so that it would seem necessary not only for a bird but even a Filipino to carry his rations while crossing it."[25] Whether as retaliation or to create a "dead zone" to protect the southern lines, it was a harsh measure that fell chiefly on people who had committed no acts of war.

On 17 March Otis reorganized the 8th Corps, breaking it into a defensive force for Manila and an offensive force to go after the Army of Liberation at Malolos. On the southern lines the newly arrived Maj. Gen. Henry W. Lawton took over the 1st Division from the departing Anderson; Ovenshine and King remained as commanders of the 2nd and 1st brigades, respectively. On the northern front, MacArthur's 2nd Division was reorganized into three brigades: Harrison G. Otis's 2,473-man 1st Brigade, Irving Hale's 3,561-man 2nd Brigade, and Robert H. Hall's 3,003-man 3rd Brigade. To add support, Wheaton's 2,240-strong provisional brigade was shifted from the 1st Division. This reorganization concentrated nearly 12,000 men in the north and freed the brigades of Otis, Hale, and Wheaton for mobile operations while retaining Hall to screen Manila.[26]

The Malolos campaign was designed not only to capture the enemy capital but also to destroy the Army of Liberation. Hall's brigade would feint a frontal assault up the Caloocan-Malolos road. With Wheaton's brigade as a pivot, MacArthur's division—Hale's brigade on the right and Otis's on the left—would drive north to Novaliches and then split into two columns, Hale's moving farther north to San Francisco del Monte and Bagbag and Otis's sweeping the area below Novaliches. The brigades would then turn westward, cutting the railroad line south of Polo, simultaneously driving in the Filipinos' left flank and blocking their retreat. At this point, Wheaton would launch a frontal attack, driving the Army of Liberation toward Hale and Otis. On paper, the plan was a good one. Unfortunately, the troops would soon discover that what Spanish maps revealed as open country with roads and bridges was trackless thicket broken by unspanned rivers and estuaries. MacArthur would later claim that "from the start" he knew "the strategical possibility of enveloping the insurgent right was viewed simply in the light of hope and not in the expectation of success," but, as with many of MacArthur's pronouncements, this was the wisdom of hindsight.[27] At the time, there is every indication he and most of his fellow commanders believed the offensive would simultaneously smash the Army of Liberation and destroy the Philippine Republic.

The Malolos campaign began on 25 March. Supported by the guns of the Utah Battery, Hale's brigade charged from its trenches and broke through the enemy line. As the enveloping force, it then had to move rapidly to the north and east but soon found its way delayed by jungle and thickets, and by dozens of enemy detachments that contested the advance. As temperatures soared, the troops discarded their haversacks, ponchos, food, and bayonets, but even so, several were overcome: a correspondent saw one delirious sunstroke victim being held down by five of his comrades.[28] At the first of the major water barriers, the Tuliahan River, Hale's advance guard of 4th Cavalry ran into a strong trench line, losing almost a dozen men in a few minutes. The Utah Battery managed to push its 3.2-inch guns up and shell the enemy, allowing troops to cross over. The supply train followed, but as it approached a narrow defile prior to crossing, the versatile Maj. J. Franklin Bell, officially the 2nd Division's engineer but more often its chief scout, became uneasy. With a small escort of the 4th Cavalry he moved forward and found a large enemy force behind three field fortifications across the Tuliahan. A sharp skirmish followed, costing the troopers seven wounded before a cannon and a Colt machine gun—firing at barely 200 yards—allowed a detachment to slip across the river and take the enemy in the flank. Bell's intuition and quick thinking had prevented the ambush of the division's supply train, a disaster that might have ended the entire campaign.[29] The incident also illustrated the hazards of advancing amid the thickets and estuaries; enemy forces could slip in behind and attack troops in the rear.

On Hale's left, Otis's 1st Brigade had an even harder time. The roads turned out to be little more than paths, and the men struggled through "dense jungles, thorny thickets, bamboo belts, difficult streams and treacherous morasses."[30] The Filipinos contested every stream and open field, inflicting sixty-eight casualties. By the end of the day, MacArthur's division was spread out over eight miles. Bamboo thickets, paddies, and jungle screened units from each other, prevented coordinated action, and rendered operations little more than "a series of detached combats."[31] A frustrated MacArthur recognized he could not reach the assigned rendezvous in time and requested permission to abandon the drive to Polo and swing farther south. Otis accepted MacArthur's suggestion, although he must have known this effectively ended any possibility of blocking the Army of Liberation's retreat to Malolos.

Resuming its march early on the twenty-sixth, the 2nd Division pushed northwest toward Polo through jungle, mud, scrub, and thickets. The air was hazy with heat and from the smoke of villages burned by the retreating Army of Liberation on Luna's orders. Reaching the railroad line, the Americans turned north and crossed the Mecauayan bridge, where they fought a bloody battle in which the 1st South Dakota, 10th Pennsylvania, and 1st Nebraska killed over ninety enemy soldiers.

The following day saw an even harder battle at the Marilao River. A charge across the damaged railroad bridge by the 1st South Dakota was halted by heavy fire, and the confused troops bunched up, taking several casualties before a major rallied them and led them across.[32] In the meantime, Funston and the 20th Kansas were making one of the most celebrated river crossings of the war. Fired on from the flanks, Kansans charged into the brush with their customary enthusiasm, only to be stopped by the eighty-yard-wide river. Raked by fire from across the river, Funston sent two companies up to the bank, and both sides blazed away at each other at almost point-blank range. Then a Colt machine gun arrived and began sending a stream of bullets over the top of the enemy trenches. A few brave soldiers tried to ford the river, but it was much too deep. When Funston called for volunteers, a lieutenant and four men stripped off their uniforms, swam across to a bamboo raft, and pushed it to the south shore. Taking twenty-two volunteers, Funston recrossed the river and attacked the enemy in the rear, whereupon they fled.[33] At the same time, a detachment of the 10th Pennsylvania swam across and drove off the enemy on their front. Once more the Volunteers' courage and initiative had paid off. The Marilao River line, which should have delayed them for days, was breached in a matter of hours.

In the meantime, the second phase of the pincer movement had begun. On the twenty-fifth, Wheaton launched a furious attack on the enemy positions past Caloocan and pushed forward to the Tuliahan. A daunting task fell to the 2nd Oregon on the extreme left: to the natural defenses of marshes, brush, scrub forest, and ravines, the defenders had added a series of trenches, strongpoints, and blockhouses, capped by a formidable earthwork, with carefully constructed rifle pits and a three-foot roof for protection against shrapnel. Worse, the attackers would have to advance across a long open field, under constant enfilading fire. Well aware of the strength of the defenses, the 2nd Oregon's officers decided to pause until the assault could be coordinated with a flank attack; but shortly after eight in the morning, Wheaton inexplicably ordered the regiment to charge the enemy position. There was no time to plan, to send detachments to work around the enemy lines, or to arrange for artillery support beyond some ineffectual shots that did little but cut down trees. As the bugle sounded, the Oregonians climbed out of their trench, formed up in a rough skirmish line, fired two volleys, and began trotting across 200 yards of open ground. One veteran recalled, "Our thin, widely spaced skirmish line lost form and order. In the deafening war, it was each man for himself, darting forward and dropping to fire behind rice paddies and ant hills."[34] Men ran until winded, then flopped down and fired their Springfields until they recovered their breath, then got to their feet to run forward again. Their right flank was raked by fire; the left wing was blocked by an enormous bog. The Filipinos tenaciously held their ground, shooting from concealed trenches and fire pits, laying down a storm of fire until the troops were a few dozen yards away, then withdrawing to another trench line. Gradually the regiment pushed its way toward the Tuliahan River and the enormous earthwork on its banks. The 2nd Oregon charged across the fields and up the earthwork's steep sides to the top. Then it was their turn: dozens of insurgent soldiers were trapped, and the Americans worked their heavy Springfields as fast as they could, firing into the packed trenches. Shattered, the defenders fled into the tall grasses on the riverbanks. There followed a deadly game of close-in fighting: "Often the pursued would rise only a few feet from the Americans, fire his gun squarely in their faces, and coolly meet the swift death that followed."[35] The attack—an unsupported frontal assault on a heavily defended position—was a remarkable achievement, but it cost the 2nd Oregon nine killed and forty-three wounded.

Crossing the Tuliahan on 26 March, Wheaton's brigade, spearheaded by the 2nd Oregon, pushed on. The defenders again fought with determination—killing another 26 soldiers and wounding 150—before pulling back. Wheaton demanded the offensive continue, but Otis still hoped to keep the Army of Liberation in the pocket until the 2nd Division could cut off their retreat at Polo. However, on receiving MacArthur's note that he wanted to abandon the drive to Polo, Otis revised his plan: MacArthur and Wheaton would now combine and drive north, catching the Army of Liberation before it could retreat to Malolos. Wheaton set off at once, his troops marching up the railroad line past villages put to the torch on Luna's orders. On 26 March, the 22nd Infantry entered the town of Malinta and found the enemy trenches deserted. They were just congratulating themselves on an easy victory when a "perfect hail of rifle fire" struck them, killing their colonel and wounding several soldiers.[36] Most of the troops were recruits who had never been under fire; now they were exposed, taking heavy casualties, and without their leader. But Capt. John G. Ballance coolly walked back and forth amid the flying bullets and rallied them; then, spotting a depression in the ground that would screen his men, he led the battalion into an attack that routed the enemy. Ballance had turned a potential slaughter into victory—an auspicious start to what would be one of the most brilliant careers of the war.

Malinta was the last major engagement of the first half of the campaign. Shortly afterward, Wheaton's flankers encountered MacArthur's advance guard. The trap had thus closed, and the Army of Liberation had escaped it; but there still remained the possibility of a decisive battle. The 8th Corps had inflicted heavy losses on its opponents and driven them out of their entrenchments; rapid pursuit might yet turn the retreat into a rout. But MacArthur was in no shape to continue: his men were exhausted and out of supplies. He could not resume until 29 March, and by that time the Army of Liberation was in full retreat. But at the Bocaue River, it showed it still had some sting, ambushing the 20th Kansas in midcrossing, inflicting twenty-nine casualties in ten minutes, and briefly throwing the regiment back. But this was a temporary check, and it became increasingly clear there would be no climactic battle at Malolos. On the morning of the thirty-first, under cover fire from four 3.2-inch artillery pieces and a Colt machine gun, the infantry advanced in long skirmish lines in echelon. But as the soldiers entered the center of Malolos, the buildings on all sides burst into flame. Luna's forces, as throughout the campaign, had ignited the town to deny its use to the enemy. When the fires were spent, the Philippine Republic's capital was "gutted; nothing but bare houses remained."[37]

For the Army of Liberation, the Malolos campaign proved only slightly less of a disaster than the February battles around Manila. In the first month, its troops had fought with courage and tenacity, but its effectiveness rapidly declined as experienced soldiers became casualties and were replaced by "yokels snatched out of their rice fields and compelled to fight."[38] Almost worse, the battles cost the army irreplaceable resources, especially Mauser rifles and ammunition. Even more disturbing was the widespread devastation inflicted on the civilian population. Luna ordered the thorough destruction of any village given up to the enemy, and his troops complied with a cruel efficiency. But the general had misread his Napoleonic history: his opponents were not living off the land as had the French. The burning of homes and fields was a minor inconvenience to the Americans but condemned hundreds of noncombatants to poverty and hunger.[39]

For their part, most American authorities considered the Malolos campaign to have been a qualified success. Otis's plan to smash armed resistance in a single stroke had failed, and at least some observers wondered whether such maneuvers could secure victory. Terming the results "disappointing," MacArthur opined that "a well-planned, slowly moving battle line directed as if to meet a well-trained enemy is not successful against a guerrilla enemy who simply moves out of the way."[40] He may have been miffed that Otis did not accept his proposal to continue the advance five miles up the railroad to

Calumpit, located at the confluence of three rivers, where he predicted the 2nd Division could establish a defensive perimeter and "view with considerable complacency the disintegration of the Malolos junta, which is almost sure to occur at a very early day."[41] As was often the case, MacArthur was speaking for the record. As Otis pointed out, a "hasty" movement north was unwise until the enemy's location was known; in any case, as MacArthur well knew, his division was incapable of further offensive action: the one-week campaign had cost it 56 killed and 478 wounded, and roughly one man in six was incapacitated by heat or disease.[42]

In addition to demonstrating again the military prowess of the Volunteers, the campaign was notable for its good conduct. Senior officers took great pains to ensure that Filipino prisoners and wounded were well treated and that the troops behaved themselves. In the 2nd Brigade, for example, there were "stringent orders . . . to the effect that there must be no burning or destruction of property by our troops; that public and private property should be put under guard; there should be no looting whatever by the troops, that perfect order be maintained throughout the captured city."[43] Save for the widespread expropriation of chickens, eggs, and other food supplies from deserted farms and villages, these orders appear to have been followed.

The campaign did reveal one significant problem: the citizen soldiers were armed with a rifle that was patently inadequate, and they knew it. The Springfield was heavy and awkward, kicked like a mule, and was woefully inaccurate at long range: when one regiment had its sharpshooters fire at flat trajectory at a target 600 yards away, many of the bullets fell to the ground at half that range. The dense clouds issued by the rifle's black powder ammunition reminded one veteran of "a straw stack afire" and earned the weapon the nickname the "Smoke Wagon."[44] When the War Department issued smokeless ammunition, the cartridges split barrels and blew out breech-blocks. Facing Mauser rifles with four times their range, the Volunteers were essentially defenseless unless supported by Krag-armed Regulars or artillery. Much of the responsibility for this disgraceful situation rested with Otis. Early in November 1898 he had requested 8,000 Krags—enough to equip roughly half the 8th Corps—but ordered only 3,000 shipped to Manila, enough to issue 300 Krags to each Volunteer regiment in late March. It was not until April that he requested more Krags, and then only 3,000. When complaints finally provoked a War Department inquiry in May, Otis responded that the Springfield was preferable at midrange fighting and that, since the Volunteers would soon depart, no further Krags should be sent out. In what was clearly a direct reprimand, Secretary of War Alger responded by ordering the immediate shipment of the 5,000 Krags available.[45] The entire incident demonstrates Washington's continued administrative and supply problems and, most of all, Otis's parsimony—his inability to shift from the narrow focus and penny-pinching of the peacetime army to the demands of war—and his lack of empathy for his soldiers.

As his northern forces rested, refitted, and planned for the next offensive, Otis shifted his attention to the deteriorating situation in the south. Provincial units drawn from the towns of Cavite, Batangas, and Laguna Provinces harassed the Pasig River–San Pedro Makati line. At Pasay, garrisoned by a detachment of the 14th Infantry, the enemy trenches were barely 300 yards from the outposts, and the soldiers were exhausted from skirmishing and guard duty. Unable to sleep amid the incessant rifle fire and alarms, they lay on their bunks fully clothed with their ammunition belts on.[46] To relieve this pressure, Otis planned a raid along the Laguna de Bay that would destroy supply centers, recapture several Spanish steamboats reputed to be in Filipino hands, and disrupt cross-lake communications. Given his manpower shortage and the primacy of the northern theater, such limited strikes were the best he could do.

Shuffling his forces, Otis scraped together a provisional brigade of 1,500 under the tactical command of Brig. Gen. Charles King. Perhaps as a result of the lessons of the Malolos campaign, there was a special 200-man reconnaissance and assault unit formed out of the best marksmen in every regiment. Loaded onto seventeen shallow-draft barges, or *cascos,* and escorted by the gunboats *Oeste* and *Napindan,* the brigade would cross Laguna de Bay at night and seize Santa Cruz, a supply and distribution center sixty miles from Manila on the southwestern shore. Then it would explore the area and distribute proclamations declaring the United States' good intentions. In what may have been an oblique disavowal of Wheaton's destructive southern foray a month earlier, division headquarters issued general orders emphasizing that one of the goals of the expedition was "to prove to and reassure the Philippinos that a campaign conducted by Americans, through hostile country, can and will be prosecuted according to the most generous rules of civilized warfare."[47]

Accompanying King, and in overall command of the expedition, was one of the most famous and popular officers in the army, Maj. Gen. Henry W. Lawton. In many respects Lawton was the ideal frontier officer: almost six and a half feet tall, handsome, courageous, physically robust, flexible, practical, innovative, a man who "fought relentlessly when he fought, but laid aside rancor and prejudice with the vanquishing of the adversary."[48] But Lawton was also a self-pitying alcoholic who was often lost in the complexities of higher command. In Cuba at the crucial Battle of San Juan Heights he

had disregarded his orders to support the main attack and spent hours re-
ducing a minor strongpoint at El Caney, deploying his troops so ineptly that
a third of them could not get into the fighting. His subsequent performance
had been even worse. Appointed military governor of Santiago, he promptly
threw the city's administration into chaos, went off on a week-long drunk,
and assaulted the police chief. Only the intercession of powerful friends saved
this self-confessed "white elephant" from retirement.[49] After a stern lecture
from McKinley, Lawton was shipped off to the Philippines, to either redeem
himself or fade away.

Setting out from San Pedro Makati on the afternoon of 8 April, the
Lawton-King expedition immediately ran into difficulties. Many of the *cascos*
ran aground in the Pasig River, and most of the night was spent forcing them
over and around mudflats and bars. The plan had called for a surprise dawn
attack, but it was not until early afternoon that the flotilla reached the landing point four miles southwest of Santa Cruz. After a brief five-minute shelling by the gunboats, the launches pulled the *cascos* bearing the sharpshooters
toward shore to cover the expedition's disembarkation. Like most such operations in the Philippines, the amphibious landing was a simple affair. Soldiers climbed from their *cascos* into rowboats; steam launches gathered up
the lines and pulled them as close to shore as possible, then cast off the lines,
leaving the men to pole themselves ashore. The most important mishap was
King's heart attack, creating temporary confusion until Lawton transferred
tactical command to Maj. John J. Weisenberger of the 1st Washington. When
all the troops except the 4th Cavalry were ashore, they formed a long skirmish line and set out for Santa Cruz. The driving rain continued; the soldiers had to pull the two 3-inch guns through mud and wallows. At 5:45 the
1st Idaho and 14th Infantry on the right flank were stopped by a defense
complex of trenches, breastworks, and bamboo obstructions. They advanced
slowly, driving the enemy from the entrenchments, but by then it was dark
and the troops camped in the fields.

The next morning, 10 April, the 4th Cavalry squadron landed to the north
of the town and began a pincer attack, aided by the gunboats' covering fire.
Driven back, the defenders made a desperate stand on the outskirts of the
town but soon broke and withdrew across an open field. Raked by artillery,
machine-gun, and rifle fire, ninety-three perished; the Americans had one dead
and nine wounded. Lawton himself was almost a casualty; as he walked in
front of the advancing lines, his towering figure made even more conspicuous by an enormous white hat, a sniper fired three shots at less than thirty
yards' range, but the general was unhurt. Such public displays of courage,
and near escapes from death, would become commonplace with Lawton.[50]

For the next few days, the troops scoured the area, marched south to occupy the town of Pagsanjan, and captured several launches. In the meantime, the Filipino forces re-formed and closed on Santa Cruz. Evidence of this resurgence came dramatically on 12 April when the North Dakota battalion had a costly skirmish north of the town that left five dead.[51] For the most part, however, there was little fighting. The troops tacked up McKinley's "benevolent assimilation" proclamation, leading some to refer sarcastically to the operation as the "Santa Cruz Bill Poster" expedition. When they could, they scrounged for chickens and collected souvenirs. With his troops running out of rations, Lawton chose to overlook his strict orders against looting. On one occasion he saw soldiers of the 1st Washington dragging a calf and ordered them to release it. The next day, served veal steaks by the regiment's commander at breakfast, he commented that meat from Manila kept exceptionally fresh. On another occasion, visiting the 1st Idaho, he remarked that all the chicken feathers in the area must mean the men were having a soft night's sleep. Such pragmatism and humor explain his soldiers' devotion, but they refute his admirers' claim that Lawton zealously protected civilian property.[52]

Perhaps planning a permanent occupation of the lake towns, Lawton advocated the capture of Calamba. Otis, unwilling to prolong operations against minor objectives he lacked the troops to hold, sent Lawton a telegram on the fifteenth calling off the expedition. Lawton was not pleased, but Otis's decision was sound, for the foray had accomplished all it could do and the troops were exhausted. On the sixteenth they boarded their *cascos* and headed back up the lake to Manila. As they pulled away from Santa Cruz, they could see enemy soldiers entering the town.[53]

The Santa Cruz expedition has generally been dismissed as "a piratical raid" or an example of Otis's "strategic vagueness."[54] Karl Faust totaled up the results—the capture of six launches and the deaths of 125 enemy soldiers—and concluded that save for showing the fine qualities of American soldiers and learning about the varied terrain of Luzon, little had been accomplished.[55] Such criticism is shortsighted. In the minor theater south of Manila, Otis had retained the initiative, demonstrating that the 8th Corps could go wherever it wished with relative impunity. As Filipino documents show, the expedition shocked the revolutionaries. Convinced the next attack would be to the south, Aguinaldo ordered the forces in Cavite, Batangas, and Laguna provinces to concentrate at Muntinlupa.[56] The expedition thus not only distracted Otis's opponents but also tied up manpower and resources that might have gone north. Moreover, it demonstrated that no town on Laguna de Bay was safe from raiders, and this in turn forced local officials

Soldiers patrolling a captured town, 1899

to keep their military forces close to home. Given the limited resources it required, the expedition was a respectable achievement.

As Otis made clear when he recalled Lawton, he wanted to "strike a hard blow at the north very quickly and while we have the volunteers with us."[57] This time, the area of operations would be Bulacan and Pampanga Provinces. MacArthur's 1st Brigade, now commanded by Wheaton, would move up the railroad as Hale's 2nd Brigade forded the Quingua River and strike up the wagon road to the west.[58] They would join at the Army of Liberation's stronghold at Calumpit on the Rio Grande, storm the fortifications, and drive the enemy northwest toward Baliuag. Meanwhile, Lawton, with a 4,000-man provisional division, would set out from Manila on the main wagon road and swing along the base of the mountains to Norzagaray, some twenty miles northeast. There he would meet another brigade under the 2nd Oregon's Col. Owen Summers, which would have established a supply line to the railroad station at Bocaue. At this point, the plans became ambiguous, and the subject of later debate. Otis intended Lawton to advance ten miles west to Baliuag, block the enemy retreat, and trap the Army of Liberation. Lawton believed he was to continue north from Norzagaray into the Central Luzon plain between the mountains to the east and the Rio Grande in the west to draw enemy forces away from defense of Calumpit.[59]

Both Otis and his subordinate commanders believed this would be a decisive campaign, and they were determined to conduct it as an example of American benevolence. For this reason, they devoted great attention to ensuring that the soldiers were aware of their obligations. MacArthur's field orders reminded his men that the United States' goals were "beneficent. It is therefore one of the most important duties of American soldiers to assist in establishing friendly relations with the natives by kind and considerate treatment in all matters arising from personal contact. To exasperate individuals or to burn or loot unprotected houses or property is not only criminal in itself, but tends to impede the policy of the United States and to defeat the very purpose which the Army is here to accomplish."[60] Similarly, Lawton declared that "straggling, looting, pillaging, burning, or the commission of any unlawful excesses on the part of any member of this command is prohibited, and the Provost Marshall will exert himself to prevent the same."[61]

For all its strategic insight and humanitarianism, Otis's plan made scant allowance for the friction of war, terrain, the primitive rural road system, or the inaccuracy of his Spanish maps. Calumpit, his target, was on the southern bank of the hundred-yard-wide Rio Grande. Approaching from the east, the Americans would have to cross two rivers, both considered unfordable. To the west, the Rio Grande wound its way southwest through a maze of estuaries, bayous, and tidal basins into the bay. The offensive would thus be confined to a narrow area along the railroad, crossed with deep rivers, dotted with bamboo and brush, and containing numerous open fields. Moreover, it carried with it the same problems as the Malolos campaign.

As if terrain and climate were not enough, Luna had deployed much of the Army of Liberation along the railroad line and river crossings. Calumpit's already formidable natural defenses had been strengthened by the efforts of thousands of laborers: some trenches were roofed by steel rails or boilerplate to withstand shrapnel, others consisted of a breastwork and several outlying strongpoints. These defenses were held by 4,000 soldiers, and another 3,000 guarded the flank at Baliuag.[62] Convinced that only he could save the republic, Luna was open in his contempt for Aguinaldo: even going so far as to disarm the Kawit Battalion, which had been raised in the president's hometown and considered itself his private guard. Aguinaldo, as the killing of Bonifacio had graphically illustrated, was not someone who would tolerate such an obvious threat, and he undermined many of Luna's efforts. The result was a divided army unsure of its commanders, riddled by factions, and increasingly torn between its president and its commander.[63]

On the night of 10–11 April, Luna launched a series of assaults on the garrisons along the railroad. The American pickets were driven back, and for much of the night there was desperate close-in fighting. Soldiers fired on shadowy forms, and on each other. A flustered MacArthur wired one post commander: "You must hold your position at all hazards. You must hold the place."[64] But this was a situation for which twenty-five years on the frontier had prepared Wheaton. With only a few dozen cavalrymen as escort, the general set out from Malolos, picked up two companies of the 13th Minnesota, and reached Guiguinto, where he found that a large enemy force had worked itself into the dense scrub near the station and was pouring fire into the confused defenders. He rallied the shaken troops; others pushed the armored train forward, and soon its cannon and machine guns—"the sweetest music I ever heard," one veteran recalled—were tearing into the attackers.[65] Wheaton and some 400 men then marched north to Bocaue and beat off another assault. The next morning, he sent the entire 13th Minnesota and two battalions of the 2nd Oregon into a counterattack on a Filipino stronghold near Bocaue. Wheaton's courage and inspiration, and the fighting ability of the Volunteers, had saved the railroad and preserved the campaign.[66]

Otis had scheduled the offensive for 24 April but began a day early when the ubiquitous J. Franklin Bell took the newly formed divisional scouts a few miles east to examine the approaches to the town of Quingua. Bell, who could be aggressive to the point of folly, pushed the patrol on until it was discovered by a far larger enemy force and pinned down. Hale dispatched two companies of the 51st Iowa and, when this proved insufficient, another two. In the meantime, responding to Bell's request, Maj. Henry B. Mulford linked up his 200-man battalion of the 1st Nebraska with Bell's small detachment. Unable to see their enemy in the dense bamboo, flames, and black powder smoke, and raked on all sides, the troops soon succumbed to thirst and heat, and could neither retreat nor advance. Hale fed more and more of his brigade into the fight and brought up the Utah Battery. The gunners tore up some shrub but could not reach the main enemy trenches for fear of hitting troops pinned down in front of them. Hale decided to pull back his brigade and let the artillery soften up the enemy trenches, but to his utter shock, Mulford's battalion rose and charged forward. Just returned from Manila and unaware of Hale's orders, Stotsenburg had rushed to the firing line and ordered his Nebraskans into a frontal assault on the entrenchments. Incredibly, the exhausted soldiers managed to stumble forward, climb the breastworks, and drive off the enemy. Other soldiers seized the two bridges over the river at Quingua. The battle cost Hale's brigade seven killed and forty-four wounded, of whom four of the dead and thirty-one of the wounded were from the battered 1st Nebraska. Among the fatalities was Stotsenburg, killed by a bullet in the heart 200 yards from the enemy defenses.[67]

With the bridge at Quingua captured, MacArthur modified his original plan. Wheaton's brigade would delay its attack across the Bagbag until the 25th so that Hale could cross the river at Quingua, reverse direction, and sweep down its banks to Calumpit. The two brigades would then launch a combined attack on Luna's stronghold.

At five in the morning of 24 April, Hale's small artillery corps began blasting the trenches across the river. After an hour, he ordered the 1st Nebraska over the main bridge while a company of the 1st South Dakota threaded its way across a small footbridge. It took three hours for Hale's brigade to cross the rickety bridges and drag the heavy 3.2-inch guns over. Hale then swung west, marching down the opposite side of the river to sweep the area and prevent any flank attack on Wheaton. Stretched out in a long skirmish line, the Nebraskans on the left flanked by the river and the South Dakotans on the right, with the 51st Iowa in reserve, the troops proceeded slowly in the face of weak but continuous resistance. Tactics were simple. Skirmishers would brush away snipers and protect the flanks; when fieldworks were encountered, the artillery would come up and the troops would spread out

U.S. artillery in action, 1899

and advance on the run, trying to forestall any escape. Thus the advance continued—leaving twenty-eight enemy dead behind one barricade, thirty-eight at another—but losing seven dead and thirteen wounded in the process. When late in the afternoon the tired soldiers charged the last entrenchments, they had almost reached Calumpit.[68]

The next day Wheaton's brigade took its turn. Advancing with the 20th Kansas on the left and the 1st Montana on the right, the armored train and field artillery firing over their heads and keeping enemy marksmen down, the soldiers marched up the railroad line to the Bagbag River. There, Funston and three volunteers tried to rush across the bridge but found it too badly damaged; however, other Kansans splashed across the river and launched a ragged attack on the trenches. On the right, Mulford's battalion waded through shoulder-deep water and swept into Calumpit, clearing out resistance and linking up with Funston. The soldiers pushed through the burning town until they reached the Rio Grande. Across the river was Luna's main defensive position.[69]

An assault across a wide river against extensive fortifications defended by 4,000 enemy soldiers supported by artillery and a machine gun was no mean assignment. Wheaton's solution was characteristically direct. With the 20th Kansas on the left and the 1st Montana on the right, his brigade moved forward in a long skirmish line to some 600 yards from the Rio Grande. As the main body, supported by artillery, laid down suppressing fire, skirmishers raced forward and took up positions behind walls, trees, and inside two stone-and-brick houses near the river that unaccountably had been left standing. Other troops filtered forward, pushing a 3.2-inch cannon up to the abandoned houses, where it soon blazed away directly at the enemy trenches. That evening, a corporal in the 20th Kansas crawled along the railroad bridge, but it had been stripped of its wood flooring and could not be crossed if the enemy offered any resistance. The energetic Funston then took two companies to ford the river a mile downstream, but alert sentries forestalled him. The next morning, his Kansans located a spot 900 yards downriver where a crossing seemed likely. As the regiment sent volleys across the river and the cannon and snipers in the abandoned house poured in an enfilading fire, two soldiers stripped off their clothes, swam the river, and fastened a rope to a stake on the enemy trenches. Two others swam across with rifles and held off the counterattack. Within a few minutes, Funston and a raft load of soldiers had joined them. With his forty-five men, he charged up the banks, taking the surprised defenders in the flank. After a brief exchange of fire, the entire line gave way: hundreds of Luna's soldiers simply walked north up the railroad, abandoning the defenses they had constructed with so much effort.[70]

As MacArthur proudly noted, the capture of the fortifications at Calumpit and the forcing of the Rio Grande in three days was a "remarkable military achievement."[71] Indeed, the operation is difficult to understand in purely military terms and must be seen as a moral victory, in the true sense of the word. Ultimately, the campaign was decided in a series of tests of will between relatively small forces, and in these contests the American citizen soldiers were consistently superior. Time and time again the Volunteers were faced with a daunting tactical challenge and inevitably a few dozen men—sometimes only one or two soldiers—would rise to the occasion. Against such aggressiveness, Luna's grandiose claim that his men had fought valiantly and inflicted crippling casualties was not simply inaccurate, but wildly so. Individual Filipinos fought bravely, and some detachments put up desperate resistance, but as a whole the defense of Calumpit marks a collective failure by the Army of Liberation.[72]

The extent of the demoralization can be inferred from a brief peace attempt on 28 April, when Col. Manuel Arguelles, who had participated in the abortive January negotiations, arrived in Lawton's camp with Aguinaldo's request for a three-week armistice to call together his scattered government and discuss terms. Lawton sent him on to Otis, who, convinced the negotiations were a cynical effort to avert military defeat, refused a truce until the Army of Liberation put down its arms, but he did wire Lawton and MacArthur to hold their positions until he was sure of the situation. After meeting with Aguinaldo's rump cabinet in San Isidro, the delegates returned to Manila on 2 May, with a proposal for a three-month cease-fire, couched in language that required Otis to acknowledge the Philippine Republic as a sovereign nation. This confirmed the general's view that the negotiations were not conducted in good faith, and he again refused an armistice. However, he gave the delegates the Philippine Commission's proclamation and a copy of McKinley's plan for a Philippine civil government, which included an advisory council and judiciary selected from Americans and Filipinos. The delegates, after conferring with Otis, the civilians on the Philippine Commission, and prominent *americanistas,* were won over. Encouraged by their report, and by Aguinaldo's wavering, the moderates at San Isidro ousted Mabini, the hard-line president of the council, and replaced him with Pedro Paterno, who sent the delegates back to Manila to discuss surrender. What might have resulted from Paterno's effort is mere conjecture, for Luna promptly arrested the delegates and substituted his own. Negotiations collapsed, and Otis resumed his offensive.[73]

From Calumpit, MacArthur's next target was San Fernando, ten miles up the railroad to the north. From there he could link up with Lawton and block the Army of Liberation's retreat, or at the very least, drive it completely out of the Tagalog-speaking provinces. Otis's maps, however, showed few of the physical difficulties the 2nd Division would face as it moved along moors, bogs, muddy creeks, estuaries, and dense grasslands on the western fringe of the Candaba Swamp. Because of the marshy terrain, Wheaton's brigade was confined to the narrow railroad embankment and had to send its guns and wagons across the Rio Grande to Hale's brigade, which was to march up the eastern, or right, side of the river along a wagon road and join Wheaton's force at San Fernando.

On 4 May Hale's brigade set out before dawn, the 51st Iowa followed by the Nebraskans and South Dakotans and the supply train. The heat beat down on the tired soldiers, and the few water holes had been destroyed or polluted, sometimes by throwing corpses in them. As the advance guard of Iowans moved through a dense cane field, their scouts spotted a large column barely 400 yards away. With great control, the soldiers withheld their fire and reported back to Hale. Following the tactics he had used so success-fully, the general ordered up his cannon and deployed the Iowans in a skir-mish line. The soldiers soon discovered what the Filipinos had been up to: hundreds of deep holes, spiked with sharp bamboo and camouflaged with mats and dirt dotted the road and surrounding area, channeling the Iowans' attack into "a muck of foul mud mixed with decayed vegetation. Its tangled, rotten dirt and grass would hold and pull at one's legs until it seemed almost impossible to go a step forward."[74] The insurgents, standing plainly in sight but out of the range of the Springfields, sent bullets splashing among the attackers. Dragging themselves forward, the soldiers finally closed within range, and for two hours Americans and Filipinos blazed away at each other; one veteran recalled it as "the best fight they ever made on the islands. . . . they stayed and gave us shot for shot."[75] Luna himself was at the front and was badly wounded. Hale sent the Nebraskans and then the South Dako-tans into the muck and flanked the Filipino left. Too exhausted to pursue, the soldiers moved up to Santo Tomas, where they linked up with Wheaton's brigade.

As Hale's brigade oozed its way forward, Wheaton's clashed with a large enemy force at Santo Tomas, five miles from Calumpit, on 4 May. With Hale's advance threatening their right, the Filipinos fell back, setting fire to build-ings as they went. Funston's Kansans pressed forward, only to encounter a large enemy force dug in near the railroad station. The combative Wheaton led his troops forward in a charge, driving the Filipinos out of their trenches. The next day, two battalions of the 51st Iowa swung out to the right, out-flanked the trenches in front of San Fernando, and caught the defenders out in the open; the result was "simply a stampede."[76] The entire line gave way, some running up the road, others tying their shirts on their rifles as flags of truce. The Americans captured over 100 rifles, many of them thrown away, others surrendered unfired by soldiers who claimed their officers had forced them into battle.[77]

With San Fernando taken, the way appeared clear for a decisive stroke, but MacArthur's division halted. Kenneth Young, the general's admiring biographer, claims that MacArthur believed he could push forward all the way to Lingayen Gulf, and that, in a typical example of meddling, the desk-bound Otis refused.[78] In fact, as the telegraphic correspondence makes clear, it was MacArthur who insisted that his "reduced force" precluded any advance and that "conservative action is necessary."[79] Since 4 February, his 2nd Division had pushed the American lines over 40 miles north, fought 18 major engagements, and lost 53 killed and 353 wounded. Its supply lines were in shambles, and barely half the troops were fit for active duty. The 1st Nebraska was the worst off—35 killed, 151 wounded, and 36 discharged for disability; another 281 were in the hospital and 125 sick in quarters. On 8 May the 395 survivors petitioned for a few weeks' rest, a request their colonel supported strongly: "There is a limit to physical endurance, I believe that limit has now been reached."[80] Although the 1st Nebraska's plight was extreme—and led to its return to Manila on 28 May—the other regiments in the division were in little better shape. Although he had accomplished a great deal, MacArthur knew his command was incapable of further offensive action.

For the rest of May, the 2nd Division recuperated and guarded the long, thin corridor along the forty miles of railroad line from Manila to San Fernando. It was a far from easy task, and the soldiers got little rest. General Tomas Mascardo directed a war of "ambuscades, surprises, capture of detachments, and incessant harassing of the American lines."[81] By the end of the month the San Fernando perimeter was under continuous attack, and patrols along the railroad had to fight off large bodies of irregulars. Although the Army of Liberation was in serious disarray, individual units continued to resist the invaders. The tenacity, resilience, and determination of these Filipino soldiers were impressive; they boded ill for army hopes that the war would be over as soon as the country was occupied.

With MacArthur's offensive stalled in Pampagna Province, attention shifted to the second half of Otis's envelopment, the offensive into Bulacan Province. Lawton's provisional division had set out from Manila on 22 April, marching on what Otis's Spanish maps showed to be the main road into Central Luzon. The soldiers soon discovered it was little more than a muddy foothill trail winding up and down steep hills, and broken at times by swamps and rivers. To increase mobility, Lawton had stripped his column: the men carried little but their rifles and ammunition, and the wagons were limited to ten days' rations and the ammunition reserve. Even so, these loads proved too much in the stifling heat. When Lawton reached the town of Norzagaray three days later, many of the carabao had died and the men were dragging the wagons by hand. At Norzagaray the column was met by a provisional brigade commanded by Col. Owen Summers consisting of two battalions each of his own 2nd Oregon and the 13th Minnesota and a troop of the 4th Cavalry. Summers, who had marched eight miles from Bocaue to establish a secure supply route from the railroad to Lawton's column, entered the town after a short skirmish on 25 April.[82]

At this point occurred one of the delays that would so irritate Lawton and contribute to Otis's reputation for timidity and meddling. On 26 April Lawton wrote Otis outlining an ambitious plan to encircle and destroy the Army of Liberation and Aguinaldo's government. Believing his force was behind the enemy's flank and facing no substantial resistance, he proposed marching his column west along the Quingua River to Baliuag for supplies, then swinging north to San Ildefonso. In the meantime, MacArthur would march from Calumpit north on the San Fernando road along the western flank of the Candaba Swamp. The Army of Liberation, pinched between the two columns and unable to retreat, "would be disintegrated."[83] To Lawton, a wonderful opportunity to end the war had presented itself, and everything must be subordinated to his advance. To Otis in Manila, the situation looked far from certain. Lawton's difficulties en route to Norzagaray had shocked Otis: "I have lost all confidence in any map which I have yet seen."[84] Nor was it clear that Lawton's course was as easy as he suggested, for his dispatches hinted that he faced a large enemy column. Moreover, MacArthur claimed that his division was incapable of supporting Lawton. Even more disturbing, the Filipino forces around Manila were stirring: between the twentieth and twenty-seventh, the 1st Washington detachment at Taguig was repeatedly attacked.[85] But even allowing for all this, Lawton's plan was unrealistic, a testimony to his assumption that everything should be secondary to his goals. Summers's brigade had been assigned temporarily to establish a supply route and was needed to guard the railroad and the Manila lines; now Lawton proposed to keep it indefinitely. With his customary disregard of logistics, Lawton had managed to kill or cripple most of his draft animals in just three days—thus effectively stranding his column in the middle of enemy territory. Unfazed and unrepentant, the general airily demanded that Manila immediately build a new line from the railroad to Baliuag—six miles—so that he could resume the attack. Not surprisingly, Otis hesitated. He urged

Lawton to remain at either Norzagaray or Angat until his logistics were in order and the situation had resolved itself.

Lawton, however, was determined to push on. His plans are uncertain, but he appears to have decided to move north to Angat on the Quingua River and then down that river to the Rio Grande, where supplies could be ferried to him. Taking Angat on the twenty-seventh and briefly establishing telegraphic connections the next day, he informed Manila he intended to press on to San Rafael. On the morning of the twenty-ninth, he sent a column under Lt. Col. William C. Treumann along the north bank of the Quingua while Summers's column approached the town from the south. As Treumann's 1st North Dakota, with some help from the 3rd Infantry, fought a brief skirmish, Summers's troops entered San Rafael. But Lawton had received a telegraphic message from Manila notifying him that Aguinaldo's delegation had just arrived to discuss an armistice. As Otis desired that "everything will be peaceful, at least while they are in our lines," Lawton was to fall back on Angat for resupply.[86] A furious Lawton pulled his troops back, only to receive new instructions to hold San Rafael if he wished. To Lawton this was another example of Otis's interference and incompetence, and he immediately made his displeasure known to the journalists in his camp. But the general's own conduct was far from irreproachable. The most charitable explanation is that at the time he received Otis's orders to withdraw, Lawton did not know that Summers had taken San Rafael. But if, as his telegram implies, he did indeed know that San Rafael had been captured and failed to give Manila an accurate report of the situation, then his abrupt withdrawal was not obedience but spite. Lawton's subsequent efforts to shift blame for his mistake—and by implication the later deaths of two soldiers in the recapture of San Rafael—demonstrate his inability to understand that taking the initiative also meant taking responsibility.[87]

Lawton resumed the advance on 1 May, recapturing San Rafael and entering Baliuag and Bustos the next day. But once again he had to stop and reorganize: he had exhausted his supplies, he was experiencing "considerable resistance" and could "expect resistance from this [point] on."[88] He may have intended his pessimistic reports to persuade Otis to shift resources to his campaign, but if so his plan misfired. Instead, Otis ordered him to remain at Baliuag and organize his supply lines, scout the surrounding area thoroughly, and destroy the vast enemy depots reported to be in the Baliuag-Maasin area. On 3 May, Lawton suddenly reversed himself. Now he was sure that he could easily take San Ildefonso: the Filipinos "have offered no determined or effective resistance. Are greatly demoralized and breaking into small parties and disintegrating."[89] Otis, however, was not to be budged, and

Lawton soon found considerable evidence that his chief was right about enemy supplies in the area. At Baliuag alone he found thirty-seven warehouses and, at Otis's suggestion, distributed nearly 150,000 pounds of rice to the needy. On the sixth Lawton sponsored a town meeting, which elected a mayor and council in Baliuag. By authorizing payment for these officials, he created the first civil government on Luzon that owed its authority to the United States. Despite these activities, the enforced stay at Maasin contributed greatly to Lawton's irritation with Otis, especially when he learned the Filipinos were fortifying San Miguel de Mayumo and San Ildefonso. He complained to MacArthur: "My movements are dictated in detail and I have not been advised of my future disposition; as a result, am not altogether happy."[90]

To Otis, Lawton's demands that everything be subordinated to his campaign must have had an air of unreality. If the experience of the last months had proved anything, it was that only by encircling the Army of Liberation could the 8th Corps hope to destroy it; otherwise the enemy would just continue to retreat up the Central Luzon Plain. Therefore, it made little sense for Lawton to advance any farther north until MacArthur's division was ready, but MacArthur insisted his division needed rest. Moreover, Otis was in the midst of negotiations with the remnants of the Malolos congress, a process that carried a possibility, however small, of ending the war. Under the circumstances, turning Lawton loose would hardly have been a sign of good faith. Even more serious, the War Department, under great pressure from Congress and the states, had all but ordered Otis to return the 16,000 State Volunteers; the longest Otis could delay beginning repatriation was the end of May.[91] To balance their loss, Otis would receive only six regiments of Regulars—barely 7,000 men—one of which he had to send to relieve the Spanish garrisons at Jolo and Zamboanga. Finally, and perhaps most seriously, Otis—like Lawton and MacArthur—badly misjudged the situation. Unaware of the virtual collapse of the Army of Liberation, he believed it was moving against Lawton. To this misapprehension was added another equally mistaken fear: 5,000 Filipino soldiers had moved up from the south and were preparing to fall on Lawton's flank. Given these problems, both real and imagined, delaying Lawton's advance north was a sound decision.[92]

Not until 11 May, after a week of waiting, would Otis allow Lawton to proceed. Because MacArthur, after much shuffling, had finally acknowledged he could provide no support, Lawton now proposed to march north, capture Aguinaldo's new capital at San Isidro, and then march down the Rio Grande, striking the rear of the forces opposing MacArthur at San Fernando. On 15 May, Lawton's crack twenty-five-man reconnaissance unit under civilian William H. Young set off at 2:00 A.M. to sketch the Filipino defenses at San Miguel and San Ildefonso. Because of the dark or their own aggressiveness, "Young's Scouts" infiltrated deep into the Filipino lines and located the main enemy position, but they were attacked; only the arrival of a relief force saved them.[93] The next day, eighteen scouts, accompanied by Lawton's aide, Capt. William E. Birkhimer, and trailed by two companies under Capt. James F. Case, investigated San Miguel de Mayumo's defenses. They bumped into General Gregorio del Pilar's 300 troops drawn up in an open field. Birkhimer ordered up Case's support force, but before it could arrive, a dozen scouts raced across 150 yards of open ground toward the enemy right flank. Faced with this audacity, Pilar's soldiers wavered and then retreated across the river, with the scouts in reckless pursuit. The scouts took the bridge, then charged into San Miguel and held the town for several hours, until Birkhimer belatedly brought up the support. Young, at the forefront of the attack, received what appeared to be a slight wound in his leg; by the time he could be moved to Manila, it had turned septic, and he died shortly afterward. Eleven soldiers, and Birkhimer, were awarded the Medal of Honor for their actions at San Miguel.[94]

On 16 May the scouts again proved their worth. As Private John Killian described it, he and his fellow scouts were reconnoitering the approach to San Isidro, eight men to the right, six to the left, and four on the road, when they saw smoke. Young's replacement, Lt. J. E. Thornton, sent three men to investigate and slowly moved the rest up behind them. The scouts cautiously moved forward until they discovered the source of the smoke—a large enemy force was burning a bridge spanning a deep creek with steep banks. Almost simultaneously, the Filipinos spotted the scouts and opened fire, joined by their companions in the trenches flanking the creek. Amid the flying bullets, Thornton and three others charged over the bridge and enfiladed the enemy trenches, shooting down the defenders at close range. The rest of the scouts forded the river, beat out the flames, and saved the bridge.[95] The next morning, Summers sent his brigade across, formed it into a long V-shaped skirmish line (the 22nd Infantry on the left, the 1st North Dakota and a battalion of the 2nd Oregon on the right), drove off the defenders, and entered San Isidro, the scouts having already rushed through the town and rung the church bell to signal possession. The soldiers were enthusiastically welcomed by dozens of wretched Spanish prisoners and several wealthy Filipinos, but Aguinaldo had already left, taking with him thirteen American captives. The seizure of yet another of the Philippine Republic's capitals was, sniffed one of the accompanying correspondents, an "easy and barren victory."[96]

In Lawton's words, the occupation of San Isidro "practically terminated" his expedition, and with it the great northern campaign.[97] He wanted to continue on to Aguinaldo's new capital at Tarlac and grew angry when Otis refused. His admirers, accepting Lawton's claims at face value, have seen the termination of his offensive as another example of Otis's meddling and caution. But the evidence suggests that Lawton was speaking for the record—or at least for the correspondents—for the campaign had all but ruined his division. Although the month-long advance into Bulacan Province had resulted in only 9 Americans killed and 35 wounded—a clear indication of the weakness of the opposition—515 soldiers required immediate medical attention. Moreover, Lawton had exhausted his supplies and had no means of obtaining more at San Isidro.[98] Otis, with a far more realistic view of the situation, ordered Lawton to march west down the Rio Grande to Arayat, where he linked up with a flying column pushing up from Calumpit on the twenty-first. Three days later, Lawton's command was officially broken up; of all the towns and villages taken on the expedition, only Candaba, Baliuag, and Quingua were retained.[99]

One participant later commented that the Pampanga-Bulacan campaign was "not conspicuous for its importance," a verdict somewhat akin to MacArthur's summation of the Malolos campaign as "disappointing."[100] In the two offensives, the 8th Corps had delivered a series of smashing blows to the enemy, both physically and psychologically, but it had neither annihilated the Army of Liberation nor convinced the revolutionary government to surrender. A combination of factors—logistics, bad roads, Filipino resistance, weather, disease, inadequate manpower—all frustrated the 8th Corps' efforts to maneuver the enemy into the one great war-winning battle. With the monsoon already beginning and Washington adamant that the State Volunteers be repatriated, Otis settled for a defensive perimeter forty miles north of Manila until better weather and reinforcements arrived in the fall. Then, once again, the 8th Corps could attempt to destroy the Army of Liberation once and for all.

SIX

SUMMER STALEMATE

The summer of 1899 witnessed some reassessment of the war. In August, Otis acknowledged that despite over half a year of continuous defeats, the "rebellion still presented a bold and defiant front."[1] He believed military victory was only a few months away, but he was intelligent enough to recognize that defeating the Army of Liberation was not enough. Armed resistance would continue until the Filipinos were convinced both that the United States intended to remain in the islands and that American colonial rule would be to their advantage. Otis urged the Executive Office and Congress to develop a clear political program for the governance of the islands after the war was over. The commanding general's views reflect the growing uncertainty within the 8th Corps about the nature of the war and the best means to carry out its mission. To some officers the conflict was simply an insurrection of Tagalogs, *ladrones,* fanatics, and adventurers who sought little more than self-aggrandizement. They persisted in the belief that an all-out offensive would rapidly resolve the issue. Other officers were far more pessimistic: arriving in Manila in August, one noted, "An air of gloom prevails everywhere and even the city is deemed unsafe. Although we have over 30,000 troops about Otis seems to have failed entirely."[2]

By May pressure from Washington, the state legislatures, and the citizen soldiers themselves severely curtailed Otis's ability to use the Volunteers except in an emergency. At least some of the citizen soldiers were thoroughly sick of the war and furious with their commander. Lewis Burlingham, displaying racial attitudes typical of the time, reminded his parents that "the volunteers never enlisted to fight these nigers [sic]" and were "forced to fight and kept here against our will because Gen. Otis (the ———) cables home that all the volunteers want to stay here."[3] A veteran of the 1st Nebraska wrote, "We feel that every man of ours that's lost is worth more than the whole damned island. . . . We don't know what we are fighting for hardly."[4] With the end of the Bulacan-Pampanga campaign in May, Otis recalled many of the Volunteer regiments to Manila for what they believed would be a short period of rest before being sent home. But Otis, parsimonious to the last, intended to extract the last nickel's worth of service from them.

In order to support the spring campaigns in the north, Otis had had to neglect the southern and western lines circling Manila. There the 8th Corps

117

had established a solid defensive position, but it was under incessant harassment by revolutionary forces from Batangas, Cavite, and Laguna. To the west, the mountainous, rugged area along the northern coast of Laguna de Bay had long been a hideout for brigands and scattered insurgent bands; now Otis's informants reported between 2,500 and 5,000 soldiers under the loose control of Brig. Gen. Pio del Pilar. These were the troops whom Otis had feared would attack Lawton in April. The concentration of the Volunteers in Manila gave him an opportunity to strike a few preemptive blows before the enemy attacked again.

Otis's plan called for two converging columns under Lawton's overall command. The first of these, 2,576 officers and men, under Brig. Gen. Robert H. Hall, was to advance southwest from the Marikina waterworks to Antipolo and then drive south to Morong. In the meantime, Col. John Wholley, with the 1st Washington and 1st North Dakota, would march east from San Pedro Makati. Ideally, del Pilar's forces would be driven into the Morong Peninsula, a narrow finger that jutted into Laguna de Bay, where they could be mopped up. It was a plan similar, on a much smaller scale, to the one Otis had tried in the northern campaigns, and, like its predecessor, it looked far better on his office maps than on the field.

Shortly before daylight on 3 June, Hall crossed the San Mateo River and pressed forward into the mountains. The next morning, the North Dakotans pushed east to Cainta—the artillery driving off the defenders easily—then on to Taytay. This movement sealed off the northwest of the Morong Peninsula. On the morning of the fifth, Wholley loaded his battalions onto *cascos* and, supported by three gunboats, crossed the lake to attack the town of Morong and drive its defenders into Hall's approaching column. But by now a familiar pattern had emerged: the Americans won the skirmishes, but their opponents escaped with little damage. As the soldiers pushed deeper into the countryside, their progress slowed to a crawl. One veteran recalled the "terrific heat of sun" and how the infantry "suffered tortures" as they waited in a steaming rice paddy for hours as the cavalry sought vainly to locate the trail.[5] From the mountaintops, snipers strafed Hall's column, forcing the soldiers to scramble up the steep slopes, only to find their opponents perched on another hill ready to resume the fight. The brigade suffered three killed and ten wounded, and another eighty-four were felled by exhaustion. Hall did not reach Antipolo until the next morning, a march that Lawton had believed would take but two hours.

On 4 June Hall linked up with the North Dakota regiment near Antipolo and entered the town without resistance; del Pilar and his phantom army were long gone. Lawton, in a vain attempt to catch his elusive foe, ordered the combined column to march south to Morong, sweeping the area. Once again, ravine and brush, heat, thirst, and exhaustion slowed progress to a crawl and left huge gaps in the cordon. A few armed insurgents were shot or captured, but the rest escaped to the north or, hiding their uniforms, became "amigos." In an effort to salvage some permanent gain out of this disappointing campaign, Otis occupied Morong and Cainta, relieving much of the pressure on the Marikina waterworks, but condemning the 1st North Dakota to a miserable, unhealthy, and demoralizing tour of occupation.[6]

With his western defenses somewhat more secure, Otis then turned south, seeking to drive Lt. Gen. Mariano Trias and the reputed 6,000 revolutionary troops in front of the Manila lines into Cavite Province. On 7 June, Lawton concentrated 4,000 soldiers into two columns—Wheaton's 1st Brigade and Ovenshine's 2nd Brigade. They were to break through the enemy line, then swing out in separate arcs, pinning the Filipinos against their trenches. Lawton arranged that navy and army gunboats would patrol both Manila Bay and Laguna de Bay, shelling any enemy formations that appeared. The attack began on 10 June, a grueling ordeal that few forgot. Even before the march began, many of Wheaton's units were exhausted—they had been rushed about from camp to camp, enduring torrential rains and temperatures so high they felt they had fevers. Marching out at 5:00 A.M., without breakfast, they quickly broke through the enemy lines. They then entered an area known as "el desierto," a barely cultivated, roadless expanse of thickets, head-high grasslands, rice fields, ridges, gullies, and wallows.[7] Snipers raked the footpaths, forcing the troops to march in extended skirmish order through ravines and scrub, so that increasingly battalions, then companies, began to separate into isolated groups. By noon everyone was out of water and most had thrown away their ponchos, rations—everything but rifles, ammunition, and canteens. Near Las Pinas the Filipinos launched a determined attack, but the 9th Infantry and the Colorado regiment beat them back. Too fatigued to go on, and with stragglers spread over the countryside, Wheaton's brigade went into camp.

In the meantime, Ovenshine was falling farther and farther behind. Lawton's plan called for him to move behind Wheaton and then swing right toward Manila Bay and roll up the Filipino forces southeast of Las Pinas. But Lawton had not anticipated the problems inherent in funneling the two brigades through a narrow breach, nor the appalling condition of the trails and paths. Ovenshine's soldiers were soon scattered over the countryside, and by the time he linked up with Wheaton late in the afternoon, his brigade was in a shambles and the newly arrived 13th Infantry was so exhausted and demoralized it had to be sent back to Manila.[8]

Over the next few days, Lawton's division pushed south, encountering little direct resistance but continually fighting with irregulars who roamed freely around his flanks and rear. However, on the thirteenth, one of the hardest-fought engagements of the war took place at the bridge over the Zapote River. This had been the site of a heroic battle against Spain, and the defenders had constructed a formidable series of earthworks on the southern bank of the river. Confronted with these fieldworks, three companies of the 14th Infantry set off to find a crossing farther up the river as two companies of the 12th Infantry and three companies of the 14th, supported by Lt. W. L. Kenly's four field pieces, attempted a frontal assault. The troops advanced by rushes, attacking over open ground as Kenly's artillerymen pulled their light guns up the road, stopping now and then to shell the insurgents' trenches. Reaching the river, the soldiers took cover along the banks and poured a suppressing fire into the trenches. They were joined by Kenly, who set up his guns on the road, less than forty yards from the enemy position. The gunners would push one gun up the slope of the bridge's ramp, let the recoil kick it back, then push up another. For over an hour the firefight raged along a three-quarter-mile front, the soldiers on the banks taking cover behind bushes and ditches while the Filipinos blasted them. Finally, the flanking force arrived, moved to within 300 yards of the enemy trenches, and opened a deadly fire. The defenders fell back, their retreat assisted by Ovenshine's orders that his troops cease firing to avoid hitting each other. The Americans counted thirty dead in the trenches and captured another twenty-nine wounded, but they had suffered eight killed and forty-six wounded.[9]

After Zapote Bridge, Lawton scoured northern Cavite, occupying towns and aggressively seeking a decisive battle, but the enemy was content to revert to harassment. Lawton wanted to push on to San Francisco de Malabon, believing he would find Aguinaldo's deputy, Trias, and a large force. Otis, on the other hand, was increasingly concerned that what he had intended as a limited raid to relieve pressure on the southern lines was turning into a major offensive. On the sixteenth he ordered Lawton to pull back. But Lawton, or his subordinate Wheaton, continued raiding into Cavite. They duly paid the price. On the nineteenth a battalion of the 4th Infantry pushing south out of Imus was ambushed and had to retreat for four miles, losing five killed and twenty-three wounded.[10] Perhaps chastened by this near disaster, Lawton pulled back.

In many respects, the Cavite campaign was a microcosm of the triumphs and frustrations the 8th Corps had endured in the first four months of war. The Americans had demonstrated their ability to fight their way through the strongest enemy defenses, but climate and terrain, exhaustion, poor logistics, and miscommunication had denied them a decisive battle. In the south, as in the north, the 8th Corps had extended its lines, inflicted heavy losses, and badly hammered its opponents. But these victories had come at a terrible cost. Lawton's division was no longer capable of any but the most limited operations: of the 1st Montana's 14 officers and 477 men, only 8 officers and 112 men were present, and out of the 44 officers and 1,216 men in the 14th Infantry, merely 5 officers and 302 men were fit for duty.[11] What was even more disheartening was that, as even the optimistic Otis recognized, these losses had succeeded only in gaining a large amount of territory "without strategic importance." A campaign that Otis had intended to do no more than relieve pressure on the southern lines had instead greatly lengthened his front and tied down an additional 2,500 soldiers when "every available man should be sent toward our true objective in the north."[12] It was a discouraging result.

By the end of May, the summer monsoon and the imminent withdrawal of the Volunteers restricted the 8th Corps to what Otis termed "minor military operations."[13] Although total manpower hovered between 26,000 and 30,000, the numbers available for active operations were barely half. For most of the summer, the American position north of Manila extended forty miles in a narrow peninsula along the wagon route east of the Candaba Swamp to Baliuag, then turned west along the swamp to Calumpit, and finally northwest along the railroad line to San Fernando. South of Manila, it followed two routes: the first extended about ten miles along the Manila Bay road into northern Cavite, with garrisons at Bacoor, Paranaque, and Las Pinas; the second followed the towns on the Pasig River, then went along the southwestern shore of Laguna de Bay to Calamba, some thirty miles from Manila. Although both the northern and southern positions were commonly referred to as "lines," they were not contiguous trench systems but small company and battalion garrisons stretched along the main roads, linked by telegraph and patrols, but with large gaps in between. This disposition had both advantages and disadvantages. Given the difficulties of Luzon's terrain, no large force could move cross-country in any sort of order, nor could it keep itself supplied. Thus by holding key points along the main arteries, the Americans effectively blocked any major offensive and made maximum use of their limited forces. But the isolated garrisons served as magnets for provincial and regular forces, who dug trenches near the outposts and, in some places, virtually besieged them. Small enemy detachments moved with relative impunity through the gaps; indeed, guerrillas operated all the way to the outskirts of Manila, harassing supply columns, cutting telegraph wires, sniping at soldiers, and, perhaps most serious, intimidating any civilians inclined to cooperate with the invaders.

For the troops of Lawton's 1st Division who pulled duty around Manila and to the south, July and August were endless misery. Forty-six inches of rain fell near Manila, turning paths into mud pits, dry gullies into raging streams; it soaked clothes, food, and bedding, and sent disease rates skyrocketing. Military operations were confined to brief reconnaissances, such as the sodden cruise of Capt. Hugh J. McGrath, who steamed up and down Laguna de Bay, sometimes greeted by white flags, other times by sniping and burning villages. Occasionally there were larger operations, such as the 26 July occupation of Calamba and Los Banos, a stiff fight that cost three dead and another eleven wounded but inflicted heavy casualties on the Filipinos. Intended as a limited offensive to solidify the southern flank, the operation had exactly the opposite effect, for both towns were soon surrounded. An August expedition under newly arrived Brig. Gen. Samuel B. M. Young sent to clear out the area near the Marikina pumping station had similar results. The troops plodded through water and mud up to their knees until they had closed to within 250 yards of the enemy trenches, whereupon their foes vanished into the underbrush or hid their weapons and became "amigos."[14]

To the north, MacArthur's 2nd Division stood on the defensive for much of the early summer as the Army of Liberation sought to break through its perimeter. But the railroad to Manila remained secure, and behind the defenses engineers restored rails, roads, and bridges, and quartermasters unloaded wagons and freight cars bulging with ammunition, rations, telegraph wire, and all the other matériel necessary for a fall campaign. In late summer, MacArthur directed a limited offensive to secure his northern and western flanks by occupying Bacolor, Mexico, and Angeles. After torrential rains caused several delays, on 9 August the attack began. As cannon and the Gatlings of the armored train pounded the town, newly promoted Col. J. Franklin Bell sent his 36th Infantry into Bacolor. The armored train then steamed up the line to provide cover for a pincer attack. Wheaton led the 51st Iowa, the 17th, and a battalion of the 22nd along the right of the rail line as Col. Emerson H. Liscum, with the 9th, 12th, and 36th Infantry, struck on the left. Against weak resistance—some companies did not fire a shot the entire day—the soldiers advanced through flooded paddies and dense sugarcane in stultifying heat. By the eleventh, the division had pushed into Angeles, which was burned by the retreating Filipinos. The soldiers dug trenches and set up outposts; engineers and quartermasters resumed their preparations, the Army of Liberation returned and hemmed in the defenders; and the miserable summer continued.[15]

In the southern Philippines, the summer witnessed one important campaign, one failure, and one draw. On Negros, a series of hard-fought engagements and vigorous patrols suppressed a Babylane-inspired uprising. On Cebu, however, Hamer's lethargic direction resulted in a wasteful campaign against an insurgent stronghold. On Panay, Hughes virtually suspended operations during the summer. Like Otis, he planned to resume the offensive in the fall. The army had far more success in Mindanao and the Sulu archipelago, the so-called Moro Provinces, where Brig. Gen. John C. Bates negotiated an important agreement on 20 August 1899 in which the Sultan of Sulu accepted United States sovereignty. In return, the Americans agreed to defend the sultan from his enemies and promote free trade. Otis was very pleased; he later commented that without Bates's efforts he would have required 15,000 soldiers to garrison the Moro Provinces.[16] With the treaty, he only had to reoccupy the old Spanish outposts at Jolo, Zamboanga, and Siassi.

With the 8th Corps essentially on the defensive, the War Department began to replace the "boys of '98" with a new army for empire. Lack of quarters in Manila, a shortage of transport, and enemy attacks kept some unlucky state regiments in the islands until the fall. Lucky units had a relatively easy, if boring, time in Manila playing baseball, shopping for souvenirs, and drinking at the beer gardens that were springing up all over the city.[17] Once on board the transports, the citizen soldiers made it known that they were having no more Regular Army nonsense. When one colonel attempted to force his troops into a routine of drills, inspections, and uniform regulations, the men refused to muster for drill and "bawled the officers out to their faces."[18] The 2nd Oregon all but rioted when the governor sought to have them discharged in Portland and deny the men their substantial travel allotment.[19]

The State Volunteers left a somewhat ambiguous legacy in the Philippines. For four months they shouldered the burden of fighting while Otis kept the bulk of the Regulars near Manila. They performed some of the most notable acts of heroism of the war: of the twenty-three Medals of Honor awarded during their stay in the islands, Volunteers won all but six.[20] Yet at the same time they conceded the Volunteers' fighting ability, some witnesses were critical of their behavior. Hughes urged that they be kept out the Visayas on the grounds they "may do our cause very great injury amongst the people by misconduct, or, as has occasionally happened, by mistreatment of Natives."[21] Correspondent Albert G. Robinson termed them "inflammable material" whose virulent racism and bellicose eagerness for a "scrap" were in sharp contrast to the iron discipline of the Regulars.[22] A recent popular work goes even further, arguing that the Volunteers "brought with them a frontier spirit steeped in an individualism that easily degenerated into lawlessness."[23]

Some State Volunteers did take a somewhat cavalier attitude both to the forms of discipline and to Filipino property. Hughes, it will be recalled, claimed they "would steal the sandals of a native who had died of small pox."[24] Another Regular officer praised their abilities in combat but deplored their "disposition to loot and destroy."[25] This accusation needs some clarification. Because soldiers were constantly operating at the end of their supply lines, virtually all officers, including Lawton, expected them to forage for food. Similarly, soldiers were well within their rights to impress civilians for work parties, to confiscate wagons and livestock for transportation, and to destroy buildings that the enemy had used. Moreover, because the U.S. Army paid compensation, civilians often accused soldiers of damages done by Filipino soldiers or bandits. Yet even with these exclusions, and despite strict orders, the torch was applied all too freely by the Volunteers. The strong prohibition against looting did not preclude a great deal of "mooching" for "relics" from deserted or destroyed houses. Nor did the mostly Protestant citizen soldiers hesitate to remove valuables from churches, for as Joseph Smith of the 1st Washington explained, "With the priests fighting on the side of the enemy and the churches barricaded as rebel strongholds this vandalism did not appear in their eyes to be particularly atrocious." Smith recalled that on one campaign a chance find of 250 pesos ($125 U.S.) touched off a frenzy of "prospecting" which yielded a total of 10,000 pesos. By the following day the entire regiment was involved, soldiers seeking out money buried in stone jars, hidden in walls, or concealed in false-bottomed boxes. Some companies went off to explore the pickings in other towns, but as the wealth increased, its finders became more and more reticent, so that the actual amount was never known. According to Smith, the officers were equally culpable: when one honest soldier turned over 150 pesos he had taken from a looter, the money duly turned up in a poker game.[26]

A more serious charge is that the State Volunteers routinely shot prisoners and civilians. There is no doubt that fighting during the Philippine War was vicious and brutal, but on closer examination, many incidents appear to be inseparable from combat. For example, during its assault on 5 February the 1st Washington crossed an open field, scaled an eighteen-foot entrenchment, and trapped the defenders against the Pasig River. According to one eyewitness, "many were shot down like sheep" as they tried to swim away: "It was a glorious victory but a horrible slaughter."[27] During the attack on Caloocan on 10 February, Kansans allegedly shot five prisoners and cited orders that there was no place to keep prisoners. Even more appalling, they insisted that Funston had made it generally understood that no quarter was to be given. An investigation exonerated Funston, and several of the witnesses recanted both the shootings and the orders.[28] Other cases are not problematic at all. One veteran recalled seeing a corporal boot a dying enemy soldier and another incident in which a Filipino who tried to surrender was shot down.[29]

Although there is much anecdotal evidence, the statistical material available on troop conduct in the Philippines does not support the contention that the State Volunteers were undisciplined. Of the 563 general courts-martial between 1 July 1898 and 30 June 1899, two Regular regiments, the 18th and the 14th Infantry, were responsible for roughly a quarter (134). Similarly, during this period two Regular regiments—the 23rd (947) and the 20th Infantry (914)—accounted for almost 20 percent of the 10,605 total summary courts-martial. In contrast, the two "worst" state regiments—the 2nd Oregon (593) and the 13th Minnesota (485)—accounted for 10 percent.[30] This suggests that Regulars were twice as likely as State Volunteers to commit breaches of discipline, but it may indicate merely that the citizen soldiers behaved as badly as or worse than Regulars but were not held as strictly accountable for their actions.

As the state regiments returned to enthusiastic popular acclaim, their place was filled by the U.S. Volunteers. If the State Volunteers were the lineal descendants of the county and neighborhood companies that made up the armies of the Civil War, then the U.S. Volunteers looked forward to the national citizen soldier armies of the twentieth century. Called into existence by the Army Act of 2 March 1899, which authorized the president to enlist up to 35,000 volunteers for service in the Philippines, they were an experiment from the beginning. The War Department wanted soldiers who would combine the best qualities of the State Volunteers and the Regulars; to the Volunteers' initiative, adaptability, morale, esprit de corps, and aggressive fighting spirit would be added the Regulars' discipline, training, and leadership.

In part owing to Otis's unrealistically low estimates, in part because recruiting for the Regular Army was of higher priority, the War Department delayed until 5 July before authorizing the first ten infantry regiments. These, numbered 26 through 35, were filled by 15 August, and eight were deployed in the Philippines by 7 November. Three more, the 36th and 37th Infantry and the 11th Cavalry, were predominantly recruited in the Philippines from State Volunteers who received a $500 bonus to reenlist. In August the War Department called up the 38th through 47th Infantry regiments, and in September two regiments of African-Americans, the 48th and 49th. These last units had white field officers but mostly black company officers. Each regiment consisted of some 1,350 officers and men, divided into twelve 109-man companies and three battalions.

The War Department took great pains to ensure that the new regiments were commanded by the finest officers available. Justly or not, Regulars believed that too many State Volunteer officers had proved to be political hacks, infirm, or unfit for combat command. In contrast, each candidate for the U.S. Volunteers was subject to rigorous screening. Most of the colonels and lieutenant colonels and a high proportion of the majors were selected from Regular Army officers who had excelled at company command. Company officers—captains and lieutenants—were chosen from proven State Volunteer officers, from recent West Point graduates, and from Regular noncoms. In recognition both of the importance of small-unit cohesion and of the ravages of tropical service, each company had, in addition to a captain and two lieutenants, eighteen noncoms.[31]

The U.S. Volunteers were intended to preserve local pride and neighborhood connections and yet still be national regiments. Each possessed a distinct regional character, which was reflected in both its officer corps and its enlisted ranks. The 33rd Infantry, for example, was headquartered at San Antonio and soon was nicknamed the "Texas Regiment"; a third of its officers and enlisted men came from Texas, and another third were from the South or Southwest. Its colonel was Luther R. Hare, a 7th Cavalry captain who had fought at Little Big Horn and, perhaps equally important, a Texan with excellent political connections. The hard-cursing Hare established an immediate rapport with his men, once boasting that he had 1,200 sharpshooters and 1,300 crapshooters. Among its company commanders were two West Point classmates, a sprinkling of Texas Rangers, and an Illinois lawyer.[32]

The U.S. Volunteer regiments were intended to go into battle immediately, and so great attention was spent on their recruitment, physical fitness, and training. Because popular enthusiasm for Philippine annexation was still high in the summer of 1899, the regiments were deluged with volunteers. A particularly eager or athletic underage volunteer, however, might slip in by writing the number "21" on a piece of paper and putting it in his shoe; he could then swear truthfully that he was "over 21." The U.S. Volunteers tended to be both more mature and better skilled than their Regular counterparts: in the 26th Infantry, for example, the average age was twenty-seven, and ninety-nine different occupations were represented. Also unlike the Regulars, the Volunteers were given a thorough and vigorous training program that stressed small-unit tactics, hiking, fieldcraft, and marksmanship with the Krag. They were closely monitored, and any who might lack the necessary physical or moral abilities for tropical service were culled out. What remained were some of the best troops man-for-man the United States has ever fielded.[33]

The army also supplemented its manpower by employing residents of the islands. Filipino nationalist scholars have long demonized the elite "collaborators" for betraying the cause of independence. This is overly simplistic and ignores the great differences among the Filipino upper classes. Some provincial elites had benefited from the revolution and had all but been confirmed in their domination over local affairs, but others, particularly those interested in trade, were sympathetic to the economic reforms and stability promised by the United States. Although some prominent upper-class *principales* served in the civil administration, the average "collaborator" worked for the Quartermaster's Office: between 1 September 1898 and 30 June 1899, this office employed 132,000 laborers in Manila alone.[34] Indeed, without native help the 8th Corps could not have even fed itself in Manila. In addition to Filipinos, the army used Chinese porters on its expeditions. One surgeon praised them for their bravery, noting that when the medical wagons could not get to the front, the Chinese would go up to the firing line and carry the wounded back. By summer, companies in Lawton's 1st Division had a permanent component of six "Chinos," and in MacArthur's 2nd Division, fifty were assigned to each regiment.[35] The successful use of laborers, police, and guides also broke down prejudices against the eventual use of Filipinos as distinct military forces.

Less visible than the laborers were the hundreds, perhaps thousands, of Filipinos and Chinese who worked as part of the U.S. Army's intelligence services. Unable to speak the local dialects, unfamiliar with terrain and local customs, unable to tell noncombatants from guerrillas, the army was, in the words of one officer, "a blind giant. The troops were more than able to annihilate, to completely smash anything that could be brought against them in the shape of a military force on the part of the insurgents; but it was almost impossible to get any information in regard to those people."[36] In the early engagements around Manila, soldiers discovered that the revolutionaries were "prone to put into writing all their official acts. . . . but they seem very generally not to have taken proper precautions to keep these records from falling into our hands upon the advance of our troops, and accordingly large numbers of such papers were captured."[37] However, 8th Corps headquarters did little to exploit this opportunity beyond creating the Insurgent Records Office, later the Bureau of Insurgent Records, to translate them. Headed by Capt. John R. M. Taylor, the bureau was understaffed but given a multiplicity of tasks; as a result, it often failed to provide up-to-date intelligence.[38] Otis preferred the Manila elite, even though their information was often self-interested and inaccurate. Finding themselves unable to rely on the corps' headquarters for accurate information, field officers began to develop their own intelligence networks, to hire guides and interpreters, and to cultivate contacts among the many Filipinos who were hostile to the revolutionaries. One of the most innovative was James F. Smith, who used a variety of agents, ranging from powerful Negrense planters to a man who "would very soon have begun to make trouble and I thought it better to secure his faithfulness by putting him to work even if it cost a few dollars extra per month. He is shrewd and sharp and has the reputation of being unprincipled."[39] The actual number of guides and agents is difficult to determine, as great efforts were taken to protect their identities. Some were paid from the Quartermaster's Office as laborers, others from clandestine Secret Service moneys, and some, such as Smith's informant, from officers' personal funds.

A far more radical step was the employment of Filipinos as military auxiliaries. In July the Americans formed a Manila Native Police of 246 constables—soon 625—which within a year made 7,442 arrests, including three revolutionary generals.[40] On Negros, Smith went even further, raising a constabulary, arming town police with rifles, and employing local and constabulary forces against Babylanes and *ladrones*. The final step was Lt. Matthew A. Batson's recruitment of a company from the town of Macabebe, Pampanga Province. The Macabebes had a tradition of military service to Spain, and hated both the Tagalogs and the Republic. With Lawton's support, Batson submitted a plan that called for Macabebes to be employed on the lower Rio Grande. Traveling through the swamps on *bancas* (canoes), they would spy on enemy forces, patrol communications, and hunt down *ladrones* and guerrillas. Otis recognized that if Lawton was to execute his part of the fall northern offensive, he would need skilled guides and scouts, and, so far, the Macabebes were the only Filipino tribe willing to serve. On 10 September the 100-man 1st Company, Macabebe Scouts was formally organized. Given a short course in drill and tactics, equipped with Krag carbines, and assigned to four-to-six men *banca* teams, they quickly reduced guerrilla attacks on army communications. Greatly impressed, Otis ordered another Macabebe company organized on 21 September, and a third on 6 October. Within a few weeks, the 8th Corps had gone from having no Filipino troops to a five-company battalion, fittingly titled Batson's Macabebe Scouts. Joined by a small Fil-American unit, the Lowe Scouts, Batson's were the first of what would eventually become a military auxiliary corps of over 15,000.[41]

If many army officers remained skeptical of using Filipinos to fight Filipinos, they were more amenable to Filipinos governing Filipinos under American auspices. This was especially true in the Visayas, where at Bacolod, Iloilo, and Cebu City the army approved local governments complete with

Matthew Batson and Macabebe scouts

mayors and town councils. On Luzon, the problem of government increased as the army pushed north. But the public execution of a mayor who welcomed American troops in the first week of war served as a stark reminder that, without permanent occupation, it was unconscionable to ask Filipinos to openly support the United States. However, as the army occupied more and more towns, garrison commanders needed the help of local political leaders in order to ensure clean water, waste disposal, and other necessities, lest their own soldiers sicken. In most cases, officers and officials worked out ad hoc measures: Lawton established municipal government on 6 May at Baliuag by the simple expedient of calling a town meeting and having residents vote for a mayor.

In July, William A. Kobbé, whose 3rd Artillery had borne heavy duty along the Manila–San Fernando railroad, developed the first practical plan for civil government. His proposal was brief, barely two pages, and very simple, consisting of only six articles. Each town would have a municipal council composed of a *presidente* (mayor), a vice *presidente,* and one headman from each barrio or ward. The council was charged with the "interest of the town, of the maintenance of public order, of the police, of hygienic measures, and of public instruction, and of the prosperity of each locality." The *presidente* had considerable powers, but "taking into consideration the misery which at the present prevails in towns" he was to impose only the "least burden- some" taxes to pay the council and establish public schools. In order to fore- stall corruption or oppression, the *presidente* was required to turn over the public accounts to the garrison commander each month.[42] MacArthur op- posed Kobbé's plan as too ambitious, but an enthusiastic Otis issued it with slight revisions as General Order 43 on 8 August 1899. For Otis, it was a logical step in the army's mission to convince Filipinos of American benevo- lence and to prepare for civilian rule.

For the U.S. Navy, the summer brought little change in duties but a marked change in command—and in the conduct of joint operations. Since the be- ginning of the war, Dewey had evinced little interest in the land campaign, or even in blockading the archipelago, focusing his attention on the Cavite naval yard and his social schedule. He had often played dog in the manger, never conceding that the navy was not the primary service in the Philippines. Nor did he contribute much to policy, absenting himself from the Philippine Commission meetings and rarely commenting on strategic issues. He seems to have disliked Otis and battled him over control of the gunboats and the credit for the capture of Manila and Iloilo.[43] But finally, on 20 May, he left for a tumultuous hero's welcome and was replaced on 20 June with Rear Adm. John C. Watson. Fortunately, Dewey's successors devoted far more time, energy, and expertise to conducting naval operations in the archipelago.

In his annual report of 1899, the secretary of the navy summarized his service's primary duty as "to cooperate with the Army and to maintain a blockade of such extent as has been determined by the general policy of cam- paign laid down by the War Department."[44] The blockade was intended to shut off all "illicit traffic," defined by Watson on 19 August as any vessel flying the Philippine Republic's flag, any vessel trading with "closed" ports, or any vessel laden with contraband of war.[45] Since for most of 1899 there were only three "open" ports—Manila, Iloilo City, and Cebu City—and since the contraband list included such necessities as matches, rice, oil, nipa, and fish, the blockade outlawed most waterborne trade.[46] Of the navy's other missions, one of the most important was reconnaissance. Warships took soundings at Lingayen Gulf, Albay, Sorsogan, and other sites where the army would later stage amphibious landings. Captains also visited several islands to secure the return of prisoners or to negotiate with local military chiefs for the release of European hostages and the preservation of private property. The navy also did its own bit for "benevolent assimilation," distributing rice to the destitute and hunting down pirates. But the blockade was by far the navy's most important contribution to the American war effort.[47]

The blockade struck at the crucial necessities of any Philippine national government: interisland communications and finances. By severing water-borne traffic, the navy isolated and localized each island's resistance movement and prevented both the transfer of reinforcements and the establishment of sanctuaries. Of equal importance was the gradual destruction of the revolutionaries' financial system, which eventually made it impossible for them to pay or feed their military forces. But the blockade also contributed greatly to the already existing food crises in much of the archipelago. Barely a month after the war's beginning, one captain reported the blockade had caused widespread rice shortages in southeastern Luzon, Samar, and Leyte. In July 1899, Vicente Lukban, Samar's revolutionary chief, complained that it had reduced him to eating little more than yams and rice. A few months later, Bates praised the navy's blockade of Zamboanga, which "had literally starved the natives into subjection" and thus allowed the army a bloodless occupation.[48]

Within the armed forces there was much ambivalence about the blockade. Admiral Watson worried about its legality. Hughes was an enthusiastic supporter, as were a number of hard-liners. But Otis noted it left many areas without food and badly undercut the revival of commerce, and thus greatly increased the problems of reestablishing order and prosperity on the islands. The military commander on Cebu protested that since only Cebu City was open, the blockade restrictions effectively precluded all waterborne trade and caused demoralization, unemployment, and smuggling. He asked that all small coastal vessels, most of them one-person *bancas,* be allowed to trade throughout the island. However, his superiors upheld the restrictions on trading with "enemy ports," pointing out that the revolutionaries were raking in substantial sums selling passes and licenses for trade, and this could be ended only by treating all trade outside the city as illicit.[49] A naval officer assigned to the Mindanao-Sulu patrol complained that the local army commander wanted him to encourage trade among the Moros, but his superiors in Manila ordered him to suppress it.[50] Such disputes were a harbinger of many between local officers seeking to address conditions in their areas and authorities in Manila attempting to create general policies.

For the blockade to be effective, the navy had to restructure its Asiatic Squadron. Instead of the large steel, big-gunned warships that had won the

Battle of Manila Bay, the navy turned to some twenty-five gunboats, many of them captured from the Spanish, ranging in size from 250 to 900 tons. Equipped with formidable batteries of cannons and machine guns, they might well be—as one captain boasted—more feared than a regiment of infantry. They were commanded by junior officers, some barely out of Annapolis. Keeping the cranky engines working, securing sufficient coal, avoiding shoals and reefs, and stalking smugglers and pirates through the archipelago was exhilarating work, and many a veteran viewed it as the best part of his naval career.[51] To administer and supply the gunboats, the navy initially assigned each one to a larger "mother ship." Later it divided the archipelago into four patrol areas, with stations at Zamboanga, Cebu, Iloilo, and Vigan, and assigned gunboats to them.

The gunboats were almost as controversial as the blockade. When Manila fell, several gunboats and steam launches fell into the hands of the army, and thirteen others were acquired by purchase from Spain. Otis planned to use the vessels to support garrisons in the Visayas and to suppress smuggling, but this proposal so infuriated Dewey that he allegedly swore to attack them as pirates.[52] After a lengthy and acrimonious debate, a compromise was worked out in June. The army kept ten shallow-draft river steamers—arming the *Laguna de Bay, Napindan,* and two others with heavy batteries of cannons and machine guns—and used them to support military operations.[53] The navy took the seagoing gunboats. A rough joint command relationship was worked out, in which army post commanders would request the services of a gunboat from the senior naval officer in the patrol zone, and in return naval officers were "instructed to work in harmony to end the war—but of course they must exercise their own judgment as to the practicality of performing the service required."[54] Although this seems a recipe for interservice squabbles, for the most part gunboat captains and post officers cooperated efficiently.

A far more lively dispute waged throughout the summer between Otis and the press corps. In June, John Bass sparked a major controversy with an article asserting that "the American outlook is blacker now than it has been since the beginning of the war." Bass argued that the "whole population of the islands sympathizes with the insurgents," the 8th Corps was inadequately manned and equipped, and Otis's military policy was undefined and poorly executed: "We have waged a harsh and a philanthropic war at the same time." Bass dismissed the 8th Corps' victories and maintained that "expeditions, lacking the purpose of holding the land conquered, alienate populations already hostile, encourage insurgents, teach them true methods of fighting us, and exhaust men." Otis never left his Manila office, but he constantly interfered with his commanders in the field; worse, his rosy predictions were

Gunboat *Laguna de Bay*

at odds with the views of the majority of his officers (read Lawton), who believed it would take 100,000 men and two years to "get even a fairly firm foothold" in the Philippines.[55]

Bass's critique exposed the ambivalent relations between the army and the press. Although individual correspondents were well liked, there was a great deal of suspicion about the press itself. Barely a month after the war began, Maj. Gen. Thomas M. Anderson complained of "detrimental" articles that provided the enemy with crucial military information and spread false accounts of American defeats.[56] Soldiers were alternately amused and enraged by newspaper accounts that claimed they had slaughtered helpless Filipinos armed with no more than bows and arrows.[57] But these complaints were mild compared with the anger they felt at newspapers that espoused the anti-imperialist position and attacked the army. Soldiers blamed such papers, and indeed the whole anti-imperialist movement, for keeping Filipino resistance alive and thus contributing to American deaths. They were also furious at personal and professional attacks: one soldier complained that according to the newspapers, he and his comrades were "nothing but murderers that march out occasionally and kill all the niggers we see!"[58] A decade after the war, Funston still fumed at the libel that he had murdered prisoners and looted churches.[59]

Most of the writers who covered the Philippine War were adventurous, intelligent, audacious, and given to view their dispatches as a bully pulpit from which to educate their countrymen. Most were also strong supporters of annexation; one later wrote that rather than seek independence, the Filipinos "should have got down on their knees every day of the year to thank God for the American occupation."[60] In the Philippines, as in Cuba, the army accorded journalists considerable freedom, and they responded by rushing to wherever the bullets were flying. James McCutcheon remembered the war as a life of a "maximum of thrills with a minimum of danger" in which "every day was a chapter of gay adventure."[61] Another correspondent, Frederick Palmer, recalled that most of his fellow correspondents participated in combat operations "out of sheer fellowship."[62] Such daredevils found kindred spirits in Lawton, Wheaton, Funston, and Bell, and their stirring and colorful descriptions of their heroes' exploits thrilled American audiences. In return, officers were remarkably open in voicing their disagreements with official policy. Wheaton, for example, told Palmer: "The reason that General Otis and I don't agree [is that] I want to lick the insurrectos first and reason with them afterward. He wants to reason with them and lick them at the same time."[63]

Most of the Manila press corps detested Otis. As noted, he was unpopular with the correspondents even before he left San Francisco, and as commander he did nothing to improve relations. Otis did not act as the press thought a commander should, being neither charismatic nor given to heroic action, and his ponderous lectures seldom yielded exciting quotes. Some believed, quite incorrectly, that McKinley intended to restrict Otis to administrative duties and place Lawton in command of the 8th Corps, and that Otis was denying their hero his proper place. There are even graphic accounts of a stormy confrontation in which—to quote one writer who could not possibly have been present—Otis dismissed one Lawton proposal with an "ironic, perverse, almost scornful guffaw."[64] Indeed, the putative Otis-Lawton feud is so widely accepted in Philippine War history that it is surprising to find that it is based almost entirely on journalistic speculation, much amplified by later writers. Otis invariably addressed Lawton as "My Dear General," praised him highly in reports, and gave him ample opportunity for distinction. Sources where one would expect to find references—such as the diary of Otis's confidant, Hughes, and the correspondence of Lawton's adjutant, Clarence R. Edwards—do not mention any ill feeling or quarrels.[65] This is not to say the men liked each other. Otis was prickly, with little grasp of the problems his commanders encountered on campaign; Lawton was insubordinate and selfish, continually blaming his superiors for his own lapses. But this is a far cry from the mutual hatred that some writers claim.

To many correspondents, Otis's treatment of Lawton was but one example of his intrusive censorship. The army controlled the only telegraph line out of Manila, and all dispatches had to be routed through the 8th Corps' censor or sent by boat to Hong Kong or some other neutral port. Even before hostilities began, the War Department instructed Otis to review all press dispatches leaving Manila, which generated an immediate accusation he was discriminating against some news services. Otis protested that he had allowed correspondents to cable the "established facts" but had censored "numerous baseless rumors circulated here, tending to excite [the] outside world."[66] But, as one bill submitted by the *Manila American* demonstrates, army censors went to ridiculous lengths, striking out news of Cuban elections, Dewey's illness, the Boer War, and even the Dreyfus Affair.[67]

The estrangement between the press and Otis was thus fueled by two issues: censorship and whether his official dispatches were reliable. The problem came to a head when the censor refused to allow a story claiming Lawton had estimated it would take at least 75,000 troops to pacify the islands. Perhaps encouraged by Lawton, the correspondents decided to sign a joint letter, much like the "round robin" the general had allowed his officers to sign protesting conditions in Cuba. At a stormy three-hour meeting, Otis threatened to court-martial or expel anyone who sent the letter from Manila. The offending document was therefore sent off to Hong Kong and soon hit the newsstands. It charged Otis's dispatches with misinforming the American people and the administration, of underestimating the "tenacity of the Filipino purpose," and of downplaying his officers' dissatisfaction with the way the war was being run.[68]

The public battles between Otis and the correspondents have been much discussed, but their impact is uncertain. McCutcheon's boast that publicity over the "round robin" precipitated Elihu Root's appointment to secretary of war and led to an increase of troop strength in the Philippines to 75,000 is incorrect. Although press criticism of Otis continued, McKinley did not waver in his support of the general. Lawton, whose indiscretions had contributed to the imbroglio, was soon in trouble again for allegedly telling a reporter: "What we want is to stop this accursed war. It is time for diplomacy; time for mutual understanding."[69] The general repudiated the interview, but the experience soured him: he prohibited his staff from talking to correspondents and later wrote contemptuously of "reporters, who appear, whenever a chance offers to misrepresent and distort the facts."[70] Perhaps the most lasting effect of the quarrel fell upon Otis's reputation. Hostile correspondents created the image of the stuffy, meddlesome, chair-bound bureaucrat, one that later historians accepted uncritically.

For the Philippine Republic, the summer continued the steady erosion of political and military power that had begun with the defeat at Manila. Aguinaldo's cabinet, reduced to a handful of ministers, moved from capital to capital. Factional disputes between the peace party, which favored negotiations, and the hard-liners under Mabini, who demanded complete independence, often paralyzed decision making. To the Americans, it appeared that the government was an empty shell, and the confused efforts to resume peace negotiations only heightened this perception.[71] And indeed, outside of north-central Luzon, the Republic exerted virtually no influence beyond that accorded by military commanders and civil officials. Apparently paralyzed by months of defeat, Aguinaldo did little to revive his moribund government.

In the military sphere, Aguinaldo moved with more decisiveness, but his actions further weakened the Army of Liberation. The president's relations with Luna had never been good, and they had grown steadily worse as the defeats mounted. Luna's early insistence that the army fight a conventional war contributed to high casualties among his veterans and depleted precious stocks of rifles and ammunition. Failure made him more irrational: he accused the Republic of failing to support him, denounced his subordinates' cowardice, and accused his fellow generals of treason. He publicly criticized Aguinaldo, threatened prominent revolutionaries, and demanded a new government—all this from a general who had yet to win a single battle.[72] By June, Aguinaldo had become convinced that Luna's Caesarism posed not only a political threat but a personal one as well. Indeed, as he reputedly told Funston, the issue had been reduced to whether Luna would kill him or he kill Luna, and he took steps to ensure the latter. On 5 June he invited Luna to his temporary capital of Cabanatuan, Nueva Ecija, to discuss changes in the government. Luna and his aide were met by the Kawit Battalion, a unit that served as Aguinaldo's bodyguard and that Luna had earlier tried to disarm. According to Aguinaldo's partisans, Luna flew into a rage, attacked the battalion's commander, and was killed in the scuffle. It is far more plausible that Aguinaldo arranged Luna's murder, and in a way calculated to send a message to his other generals. Aguinaldo's subsequent efforts to distance himself from the assassination, as with Bonifacio's, cast grave doubts on his veracity.[73]

In death, as in life, Luna cast a long shadow; he is now firmly installed in the pantheon of Filipino heroes. Mabini and Jose Alejandrino praised his patriotism and attacked Aguinaldo's opportunism and ambition. Luna's biographer went even further, claiming he was a dedicated revolutionary "whose final act of magnificence consisted of leaving off his ilustrado commitment to fight heart and soul with the revolutionary masses."[74] Bell called Luna "one of the ablest, but most arbitrary and arrogant generals of their army," whose assassination proved the "dismal incompetence" of Filipinos for self-government.[75] But the evidence suggests that Luna was a creation of the revolution, a self-professed expert who in ordinary times would never have been given an important command. His power came from his ability to convince others of his military genius, something he manifestly lacked. Moreover, there was in Luna a streak of vicious cruelty—revealed in his physical abuse of the wounded and defenseless, in his orders to burn houses, and in his summary executions of soldiers for minor offenses—that hints at deep mental or moral imbalance.

Perhaps the most serious result of Luna's death was Aguinaldo's inability to revive the fighting spirit of the Army of Liberation. Logistical constraints kept the army small—about 4,000 soldiers—and tied it to the railroad. But by the end of the summer it had become little more than a collection of free companies, each loyal to its commander but seldom able to work with others. An outsider would have had difficulty distinguishing this army from the provincial "zone" commands that existed outside the main theater of operations: Pampanga was shared by generals Tomas Mascardo, Servillano Aquino, and Luciano San Miguel; Bulacan was under Pio del Pilar and Urbano Lacuna; Francisco Macabulos dominated Tarlac; Gregorio del Pilar was in Pangasinan; the Ilocano provinces were led by Manuel Tinio; and in the Cagayan Valley there was Daniel Tirona. There was little cooperation among the generals, and their independence set the tone for the entire officer corps.

In retrospect, Aguinaldo would have been far better advised to use the summer to prepare for guerrilla war. Recurrent defeat on the battlefield had led some to urge the abandonment of conventional warfare and the adoption of guerrilla tactics. The change would have meant a shift in war aims but not in methods. From the outset of fighting, regulars and militia had worn civilian clothes, operated in small bands behind American lines, avoided pitched battles, and attacked sentries, supply wagons, and small detachments. Moreover, an organizational structure for guerrilla units had existed since Aguinaldo's February decree that created zone commands under political-military chiefs. As the U.S. Army occupied their territories, each zone's military forces had shifted to guerrilla tactics: outwardly friendly "amigos" pursuing their peacetime occupations, they formed guerrilla bands that attacked isolated detachments and supply wagons, cut communications, intimidated collaborators, and otherwise plagued the occupation forces. In the occupied towns, revolutionary agents, often the same civic officials the Americans had appointed, continued to collect taxes and serve the zone commanders.[76] But Aguinaldo remained curiously passive throughout the summer, and again let opportunity elude him.

SEVEN

THE NORTHERN OFFENSIVE

In his annual report at the end of August, Otis summarized the 8th Corps' accomplishments as well as the military and political difficulties that lay ahead. Somewhat reversing his earlier assessments, Otis believed that even had the Army of Liberation been decisively defeated in February 1899, there would have been continued resistance to American rule, "for the mass of people were intoxicated with the cry for independence and self-government." The spring campaign had proved that "little difficulty attends the act of taking possession of and temporarily holding any section of the country. A column of 3,000 men could march through and successfully contend with any force which the insurgents could place across its route, but they would close in behind it and again prey upon the inhabitants, persecuting without mercy those who had manifested any friendly feeling towards the American troops." As a result, despite recurrent defeats, the "rebellion still presented a bold and defiant front."[1] However, with the arrival of the U.S. Volunteer regiments and the end of the rainy season, he intended to launch an offensive that would shatter Aguinaldo's government and army once and for all.

Otis's greatest concern was that his victory would be indecisive. He feared that the Army of Liberation would withdraw into the mountains that flanked the Central Luzon Plain and continue the war as guerrillas. Accordingly, he planned a campaign that would encircle it completely and smash it between three fast-moving columns. Behind the newly created Cavalry Brigade commanded by Brig. Gen. Samuel B. M. Young, Lawton's 1st Division would advance up the Rio Grande to San Isidro, sixty miles from Manila, and then seventy miles farther north to Lingayen Gulf, simultaneously flanking Aguinaldo's army and sealing off the passes to the east. Once Lawton was well under way, Wheaton would make an amphibious landing on the southeast corner of Lingayen Gulf to block the coast road leading north. The third column, composed of MacArthur's 2nd Division, would thrust up the railroad from Angeles to Dagupan on Lingayen Gulf, a distance of some eighty miles, and force the Army of Liberation into the pocket created by Lawton and Wheaton. With the Philippine

Central Luzon

Scale 1:267,200

Republic's government and army captured or dispersed, the 8th Corps would turn south and clear out the Tagalog provinces of Cavite, Laguna, Batangas, and Tayabas. Once the "Tagalos" were overpowered, Otis believed that all "organized armed opposition" would end.[2] The army could then peacefully occupy the rest of the archipelago and shift to civil duties, preparing the presumably compliant inhabitants for their transition to

Northern Luzon

Scale 1:2,027,520

colonial rule. Meanwhile, the real problem was protecting the lives of those
Filipinos who accepted the United States' authority.[3]

Otis's immediate task was to avoid the major weaknesses of earlier campaigns, in which his soldiers won battles but invariably advanced beyond
their supplies, whereupon they succumbed to disease, malnutrition, and exhaustion. They could not live off the land: army discipline, McKinley's de-

mands for benevolent assimilation, and the poverty of the countryside all precluded it. Otis hoped his commanders could purchase draft animals and some supplies en route, but his concern over looting led him to impose very strict controls on requisitions.[4] Accordingly, virtually everything had to be unloaded in Manila, carted to the railroad, and then sent up north to be stored in supply dumps. Because MacArthur would be advancing directly up the Manila-Dagupan rail line, the 2nd Division could be supplied as long as that line remained open. But Lawton's column, which alone would need 650,000 rations, would be traveling over muddy wagon tracks during the rainy season. Logistics dictated that Lawton proceed in a series of caterpillar-like advances and contractions. Young's brigade would push ahead and seize San Isidro on the Rio Grande; behind it, engineers and road crews would make the river road suitable for supply wagons. Once a supply line was established and sufficient supplies for ten days concentrated at San Isidro, Young would swing north to block off the mountains and Lawton could go after the enemy forces. As the first step, Otis had MacArthur's division repair the damaged rail line between San Fernando and Angeles, using the latter town as its supply center. He sent Young to repair the road from San Fernando to Arayat and to forward Lawton's supplies up the Rio Grande to the town of Santa Anna.[5]

As in the spring campaigns, Central Luzon's terrain and climate soon ruined Otis's careful logistical plan. Heavy rains, mud, the rise and fall of the rivers and creeks, and enemy harassment all slowed Young's efforts to collect supplies. Although only ten miles long, the road from San Fernando to Santa Anna contained numerous stretches, some over 100 yards, that were covered by a foot of water and had to be rebuilt; most of the bridges were destroyed; and many of the rivers threatened to break their banks. Young complained that quartermasters in Manila had hired or impressed every wagon and draft animal in the area; on 26 September he wrote Lawton, "I am crippled for lack of transportation."[6]

Other problems arose. Perhaps as a diversion, the Filipino forces south of Manila attacked Calamba, Los Banos, Imus, and Bacoor. In order to free troops to join the advance north, Otis found it necessary first to "attack and severely punish these Cavite insurgents."[7] With three columns, Lawton crossed the Imus River and swept the lines between Imus and Bacoor and along Laguna de Bay. On 7 October a second column composed of Col. William Bisbee's 13th Infantry and detachments from the Manila garrison under Otis's chief of staff, Brig. Gen. Theodore Schwan, moved along the west shore of Manila Bay. Warships provided fire support, and a battalion of U.S. Marines advanced down the narrow peninsula from the Cavite

Naval Station toward Novaleta. In a disorganized, messy skirmish in dense undergrowth and stultifying heat, the marines broke out of an ambush and drove the enemy back. At the same time, Schwan's column pierced the defenses at Aguinaldo's hometown of Kawit. Lawton joined Schwan, and the combined column then proceeded toward San Francisco de Malabon, where the commander for southern Luzon, Mariano Trias, was reputed to be entrenched. The expedition struggled through bamboo and jungle, crossing swamps and cane fields, and following roads so deep in mud that the horses' heads had to be held up to prevent suffocation. Well guided by the Tagalogs in Lowe's Scouts, the expedition avoided ambush, drove off snipers, and entered San Francisco on the tenth. Unable to move his wagons and artillery farther, Schwan returned them to Kawit and then marched off to Dasmarinas. There was little resistance; the Caviteanos had hidden their arms and "present[ed] themselves to any passing American troops as the most consistent of 'amigos.'"[8] Otis pulled his troops back to the Bacoor-Imus line and went on the defensive. The expedition had cost the Americans 2 dead and 23 wounded; Schwan claimed he had killed over 100 insurgents.

With the southern front quiet, on 9 October Otis began the northern campaign by ordering Young to advance sixteen miles up the Rio Grande to San Isidro. In retrospect, this decision seems a poor one. The Army of Liberation was quiescent; even if given a few weeks, it was not going to revive sufficiently to offer a serious check. In contrast, Otis had substantial reasons to delay. By his own estimate, he required 50,000 frontline soldiers to conquer and hold the archipelago, but the 8th Corps' effective strength stood at 26,400. By waiting until the end of the month, he would have gained another 10,000. The 8th Corps' logistics were already strained. MacArthur's division was still repairing the San Fernando–Angeles rail line, Lawton's Cavite expedition had delayed his own preparations, and Young had been unable to collect sufficient supplies at San Fernando. Ever parsimonious, Otis had badly underestimated his need for draft animals, and the loss of 312 mules in a typhoon on 1 October virtually crippled his supply trains. Otis's plan called for Young's Cavalry Brigade to move rapidly through the flooded countryside, but half the troopers in the 4th Cavalry were dismounted, and the recently arrived 3rd Cavalry, which was being rushed north to join him, lacked many of its horses. Otis's decision to proceed with the northern offensive must be seen as yet another example of his trying to accomplish too much with too little. As always, his soldiers suffered for their general's parsimony.[9]

Young's march to San Isidro gave some hint of the difficulties to be expected. On 10 October, Batson, with two companies of his Macabebe Scouts, swung west to the Rio Grande, then north toward Arayat. The next day, Young took the wagon road from Santa Anna for the same destination. His misnamed Cavalry Brigade consisted of the 24th Infantry, two squadrons of the 4th Cavalry (one dismounted), and a mountain battery from the 37th Infantry. Ahead, an engineer detachment and dozens of laborers laid down bamboo over the muddy road to allow the artillery and wagons through. Brushing aside light resistance, on the twelfth Young entered Arayat, which had been fired by the defenders. Already the heat, rain, and mud were affecting his command, and many men fell out on the march. Young remained in the smoldering town as engineers repaired the road and the first *cascos* of supplies came up the Rio Grande from Calumpit. With two battalions of the 22nd Infantry and Batson's Macabebes, on the seventeenth he crossed the Rio Grande and moved up the east bank toward Cabiao, where he fought a sharp skirmish the next day. Faced with a strongly fortified position, Young sent the Macabebe and the Lowe Scouts to outflank the breastworks. But the Macabebes were bogged down in mud, and it was left to Maj. John G. Ballance's battalion of the 22nd Infantry to make a "screaming bayonet charge" over the entrenchments.[10] In a pursuit past Cabiao, Ballance's infantry caught up with the fleeing enemy and struck them again, driving them back in a rush. In the dark and rain, the Filipinos across the river became confused and fired indiscriminately into the press of their comrades, only to be shot down in turn by Batson's Scouts, who arrived at the last minute and poured in volleys at close range.

After a short rest at Cabiao, on 19 October Young resumed the drive for San Isidro. The Scouts were in the advance, followed closely by Ballance, leading his battalion and a mixed cavalry and artillery detachment. A few miles outside of town, the Scouts found a group sabotaging a bridge. Rushing across on the stringers, they held it until Ballance brought his infantry up and drove off the enemy. The advance resumed along the muddy track, flanked by submerged rice paddies. Snipers fired into the column from bamboo thickets and brush. The cavalry could not drive them off, for the mud came up to the horses' bellies whenever they left the road. So it fell to Ballance's weary soldiers to advance in a long skirmish line, floundering through the quagmire on both sides of the road. Early on the morning of the twentieth, Young entered San Isidro. It had taken him eleven days to advance sixteen miles, and the rains began to fall ever more heavily.

Young's push north had an immediate effect on MacArthur's front. Filipino forces had been pressing on the garrison at Angeles, and early on the morning of 16 October they launched an attack on the outposts, complete with artillery barrage. Fighting raged along the line for miles, but the experience of Company H, 17th Infantry, was typical. Roused from their cots before dawn, the company rushed forward to the outskirts and took up a position across a road facing a large cane field. Above them, their own artillery shells passed so close the men joked that they could reach up and touch them. Faint shapes filtered into the field, and the dark was suddenly broken by the blaze of rifles. Bugles sounded the charge, and Filipino infantry came crashing through the cane directly toward the waiting company. The soldiers worked their Krags as rapidly as they could, but their opponents doggedly stood their ground; for over an hour both sides blazed away until daylight brought the battle to a close. Filipino dead were heaped throughout the field. All along the line the attack proved a costly fiasco, inflicting terrible casualties on the Army of Liberation and further demoralizing the survivors.[11]

Following behind Young, Lawton experienced innumerable difficulties. His expedition totaled about 3,000 soldiers, but, as he explained on 28 October, "my command is strung along the road from Manila to this place [San Isidro] because I can not subsist them here."[12] Heavy rains caused the Rio Grande to rise and fall, sometimes ten feet at a time, so that when the soldiers were not loading and unloading supplies and pulling barges across the river, they were digging the landing piers out of the mud. As whenever things went wrong, Lawton blamed Manila and bombarded headquarters with barely civil demands for more wagons and river transportation. Although Otis certainly deserved some censure, Lawton was responsible for most of the confusion and delay. Although with several weeks to prepare, he had done little to organize transportation or supplies for the offensive. The death of his quartermaster on 22 October threw the burden on Lawton, who appears to have regressed to his habits as frontier captain. He arbitrarily held up convoys, overruled the officer in charge of bridge building—and saw his own effort promptly swept away by the river—and drove his already overworked men mercilessly. Young's supply officer commented acidly that Lawton's logistical talents were those of "a good section-boss or stevedore" and that he was "a great hindrance to good work."[13]

As Lawton's division toiled its way up the Rio Grande, on 27 October Young's column pressed northeast into Nueva Ecija Province.[14] His target was Cabanatuan, twenty miles away, a city reputed to hold two dozen American and 4,000 Spanish prisoners of war. Young's route took him along the east bank of the Rio Grande de Nueva Ecija through flooded rice paddies and cane fields. With the cavalry helpless in the mud, and the artillery and wagons hauled by hand, the advance was again led by Ballance's hardworking infantry. For seven miles they fought their way up the muddy trail, crossing six flooded streams, outflanking entrenchments, driving off snipers, and winning a sharp skirmish at the Tabaotin River. Behind them, the engineers and laborers built temporary bridges and matted the road with bamboo. The next day, Young entered Santa Rosa, halfway to Cabanatuan. There he had to call a three-day halt: his supply wagons and cavalry were bogged down in mud or stranded before raging streams, and his engineers had to repair the road and build bridges and ferries. Then, pushing on to Cabanatuan, he found the trail north in even worse shape; once again he halted, sending the Macabebes and the cavalry to scout the roads to the north.

By the end of October, it was clear that Otis's plan for Lawton's division to carry out a sustained offensive by sending Young forward to establish a supply line and then following with the main force was unrealistic. The campaign was now almost in its fourth week, but Lawton had advanced barely twenty miles from Young's point of departure. Even with the advantages of operating near the river, Young could not move rapidly and also repair the road for Lawton to follow. Clearly a choice must be made. Lawton could either delay until he had sufficient supplies at San Isidro to sustain an advance by 3,000 soldiers, or he could try to send a detachment north in a rapid march to close off the passes and link up with Wheaton. Both options carried considerable risk. If Lawton delayed much longer, Aguinaldo and the Army of Liberation might move east from Tarlac through the passes and into the mountains. But sending a small column deep into enemy territory might be even more hazardous. Young believed he had discovered the solution to this dilemma in his march to Cabanatuan. If Lawton would let him keep his existing force and a mule train with eight days' rations, he could push north rapidly enough to link up with Wheaton and block the passes. Lawton was less than enthusiastic. Young might encounter the entire enemy army, and even if he avoided defeat, his detachment might succumb to mud, disease, and starvation. At most Lawton would permit the dispatch of the cavalry and Macabebes eight miles north and west to Talavera and Aliaga, respectively.

No sooner had Lawton agreed to this limited advance than news from MacArthur radically altered the entire pace of the campaign. On 31 October, 2nd Division scouts intercepted a message from Aguinaldo, dated the fifth, declaring he was shifting his capital 110 miles northeast from Tarlac to Bayombong, a mountain town deep in Nueva Vizcaya Province. Liberated Spanish prisoners told Young that Aguinaldo's route would skirt the northern end of Young's perimeter, taking him east through Umangan to the pass at San Nicholas and then north to Bayombong. The news persuaded Lawton that Young should move north as rapidly as possible to intercept Aguinaldo and shut off any escape route through the northeastern passes to Nueva Vizcaya. But Otis could not believe that Aguinaldo would give up the railroad without a struggle, for to do so would effectively break up the Army of Liberation and force him to leave the Republic's treasury. Lawton was ordered to dispatch troops to seal off the passes due east but to advance no farther north than the twenty miles to San Jose, twelve miles south of Umangan.[15]

In retrospect, Otis's decision seems almost perverse. Perhaps he was still dazzled by the elegance of his original plan, with Lawton, Wheaton, and MacArthur uniting in concert. Perhaps Lawton's incessant complaining and manifest inability to supply his troops had persuaded Otis that a rapid advance up the Rio Grande was impossible. He may have feared that Young's small force would leave gaps for the Army of Liberation to slip through, or even that it would be surrounded and annihilated. Or he may have simply hoped blindly that Wheaton's imminent landing would block the passes north of San Jose. Whatever the reason, he showed poor judgment in ordering Lawton to halt.

Young could not accept Otis's decision. Spanish prisoners assured him that Aguinaldo intended to retreat to Tayug and then through the San Nicolas pass. If so, there was a good chance the president would elude Wheaton's southern patrols. Young must move north, seize Tayug, and block the escape route. The "great drag anchor" to such a plan "was the apparent impossibility of transporting supplies for rapidly moving columns."[16] Young's solution was both logical and daring: he would take the Macabebes, Ballance's 22nd Infantry battalion, three troops of the 3rd Cavalry, and the 37th Infantry's mountain battery and drive directly to Tayug and San Nicholas. There would be no further effort to maintain a supply line: each company would be restricted to four bull carts. Young believed his cavalry could live off rice plants; the men would either find food or go hungry. With permission from Lawton, Young's small force left Cabanatuan and struck out north on 7 November.[17]

The ensuing march by Young, Ballance, and the 1,100-man Cavalry Brigade became celebrated in the annals of Philippine service, where hard marches were the norm. The column moved in stages. Scouts and wide-ranging patrols would sweep the countryside ahead, occupying towns and villages until the main body passed through, then moving out to begin the process again. Young later commented that nothing in his four decades of active service had prepared him for the "tropical deluges, mud and water, the swimming, bridging and rafting of innumerable streams, most of which were not on the map."[18] Rain fell incessantly, and the mire was so deep that soldiers had to cut brush and bamboo continually so that the wagons could pass. The men subsisted on soggy bacon, barely cooked rice, carabao meat, and whatever they could scrounge. They were infected with tropical ulcers, dysentery, fevers, and a variety of other ailments. Nevertheless, Young reached San Jose on 12 November—the point where Otis had ordered a halt—and then set out for Umangan, reaching it the next day. From there he sent his cavalry to Tayug and San Nicholas, closing off two more passes.[19]

As Young's brigade trekked north, its far-flung scouts found increasing evidence that Aguinaldo was fleeing toward them. Retreating before Mac-Arthur's advance, the president had left his capital of Tarlac and moved north thirty miles up the railroad to Bayambang in Pangasinan Province. At a 13 November conference he decided to disperse his army and begin guerrilla war. Leaving that evening, Aguinaldo's party rode the train north twenty miles and then set out across country for Pozorubio, twelve miles to the east. En route, they were met by Brig. Gen. Gregorio del Pilar's force, swelling the party to over 1,200. Aguinaldo made good time. Late on the fourteenth he reached Pozorubio, but his rear guard was attacked by Maj. Samuel M. Swigert's 3rd Cavalry, and his mother and son captured. In a decision that may have owed much to the fatigue, disease, and debilitation suffered by all of Young's troops, Swigert halted his troops on the outskirts of the town for the night. When he rode into Pozorubio the next morning, Aguinaldo had already left. Recognizing that the Americans had blocked his escape east and that Bayombong was no longer an option, on the fifteenth Aguinaldo turned north and west, crossing the mountains into La Union Province. From there he could head north along the coast road on the eastern side of Lingayen Gulf and either take shelter in the Ilocano provinces or turn east, cross the Cordilleras, and link up with Maj. Gen. Daniel Tirona in the Cagayan Valley.[20]

Having reached the San Nicholas–Tayug area on the sixteenth, Young now faced a dilemma. For the last few days his troops had been fighting Aguinaldo's rear guard, in the process all but destroying it. Out of contact with Lawton, he was far past his destination, and his command was so stretched out and exhausted it might not survive a strong attack. His best unit, Ballance's infantry, was unfit for further service: three-fourths of the soldiers would soon be placed on sick report. But the general was convinced that with one more effort he could still catch the president. He believed that Aguinaldo had less than 150 soldiers left and was fleeing north. With commendable, if breathtaking, initiative, Young decided he could not wait for orders, and on 17 November he set out after the fleeing president.[21] By now he knew that something had gone seriously wrong with Otis's plan. Aguinaldo's escape route north from Pozorubio should have been shut off by Wheaton's forces. Where was Wheaton?

Wheaton, with Bisbee's 13th Infantry and Hare's 33rd Infantry had sailed from Manila on 6 November and arrived off the Lingayen Gulf town of San Fabian, east of Dagupan, the next day. At four in the afternoon, under cover of naval gunfire from the six warships, the troops disembarked from their transport into *cascos* and were towed ashore, screened by small steam launches that raked the shores with machine-gun fire. The defenders had strengthened a natural sand ridge some twenty feet high with parapets lined and riveted with bamboo and loopholed for rifles and artillery. But the naval bombardment was so destructive that they abandoned their entrenchments, and within three hours Wheaton put ashore his entire force. The ease of his landing was deceptive. For the next week high surf hampered the landing of supplies, and on the twelfth a typhoon struck, flooded the countryside, and made marching almost impossible. Wheaton pushed out patrols, primarily to the south and west toward Dagupan. But he did not send troops to Pozorubio until the sixteenth, a day after Aguinaldo had left for La Union.[22]

The escape of Aguinaldo still excites controversy. According to William T. Sexton, Otis's caution warped his subordinate's judgment; had Wheaton "displayed even a modicum of initiative, Aguinaldo undoubtedly would have been captured, or at least kept out of the wild mountain regions to the north, and the pacification of the Islands with its attendant loss of American and Filipino lives . . . would probably have been shortened by two years."[23] However, Otis maintained that "no blame can attach to either Wheaton or Young, and no line could have been made sufficiently strong to prevent the escape of a small body of the enemy."[24] Which is the better judgment? Otis's view of the situation was shaped by his conviction that Aguinaldo would remain close to the railroad with his cabinet, army, and treasury, and would not move east across Lawton's route until the last moment. This meant not only that MacArthur's offensive was the critical one and that Lawton had more than enough time to extend his blocking line north but also that every detachment on Lawton's line should be strong enough to hold off an assault by a large contingent of the Army of Liberation. When MacArthur intercepted Aguinaldo's proclamation that he was relocating his capital to Bayombong, Otis interpreted this to mean the president still planned to withdraw with the army and his cabinet. This would have limited his route to a few major trails, most of which were already blocked by Lawton. Only very late in the campaign did Otis become aware of Aguinaldo's 13 November decision to disband the Army of Liberation and begin guerrilla war. Rather than remaining limited to a few routes, the president now could travel rapidly, and his ultimate destination was no longer certain: it might still be Bayombong, or the Ilocano provinces, or even southern Luzon. Predictably, Manila's efforts to direct the columns and capture the president were unsuccessful: from 14 to 17 November, the critical period when Aguinaldo slipped between Young and Wheaton, there was virtually no direct communication among the various American commands; Otis did not hear from Wheaton from the fourteenth to the twenty-fifth. To add to the confusion, there were a number of misleading Aguinaldo sightings, including a persistent rumor that he had fled in disguise to Cavite.[25]

A second major issue is the nature of Wheaton's orders. No copy of Otis's original plan has been found, but it appears that he failed to establish a timetable, to outline clearly who was responsible for blocking which passes, or to fix the point where the three commands would meet. Otis told Lawton he expected Wheaton to operate to the east as far as Tayug and to "shut up" the northern routes, but left unclear what these routes were being "shut up" against.[26] Lawton, Young, and later critics assumed it was against Aguinaldo's escape, but this is not supported by the evidence. Rather, Otis's instructions were for Wheaton to place troops "on the roads leading north and near the coast, to prevent the retreat of the insurgent army to [the] north along the roads or trails leading in that direction."[27] Both this directive and Wheaton's later summary of his accomplishments indicate that his mission was to block the Army of Liberation's "retreat into the mountains of Northern Luzon."[28] The capture of Aguinaldo, while of high priority, was, at least to Otis and Wheaton, far less important than the destruction of the enemy's conventional forces.

In one of the ironies of the war, Wheaton's mistaken conviction that he should keep his command concentrated near San Fabian to face the Army of Liberation approaching from the southwest was apparently vindicated by the Battle of San Jacinto on 11 November. San Jacinto, four miles to the south of San Fabian, was occupied by a 1,200-man brigade under twenty-three-year-old Brig. Gen. Manuel Tinio. In early November he had marched his brigade down from the Ilocano provinces and established his headquarters at San Jacinto, a natural stronghold, surrounded by flooded rice fields and approachable by only one road that passed through the paddies. To these defenses, Tinio had added a strong barricade across the road and an intricate series of trenches, ditches, and water obstacles on the flanks. The general planned to ambush the attackers on the road and force them into the paddies, where they could be shot down by his concealed riflemen. The plan worked well at first. Approaching the town in battalion column, the 33rd's advance company was hit by frontal fire at the barricade and by snipers on the flanks. But the inexperienced Volunteers recovered quickly. The lead companies scattered into the muddy paddies on the right, and Maj. Peyton

C. March's battalion deployed to the left and toward the rear. Although protected, Tinio's untrained troops were no match for the 33rd's marksmen, who sprayed the trenches with Krag fire, picking off anyone who showed his head. While a prolonged firefight raged in the paddies, March's battalion managed to turn the left flank and fight its way into the town. The Tinio Brigade fell back, leaving 134 dead. The battle was costly for the "Texas Regiment" as well: eight soldiers were killed or died of wounds, and another thirteen were badly wounded.[29]

The battle appears to have galvanized Wheaton into action, and he began sending columns farther from San Fabian. But much of his attention was still focused on the south and west, whereas by this time Aguinaldo was north and east. Moreover, there was little coherence to Wheaton's dispositions; units were thrown out in a porous net. The experience of Capt. Godfrey Fowler's Company F, 33rd Infantry, is perhaps not untypical of the fragmented small-unit actions that occurred in northern Pangasinan Province in late November. Fowler's company set out on the twenty-second to patrol southwest of Dagupan. Learning there was a large force at Mangatarem, he marched all night, and on the morning of the twenty-third sent his company into the attack. Unbeknown to Fowler, Mangatarem was occupied by Brig. Gen. Jose Alejandrino with between 500 and 1,000 troops. But the audacious captain was up to the challenge: by shifting formations and sounding bugle calls, he gave the appearance that the company was a much larger force, and the deadly marksmanship of his soldiers swept the enemy trenches. Alejandrino's forces barely resisted, abandoning their artillery, vast supplies of stores, and a hundred Spanish prisoners. Fowler's men were joined on the twenty-sixth by the 36th Infantry, linking Wheaton and MacArthur's forces and closing off the western half of the circle.[30]

The physical obstacles to Young's advance and the controversy over Aguinaldo's escape have overshadowed MacArthur's operations. After the capture of Angeles, MacArthur reequipped and rationed his division—the 9th, 12th, 17th, and 36th Infantry, two troops of the 4th Cavalry, and two light artillery companies—for a three-month campaign. In late October, as Lawton struggled toward San Isidro, MacArthur sent Bell's 36th to harass a large enemy force under Gen. Tomas Mascardo operating to the west near the Zambales Mountains. Bell effectively sealed off the southwest entrances into Bataan Province by taking Florida Blanca at the edge of the Zambales. MacArthur may have learned too well the lessons of the spring campaigns, when his 2nd Division had been decimated by hard marching, disease, and lack of supplies. He now planned to move up the railroad in short, limited stages, ensuring that his rear was secure and stopping frequently to build supply depots. His passivity worried Otis, who on 3 November urged MacArthur to advance up the railroad, noting that the Army of Liberation had begun destroying the rails, engines, and stations along the route. It was the first of several messages Manila would send to prod the methodical general forward.[31]

MacArthur began his advance north on the fifth, clearing out the countryside between Angeles and Arayat. His division advanced with Col. Jacob H. Smith's 17th Infantry on the left and Bell's 36th on the right. As he moved north, Bell tried to establish and maintain contact with Lawton's forces pushing northwest. MacArthur took three days to get to Mabalacat, barely seven miles up the track from Angeles, then wired Manila he would need two more days to rest his men and secure supplies before he could "develop" a strong position at Bamban, some three miles up the road.[32] Otis and Schwan became impatient, for if MacArthur's advance did not engage the main body of the Army of Liberation, whose strength and efficiency they seriously overestimated, Aguinaldo could shift troops to oppose Lawton and Young and retreat to the east. They urged MacArthur "to move up the railroad with celerity" and pointed out that with his four regiments and three others to guard his rear, he had more than enough to withstand any enemy force.[33] Thus prodded, MacArthur started forward, only to be halted by the typhoon that struck on 12 November, causing the rivers to rise ten feet and washing out a half-mile section of the road.

MacArthur's problems were exacerbated by the presence of the irrepressible Brig. Gen. Joseph "Fighting Joe" Wheeler, a sixty-three-year-old Confederate cavalry officer turned Alabama congressman. In 1898 McKinley made Wheeler a general in an attempt both to bind up the emotional wounds of the Civil War and win over Southern voters. Wheeler achieved a checkered career in Cuba: the correspondents and public loved him, but his impetuosity and negligence appalled professional officers. Excitable and disorganized, he often abandoned his headquarters and rushed to the front to lead a charge. In the Philippines he often treated the bewildered natives as potential voters, stopping to lecture young Filipinos that they could become president of the islands. Given command of a brigade composed of the 9th and 12th Infantry, the free-spirited and fiery Wheeler soon clashed with the haughty MacArthur. On 11 November, as part of the division's crossing of the Paruao River in front of Bamban, Wheeler was directed to distract the main enemy force while other units flanked it. But once the firing began, Wheeler could not restrain himself and ordered a charge. MacArthur directed him to halt his advance, but Wheeler, his blood up, sent his entire brigade into the assault. Fighting their way across the river, his companies became a disorganized mob, pressing forward miles beyond their support. Had the defenders held their ground, the result could well have been a massacre; instead it was a notable victory. MacArthur sent Wheeler and his brigade to the rear to maintain the supply line. This he did with commendable skill, constructing a bamboo bridge over a half-mile washout at Tarlac and bringing up 25,000 rations to maintain the advance. But despite Wheeler's protests, MacArthur kept him in reserve.[34]

Wheeler's banishment left most of the fighting, and the hard marching, to Bell's Volunteers and Smith's Regulars, who ranged out on the flanks and swept the front. The 36th entered Tarlac on 12 November, but MacArthur then delayed for four days as his engineers struggled to repair a washed-out bridge and bring up supplies. On the seventeenth, a 900-man task force crossed a half-mile washout and pushed up the trail, and two days later occupied Bayambang. From there MacArthur reconnoitered to the railroad's terminus at Dagupan and entered that town on the twentieth. As his regiments pushed into Pangasinan Province, armed resistance seemed to melt away. The soldiers marched through small villages lined with Filipinos waving white flags and shouting "Viva Americanos!" But the old challenges remained: the swollen streams, washed-out trails, glutinous mud, broken bridges, torn-up track, and other obstacles. Perhaps the true heroes of the campaign were two engineer companies and hundreds of Filipino and Chinese laborers who repaired the railroad and literally pushed forward the supply trains. Once linked up with Wheaton's forces, MacArthur's troops scoured east and west of the railroad, but they found few enemy forces. Convinced that the enemy had escaped into Zambales, MacArthur pressed Otis to allow him to go after them.

With the exception of Young's expedition, Lawton's campaign also finished by the end of November. Moving up two trails, one Young's and the other along the Nueva Ecija–Tarlac border, Lawton's command—more a collection of companies and battalions than a coherent tactical unit—worked its way north to enter San Fabian on the eighteenth. By then, the majority of his troops had been dropped off along the route, to garrison strategic towns and keep the logistical lines open. The major obstacles remained—rain, mud, broken bridges, and lack of supplies. There was no resistance beyond hit-and-run raids and sniping; indeed, many nationalists were eager to capitulate. The provincial commander of Nueva Vizcaya, for example, surrendered 800 soldiers to 50 cavalrymen and 3 native scouts.[35]

On 22 November Lawton ordered Capt. Joseph Batchelor, commanding three companies of the African-American 24th Infantry, to Bayombong. What else Lawton ordered is unclear, but Batchelor conceived his mission as a strike northeast from Nueva Vizcaya over the mountains into the Cagayan Valley, where Tirona and a reputed 1,100 soldiers awaited Aguinaldo's arrival. It is difficult to imagine Lawton giving such a bizarre order, but if he did so, he soon changed his mind and sent orders for the captain's recall. Batchelor, however, had hooked up with the Lowe Scouts and, already on the trail for the Cagayan, pressed on in what one exasperated naval officer termed "an independent expedition of his own, resembling Sherman's march through Georgia."[36] For some 200 miles the tiny force trekked through the mountains, fighting a number of engagements, before it reached the Cagayan Valley. At the request of Otis, Admiral Watson dispatched Comdr. Bowman McCalla with a small squadron to Aparri, at the mouth of the Cagayan River, where he quickly established contact with Tirona. Although a close friend of Aguinaldo, the general had decided that resistance was futile, and on 11 December he surrendered 1,200 precious rifles and all the forces in Isabella and Cagayan Provinces to McCalla. McCalla immediately appointed him governor of the surrendered territory and confirmed all the existing office-holders. He also sent a steamboat up the Cagayan, and two days later, and eighty miles upriver, it found Batchelor's battered command. Instead of being grateful for his rescue, Batchelor, who may have become unhinged by the ordeal, immediately began bickering with McCalla over credit for Tirona's surrender. It had been a march of epic hardship, though to little purpose. The battalion was all but destroyed by the march, and Batchelor was invalided out of the army and would die in 1902.

A far more significant campaign was that of Young on Aguinaldo's northern trail. By forced marches, Aguinaldo had avoided Wheaton's patrols and on 17 November reached Naguillian, La Union Province, on the east coast of Lingayen Gulf (the Ilocano coast) about twenty miles up the road from San Fabian. That day, Young set out from Pozorubio. The only soldiers that remained from his original flying column were eighty troopers from the 3rd Cavalry and the remnants of Batson's Macabebes. Recognizing these forces were insufficient, Young requested that a battalion of infantry be sent after him. Crossing the mountains, he reached the coast on the nineteenth. There he made contact with the *Samar* and, assisted by the gunboat, routed the defenders and took the provincial capital of San Fernando de la Union the next day.[37] By now, Young's force was breaking down. Batson had been badly wounded in a skirmish, most of the Macabebes could go no farther, and even the daring Young hesitated to push into unexplored territory with the handful of men who remained. Moreover, he now faced a choice of targets. The location of the American prisoners was unknown, but it was likely they were being hurried north into the mountains. Aguinaldo was moving up the coast road, his final destination assumed to be the Cagayan Valley. He might turn inland at Candon through Tirad (Tila) Pass or push on to Vigan, and then cross Tangadan Pass or raft up the Abra River to Bangued. In a remarkable achievement, Tinio had pieced together a 600-man force outside of Namacpacan. Young sent his aide, Lt. Col. James Parker, to San Fabian to ask Wheaton to occupy Vigan. Wheaton refused, for reasons that are not difficult to guess. Young's dash up the Ilocos coast had been completely unauthorized, and Wheaton was under no obligation to support it. Moreover, he was convinced he needed all his troops to block the Army of Liberation, which he still expected in the southwest. Most important, Wheaton may have been piqued by Lawton and Young for blaming him for Aguinaldo's escape.

A frustrated Parker returned to San Fernando on the twenty-fifth and found March's battalion of the 33rd had just arrived from San Fabian. Parker ordered March to leave immediately to support Young. March refused, claiming he was under Wheaton's authority. A heated discussion followed, doubtless to the amusement of the soldiers, and Parker stormed off. Fortunately for Young, the navy proved more cooperative, and the captain of the *Oregon* readily agreed to occupy Vigan. After a brief bombardment intended to discourage any resistance, a landing party of marines and sailors went ashore, where they were greeted with brass bands and a great deal of popular enthusiasm.[38]

March arrived at Namacpacan on the twenty-sixth and immediately put himself under Young's command. The general sent March's battalion toward Candon to block Tirad Pass. On 2 December, as they moved up the zigzag trail over the pass, they ran into Aguinaldo's rear guard, a sixty-man picked force under twenty-two-year-old Gregorio del Pilar. Pilar had built a strong barricade across the narrow trail; his troops held their fire until the Americans were close. Their first volleys from their Mausers drove the lead company to the ground. March ordered another company to an attack, but they too were quickly driven back. Settling down for a long fight, March dispatched a noncom and ten sharpshooters to an adjoining hill, where they covered Pilar's rear and picked off anyone who raised his head. After further thought, he sent Company H on a long trek up a ravine to find a route up the cliffs next to the pass. The rest of the battalion remained on the trail, amusing themselves by putting their hats on sticks to draw fire. The clouds pressed in, muffling shapes and noises, and a rumor spread that Aguinaldo and a large force were in their rear. March, dodging fire, went up and down the trail reassuring his men. As the morning dragged on, Company H worked its way up the steep cliffs, the men hauling each other up by belts, rifles, and ropes cut from their blankets. Shortly before noon they emerged above Pilar's position, charging down at the same time the rest of the battalion rushed the barricade. The Filipinos fell back, and were blasted by the marksman on the hill. Of del Pilar's sixty defenders, fifty-one died, but they bought Aguinaldo five precious hours to escape. The next day, March resumed the advance, but by now exhaustion and disease were winnowing his command. Two days after the battle, only 100 men were able to continue. March pushed deep into the mountains until his entire command collapsed and he had to turn back.

One of the most famous battles of the war, the "Filipino Thermopylae" is known for a variety of reasons: its Last Stand aspects; the engagement of the already famous "Fighting 33rd"; the brilliant leadership of March, future U.S. Army Chief of Staff; the death of the "boy general" del Pilar—and, not least, the presence of several journalists. In an oft-quoted article, correspondent Richard Henry Little described how del Pilar could be plainly seen at the front, his voice carrying clearly as it exhorted and threatened his men. Finally, as the soldiers closed in and all his troops had fled, he mounted a white horse, only to be felled by a sniper. Maintaining its Homeric theme, Little's account ends with del Pilar's corpse stripped by thuggish soldiers and left all but naked on the battlefield.[39] Perhaps because Little's piece is such a stirring example of combat journalism, few have noticed that it is flatly contradicted by every other eyewitness in nearly all its particulars. According to Lt. Telesforo Carrasco, the only participant actually with del Pilar, the general was initially in the rear and had walked down to join a squad assigned to defend the left side of the mountain. As he arrived, enemy soldiers appeared at the crest. There was a confused exchange of fire; del Pilar raised his head to see over the tall grass and was shot in the neck, dying instantly.[40] Carrasco's version is corroborated by two members of the 33rd, far closer to the action than Little, who fail to mention seeing or hearing del Pilar, much less a white horse. As for the stripping of del Pilar's corpse, this is at some variance with the account of correspondent James McCutcheon, who identified the body by its silver spurs, lockets, and a twenty-dollar gold piece in its pocket, and by March, who mentions he confiscated items of military value.[41] In short, the widely accepted version of the death and desecration of Gregorio del Pilar, like so many other colorful Philippine War accounts and atrocities, has little substance in fact.

As March's battalion turned inland to continue the pursuit, Hare sent Company B and the 33rd's sick to Vigan on 3 December to relieve the navy landing party. Young had designated the city as his supply depot, and thousands of rations and 50,000 rounds of ammunition were stored there. Stationed in the large municipal buildings around the plaza, the soldiers and townspeople mingled happily. Among the visitors were Tinio and several other revolutionary leaders. As one soldier recalled, "They seemed so polite and refined. Well anyway, they sure pulled a good one on us."[42] That night, some 400 insurgents rowed *bancas* down the Abra River, which all but encircled Vigan, and moved silently through the town until they reached the plaza. A large force of bolomen hid in Vigan's famous cathedral, waiting for the order to charge. Shortly before 4:00 A.M. one of the 33rd's patrols saw armed men moving through the streets and opened fire. Soldiers stumbled out of their quarters, some dressed in nothing but underwear and ammo belts. A confused and desperate fight flared across the plaza, as Filipinos and Americans traded volleys at ranges so close they could hear each other's commands. The volume of fire was perhaps the most intense of any engagement in the war. With a virtually unlimited supply, the 120 defenders fired 15,000 rounds in less than three hours; some rifles became so heated that bullets exploded in the chambers. Terrified civilians called "Amigo, amigo," a cry taken up by some insurgents who then fired at their rescuers. Fighting raged in and around the cathedral, as soldiers shot down the bolomen. Dead and wounded lay in heaps in the plaza and along the city's streets. At daylight, the tired Americans waited for the final charge, but except for the occasional shot the town was quiet. With Young's cavalry en route from the south, Tinio's men had melted away.[43]

Colonel Hare, with the rest of the 33rd, had hiked up the east coast of Lingayen Gulf, dropping off companies to garrison the main towns in La Union and Ilocos Sur Provinces. Marching twenty miles in one day, Hare and 270 men caught up to Young at Tangadan Pass on 4 December. With barely 250 men, the impulsive general had attacked some 700 enemy soldiers under the leadership of two highly competent cousins, Juan and Blas Villamor. Young had dispersed his forces in such a way that he himself was in some danger of being overrun. Hare's men succeeded in scaling the adjoining hills and arrived on the flanks at about the same time the Filipinos ran out of ammunition. The Villamors managed a skillful withdrawal. As the Americans would soon learn, they were far from finished.[44]

Young assigned Hare's 33rd and Lt. Col. Robert L. Howze's battalion of the 34th to pursue the retreating enemy forces and to release the navy's Lt. James Gillmore and other American prisoners. Splitting into two separate commands, Hare and Howze pushed into Abra Province, supplying themselves from captured stores and contributions, and releasing hundreds of Spanish. On the eighth, three prisoners stumbled into Howze's camp and told him where Tinio was taking their comrades. Howze caught up with the Tinio Brigade later that day; the ensuing three-hour running battle virtually ended it as a fighting force. Howze's men destroyed 200 rifles, 60,000 rounds of ammunition, and most of the arsenal, an irreplaceable loss to the Filipino forces in northwestern Luzon. By now both Hare and Howze were deep in the main mountain range of northern Luzon, and the soldiers were suffering from exposure and disease; Hare's troops had marched over 300 miles from San Fabian, Howze's even farther. Uniting on 14 December and securing a small supply of shoes from the navy, the two commands pushed still farther into the mountains. To save the remnants of his force, Tinio turned the prisoners over to a subordinate with orders to execute them rather than allow their recapture. The lieutenant took the easier, but no less morally reprehensible, step of abandoning his charges without food or water in country peopled by headhunters. Hare and Howze found Gillmore and the others on the eighteenth, but their own situation was also critical. They had 150 soldiers and 26 rescued prisoners, all of whom were malnourished and suffering from a variety of ailments. Convinced they would starve if they retraced their route, they decided to press on to the Cagayan Valley and the town of Aparri on the northwest coast. They subsisted on one meal of rice a day, beaten out of its husks every night, and supplemented by the occasional coconut. The men could hardly limp on feet that were cut and bleeding from rocks and repeated immersion in rivers; some were delirious; others staggered on like zombies, and one died during the ordeal. On 2 January they reached the town of Abulug on the Cagayan River and soon made contact with a scouting party from the *Princeton*. The navy rushed supplies and medicines upriver and brought the expedition down to Aparri. All but forgotten today, the Gillmore Expedition was one of the most heroic marches in American military history, an epic of exemplary leadership, courage, and endurance.[45]

While Young was mopping up resistance in the Ilocano provinces, MacArthur sent Brig. Gen. Frederick D. Grant after the remnants of the Army of Liberation, which had escaped into southwestern Pampanga, Bataan, and Zambales. Grant divided his forces into a 400-man northern column of the 25th Infantry which, accompanied by 100 porters, climbed through the mountains and occupied Iba. Resupplied by the navy, it then marched south to arrive at Subic Bay on the twelfth. The southern column, of 750 soldiers from the 32nd and 3rd Infantry and the 3rd Artillery, left Florida Blanca and marched to Balanga, the capital of Bataan, and then returned and took another route to Subic. Faced with little resistance and worried about supplies, Grant broke the column into three detachments and rushed it through the mountains. Arriving at Subic on the tenth, they drove a small garrison out of Olongapo and captured the naval station and its arsenal. With assistance from the navy, Grant then launched a series of amphibious landings up and down the coast. Most of the troops returned to Pampanga; the rest garrisoned the major towns. Grant was pleased with the expedition's result: it had killed several enemy soldiers and captured a great deal of military ordnance, but it had also been conducted "with a view of aiding the pacification of the country, and strict orders were issued against looting, and against offending or intimidating the natives, and especially against interfering with women."[46]

Grant's emphasis on the nonmilitary benefits of the expedition and his choice of the word "pacification" are significant, for they showed the shift in army priorities. On 24 November, Otis informed Washington that the claim of an independent Philippines "can be made no longer under any fiction." The Philippine Republic had collapsed, many of its officials were prisoners, and its army was broken "into small bands scattered through these provinces, acting as banditti, or dispersed, playing the role of amigos with arms concealed."[47] Otis's assessment was shared by his division commanders. Lawton had decided the war in the north was over as early as 19 November, and turned his attention to planning a sweep into the provinces south of Manila.[48] MacArthur wrote on 20 November that it was impossible to determine if the revolutionaries had "any armed forces at all . . . with sufficient organization left to be regarded as an army."[49] Otis began shifting his resources from military to occupational duties. Both in Manila and in the field, it was hoped that good government, humane treatment, and the restoration of peace would soon pacify the area.

EIGHT

THE OCCUPATION OF
THE ARCHIPELAGO

The dispersal of the Army of Liberation and Aguinaldo's flight to the north removed the 8th Corps' primary opponent. From Otis's perspective, all that remained was to mop up the remaining enemy military forces and occupy the major municipalities of the archipelago. Otis put MacArthur in charge of the area north of Manila and brought Lawton back for the next campaign: the southern Tagalog provinces of Cavite, Laguna, Batangas, and Tayabas. But first Otis had to hurry supplies to the garrisons in the north and assemble troops, supplies, and transport. Not content with preparing for his next assignment, Lawton sought a new opportunity for action.[1]

What prompted Lawton to assume command of the small punitive expedition against Montalban and San Mateo is unclear. Located in hilly, easily defended country on the Marikina River roughly twenty miles northeast of Manila, the two towns were controlled by Brig. Gen. Pio del Pilar, who was reputed to have over 1,000 well-armed troops. Filipino soldiers and supplies could move from south to north by skirting the east shore of Laguna de Bay and then taking the trail along the river through San Mateo and Montalban. From the two towns, del Pilar could easily strike at the Marikina waterworks, barely two miles away, or cut the main wagon road leading from Manila to the north. Lawton may have had a personal reason to clear the area: on both his northern campaigns he had been distracted by reports that del Pilar would cut this route and attack him from the rear. Nevertheless, such a campaign was clearly a sideshow and hardly worth the attention of the senior field general in the 8th Corps.

On 18 December, in the midst of a monsoon, Lawton moved up the Marikina River for San Mateo. His plan called for a battalion each of the 27th and 29th U.S. Volunteer Infantry, and two squadrons of Col. James Lockett's 11th U.S. Volunteer Cavalry, to converge on a bluff outside the town early the next morning. Delayed by rain, mud, and the rapidly rising river, only Lt. Col. H. H. Sargent's 29th battalion and a mounted squadron of the 11th reached the rendezvous point on time. James A. LeRoy describes the ensuing skirmish as "directed with the precision and care which always characterized Lawton," but this may be unintended irony: San Mateo was a botched engagement in which no one distinguished themselves.[2] Although half his force was still marching up the trail, Lawton sent the cavalry squadron up the river to find a ford, cross over, and come down on the enemy flank. But the monsoon had turned the Marikina into a torrent and the trail into a quagmire, and Lockett rode all the way to Montalban before he found a crossing. The 11th fought a successful skirmish, complete with mounted charges, and occupied Montalban, but removed themselves completely from the fight for San Mateo. In the meantime, Sargent's battalion stumbled down the bluff to a 300-foot open floodplain broken into inundated rice paddies. Mist and rain allowed them to approach almost to the river's edge before the defenders noticed them. The Filipinos began a heavy, if inaccurate, fire, and the infantry, unable to find a crossing, took cover behind the paddy dikes. As more troops staggered up the trail, Lawton pushed them onto the firing line with little regard for tactical coherence. Standing out in the open rice field in his white rain slicker and pith helmet, the towering general made an inviting target. When his aide was struck down beside him, Lawton told the others he would go back up the bluff, where he would be less conspicuous; but he continued to walk along the firing line and was soon struck by a bullet in the chest. He died almost instantly, the only American fatality of the day. Shortly afterward, Sargent located a ford and sent his men across it, driving the stubborn defenders out of San Mateo.

Both to the soldiers he commanded and to the American public, Lawton was a living monument, and his death prompted an outpouring of grief in the army and the nation. At his funeral, Professor M. Woolsey Stryker compared him to Bayard, and opined that in the near future "our brown brothers" would proclaim, "He was America's; but he was ours too—LAWTON! He was slain by us ignorantly in unbelief; but he has forgiven."[3] Indeed, Lawton was, in many respects, one of the most admirable officers of the war: kind, generous, chivalrous, and able to inspire his troops to almost superhuman efforts. Disdaining cover, always at the firing line, he was so conspicuously brave that it was rumored he sought a quick death from a bullet to avoid a lingering one from tuberculosis. Certainly his insistence on unnecessarily exposing himself to enemy fire raises some questions about his physical or mental soundness.[4] To his credit, Lawton recognized the political dimensions of the conflict: his efforts to hasten local government, to employ Filipino soldiers, and to prevent abuses against civilians all indicate an ability to transcend purely military considerations. But he lacked strategic ability and never rose above the role of critic to articulate a coherent plan for ending the war. His renown as the war's consummate field general is also overdrawn. Essentially a charismatic warrior, he remained a commander whose heroics—and those of his men—were far too often the result of his own poor planning. Much of Lawton's reputation was established by an uncritical press, and by historian–policy makers LeRoy and Dean Worcester, who attributed to the deceased hero their own views on the war and army pacification policy.[5]

Following Lawton's death, the Americans mopped up the San Mateo–Montalban area. On 27 December converging columns of the 45th and 27th Infantry and the 11th Cavalry attacked the stronghold across a gorge on the San Mateo River. Under cover of an artillery bombardment, they launched a furious assault across open ground into the enemy trenches. Although it was the 45th's baptism, "the men acted as if they were on a field day, volleys were fired as one man."[6] Cheering, they advanced by rushes, one company running forward fifty yards, then dropping to the ground to fire its Krags while the next company sprinted forward. One veteran reflected that had the Filipinos been able to maintain a disciplined fire, the losses would have been catastrophic, but "the officers in command knew that the enemy could not shoot well and that our loss would be small."[7] The soldiers killed twenty-five insurgents and captured 10,000 rounds of ammunition. More important, they closed off the narrow north-south corridor around Laguna de Bay.

On 4 January Otis turned command of Lawton's 1st Division over to the newly promoted Maj. Gen. John C. Bates. Almost the complete antithesis of Lawton, Bates was a competent but cautious commander who owed his promotion to the iron law of seniority. His field officers would find that he did little to implement innovative measures but equally little to check their initiatives. Bates's division consisted of 8,000 soldiers in two brigades and a reserve force of the 37th and 39th Infantry. The first brigade—the 4th, 28th, 38th, and 45th Infantry and small detachments of cavalry and artillery—was commanded by Wheaton, brooding because he had been bypassed for promotion to brigadier general in the Regular establishment.[8] For much of the campaign, Wheaton exercised little direction or control. His fellow commander, Brig. Gen. Theodore Schwan, behaved far differently. Born in Germany, Schwan had begun his four-decade military career as a sergeant and slowly risen through the ranks. As Otis's chief of staff, he had served as a buffer between his commander and the field officers. Now, his rivals whispered, Otis had given his loyal assistant a 2,500-man brigade and an easy mission so as to gain him a general's star in the Regulars.[9] In turn, Schwan was determined that nothing would interfere with a glorious culmination to his military service. He tried to maintain strict control over his officers and prevent any unauthorized departures from the overall campaign strategy.

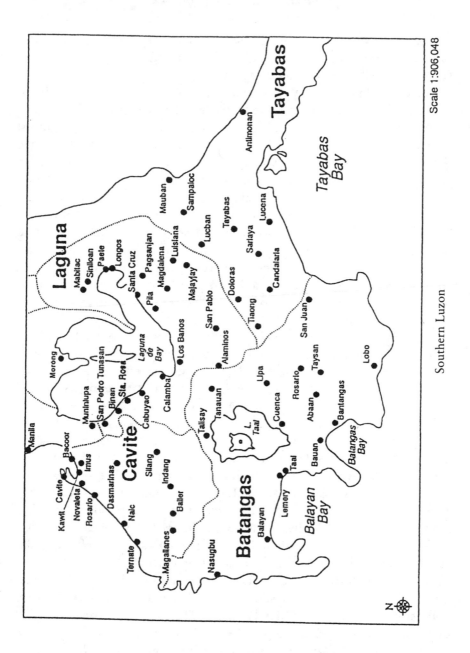

Southern Luzon

Scale 1:906,048

No sooner had Bates assumed command than his forces began Otis's final campaign to occupy the southern Tagalog provinces. The first target was Cavite, Aguinaldo's home and reputed to be "the strongest insurrecto province in the Philippines."[10] Wheaton was to concentrate his brigade at Imus, near Manila Bay, as Schwan moved from San Pedro Makati down Laguna de Bay and westward across Cavite, establishing a line running southwest from Binan to Indang and then northwest to the coastal town of Naic. Then Wheaton would drive south, forcing Mariano Trias, the political-military commander for southern Luzon, and his estimated 3,000 soldiers back into Schwan's cordon.[11] The plan had all the strengths, and all the weaknesses, of Otis's earlier campaigns to the north. If it succeeded, it would completely encircle and destroy the only major enemy concentration in the area. But to prevail, the Americans would have to move rapidly through broken country on primitive roads and to integrate maneuvers between two widely separated columns so as to form an impenetrable cordon. Most important, the Filipinos would have to cooperate and remain concentrated and immobile as the trap closed around them.

The difficulties inherent in coordinating scattered commands surfaced almost at the outset in the minor operations around Calamba, Laguna Province. Thirty miles south from Manila, this Laguna de Bay town had been occupied the previous summer by Col. Jacob Kline's 21st Infantry. Subjected to constant sniping and attacks and racked by disease, the 21st had barely held it against Brig. Gen. Miguel Malvar's Batangas militia. In late December they were replaced by Col. Robert L. Bullard and the eager Volunteers of the 39th Infantry. Aided by Lt. Charles P. Summerall's artillery battery, Bullard quickly moved to break Malvar's forces into two sections and destroy them in detail. On New Year's Day he loaded a battalion under Maj. John H. Parker on to *cascos* and had them towed across the lake, where they landed and attacked Malvar's left flank. The rest of the regiment drove through the Filipino lines. Hit in the front and flank, Malvar's forces disintegrated, and Bullard's "Indians" chased them northward nine miles down the bay toward Binan. The next day, Bullard continued the pursuit. The Filipinos had taken up a good position across a stream, but Summerall's guns battered down the defense, and Bullard, in Parker's admiring terms, "pounced on the flank of the fleeing fugitives. . . . it was a complete rout."[12] At a cost of four wounded, Bullard had killed thirty of the enemy and broken the siege of Calamba.

Otis was not impressed with the magnitude of the victory. Bullard's unauthorized attack had driven enemy contingents right into Schwan's intended path. Bullard received an immediate order to explain his actions and to desist from all further offensives. Undeterred, the following day he launched a reconnaissance that struck a large force under Malvar's chief subordinate, Mariano Noriel; Bullard happily reinforced it with the rest of the 39th and drove Noriel's forces back in confusion. This time, Manila made it clear that Bullard was to remain in Calamba and not to venture out again without orders.[13]

Had Otis and his staff been less miffed at Bullard's insubordination, they might have noticed that his campaign closely approximated on a small scale their own plans for Cavite. Bullard had successfully placed a cordon across the enemy rear and then driven the Filipinos into the pocket. But as Parker soon recognized, his boast that Malvar's command was "annihilated as an organized force" was misplaced: "We did not know it then, but the capture of rifles was the important thing; not the scatterment of Filipino organizations."[14] A second lesson was to be learned at greater cost: Manila's inability to control one headstrong colonel boded ill for its planned coordination of a complicated offensive involving several equally ambitious field officers eager for glory and promotion before the war's end.

But even hampered with unruly officers, Bates's expedition was well ahead of its opponents. Not only did it have far superior weapons, training, and logistics, but it faced opponents ill prepared to resist. Most of Trias's 3,000 soldiers were poorly armed militia, and he himself was distracted by a fanciful plan to stage an uprising in Manila. The result was that despite ample warning of the American advance, the insurgents were unready.[15]

On 4 January Schwan's 2,500 infantry marched twenty miles south from San Pedro Makati to the town of Muntinlupa on the lakeshore. Over the next few days, they brushed aside Noriel's delaying force and swept west through Binan and then Silang. Schwan's cavalry under Lt. Col. Edward M. Hayes took Indang on the seventh and Naic the following day. In four days, Schwan's brigade had sliced through Cavite from Laguna de Bay to the coast, stringing a loose cordon across the province. Now they marched over a largely deserted countryside. When the 30th Infantry entered one town they found only a terrified young girl waving a white flag; the bemused soldiers calmed her and assured her they meant no harm. To Col. Walter S. Schuyler, commanding the 46th Infantry, the campaign consisted of little but long marches and "many halts and tedious waits."[16] Sent to attack the stronghold of Carmona on the seventh, Schuyler found the bridge intact, the defenses deserted, and the road littered with ammunition carts and guns. By the ninth, the 46th was divided into battalions and assigned to occupation duties. The soldiers immediately dug rifle pits and other defenses, built a telegraph line, and then began scouring the area for discarded weapons. Schuyler met the priest at Silang and urged him to spread the word that it was safe to return. As civilians trickled back in, Schuyler's provost marshal sent the women and children back to their houses and put the men to work cleaning up the town and repairing the roads.[17]

Meanwhile Wheaton, who according to Otis's plan was supposed to wait until Schwan had closed off Trias's escape route, allowed his subordinates to draw him into a premature attack. On the sixth, barely two days into Schwan's campaign, Col. William E. Birkhimer's 28th Infantry broke through the Filipino lines southeast of Imus. The next day, a Filipino spy informed Birkhimer there was a strong enemy force entrenched behind a river crossing at the village of Putol on the road to Novaleta. The colonel sent two scouts to find the enemy position, but they were spotted and one was badly wounded. Birkhimer promptly sent his regiment into the attack. According to one participant, the Caviteanos "certainly were confident of defeating us, and sent the bullets around our ears in lively style."[18] Birkhimer was also impressed: the enemy was "confident and defiant; cheers arose from their whole line. . . . They kept sounding the charge, 'Viva las Filipines' arose throughout their line."[19] Birkhimer moved his artillery up to within 300 yards of the barricade and sent his scouts out along the flanks to draw an attack. He directed two companies to take up a position out of sight and prepare to counterattack; two other companies swung around the Filipinos' exposed right flank. Creeping undetected to within 150 yards, the soldiers "sprang from the bushes and with bloodcurdling yells charged the enemy driving everything before them. . . . the retreat became an utter rout and slaughter."[20] Birkhimer claimed the 28th killed sixty-five insurgents, wounded another forty, and captured thirty-two rifles.

Over the next few days, Wheaton moved across northern Cavite, his cavalry linking up with Hayes's troopers at Naic on the tenth. There were some sharp skirmishes in which soldiers were wounded or killed, but resistance was disorganized and ineffectual. Trias went into hiding near his hometown of San Francisco de Malabon; his officers and foot soldiers took their weapons and returned to their barrios and villages. To the disappointment of most Americans, there was no climactic battle of annihilation. Indeed, Col. George S. Anderson's 38th Infantry did not fire a shot in anger during the entire Cavite campaign, for "nothing was seen of the enemy."[21] As had happened in the north, the elaborate trap closed on empty air.

With Cavite apparently quiescent, Bates turned to Laguna and Batangas. He ordered Bullard with the 39th and a battalion of the 37th south to Malvar's headquarters at Santo Tomas on 9 January. The Batanguenos had built a series of defensive lines, culminating with a strongpoint at Biga, where the gorge of the San Juan River crossed the road. The position was formidable: tiers of loopholed earthworks swept the bridge and the approaches twenty feet below. However, Malvar had fewer than 1,000 men at Biga; most of his troops were in the south guarding against attack from the sea. Bullard deployed his forces skillfully. Summerall's small battery pounded the entrenchments, and the infantry picked off the poorly armed militia. After an hour the defenders had had enough and retreated, leaving twenty-four dead and sixty captives. Bullard crossed the gorge and continued on to Santo Tomas.

As Bullard's troops cut south, Bates pulled Schwan's brigade out of central Cavite and sent it into Batangas. Anderson's 38th left Dasmarinas on the tenth with little direction from Wheaton except to attack any enemy concentration they found. In a series of forced marches across thirty-three miles of mountains around the north of Lake Taal, the 38th arrived in Tanauan on the twelfth and linked up with Bullard's 39th. The two colonels, and Anderson's equally aggressive second in command, Lt. Col. Charles J. Crane, decided to attack Malvar's new headquarters at Lipa, eight miles to the south, the next morning. Since Anderson was senior, the 38th led the advance, brushing aside a small roadblock and entering Lipa with the loss of one soldier killed and another wounded. The town was deserted except for 130 exultant Spanish prisoners, one of whom informed the two colonels that several American prisoners were less than six miles farther south in Rosario. Without much thought, Bullard, Anderson, Crane, and four other officers, escorted only by four orderlies, galloped off to glory. Charging into town and firing their pistols like Wild West desperadoes, they sent soldiers and civilians fleeing in terror. Much to their disappointment, the only prisoners were another 170 Spaniards. However, one revealed a treasure trove of 20,000 pesos; with prisoners and treasure, the small detachment returned to Lipa in triumph. The feat attracted a great deal of popular enthusiasm in the United States, but Bates and Schwan were not amused. They had little patience with officers who left their regiments to go grandstanding, especially after Col. Cornelius Gardener reported that soldiers from the unsupervised regiments had looted Lipa.[22]

Much of the generals' irritation sprang from their recognition that the campaign was getting out of control. Brigade boundaries had broken down, regiments were mixed up, and ambitious officers like Anderson and Bullard were acting on their own. Even more disconcerting, there were increasing signs of resistance in supposedly secured areas. Supply wagons and reinforcements were routinely sniped at and occasionally ambushed. These attacks compounded problems in the overburdened logistical system, and hungry soldiers disregarded strict instructions against foraging and took what they could find. In an effort to regain control, on 12 January Bates reorganized his division, transferring the 38th and 39th to Schwan and putting him in charge of operations east of Lake Taal. Wheaton got Schuyler's 46th Infantry and took over operations in Cavite and Batangas west of Lake Taal. The two brigadiers immediately sent out columns to clear out any remaining pockets of resistance and to occupy the major towns. They would link up at the southern border of their commands—the twin towns of Lemery and Taal, separated by the Pansipit (Taal) River, which feeds Lake Taal.[23]

Wheaton quickly pushed his troops from northern Cavite into southwestern Batangas. On the fifteenth, Col. Joseph Dorst, with Lt. Col. James Parker's battalion of the 45th Infantry and three troops of 11th Cavalry, left Naic and set out across the mountains for Nasugbu, thirty miles down the coast on the Batangas border. Although they left at night, their approach was signaled by fires that blazed along the hills. The mountainous terrain was hellish; at one point the cavalry filed through a pass so narrow that their saddlebags scraped along the sides, at another they led horses along a trail with a 500-foot drop. But despite the fact that, as one soldier noted, 100 defenders could have held off 5,000, the only resistance they encountered was from monkeys, which dropped coconuts and kept them awake all night with their howling. As the cavalry approached Nasugbu the next day, they surprised a religious procession. The priest and his parishioners fled, leaving seventy armed men who immediately opened up at barely 150 yards' range. The 11th lost several horses in the desperate fighting but killed four insurgents. Eager for further glory, Parker urged Dorst to push on to Lemery, but the colonel had no intention of being chastised for exceeding his orders. He returned to Naic, fighting off a well-placed ambush at a river crossing.[24]

Meanwhile, another of Wheaton's units, Maj. William H. Johnston's battalion of the 46th Infantry, had left Indan on 16 January to strike out across the mountains to Balayan, twenty-four miles to the south, and then eastward thirteen miles along the coast road to link up with Schwan's brigade at Taal. After a long, arduous march, Johnston reached the outskirts of Lemery, across the Pansipit River from Taal, on the eighteenth, where he found Brig. Gen. Martin Cabrera and 1,000 Batangueno militia dug in a strong position across the river. Flanked by Lake Taal and the sea, the 46th's only access was over a 150-foot bridge swept by artillery and blocked by a breastwork of brush and earth. A prudent officer, Johnston called for support. The gunboat *Marietta* shelled the trenches, and Maj. Charles Muir's battalion of the 38th, from Schwan's brigade, marched fifteen miles and fought its way in to Taal from the east. Johnston sent his best soldiers rushing across the bridge. They tore a hole in the breastwork, and the rest of the battalion followed. Johnston linked up with Muir, establishing contact between the Wheaton and Schwan brigades as planned, and in the process fighting the last significant engagement of the southern Luzon campaign. With his forces in control of most of the main towns and the enemy scattered, Wheaton turned his attention to pacifying Cavite and western Batangas.[25]

In the meantime, Schwan was pushing into southeastern Batangas. He broke his force into three columns and set out on the fifteenth from Lipa to Batangas City. He intended them to arrive together on the seventeenth, but Muir's battalion hiked so rapidly through the mountains that it reached Batangas City a day early. Sending Muir to link up with Johnston at Taal, Schwan turned the rest of his brigade east, marching across Batangas into Tayabas Province and then north into Laguna. Hayes's cavalry swept ahead, followed by Gardener's 30th Infantry, which occupied the main towns in Tayabas. On the twenty-second the soldiers encountered an impressive series of entrenchments across an almost impassable gorge near Majayjay, Laguna. But as had happened throughout the campaign, virtually impregnable defenses were useless without determined soldiers to hold them. Two companies of the 39th lowered ropes and managed to scale the steep cliffs, and the defenders fled. Two days later, Hayes's troopers rode into Santa Cruz on Laguna de Bay, completing Schwan's circuit through Cavite, Batangas, Tayabas, and Laguna.[26]

The southeastern Luzon campaign of January 1900 shared many similarities with the great northern campaign of the previous three months. In both, the army had shown an impressive ability to move through rugged terrain; it had occupied most of the major towns, setting the stage for the imposition of political control over the populace. In both north and south, there appeared grounds for cautious optimism. Returning to Naic after a long hike in early February, one soldier reported that the "market place was booming and twice its former size," and that saloons, cafes, and even a modern drugstore with a soda fountain had all opened. The streets and docks were filled with people, there was a constant stream of carts bringing in hemp and produce to the wharf, and "squads of natives hired by the government could be seen everywhere busily engaged cleaning the streets and gutters and things began to look as if peace was near [at] hand."[27]

Nevertheless, the expedition had not succeeded in defeating, or even crippling, the revolutionaries' military organization. For all of Schwan's boasts that he had destroyed the "cream" of the enemy forces and that only "predatory bands" remained, his accomplishments were relatively modest: 180 enemy dead and, equally significant, only 154 rifles captured.[28] Even more ominous were the continued indications that local resistance was far from over: guerrillas ambushed patrols that strayed too far into the mountains or brush, and most supply trains ran a gauntlet of sniper fire. The fighting was relatively minor, but it caused a steady trickle of dead and wounded that soon passed the number of casualties for the entire campaign. This harassing, hit-and-run guerrilla war both puzzled and infuriated the soldiers. One veteran commented that when his comrades captured two Filipino soldiers, they "gave them a good hammering and a little good advice, [then] turned them loose." But after he learned of Aguinaldo's declaration of guerrilla war, he wrote: "If they intend to resort to bushwhacking methods and fight like savages, we shall treat them as such when we capture any of them."[29]

Concurrent with the final campaigns on Luzon, Hughes broke the long stalemate on Panay. Throughout the summer the general had remained on the defensive, unable to overcome the combination of insufficient manpower, Delgado's defensive lines outside Iloilo, and the monsoon, which, as Hughes complained, precluded all military operations: "We could chase [the insurgents] all around the place if we could move, but the mud and water is breast deep."[30] Hughes tried a variety of means to break the deadlock and damage his opponents. He conducted extensive negotiations with the junta of the Federal State of the Visayas to swing them over to the American side, but these collapsed in September when Delgado declared himself political-military governor. Hughes increased his efforts to starve the revolutionaries out by shutting off trade from Iloilo City to the interior. Assisted by the navy's gunboats, he banned coastal sailing boats from trafficking in food. To lure them from areas controlled by Delgado, he issued all civilians who moved within the American lines with a daily rice ration; the population doubled between July and August. He located these new arrivals on the outskirts of his lines, cynically reasoning that they were all relatives of the insurgents and their presence would discourage attacks and sniping. Suspecting that guerrillas were coming into his lines to rest and recuperate, in October Hughes authorized sweeps of the occupied zone, arresting and expelling all males of military age who lacked registration papers. These measures had a devastating effect. One soldier described the population around Iloilo as on the verge of starvation; the children fought over the troops' slop buckets, and the old people picked up scraps around the camp. Nevertheless, he felt Hughes's policies were justified, for, "If we even give a small child anything to eat they take it home with them and divide it with one of their soldiers."[31]

In October the arrival of Col. Edmund Rice's 26th Infantry and two battalions of the 19th Infantry, coupled with the end of the monsoon season, finally gave Hughes his opportunity. He planned to encircle Delgado's forces by first driving down Panay's west coast and then swinging north and east to block off the mountain passes to Capiz and Antique Provinces. By means of heliographic signals, Hughes would direct converging columns, some landed by water, to trap Delgado's 2,000 troops at Santa Barbara, ten miles north of Iloilo. Like many American operations, the general's ambitious objectives were thwarted by weather, terrain, and the near impossibility of coordinating separated commands. On 9 November the first column broke out of Iloilo and drove west, but heavy rains, swamps, and mud soon slowed its march to a crawl; supplies failed to arrive, and high winds prevented some landings. On the twentieth, believing his troops would soon seal off the mountain passes, Hughes ordered the 18th Infantry's Col. Gilbert S. Carpenter to strike out from Iloilo to Santa Barbara. But the message had hardly been sent than Hughes's column halted while his engineers bridged a ravine. Thus when Carpenter's force attacked Santa Barbara on the twenty-first, Delgado, after perfunctory resistance, slipped away. Carpenter, an aged and infirm mediocrity, proved unequal to the challenge of independent command, losing track of his men and tangling up his logistical lines. Uniting the two columns, Hughes drove his men ruthlessly in pursuit to Passi, arriving on the twenty-seventh. Delgado's men scattered, a small contingent retreating north to Capiz Province across narrow mountain trails. Pausing briefly to supply his exhausted troops, Hughes set off in pursuit. After a heroic struggle over the mountains, which included marching through a typhoon, they reached the capital town of Capiz on 9 December, but once again a decisive battle eluded them. As had happened on Luzon, most of the insurgent forces had already broken into small parties, which filtered through the porous American lines and made their way home. Still seeking battle, in December Hughes sent expeditions to Antique Province and the island of Romblon, but they encountered only skirmishers. Although his forces had scattered the enemy, Hughes had few illusions that the war was over: after meeting the officials of Capiz Province he sourly noted he had "made them quite a speech in which the utter uselessness of their continuing the unequal struggle was fully explained to them and they were told to quit their fooling and 'play ball,' but I do not suppose it will do much good."[32]

Hughes's campaign on Panay had serious effects on Negros, where it contributed to what the military authorities called, with some exaggeration, the "December Uprising."[33] Three revolutionary agents arrived in late November and through a skillful propaganda campaign convinced many that William Jennings Bryan would become president and that Congress would soon recognize Philippine independence. Under their direction, some municipal officials raised a force of bolomen in preparation for a rebellion. They were soon joined by ninety armed men—referred to as "Tagals"—who had escaped Hughes's campaign on Panay.[34] According to the island's governor, Brig. Gen. James F. Smith, the putative insurrection was exposed by a loyal municipal official, with the result that the conspirators fled the towns and took to the hills. Patrols promptly went in pursuit, and on 7 December a detachment of 15 soldiers, 4 police, and 6 militiamen under Lt. Augustus C. Ledyard was attacked by 60 riflemen and 320 bolomen. After a hard fight in which Ledyard was killed and 2 soldiers wounded, the outnumbered patrol made its way back to safety, having killed 17 opponents. The next day, another isolated detachment was attacked.

Shocked, perhaps even panicked, by the outbreak, Smith reacted quickly and drastically. He telegraphed Hughes that his troops were facing twenty-to-one odds and that if he did not obtain reinforcements he might have to order the population moved into protected zones. He ordered each sugar plantation to collect all its food supplies and bring them to a central location where they could be placed under military guard. He summoned provincial and municipal officials as well as families suspected of assisting the rebels, forced them to post bonds for good behavior, and warned them "they had better not make fools of themselves unless they wanted to get badly hurt."[35] He fined individuals and towns that had harbored revolutionary agents and, most drastic of all, issued a circular authorizing summary execution of any person caught in insurrection. Assisted by six companies sent by Hughes, Smith dispatched small patrols of infantry, local police, and militia, which skirmished with guerrillas and Babylanes, inflicting few casualties but destroying storehouses and camps. The American response demoralized the resistance, and by 3 January Smith declared the insurgents were in their "death flurry," and he expected them cleared out completely in the near future.[36]

Although a relatively minor affair in terms of combat or casualties, the "December Uprising" revealed significant differences within the army leadership over the proper pacification policy to follow in the occupied provinces. Hughes, who already viewed Smith as an alarmist and too conciliatory, was confirmed in his prejudices.[37] For his part, Smith reasserted his belief that the Negrenses were happy under American rule: "All would be serene here if there were no outside interference, no landings of the dreaded Tagals, and no fear that Aguinaldo may come into power and punish Negros for what it has done." But in Smith's explanation that "our friends are timid and only come valiantly to our sides when the storm has passed" underlay a serious dilemma for the United States.[38] Negros, and especially those influential Negrenses who had cooperated, had gained the full benefits of benevolent assimilation. Yet three revolutionary agents and a small force of riflemen had been able to gather sufficient support there for an uprising. Worse, instead of depending on the Negrenses to rally for their own defense, the army had been forced to send in reinforcements to protect them.

The problem underlay a large part of the controversy between Smith and the 6th Infantry's Col. Charles W. Miner, the military commander on Negros. The two men disliked each other. Smith was a brilliant jurist, a prominent political leader, and an amateur soldier who tended to view the 6th as his own private army. Miner was an all-too-typical example of the senior Regular Army officer—a sexagenarian veteran of the Civil War and Cuba whom seniority and his predecessor's ill health had rewarded with a colonelcy in 1899. He was deeply suspicious of the civil government and the Negrenses, and believed he should be consulted on all important issues. But beyond their personal antipathy, the two men had substantial differences on pacification policy. To ensure the legitimacy of the civil government and because of his own legal training, Smith wanted to work within the law. He favored selective punishments—fines, removal from public office, and imprisonment of individuals who had been compromised in the recent disturbances. In contrast, Miner viewed the destruction of enemy forces as the paramount object and believed Smith was overly concerned with the civil and property rights of those in rebellion against the United States.

The disagreements eventually culminated in a struggle for control of policy. Both men recognized that many plantation owners supplied the guerrillas with food and shelter as a form of protection. Accordingly, Smith ordered plantation managers to make an inventory of all their supplies and bring them to a central storehouse, where they could be guarded by soldiers. Field officers viewed this as cumbersome and impractical; they had no time to check supplies and no extra soldiers to guard them. Instead, when they found foodstuffs they suspected of being used by the enemy, they confiscated or burned them. In December, Miner's chief field officers began a more drastic policy of removing rice from plantation storehouses to occupied towns and arresting anyone suspected of assisting the insurgents. When Smith learned of this and other abuses, he was furious. In a sharp reprimand, he lectured Miner that "the policy of destroying private property or taking the life or punishing unarmed citizens on denunciations and ex parte statements, without a trial, will not be countenanced and any attempt to introduce it will bring disaster on those engaged in the interprise [sic]."[39] On 20 January, Smith issued G.O. 1. Quoting extensively from G.O. 100, it mandated that "every effort should be made by the American forces here to gain and merit the friendship and good will of the People."[40] For a variety of reasons—Manila's interest in benevolent pacification on Negros, the virtual end of fighting on the island after January, and Smith's considerable personal influence—the controversy ended and Smith found no more reason to complain. Nevertheless, the confrontation foreshadowed many future ones between those military officers committed to long-range goals of benevolence and conciliation, and others who thought only in terms of practical, immediate military necessity.

At the very time the Tagalog heartland was being occupied and the western Visayas cleared up, Washington directed Otis to occupy the "hemp ports" in the Bicol-speaking provinces of southeastern Luzon—Sorsogan, Albay, and Ambos Camarines (later divided into Camarines Norte and Camarines Sur)—the eastern Visayan islands of Leyte and Samar, and northern Mindanao. Philippine hemp made the best cordage in the world, but four years of war and the navy's blockade had sent prices skyrocketing by 300 percent.[41] American farmers and businessmen predicted that without sufficient hemp for twine and rope an agricultural depression might result. Certainly it would increase the farm vote for Bryan in the forthcoming November elections, as the McKinley administration was quick to recognize. There were also strong military reasons to secure the hemp provinces: taxes on the crop and contributions from merchants channeled thousands of dollars to the revolutionaries.[42]

Amphibious landing during the "Hemp Expedition," 1900

However clear the objective, it posed a considerable dilemma. On the one hand, the occupation of a few key ports and the resumption of the hemp trade would win over the elite, who presumably dominated the masses. Given Otis's underlying assumption that resistance stemmed entirely from Tagalogs and brigands, it made sense to station troops throughout the Philippines where they could best protect the peaceful population. On the other hand, the occupation would take precious resources, and even more precious manpower— over 5,000 men—out of the strategic areas of Luzon and disseminate them in areas of negligible military importance. It would also strip Otis of his reserve and prevent any sustained large-unit military operations. Scattered into small garrisons throughout the archipelago and with no reinforcements, the army ran the risk of being overwhelmed by local guerrillas and defeated piecemeal. But because he did not appreciate the consequences, or because he failed to comprehend the strength of the independence movement, or simply because he unquestioningly accepted Washington's authority, Otis did not challenge the directive to send troops to the hemp provinces. However, MacArthur believed Otis had made a terrible blunder; the army should have first pacified Luzon, then the rest of the archipelago.[43] Certainly the decision was a momentous one, for it turned the entire archipelago into a battlefield, where the Philippine War could only be won or lost island by island.

The revolutionaries faced even greater problems in the hemp provinces. Geography favored the defenders, particularly if they abandoned the coastal towns and took to the mountains. But for the resistance to succeed, the revolutionaries had to bridge the deep social divisions between the impoverished hemp growers in the interior and the townspeople and merchants on the coast. Often cheated and exploited, some peasants had become brigands or joined militant sects such as Samar's Dios Dios. The merchant and planter elite who dominated the revolutionary committees that seized power from the Spanish sought to maintain control over their labor force but were suspicious of outside interference. Like their compatriots in the Visayas, the elite in the hemp areas tended to favor a federal system of government, in which provinces retained considerable autonomy. Many of them depended on foreign trade. Badly hurt by the navy's blockade of abaca shipments, they soon discovered the insular and impecunious Republic was unable to protect their interests. Their suspicions were not assuaged by the Philippine Republic's tendency to treat all areas outside the Tagalog region as colonies. Aguinaldo and the Malolos government had appointed political-military jefes—invariably Tagalogs—for each island; then demanded money, food, and recruits, and in return sent a minuscule number of troops and arms, fewer than 200 rifles for the entire Bicol region. They sowed further confusion by establishing overlapping jurisdictions, creating a bitter feud over who commanded in Leyte. Not surprisingly, in the year and a half between the expulsion of the Spanish and the coming of the Americans, little had been done to prepare for invasion.

The generals who represented the Philippine Republic—Vicente Lukban on Samar, Ambrosio Moxica on Leyte, and Vito Belarmino in the Bicol area—each had to tread a cautious path between local demands and Aguinaldo's directives. The most capable and energetic was Lukban, who sought to win over the population by exhortation and example, even to the point of marrying a Samareno. He built his resistance around a few riflemen, supported by village militias, and sought to impose a uniform strategy on his local commanders. He made an uneasy alliance with the Dios Dios sect, which not only provided him with several hundred fanatical bolomen but also ensured that the mountaineers would not attack Lukban's partisans. Unfortunately, his energy was often misdirected; his repeated interference in Leyte, his tampering with elections, and his virulent anticlericalism provoked a reaction that led Aguinaldo to restrict him to Samar. A ruthless patriot, Lukban had no compunction about burning the houses and property, or taking the lives, of those who collaborated.[44] Belarmino was less successful in dominating the Bicol provinces: a navy officer who visited him in 1899 reported the general admitted he could not control his forces.[45] Prematurely aged and losing his sight, he confined himself to a largely inspirational role and to raising money. Moxica formed a 400-man "Battalion de Leyte," which provided a solid nucleus of riflemen and officers for mobile guerrilla war. But, like Lukban, Moxica's main resources were the town militias, each of which was raised and commanded by the local elite. Distance, poor communications, personal disagreements, and the naval blockade prevented these commanders from aiding each other, even had they wanted to. Therefore, in the hemp provinces there would be no central control or even direction to the resistance. As the Americans advanced, each island, and sometimes each locality, would conduct its own war.

The "hemp expedition" was mounted with great haste and little preparation. Although naval warships had made a thorough reconnaissance of the bays and landings, the 47th's historian recalled "the topography of the country was absolutely unknown in Manila," and the little available information was "absurdly incorrect."[46] Troops and supplies were crammed into the transports anywhere they could fit. That the expedition succeeded as well as it did was due in no small measure to the cooperation of the army and navy. William A. Kobbé, recently promoted to brigadier general, was placed in charge of the Volunteers of Col. Arthur Murray's 43rd Infantry and Col.

Walter Howe's 47th Infantry, as well as a detachment of his old command, the 3rd Artillery. Commodore Raymond P. Rodgers commanded the *Helena*, *Nashville*, and *Mariveles*. In sharp contrast to the impasse at Iloilo, the two commanders developed joint tactics for landings and cooperated throughout the campaign.[47]

Departing Manila on 18 January 1900, the expedition sailed south and then west, arriving off the long tip of the Bicol Peninsula on the twentieth. At Sorsogan City the Americans were met by a group of merchants who had appointed their only English-speaking member as official greeter—a small, rotund individual who stood alone on the pier and invited the landing boats again and again to "Come to Yee-sus, Come to Yee-sus!"[48] The troops landed and quickly occupied the town, although without meeting their divine host. On the twenty-third the expedition reached Albay Province's main port, Legaspi. Belarmino had assembled between 800 and 1,000 militiamen and constructed an impressive line of earthworks and firing pits. But Kobbé saw that the defenses were poorly designed: intended to repel a frontal attack, they were open on the left flank. Cramming seventy-five soldiers of the 47th into his few landing craft, he ordered them ashore. As they approached the beach, the warships opened up with their heavy cannon and machine guns, sweeping the entrenchments. With the enemy fire effectively nullified, the 47th charged the left flank, firing into the crowded trenches with deadly effect. The defenders, many of whom had been given amulets for invulnerability, made desperate but futile bolo charges. Soon joined by reinforcements, the soldiers forced their way through Legaspi and drove the insurgents back through the neighboring towns of Albay and Daraga. The fierce fighting left fifty-three Bicols dead and another eight severely wounded; Kobbé had three wounded.[49]

Leaving Howe and the 47th to garrison the ports of Albay and Sorsogan Provinces, Kobbé steamed off with Col. Arthur Murray's 43rd for Samar. Arriving off Calbayog on the twenty-sixth, Kobbé landed Maj. John C. Gilmore's battalion unopposed. Lukban had ordered the town commander to torch the town, but he disobeyed and instead pulled his troops out to the surrounding hills. Gilmore occupied the town, pushed out patrols, and skirmished with the militia, killing two and capturing eleven primitive bamboo cannon. In the meantime, Kobbé sailed down the coast to Catbalogan, arriving early on the twenty-seventh. Determined to avoid unnecessary violence, Kobbé sent Maj. Henry T. Allen ashore to promise the defenders a full pardon. The local commander, perhaps emboldened by Lukban's presence, refused to surrender and, as Allen's boat pulled away from shore, ordered Catbalogan burned. To the surprise of the defenders, Allen immediately sent his four companies ashore. The troops splashed through 300 yards of water and stormed into the burning town. The troops were "keen for the fight and rushed forward with such disregard of the insurgent fire as would have brought upon themselves much greater loss in front of a more effective enemy."[50] They drove the defenders off after a brief engagement and then set to work fighting the fires. With Samar's two chief hemp ports secured by seven companies of the 43rd, Kobbé's flotilla steamed across the Surigao Strait to the neighboring island of Leyte, landing Murray and a battalion at the capital city of Tacloban and sending a small garrison of the 43rd to the west coast port of Ormoc. Both these landings were virtually unopposed.

Kobbé's expedition left only the western Bicol province of Ambos Camarines and northern Mindanao unoccupied. The Camarines had become a sanctuary for insurgents fleeing east from Schwan's expedition into Tayabas and west from the 47th's operations in Albay. Otis dispatched Brig. Gen. James M. Bell and a provisional brigade of Col. Edward A. Goodwin's 40th Infantry and Dorst's 45th. Once again, army and navy commanders demonstrated close cooperation. Arriving at San Miguel Bay on 20 February, the Americans discovered that silt and sediment forced them to unload the troops five miles out. Under the authority of two navy beach masters, steamers towed the troop boats as close as possible, then cut loose the lines, turning the task over to sailors who rowed until they grounded. The troops then struggled ashore through waist-deep mud. The initial plan had called for a small steamer with a battalion of the 45th aboard to move up the Bicol River to Nueva Caceres (now Naga) while the rest of the troops slogged along the riverbanks to cut off the enemy escape. However, the steamer soon ran aground, and it was not until the twenty-second that, accompanied by the gunboat *Paragua*, the Americans reached the capital city and took it without resistance. That day also saw the most serious fight of the campaign, at Libmanan. The 40th had sent Filipinos into the town to negotiate a surrender, promising no harm would come to the town or its people, but the offers were rejected. Advancing across a marshy plain, the soldiers were repeatedly attacked by individuals who rushed out of the high reeds, slashed and stabbed with spear and bolo, and then vanished. The officers reacted quickly, ordering the men to tighten up formation, fix bayonets, and sweep the area. Against such countermeasures, the attacks proved suicidal: sixty-four Bicols were killed at a cost of eight wounded by the time the troops reached Libmanan.

With Libmanan and Nueva Caceres taken, Bell sent his five companies of the 45th on a forced march to seal off the Albay border, trap Belarmino's forces, and release Spanish and Chinese captives. The grueling mountain hike along narrow, broken trails and rushing streams exhausted the men; luckily, they encountered only poorly armed irregulars who melted away after a few shots. By the end of February they had reached Albay's borders and interdicted the major routes between the Camarines and its neighbors. Resistance collapsed; there were so many surrenders that Bell ordered all but those charged with criminal activity turned loose.[51]

As each hemp port fell under American control, Otis declared it open for trade, touching off a frenzy of speculation. Merchants and their factors converged on the ports and soon bought up all the hemp in the towns; then they petitioned the post commanders, and Manila, to push troops into the countryside and to open new ports. Their demands reached a new urgency when insurgents in Samar and Albay burned towns and hemp warehouses. Post commanders stretched their already small detachments dangerously thin to send out patrols to protect hemp gatherers and convoys. But these same merchants were paying substantial sums to the guerrillas to protect their fields and workers. To make matters worse, officers discovered that the insurgents were collecting taxes on hemp going through the ports or smuggling it aboard coastal steamers and *cascos*. Indeed, Kobbé himself inadvertently assisted this illicit traffic by removing most of the restrictions on coastal trade; all a skipper needed was to have his boat registered in an occupied town and a pass stating the nature of his cargo. Far from cutting off the illicit hemp trade and the revolutionary funds, the opening of the hemp ports may have increased them.[52]

Although smuggling had not been reduced, the amphibious operations in the Bicol Peninsula and eastern Visayas were a strong demonstration of the flexibility the U.S. Navy lent to military operations. The Americans had obtained excellent intelligence and were well informed of the conditions they would encounter. Navy and army officers had scouted prospective landing sites, and hemp merchants served as interpreters and envoys. One correspondent who accompanied the expedition noted that soldiers and sailors were so accustomed to working together that landing operations "had become conventionalized."[53] Tactics were relatively simple. The Americans would arrive at a port at dawn, inducing an exodus of civilians. Under a flag of truce, an officer would go ashore, often with a representative of the hemp trade, to persuade the locals to lay down their weapons. If this failed, the steam launches would tow a line of boats up to the transports, and the soldiers would disembark into them. Then, with the warships providing a cover fire, the launches would race toward shore. This was the most critical time, for the troops were crammed into the boats and unable to defend themselves. Once they reached shallow water, they would scramble ashore, form a skirmish line, disperse the defenders, if any, and occupy the town. They would then set up a defensive perimeter, unload supplies and ammunition, chase off any lurking snipers, and send townspeople into the countryside to encourage refugees to return home. Usually within a week the town would be almost full again, with trade flourishing under a temporary government appointed by the commanding officer.

The campaigns of late 1899 and early 1900 stretched U.S. military power farther into the provinces, and Otis soon pushed it even farther south. Following his agreement with the Sultan of Sulu, Bates had remained in the Moro provinces, his forces consisting at first of a few companies of the 23rd stationed at Bongao, Siassi, and Jolo in the Sulu archipelago. In November the 23rd occupied Zamboanga on Mindanao, and a month later Col. James L. Pettit's 31st Infantry arrived, relieving the 23rd at Zamboanga and garrisoning Davao and Cotabato on the southern coast. After taking over from Lawton and commanding the invasion of southwestern Luzon, Bates briefly returned in March to station the 40th Infantry on Mindanao's northern coast at Surigao, Iligan, Misamis, and Cagayan, before turning over the newly formed District of Mindanao and Jolo to Kobbé.

With the exception of the Christian settlements in northern Mindanao, there was little organized military resistance in the southern Philippines; but tribal, ethnic, and sectarian unrest and banditry kept the region in turmoil. In the Sulu archipelago, Kobbé ordered post commanders to stay out of Moro affairs and conduct operations only to ensure the Bates Agreement was followed.[54] Mindanao was a much tougher theater. The simmering Muslim-pagan-Christian rivalry threatened to erupt into open warfare and served to cover a great deal of banditry, rustling, and violent crime. Unlike the small islands of the Sulu archipelago, where the sultan's authority was recognized, if not obeyed, and where powerful *datus* (chieftains) could cow recalcitrants, Mindanao lacked any strong governing authority. The tribes were many and fractious, touchy of their honor, and accustomed to settling disputes with rifle, kris, and spear. Most of the richer *datus* welcomed the Americans, if only because stable government would confirm their authority, but the friendship of one could mean the alienation of a lesser, rival *datu*. Although he recognized the difficulties in his position, Kobbé was confident that a combination of patience, scrupulous regard for religious rights, and respectful treatment would win over the population and prevent serious fighting.

These sentiments accorded with those of the army high command in Manila. Convinced that, by December 1899, "war in its proper meaning had ceased to exist," Otis began to break up his divisions and brigades into smaller forces to provide a "very extended police system for the protection of the inhabitants."[55] His chief of staff, Schwan, told his powerful friend Henry C.

Corbin, the army's adjutant general, that the revolutionaries were dispersed into "predatory bands" and "will be extirpated in short order."[56] But, as so often before, the high command's optimism was misplaced, for there were disturbing signs that the Philippine War was entering a new phase. In January, MacArthur's headquarters reported a "secret local government has been or is being established by the natives in all towns occupied by American troops . . . in the name of the so-called Philippine Republic, the purpose of which is to maintain a military as well as a civil organization." Many townspeople were active allies of the guerrillas in the field, hiding weapons and providing food and shelter, ready at any time to attack the garrison. "For some time to come it will be impossible to make an error on the side of prudence."[57] From Cebu, an officer wrote to the *Army and Navy Journal* that the insurgents were having far more success with guerrilla war than they had had with conventional operations. If this was correct, warned the editor, "the adoption of bushwhacking tactics may not after all be a hopeful sign of the extinction of bellicose feeling among the natives as one may have been led to think."[58] With the shift to guerrilla warfare, dazzling military victories were no longer attainable; from now on there would be few opportunities for glory.

PART TWO
The Archipelago
1900–1902

NINE

THE GUERRILLA WAR

With the revolutionaries' adoption of guerrilla war and the army's occupation of the archipelago in early 1900, the Philippine War became a series of regional struggles, bewildering in their complexity. Confronted with the problem of drawing comparisons with what appear to be little more than dozens of separate local struggles, most historians have kept their eyes fixed firmly on Manila and the development of pacification policy, citing a few incidents as typical of the war in the boondocks. However effective at providing some coherence, this method cannot supply a suitable way of studying the war, for generals and jefes might decree, but to enforce their directives in the field was often beyond their means. An equally unbalanced perspective is gained by extrapolating from a few particularly savage campaigns any broad conclusions on the nature of the entire war. Even within an individual province or regiment, the diversity of experiences precludes sweeping generalizations. It was not unusual for soldiers in one town to be under constant attack, and for their comrades a few miles away to go for months without a fight. Moreover, in thirty-four of the seventy-seven provinces (44 percent) the total of military operations between United States troops and supporters of the Philippine Republic was zero; that is, in nearly half of the provinces there was no fighting at all.[1] The best that can be done is to provide a broad overview of both the resistance and the development of American pacification policies, and then in following chapters to discuss the conduct of the war region by region.

Perhaps the most important factor in the Filipino resistance to American military occupation was that it lacked a centralized political or military organization. For almost a year after he dissolved his government, Aguinaldo lived a peripatetic existence in the mountains of northeastern Luzon. Much of his time was spent avoiding patrols and securing food and shelter, often by contributions levied on hostile inhabitants. Not until September 1900 could he establish a permanent headquarters at the remote village of Palanan, Isabella Province. Isolated, reduced to a few dozen companions, his location known to only a few, Aguinaldo could not exercise effective control over the islands' diverse resistance movements. Beyond outlining general policies— to pursue a war of attrition through guerrilla tactics, to keep the population

from collaborating with the Americans, to launch an offensive in the fall of
1900 to influence the U.S. elections—he did very little to determine the course
of the war. That is not to say that Aguinaldo did not issue decrees, orders,
and exhortations, but many never reached their destination, others arrived
after delays that outwore their relevance, and others were flatly disregarded.
Thus when he revitalized the Katipunan society, he was far behind the actions of his subordinates, and when he appointed a new supreme commander
for Central Luzon, he was simply ignored. In February 1901 a guerrilla major
told his captors that Mariano Trias, supreme commander of Southern Luzon,
had received no word from his president for six months. What limited information Aguinaldo received was incomplete and often incorrect. For example,
in late July he was just learning of April's events from newspapers and couriers, including the erroneous report that the Americans had abandoned
Samar. Throughout the guerrilla war, Aguinaldo's most important role was
not military but symbolic: like no one else, he personified the independence
movement. As long as he remained free, his supporters could still maintain
they fought for a legitimate national government.[2]

With Aguinaldo effectively neutralized as commander in chief, military
authority devolved on the virtually autonomous regional political-military
jefes. Roughly analogous to the U.S. Army's departmental and district commanders, they were responsible for directing major military operations, distributing rifles and ammunition, developing both military and political
strategy, and a host of other duties. Constantly on the move, the jefes' personal forces seldom exceeded a few staff officers and a handful of guards.
Each had to overcome primitive communications, dispersed military forces,
fragmented commands, and regional jealousies. In the Visayas there was no
supreme jefe; each island, and occasionally each province on each island, was
the fiefdom of one or more local commanders such as Martin Delgado in
Iloilo Province, Vicente Lukban on Samar, and Moxica on Leyte. In some
provinces even this much centralization was impossible: on Negros in a span
of three months a total of five generals were captured or surrendered in the
Dumaguete area alone. Although they might claim their authority stemmed
from Aguinaldo or the Philippine Republic, successful jefes were coalition
builders who relied more on persuasion than on domination. Challenges to
their authority were common—in part because of the continued overlapping
and competing areas of responsibility—and prewar rivalries often distorted
military decisions.[3]

From the very outset, Americans had commented that the insurgents'
preferred style was "that of the Indian or the guerrilla."[4] But, as Glenn A.
May has noted, for most of 1899 the revolutionary leadership had viewed

guerrilla warfare as a tactical option; strategically, it was seen only as a final recourse, and not as a way of waging war that might allow poorly armed irregulars to defeat an occupying army.[5] But on 13 November 1899 Aguinaldo decreed that guerrilla war would now be the strategy. Henceforth, the revolutionaries would avoid enemy strength and attack its weakness, prolong warfare rather than seek a rapid decision, preserve troops and weapons, and fight only when they had overwhelming superiority. As Gen. Francisco Macabulos explained, the objective was "not to vanquish [the U.S. Army], a difficult matter to accomplish considering their superiority in numbers and arms, but to inflict on them constant losses, to the end of discouraging them and convincing them of our rights."[6] This was therefore a war of attrition, of wearing down an opponent over a long period through exhaustion, disease, and steady bloodletting. Unfortunately for their cause, the insurgents used a strategy suited for a protracted war to achieve an immediate goal: to convince the American public to repudiate McKinley and elect the anti-imperialist Bryan in November 1900. Typical was the August appeal of Gen. Tomas Mascardo: "Let us for a little while longer put forth heroic deeds of arms," because "McKinley falls by the way side, the people abandon him and incline to the political party of Mr. Bryan whose fundamental teaching is the recognition of our independence."[7] As John M. Gates has observed, by tying independence to the election, the revolutionaries increased their short-term appeal, but at the cost of widespread demoralization when McKinley was reelected.[8]

The revolutionaries' military organizations were diffuse and shared only the most general characteristics, but the resistance movement in northwestern Luzon indicates how the system could work in practice. The armed forces were divided between regulars and militia. Both forces were organized along territorial lines and usually consisted of people from the same ethnic group, and often from the same village, plantation, or extended family. The regulars often bore the title of an Army of Liberation unit or of their commander and had a higher proportion of firearms. Their officers tended to be drawn from landowners and influential families, the rank and file came from their retainers, clients, and tenants. Seldom numbering more than a few hundred in any province, they usually remained itinerant bands of ten to sixty riflemen and an equal number of bolomen, holing up in barrios or strongpoints in the mountains. The militia—sometimes sworn in as members of the Katipunan—consisted of all males of military age, armed mainly with bolos and spears. They remained in the towns and barrios and provided village security, built field fortifications and mantraps, cut telegraph wires, collected taxes, and intimidated collaborators and *americanistas*. Theoretically, the

Guerrilla officers

regulars served as a core around which the militia coalesced; and the combined force would then attack isolated patrols and garrisons, logistical lines, communications, and collaborators, whether towns or individuals. In many provinces, however, the distinction between the two forces was merely the ratio of farming and fighting.[9]

As described by one jefe, the guerrilla's tactics should be to "constantly harass the enemy, causing him losses and avoiding such to our people, . . . to prepare ambushes avoiding combats, and to take rifles, ammunition, and prisoners."[10] Manuals and field orders instructed officers to keep their forces small and mobile, to preserve their weapons and ammunition, to maintain close contact with local political leaders, to eliminate spies, and to remain active, even if this meant little more than sniping or wire cutting. One handbook emphasized that the preservation of rifles and ammunition was all-important; if given a choice between saving a rifle or a wounded comrade, the rifle came first. When fighting, guerrillas were to conceal themselves and fight behind entrenchments, and to fire three or four volleys at close range—no more than fifty yards—and then to withdraw.[11] They were also to leave a multitude of traps and snares—spring-loaded arrows, pits filled with sharpened stakes, deadfalls—all of which made rapid pursuit, night marches, and surprise attacks by their enemies almost impossible. In a long letter to President McKinley, one district commander acknowledged the effectiveness of these tactics: "the guerrillas are scattered among the mountain barrios, in peasant dress with arms hidden, subject to call at any minute. In the meantime, certain daring ones keep our communications cut either north, south, or east, almost every night, while the necessity of protecting the people in every pueblo where they have shown us friendship, limits materially our scouting and patrolling policies; and the floods at this season confine to stall our active operations."[12]

In practice, guerrilla tactics inflicted (and incurred) few casualties but caused their opponents much frustration. John D. LaWall recalled an incident he felt best described "the insurgents' mode of warfare": fifty irregulars surrounded an outpost and threw stones until they determined its layout, then fired a volley into the guards' tent that killed one and wounded another; but "before a relief force could arrive to punish their cowardly work, the insurgents were miles away."[13] Captain James L. Anderson was on a routine "hike" in the quiet island of Bohol when suddenly his patrol was overrun by bolomen "who cut, stabbed and slashed at those front and rear"; in ninety

Guerrillas, Laguna, 1901 (National Archives)

seconds, his command suffered three killed and several wounded.[14] But such successes were unusual; life as a guerrilla consisted of long periods of flight and recuperation. The journal of Lt. Telesforo Carrasco, who served in a guerrilla unit in Cagayan Province between August 1900 and April 1901, shows he participated in fewer than ten skirmishes, only one of which was initiated by his men. Carrasco's journal also shows another weakness of the guerrillas' hit-and-run tactics: neither he nor his fellow officers could make more than a rough guess of their success, and they invariably overestimated the casualties they inflicted.[15]

The most effective aspect of such tactics was the guerrillas' ability to blend into the population. Both officers and soldiers often lived in or near the occupied towns and were, to all outward appearances, friendly noncombatants going about their peacetime occupations. As Capt. John L. Jordan explained: "Get after them [and] they scatter, hide their uniform and rifle, don [a] white suit they carry with them and meekly claim to be amigos (friends)."[16] To Birkhimer, this was the vital issue: "I owe it to our rebel enemy to say that, from their standpoint, I regard their scheme of warfare [as] nearly perfect. In the facility with which they can play the insurrecto-amigo act they have an immense advantage. Their facilities for recruitment, and their plans of securing money and supplies are not to be despised. Their preeminent advantage, however, lies in their chameleon act—insurrecto or amigo—as suits them."[17]

The primary obstacle to the guerrillas was their lack of weaponry. Major Leonicio Alarilla's plaintive letter begging just ten cartridges apiece for his dozen rifles in order to attack the weak American escorts encapsulates their problems.[18] The navy's blockade prevented arm shipments, and the insurgents' existing rifles were often old, badly maintained, or damaged—conditions that were not improved by firing homemade shells made from black powder and match heads, melted-down brass and tin fittings, and lead slugs. In one instance guerrillas armed with twenty-five rifles fired at point-blank range into a group of soldiers bunched up on native canoes, but they wounded only two. An officer who inspected the site estimated 60 percent of the Filipinos' ammunition had misfired.[19] Advising a subordinate on organizing a Katipunan militia, Col. Luciano San Miguel suggested using "knives, arrows, and lances"; such primitive weapons—along with their ubiquitous and ingenious obstacles and traps—were all that many insurgents possessed.[20] Hopes that rural guerrillas could use their bolos to attack sentries and patrols proved chimerical. Writing after some two years of warfare on Panay, Hughes noted of one bolo attack: "It is the first successful effort of that weapon here and I am afraid that it proved fatal by reason of the absolute contempt our people have for the thing."[21] The lack of firearms and the failure of the bolo led some to advocate poisoning soldiers, and there are several cases of soldiers who suffered serious consequences from food and drink, especially liquor, but whether this was caused by poison, improper preparation, or methanol is impossible to know. Nevertheless, despite their unsuitability for conventional warfare, soldiers conceded that in 1900 the insurgents possessed sufficient weapons to intimidate the populace and sustain a guerrilla war.[22]

Years of clandestine activity against the Spanish had made many revolutionary commanders aware of the importance of intelligence. Tactical instructions placed great emphasis on security: commanders would issue orders in code, refer to each other by aliases, and use women as messengers. Much attention was devoted to protection and camouflage: one ten-acre camp escaped detection even though three American expeditions walked right past it. Sentinels, both in and outside the occupied towns, warned of the departure of army patrols by church bells, conch shells, bamboo drums, or couriers: one American officer complained, "I cannot send out 10 men in the middle of the night without it being known before they have gone a mile."[23] The guerrillas also specialized in disinformation. They would forge documents that led post commanders to arrest *americanistas* or to dispatch debilitating hikes into the boondocks. Ironically, they also misinformed each other. Mendacious communiqués boasting of rifles captured and imperialist soldiers slain, of towns rising in rebellion, of widespread popular support, and of imminent foreign intervention flowed up from guerrilla chiefs to their superiors. Despite an equal amount of correspondence the other way demanding a strict account of men and weapons, it is unlikely that any provincial jefe had more than a vague idea of the strength of his own forces or the military situation in his area.[24]

Particularly in the first months of 1900, soldiers assigned to occupation duties in towns throughout the archipelago usually viewed the guerrillas as external threats. Only a few recognized that often "the towns, regardless of the fact of American occupation and town organization, are the actual bases for all insurgent military activities; and not only in the sense of furnishing supplies for the so-called flying columns of guerrillas but as affording secure places of refuge."[25] In some—but by no means all—towns a clandestine "shadow government" served the revolutionaries under the very noses of the post authorities. At its most successful, it could function as the "real" government, collecting taxes, recruiting soldiers, maintaining morale, and administering justice far more efficiently than could its American-sponsored counterpart.[26]

Unfortunately for their cause, in its efforts to stop the United States from creating municipal governments, the revolutionary leadership often hampered the development of its own infrastructure. Virtually every major revolutionary jefe insisted that no Filipino accept public office, and a host of proclamations threatened summary punishment to all who did. In some places, such as southeastern Luzon and Samar, the insurgents even required the population to leave any occupied town. This policy may have caused a short-term gain, but in the long run it was a serious blunder. Colonel Buenaventura Dimaguila astutely noted a key weakness: if patriots did not hold public office, then the "bastard sons of the Philippines" would. Dimaguila believed, as did many local commanders, that it was far better to have mayors, town councillors, and police who publicly aided the Americans but secretly assisted the guerrillas. This often appears to have been the practice, for the U.S. Army's correspondence is filled with reports of *presidentes* and police chiefs who served as double agents. Nevertheless, the revolutionary leadership continued to insist on complete noncooperation and to impose draconian sanctions not only on officeholders but also on their townspeople. This hard-line policy ensured that once a *principale* took office he and his followers often became totally committed to the Americans, for only through the complete defeat of the *insurrectos* could they guarantee their safety. As Dimaguila poetically observed, the noncooperation policy virtually forced Filipinos to "appeal to the forces of the powerful enemy to tear from their hearts a thorn planted there through the absolute intolerance of our people."[27]

Much of the shadow government's effort went to supporting local military forces. As is true in most guerrilla wars, and in contrast to conventional armies, the guerrillas' logistics were at the front. But unlike in Vietnam, there were no key supply routes for the Americans to interdict or sanctuaries to invade. Food and stores were collected in the towns and then transported, kilo by kilo, in carts or by porters to camps and supply dumps. As part of their political duties, some provincial jefes authorized taxes and created a bureaucracy responsible for collections. In practice, however, the supply system remained largely ad hoc; each guerrilla unit either developed or was assigned its own supply network.[28] Joaquin Luna, the revolutionary commissary in the Ilocano provinces, described the supply system as heavily bureaucratized, with a hierarchy of rank, clearly defined responsibilities, accounts, even contracts. However, he complained it was riddled with waste and dishonesty, and this certainly appears true. Indeed, the clandestine collection of money and supplies invited corruption. On Panay, supply officers stole thousands of pesos and sent only a pittance to the guerrillas; in southeastern Luzon, the Americans estimated tax collectors pocketed half their takings. Despite collecting sufficient funds and supplies to keep the war going in 1900, the revolutionaries were increasingly unable to distribute them efficiently, with the result that their forces grew hungry and demoralized.[29]

One of the primary functions of both the infrastructure and the guerrilla units was the administration of justice. In most of the archipelago, law and order had effectively broken down, and the only institutions that could prevent banditry, murder, and civil war were the revolutionary forces and the U.S. Army. To support their claim to serve a legitimate government as well as to refute American accusations that they were little better than *ladrones,* or outlaws, the insurgents had to show they could enforce order on the lawless. This posed a dilemma, for some of the worst offenders were guerrillas themselves. Revolutionary correspondence is filled with decrees denouncing soldiers for extortion, mistreatment of civilians, sexual abuses, and other crimes, and threatening swift and terrible punishments. Some particularly vicious or unpopular guerrillas were punished, as, for example, when the jefe of Laguna, Juan Cailles, publicly executed an officer for robbery. But the very fact that so many decrees denounced such criminal activity indicates serious problems with discipline, as well as the inability of superior officers to enforce their authority on insubordinate commanders.[30]

The brigands who flourished in much of the rural Philippines presented another problem for the leaders of the resistance. Having been outlaws for years, they were very useful allies: they knew the best hideouts, had a paramilitary organization, were familiar with weapons, and were adept at hiding among the population. Moreover, as Glenn May has pointed out, in their actions guerrillas and *ladrones* were all but indistinguishable—so much so that some American officers insisted they were two sides of the same coin. But despite the brigands' expertise at irregular warfare, the revolutionary leaders tended to view them as a serious threat and devoted a great deal of effort to hunting them down. Part of this was due to traditional animosities. The guerrilla leadership was drawn overwhelmingly from the landowning, locally powerful *principales,* and they recognized the largely peasant-based bandits as a serious threat to their socioeconomic interests. Many, such as Miguel Malvar and even Aguinaldo himself, had gained their baptism in irregular warfare leading antibanditry forces under the Spanish. Moreover, as Col. J. Milton Thompson pointed out, the bandits were undisciplined and seldom able to restrain their thieving proclivities, and "the insurrecto forces would not receive the cooperation of the natives, if certain of their leaders were permitted to prey upon their own people."[31] The fate of the Cagayan Valley's Andres Banlad is instructive. A brigand who joined the insurgents in return for a pardon, he proved a brave and capable fighter. But when his continued robberies alienated the local political leaders, the revolutionary leadership promptly captured, tried, and shot him.[32]

To their credit, Aguinaldo and most of his jefes were well aware of the potential for revolutionary justice to degenerate into random terrorism. In February 1900 the jefe of Central Luzon, Pantaleon Garcia, authorized his subordinates to kidnap *presidentes* who served the Americans, but he insisted they be well treated, "as it only desired to make our enemy believe that they have been assassinated."[33] But as benevolent assimilation won converts, and as these converts proved increasingly aggressive, the guerrillas' threats became more and more vehement. By July, Garcia's successor, Jose Alejandrino, ordered all *americanista* civil officials to be dealt with summarily as traitors. Lukban authorized the death penalty for a variety of offenses ranging from spying to leaving camp without permission, and virtually identical proclamations, sometimes under the aegis of the Katipunan or other secret societies, appeared in nearly every combat area in the archipelago throughout 1900.[34]

For those who disregarded these warnings, retribution could be swift and gruesome. The dry, brief accounts of robberies, tortures, mutilations, stabbings, shootings, and other crimes that appear in the army general orders—and were reprinted in nearly 400 pages of a U.S. Senate investigation—give

Soldiers with assassinated *americanista*

only the most sanitized account of the horrific internecine war that raged throughout the archipelago.[35] May has noted that guerrilla organizations seldom had recourse to most of the normal sanctions available to the state, such as fines and imprisonment, and thus had to rely on corporal punishment and death.[36] This might justify the actions of Cailles, who personally ordered the assassination of twenty-nine people in an eight-month period. But it does not justify the cruelty of some guerrillas. In slightly over two months near Vigan, Ilocos Norte, a murder ring slaughtered as many as thirty people, dragging them to open graves and then hacking them to death. Samar's guerrillas buried three collaborators alive, butchered one suspect's family, and lashed another man to a tree and chopped him to pieces. Such actions speak of individual sadism or of a policy of deliberate terrorism more than of the implementation of justice. Certainly William H. Taft maintained that in a systematic effort to terrorize the population the guerrillas made "cruelty deliberately part of their policy," and that "without that system of terrorism the guerrilla campaign would have ended very quickly, because the people wanted peace."[37]

In contrast, the revolutionary leadership tried to ensure humane care for captured Americans. From the beginning, Aguinaldo insisted that prisoners be treated well, and on 3 August 1900, in a somewhat mystifying gesture, he ordered that they all be released. Only late in the war, as more and more Filipinos began cooperating with the invaders, and as the Americans began executing guerrillas for war crimes, did his attitude harden. On 17 January 1901, he directed that henceforth all prisoners would be exchanged for captured revolutionaries, but if this was refused and the army continued to execute guerrillas, then they were to be shot.[38] Guerrilla leaders such as Urbano Lacuna, Simon Tecson, and Juan Villamor won a great deal of respect for their good treatment of prisoners; Alejandrino ordered wounded Americans released; Malvar issued strict orders against mistreating prisoners of war. Lukban also treated prisoners well, although before they reached his camp two captives were terribly abused.[39]

Despite these directives, in some instances guerrillas subjected captives to barbaric cruelty. Sergeant Bernard Lichtig of the 30th Infantry recalled that captured soldiers were treated "very, very badly—some were buried and molasses applied to [their] head so ants would eat."[40] Another soldier in the same regiment reported that the insurgents "mutilated the boys they captured."[41] Veterans of the 45th Infantry knew of similar barbarities: one wounded captive had his eyes put out, and another had his feet cut off. On Panay two prisoners were butchered with knives; another was tortured over a slow fire for hours. On Luzon during an assault on his headquarters, Gen.

Servillano Aquino had five prisoners shot and stabbed.[42] It must be emphasized that these were isolated atrocities—much like those perpetrated against Filipinos by individual Americans. There is no evidence that the revolutionary high command advocated, or even considered, systematic terrorism against the invaders as a strategic option.

Given that any informant in a village could denounce the guerrillas and their agents to the pursuing local garrison, the guerrillas' survival depended on popular support, or at least compliance. This raises one of the thorniest issues of the war: Did the general population support the guerrillas and, by extension, the cause of Philippine independence? Some scholars argue that the very durability of the resistance implies, if not demonstrates, the willing support of the population. But if this were so, why did the guerrillas devote as much attention, or more, to discouraging collaboration as to fighting the occupying forces? Moreover, modern writers often assume a degree of political awareness and democratic participation by the "masses" that simply did not exist in most of the archipelago in 1900. With the exception of Malvar and a few others, the insurgent jefes refused to countenance a social revolution or to advocate radical policies—such as land distribution—that might have attracted the peasantry. Similarly, with one conspicuous exception, there was almost no effort to enroll women into the guerrilla forces. In one of the few in-depth studies of the resistance, May concluded that in Batangas Province, at least, "the indigenous lower classes were not necessarily dogged and enthusiastic supporters of the resistance."[43] Most observers accepted the argument that the local elites were the real opponents of American rule and the peasantry merely obeyed them, and there is some Filipino documentation to support this view.[44] But the Americans were wrong to assume that the peasantry's allegiance was tendered only through fear. For the vast majority of people, the transition from Spanish to revolutionary government in 1898 meant little more than a continuation of rule by the local elite. Unless the local government and the military commander were oppressive, there was no reason to oppose them, and it is logical to suppose, even if it cannot be demonstrated, that there was widespread, if lukewarm, acceptance of the revolutionary governments. Only when the Americans occupied the towns did the population became subject to taxation, looting, physical coercion, and death from both sides; and at that point the decision of an individual to support one or the other can be explained only case by case.[45]

It is important to note that the guerrillas' ascendancy was greatest at the start of 1900 and thereafter declined. The very diversity of the resistance meant there was no single target—human or geographic—whose destruction would end the war. The defeat of a guerrilla band, the loss of rifles, the capture of a tax collector, the betrayal of a town's shadow infrastructure could have limited impact outside the immediate area. The guerrillas' knowledge of local conditions allowed them to secure supplies, taxes, shelter, recruits, and information. Their leaders enjoyed extensive social contacts among their fellow *principales* and were accorded almost unquestioning obedience from their tenants and clients. Their weaponry, patently inadequate against enemy soldiers, was more than sufficient to enforce their authority on their fellow citizens. But all these advantages became attenuated as the American forces created a colonial government, established social and intelligence contacts, and learned the terrain and sufficient "bamboo" dialect to communicate with the inhabitants. Over time, patrols and raids disrupted the guerrillas' logistical system, destroyed their supply depots and camps, and forced their bands to disperse and keep constantly on the move. Once driven out of their home area, they became outsiders elsewhere.

The guerrillas' relationship with the population—one of their greatest strengths—was also a source of weakness. They were dependent on the populace for shelter and supplies, and if these were not given willingly, they had to be taken by force. But if the guerrillas became too coercive, or if they could not protect the peasantry from coercion by the occupiers or brigands, then they became merely a burden, if not a menace. As one guerrilla jefe warned a subordinate, "You must remember that the pueblos are sick of arbitrary acts and sick of the abuses committed by we military men; we must not add new arbitrary acts to those which we have already committed, especially now when we need the spontaneous and voluntary support of the people."[46] Sooner or later, whether because of a personal grievance or American blandishments (or abuse), someone would inform on them. Last, the local elite who led the resistance eventually found the cost of guerrilla war too high to bear: theirs were the lands sequestered, theirs were the tax assessments from both sides, and theirs were the families and fortunes at risk. Class cannot be denied as a factor in explaining the growing disenchantment of the guerrillas' predominantly *principale* officer corps as well. The ordeal of military life in the boondocks wore down the old and unfit and led to the rise of more charismatic or more ruthless commoners with a natural affinity for irregular war. Faced with increasing challenges to their position, more and more leaders found their personal and class interests better served by the Americans.

Both the McKinley administration and its senior commanders recognized that they could not hope to conquer and rule an archipelago of 500,000 square miles and over 7 million people without substantial cooperation from the Filipinos themselves. Therefore, an essential—perhaps even the most essential— mission was to establish an environment in which Filipinos could carry out

Benevolent assimilation (3rd Cavalry Museum, Fort Bliss, Texas)

most of the functions of the colonial government; in the words of one officer, soldiers must "cultivate in the peaceful natives a confidence in our intentions to protect them, and treat them kindly while dealing relentlessly with armed bands."[47] The U.S. Army's experience during Reconstruction and on the Western frontier provided an administrative structure—the department-division model—under which territory was divided into semiautonomous geographic commands, each with a garrison force. Otis implemented this system as early as March 1899 when he created the Visayan Military District to administer Panay, Cebu, and Negros. Three months later, at the War Department's request, he outlined a plan to divide the entire archipelago into four geographic departments. This system was set firmly in place on 20 March 1900 when Otis dissolved the army's tactical organizations—the 8th Corps and the brigades—and created the Military Division of the Philippines, with its four departments of Northern Luzon, Southern Luzon, Visayas, and Mindanao-Jolo, and each divided further into districts and subdistricts.[48]

The department-district organization established two parallel chains of command that culminated with Otis himself, who was both commanding general of the Military Division and military governor of the Philippines. In his first role, he coordinated operations against those who continued armed resistance. In his second, he headed the Office of the Military Governor (OMG), which established civil government, built schools and roads, developed codes and procedures, and in numerous other ways oversaw the transition from military to civilian. These dual responsibilities extended down to the smallest detachment commander, becoming official policy in May 1900 when Manila directed that "not even those left on duty with troops can wholly escape the character of civil administrators. . . . As the work of reconstruction of civil government advances the performance of civil duties must become more and more exacting and ultimately assume a first importance."[49]

The department and district commanders responsible for executing both the military and civic action pacification programs were permitted, and assumed, considerable independence.[50] With this freedom went considerable responsibility. Brigadier General J. Franklin Bell commented that as district commander, he was charged with the "apprehension, collection of evidence, trial, disposition, and imprisonment of criminals; the re-establishment of civil government, of schools, mail, and telegraphic communications; the reconstruction of roads and bridges; the collection of revenue taxes and insular statistics; supervising the affairs of provincial and municipal governments; the investigation of claims of all descriptions; and the discharge of all other duties heretofore performed by civil officials." This was, of course, in addition to his military tasks of hunting down guerrillas and bandits, breaking up their supply system, developing intelligence, and ensuring the health and welfare of his troops. Thus, as district commander his duties were "far more onerous . . . than they were when the insurrection was in its greatest activity."[51] Moreover, all this work had to be done with an infinitesimal staff: Brig. Gen. Frederick D. Grant, for example, administered an area of 3,000 square miles and a population of 500,000 with a quartermaster, an engineer/ topographical officer, and two aides.[52]

Below the district commanders were the provincial civil-military governors—usually regimental commanders—and hundreds of battalion and company posts. The number of garrisons expanded rapidly, from 53 on 1 November 1899 to 413 stations on 1 October 1900, then to 502 in March 1901, and to 639 by the end of that year.[53] Many officers bemoaned the army's policy of occupying the entire archipelago, for it tied down thousands of troops and eliminated a mobile reserve. But others believed garrisoning was absolutely necessary to protect the population. Moreover, as Bell acknowledged, the key to pacification was learning the identities and securing the weapons of those who continued armed resistance, and this could not be done without troops living among the population for some time.[54]

In the first six months of the guerrilla war, the army's pacification program was heavily weighted toward civic action. Otis and many of his subordinates maintained that Filipinos would welcome the benefits of American rule—law, education, peace, trade, honest government, financial responsibility—once they had a chance to experience it. Thus he downplayed the military side of pacification and emphasized the importance of municipal government, health, education, roads, and police as the practical application of McKinley's policy of benevolent assimilation. Otis's expertise can be seen in the criminal code of 1900, which incorporated such American guarantees as an expeditious trial and repudiated practices such as secret testimony. Otis and the OMG also revised the tax codes, simplifying the cumbersome Spanish system and eliminating a number of oppressive impositions that fostered monopoly and hindered trade and development. The military government took an active interest in public health; it instituted vaccination programs, distributed funds to army officers for the treatment of disease, and established clinics. It also created a Department of Public Instruction, which distributed books and paid teachers' salaries; ultimately the army helped support 1,000 schools, with an enrollment of 100,000 pupils.[55]

The centerpiece of Otis's pacification program was municipal government. He believed that the 1899 directive, G.O. 43, and its successor in 1900, G.O. 40, provided a clear blueprint for municipal organization. With these as guidelines, post commanders could quickly revive local government, put municipal finances on a sound basis, sanitize the towns, win over the population, and put an end to disorder in the countryside. Once this was done, the army could begin to implement the numerous other social reform projects— schools, roads, clinics, markets, courts—that would demonstrate the benefits of United States rule. Accordingly, Otis pestered his department and district commanders to begin civil government forthwith, and he demanded reports of their progress.

In practice, municipal government was seldom organized along the lines Otis and the OMG envisioned. In some areas, such as northwestern Luzon, virtually every town had its own government in the first month of occupation, but in other regions district commanders delayed until 1901. Despite the widespread circulation of G.O. 43 and G.O. 40, many town governments were ad hoc creations of the post commander and the local authorities. Some officers made sincere efforts to hold democratic and fair elections; others merely went through the motions. Major Robert E. Spence, for example, advised a post officer to "let the natives establish [the] same kind of government they had, interfere as little as possible with their customs, exercise a mild and gentle policy, encouraging them to return to their houses and work."[56] However, when he himself organized a town, he could only round up "a few boys, old men, and fishermen, with which to have an election."[57] At Marikina so few people showed up to vote that the commanding officer simply appointed the officials he wanted. Reporting from Laguna Province, Col. Benjamin F. Cheatham noted that since no one would take public office for fear of assassination, the towns were governed by a provost marshal, an arrangement that seemed to please everyone. In neighboring Tayabas Province, Col. Cornelius Gardener ordered one subordinate to lock the prominent residents of his town in a room until they agreed to serve. The district commander in southeastern Luzon discarded both G.O. 43 and G.O. 40 as unworkable and drew up and implemented his own plan.[58]

For civil government to work, officers had to maintain close personal relations with the municipal officials. This often required a great deal of discretion, for many post commanders, with good reason, suspected their municipal officials of serving both sides. Writing to an officer who had captured his town's *presidente* in a guerrilla camp and wanted to punish him, Bell commented: "I am not yet ready to demand loyalty as a condition of liberty, from all civil officials. It would render it impracticable for me to get the best men to accept official positions. If they voluntarily render us assistance and demonstrate [this] so much the better, but if not, forcing them or punishing them for failure to do so would do no good . . . but would do harm."[59] A similar practical viewpoint was found in the post officer who appointed a former guerrilla as mayor on the grounds that "he is as good or better than a prisoner now. He is confined here by his duties—is known to us—under constant surveillance and has openly attached himself to the peace faction."[60]

The town of Indan, Cavite, offers a good example of how an army civil government functioned in practice. When Maj. William H. Johnston's battalion of the 46th Infantry occupied Indan in January 1900, the 13,000 townspeople had fled; the town was bankrupt; there was no functioning government; and the schools and markets were closed. Schwan appointed a town council, and Johnston sent its officials into the countryside to bring back the townspeople. The council and Johnston met and established duties on liquor, businesses, markets, and gambling; these taxes were collected by an army officer. Using corvée labor from citizens, the army and council cooperated on a thorough cleaning of the houses and streets, the repair of culverts and walls, and rebuilding the marketplace. Johnston arranged to distribute captured medicines to the poor and purchased books for the municipal schools, which by April taught 600 pupils. Indan's successful government resulted from the working relationship Johnston established with the city council; it had no basis in army regulations. Indeed, in authorizing taxes and drafting labor, Johnston violated official policies. But when his district commander sought to reorganize the town to conform to G.O. 43, Johnston protested that Indan's government was functioning well and that if the regulations were enforced all sources of revenue would be cut off. His superiors chose not to press the issue.[61] Such improvisation and flexibility, instead of rigid adherence to OMG directives, characterized the U.S. Army–sponsored municipal governments until late in the war.

In his annual report of 1900, Secretary of War Root listed road construction as one of the four highest priorities of the U.S. Army's pacification effort.[62] James Parker considered the roads to be among the worst obstacles soldiers faced; many consisted of little more than a narrow trail that could be traversed only in single file, spreading a regiment out over more than 1,000 yards and rendering it vulnerable to ambush.[63] Weather, particularly the months-long monsoon season, virtually dissolved some roads and all but marooned some garrisons. One officer noted that when the rains came, the number of river crossings his troops had to make on one patrol route tripled, and at any time each river might vary from 100 to 1,000 feet across.[64] Accordingly, in the Department of Northern Luzon, for example, headquarters dispatched topographical officers to make inspections and also required each post, province, and district commander to make estimates of essential repairs: by August 1900 over 1,000 miles of roads were built or improved. A visiting naval officer was amazed at the rapid progress: one modern five-mile road was built by 2,000 local laborers in less than a week.[65] Such improvements allowed the army to sustain and coordinate military forces in areas that previously had been inaccessible, and were a decisive factor in its success in 1901.

Closely related to the road-building was the construction of telegraph lines. Although mail service had improved, it remained slow and uncertain: the chief signal officer reported in 1901 that even high-priority correspondence took at least thirty days to deliver on Luzon and twice as long for half of the posts in the archipelago.[66] Therefore, despite intensive efforts by the guerrillas to cut or destroy wires, telegraphic service grew dramatically: in June 1899 only 139 miles of line connected 8th Corps headquarters with military commands; a year later the figure was 3,000 miles, and by the end of the war, 10,000 miles. The telegraph allowed department and district commanders to direct operations instead of merely advising. In the Department of Mindanao and Jolo, for example, in early 1900 headquarters needed at least two months to respond to any message, and Manila did not receive word of one serious engagement for three months. But by early 1901 cable and telegraph put the department commander in daily contact during surrender negotiations. Small wonder that MacArthur stated that without the telegraph the army could not have pacified the Philippines with 150,000 soldiers. Small wonder also that commanders were ruthless with guerrillas who damaged the lines.[67]

"One of the greatest principles of the American government is the education of her people."[68] With these words the post commander of Orani, Bataan, emphasized not only the army's commitment to establishing public schools but also, indirectly, to its assumption that through education Filipinos would recognize their new role and responsibilities as United States subjects. The eighteen soldiers Maj. John H. Parker assigned to teach schools in Laguna "were worth more as teachers than as soldiers and it was plainly evident that every new school established out in any outlying barrio meant an effective extension of lawful authority deeper not only into the territory, but also into the hearts of the Filipinos."[69] Similarly, Parker boasted of his wife—who supervised schools teaching almost 2,000 students—that "her presence was worth more toward tranquilizing the country than a thousand men, for it indicated permanence of occupation and friendship for the people."[70] Visayan commander Hughes took a shorter view; English-language education was essential for American rule: "The most important step to take with these new subjects of ours is to put them in the way of communication with our people directly and not through a third person or through signs. . . . As our affairs now stand one half of our difficulties would disappear if our men could communicate directly with whom they are dealing."[71] Support for education united hard-liners and moderates: Governor James F. Smith and Col. Charles W. Miner clashed on numerous issues, but they both took great pride in Negros's public schools and the 6th Infantry soldier-school-teachers.[72] The public school was unique in its ability to transcend intra-army disputes and Fil-American problems. Indeed, the major drawback in army education was the OMG's inability to meet the demand for books, supplies, and teachers.

In contrast to the unanimity of support for education, officers remained deeply divided on both the utility and the trustworthiness of the Filipino police and scouts. For some, the more efficient the police, the stronger the tendency to use them in military operations against the insurgents. In some areas the small size of the garrisons forced post officers to incorporate police into their patrols. But this in turn created problems of its own: the police of San Miguel de Mayumo, for example, were adept at hunting down guerrillas, but their methods were so brutal that the post commander was warned, "If native police or any other natives are used as scouts, guides, or in any way as part of your force or command, you will be held responsible for their conduct and behavior under G.O. 100 of 1863, and laws of war generally."[73] The commander at Pasay praised the police for their courage and loyalty, but one officer claimed the "natives are terrorized by them" and accused them of conducting blackmail, arbitrarily holding people for trial, and practicing "certain methods of torture."[74] Although Washington prodded Manila to organize native forces, and although both G.O. 43 and G.O. 40 included municipal police as part of each town's government, Otis opposed arming the police or paying them out of OMG funds. Similarly, although he had allowed Batson to form the Macabebe Scouts and Smith the Negros constabulary, he squelched a number of proposals to raise large contingents of indigenous troops. The result was that many police and irregular units were badly paid, poorly armed, and unreliable. Only where officers ignored Manila's regulations and provided weapons and compensation were Filipino auxiliaries effective allies in the war against the guerrillas.

When MacArthur succeeded Otis in May 1900, one of his first actions was to issue G.O. 87, which directed the arming of municipal police and the creation of mounted "constabulary bodies," which henceforth would be the "conservators of the peace and safety of districts, instead of confirming [*sic*] their operations to areas limited by the boundaries of towns and barrios."[75] But MacArthur could not overcome his concern that auxiliaries might abuse civilians or turn traitor. He did little to enforce his orders—refusing to allow local officers to equip police and auxiliaries with rifles—and limited the police to revolvers and shotguns. To some officers, his reasoning made no sense: shotguns were ideal for ambushes, required no marksmanship, and were better suited for the guerrillas' homemade ammunition. The point was somewhat moot, as it soon developed that Manila had virtually no stocks of suitable weapons available.[76] Only in December, when the imminent departure of the U.S. Volunteers forced his hand, did MacArthur finally shake off his doubts and order department commanders not only to recruit and arm many more police and scouts but also to transfer much of the pacification mission to them. Despite strong resistance from conservative officers and continued internal problems, in 1901 local police proved some of the more effective counterinsurgency forces the army raised.[77]

Although most post commanders boasted of the benefits of military efficiency and benevolent paternalism, army civic action was neither completely altruistic nor democratic—nor free of coercion. The rigid enforcement of sanitation, the construction of sewers and drains, the regulation of brothels, gambling, and saloons, even the free distribution of medicines—all these were

Major General Arthur MacArthur

essential to protect soldiers' health. Officers used municipal government to impose their authority on the population. By refusing to organize a town, a post officer could deny it public funds and, more important, any legitimacy in land or jurisdictional disputes. Through a variety of ways, ranging from inspecting the books to cutting off funds, he could ensure that his municipal government remained compliant. Even the most humane commanders acted in an authoritarian and autocratic manner: Johnston, despite his concern for the people of Indan, advocated impressing laborers and keeping them under military guard until a crucial road was completed.[78]

Under army rule, municipal office offered local politicians great rewards and great responsibilities. Civic officials could use their position to secure employment for their friends and families, award themselves lucrative contracts and licenses, and punish their enemies with the full force of the law. But just as army officers were assigned civil tasks, so municipal officials were pressed into military duties. Throughout the archipelago, they were expected to investigate any stranger arriving in their jurisdiction, to check passes, and to make arrests. They might also be called upon to furnish laborers for military projects or guides for counterguerrilla expeditions. If they met such requirements, civic officials became vulnerable to retaliation from insurgents and bandits, and a disproportionate number of them were victims of assault and assassination. But if they refused to follow the post commander's directives, they could be dismissed, fined, and imprisoned. Some post commanders were morally troubled by this, even to the extent of refusing to organize civil governments until their leaders' safety could be guaranteed. Others, such as Johnston, were more callous: his municipal officials had become "targets for any ladrones in hiding, and especial objects of the latters' hatred . . . and their own protection demands [our] discovery of arms and ladrones."[79]

In his enthusiasm for civic action, Otis soon became blind to the necessity of a complementary military policy. When the War Department inquired about the guerrillas' resurgence, and about complaints from field officers that the situation was deteriorating, Otis replied, "We no longer deal with organized insurrection, but brigandage; to render every town secure against [the] latter would require [a] quarter million men."[80] So convinced was he that the war was over that on 3 April he requested his relief no later than 1 May. A few days before he left, Otis gave a long interview in which he emphasized that the army's civic action was pacifying the countryside and that peace was at hand. He concluded with the optimistic, and woefully mistaken, prediction: "I cannot see where it is possible for the guerrillas to effect any reorganization, concentrate any force, or accomplish anything serious."[81]

In the words of one senior commander, "The naval part of the campaign against the Insurrectos in the Philippines was practically finished in March, 1900."[82] With soldiers holding all of the archipelago's ports, there was no need for large-scale joint operations. Moreover, the narrow seas and shallow harbors precluded the use of any but the smallest vessels. Nevertheless, fueled in part by Dewey's fears of German intervention and in part by a growing desire to acquire naval bases in China, the Navy Department continued to send warships to the East, so that in 1900 the Asiatic Squadron consisted of a battleship, six cruisers, two monitors, and thirty-one gunboats. Although it numbered almost 6,000 officers and men, blockade duty, disease, and high turnover—in a two-year period the cruiser *Newark* had eight navigators, fourteen executive officers, and twenty-four watch officers—caused several ships to lose their crews to other warships. This problem became even more servere in the spring of 1900, as the Boxer Rebellion drew more and more ships north. By April so many ships were in China that the commander in chief, Rear Adm. George C. Remey, created a separate squadron under Rear Adm. Louis Kempff to handle affairs there. By July, the situation was serious enough that Remey himself went north, and the Philippine War reverted to a distinctly secondary priority to the navy.[83]

Owing both to the Boxer Rebellion and to the inability of large warships to operate in the narrow, shallow waters of the archipelago, the "real war" in the Philippines was fought by the gunboats. Ranging in size from the 600-ton *Elcano* to the tiny *Basco*, with its twenty-seven-man crew and single gun, they convoyed troops to isolated coastal villages, protected garrisons and patrols, and ferried supplies and reinforcements. From Mindanao to Luzon, local officers and gunboat captains hammered out procedures, transport, logistics, and fire support arrangements for dozens of raids along the coasts and rivers. The most famous single exploit of the Philippine War, Funston's capture of Aguinaldo in March 1901, was itself a masterful example of these informal joint operations. Transported by Comm. Edward B. Barry on the *Vicksburg* to Casiguran Bay, Funston and a party of Filipino scouts marched inland, seized the Filipino president, and spirited him back to Manila.

Although by 1901 the marines had some 64 officers and 1,934 men in the Islands, roughly a third of the corps' total manpower, they did not—with one notable exception—play a significant combat role in the Philippine War. The majority of naval operations during the war involved blockading and patrolling, which seldom required marines as a landing force. Nevertheless, the navy insisted on complete control over its naval bases; accordingly, on 23 May 1899 the 1st Marine Battalion, consisting of 16 officers and 260 men, was dispatched to take over from the army garrison at the Cavite naval base. Marine strength steadily increased, and on 10 December another detachment occupied the Spanish naval base at Olongapo on Subic Bay, Bataan Province. Eventually the marines garrisoned fourteen naval stations throughout the archipelago as well as serving as ships' guards.

The transfer of many marines to China in 1900 left the Philippine contingent stretched thin and barely able to meet its commitments. Fortunately, there was little serious resistance at Olongapo, and although Cavite Province was not pacified until early 1901, the clearing operations around Manila Bay in 1899 had ended most opposition in the marines' immediate area. Far more common were pacification activities related to civil government and social reform. In keeping with American military policy in the archipelago, the marines held civic elections in the towns they occupied, recruited police forces, cleaned streets, issued rations and medicine to destitute Filipinos, and taught in the local schools. It was only after the Boxer expedition returned, in mid-1901, that the marines would play a significant role in the Philippine War.[84]

Arthur MacArthur, who succeeded Otis as commanding general and military governor on 5 May, was to become even more controversial. To some admirers he was a military genius—the general who won the war, only to be consigned to obscurity through the machinations of William H. Taft and the McKinley administration. To others he was a sanctimonious, verbose humbug. The son of a prominent Wisconsin judge, he had an impressive record in the Civil War and, after a decades-long campaign, was among the seventy-odd officers retroactively awarded the Medal of Honor in the 1890s. He became a captain in the postwar Regular Army, a rank he held for twenty-three undistinguished years, despite his unrelenting and often insubordinate efforts to gain promotion and better postings. Like his son Douglas, Arthur MacArthur often stated his intuitions as absolute certainties and obscured his mistakes in circumlocution. Nevertheless, with Lawton dead, he was clearly the outstanding senior officer in the islands, and both Washington and Otis supported his appointment to supreme command.[85]

The new supreme commander recognized he had inherited an unbalanced pacification program. The benevolent civic action component so beloved by Otis was making substantial gains. Numerous towns now had municipal governments, thousands of Filipinos had acknowledged United States sovereignty, and most of the government services that had disappeared during the war were being replaced. Roads and bridges, schools, new marketplaces, improved drainage and sanitation, and other signs of progress were everywhere.[86] But MacArthur was convinced that the military side of pacification—the suppression of those in armed resistance—was degenerating rapidly.

Not only had casualties and engagements increased after the destruction of the Army of Liberation, but they showed no sign of diminishing. Further, as MacArthur began the transition to his new command in April, conditions dramatically worsened. Throughout the archipelago the level of fighting—in number of troops engaged and casualties sustained—approached the level of the conventional operations of 1899. Cagayan, Mindanao, was attacked by over 1,000 insurgents; at Catubig, Samar, a detachment was besieged for five days and suffered heavy casualties; on Leyte there were several engagements; there was a series of attacks and ambushes in Bataan; and in the Ilocos Norte Province there was a full-fledged rebellion. Manila was deluged with requests for immediate reinforcements from field officers claiming they would soon be overrun.[87]

MacArthur feared he would be blamed if he did not fulfill Otis's rosy predictions. Having convinced themselves, however mistakenly, that Bryan would defeat McKinley and acknowledge Philippine independence, the insurgents would not consider surrender until the results of the elections were known. Even those Filipinos who benefited from the army's rule were unlikely to commit themselves openly until McKinley had been reelected.[88] Nor did MacArthur see much hope of launching hard, sharp strikes at particularly troublesome districts, for Otis had scattered the reserve; worse, the summer monsoon was about to begin, and MacArthur knew too well the difficulties of campaigning in the rain and mud. To complicate issues further, in June the Boxer Rebellion erupted, and he had to divert two regiments to China and hope he would not be drained of more. He knew he could not expect to see the benefits of the increased manpower authorized by the 1900 army bill until the fall. Moreover, this would be only a temporary increase, for as the War Department reminded him several times, by mid-1901 the U.S. Volunteers would be demobilized, and he would have lost half his active forces.

Unlike Otis, MacArthur recognized both the significance of Aguinaldo's 13 November declaration of guerrilla war and the symbiotic relationship between the guerrillas and the towns. In January, MacArthur had warned officers in Northern Luzon of the existence of "secret local government[s]" in the towns, which gathered supplies, collected taxes, and provided recruits.[89] This suspicion became a certainty in June, when he received a lengthy analysis of the resistance movement in the occupied towns of La Union Province from Lt. William T. Johnston. Johnston painstakingly dissected the various components of the infrastructure, showing how taxes were collected, guerrilla units protected, and civic records falsified. The report gave a structure and coherence to MacArthur's suspicions and led him to conclude that the guerrillas "could not exist for a month without urban support."[90]

Understanding the guerrilla war was not quite the same as developing a solution, and MacArthur clearly had no master design when he took office. Indeed, in his first months as commanding general, he did comparatively little beyond continuing Otis's emphasis on conciliation and civic action. He may well have been suffering from a serious illness that sapped his energy and left him irritable and moody.[91] His initial strategic plan, outlined in a cable of 28 May, showed little originality. Based on holding the archipelago with a force of 45,000 by 1 March 1901, it advocated the gradual concentration of troops into a few "central stations" whence they could rapidly move into the countryside.[92] His chief requests were for funds and engineers to build more roads. In response to Washington's pressure to raise Filipino forces, he proposed a very modest 2,000-man local constabulary and maintained the Native Scouts at about 1,400. In June, he authorized the armistice he had urged so strongly on Otis, but, by his own admission, it had a "meager result": only 5,022 took advantage of the offer, none of them senior leaders.[93] Meager may also describe MacArthur's changes to Otis's policies. Despite his anger at Otis for extending garrisons outside of Luzon, he permitted the number of military posts to rise by almost a third, and he did little to scale back commitments in areas he deemed of minimal strategic importance. By the end of August, he appears to have conceded that little could be done until after the presidential elections. In a typical mixture of dire foreboding, guarded optimism, and equivocation, MacArthur cabled Washington: "Week by week, situation shows little improvement; month by month, progress slow, but quite apparent. Unless rapid improvement sets in after election, which fortunately now seems very probable, it will not be possible to materially reduce present force for a long time."[94]

In September, in one of their few efforts at concerted action, the guerrillas in much of Luzon shifted tactics. Hoping to secure Bryan's election, and with it their independence, they concentrated their scattered forces to launch attacks on garrisons and patrols. Somewhat assisted by incompetent American leadership, in less than a week they inflicted two of the worst defeats of the war. On 13 September on Marinduque Island, Capt. Devereaux Shields led 51 soldiers of the 29th Infantry into a well-constructed ambush; Shields was badly wounded, and his demoralized command surrendered. Four days later, Capt. David D. Mitchell, a recently arrived Regular, led 130 soldiers on a frontal assault over a narrow causeway against a well-entrenched enemy. Cailles's veterans coolly picked them off, killing or wounding a third of them. Although the strength of the fighting in September shocked the Americans, the revolutionaries were unable to sustain the pressure except in a few areas, and began in turn to take heavy losses from counterattacks.[95]

The fall resurgence, and its possible effect on the presidential race, led to open questioning of MacArthur's ability. Much of the censure was unfair, for as MacArthur pointed out, he had predicted, or at least suggested, that the revolutionaries would go on the offensive in an effort to influence the election.[96] Nevertheless, his apparent passivity and his failure to communicate his plans encouraged criticism. Washington insider Clarence Edwards wrote a friend serving in the islands: "Confidentially the powers that be are chafing—The yellow journals are jumping on us fearfully. . . . A little throttling is necessary. General killing."[97] Ominously, McKinley's closest military adviser, Adj. Gen. Henry C. Corbin, denied that the administration intended to recall MacArthur—no doubt encouraging speculation that it did—but added that it was time the army took the offensive.[98] Perhaps even more disturbing, some of this criticism reflected back-channel communications from disenchanted field officers. Even those who supported civic action and conciliation believed it was time to shift emphasis. As Captain Jordan explained, "This business of fighting and civilizing and educating at the same time doesn't mix very well. Peace is needed first."[99] To Brig. Gen. Samuel B. M. Young, the fault lay with army policy: soldiers treated the Filipinos as if they were civilized, when what was required were "the remedial measures that proved successful with the Apaches."[100] From Laguna, Parker complained to his old Cuba companion Theodore Roosevelt that MacArthur and the staff in Manila were trying to fight the war in "white suits and collars."[101]

Like many other officers, Parker believed he had the solution: if the punishments authorized in G.O. 100 against guerrilla warfare were actually enforced—including suspension of civil rights, trial by provost court, confiscation, deportation, property destruction, and summary execution—the war would be over in a few months. The humanitarian provisions of G.O. 100, which imposed strict standards of conduct on the occupation forces, had been in effect since the arrival of the first expedition. Specific sections of the orders were reissued periodically to ensure that all soldiers were familiar with the laws of war. Thus in May 1900 post commanders in Wheaton's Department of Northern Luzon were informed that "in the treatment of natives the requirements of G.O. #100, A.G.O. 1863 be observed and that care be taken that in all efforts to obtain information from natives there be no action not in accordance with the order mentioned."[102] In June the Judge Advocate apparently justified the application of G.O. 100 when it ruled that "martial law applies throughout the archipelago."[103] But neither Otis nor MacArthur took the final step of authorizing the enforcement of the orders in their entirety.

Despite Manila's failure to confirm its legality, throughout 1900 many departmental and district commanders issued all or part of the code, sometimes accompanied with instructions that "the utmost severity consistent with G.O. 100 of 1863 is desired."[104] In March, Funston cited the orders to justify his summary execution of two men he caught in the act of killing Macabebes, and his superiors confirmed his action. In October, following the arrest of several civilians whose bloody bolos implicated them in a particularly brutal attack on five soldiers, district commander Brig. Gen. Jacob H. Smith wrote: "I only wish that I could have been there to have summarily dealt with them, but it is difficult to get Officers to take prompt measures under G.O. 100. . . . A few killings under G.O. 100 will aid very much in making the enemy stop these assassinations."[105] But two months later, in a neighboring district whose commander had authorized G.O. 100, Lt. Arthur G. Duncan narrowly escaped a court-martial when he summarily executed a spy.[106] No wonder officers expostulated that they had no guidelines for their rights and obligations. As one soldier in Duncan's province complained, "We have imposed all measures short of [the] death of [the] persons thought to be implicated. The par[agraphs in] G.O. 100 [are] plain to me, but I do not believe my action would be approved were all guilty who may be captured immediately put to death."[107]

By late 1900, there were disturbing indications that soldiers increasingly were enforcing their own interpretation of G.O. 100, and that their superiors were collaborating in their activities. In Wheaton's department, for example, crop and property destruction increased, and in directing the burning of buildings and supplies, officers were told to "exercise such methods as are authorized by G.O. 100 of 1863."[108] The general reminded subordinates that guerrillas, spies, and others who violated G.O. 100 lost the right to be treated as prisoners of war.[109] In November, after Wheaton had convicted a guerrilla of three murders and sentenced him to hang, MacArthur had followed his usual practice of commuting the sentence to imprisonment. Wheaton promptly held another trial, convicted the man of three more murders, and hanged him. Almost as dismaying as this action was the gloating approval of one prominent civic official: Wheaton had "played a pretty sharp trick on General MacArthur."[110] Clearly, when even senior generals were winning approval for defiance, the benevolent policy was in trouble.

On 1 October, MacArthur offered an acute analysis of the war in his annual report to Washington. Unlike Otis, he stressed the revolutionaries' shift to a guerrilla strategy and the difficulties of fighting enemies who "at one time . . . are in the ranks as soldiers, and immediately afterwards are within the American lines in the attitude of peaceful natives, absorbed in a dense mass of sympathetic people, speaking a dialect of which few white men, and no Americans, have any knowledge."[111] Although he did not openly break with Otis's and the McKinley administration's benevolent assimilation policy, MacArthur questioned the assumption that the Filipinos were eager to accept United States rule. They cooperated enthusiastically with the civic action aspect of pacification—the roads, schools, sanitation projects, improved trade—but they resisted all efforts to use these municipal governments for the purposes of military pacification, and they continued to support the guerrillas with contributions, recruits, and shelter.

Indicative of MacArthur's new direction were his orders in early October to Brig. Gen. Luther Hare on Marinduque, scene of the recent disaster, to treat all males as hostile and to arrest and hold them hostage. Later that month, he cabled Washington that on 15 November he would begin a four-month campaign. The arrival of substantial reinforcements, which brought his manpower to 70,000 by the end of 1900, and the cessation of fighting in some provinces allowed him to shift troops to the most troublesome areas. Even more important was McKinley's reelection in November. Revolutionaries and soldiers alike had been awaiting the outcome of the presidential race with a mixture of hope and trepidation. Some officers believed that for months MacArthur, and U.S. Army policy, had been "much influenced by fear of what the newspapers may say and its possible effect upon the election."[112]

On 19 December, MacArthur notified his department commanders of a "new and more stringent policy" and directed them to focus on the "organized system by which supplies and information are sent to [the guerrillas] from the occupied towns." Abandoning Otis's cultivation of the elite, he declared that "all prominent families" who had not publicly committed themselves were to be assumed guilty of aiding the guerrillas. He concluded with the grim notice that "whenever action is necessary the more drastic the application the better," though he softened this by forbidding "unnecessary hardships and personal indignities" or violations of the laws of war.[113]

The following day, MacArthur issued a proclamation to the Filipino people. Couched much like a legal brief, it pronounced the guerrillas and their supporters guilty of violating the laws of war, or G.O. 100. In particular, he referred to those guilty of the abduction and assassination of people who cooperated with the authorities, to the "secret committees" in the occupied towns that collected contributions for armed bands, and to those who conducted hostilities without belonging to an organized, uniformed military force. These deeds, and others he specified, were criminal actions under the law of war and subject to "exemplary punishments." The military authorities had previously chosen not to hold perpetrators to a full accounting for their crimes, but from now on they intended to do so. With the proclamation of these orders in English, Spanish, and Tagalog, neither guerrillas nor their supporters could pretend to be unaware that their actions were, in the eyes of the conqueror's law, criminal.[114]

MacArthur would later claim, "Rarely in a war has a single document been so instrumental in influencing ultimate results. The consequences in this instance, however, . . . seem to preclude all possibility of doubt, and also seem to justify the conclusion that the effective pacification of the Archipelago commenced December 20, 1900."[115] This is largely hyperbole. The proclamation did signify a shift in strategy, but not because it established a clearly defined, centralized pacification policy or because of the issuing of G.O. 100. Rather, MacArthur rectified the long-standing disjunction between Manila's emphasis on civic action and conciliation, and regional commanders' counterinsurgency policies, including their use of methods sanctioned in G.O. 100. Benevolent assimilation would remain, but it would now take second place to punitive measures against those who continued to resist. Thus within the army the proclamation was widely interpreted to mean that Manila was removing most of the restrictions on local commanders. In this respect, it may be argued that the general's action was a classic example of the adage that those who wish to lead must rush to the front of the crowd.[116]

Although the formal declaration of peace would not occur until 4 July 1902, the collapse of Filipino resistance gives credence to John Gates's contention that 1901 was the "year of victory."[117] Between December 1900 and MacArthur's departure in mid-July 1901, the army conducted a series of regional campaigns that ended armed resistance in twenty-one of the thirty-eight unpacified provinces.[118] There were far larger and more effective sweeps into the mountains and swamps, better use of mounted forces, and increased efforts at trapping and destroying guerrilla bands. Officers purged municipal governments and broke up the guerrillas' shadow governments. Instead of being released, prisoners were now held until they, their companions, or their relatives surrendered weapons and furnished information. In some areas, post commanders suspended payment of rents to people suspected of insurgent sympathies, or confiscated their crops and buildings. Despite MacArthur's injunctions to avoid unnecessary hardship, he tolerated, even encouraged, campaigns that can only be described as punitive. Crop and property destruction, euphemistically called "burning," became far more common; and there was less effort to ensure that only property clearly in use by the insurgents was torched. Marinduque, Abra, parts of Panay, and other areas were systematically devastated to deprive the guerrillas of food and punish their supporters. In some places, the army imposed, or local residents suggested, "concentration," the separation of civilians into towns or "protected zones," outside of which everyone was regarded as an enemy. MacArthur also removed many of the restrictions on the courts, which now proceeded with far more dispatch and sent prisoners to the gallows with far more regularity. Harsh as these methods were, they worked. By September, MacArthur's successor, Maj. Gen. Adna A. Chaffee, considered only three areas—southwestern Luzon, Samar, and Cebu—still actively hostile.

The early months of 1901 saw several of the most recalcitrant revolutionary leaders capitulate. The first was Martin Delgado, the primary leader on Panay, who surrendered on 10 January with 30 officers, 140 riflemen, and a large number of militia. By March, all but one of Panay's major chiefs had either capitulated or been captured. That month also saw the surrender of Nicolas Capistrano, the leader of the resistance in northern Mindanao. In Aguinaldo's home province of Cavite, only 2 Americans and 5 guerrillas were killed in February, but 376 of the latter were captured or surrendered, and, perhaps even more important, 305 rifles were turned over. The next month, only 2 Americans and 1 guerrilla died, but 640 guerrillas surrendered, and 776 rifles were captured or turned in. The jefe of Southern Luzon, Mariano Trias, capitulated late in March and then published an appeal to his compatriots to abandon resistance. A month later, Aguinaldo was captured in a daring raid, and he too issued an appeal for peace. By July, only Miguel Malvar in Batangas and Vicente Lukban on Samar still maintained forces capable of resisting American control.[119]

As the district commander in the Ilocano region acknowledged, much of the Americans' military success came from Filipinos.[120] The Federal Party, organized by Manila *ilustrados* and former revolutionary officers on 23 December 1900, and supported by Taft and MacArthur, called for the recognition of United States sovereignty as a precursor to the establishment of a representative government. At considerable risk of their lives, Federalists visited dozens of towns and sponsored rallies to urge the acceptance of American rule. Some went into the mountains to persuade guerrilla leaders to surrender. Although many officers were initially skeptical of the party, most came to appreciate its contributions to their success. One went even further: to the local Federal Party representative "more than any other influence is due the complete pacification of this province."[121]

In a similar acceptance of common practice in the field, MacArthur abandoned his stubborn opposition to recruiting Filipino military forces. On 6 January 1901, his chief of staff reminded department commanders of the imminent departure of the U.S. Volunteers, and authorized them to recruit Native Scouts "to any extent you deem expedient in any manner you regard best."[122] This led to a huge expansion of auxiliaries—in some provinces the numbers doubled in less than a month—and by June there were 5,500 Native Scouts. Thousands more Filipinos served in paramilitary forces such as the militia, town security, porters, police, and guides.[123]

MacArthur's pride in the success of the military effort was somewhat diminished by his continual bickering with William H. Taft, the man designated to take over the civic action part of the pacification policy. Perhaps influenced by Otis's view that the war was over, McKinley had appointed a second Philippine Commission to establish municipal and provincial governments and to oversee the transfer of power from the military governor to colonial rule. His instructions set a timetable for this transition, starting with the assumption of legislative power in September 1900. Thereafter, as each province was declared pacified, the army would turn over its governance to the commission. Eventually, when all was at peace, the commission would replace the OMG, and Taft would become the new governor.[124]

The arrival of the commission on 3 June, and of the well-connected and ambitious Taft, put MacArthur in a very difficult position. He had inherited Otis's administration and organization, which concentrated all powers in the OMG, and the commission soon challenged his judicial and administrative prerogatives, and ultimately his executive powers. But MacArthur's personal failings made the situation far worse. Like his son, and with similarly disastrous consequences for his career, MacArthur could not accept his subordination to civilian authority. For his part, Taft viewed many of the senior military leaders with contempt, and suspected they distorted the situation to retain power. He found MacArthur's lectures tedious, his rhetoric ludicrous, his legal views alarming, and his personality unpleasant. Their relations never recovered from their first meeting: the general kept the commission members sweltering on their transport for a day and then had them brought before him as if they were barbarian dignitaries seeking audience with the emperor. He told them that he viewed their very existence as "humiliating to him personally" and that he could discharge all their duties by himself.[125] This and subsequent behavior would have nettled even an exceptionally charitable person, and Taft was anything but. He responded to MacArthur's obstructionism with a very effective letter-writing campaign to Washington detailing the general's foibles.

Their mutual detestation aside, there were important differences between Taft and MacArthur, both on the nature of the war and on the proper way to end it. MacArthur was often pessimistic and convinced that "ethnological homogeneity" contributed to an "almost complete unity of action of the entire native population" in support of Aguinaldo and the guerrilla leaders.[126]

Taft dismissed this statement completely; he and the rest of the commission had conducted a two-month tour of the archipelago, and he was confident that the "great majority" of the population had accepted United States rule and that, "without the system of terrorism and assassination and murder," it would have been "utterly impossible to continue the guerrilla war."[127] Taft believed, with some reason, that a civil government supported and aided by Filipinos, and with the army firmly under its control, would be far more effective in securing law and order than autocratic military rule.[128]

As armed resistance ended in more and more areas, the Philippine Commission quickly—precipitously, in the army view—assumed responsibility for the organization and maintenance of civil governments. Despite the objections of many field commanders, on 20 July army headquarters issued G.O. 179, which transferred twenty-three formally hostile provinces from the army to the commission.[129] To their chagrin, officers who had carefully nourished their civic creations were pushed aside, and new institutions were substituted, often peremptorily. Writing from Samar, one officer complained that the Filipinos "cannot be conquered, civilized, and taught to love us in a year, and are not yet fitted for the civil government which is being forced upon them by the impetuous American." He noted sarcastically that inasmuch as the commissioners still required "a strong guard around their Manila residences it hardly looks like time for civil government throughout the islands."[130] But although army officers lambasted Taft, according to one commissioner, it was MacArthur who was to blame: in May the general, who had "got himself into a precious scrape" over his intransigence, "suddenly went to the other extreme and advocated the establishment of civil governments all over the islands, even in provinces which in our judgment were wholly unfit for it."[131] MacArthur even insisted the commission take over such clearly rebellious provinces as Batangas. Whether he did so because he honestly believed this would lead the guerrillas to surrender or because he cynically hoped it would demonstrate the need for continued military control is impossible to determine.

On 4 July 1901, MacArthur officially surrendered the OMG to Taft, and his responsibilities as commanding general to Maj. Gen. Adna R. Chaffee. Secretary of War Elihu Root had decided in February that MacArthur had to go, and that Chaffee would replace him, but he avoided telling the general, who learned of it through the Washington papers.[132] The implicit censure may have been the product of bad timing: by the end of March, it was clear that MacArthur's "new and more stringent policy" had succeeded. But even discounting Taft's implacable hatred, the general had become a political liability. In his last report, MacArthur emphasized that the revolutionary leaders had "enjoyed a very extensive cooperation of the whole mass of the Filipino people" and credited his 20 December proclamation as the start of the "effective pacification of the Archipelago."[133] This was not only monstrous egotism, it was simply untrue. More important, it contradicted the administration's cherished dogma that the Filipino people wanted United States rule and opposed it only out of fear and ignorance. Clearly an officer so out of step could not continue in such a sensitive position, and MacArthur's subsequent outspoken opposition to administration policies confirmed Root's foresight.

Within the army, there was little support for retaining MacArthur. Many of his mentors were long retired, and his arrogance and selfishness—not to mention his belief that the army should be dominated by Civil War veterans such as himself—gave him no following among the younger reform-minded officers who had captured Root's attention and were transforming the War Department. Like Otis, he was a distant and unloved figure: after his brief tour in 1900, he rarely ventured from Manila and seldom met even his senior commanders. Field officers applauded his December policies, but there was a general feeling that they came too late. Most local officers had become intensely parochial and tended to view Manila as an obstruction more than a help. A hostile witness noted that after a curt, ungracious speech at the ceremony transferring executive authority to Taft, MacArthur received few cheers from the assembled soldiers.[134]

MacArthur's successor was a tough Civil War veteran cavalryman who had distinguished himself in Cuba and the Boxer Rebellion. Although often portrayed as little more than a simpleminded and brutal Indian fighter, Chaffee was a shrewd and capable officer much admired by reformers. He was more adroit politically than MacArthur—as is evidenced by his appointment to chief of staff shortly afterward—and although Taft did not like him, at least he could work with him.[135] This is not to say that Chaffee approved of the civil government. In a September letter to his friend Corbin, he noted a deep gulf between the military and the commission over whether the islands were pacified, opining that without the police, civil government would soon collapse.[136]

Root had made it clear to Chaffee that his primary task was to divorce the army from its civil functions so as to restore the Philippine army to military efficiency. Four years of imperial warfare in disease-ridden islands had cost the Regulars thousands of veterans, and the recruits badly needed training and discipline. Moreover, there were hundreds of newly commissioned officers whose entire experience in the past three years had been in civil government or small-unit command.[137] To symbolize both the army's withdrawal from civil affairs and the reinstitution of conventional military duties, in the fall Chaffee abolished the department-district system and divided the Division of the Philippines into a Department of Northern Philippines (Luzon) and a Department of Southern Philippines (everything else). Within these departments, troops would be placed in seven "Separate Brigades." But his efforts to bring the army into a better state of discipline were frustrated by the continuation of military operations and by a scarcity of manpower: beginning in October, each month the Philippine garrisons lost 2,000 Regulars whose enlistments had expired.[138]

Chaffee at first made few changes to a pacification effort that was already proving very successful. The number of provinces turned over to civil government steadily increased, and by fall his only serious concern was Batangas Province, where, he complained, "a vast majority of the people profess friendship for us, while we know that without a doubt they are intensely hostile," and where the guerrillas hid in the towns and went out to fight "at their desire."[139] In September he reorganized Luzon's command structure preparatory to bringing in the army's premier counterinsurgency expert, Brig. Gen. J. Franklin Bell, to clean up Batangas once and for all. Then, on 28 September, villagers and guerrillas attacked the seventy-four officers and men of Company C, 9th U.S. Infantry at the town of Balangiga, Samar, killing forty-eight soldiers in what was the worst single American disaster of the war. The "Balangiga Massacre" panicked Chaffee into authorizing the most extreme measures against the remaining centers of armed resistance. In particular, he sent Brig. Gen. Jacob H. Smith to conduct a punitive campaign on Samar—to be described later—that was conspicuous for its brutality and excess. At the same time, with Chaffee's and Taft's blessings, Bell imposed severe sanctions in Batangas. These two campaigns, and the revelation of atrocities that accompanied them, prompted a Senate inquiry into army misconduct and badly tarnished its reputation. Nevertheless, they succeeded. Lukban was captured in February; on 16 April, Malvar surrendered, followed eleven days later by the last of the Samareno revolutionaries. On 4 July 1902, President Roosevelt officially declared the "insurrection" over and thanked the U.S. Army for pacifying the islands.[140]

Roosevelt's announcement of the end of the Philippine War took place amid enormous public outrage over the conduct of U.S. forces in the islands. Rumors of widespread burning, of prisoners executed, and of torture had appeared within a few days of the start of the war. In the years since, the issue of atrocities has so dominated textbooks and popular accounts that it needs to be addressed in some length. That soldiers committed war crimes is true, but that "race hatred brought American forces in the Philippines to the brink of genocide" represents a caricature of the historical truth.[141] The entire "atrocity issue" itself is too often seen in the context of present moral and behavioral standards, and not by the legal and ethical standards of the time. And even at the time, outraged public figures and the press rather sanctimoniously held soldiers to higher moral and legal—and especially racial—standards than those they condoned in their fellow citizens. Even so, this distinction between legal and illegal acts, although often overlooked by the army's critics, is enormous: when historian Richard Welch applied the legal definition of atrocities to U.S. actions—rape, the systematic burning of civilian property, torture, and murder—he found only fifty-seven cases during the entire Philippine War.[142] Similarly, critics have been too quick to ascribe sinister motives—most often racism—to behavior that has been typical of combat soldiers for hundreds of years.

Otis, and initially MacArthur, insisted on a very high standard of troop behavior. Soldiers were threatened with dire punishment for misconduct and exhorted to remember always: "*The purpose of the United States* in these islands is *beneficent*. It is therefore one of the most important duties of American soldiers to assist in establishing friendly relations with the natives by *kind and considerate treatment* in all matters arising from personal contact."[143] Although the army court-martialed very few officers for war crimes and convicted only a handful, these trials had chastening effects: one commander complained that his officers were "frightened; they dare not do anything beyond making a request to persons who may know [the guerrillas' whereabouts] very well and are thoroughly informed. They have to take a denial and be satisfied with it, as they are afraid to force parties to give the information."[144] But as benevolence and civic action proved inadequate, soldiers in the province turned increasingly to repression, or what Andrew Birtle terms "the policy of chastisement."[145]

One coercive measure that grew increasingly popular was property destruction, for it not only deprived the guerrillas of food and shelter but also punished their supporters. Indeed, some senior officers, such as Samuel B. M. Young, came to believe that "the judicious application of the torch is the most humane way of waging such a war."[146] General Hughes recalled that in 1899 there were strict orders that no harm must be offered to civilians and that everything taken must be paid for. However, as his troops endured sniper fire or discovered guerrilla storehouses in the midst of supposedly loyal villages, there was a growing tendency to "burn the place."[147] Similarly, Lt. Col. Charles J. Crane justified the destruction of a village after an attack on his regiment: "The burning of their houses was most just retribution and retaliation, and it had a fine effect."[148] This shift toward hard war was apparent even in officers known for their support of civic action. Shortly after his arrival on Leyte, Col. Arthur Murray maintained, "I am very much opposed to the burning of towns or villages when it can possibly be avoided, as it not only causes innocent people to suffer, but also makes enemies of people who would otherwise be friendly."[149] But by 1902, Murray's views had changed: "If I had my work out there to do over again, I would do possibly a little more killing and considerably more burning than I did, though I was accused by Gen. Otis in his report of doing possibly more killing than was necessary."[150]

Even more controversial is troop violation of what would now be termed civil rights. In imposing their own values on the past, critics often ignore or dismiss the fact that neither civil nor military law in 1900 restricted physical coercion in the way they do now. American soldiers were subject to brutal punishments that are unthinkable today. One battalion commander wrote to a subordinate that instead of pressing charges he should "administer summary punishment, such as standing a man on a barrel, in the sun for a couple [of] hours, or putting him in stocks for a while, or something of that kind your ingenuity may devise."[151] Occasionally such measures got out of hand: Lt. William S. Sinclair of the 29th Infantry tied the hands and feet of a drunken private, gagged him, and then supervised his dousing with buckets of cold water. The soldier died of this punishment, but Sinclair was acquitted of using excessive force.[152] Given the degree of physical punishment they endured, it would be surprising indeed if soldiers regarded slapping or punching people, tying them up, or threatening to shoot them as illegal or illegitimate actions. More important, the soldiers may have had a far better grasp of what was legal and legitimate than their critics. According to the standard army text on small-unit tactics, soldiers were within their rights to impress guides, and "if they are contumacious, they must be threatened, and sometimes roughly handled. It may be necessary in some cases to tie them to trees or posts, or even gag them and threaten them with death if they cry out; but it shall be the invariable rule never to resort to harsh measures when gentler ones will secure the same end."[153]

Psychiatrist Jonathan Shay argues that combat soldiers have a strong sense of moral order or "what's right"; any betrayal of this, either by their officers or the enemy, creates severe trauma and "rage."[154] To many Americans the insurgents' actions—the early and flagrant violation of flags of truce, the surprise attacks by guerrillas in civilian dress, the grisly killings of civilians, and especially the torture and mutilation of American prisoners—were all clear violations of "what's right" and justified the most severe retribution. Virtually every soldier knew a victim personally or had heard of some horror visited on his comrades or on a friendly Filipino. During the 26th Infantry's one-year tour on Panay, for example, one officer was assassinated by men wearing U.S. Army uniforms, another was lured into an ambush by guerrillas under a flag of truce, a soldier's corpse was disinterred and mutilated, three privates were murdered by officials of a town that had proclaimed its loyalty, and three captive soldiers were tortured and killed.[155]

Soldiers who discovered the scenes of such crimes were enraged and might, as Taft argued, exact revenge "under circumstances they regarded as more or less justified."[156] Thus Lt. Preston Brown shot a prisoner of war after the man failed to help a drowning soldier. The investigating officer concluded that Brown killed the prisoner in part because of the demands of his troops and that officers and men approved of his action.[157] In another case, five soldiers were attacked and two murdered while talking to apparently friendly Moros. A patrol immediately went out, surrounded the village where the incident had occurred, and arrested forty-five men, all of whom were subsequently shot "attempting to escape."[158] On Samar, the commander of a small outpost charged with guarding hundreds of prisoners believed they were planning a revolt; after a sentry was killed during an escape attempt, he selected four prisoners and shot them as a warning to the rest.[159]

Unlike executions, which usually were retaliatory, torture had a very practical motive—it was used to secure information or extort confessions. The guerrillas' practice of concealing their weapons and hiding among the population placed troops in an impossible dilemma. Soldiers were well aware that the villagers knew the identities of the guerrillas and the location of their arms, but they also recognized that unless protected, any informant would be kidnapped, tortured, or killed. As one officer noted, although they were unable to challenge the army in the field, the insurgents could exert substantial influence over the population "for the simple reason that their punishments for failure to comply are much more severe than any practiced by us, or permitted to us under the laws of war."[160]

From operational records and personal accounts, it appears that a disproportionate number, perhaps even the majority, of American atrocities involving torture were the result of small groups of men under junior and noncommissioned officers searching for weapons or information. Because garrisons were so isolated and undermanned, virtually all regiments formed elite units, often mounted, which had both a defensive and an offensive mission. These troops provided a quick relief force for any outpost under attack and a prompt application of tactical intelligence against guerrilla concentrations and supplies. Their isolation and distance from support, their frequent and prolonged exposure to combat, and their dependence on immediate information made these elite forces especially quick to abuse. Such a unit was

Gordon's Scouts, formed from the 18th Infantry, which became famous on Panay for its fighting ability and infamous for its misbehavior.[161] Gardener's concern for Filipino civilians did not prevent him from organizing a special unit under Maj. Charles P. Newberry, an officer known within the regiment as "being perfectly unscrupulous as to his methods of gaining information."[162] A veteran of the 33rd Infantry's mounted force recalled, "Sometimes we would take some hombre out and give him a good hanging, hang him until he was dead or ceased to move and then take him down and pour water until he came to and repeat the remedy." He also remembered that the process was not foolproof, for sometimes the informant "would send us into a death trap and get the devil shot out of us."[163]

The most notorious method of interrogation was the "water cure," described by one witness thus: "The victim is laid flat on his back and held down by his tormentors. Then a bamboo tube is thrust into his mouth and some dirty water, the filthier the better, is poured down his unwilling throat."[164] Macabebe scouts allegedly taught the Americans this method, and some intelligence officers, such as Edwin F. Glenn, were eager practitioners. Others, with more delicate sensibilities, turned their prisoners over to Filipino interrogators, some of them former guerrillas. Investigations into the scale of its use by American troops produced such contradictory testimony as to preclude any reliable conclusions, but it appears that the use of torture steadily increased. Colonel C. M. Foote, who investigated allegations of mistreatment in Batangas Province in 1902, found only a few cases where officers were present. According to Foote, many "water cures" actually were instances in which people had their heads ducked in water, and others were exaggerations: one victim claimed he had been tied up for an entire week without any food. When told that a man would starve in that time, he replied that he had eaten his clothes.[165] In contrast, Edmund Block, who investigated troop misconduct in neighboring Tayabas Province during this same period, reported seventeen separate incidents involving eight officers.[166] Block's report may have underestimated the extent of torture in this campaign. In a revealing letter written when accusations about troop misconduct were just surfacing, Henry T. Allen told a fellow officer: "You, as well as I, know that in bringing to a successful issue war measures out here certain things will take place not intended by the higher authorities; that the 'watercure' and other unauthorized methods will be resorted to in spite of the strictest instructions. I have heard that under me, although against my orders, the 'watercure' and other measures just as bad, or worse, were adopted, and probably under you the same; moreover, it can be said that such things have taken place under all commanders out here."[167]

No district commander—with the possible exception of Smith on Samar—ever implemented a counterinsurgency policy based on extralegal repression. But they found it very difficult to control the behavior of their isolated commands, and many were willing to tolerate a considerable stretching of the laws of war in order to secure results. Bell's comments to the 13th Infantry's Col. William Bisbee are perhaps the best summation of the attitudes of senior commanders. Bell wrote to Bisbee to warn him that many of his reports were couched in language that might be construed as sanctioning property destruction and physical coercion. More alarmingly, recently a high-ranking officer on Otis's staff had visited Bell and related an incident in which

> a young officer of the 13th Infantry told him that he once went to a man's house to get some rifles which he was absolutely certain he had hid there. That he demanded the rifles and indicated clearly to the man's mind that he knew he had them, but notwithstanding this the native persisted in lying and denied having any arms. That he then strung him up by the neck, whereupon the rope broke. That he then threatened to shoot him and did actually fire his pistol very near to him as if he were trying to hit him, but still the native persisted that he had no guns. That he then raked up some leaves against his home and lit a match preparatory to setting the leaves on fire whereupon the native weakened and disclosed the hiding place of 13 guns.

Bell emphasized that, although "I fully believe that such methods are necessary and justifiable under the circumstances, I have no authority in the matter and therefore would not be able to protect any officer whose employment of such methods became a matter of complaint or scandal."[168] As Bell's letter indicates, in considering possible violations of the laws of war, most senior officers preferred a policy of "don't ask, don't tell." They zealously published Manila's orders against physical coercion while at the same time conceding that conditions in the field often precluded compliance.

TEN

MOROLAND
AND THE
EASTERN VISAYAS

From the perspective of the supreme command in Manila, the main theater was Luzon; the western Visayan islands of Panay, Negros, and Cebu a distant second. The least important were the eastern Visayan islands of Leyte and Samar, and the southern islands of Mindanao and the Sulu archipelago. Indeed, the fact that there was an army presence at all was the result of outside pressure. Mindanao, Jolo, and the small post of Siassi received a few companies in 1899 because Washington insisted that troops replace the departing Spanish. Samar and Leyte were occupied in late January 1900 because of McKinley's insistence that the hemp ports be opened. Otis believed these regions were unaffected by independence sentiment—except from dissident Tagalogs and brigands—and that a few thousand soldiers would be enough to hold them. MacArthur begrudged even these paltry numbers. For both the army and the navy, the southern and eastern Philippines marked a frontier, the farthest extreme of their organizational and operational borders.[1]

For the navy, the southern Philippines was an exciting, picturesque station. Based at Zamboanga on Mindanao, a flotilla of gunboats roamed the Sulu, Philippine, and Mindanao seas. The Moros were not much interested in trading with the revolutionaries, and patrols turned up little contraband. Indeed, the senior naval commander urged that the blockade be lifted in the Moro areas.[2] With the army largely confined to the coast of Mindanao and the Sulu islands, the navy played a major role in military operations. For the most part, the services cooperated, but rivalry was rarely suspended for long. After a gunboat bombarded a Moro village, the furious district commander wrote in his diary: "I do not understand under what authority the Commanding Officer of a Gun boat can proceed with a Post Commander and fire at a native village in my Department, or how the Navy can co-operate with the land forces unless doing so through the Department Commander."[3]

Brigadier General William A. Kobbé's Department of Mindanao and Jolo was the largest department in area, and the smallest in terms of manpower.

In 1900 he was assigned barely 2,600 soldiers to hold Mindanao's 36,500 square miles and the Sulu archipelago's 160 inhabited islands. Kobbé recognized that because of the "diversity of race, religion, and habitat"—the population included pagans, Muslims (Moros), and Christian Filipinos—"it was necessary to adopt a military and civil policy varying with the locality."[4] He divided his department into four districts: the first, headquartered at Cagayan, was held by Col. Edward A. Goodwin's 40th Infantry and covered northern Mindanao; the second, under Col. James S. Pettit's 31st Infantry, was headquartered at Zamboanga and covered the south of that island; the third, under Maj. Owen J. Sweet and six companies of the 23rd Infantry, was headquartered at Jolo and responsible for the Sulu archipelago; the fourth was the island of Paruga, which was not occupied until 1901. Kobbé then subdivided each area into virtually autonomous subdistricts and post commands and allowed each commander considerable flexibility.

Policies in the Sulu archipelago were guided by the Bates Agreement, and although most officers found much fault with it, they followed it closely. The agreement gave the Sultan of Sulu jurisdiction over intra-Moro affairs and the army control over all external affairs. As a result, officers remained uncomfortably neutral in the face of local practices they found grossly offensive—slavery, blood feuds, polygamy, and draconian punishments for trivial offenses. After a brief effort to pry the garrison of Siassi out by embargo and control the island himself, the sultan supported the American presence, recognizing that it enhanced his weak position among his *datus*. As district commander Sweet noted, the district was "outside of the zone of disturbances from insurgents," and military operations were thus restricted to enforcing the Bates Agreement.[5] In the only incident that resulted in bloodshed, ostensibly friendly Moros attacked five soldiers from the Bongao, Tawi Tawi garrison, killing two. Retribution was swift: the post commander surrounded the offending village, arrested forty-five suspects, and shot them when they tried to escape.[6]

Initially, the Moros appeared enthusiastic about United States sovereignty, for it protected both Islam and their traditions from their hereditary enemies, the Christian Filipinos. But relations deteriorated over time, a harbinger of the Moro Wars that would break out in 1903. In May 1900, Sweet emphasized the study of the Koran as a means to provide "enlightened control."[7] But by 1901 he was disenchanted: "I have no confidence in the natives. I do not trust them," and he was emphatic that "military domination must prevail among the Sulu Moros for years to come."[8] Like many officers, he concluded that the Bates Agreement—or at least the provisions that allowed slavery and *datu* rule—would have to be abrogated before the United States could introduce order and civilization. Much of this disenchantment may have been due to the Americans' isolation and their primitive living conditions. At Bongao, "a desolate, silent post with but small opportunity for work other than fatigue," the garrison suffered from sickness, "moping," and "mental anoemia."[9] Supplies arrived infrequently, and salt water, spoilage, and waste ruined as many as two-thirds of the perishable food items. At Siassi, morale became so bad that soldiers shot an officer, and Sweet found it necessary to withdraw the company.[10]

In southern Mindanao, as in Jolo, there was no strong sentiment to aid the Philippine Republic: as Kobbé noted, the most powerful *datus* had already seized whatever the area possessed and were now eager for peace and security. Indeed, by the time the 31st Infantry arrived in December 1899, the local nationalists had been all but exterminated in vicious internecine conflicts. In its eighteen-month tour of duty, the regiment saw only one military engagement, and even that was unnecessary. Responding to a complaint that Datu Udasan had raided a town and stolen slaves, on 24 April 1900, Maj. L. M. Brett and twenty-five soldiers, accompanied by 100 Moros under Datu Piang, marched to Udasan's village. Both sides claimed the other fired first, but the result was a sharp fight between the two Moro factions in which between sixteen and thirty of Udasan's people were killed. The 31st's historian proudly noted that "thereafter the Malabon area enjoyed perfect peace," but Kobbé believed the affair had aroused needless antagonism. He

Troops on patrol, Mindanao

appears to have been correct, for in the Malobon area, as in Sulu, relations between Moros and Americans declined in the following years.[11]

Northern Mindanao's three provinces of Cagayan, Misamis, and Surigao contained the only significant resistance groups with any commitment to Philippine nationalism, and thus were the site of the only substantial military operations in the department. The area had been a battleground among Moros, pagans, Spaniards, and Christian Filipinos for years, and the independence movement exacerbated the violence. In Surigao, a local militia under Prudencio Garcia drove out the small Spanish garrisons and established a revolutionary government. However, in January 1899, the brothers Simon and Wenceslao Gonzalez arrived with a commission from the Philippine Republic to form a new administration. They swiftly alienated the locals; Garcia deposed them, and both sides proceeded to raise troops, capture towns, collect taxes, and raid the countryside. To the west, Jose Roa, another Malolos appointee, declared himself president of Cagayan and Iligan Provinces, but, as he plaintively wrote Aguinaldo, he was beset by the Moros—"our mortal enemies since time immemorial"—as well as a brigade of convicts and self-styled revolutionaries who held towns hostage for "taxes."[12] Thus, when the 40th Infantry arrived in March 1900, many inhabitants looked to the soldiers to restore order.

Most of the military operations in northern Mindanao centered in the Cagayan Valley, where a force of some 500 armed rebels were under the loose control of Gen. Nicolas Capistrano. On 7 April, Capistrano, with perhaps 150 riflemen and 1,000 bolomen, launched a ferocious but badly conducted attack on the 400-man Cagayan garrison. Taking advantage of dense cane-brakes, they approached to within 200 yards of the outposts, then charged. The sleepy sentries believed they faced a cattle stampede and delayed firing until too late. The insurgents broke into the town, but after much confusion the defenders organized a firing line and counterattacked, pursuing the guerrillas for six miles. Four soldiers were killed or died of wounds, and another seven were badly wounded; but the insurgents left fifty-two dead in the streets and surrounding fields.[13] On 7 May a forty-man garrison near Misamis incurred a similar attack. A large group of apparently harmless civilians approached the outposts, then suddenly drew weapons and charged, followed by an all-out assault of hundreds of bolomen. In desperate house-to-house fighting, the solders rallied and beat them back, killing over fifty but losing seven dead and four wounded. Having learned the power of modern firearms, the insurgents retreated to the mountains and thereafter fought on the defensive. Henceforth, their attacks were sporadic incidents, as when a party passing an outpost suddenly drew its bolos and killed the sentry.[14]

With the 40th Infantry's 1,200 Volunteers the lone force available for most of 1900, punitive expeditions could be mounted only at the cost of leaving the garrisons vulnerable to attack, and the jungles and mountains of Mindanao's backcountry inflicted considerable hardship on the men. The guerrillas proved adept at building fieldworks, improving on the traditional Moro stone-and-wood fortress *(cotta)*. Major James F. Case described one such strongpoint: its sole approach was by an arduous, narrow trail that, for the last 400 yards, could be swept by fire from a breastwork. The nearby area was "thick with traps, spear pits, and pit-falls, etc. Twenty resolute men could have held the place against any force making a frontal attack."[15] An assault on 14 June demonstrated that this was no exaggeration. From behind concealed trenches Capistrano's guerrillas raked the attackers, killing nine soldiers instantly and badly wounding nine others. The command fell back in confusion, abandoning their dead and their weapons. To Kobbé, it was a textbook case of "palpable mismanagement."[16] With neither side able to defeat the other, the situation in northern Mindanao remained stalemated.

On November the department received some badly needed reinforcements in the form of Birkhimer's veteran 28th Infantry. Kobbé put Birkhimer in charge of the area stretching from Cagayan to the east, with Case's battalion taking the area to the west, and ordered them to rotate battalions, keeping constant pressure on Capistrano. There were few battles: in December Birkhimer complained that in two months his regiment had marched 165 miles without a fight; and the 28th's history shows that in its five months in Mindanao the average company had but two engagements and none had more than four. But whereas previously the insurgents had been able to retreat to their *cottas,* the army now could sustain large expeditions, complete with mountain guns that could drop shrapnel into the *cottas* at 2,000 yards: defenseless against the flying steel splinters, the defenders would soon abandon the fort. Birkhimer made good use of mounted infantry companies and formed special sharpshooter units, which gave him mobility and a fast-striking reconnaissance force.

Gradually, the continual pressure from sweeps and raids and the steady destruction of *cottas* and supply dumps left the insurgents hungry, dispirited, and scattered. Kobbé encouraged noncombatants to enter the occupied towns but refused admittance to men of military age until they surrendered their weapons: "Let this class either surrender their arms in good faith, or take them with them into the mountains and fight us with them as they wish, but do not permit them while concealing their arms, to come into our lines, playing the perfidious pack of war traitors because it suits their convenience or is congenial to their natures."[17] In February 1901, with many of his lieutenants already captured or surrendered, Capistrano sought terms but balked at the requirement he surrender his guns. Kobbé was sympathetic—he admired the rebel leader as "a man of considerable education and honorable character" but who lacked the power to compel his subordinates to turn in their weapons.[18] Nevertheless, he freely authorized "drastic measures"— widespread crop destruction, the closing of most ports, and unrelenting military operations—until Capistrano surrendered on 27 March. Although northern Mindanao remained infested with brigands, and although the Moros in the Iligan region grew steadily more restless, no organized resistance with any connection to the Philippine independence outlasted this capitulation.[19]

Kobbé, an outspoken supporter of benevolent policies, encouraged his officers to bring to the population the benefits of American rule. Perhaps the greatest proponent of this was the 31st Infantry's Capt. John A. Wagner, post commander of Baganga, Mindanao. When he arrived, Wagner found "a pitiable condition of affairs. Families shared their miserable huts with pigs, dogs and chickens. Few roofs offered protection from the rain and the loose bamboo floors allowed the foul odors of rotting vegetation and hog wallows to enter from below. Each house contributed its part to the general conditions of ignorance, indolence, wretchedness and filth."[20] Wagner's military problems were negligible—the area was so safe he could station a four-man garrison at a neighboring town with equanimity—and he threw himself into cleaning up the town, opening a school, and revitalizing agriculture and trade.[21] Whereas previously the population had been largely subsistence growers, Wagner worked to create a market economy both through the cultivation of cash crops and the regulation of the prices charged by coastal traders. Eventually, he encouraged the formation of a local consortium to sell hemp, rice, and other products at the best price. But Wagner's paternalism was autocratic. He required every male between the ages of fourteen and fifty to contribute two days' public labor a month, because the population were "vassals" who "will only work through fear for men whom they seem to consider their masters, otherwise I think most of them would starve; they do not understand making a living for themselves, nor do they care to do so." What was needed most of all was strong government to "compel them to work to raise and sell their own crops."[22] Within nine months of his arrival, Wagner was confident that he had found civil officials able to act in a suitable manner and that the entire garrison could be withdrawn.

Kobbé's mixture of military operations, civic action, and benevolent government was very successful in the short term: resistance from rebels claiming to serve the Philippine Republic had all but ended by the time the U.S. Volunteer regiments left in mid-1901. In part, this reflects the relative ease of his task. The insurgency was confined to three provinces, torn by internal conflicts, with few weapons, and little popular support. Indeed, in several areas the local *datus* had already suppressed the dissidents before the troops arrived. Nevertheless, Kobbé shrewdly played on his advantages. Although he had few troops, he maximized their effectiveness by creating close relations with the populace. This required holding soldiers to high standards of conduct and encouraging his officers' civic action programs. No better example of Kobbé's influence can be found than in the answer one officer gave to the bewildered Paruga islanders when they asked him what the United States required from them: "Cleanliness and schools is all we want."[23] The department commander also worked hard to conciliate the Moros, a policy that was helped by his belief that they were "very like the best North American Indians—as the Nez Percé and Northern Cheyenne—in features and manners, in their love of independence, and in personal dignity and pride."[24] Depressingly, Kobbé's efforts to establish a peaceful basis for army-Moro relations were not followed by his successors, and by 1902 there was notable estrangement between the two.

On Samar, the U.S. Army pacification effort was begun with promise in 1900 and suspended in frustration. Samar is a large island—5,200 square miles—surrounded by treacherous reefs and shoals, and subject to heavy monsoons and recurrent typhoons. Outside of the coastal towns the terrain was so rugged—swamps, mountains, cane fields, jungles—and so filled with disease-bearing fauna that all communications went by water. The island's chief crop was hemp, which in turn meant it was dependent on imports to supplement its meager food production. By 1900, the effects of war, drought, and the navy's blockade had intensified food shortages among the island's 195,000 inhabitants to critical proportions. Economic difficulties exacerbated Samar's social conflicts—pitting highlander against townsman, orthodox against sectarian, merchant against hemp grower, landowner against peasant. Despite these considerable difficulties, Samar's political-military leader, Vicente Lukban had mobilized a formidable resistance movement. Headed by local officers such as Claro Guevara and Eugenio Daza, and bolstered by brigands and the Dios Dios sectarians, the Samareno guerrillas would prove among the toughest the Americans faced.

After the army occupation of the hemp ports of Catablogan and Calbayog in January, Lukban established a new headquarters some fifteen miles from the west coast up the Gandara River. Although a Tagalog and an outsider, he retained strong local support. Lukban recognized that the key to the struggle was convincing the Samarenos of the inevitability of Philippine independence, and he sent forth a steady stream of propaganda describing

American outrages, revolutionary triumphs, and the terrible fate of collaborators.[25] Samar's guerrillas took advantage of their island's rugged terrain and compensated for their lack of modern weapons with mantraps and their deadly bolo knives.[26]

His attention distracted with running a department that stretched from Luzon to Mindanao, Kobbé did not pay sufficient attention to Samar. He intended that Maj. Henry T. Allen occupy only the two ports and begin exporting hemp as rapidly as possible. Although Allen assured Kobbé he intended to remain on the defensive, he soon garrisoned eight towns, including several on the north coast, and initiated a series of campaigns on the Gandara River. These early operations yielded encouraging results: in all of February there were only three skirmishes on Samar, and everywhere the population appeared enthusiastic about the restoration of the hemp trade. Allen's principal field commander, Maj. John C. Gilmore, reported after one hike: "The people in the interior saw the American troops for the first time, and realized that they had come to protect people's lives and property and establish peace, and that they did not murder and pillage as they (the natives) had been told they would do."[27] Kobbé, however, was dismissive, describing Gilmore's expedition as "a flat failure"; beyond marching into a burned-out town, he had done little more than prove the interior was impassable.[28]

Much of Allen's enthusiasm was based on his conviction that the Samarenos were an "intelligent and naturally peaceable people who would never have offered any resistance had not the Tagalog influence been forced upon them."[29] He made earnest efforts to assure the population, or at least the elite, of the United States' benevolent intentions by proclamations, by meeting with town officials, and by encouraging the resumption of trade. In April, at Allen's urging, seventy-seven prominent Samarenos denounced Lukban's "savage and barbarous acts" and promised to embargo rice shipments to unoccupied towns and to furnish volunteers to garrison the interior villages.[30] Allen's solicitation of the elite even extended to his efforts to enlist a paramilitary force "composed of men picked from the most intelligent and influential families."[31] As a result of Allen's efforts, and Hughes's support, on 28 April Manila authorized two 100-man companies of "provincial police."[32] Ironically, no sooner had the first of these companies been recruited than it was transferred and renamed the Leyte Scouts; it did not return to Samar until mid-1901.

In March and April, Allen's pacification campaign began to disentangle. His isolated garrisons, stretched along the coast and the interior, were surrounded and virtually besieged. At Calbayog, 5 bolomen stabbed a sentry, then slipped inside an officer's house and hacked his cook to death before being discovered and killed. Catarman was surrounded by 600 insurgents; but the garrison managed to flank the trenches and catch the bolomen in a cross fire, killing 152 at a cost of 2 dead. The Samarenos proved more adept at guerrilla fighting in the mountains and grasslands, severely mauling isolated patrols. On 8 March they ambushed a group of soldiers near Mataguinao, killing 2 and wounding 4 others. Three days later, at Paranas, 8 soldiers were overrun by 200 bolomen, and 3 were badly wounded. Although the Americans inflicted far more casualties—killing 20 at Mataguinao and 30 at Paranas—the ferocity and determination of the Samarenos astonished the soldiers. One officer saw a boloman hit five times at close range by pistol bullets, but the man continued to attack until shot directly in the head with a rifle. Incidents such as this soon endowed Samar's warriors with a fearsome reputation, which was to grow in soldiers' tales until they became almost superhuman.[33]

Early on a Sunday morning, 15 April, the 31 soldiers stationed at Catubig were attacked by an estimated 600 guerrillas and soon trapped in the church buildings. By Tuesday, subjected to unrelenting fire from all directions and numerous efforts to burn them out, the soldiers decided to make a break for the river, where they had moored several boats. Loading their packs with ammunition, they set fire to their barracks and made for the water, but their attackers were waiting and unleashed a torrent of musketry. What was supposed to be an orderly withdrawal turned into a panicked rush: 13 soldiers were killed and 3 others wounded. The survivors, under a corporal, managed to dig a shallow trench along the riverbank with their bayonets. For the next two days they held out against an enemy less than 100 yards away. Finally, on 19 April, a patrol fought its way through and rescued the garrison. The Americans estimated they had killed over 150 insurgents; but of the garrison's 31 original members, 19 were killed and another 5 were badly wounded.[34]

Catubig was an exceptionally bloody battle by the standards of the Philippine War and was given graphic coverage in American newspapers, much of it critical of Allen. Otis and Kobbé also condemned Allen's actions, but Hughes, the Visayan commander, supported his subordinate and Allen avoided censure.[35] Nevertheless, the attack convinced Allen that conciliation was not working. On 25 April he issued a new proclamation that, although blaming Tagalogs and bandits for the continued fighting, warned Samarenos that if they failed to act against the common enemy they would suffer severe consequences.[36] Five days later he reported he had directed Gilmore to "see that a proper punishment be effected on the Catubig Valley" and that the "good effects of drastic measures employed by the several detachments sent to numerous places along the West Coast . . . are very marked."[37] By his own admission, Gilmore "destroyed thousands of bushels of rice and palay, burnt Catubig, and several visitas [hamlets]."[38] This devastation exacerbated Samar's already critical food shortages and compounded the effects of a drought: Calbayog's commander reported that the "insurgents had been driven to such a state of frenzy by the effective cutting off of their food supplies that they intended at all hazards to made a night attack on the town."[39] But the real sufferers were noncombatants, for, as Allen soon recognized, the guerrillas simply appropriated the peasantry's foodstuffs. By 21 May, Allen admitted, "Unless the situation changes soon the outlook here as regards the weaker part of the population will become serious."[40]

In May, MacArthur arrived in Samar and declared that the "future military policy would be to simply hold the insurgents in check on the other Islands than Luzon and crush the rebellion of that Island when it would cease of itself on the others."[41] He ordered Allen and the rest of the 43rd to join their comrades in Leyte, and brought in four companies of the 29th Infantry to hold Catbalogan and Calbayog. At the same time, he transferred Samar to the 4th District, Department of Southern Luzon. This arbitrary, and completely bizarre, organization meant that the commanders on islands barely two miles apart were unable to coordinate their pacification efforts.[42]

Between the withdrawal of the 43rd in July and the island's transfer back to the Department of the Visayas in May 1901, Samar remained a military backwater. With the exception of an abortive campaign in December 1900 and January 1901, the army undertook little offensive action beyond punitive raids to destroy villages, crops, and hemp.[43] Lukban and his local jefes had ample time to mobilize the population against the invaders, to store food and weapons, to encourage the cultivation of crops in the mountains, and in other ways to prepare for the resumption of the struggle.

Across from the southwestern third of Samar, separated from it by a narrow strait, was the island of Leyte. Roughly 120 miles long and 52 at its widest, 3,800 square miles in all, it is smaller than Samar; but its population, then 270,000, was larger. Like Samar, it is divided by high, rugged mountains into a number of river valleys and coastal settlements, but unlike Samar, land transportation along its coast was possible. It was a much richer and more productive island, with some 50 percent under cultivation. Although hemp was the most important crop, the island grew much of its food and was not as dependent on imports. On both islands, Aguinaldo's political-military jefes had over a year to energize the indigenous revolutionary movements. Like Lukban, Brig. Gen. Ambrosio Moxica sought to mobilize the entire population: he ordered all males aged sixteen to fifty to join the militia, directed the population to grow crops, and organized town government in conformity with Aguinaldo's 18 June 1898 directive. After the American invasion, he first tried to concentrate his forces and overwhelm isolated detachments; when this failed, he retreated to the interior and adopted guerrilla tactics.[44]

The early months of military operations in Leyte also bore a strong similarity to those on Samar. Both Manila and Kobbé viewed the 43rd Infantry's task as opening up the main hemp ports on each island, but doing little more until Hughes had pacified Panay and could turn his attention to the rest of the Visayas. But Col. Arthur Murray, like Allen, was an ambitious, intelligent officer who believed his superior's directions were both militarily and ethically wrong. He was convinced the revolutionaries were demoralized and that, under enlightened rule, the Leyteanos would soon join his 43rd Infantry in hunting down the Tagalogs and bandits who opposed occupation. In a letter to Moxica, he emphasized the United States' benevolent efforts to raise the Filipinos from their "semi-barbarous condition" and pointed out that "the Philipino [sic] Army exists but in name, and consists chiefly of guerrilla bands who are doing more harm to their own people through pillage and robbery than to the armed forces of the United States."[45] Thus, although he initially had only five companies on Leyte, he embarked on an aggressive campaign, sending patrols into the interior to seize the major rice-growing areas and increasing his garrisons from three to twelve towns.

As in Samar, the 43rd's overextension left its garrisons vulnerable; guerrilla bands several hundred strong surrounded the towns, harassed patrols, and drove much of the population into the hills: from February to June, there were 125 engagements on Leyte. The strain on the outnumbered soldiers was immense. One officer reported that half his troops suffered from "nervousness" and could not be relied on; the least alarm caused them to jump for their Krags.[46] The unexpected resistance and the decline in his soldiers' effectiveness led Murray to urge that the rest of the 43rd be sent over from Samar at the same time Allen demanded reinforcements for that island. In April, Hughes resolved this conflict by deciding that the situation on Leyte was so critical it was necessary to "over run that Island at once to crush the life out of the effort."[47] By juggling his forces, Hughes freed two companies each of the 44th and 23rd Infantry for a brief campaign on Leyte.

Thus reinforced, Murray went on the offensive in late April. Unlike Lukban, Moxica and his war chiefs did not withdraw to the mountains but instead tried to defend their strongholds and supply depots. The result was a series of one-sided defeats. On 26 April, Maj. Lincoln C. Andrews stormed one of the insurgents' largest camps near Ormoc. After a stiff battle in which three died and another thirteen were wounded, the soldiers scattered the defenders and destroyed tons of precious supplies. On 6 May at Hilongas, a composite force of the 43rd and 23rd, aided by the cannon and machine guns of the gunboat *Pampanga,* killed seventy-four and captured another sixty, at a cost of four wounded. But to Hughes's chagrin, Murray reoccupied most of the towns he had previously abandoned, a "situation [which] rather invites attack [as the] small detachments do not impress [the] inhabitants of our ability to hold."[48] In late May and June, the tide turned again, and once more the outnumbered garrisons were virtually besieged. Frustrated, Hughes asked Manila whether he was expected to occupy all of Samar and Leyte or only the hemp ports. If the former, he needed at least a regiment for each.[49] MacArthur responded by shifting Samar out of Hughes's jurisdiction and emphasizing that the Visayas were a secondary theater. Making a virtue of necessity, Hughes abandoned Leyte's interior towns—where he reasoned the inhabitants could safely return without retaliation—and garrisoned the principal ports and the major agricultural valley in the north.[50]

The addition of Allen's six companies, plus the retention of two companies of the 44th, gave Murray sufficient strength to implement his views on pacification: "Where the natives are friendly they should be treated with the utmost kindness. . . . when armed parties of the enemy are encountered they should be hit and hit hard."[51] Like Allen, Murray sought to conciliate the *principales* and "cause the better class of natives to unite and aid us in our search for the [guerrilla] bands."[52] Moxica had taxed the hemp crop heavily, so the army's directives that products be shipped duty-free pleased businessmen and planters. Murray also developed close relations with the clergy, enlisting their support to restore order and to convince the population to return to the towns.

Murray viewed civic action, and especially municipal government, as an excellent way of securing popular support, and he directed that "commanding officers of occupied towns do all they can towards inducing friendly natives to remain in their homes and give them all possible protection."[53] Most of Murray's subordinates enthusiastically concurred. As a subdistrict commander on Leyte, Allen developed a comprehensive program to improve civil government. He advocated that teachers' pay be increased, that the best Filipino students be sent to American schools, that the police be better paid and trained, and that the army provide free health care to the urban destitute and the rural population.[54] Other post commanders encouraged cooperation through joint activities such as the Fil-American Fourth of July festival at Carigara, with dinner for hundreds of people and a concert by the regimental band. Murray believed "a proper fostering of the schools of the island will prove one of the potent factors in securing for us the friendship of the natives," and most of his officers agreed.[55] One officer wrote that the school, and the support of the *presidente,* were major factors in doubling the population of his town; another proudly reported that the 300 pupils in his area "eagerly and quickly learn American ways."[56] Murray's faith in civil government also bore fruit. In the town of Palo, for example, one insurgent officer reported shortly after the Americans' arrival that the townspeople were "wild about the new elections," and another complained that the population denounced guerrillas and assisted the soldiers on patrols.[57]

But Murray was also a pragmatist who never forgot that his primary goal was the pacification of the island. When one town requested a garrison, he made it a precondition that it first clear the area of insurgents, and proudly noted this prompted "a little civil war" between townspeople and guerrillas.[58] In every town the 43rd garrisoned, post commanders established police forces that guided patrols, gathered intelligence, interrogated suspects, arrested guerrillas posing as "amigos," and even fought as infantry. At Jaro the police prevented guerrillas from burning the town, and at Barugo, police and townspeople joined to fight off a guerrilla attack. Not surprisingly, the police became special targets of retaliation.[59] Murray believed that Filipino soldiers "would be worth three or four times the same number of soldiers in bringing about good order in the Islands," and he strongly supported the Leyte Scouts.[60] Formed from a company each of Leyteanos and Samarenos, by late 1900 they were being used on military operations and as garrisons for outlying towns.[61]

The second part of Murray's pacification policy specified that "when armed parties of the enemy are encountered they should be hit and hit hard." The first "Moxica Expedition" of 13 July to 3 August kept two columns of scouts and infantry scouring the mountains in the northeast, although with little result. The second, of 27 August to 3 September, was more successful, covering 150 miles, destroying four storehouses, and capturing Moxica's archives, treasury, supply officer, 143 prisoners, and seventeen firearms. The effect of such activity was cumulative, as more and more combatants decided to give up the struggle. For example, on 12 September a patrol managed to work its way into the rear of a stronghold, cutting off retreat and killing nineteen bolomen in a sharp skirmish, Within a week, sixty more guerrillas had surrendered, and 195 people who had been living in the mountains had come in to take an oath of loyalty. To those who moved to the occupied zones, Murray offered good treatment, but by the fall he was adopting harsher measures against those who remained out. In November he both approved Allen's orders authorizing that telegraph wire cutters be shot on sight and recommended further the deportation of anyone "reliably but secretly reported to be secretly engaged in aiding the enemy and undermining American authority."[62]

A good example of a post commander who fulfilled Murray's balance of conciliation and coercion was Capt. Washington L. Goldsborough, whose modest goal, stated without a hint of irony, was to make his town of Dagami "as safe for the natives as New York City would be." When he arrived he found the town almost deserted: the insurgents had forced the population into the hills to grow crops. Goldsborough imported rice to encourage resettlement, organized a government, and began a school: within three months, the population increased from 900 to 4,000. But benevolence alone was not enough: "The insurgents are well housed and well fed, and when we pass near them they only disturb themselves to the extent of going a few yards out of the road or trail into the dense cover. My men march miles to make them walk yards, and as we pass the empty towns we know that five minutes before we reached them they covered our enemies who return to them as soon as we have left the neighborhood."[63] Accordingly, he began restricting food transfer into the countryside, brought all rice and livestock into Dagami, and proposed the total destruction of the rice crop in the unoccupied areas.

Not all officers could achieve such standards, and some did far more harm than good. Lieutenant Jonathan Cilley, assigned to the port of Ormoc—described as one of the friendliest towns in the island—promptly got drunk, chased the officials out of the municipal building, and terrorized the town.[64] An even greater problem was Capt. John Ketcham, post commander at Hilongas, who rebuilt the destroyed insurgent fort and cleared the entire area for a hundred yards on each side. He discouraged people from living in the destroyed town and boasted to Murray that when town officials had greeted him: "I did not want any *d——d nigger* to put his hands on me, so I drew my revolver and called the detachment which had stacked arms outside. As the detachment rushed for the guns, the niggers fairly fell over getting out of the second story window; and those who remained promised to do all I asked."[65] As an officer in the 44th Infantry, Ketcham was outside Murray's direct command, and thus all the colonel could do was petition Hughes to put the man before a medical board to determine his sanity. Hughes ignored this request, perhaps because Ketcham was a tough combat commander who killed one of Moxica's zone commanders and quickly ended resistance in his area.[66]

Murray's problems with such subordinates were mild compared with his struggles with his superiors and the navy. Hughes never understood the importance of a pacification program that balanced civil and military concerns, and pressured Murray to pull most of his troops out of the towns and send them on expeditions into the hills. An even touchier issue was the blockade. Shortly after his arrival, Murray, following the instructions of his then commander Kobbé, declared all occupied towns open for trade, a measure he viewed as essential to reviving Leyte's economy and winning over the "better class." But patrolling gunboats, following navy orders, interdicted all trade from Leyte; especially galling, they burned or confiscated boats and cargo carrying passes issued by post commanders. Murray was so furious he threatened to fire on gunboats off the Leyte coast. But Samar's new commander, Col. Edward E. Hardin, supported a strict blockade, for he believed the restriction of trade was essential to starve Lukban out. Hughes also was unsympathetic, advising Murray, "Let us get the islands in hand before we begin to give full swing to smuggling."[67]

Despite these disappointments, overall Murray's pacification policies were successful, and Moxica's dispatches reflected a diminishing control of the population. His proclamation of 20 May strictly forbade people from living in occupied towns or aiding the United States, but it imposed equally drastic penalties for those who demanded contributions or abused their authority. Captain Jorge Capili, a guerrilla commander, not only defied Moxica's orders, but also cut the hair off a seamstress and beat her husband to death, as well as committing numerous other outrages. On 1 August, Murray reported that surrendered insurgents told him Moxica was sick, lacking a permanent headquarters and an organized force of his own; the guerrillas were dispersed throughout the island under regional commanders. Ten days later, Moxica sent a letter and his chief subordinate to Murray requesting a suspension of hostilities to allow him to consult representatives of the revolutionary movement in Leyte. With Allen's troops in the midst of operations, Murray would not accept any suspension, and so the negotiations fell through. By November, Moxica's spirits appear to have revived, and he issued a strong exhortation to the Leyteanos reaffirming his commitment to "wage a war without quarter on the invading enemy."[68]

Toward the end of 1900, even the skeptical Hughes told Manila that the 43rd controlled Leyte's food-growing areas and that the insurgents were scattered in the mountains, "roving bands of vigorous young bucks who have about one hundred rifles and an abundant supply [of] long knives."[69] With most of the towns under civil government, and local police handling routine duties, Murray could concentrate his military forces for sustained operations in the mountains. Squeezed into smaller and smaller areas, their sanctuaries burned, unable to secure food from an increasingly hostile population, the guerrillas were kept continually moving. For their part, the soldiers had learned much about fighting in the jungles, mountains, and rice paddies. When they caught the insurgents, they made them pay a terrible price in killed and wounded. Even more revealing were the growing numbers of guerrillas who surrendered. Murray increased pressure on those prominent Leyteanos who had still not publicly committed themselves to the United States: "Kindness and consideration I regret to say appear to me largely if not wholly unappreciated by these people, who seem to regard our lenient and humane treatment as an evidence of weakness on our part."[70] Those who refused to take an oath of allegiance were now treated as enemies and subject to arrest and fines. On 9 April, Moxica's final headquarters was located and attacked, and his forces scattered. That was enough. The general opened negotiations, and on 18 May surrendered with forty-three officers and 1,386 men.[71]

ELEVEN

PANAY

The Department of the Visayas, headquartered at Iloilo City, comprised five major and numerous small islands totaling 25,300 square miles and a population of 2.5 million. To impose a coherent pacification policy over such a wide and diverse area with an occupation force that averaged some 8,600 soldiers was an awesome challenge. For someone as volatile as Brig. Gen. Robert P. Hughes, it was next to impossible. In his sixties and suffering from a variety of ailments that would force his retirement in 1903, Hughes was often frustrated by the guerrilla war in the Visayas. Depending on his moods, he alternately ascribed his problems to Tagalog outsiders, to the "absolutely ignorant" local population, or to the incompetence and lethargy of his officers.[1] After weeks of inaction he would suddenly become interested in—or, more often, impatient with—some area or policy and would send a flurry of querulous and sarcastic demands for immediate attention. When placated, he would relapse into quiescence until the next provocation.

Hughes considered Panay the most important and most difficult island in his command. Because of the high mountains across the interior of the island, it was almost impossible to move from province to province except by water. Even sea communication was hazardous: Capt. Francis H. French left on a supply boat from San Jose, Antique Province, to Iloilo. Six days later, after battling contrary winds and currents, the boat put back into San Jose.[2] Iloilo Province's relatively good road system allowed troops to move rapidly during the dry season, but even there the summer monsoon halted campaigning and sealed off the interior towns. Even more isolated were the garrisons in Antique, Capiz, and the northeast area around Concepcion, which could be reached overland only by narrow, treacherous mountain trails. Accordingly, Hughes kept twenty-seven of his sixty-eight companies on Panay. Colonel Edmund Rice's 26th and five Regular companies of the 18th Infantry were assigned to Iloilo, the most important province. Antique, initially held only by Maj. J. F. Huston's battalion of the 19th, was later reinforced by Lt. Col. Walter S. Scott's battalion of the 44th Infantry. Clearly isolated were the other two battalions of the 18th: one in Capiz Province, the other at Sara and Concepcion in the northeast.[3] But isolation was a relative term: beyond Iloilo City, post commanders and

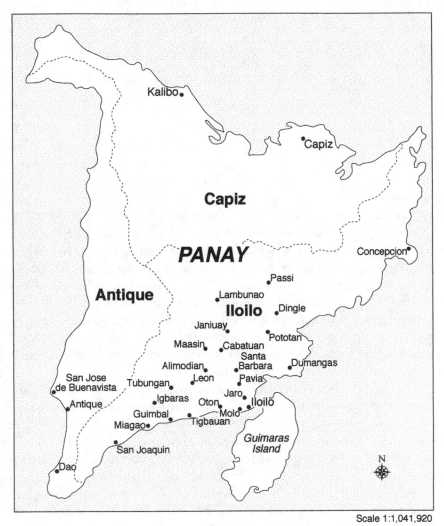

Scale 1:1,041,920

Panay

their garrisons, usually no more than 100 men, had to fight the war virtually on their own.

Following the breakup of Delgado's army during the December 1899 campaign, Hughes was certain that the remnants had fled to the mountain ranges along the Iloilo-Capiz-Antique borders. Convinced that "we must bring these mountain bands into some kind of subjection or break them up in this season or they will give us no rest during the season of rains," he was insistent that his soldiers keep up the offensive.[4] On 2 January 1900 a com-

U.S. mounted patrol on native ponies, 1900

posite column of Gordon's Scouts, a mountain battery, and two companies of 6th Infantry set out along the coast road from Iloilo to approach Antique from the south. Meanwhile, a battalion of the 19th under Huston landed at San Joaquin as Scott's battalion of the 44th marched over the mountains from Igbaras. Hughes intended Huston to drive the enemy out of San Jose de Buenavista into Scott's waiting cordon. But Huston moved slowly, and the local guerrillas under the command of Leandro Fullon dispersed; barring a few skirmishes the campaign accomplished little. No sooner had Gordon and Scott's commands returned to Iloilo—fighting a sharp engagement on the way out—than Huston's battalion was virtually besieged in San Jose. Antique's 120-mile long coast and mountain ridges allowed the guerrillas to spot enemy movements easily, and to choose whether to ambush or to flee. Huston, an unpopular, hard-drinking officer, wanted reinforcements so that he could occupy more of the province. Instead, Hughes sent him singularly unhelpful advice such as "Hold your force well in hand so as to be able to give the insurgents a good whipping" and "Keep them well stirred up and they will have to give it up soon."[5] In March a composite battalion arrived for a brief campaign, but again Fullon's guerrillas scattered, only to reappear once Huston fell back to San Jose. In April and May Hughes tried another tack. From its stations in northwest Iloilo Province, Anderson's 26th battalion tried to drive the guerrillas into Scott's battalion, which had established a supply depot on the coast. Hughes expected great things; if Scott could keep "rattling" the *insurrectos* for a month and "roast them wherever you find them," he could "bring these beggars to terms."[6]

The impact of these large-scale sweeps is difficult to assess. Certainly, they harried the guerrillas and prevented their concentrating on any town and overrunning its garrison. There are some indications that both Fullon and Ananias Diocno in Capiz considered surrender, for on 15 May they sent commissioners to Hughes to discuss terms. The pressure from these operations may also have contributed to a mutiny by Fullon's officers, which was put down with some bloodshed.[7] The soldiers, particularly the Volunteers of the 26th and 44th, gained valuable experience; and Gordon's Scouts, a tough forty-five-man unit of mounted infantry under Capt. Walter H. Gordon and Lt. Arthur Conger, became especially adept at small-unit tactics and locating guerrilla bands and supply depots. The district's capable subsistence officer, Capt. Briant H. Wells, developed a highly effective logistical system that sustained columns operating in the most difficult terrain for weeks. Nevertheless, Hughes's persistence in sending his few available mobile forces into the mountains did little to ensure the pacification of the countryside. Moreover, by tying up troops and logistics in mobile operations, he weakened his efforts to establish a "cordon" of towns in the main agricultural region, which would keep the guerrillas confined to the hills and prevent them from obtaining supplies.[8] Instead, he ordered more towns occupied, stretching his scanty forces even further. He even committed his departmental reserve to garrison duty so that, in April, when a detachment was briefly cut off, the only force available was Gordon's Scouts, who had to make a thirty-six-hour march to the scene.

Having been scattered by Hughes's winter campaign, the revolutionaries abandoned active operations until May. Their ostensible reason was to wait while the U.S. Congress debated the issue of Philippine independence, but a far more important consideration was that Delgado and his subordinates desperately needed to reorganize after the mauling they had received. Although born in Antique, Fullon had spent much of his adult life on Luzon and had great difficulty controlling the province's independent-minded jefes. The resistance in Capiz Province was in even worse shape and was dealt a heavy blow on 21 February when 146 officers and men surrendered, soon followed by 81 others. Thereafter, there remained only scattered forces with a combined strength of a few hundred rifles. In Iloilo Province, Delgado had about 900 rifles, divided among the commanders of five subzones; the most powerful was Quintin Salas, well hidden in the Dumangas swamp some fifteen miles northeast of Iloilo City.[9]

An anonymous *insurrecto* manual circulated on Panay entitled "Guerrilla Warfare" defined it as "made in infinitesimal fractions," a prolonged war that avoided battles and slowly wore down the enemy. The manual emphasized speed, deception, and flexibility. Guerrilla units would be built around ten-man sections, each with eight riflemen, which could be combined for major operations or rapidly dispersed. Tactics were based almost entirely on firearms; the bolomen were there purely to carry supplies, act as scouts, and maintain the camp. The manual noted that since the Americans usually marched in three files—one on the trail, and detachments on each flank—ambush positions had to be situated to avoid envelopment. It offered detailed instructions on scouting as well, recommending that each band keep watch on the enemy with as many as a dozen scouts, both mounted and on foot, disguised as peasants, merchants, and priests.[10]

In practice, however, few of Panay's guerrilla bands had either the firepower or the discipline to execute these tactics. Many of their rifles were in poor condition, having been hidden in trees or buried, and ammunition was in such short supply that guerrilla chiefs were ordered to count each man's cartridges before and after a march. During the summer monsoon, the revolutionaries built camps in inaccessible areas where they could concentrate several bands and attack isolated garrisons. During the dry season, the regulars were broken into small detachments of perhaps a dozen who lived in towns and barrios and were indistinguishable from the peasantry. When summoned to attack a supply train, patrol, or occupied town, the insurgents would fire a few volleys at extreme rifle range and then take to the brush. This had the advantage of surprise and avoiding casualties, but it prevented a close-quarters ambush which would have allowed both more accurate fire and the possibility of a charge.[11]

In the words of Iloilo Province's revolutionary council: "The greatest solidarity must be secured between these two factors, 'The People' and its 'Armed Forces' in order that they may proceed hand in hand to secure our common desire."[12] Despite the occupation of most of the island's towns, the rebels had to sustain the civic organizations and continue to draw food, recruits, money, and shelter from them. Both Fullon and Delgado ordered their commanders to avoid abuses and to send suspected collaborators and criminals to headquarters rather than execute them. Throughout the first half of 1900, they appear to have succeeded; Hughes commented in June that although the guerrillas lived among the population, "as the people of the island are a unit against us, no case of betrayal has yet occurred. . . . no Judas has been found in the million of people."[13] However, in the latter part of the year a combination of factors—widespread food shortages, more rigorous and effective army counterinsurgency methods, and exactions and abuses by the revolutionaries—caused a progressive alienation of popular support.

A shadow government, or infrastructure, supported the guerrilla bands and ensured popular compliance. In order to feed and pay their men, the revolutionaries raised money through both regular taxation and special duties. Upon moving to a new zone, a guerrilla chief would contact the *presidente* or commissary agent, who would then assign soldiers to homes in the pueblo and assess a contribution of rice and labor from each barrio. In much the same way, the town's militia might be drafted for wire cutting, sabotage, or military operations. Whether correctly or not, the Americans believed that Chinese traders smuggled food, weapons, and military necessities between towns.[14]

The revolutionary taxation system on Panay had been under development for almost two years by the time the Americans occupied the island. Ideally, taxes supported both local guerrilla units and the "state," which in wartime meant the provincial military headquarters. The *presidente,* curate, or local agent collected taxes and contributions, which were stored in hidden warehouses to be turned over to the guerrillas or the zone commissary officer. Delgado, as self-proclaimed head of state, demanded the payment of all the old Spanish taxes and fees and also imposed a weekly and an annual war tax, based on a sliding scale of income. Local chiefs also taxed funerals, fiestas, and luxuries, as well as imposing "voluntary" donations on towns and on wealthy citizens: thus, one *presidente* and other prominent members of his town were given the opportunity to buy 1,800 war bonds—or face execution.[15]

Captured correspondence indicates numerous complaints by revolutionary leaders about the "precarious state of the funds for the maintenance of our forces."[16] Problems seem to have been especially bad in Antique, where an exasperated Fullon declared the entire logistical effort was characterized by "much stupidity."[17] He was especially incensed that local officials hoarded "federal" taxes rather than forward them to his headquarters. He also denounced local guerrilla forces for collecting funds on their own and taking food from warehouses reserved for other units. Throughout Panay, the insurgents faced continual problems with skimming, corruption, unauthorized or duplicate collecting, and forced exactions. One army investigation turned up a commissioner who embezzled 8,000 pesos and two others who had stolen 10,000 pesos each, which they prudently kept in foreign banks.[18]

To ensure compliance, if not loyalty, the guerrillas depended heavily on Panay's elite. This was especially true in Iloilo Province, where Delgado's and Salas's social position and extensive prewar contacts gave them each a considerable personal following. So dependent was the revolutionary leadership on elite participation that one guerrilla leader prohibited anyone but the *presidente* to meet with the Americans; peasants and Chinese were forbidden to speak to soldiers on pain of death.[19]

In October 1900 the Iloilo revolutionary council decided to form secret societies in the occupied towns to oppose the civil governments, distribute propaganda, and strike down traitors.[20] The formation of these societies reflects the enormous importance Panay's revolutionaries attached to preventing collaboration. In October, Delgado's headquarters decried the "disastrous moral effect produced . . . by the innumerable voluntary and other surrenders of prominent persons who filled important offices under the revolution, is undeniable."[21] Officials who took an oath of allegiance to the United States were a special threat, for when they went over, so too did the town, and with it the guerrillas not only lost a source of supplies and manpower but also gained dozens of new enemies. To suppress collaboration, the revolutionaries offered periodic amnesties to those who repented, threatened destruction to towns that cooperated with the Americans, and struck at defectors, spies, and guides whenever they could. Although Delgado was a humane man who tried to maintain some semblance of trial for the accused, some of his subordinates were, in the words of a naval officer, "as inhuman and cruel to their own people as they are to ours."[22] Soldiers encountered gory reminders of summary justice: one friendly old man was beheaded and "all the flesh carved from his frame."[23] Such atrocities gave the guerrilla war on Panay a particular viciousness, in which, shamefully, some American units participated.

The attacks on *americanistas* and others who cooperated, particularly town officials, indicates the growing effectiveness of the U.S. Army's civic action program in late 1900. Following the occupation of the island, the army had moved rapidly to establish municipal governments, and by June had organized twenty-seven municipalities in Iloilo, eight in Capiz, and three in Antique.[24] However, many of these were not in compliance with G.O. 40 or G.O. 43, but rather were temporary governments worked out by the commanding officer and the local officials. The department's pragmatic approach can be seen in the instructions to Capt. Alvin A. Barker of the 26th Infantry, a subdistrict commander in Iloilo Province, that "it is not considered advisable to raise obstacles in the way of either business or social intercourse, and it is very desirable that the people should become acquainted with our people." At an appropriate time, Barker could appoint tax collectors, but he should "go very slow and employ all possible patience and tact, as we do not wish to excite the animosity of our new people through premature efforts to get the legitimate revenues."[25]

In a revealing letter to Otis in March, Hughes explained that the few existing municipal governments on Panay were unsatisfactory, and as a result he had halted their organization: "I use the enemy as an excuse for not doing anything. [I t]ell them there are too many rifles still in the brush to justify my considering the island in a fit state for anything but military rule."[26] Unfortunately, guerrilla opposition, public apathy, and the ineptitude of some of his officers all too often bore out Hughes's dim view of civil government. The dipsomaniac Huston visited the island of Cuyo to investigate reports of starvation. Moved by either alcohol or humanitarian impulses, he organized a civil government and appointed a governor. The governor promptly gathered all the firearms on the island, formed a guerrilla band, and sailed off to Panay to join Fullon. To Hughes, the entire incident demonstrated that "it is useless to help such people. The best visitor there is a gunboat."[27] In a few months, however, he had reversed course and authorized elections for municipalities throughout the department. The results were ambivalent: in the departmental headquarters of Iloilo City, only sixty-five voters braved insurgent retaliation and cast ballots.[28]

Post officers encountered a variety of problems in implementing civic action. The dislocation of agriculture and trade, the ravages of years of war, the death of livestock, poor harvests, banditry, and robberies had impoverished most municipalities. Some towns had lost everything through patriotic donations or revolutionary exactions; others had tampered with their books to avoid this fate. Trying to sort out the provincial records, the department's engineer officer complained that "land is held by the most flimsy titles"; he could not even determine where one municipality began and another ended.[29] It also took time for officers to adjust to local customs. One post officer was surprised when at the end of the first market day his servant presented him with the traditional bribe given to local officials.

Like the problems, the results of civic action varied greatly. Major Edward D. Anderson, who inspected several governments in Iloilo Province, reported that the elections had gone well, good officials had been appointed, schools were set up, and the population was happy to be free of revolutionary exactions. However, Capt. Francis H. French, stationed in Antique Province, commented that the elections for town officials were "a big farce."[30] Along the southern coast, Capt. Barker's inquiries revealed a dramatic contrast between the areas assigned to Capt. John Boardman and Capt. Fred McDonald, both of the 26th Infantry. Boardman worked closely to create local governments and to restore schools, public buildings, and roads and bridges. But McDonald virtually abolished the town councils and governed through the *presidentes*. Barker was also disturbed by evidence that few of McDonald's soldiers were interested in benevolent assimilation; many were guilty of "bullying and petty oppression," which "savors too much of the oppressive methods of the Spaniards we have supplanted."[31] Led by the town police from Guimbal, McDonald claimed to have burned a brigand stronghold near Igbaras, killing fourteen bandits. Barker, however, found evidence that the barrio had been peaceful and the soldiers had opened fire without warning, shot people indiscriminately, and then looted the place.[32]

On Panay, the municipal governments served almost as much as a way to control the population as to protect it. As part of their duties, *presidentes* were required to inform post officers of the location of *ladrones* and insurgents, and the police were expected to serve as guides and auxiliaries. In March, Hughes ordered civic officials to report the arrival and departure of any stranger and to write reports on the character of each inhabitant.[33] In the fall, as part of a concerted campaign against the guerrillas and their sympathizers, the army made the governments even more coercive. Municipal officials and wealthy citizens, who had previously not been required to take an oath of allegiance to the United States, now had to do so or risk prosecution. Those who had taken an oath and were found guilty of assisting the insurgents were subjected to heavy fines and imprisonment. The oath itself became part of a mass declaration of allegiance; in Iloilo City alone, 41,000 people were sworn by January. Having thus committed themselves—and well aware of the drastic penalties the insurgents meted out to collaborators—the population had a vested interest in assisting the army. The revolutionaries denounced the policy of waging war "against the unarmed principal citizens of the town" and claimed further that many of these oaths were exacted under threats of torture or death.[34]

In a well-researched study, John Reed has found a "dark side" to army pacification on Panay: troops burned property and physically abused Filipinos to an extent unusual in the southern Philippines.[35] As noted earlier, property destruction had begun with the burning of Iloilo City during the landings, and Hughes had begun cutting off food to the interior shortly after taking command. But the devastation and mistreatment that occurred on Panay after the occupation of the island were due less to official policies than to the failure of senior commanders to set clear limits on retaliation. Thus, for example, by mid-1900 the 26th Infantry had standing orders to burn any town or barrio from which snipers fired, and to destroy crops and houses used by guerrillas. Officers could confiscate or destroy the property or crops of known or suspected guerrillas. These retaliatory practices not only were authorized army policy and common in the rest of the archipelago but also were quite legal under G.O. 100 and international military law. But on Panay, there were wide variations in how officers chose to enforce the right of retaliation. Some were scrupulously fair: thus Anderson ordered that the houses of two *ladrones* be pulled down "without injury to the rest of the barrio. . . . it will be an object lesson, injuring only those who should be punished."[36] Unfortunately, Anderson appears to have been an exception; in other units it was standard practice to destroy entire villages if contraband articles were found in one or two houses. Troops also burned property in response to specific acts of resistance, such as wire cutting, a tit-for-tat form of retribution that seldom struck at the actual culprits. However, in the Dumangas region—an area characterized both by exceptionally difficult terrain and by a very strong resistance movement—destruction appears to have been adopted as a general policy. In May and June, in response to guerrilla attacks, soldiers began the first of several sweeps of the area, destroying crops, boats, fishing weirs, and houses. This devastation, on an island already suffering from livestock disease, food shortages, and drought, was to have terrible consequences, Nevertheless, Ken De Bevoise overstates in claiming the army engaged in "the wholesale and wanton destruction" of Panay's countryside. Destruction there was, and far too much, but it was hardly wanton; it was directed, albeit with a free hand, at centers of resistance.[37]

Like most of the archipelago, with the exception of a few sweeps or expeditions, the war was restricted to a few dozen square miles—a contest between the garrison and the local guerrillas. The soldiers patrolled the surrounding area, sought *insurrectos* and their agents, guarded against supplies going out of town, and tried to overcome boredom and isolation. Over time, they developed a variety of practical methods to deal with the specific military opposition in their immediate areas. Perhaps typical of this process was the experience of Sgt. Emil Speth, 18th Infantry. Stationed at Dao in Capiz Province, his company had little overt military opposition from the local guerrillas, who were unpopular because of their depredations. In order to augment the infrequent supplies of meat, Speth was ordered to hunt the wild cattle that roamed the hills. Speth selected four guerrilla prisoners and brought them along to transport the meat, allowing them to keep a portion to sell or give to their families. He noted with amusement that they began taking on the Americans' mannerisms and speaking disparagingly of their former comrades. The hunts quickly turned into scouting expeditions; so Speth armed his bearers with rifles and began harassing the local insurgents. Pleased with the results, Speth's commander turned a blind eye to these unauthorized irregulars.[38]

The second phase of the Panay campaign began in late May 1900 with the onset of the rainy season. Guerrillas attacked several towns, but the most se-

U.S. Army patrol

rious fighting occurred in the ten miles of swamps, marshes, tidal streams, and bayous around Dumangas. Garrisoned by an undermanned company of the 26th, this area had long been a source of trouble: in February, Hughes reported it in a "dreadful state" and suggested concentrating the population.[39] On 2 June the guerrillas attacked Barotac Nuevo, wounding three soldiers and setting fire to part of the town before they were driven off. A day later, a neighboring detachment was almost overrun. On 5 June, when it became clear that the town of Dumangas would soon be next, Capt. F. H. Peck and sixty-three soldiers marched to reinforce it. En route, he was fired on, and, following the 26th's standing orders, he set fire to Dumangas. This immediately provoked an attack at close range, which drove the soldiers back into the church and kept them pinned there throughout the night. The next day, the defenders found themselves surrounded by an estimated 1,000 insurgents. Peck sent two detachments with a request for assistance, but when they were both driven back, he decided to break out. He burned everything he couldn't take and, after a one-and-a-half-mile fight, reached Barotac Nuevo, having lost one killed and two wounded, and having expended 4,000 rounds of ammunition.[40]

The response to Peck's ordeal was fast and brutal. Lieutenant Colonel Joseph T. Dickman led a large force back to Dumangas and found that the insurgents had dug up a soldier's grave and burned the corpse. In retaliation, Dickman burned the remainder of the town.[41] Gordon's Scouts arrived and proceeded to conduct a series of "roundups." They surrounded villages and inspected the identification papers of all males of military age; then all suspects would be interrogated or lined up before a concealed defector who would point out guerrillas.[42] On 26 June two companies of the 26th arrived from Iloilo by steamer. They broke through a bamboo barricade at the mouth of a river, fought off an ambush on the riverbanks, and linked up with the scouts; then for a week the combined units moved through the countryside, destroying supplies and skirmishing with the guerrillas. By this time rain and floods had made the countryside virtually impassable, and Salas's irregulars had scattered and hidden; in early July the expedition departed.[43]

In retrospect, the revolutionary resurgence achieved very little beyond harassing several garrisons and bringing down a great deal of destruction on the Dumangas area. The fighting did not spread to Antique or Capiz, and although so stretched out he had to commit most of the Iloilo City garrison, Hughes was able to shift sufficient troops to hold on.[44] Moreover, in at least some towns, the attacks may have alienated the population. On 3 June in Pavia, a town near Iloilo City, the *presidente* was hacked to death. Responding to cries for help, soldiers rushed to the spot and killed four of the attackers and captured a fifth, who divulged they had meant to kidnap the *presidente,* but if he would not cooperate, to kill him, burn Pavia, and then ambush the relieving force. This would, he believed, not only serve a military purpose but "show the people of the U.S. and other countries that the Filipinos were organized and should be recognized." But the population of Pavia was incensed by this attack and, according to the post commander, was now "glad to cooperate with the Americans."[45] This quick-thinking officer destroyed the guerrilla chief's house and donated his land and goods to the residents.

Following the resurgence of fighting in June, Panay reverted to desultory guerrilla war during the monsoon, and it was not until fall that the Americans began their counteroffensive. Reinforced by Col. George S. Anderson's 38th Infantry in November, Hughes concentrated on the troublesome Dumangas area and the mountains on the provincial borders. By rotating in fresh troops, and by dint of Wells's efforts as supply officer, the Americans could keep large columns in the field and thoroughly cover an area. Anderson formed a composite command of artillery, infantry, and cavalry and began cordoning off and attacking guerrilla strongholds. On 22 December, his troops surrounded

Delgado's mountain headquarters and fought their way to the top, destroying large quantities of supplies and ammunition and "completely disorganizing and disintegrating the forces of the enemy."[46] Other mobile forces struck at local jefes. Typical of such units was a 100-man composite company of the 26th, a pack train, a mounted detachment, and a section of local scouts that operated in the Maasin-Leon area in late December. In three columns, it attacked the mountain bases of the zone commander, and on Christmas Day closed in on his main stronghold. At midnight, one detachment began a six-hour climb up a mountain to make the assault; another moved into position to block the retreat; and at daybreak the two columns converged. There was a short skirmish, and the guerrillas broke and fled. The company continued to burn storehouses and supplies in the area until relieved by another mobile column on 3 January.[47]

In addition to the stick of military repression, the Americans also made a strong effort to encourage surrenders. Delegates from Manila and the Committee of the Citizens of Iloilo Province went into the mountains and swamps to negotiate the capitulation of revolutionary leaders. The army established neutral zones for meetings and ordered officers to "take all necessary precautions to prevent any injury or discourtesy shown to the representatives of Sr. Delgado while there."[48] However, there was a limit. When Delgado's lieutenant demanded a suspension of hostilities to discuss terms, Hughes refused: "It is simply a question of submission of persons and arms or the fight goes on."[49]

An important part of the pacification campaign was the dismantling of the guerrilla infrastructure. Well before MacArthur's December proclamation, Panay's officers had recognized the link between the guerrillas and the towns. In the fall, the departmental provost marshal, Capt. Edwin F. Glenn, and several post commanders conducted a series of investigations that rounded up much of the collection network.[50] In October the denunciation of a purchasing agent led to the complete unraveling of the organization in Iloilo City and its environs.

Unfortunately, the army's counteroffensive was accompanied by a great deal of brutality. Although a highly effective intelligence operative, Glenn was completely unprincipled in the means he used. On 27 November, he and a detachment of Gordon's Scouts tortured the *presidente* of the town of Igbaras with the "water cure." They held the man down and forced water down his throat until he confessed that he had warned the guerrillas. Glenn's squad then burned Igbaras, destroying some 5,000 houses, and took the *presidente*, priest, and other civic officials into custody.[51] In January 1901,

Gordon's Scouts went on a rampage near Dumangas, burning much of the area and prompting a flurry of telegrams from Hughes, who wanted property destruction stopped in order to assist negotiations.[52]

By the end of 1900, the combination of negotiations and unremitting military pressure had swung the balance. In December, Delgado received a joint letter from a number of onetime revolutionary leaders, including his chief of staff, urging him to capitulate because further resistance was useless and harmful to the people. Father Praxedes Magalona, his former secretary, shuttled back and forth between Delgado and Hughes until 9 January, when the final negotiations were concluded. On 2 February, Delgado surrendered with 30 officers, 140 riflemen, and a large number of militia. He was quickly followed by most of his zone commanders.[53] Fullon sought terms in February and capitulated on 21 March. Diocno also sought to surrender, but he prevaricated so often that departmental headquarters informed the negotiating officer that much of the population in Iloilo was "ready to go over to Capiz to avenge some of the outrages he and his soldiers committed while he was here and we have plenty of Americans to go along and kill the last Tagalog that is left."[54] This was no bluff, for in late February, Hughes dispatched a large expedition of mounted troops and infantry, complete with supply train, which swept through Capiz Province, captured Diocno, and smashed his guerrilla band.[55] Virtually alone, Salas remained in the Dumangas area until October, when, harried incessantly, he fled to Guimanas Island and surrendered, ending the war on Panay.

TWELVE

NORTHERN LUZON

No matter how rapid or thorough the pacification of the other islands, both Americans and revolutionaries recognized it was on Luzon that the war would be won or lost. It was the largest island, home of half the archipelago's population, the richest and most economically diverse, and the site of the capital city. It was also the home of Aguinaldo and of the strongest military resistance to United States authority. Thus for most of the war, Luzon got the vast bulk of resources—at any one time about four out of every five soldiers in the Philippines were posted there—and the greatest attention by the high command. Indeed, one Visayan officer summed up MacArthur's policy as "simply [to] hold the insurgents in check on the other Islands . . . and crush the rebellion on [Luzon], when it would cease of itself on the others."[1]

Of Luzon's two departments, the more important was the Department of Northern Luzon, an area of 30,000 square miles and nearly 2 million people, and, for much of the war, the home of almost 25,000 officers and men, a grossly insufficient number, but one that represented half the total military forces in the Philippines. Geography divided the department into three virtually autonomous regions—northwest, north, and central—and cultural and linguistic differences further divided the population in each area. The primary question for the department's commander was to which region must he devote the bulk of his limited resources. For most of the war, the top priority was the heavily populated, agriculturally rich Central Luzon Valley, which received over half the total forces. On balance, this was a sound decision, but it was achieved at the cost of leaving peripheral areas such as the north and west drastically undermanned. The dangers of this policy became clear in the fall of 1900, when the revolutionaries launched a series of attacks in an effort to secure victory for William Jennings Bryan.

Northern Luzon's first commander, MacArthur inherited a chaotic situation after the fall 1899 offensive. Much of his five-month tenure was spent trying to reorganize and reconstitute scattered units, link garrisons with roads and telegraphs, establish the department's administration, organize municipal governments and schools, and initiate and monitor a host of other civic action projects. Perhaps distracted by the enormity of his managerial tasks,

U.S. patrol crossing a river

MacArthur noted the growing threat of guerrilla resistance but did not establish a clear pacification policy to deal with it.[2]

Wheaton, who took command of the department on 19 April, is something of a cipher. In contrast to those of his orotund predecessor, Wheaton's annual reports are models of brevity, barely a few pages of summation and a chronology. Never, either during or after the war, did he articulate a broad strategic overview, nor can one be found in the voluminous correspondence sent out from department headquarters. He appears to have had virtually no understanding of the dynamics of Filipino resistance. Indeed, in his final report he made the completely mistaken claim that Northern Luzon's guerrilla resistance had been sustained by the Katipunan and "a system of terror by assassination."[3] From private accounts, it is clear he favored repression over conciliation, telling one correspondent, "It's no use going with a sword in one hand, a pacifist pamphlet in the other and trailing the model of a schoolhouse after you. . . . You can't put down a rebellion by throwing confetti and sprinkling perfumery."[4] Nevertheless, in his first annual report in August 1900 he toed the official line: "The natives, other than the Tagalos, are generally well disposed toward the American occupation, and if protected will aid in the establishing of such form of self-government as they may be able to understand. The mass of the Tagalos, when convinced that we are here to stay and

Troops on patrol, Luzon

that the authority of the United States is to be maintained, will acquiesce, provided they are protected from the men who have dominated them as leaders of the insurrection."[5]

Wheaton's equanimity may have been encouraged by indications that the war was going well: in the six months between April and August, the occupation forces in the department suffered only 41 killed, 73 wounded, and 41 captured or missing, while claiming 1,053 killed and another 1,312 insurgents and 3,412 rifles captured or surrendered. But after a pause during the summer rainy season, the guerrillas resumed their attacks in September, and the number of engagements soared. Not only was there more fighting; it also was far more costly: 34 soldiers were killed and another 103 wounded between September and November alone.[6] Wheaton juggled his forces, stripping one province to rush troops to another, but his options were limited. Frustrated, he responded to his subordinates' demands for reinforcements with a mixture of apology and sarcasm, but with little constructive advice. Like most officers, he viewed MacArthur's December decrees as condoning harsh warfare: one of his first actions was to order all who made contributions to the "Chiefs of Assassins" to be arrested and either tried or deported to Manila.[7] Although the numbers of engagements in the department reached a high of sixty-three in January, American casualties decreased dramatically—

only two soldiers were killed and three wounded that month.[8] Through a variety of measures, ranging from imprisonment, confiscation of crops, destruction of fields and buildings, and forced resettlement of populations, the army quickly stamped out resistance, province by province. By the time Aguinaldo was captured on 23 March, the guerrillas were everywhere on the defensive. In the next two months, 12,000 guerrillas surrendered, turning in 6,000 rifles, and Wheaton declared the department pacified in mid-May.[9]

Since Wheaton believed that the solution to guerrilla warfare was aggressive military operations, he left the imposition of the benevolent aspects of army pacification to the individual district commanders. But with the exception of the 1st District, where civic action programs began virtually at the same time as occupation, most district commanders inherited a patchwork of local governments, schools, municipal engineering, and other civic action efforts. As was often the case, officers from the department commander down to the post officer tended to support most strongly those projects that had military utility. In particular, MacArthur, Wheaton, and district commanders emphasized the construction of roads and telegraph lines before the arrival of the summer monsoon. This was no easy task, for supplies and equipment were so short that one district commander complained: "I have seen natives working with their hands and sharpened sticks on the road. It is not only pityable [sic], but a great waste of labor."[10] But by August Wheaton could report that over 1,000 miles of road had been built. Although they were primarily a means for troops to move rapidly and to obtain supplies, officers believed the roads were vital not only for economic resuscitation but also to "increase [Filipino] interest in civil affairs, especially the better class."[11]

Of the benevolent civic action programs, as opposed to the strictly utilitarian, education was by far the most popular. Perhaps the greatest proponent was Brig. Gen. Samuel B. M. Young. Within six months of taking command of the 1st District, he had established 203 schools serving 10,714 students, roughly 25 percent of the district's total school-age population. His subordinate officers worked closely with civil officials to build schools, to hire teachers, and even to produce a primer in English and Ilocano. As with most army social reform, there was a strong element of enlightened self-interest: education offered the best opportunity to "Americanize the people" and to explain to them their obligations as subjects of the United States.[12]

Municipal government was a far more controversial issue, in part because there was such wide variety in town organization. In 1899 many of the towns along the Manila-Dagupan railway had been created under G.O. 43; others had been formed by ad hoc arrangements between post officers and local officials during the first months of occupation. Although Manila, and periodically Wheaton, urged reforming all municipalities along G.O. 40, many post officers thought it too complicated and inappropriate for their impoverished and depopulated towns. Moreover, there were great divisions among officers over whether the army should organize the towns at all. Some believed their local officials "utterly corrupt" and recommended town government be suspended until armed resistance had ceased; others supported civil government, but only if they were given a completely free hand to organize it.[13] One district commander was appalled when the most promising candidate for provincial governor proudly stated that "he made it a point to be loyal to whatever government actually existed in power, Filipino or American."[14] As with so much of the Philippine War, personal experience colored perception, and garrison commanders only a few dozen miles apart might have very differing views of the benefits of civil government. The conclusion of one district commander—that if the garrison was strong, local governments succeeded "pretty well," but if the area was contested, they "failed utterly"—may be taken to apply to most of Northern Luzon in 1900.[15]

A similar ambivalence characterized the use of Filipinos as auxiliaries. As with municipal government, individual post commanders developed a variety of local police and paramilitary units. Because MacArthur did not clarify the difference between police and scouts until 22 December 1900, it was largely up to post commanders to determine the duties of their local auxiliaries. Some were content to create a token police force, issue it billy clubs or bolos, and limit it to enforcing curfew and sanitary regulations. Others created paramilitary units armed with captured rifles and employed them as infantry or cavalry. In June 1900, MacArthur informed Wheaton of his intention to arm the town police with revolvers and to create a departmental mounted constabulary. But obstruction from district and post commanders and Manila's inability to provide the promised weapons forestalled everything but the most haphazard implementation. The 6th District was typical. In accordance with departmental directives, post commanders dutifully submitted plans for arming their police, but there was such variability in numbers, pay, armament, and responsibilities that no coherent system for the district could be devised. Moreover, Manila's insistence that the police be paid by the towns meant that impoverished and isolated rural areas—the very places where control was most contested—could not afford efficient or reliable police. Even after a great deal of effort, the district commander reported that although some towns had good police forces, throughout the district there had been "little, if any, progress."[16]

The army had far better success with both organized and irregular Filipino paramilitary forces. Of these, the most famous and efficient were the
Macabebes of the Philippine Cavalry. Some commanders trusted them implicitly. After one successful operation, Grant commented, "In the Macabebe
scouts the United States has a loyal servant who can be depended on to pick
out of a crowd of natives, however large, all the insurgents masquerading as
'amigos' and the culprits from other provinces."[17] Others, however, deplored
the "Macs'" penchant for brutality and believed they created more enemies
than they killed. Following a series of rapes and robberies, Lt. Col. E. H.
Plummer asked that the Macabebes be withdrawn from his area, and even
Wheaton, who was not adverse to severe chastisement, became so angered
at Macabebe excesses that he ordered a district commander "to enforce discipline on these savages at all hasards [*sic*]."[18] But such professions of shock
must be taken with a grain of salt. Within a month of demanding the recall
of the Macabebes, Plummer threatened residents with their return if they did
not cooperate against the guerrillas.[19] For their part, Batson and his fellow
officers defended the Macabebes and deplored the credulity of post officers
for accepting insurgent-generated tales, "as though this was simply a horde
of savages we have turned loose on the country."[20]

Departmental officers also raised a number of other scout units. Some
were recognized by Manila, whereas others were entirely due to the initiative of local commanders and were, in some cases, in direct contravention of
existing orders. In the 1st District, for example, Young and his officers employed the Guardia de Honor sect to hunt down guerrillas but pretended
ignorance when queried by Manila. The commander of the 2nd District, Col.
Charles G. Hood, raised several detachments and finally persuaded Manila
to recognize them as the Cagayan Scouts. In the 4th District, Brig. Gen.
Frederick Funston, its commander, and Col. Lyman W. Kennon overcame
the reluctance of Wheaton and MacArthur and obtained permission to raise
100 Ilocano Scouts, increased to 240 in January 1901. Kennon, the self-
proclaimed "Father of the Ilocanos," moved far beyond Funston's own directives and used large numbers of Ilocanos on military operations as porters,
boatmen, and guides, as well as forming an armed militia in the Ilocano towns.
Other officers, if not as enthusiastic as Kennon, were quick to use captured
insurrectos to identify their former comrades and to rely on *americanistas*
for information. In general, the longer an officer was assigned to a particular town or province, the better his contacts with the local population and
the more willing he was to raise auxiliaries.[21]

Such generalizations about the overall pattern of the army's pacification
efforts in the Department of Northern Luzon—and especially their civic action

aspect—need to be examined in light of the separate regional campaigns in the three major areas: the northwest, north, and center. As noted earlier, terrain and ethnic differences ensured that there would be three virtually independent wars, each of which must be studied in turn.

The war in the 1st District in northwestern Luzon has been covered extensively in other works, and thus can be dealt with only briefly.[22] The district comprised the four Ilocano provinces of La Union, Ilocos Norte, Ilocos Sur, and Abra and three ungarrisoned mountain provinces of Benguet, Bontoc, and Lepanto—an area of 8,000 square miles and a population of 530,000. Otis assigned Young a modest 4,000-man occupation force—the 3rd Cavalry, the 33rd Infantry, a battalion of the 34th, and, after March, the 48th Infantry—and ordered him to begin organizing civil governments immediately. Both Otis and Young believed that the reputed antipathy between Tagalogs and Ilocanos and an immediate demonstration of benevolence would quickly convert the population, and thus the district would serve almost as a laboratory for civil action. Young and his brilliant chief of staff, Maj. John G. Ballance, embarked on a comprehensive effort to build roads and schools, establish financial solvency, and bring order and good government to the population. These efforts were contested by Manuel Tinio, ably seconded by local commanders such as Juan and Blas Villamor, who established shadow governments, revived the militia, and coordinated the guerrilla regulars. Within a few months of Young's arrival, his patrols were ambushed, his supply lines raided, his communications destroyed, and his contacts among the population kidnapped and killed. The sanguine Otis dismissed Young's demands for reinforcements as pessimistic, but MacArthur considered the area the worst in Luzon.[23]

In March and April the army achieved two crucial breakthroughs. The first occurred in La Union Province, where Lt. William T. Johnston formed a close alliance with Crispulo Patajo and his Guardia de Honor sect. In a series of campaigns, combined Fil-American patrols rounded up both the guerrillas and the *principales* in the town who provided clandestine support. Equally important, Johnston's report on his investigations provided the first comprehensive study of the nature of Filipino guerrilla resistance and had a profound influence on MacArthur's policies.[24] The second was in Ilocos Norte, where in April Father Gregorio Aglipay organized a Katipunan society and appealed to Ilocanos to take up arms to defend their faith. Lieutenant Colonel Robert L. Howze, the province's commander, learned of the revolt and launched a series of preemptive strikes that dispersed the guerrilla regulars. Lacking firearms and discipline, Aglipay's followers launched mass assaults on two towns on the nights of 15 and 16 April: more than 300 were killed, with negligible American casualties. After a short grace period to allow hundreds of demoralized Katipuneros to surrender, Howze's soldiers, aided by Filipinos outraged by the attacks on their homes, drove most of them out of the province.[25]

Drawing on the lessons of these two campaigns, 1st District headquarters developed a series of effective counterinsurgency policies. A pass system restricted all travel, and civil officials were required to report any visitors—measures that severely restricted the guerrillas' movements and hampered their suppliers. In June, headquarters issued those provisions of G.O. 100 that outlined the penalties for guerrilla activity. A 250-man unit of Ilocano Scouts was raised, and hundreds of other auxiliaries, some of them Guardias, were employed as paramilitary forces. Nevertheless, in the fall of 1900, the 1st District was the scene of some of the heaviest fighting of the guerrilla war. In an effort to influence the elections, the insurgents launched a series of attacks, striking at garrisons, supply lines, and patrols. The fighting was particularly serious in previously quiescent Abra Province, where Juan Villamor had developed a well-armed guerrilla band and an impressive logistical network. In a series of well-executed ambushes, he all but cut off traffic on the Abra River, the main route into the province, and besieged the towns. The renewal of fighting pushed the already frustrated Young to the edge. After first claiming he was in danger of being overwhelmed, he urged his superiors to implement a policy of blanket repression, including eye-for-an-eye retaliation, the relocation or expulsion of civilians from hostile zones, the devastation of crops and homes, and summary execution of guerrillas. Although his superiors would not countenance these measures, they were sufficiently alarmed to rush reinforcements, so that troop strength increased to almost 6,000. Disturbed by Young's open challenge to the army's policy of "benevolent assimilation," they arranged for his replacement in February by Brig. Gen. J. Franklin Bell.[26]

By December, Young had recovered his spirits and was conducting a highly effective, if brutal, pacification campaign. Columns scoured the mountains, scattering detachments, burning storehouses, and driving the partisans out of their sanctuaries. Johnston and Patajo, now promoted to chief of detectives for the district, investigated the shadow governments in the towns and arrested numerous agents. Young secured the support of the clergy to stage quasi-religious ceremonies in which hundreds swore to accept United States authority. Soldiers confiscated the property of rebel sympathizers or turned it over to the population. The most rigorous campaign was in Abra, which was placed under a commercial interdict. In areas where guerrilla activity was especially strong, the army forced the population in outlying areas to move to protected zones and then destroyed crops and buildings, effectively starving out Villamor's partisans and forcing his surrender on 29 April. He was soon followed by Tinio, Aglipay, and dozens of guerrilla soldiers. By May, resistance was effectively over, and Villamor was being cultivated to assume the governorship of Abra.

The 2nd District comprised the northeastern provinces of Cagayan, Isabela, and Nueva Viscaya, an area of 11,800 square miles but with a population of little more than 200,000. The inhabitants were divided between peaceful farmers and warlike mountaineers, collectively termed Igorrotes. Convinced that Tirona's surrender in December had virtually pacified the area, Manila assigned Colonel Hood his own 16th Infantry and eight companies of African-American Volunteers from the 49th Infantry, roughly 2,000 soldiers. Hood stationed the bulk of the 16th at his headquarters at Aparri and in the coastal towns, and the 49th in towns along the Cagayan River and its tributaries. The vast distances—the 49th's posts extended over 170 miles—and the absence of roads, transport, and telegraph lines all inhibited command and control. Hood accepted these limitations and did little to impose district-wide policies on his scattered forces.[27]

Believing the area was essentially peaceful, the Americans devoted much of their attention to establishing the framework of colonial government. Because of distance or Manila's oversight, post officers often failed to receive the orders specifying the forms for local government and had to create their own institutions. At times, they found their views of proper conduct challenged by local customs. In one bizarre case, a mother and daughter assisted the murderer of the mother's lover. The post officer concluded that they were undoubtedly guilty, "but considering their state of civilization, they have perhaps conformed to their code of honor in shielding the accused," and recommended they not be prosecuted.[28]

As in most other areas, civil action had a practical as well as a humanitarian side. Colonel William H. Beck was furious when soldiers from his 49th Infantry stole two of the ritual axes the mountaineers used to decapitate their enemies, for it threatened to alienate a group who would be "invaluable as guides and scouts" and who could supply American expeditions into the mountains.[29] Similarly, Maj. Carter P. Johnson urged the construction of roads, both because they were "productive to the civilization of the country" and because they would allow troops to move rapidly.[30] He also recommended that civic officials be allowed to arrest "Tagalos and other natives of Bad character" and either deport or imprison them.[31]

Although the Americans faced a disorganized and dispersed resistance in the 2nd District, their manpower shortage allowed guerrillas to operate with relative impunity in the mountainous upper regions of the Cagayan River. For the most part, the irregulars confined their activities to recruiting, occasional sniping, and collecting contributions, and the district's soldiers could do little to stop them.[32] In April, however, captured correspondence revealed Aguinaldo planned to link up with Tinio on the borders of Cagayan and Abra Provinces. From mid-April to early June, hundreds of soldiers from the 1st and 2nd Districts swept this mountainous border area in a series of poorly coordinated expeditions. They narrowly failed to capture Aguinaldo but broke up the guerrilla concentration, inflicted a number of casualties, and forced the ex-president back into the wilds of Isabella Province.[33]

For most of 1900, conditions in the 2nd District remained in equilibrium, with neither side able to inflict much serious damage; entire months went by without any fighting. However, in the fall there was a dramatic upsurge as the district's guerrillas joined in the campaign to assist Bryan's election. Guerrilla wire cutting virtually isolated the 49th's garrisons in the upper Cagayan and its tributary, the Chico. Lacking cavalry to patrol the area or maintain communications among the garrisons, the regiment was in a perilous position indeed. The most serious fight was at Tuao (Santo Nino), located in the Rio Chico Valley, where 250 insurgents infiltrated the town and attacked the nineteen-man garrison. The assault began at midnight when a five-pound stone cannonball crashed into the troops' barracks, followed by a wave of bolomen. Under the leadership of their noncoms, the Volunteers beat off attacks with Krag volleys, rendering the barracks "as bloody as a slaughter pen."[34] Major Johnson interviewed the prisoners and found them all "laboring men" who said the attack was to have been the signal for a general assault on the Chico River garrisons. Although convinced that the "influential people" were behind the uprising, Johnson despaired of securing adequate testimony for conviction because any witnesses "would have their mouths cut off if they told anything they knew to an American."[35] Nevertheless, he believed the defense of Tuao had aborted insurgent plans to attack the garrisons along the Chico and that the refusal of many Filipinos to participate showed the fragility of the movement.

With McKinley's election, the guerrillas' small offensive petered out: in December a twenty-one-man patrol swept the Chico Valley, fought only a few skirmishes, and reported the insurgents had all but disappeared. In January there was only one minor engagement in which a twelve-man patrol stampeded a guerrilla band and destroyed its stores, and in February there were none of any kind. The last serious fight was on 9 March, when a paymaster's escort was attacked—perhaps by insurgents, perhaps by bandits—and one soldier was killed. Thereafter, armed resistance was all but abandoned. The

Americans could not force the guerrillas into battle, but, by making good use of mounted infantry and local guides, they were able to keep their opponents dispersed, to destroy storehouses and depots, and, through the capture of lists of contributors, to dismantle the guerrillas' supply organization. The entries in the journal of guerrilla Telesforo Carrasco during this period offer a grim view of the collapse of resistance. Unremittingly pursued for weeks at a time, surprised when they attempted to rest, ambushed on trails and in villages, driven from their supply depots and local connections, their supporters' homes and crops burned, Carrasco's company disintegrated in March. In May, after meeting with members of the Federal Party, Carrasco himself surrendered, by which time resistance had all but ceased throughout the 2nd District.[36]

The victories in the northern provinces were gratifying, but for Wheaton the most important districts were the 3rd, 4th, 5th, and 6th, which ran from Manila up the Central Luzon Plain and included the provinces of Morong, Bulacan, Pangasinan, Tarlac, Pampanga, and Nueva Ecija. Flanked by mountains to the east and west, the plain was watered by three major river systems: the Agno, which flowed north into Lingayen Gulf, and the Rio Grande and Rio Chico, which flowed south, joining near the towering volcanic cone of Mount Arayat and emptying into Manila Bay. The population of over 1 million was divided into four semihostile linguistic and cultural groups—Tagalogs, Pampangans, Pangasinans, and Ilocanos. In the last decades of the nineteenth century, the region had undergone rapid agricultural development: new areas had been brought under cultivation, immigrants had poured in, and agriculture had shifted from subsistence to large commercial rice and sugar cultivation. With economic change came social change: a new trading class emerged, many of the peasants were uprooted, and many others were forced into debt peonage. Some fled into the swamps and mountains, where they joined the bands of *ladrones* who had flourished for decades. By the beginning of the Philippine War, Central Luzon was torn by ethnic and socioeconomic strife. As Gen. Luciano San Miguel complained, in their efforts to mobilize popular support, the revolutionaries were often caught between "the policy of attraction employed by the enemy on one side and . . . brigandage on the other."[37]

The guerrillas in Central Luzon were further hampered by disorganization, decentralization, and outright insubordination. In November 1899, as part of his shift from conventional to guerrilla war, Aguinaldo made his friend and chief of staff, Maj. Gen. Pantaleon Garcia, the supreme jefe of Central Luzon. Garcia had gained a distinguished combat record dating back to 1896 and was a strong proponent of irregular warfare, but he was also a Manilero with no local base of support. Moreover, much of his new command was already occupied, and the rest would soon be overrun by MacArthur's and Lawton's forces. The American offensive, the rapid disintegration of the Army of Liberation, and the return of its soldiers to their native villages meant Garcia inherited a resistance movement that was demoralized and in disarray. A stronger personality might have risen to the challenge, but Garcia was exhausted from years of warfare and suffering from lingering illness. One of his first actions was to suspend all military operations until guerrilla forces could be reorganized. He then implicitly confirmed his lack of real authority on 9 January 1900 by recognizing as virtually independent the *jefes politico-militars* of each province: Francisco Macabulos for Tarlac; Jose Alejandrino for Pangasinan; Maximo Hizon for Pampanga; Pablo Padilla for Nueva Ecija; Isidro Torres and Pio del Pilar for Bulacan. By the time he declared a resumption of hostilities, he had almost no authority at all. In May, after an abortive attempt to organize attacks on garrisoned towns, he and most of his staff were captured.

Garcia's authority was assumed by Alejandrino. A native of Pampanga and a European-trained engineer, Alejandrino was a protégé of Luna and very much outside the Aguinaldo circle. The president, who apparently did not learn of Garcia's capture until October, was furious at what he viewed as an usurpation. He appointed his cousin, Baldomero Aguinaldo, the new jefe of Central Luzon and ordered Alejandrino arrested. But, as with many of the fugitive president's decrees, his writ carried no power. Apparently unwilling to press the issue, Baldomero remained in Cavite and Alejandrino remained the titular head of Central Luzon. Although MacArthur and Wheaton were convinced Alejandrino was the heart of the resistance, he himself felt it merited only a page in his autobiography. Traveling constantly and accompanied by a small entourage, he never participated in military operations, and his authority was dependent on whether his subordinates chose to accept it. Some, such as the Tecson brothers, remained loyal, but others, most notably Tomas Mascardo, the jefe of Zambales and Bataan, refused to accept any direction at all.[38]

The disagreements at the top of the guerrilla ranks percolated into the lower levels, where they were intensified by the death or capture of several leaders. Resistance in Nueva Ecija was badly damaged by the capture of Garcia in April and of the two provincial jefes the following month. Although Brig. Gen. Urbano Lacuna arrived from Bulacan to revive the movement in that province, he and his 200 regulars remained outsiders who had great difficulty establishing a supply system and securing recruits. A somewhat similar situation occurred in Tarlac, in the northwest, where the two major local leaders, Servillano Aquino and Macabulos, surrendered in June 1900. Alejandrino appointed Alipio Tecson as the provincial jefe, but the movement never recovered. In Bulacan Province, site of Lawton's earlier campaign, the surrender of Pio del Pilar in June removed a popular and effective leader. The insurgents in Pampanga Province also encountered severe problems in winning over the public, in part due to the Macabebes' opposition and to the apathy of the Pampanguenos. Their jefe, Hizon, was captured in June, and none of his subordinates succeeded in welding together that province's military forces.[39]

Because of the fragmentation at the top, it is difficult to evaluate the resistance movements' military forces, clandestine supply networks, and popular support. Guerrilla bands tended to remain small and mobile: Colonel Pablo Tecson, one of the best commanders, described his unit as some twenty-five regulars; "the main part are laborers and return to their work after a battle."[40] Weapons were in very short supply; one column leader had only thirty cartridges for his twelve rifles and confessed he was incapable of attacking even weak enemy patrols. Recognizing their weakness, the guerrillas relied on tactics that emphasized fighting from ambush, firing only a few volleys before retreating: the goal was not to defeat the Americans but to inflict casualties and wear them down.[41] The revolutionary jefes made numerous appeals to patriotism and self-interest, promised that McKinley would be defeated and Bryan elected, and exhorted Filipinos to remember that death was better than slavery. Decrees forbade officeholders from serving in the American-sponsored civil governments and threatened increasingly dire consequences.[42] In July, Teodoro Sandico issued detailed instructions for the formation of a "national committee of patriots" in each province, town, and barrio, which would ignite patriotism in the population, recruit a militia, assist the guerrillas with money and supplies, organize guides and saboteurs, and organize a secret police to hunt down *americanistas*.[43]

As in most of the Philippines, the revolutionaries' efforts to establish shadow governments met with uneven success. In some places clandestine agents and Katipunan societies provided support and succor for local guerrilla bands. This was particularly true in isolated, mountainous, swampy, or border regions. But in many other areas the guerrillas remained marginalized outsiders who were viewed by the inhabitants as another foreign oppressor to be placated or, eventually, to be hunted down and destroyed. The incessant reissue of decrees encouraging patriotism and forbidding collaboration implies their failure as either motivators or deterrents. To secure popular support, the predominantly Tagalog revolutionaries had to overcome decades of mistrust from Pampanguenos, Ilocanos, and Pangasinans, and all too often they failed. In Pampanga the Macabebes remained implacably hostile, and many other Pampaguenos were indifferent. In the 4th District, Tagalog guerrillas murdered a prominent Ilocano leader, opening a bitter conflict that the Americans exploited to the full, recruiting 400 Ilocano Scouts and hundreds of auxiliaries. Tarlac and Pangasinan were ethnically divided; in both provinces the Guardia de Honor continued its long war with the revolutionaries.[44]

The lack of consistent popular support presented the revolutionaries with a dilemma. They recognized, as Garcia wrote to Torres, that "if we do not endeavor to gain the good will of the people our efforts will have been in vain."[45] But at the same time, guerrilla bands needed food, money, recruits, information, and shelter, whether granted willingly or unwillingly. Driven by such practical necessities, guerrilla leaders interfered in civil affairs, demanding supplies and taxes and dismissing officials whom they considered inefficient or disloyal. But such actions, although meeting immediate needs, alienated the population and imperiled resources in the future.[46] Nevertheless, in some areas the population was so apathetic or hostile that one guerrilla leader predicted "it will be necessary that four or five lives be taken in each town" before clandestine governments could be established and popular compliance assured.[47]

Although neither Garcia nor Alejandrino authorized terrorism as a strategy, the evidence suggests that it was increasingly employed in the battle for control of the population. Guerrillas routinely sent rifle fire crashing into occupied towns or burned houses to create a climate of fear and anxiety, and to demonstrate that the Americans could not protect the inhabitants. Such indiscriminate harassment was supplemented by attacks on selected *americanistas* and civil officials. In 1900 in the four districts that shared Central Luzon at least 204 Filipinos were killed for cooperating with the Americans and another 167 were assaulted.[48] Such appalling statistics led Wheaton to refer to "an insurrection of assassins," and James A. LeRoy to claim that "coercion and brutality were, from first to last, more in evidence in Central Luzon, the chief theater of warfare, than in all other regions of the archipelago combined."[49] Terrorism was initially effective in isolating the garrisons, hindering civic action, discouraging cooperation, and denying information. But repeated threats and atrocities ultimately provoked the courage of despair: in order to protect themselves, noncombatants had to provide information and support to the Americans.[50]

Against this fragmented resistance, army pacification consisted primarily of garrisoning the most important towns and "the extension of a vast police system for the protection of the inhabitants."[51] Most of the troops' duties were tied directly to security. With the assistance of police and civil officials, they kept order in the municipality and investigated any suspicious activity. They manned outposts that inspected traffic along the roads, patrolled the surrounding countryside, searched houses, and conducted sweeps of neighboring barrios. Mounted infantry, elite scout detachments, and the Macabebes of the Philippine Cavalry operated as long-range reconnaissance and strike forces, scouring the mountains and swamps to locate guerrilla camps, disrupt their supply system, and capture couriers. After obtaining sufficient information, district commanders worked together to create expeditionary forces of several hundred soldiers and launch cordon-and-sweep operations. Large battles were uncommon, and there were relatively few casualties on either side. In its entire sixteen months of service in the 5th District's Pampanga Province, the 41st Infantry lost only two soldiers killed in action, and its official history reveals that entire months went by without inflicting a single fatality on the enemy. Yet despite its lack of combat activity, the regiment received a steady stream of rifles captured or surrendered—thirty-six in March 1900, twenty-two in April, ninety-eight in May—telling evidence of both the demoralization of the guerrilla opposition and the progress of pacification.[52]

Because of the weak resistance they faced in early 1900—a result of the disorganization following the 1899 offensive and the guerrillas' suspension of military operations—army officers were initially quite optimistic about the situation in Central Luzon. A survey of conditions in the 6th District, immediately north of Manila, concluded that the population was friendly and that opposition came only from small groups of bandits. The 35th Infantry, stationed in Bulacan Province, had but eleven skirmishes and not a single casualty between 3 December 1899 and 7 April 1900. Conditions were so peaceful in the 4th District that in January the district commander rode across much of it accompanied by only two escorts. That same month, the 3rd District commander reported that the "better elements" of the Army of Liberation had all returned home and that the first priority was to protect the population, even if that meant stretching troops dangerously thin in order to garrison each town. But he also warned that north Central Luzon was "infested by small bands of 'Tulisanes' [brigands] partly armed and largely composed of flotsam and jetsam from the wreck of the insurrection" and that terrain and logistical difficulties precluded active military operations against them.[53]

During this period of relative inactivity, the army attempted to mop up the few remaining bands that remained from the Lawton-MacArthur offensive. The most serious fighting was against Gen. Servillano Aquino's guerrillas, who operated along the western mountains of the Bataan-Zambales border and in Pampanga Province. On 5 January a combined force of some 300 soldiers from the 25th Infantry under the overall command of Capt. Harry Leonhaeuser swept the area near Mount Arayat. Dividing into two columns, the men pushed on along narrow trails obstructed by felled trees and traps. The skirmishing gradually increased to a full-fledged firefight, with soldiers and guerrillas blazing away at shadowy figures in the brush. Leonhaeuser sent Lt. William T. Schenck's scout detachment to climb a hill on the left from which much of the firing was coming. The men crawled up the steep slope through brush and vines so thick that they often were on their stomachs, all the time taking heavy fire from the crest. When Schenck was close to the top, he spotted an *insurrecto* only fifty feet away. A close-range sniping contest ensued, which became desperate when the entire enemy force—some seventy soldiers—realized that Schenck had only five soldiers with him and poured on a heavy fire. To make it worse, Leonhaeuser's men fired back from below, catching the scouts in a terrible cross fire. As Schenck recalled, "I curled up like a worm to make a small target . . . and yelled like a stuck pig to cease firing."[54] After several hectic minutes, he managed to crawl down the hill, scrape together a small force, and drive the stubborn guerrillas off. Scouting the area, Schenck discovered he had fought his way into Aquino's main camp. He also saw something that enraged him: Aquino, or his subordinates, had forced five American prisoners of war to kneel and then shot and stabbed them, killing all but two. Perhaps aware of the consequences of his crime, Aquino and his men vanished, emerging only to surrender a few months later.

The tempo of the war escalated in March as both sides became more aggressive. Alejandrino, Garcia, Lacuna, Torres, and Padilla combined their forces for an attack on Penaranda, Nueva Ecija, in Funston's 4th District. But as he did so often, Funston struck first. On 18 March he sent a mixed force of soldiers and Macabebes against the guerrilla camp at "Fort Rizal"; after a stiff battle he routed them with heavy losses, broke them into small detachments, and drove them into the hills.[55] To the southwest in the 5th District, Brig. Gen. Frederick D. Grant put together a composite force of two gunboats, several hundred soldiers, and Lt. Col. William E. Wilder's Macabebes and swept the Rio Grande delta to Manila Bay. Macabebe *bancas* successfully traversed the otherwise impassable swamps and forced the heretofore protected guerrillas into the towns, where they were quickly identified and arrested. Several rifles were captured, and many others were surrendered. Unfortunately, the operation also revealed a less savory aspects of Macabebe behavior: on 23 March the scouts' 130 prisoners "were all killed in an attempt to escape."[56] That same day, a captain in the 41st Infantry returned from a patrol and reported: "I found the natives every where terror stricken at the approach of the Macabebes, the natives charge these troops with indiscriminate slaughter of inoffensive citizens, the rape of women and [the] burning of barrios without cause or provocation. From my personal observation these charges seem to be true in part at least."[57] Both Wilder and Grant defended the scouts and claimed their accusers were known *insurrectos,* some of whom had made complaints even before the scouts arrived.[58]

April and May witnessed a number of engagements, as both sides sought a military advantage before the start of the monsoon. In Tarlac the 9th and 17th Infantry achieved a major success when they assaulted Macabulos's camp on 7 April. Aggressive patrolling swept up the scattered survivors, including Macabulos's wife, who was prominently lodged in the capital city, presumably as a symbol of American benevolence.[59] The Bulacan–Nueva Ecija border, shared by the 4th and 5th Districts, was the site of particularly heavy fighting. On 25 May Col. Pablo Tecson's Bulacan guerrillas surprised Capt. Charles D. Roberts and a six-man 35th Infantry patrol as they ate lunch, killing three and capturing Roberts and two others (in a humanitarian act, Tecson released a severely wounded soldier). Wheaton reacted with considerable speed. Grant and Funston stripped their garrisons to token forces—the 35th even assigned its regimental band to guard the supply train—and sent cavalry and infantry in pursuit. The result was a series of bloody confrontations. With 200 well-armed regulars, the Tecson brothers—Pablo, Alipio, and Simon—had constructed a number of fortresses in the mountains, and these they defended with considerable skill. On 4 June Company E of the 35th was ambushed as it crossed a river; a few miles away, Maj. Albert Laws's battalion of the same regiment encountered a strong force dug in on a steep hill. Laws ordered Lt. Grover Flint to flank the enemy, but this detachment also was ambushed by guerrillas who waited until the soldiers were thirty yards away, then rose from their concealed trenches and wounded Flint and two others. A relief party stumbled on yet another concealed trench line and was itself pinned down. Eventually a third detachment found that flanking was impossible: the guerrilla position was protected on both sides by gorges. Unable to withdraw or attack, the battalion was pinned down until the guerrillas withdrew. The two engagements cost the 35th one killed and ten wounded—30 percent of the regiment's casualties during its tour of service. The campaign destroyed supply dumps and broke up guerrilla concentrations, but it failed to recapture Roberts.[60]

Unfortunately for the guerrillas, the success of 4 June was not typical, and the summer witnessed a steady deterioration of their strength. In Nueva

Ecija, Lacuna's band was ambushed on 14 June and lost twenty-two killed; the Tecsons' assaults on three towns were beaten off with heavy casualties in July. The capture of Lacuna's chief tax collector—along with the names of his major contributors—dealt a shattering blow to the Nueva Ecija resistance. In Pampanga, garrisons drove off a series of attacks in May and June and captured Aquino's personal correspondence. Even more significant, captures and surrenders removed much of the revolutionaries' upper leadership. On 11 June a patrol from the 41st Infantry captured Hizon, the jefe of Pampanga, and shortly afterward, following extensive negotiations, Aquino surrendered as well, virtually ending resistance in that province. The tiny resistance movement in Pangasinan was badly damaged when Lt. Col. Roberto Grassa surrendered in June. In May, a captured guerrilla officer whom the Americans had appointed *presidente* of Tarlac City negotiated the surrender of Maj. Geronimo Velasco with 178 men and 168 rifles. Impressed by his good treatment and by the thirty pesos he received for each rifle, Velasco returned to the bush and on 26 May brought in another forty-nine guerrillas and fifty-five rifles. Velasco's surrender prompted a rash of capitulations in Tarlac. Discouraged by a string of defeats and the capture of his wife, Macabulos began negotiating through his wife with Col. Emerson Liscum of the 9th Infantry. After the colonel promised to pay thirty pesos a rifle and, perhaps most important, reported Macabulos had been cleared of complicity in the murder of a soldier, the general surrendered 174 guerrillas and 200 rifles in June.[61] Even the Tecsons opened negotiations with the Americans, releasing Roberts and his men on 13 June as a sign of their good faith. Their envoy reported that they had only 200 men with them and that "there is at present a feeling of great hopefulness among the Filipinos that the insurrection will be brought to a speedy end by amicable arrangements between the American and Filipino authorities."[62] Only the July to October monsoon, which washed out roads, disrupted supplies, sent sick rates soaring, and ended military operations, prevented further surrenders and perhaps the end of resistance.

In September and October, in an effort to influence the presidential elections in the United States, the guerrillas made one last attempt to regain the initiative. They ambushed isolated detachments and supply trains and stepped up their attacks on towns, firing into them at night, burning houses, and otherwise seeking to demonstrate that the army could not protect the populace.[63] But as in the 1st District, this incited a far more thorough counteroffensive from the Americans when the rainy season ended in November. In retaliation, soldiers destroyed the houses and confiscated the property of revolutionary leaders. Indicative of a new, harsher attitude, Wheaton directed one regimental commander about to undertake operations that "guerrillas . . . will be attacked, hunted down and shot or dispersed."[64] Among the more vociferous in urging that "the time has arrived when punishment must be meted out to the hostiles in order that decisive actions may shorten our work in the field" was 3rd District commander Brig. Gen. Jacob H. Smith.[65] He bitterly complained that his officers were overly lenient and cautioned them to remember that "many who apparently are friendly to the Americans rule are guilty of the blackest treachery and all officers are warned not to allow their suspicions to be lulled to sleep by friendly association and social intercourse with the native inhabitants."[66] His solution would become all too clear on Samar.

By November, the American counteroffensive was in full swing as district commanders pursued the guerrillas into previously inaccessible areas. Typical of these was an operation staged on the border of the 5th and 6th Districts. Early in the month, a patrol captured the correspondence of the local *jefe*, Licerio Geronimo, which revealed both his civilian contacts and the location of many of the *insurrecto* camps. As a result, a number of civil officials were arrested, and others were put on notice that their continued freedom depended on their cooperation. On the sixteenth, Grant began sweeping the mountainous area in southeast Bulacan, driving guerrillas south toward Col. J. Milton Thompson's 6th District. A few days later, Thompson sent an 823-man provisional force of 27th and 41st Infantry in four columns to the northeast. On the twenty-second, 350 soldiers attacked Geronimo's stronghold and after a two-hour fight broke into the camp and destroyed fifty buildings and vast quantities of rice, meat, and other supplies. Geronimo's partisans scattered, only to find that the arrest of most of the infrastructure had cut them off from food and shelter. In the following weeks, the district troops conducted a series of patrols and roundups, marching late at night, surrounding isolated barrios, and searching them for guerrillas, weapons, and supplies.[67]

In the fall campaign, district commanders devoted great attention to cutting the guerrillas off from supplies and destroying their storehouses. Encouraged by MacArthur's 23 December declaration, post officers purged their towns, breaking up the clandestine supply system and arresting civilians "where even a suspicion exists of the questionable loyalty of the suspect."[68] As army efforts expanded, guerrillas who sought food and shelter found themselves increasingly unpopular. A post officer in Pampanga reported in February: "There is nothing of importance going on in this district, only small detachments of collectors of rice and money can be found and they treat the people very harshly and are doing our cause good."[69] Caught between the army and the guerrillas, some villagers requested they be allowed to store their foodstuffs in the town. The Americans encouraged this form of population concentration: "I think it is necessary that these people be given a chance to bring their rice in otherwise it will cause great hardship and privation to a large number of people who are not taking part in the Insurrection and will necessitate the Govt aid in feeding them."[70] In January, Grant ordered troops to accompany villagers on expeditions to seize rice and other crops and bring them into towns to distribute to the destitute. The following month, he directed his troops into the field to confiscate or destroy all remaining crops in areas of guerrilla activity, especially foothills and mountains, on the grounds that the "residents are either insurgents or working for insurgents."[71] Unable to tend their fields and facing the prospect of famine, entire villages turned on the guerrillas and attacked them.

The resistance in Central Luzon collapsed more with a whimper than a bang. By early 1901, commanders in Pampanga Province were reporting that "it seems to be the only object now of the insurgents to collect money and gather rice."[72] Hungry, constantly on the run, and denied shelter, the guerrillas simply quit fighting. Indeed, throughout Central Luzon *insurrecto*-initiated engagements had virtually ceased by the end of January. The last military engagement in Pangasinan was on 28 November, and the capture of Alipio Tecson in January ended fighting in Tarlac. On 28 December, 5th District soldiers located one of Alejandrino's camps, and although the jefe escaped, they destroyed buildings and a great deal of supplies.[73] The increasing pressure fragmented guerrilla bands, as some sought to surrender, others to disperse, and still others to continue the fight. Lacuna had to threaten his officers with death for their failure to fight, and in February Pablo Tecson attacked and captured several of his brother Simon's men as they gathered to surrender. On 12 February, MacArthur proclaimed the virtual end of resistance in Central Luzon, a claim that was only off by a few months. By March the entire 6th District was cleared, and fighting was over in the 3rd and 5th by the end of April, a month that saw Alejandrino surrender as well. The last holdout was Lacuna in the 4th District, who brought his men in on 19 May, a day that also marked the end of resistance throughout the Department of Northern Luzon.[74]

Somewhat ironically, the army's pacification campaign in the Department of Northern Luzon is remembered not for any of the regional campaigns but for an event that is often cited, somewhat mistakenly, as the turning point of the war: Funston's capture of Emilio Aguinaldo. Like many Philippine War incidents, this episode is shrouded in myth and controversy, with Funston alternately a daring hero and a duplicitous publicity seeker.

After his unsuccessful attempt to link up with Tinio in April 1900, Aguinaldo had retreated into Isabella Province, and in September settled at Palanan, a village about ten miles from the coast. A network of spies, informants, couriers, and watch posts provided ample warning against any army patrols. Early in February 1901, as a result of an investigation that had begun six months earlier, Lt. James D. Taylor secured the surrender of several guerrillas, one of whom confessed to having met Aguinaldo at Palanan in December. A few days later this man brought in another insurgent officer, Cecilio Segismundo, who surrendered enciphered correspondence from Aguinaldo to several guerrilla leaders. On the tenth, Taylor sent this correspondence to his district commander, Funston. Two days later, Funston, having broken Aguinaldo's coded message requesting 400 soldiers, submitted a plan to Wheaton: an eighty-man Macabebe detachment guided by Segismundo would pose as the reinforcements, and Funston and four other officers would act as their prisoners. To maintain the cover story it was vital that no gunboat be seen in the area; so Funston decided to land at Casiguran Bay, some sixty miles in a straight line to Palanan, and then hike up the coast road. MacArthur approved the plan, and on 6 March the *Vicksburg* left Manila, steamed around to the east coast of Luzon, and put Funston ashore. The ensuing march, closer to a hundred miles in actual distance, was a terrible ordeal and the expedition came very close to starving to death. Finally, on the twenty-third, a day after Aguinaldo's birthday, the Macabebes marched into his camp and at a signal from the interpreter, dispersed his bodyguard and seized the president. Arriving in Manila on the twenty-eighth, Aguinaldo was well guarded but given every courtesy, even to taking his meals with MacArthur's staff. After a few days he began to discuss terms, and on 19 April he issued a proclamation calling on the guerrillas to lay down their weapons and the Filipino people to accept United States authority.[75]

Both MacArthur and the War Department trumpeted Aguinaldo's capture as the "most important single military effect of the year," a coup that all but ended the war.[76] However, a number of contemporary observers and historians believed it was important, but not crucial, for it occurred at a time when resistance was collapsing throughout the archipelago. The documentary evidence supports this latter argument: in the same one-week period MacArthur informed Washington of the details of Aguinaldo's capture, he also reported the end of resistance on Panay and Mindanao and the surrender of the jefe of Bulacan Province.[77] As noted in other chapters, Aguinaldo's influence, even in northern Luzon, was very small, and some of his commanders had not heard from him for months. Many had already surrendered before his capture, many others were negotiating, and still others were fugitives, hunted from place to place by American and Filipino patrols. Those leaders who were determined to resist went right on fighting. However, it is probable that Aguinaldo's acceptance of United States authority removed much of the stigma from surrender and may have contributed to later capitulations.

THIRTEEN

SOUTHERN LUZON

The Department of Southern Luzon (DSL) encompassed the 10,000 square miles and 1.2 million people of Luzon south and east of Manila and a roughly equal area in the islands of Marinduque, Masbate, Mindoro, and Samar. Like Northern Luzon, geography and culture divided the area into three autonomous zones. Directly south and west of Manila was the most important area: the Tagalog-speaking 1st District (Cavite) and the 2nd District (Batangas, Laguna, and Tayabas). Separated from the rest of Luzon by a narrow, rugged peninsula, the 3rd District comprised the Bicol-speaking southeast provinces of Sorsogan, Albay, and the Camarines. The 4th District was a military backwater, consisting of Samar, Marinduque, and several other islands and a population of 400,000, but garrisoned by barely 1,000 soldiers.[1]

It would have taken a very strong leader to impose his authority on such an attenuated area, and neither the Americans nor the revolutionaries produced one. Major General John C. Bates, the officer who commanded the department until April 1901, conformed to a type seen all too often in the war: a capable Regular field commander promoted beyond his abilities by the iron law of seniority. Joining the army in 1861, he had nearly thirty years of undistinguished service, and appears to have sought a similar anonymity in the Philippines. True, he did negotiate the Bates Agreement, which neutralized the Sulu Moros, but he exercised little direction of the Wheaton-Schwan invasion of southwest Luzon in early 1900. Thereafter, as department commander, he was inactive to the point of passivity. He remained in Manila, rarely visiting even the nearby Tagalog provinces and never going to the Bicol region or the islands offshore. Unfamiliar with conditions in the field, he vetoed a number of creative and original ideas. Taft commented that after only a few months Bates was depressed at the prospects of pacifying "the worst provinces in [the] archipelago" and did not seem to understand the guerrilla war.[2] His successor, Maj. Gen. James F. Wade, was more conversant with irregular warfare and a more active commander, but he failed to support his more competent subordinates or to push Manila to commit sufficient resources. All in all, for most of 1900 and 1901 the American supreme command was mediocre at best.

Mediocrity also characterized the revolutionary high command in the area. The veteran revolutionary Mariano Trias was one of Aguinaldo's most loyal subordinates and had been in charge of the forces in Southern Luzon since mid-1899. But, like his mentor, Trias was an indifferent military chief: unable to coordinate an assault on the southern lines, he wasted much of his time on fruitless plans for retaking Manila, a chimera that contributed to his mishandling of the defense of Cavite during the Wheaton-Schwan invasion. Thereafter, Trias focused on Cavite and left his provincial commanders— Miguel Malvar in Batangas, Juan Cailles in Laguna, Vito Beleramino in Albay and Sorsogan—virtually independent. This acceptance of regional warfare may have been due to Trias's recognition that terrain and the turmoil left by the invasion precluded his direct control. Nonetheless, compared with other senior commanders, his captured correspondence is remarkably silent on strategy, tactics, policy, taxation, command relations, and most other issues. Other than threatening collaborators with death and urging good conduct on the revolutionaries, he exercised his authority very rarely.[3]

The 4th District has always been easy to disregard. A catchall of islands with almost nothing in common but their mountainous terrain and their dependence on waterborne transport, it appears to owe its existence largely to Manila's efforts to relieve the Department of the Visayas of administrative responsibilities. District commander Col. Edward E. Hardin had little option but to split his 29th Infantry into companies and use it to hold the major ports of Samar, Mindoro, Masbate, and Marinduque. Spread over such a vast distance, it is not surprising that the 29th had mixed success. On each island the occupiers tried to form municipal governments, improve roads, and institute other civic action projects, but they had varied results. The troops on Samar did little to pacify that island and may have contributed to the viciousness of that war. In contrast, on Masbate, Hardin quickly negotiated the surrender of the revolutionary leader and ended opposition by June. On Mindoro the small garrison did comparatively little, and guerrillas and brigands moved through the island's high mountains and densely forested interior with impunity.[4]

The 29th's greatest challenge was Marinduque, where the two-company garrison proved totally unable to overcome the Fabian tactics of Lt. Col. Maximo Abad's guerrillas and the antipathy of the island's elite. Holed up in the two principal towns, they did little until 11 September, when Capt. Devereaux Shields took fifty-one soldiers and a hospital corpsmen on a hike from the east coast back to Santa Cruz. Two days later, the command was ambushed by Abad's massed force—an estimated 250 riflemen and 2,000 bolomen—and, after Shields was wounded, it surrendered. This shocking defeat gained an energetic response. MacArthur sent the tough, no-nonsense hero of the Gillmore expedition, Brig. Gen. Luther R. Hare, with orders to treat the entire male population over fifteen as potential enemies and to arrest as many as possible and hold them as hostages until Abad surrendered. Hare secured the release of Shields and his men, destroyed houses and fields, and arrested 600 suspects, but Abad remained at large.

Hare left in December, and the island was turned over first to Lt. Col. A. W. Corliss and then to Maj. Frederick A. Smith, both of whom continued the destruction of food and shelter in the interior, arrested numerous officials for aiding the insurgents, and kept patrols combing the countryside. In February 1901, Smith directed all civilians to move within the boundaries of the occupied towns: anyone who remained in the countryside was presumed hostile. With the countryside clear, army patrols pursued the guerrillas vigorously and continued to destroy crops and houses in the interior. These harsh tactics worked. Many landowners and merchants, appalled at watching their businesses and farms go up in smoke, turned against Abad and joined the Federal Party or sent emissaries demanding he surrender. This pressure increased after Taft visited the island in March and offered the prospect of civil government if there was peace, and even worse punishment if war contin-

U.S. troops in quarters

ued. Abad stubbornly held out until April, when he finally capitulated, and on the 29th the island was officially declared pacified. Both for the "concentration" of the population and for the enormous destruction of crops and houses, the Marinduque campaign was a grim harbinger of later pacification campaigns.[5]

The 3rd District stretched almost 200 miles along the Bicol Peninsula from Tayabas Province almost to Samar. At its widest barely fifty miles across, and in some places less than fifteen, the peninsula contained a few coastal and valley flatlands, towering volcanic cones, and rugged foothills covered with almost impenetrable abaca groves. Roads to the interior were few and often rendered impassable by mud and rain. Colonel Walter Howe, whose 47th Infantry occupied Albay and Sorsogan Provinces, had no means of communication with district headquarters except by dispatch boat or via Manila. Both Howe and Col. Joseph Dorst, whose 45th Infantry garrisoned the Camarines, complained their regiments were so spread out it took weeks for directives to reach some companies. Alone at the end of the army's makeshift supply line, for most of 1900 the roughly 2,600 soldiers in the 3rd District were denied adequate food, supplies, or medicine.[6]

The resistance in the Bicol area was under the overall direction of Maj. Gen. Vito Belarmino, a native of Cavite and a longtime Aguinaldo partisan who arrived in late 1898. Belarmino confined himself to the more populous and prosperous provinces of Albay and Sorsogan and left the Camarines in the hands of local jefes. As with most of the non-Tagalog areas, the Philippine Republic treated the Bicol area as a dependency, extracting taxes but sending fewer than 200 rifles to the area. The lack of armament and the severe economic distress caused by the navy's blockade hampered Belarmino's efforts to develop the region's defenses, and his mistaken decision to oppose the invaders on the beaches cost him heavily. Shocked by a series of defeats, in February 1900 Belarmino wrote Trias that although inflicting 150 casualties on the enemy (actually only three wounded) he had suffered over 100 himself, and that with Bell's invasion of the Camarines his forces were "hemmed in" along the Camarines-Albay border and in danger of starvation.[7] In March, following the surrender of his chief subordinate, he opened negotiations with the Americans. But Belarmino recovered his spirits and developed a new strategy that, in the short run, proved highly effective against the occupiers.

In the first days after the January invasion, Belarmino maintained that the best course was to pursue "a stratagem of friendship" toward the invaders and then "to entrap them treacherously."[8] But he soon reversed this course and instead ordered all civilians out of the occupied towns. In the interior, they would plant crops and harvest abaca, the first to feed the guerrillas and the second to provide income through taxes and smuggling. To ensure popular cooperation, Belarmino combined exhortation with coercion, the latter predominating as the war went on. Guerrillas fired into occupied towns and set their suburbs on fire, and assassinated civil officials and prominent *americanistas*. Army officers found it almost impossible to stop these attacks: one complained that "the insurrectos are venting their rage upon the helpless natives, but do not dare show themselves to the troops."[9]

Initially, Belarmino's strategy worked, frustrating army efforts to win over the population and diverting a great deal of money from the hemp trade. But as time went on, it proved increasingly difficult to sustain, for the revolutionaries simply could not provide, or force the population to provide, sufficient food to sustain life in the hills. The death of carabao due to rinderpest, the naval blockade of the coast, and the American devastation of fields and storehouses further decreased the supply of food in the interior. People were forced to return to the towns simply to live. Once there, they became victims of insurgent sanctions, so that sheer survival forced them to cooperate with the army. As a result, the towns became, by and large, centers of pro-American sentiment and remarkably free of the shadow governments or infrastructures that appeared elsewhere. Although some *presidentes* did straddle the middle and worked for both sides, most civil officials in the Bicol region served loyally. Only in October 1900 did Belarmino realize his mistake and order the formation of clandestine committees "to raise the courage of the citizens and make them steadfast and energetic in contributing to the near triumph of our ideals."[10] By that time, it was too late; the Americans had won over the population in the towns.

On the military side, the Bicol region's guerrillas followed the familiar pattern of dispersing into zones and subzones, each with a small force of regulars and a larger number of locally raised bolomen in what Belarmino called the National Militia. The militia was supposed to be summoned only when needed, but, in practice, militiamen complained they were retained on active service at the same time they were required to grow crops.[11] Both groups adhered to guerrilla tactics, fighting only when at a numerical advantage, avoiding the loss of their small stock of firearms, and taking advantage of the region's dense vegetation, so that army patrols and supply wagons often had to run a gauntlet of sniper fire along the narrow trails. Both groups also proved highly adept at building traps and snares, which severely restricted American night operations and surprise attacks. But efforts to drive the occupying garrisons out of the towns or to conduct large-scale operations were generally ineffective. Although Belarmino called for an offensive in the fall of 1900 to influence the presidential elections, there was little increase in fighting. The lack of weapons greatly reduced combat effectiveness; at one point Belarmino ordered the militia to arm themselves with poison-dipped arrows and poison-filled squirt bottles. Moreover, the scattered bands seldom had sufficient security or food to concentrate for any length of time, much less execute one of the overly complex plans of Belarmino's staff. He in turn was often ill and could not travel, and it took days, even weeks, for his lieutenants to disseminate orders to the scattered commands, so that to all intents and purposes the Camarines' guerrillas were virtually autonomous. The great strength of the Bicol resistance movement was its ability to deny the soldiers control over the population and thus to delay pacification; militarily, its operations seldom rose above harassment.[12]

For the Americans, the war in the 3rd District proved especially frustrating. Convinced that armed resistance was maintained only by Belarmino and a small force of Tagalogs, they ascribed Bicolano hostility "to ignorance, and to the influence of their leaders who have told them wonderful lies of American outrages and brutality."[13] The initial orders to the occupying forces emphasized the importance of restoring the hemp trade, establishing civil government, and, in the words of one post commander, "to do nothing to alienate the people who might be friendly but afraid to return to this town."[14] These latter orders, at least, were generally obeyed within the American zone, where there were unusually harmonious social relations between soldiers and civilians. But fraternization was not enough to overcome the problems of inadequate manpower, inhospitable terrain, limited supplies, and armed resistance. Although the army could hold the main towns, it could not convince the majority of the population to return, nor could it force the guerrillas into battle. The result was that within a few months of the landings, the war in the 3rd District became a stalemate. The army controlled the towns, the guerrillas the interior, and although both sides could wreak considerable discomfort on each other through raids and property destruction, neither could inflict a decisive defeat.[15]

Headquartered in the Camarines city of Nueva Caceres (now Naga), 3rd District commander Brig. Gen. James M. Bell sought to impose coherent policies on his scattered command. Often sick and forced to take extended leave, Bell was further hampered by a scarcity of waterborne transport and communication facilities. With barely 2,600 soldiers to pacify an area of 5,600 square miles and 600,000 people, Bell made a virtue of necessity by establishing subdistricts, turning Albay and Sorsogan over to Howe's 47th Infantry, dividing the Camarines among Dorst's 45th, and splitting the eight troops of the 11th Cavalry among garrison duty, escorts, and a mobile strike force.

For the most part, Bell left his subordinate commanders alone and contented himself with nagging Manila for more supplies, reinforcements, and the authority to raise local forces. Although some of the officers who ran the department during Bell's illnesses tried to impose more centralized control over pacification policy, they were seldom successful. Only in 1901, when the guerrillas had been compressed into a few areas, were district commanders able to restore hierarchical authority and to plan and execute extensive military operations. Although they imposed considerable hardship and frustration on the troops in the theater, in many ways isolation and decentralization worked to the army's advantage. Over the course of 1900, officers developed a mixture of district-wide and local counterinsurgency practices to counter the guerrillas' tactics.

Lacking sufficient resources to garrison and patrol the district, the army was forced to rely on the population. Convinced that Manila's plans for civil government were impractical, Bell issued his own, which called for the post commander and the mayor, or *presidente,* to create a town council and a police force. The *presidente* thereby assumed a pivotal role: in return for business contracts, patronage, and considerable autonomy, he encouraged people to return to the town, recruited guides and local auxiliaries, and identified insurgents. The guerrillas' efforts to capture or kill civil officials only increased their commitment to the American cause. Bartolome Roa, the *presidente* of Oas, for example, formed a militia and raided the countryside, destroying guerrilla supply depots. Roa offered those who remained in the mountains a simple choice: they could suffer the loss of their homes and fields to his militia, or they could move to Oas and be treated by American doctors, pay a token tax, and attend Mass.[16]

With these new allies, district officers organized police, scouts, and local security forces. Post commanders armed paramilitary units in the Camarines that not only served as guides and porters on expeditions but also defeated a guerrilla assault on their town. Bell and several of his subordinates pressed for the enlistment of Bicol troops, but despite enthusiastic support—one officer wrote "I feel sure this is the only method of breaking the insurrection in this section"—Bates and MacArthur refused to authorize a Bicol Scout unit until February 1901.[17] Manila displayed similar caution in arming municipal police, despite some impressive successes in the Bicol area. Innovative post officers used their police to ferret out guerrillas hidden among the civilian population, and at least in some towns it appears that virtually all patrols and expeditions were joint army-police operations.[18] Impressed with these achievements, Bell first requested Manila to send him a few hundred rifles to arm the police, and, when Bates refused, to send revolvers. MacArthur delayed approving either request for several months and then sent a completely inadequate, and inappropriate, supply of shotguns. In the face of Manila's tepid support, amounting almost to deliberate obstruction, post officers continued to arm their police with whatever weapons were available and to rely on them not only for law enforcement but also as paramilitary auxiliaries. When the weapons finally arrived in 1901, the police became an even more effective agent of army pacification.[19]

In part because of their belief that the Bicols were peaceful, in part because they relied on them to assist in pacification, most army officers strongly supported civic action programs. Municipal government was accorded a high priority and, as noted earlier, was generally successful. So, too, was education, which was among the most popular of army initiatives; a May meeting of the district's *presidentes* revealed that they "were all in favor of an early starting of the schools."[20] Bell had a progressive's belief in the power of the schoolhouse and urged Manila to send teachers, books, and funds. Post officers were equally enthusiastic and secured supplies, funds, and schoolhouses through a variety of ingenious means. By October 1900, every occupied town had a school, and in his last report in March 1901, Bell stated proudly that in the Camarines alone there were fifty schoolhouses with a student body of 12,000. Such social reform projects, when combined with the generally good conduct of soldiers, did much to win over the population.[21]

The army's slow but growing progress in civic action was complemented by increasing military effectiveness. Save on those rare occasions when they gathered to attack a town, the *insurrectos'* Fabian tactics and the rugged terrain inhibited large offensive operations. Warned by a cordon of spies and outposts, the guerrillas would simply fire a few rounds into the toiling columns and vanish, reappearing as peaceful "amigos." Soldiers had far more success when they broke up into small squads and left the trails, surrounding and searching the rural barrios that sheltered guerrillas. In July the 11th Cavalry's Lt. Col. Charles G. Starr selected Lt. George M. Wray, an officer who had already demonstrated his proficiency as a hard-hitting small-unit commander, to head an elite twenty-five-man strike force. In its first three months, Wray's Scouts conducted half the 11th Cavalry's expeditions, fought four of its six engagements, and was responsible for all but one of the casualties inflicted by the regiment.[22]

With the main ports occupied and the lowlands under continuous patrol, the army now proceeded to starve the remaining guerrillas out. Bell's prolonged illness had hampered the development of district-wide policies in 1900, but post officers, largely on their own initiative, soon began to restrict the amount of rice and other staples that could leave the towns. Some officers imposed a pass system to limit purchases and ordered merchants to convoy food shipments under army escort. One commander ordered all large quantities of rice moved within municipal boundaries; another forbade the sale of food outside the town market. In the meantime, patrols stepped up the confiscation or destruction of foodstuffs in enemy-controlled areas. The effect was almost instantaneous: Howe claimed that within two months of his adopting food deprivation policies, Belarmino's guerrillas had ceased their attacks on the main towns and withdrawn to the mountains. By August the guerrillas were spending much of their time in search of food, and many people had moved into the garrisoned towns "because they can get nothing to eat outside."[23]

In the fall of 1900 and spring of 1901, a combination of military operations and popular cooperation led to a rapid decline in the guerrillas' position. With the towns now secure, columns and amphibious expeditions pushed farther into guerrilla strongholds, including Belarmino's main camp. Smaller patrols, traveling at night and supported by local auxiliaries, raided isolated barrios and maintained constant pressure on the irregulars. In order to feed themselves, Belarmino's partisans increased their exactions on the peasantry, with the result that more and more fled the mountains for the towns. From these victims, post commanders developed a network of spies and informants who could identify the "amigos" when they took refuge in the barrios. The Federal Party and the clergy actively took on the role of peacemakers, urging people to return to the towns and negotiating with guerrilla officers. Army officers also took great pains to assure their opponents that they would be treated with all honors of war and staged impressive surrender ceremonies. Unfortunately, this pacification effort also was characterized by an increase in destruction as columns devastated previously untouched areas.[24]

In January the provincial jefe in Sorsogan gave up, and in March the last organized guerrilla unit capitulated. Among the almost 400 who surrendered there were only twenty-five rifles—an indication of the paucity of insurgent military strength in that province. March also saw the end of organized resistance in the Camarines, where 800 irregulars yielded. Only Belarmino's partisans remained at large, and in May they launched an abortive raid into Sorsogan, apparently in an effort to revive the war in that province. It is difficult not to see an element of petulance in Belarmino's actions, as if he sought to punish the Bicols for deserting the revolution. If so, he succeeded. The army's response was rapid and relentless. A three-week campaign brought the hard hand of war to the region. Almost twenty barrios and towns were destroyed, hundreds of storehouses were torched, 150 guerrillas were killed, and another 900 surrendered or were captured. Belarmino's forces simply dissolved, and on 4 July he capitulated. Mopping-up operations against scattered guerrilla bands, bandits, and religious rebels continued for several months, but organized resistance ended with Belarmino's surrender.

Both sides had recognized that the conflict in the Bicol provinces was a sideshow and that the war would be decided elsewhere. Given the difficulties of the terrain and Belarmino's Fabian tactics, it would have been understandable if the small American forces had done little but hold on to their port enclaves. Instead, largely at the initiative of post officers, they carried out a highly effective local counterinsurgency campaign. Realizing the weakness of the insurgents' strategy of keeping the population out of the occupied towns, army officers developed a variety of countermeasures: food deprivation and destruction; the use of small, mobile forces; and conciliating the population and turning them against the guerrillas.

In contrast to the undermanned, and largely ignored, campaigns in the 3rd and 4th Districts, the Tagalog 1st and 2nd Districts were clearly recognized as a crucial area; and for most of 1900 all but 3,000 of the 11,000 troops in the department were concentrated there. It was here that the revolution against Spain had begun, and here that the army would encounter some of the fiercest resistance. As in most of the Philippines, there were rugged mountains and foothills, jungle, bamboo groves, and scrub brush, and large expanses of lightly settled countryside, all of which provided sanctuaries for the guerrilla bands. But there were also densely populated areas with numerous villages and towns, croplands, and cattle, to provide food and recruits. Worse, it was "an awful region of known contagious and tropical diseases."[25] One district commander complained that when his troops engaged in extended field operations, "sick reports go up alarmingly, often averaging over fifty percent, and a considerable proportion of this number are permanently incapacitated from further duty."[26] But American soldiers overcame equally harsh terrain elsewhere. What distinguished the resistance in southwestern Luzon was the skill of the regional commanders and the depth of the elite-led popular resistance. More than anywhere else in the archipelago, the occupiers found that "the great majority of the people are violently opposed to American rule, and both hate and fear the Americans."[27]

Unfortunately for the army, the majority of its high command did not display equal determination. Bates was largely a negative influence, thus throwing most of the burden for policy on the district commanders, who proved a rather mixed lot. The 1st District was initially under Brig. Gen. Robert H. Hall, an old, lethargic officer who confined himself to administrative duties. The 2nd District was commanded by the energetic, driving Col.

William E. Birkhimer, whose constant exhortations led one officer to write, "Old Birkhimer is about the biggest old ass that anybody ever saw wearing boots and spurs. The officers and men of his regiment hate him as they do the devil. . . . He keeps the telegraph line hot sending long, prosy, asinine orders to everybody."[28] In June 1900, Hall was shifted to the 2nd District, which he listlessly held until the following April, and Hare was transferred to the 1st District. Hare had made an outstanding reputation with the 33rd Infantry in Northern Luzon, but now he was suffering from a variety of physical ailments and "nervous debility," which would force his retirement in 1903.[29] Determined to be a hands-on commander, Hare soon alienated most of his officers; he was shifted to the 4th District in October 1900, to be replaced by Col. Walter S. Schuyler. After Schuyler fell sick in December, the army's luck changed with the appointment of Col. Samuel S. Sumner, a competent and intelligent officer who achieved impressive results. With Hall's departure in April, the two districts were combined under Sumner and re-titled the 1st District.

On the Filipino side, the differences in leadership were more dramatic. Although Trias, the supreme commander, was ineffectual, both Batangas's Miguel Malvar and Laguna's Juan Cailles were two of the most capable and most independent provincial jefes of the war, and both retained considerable popular support. A successful businessman and official before joining Aguinaldo, Malvar had imposed his stamp on his native province's resistance movement in a way few other leaders were able to do. He had handpicked the top guerrilla officers and established "shadow governments" in most towns. His counterpart in Laguna, Cailles, was an intelligent, forceful, and charismatic commander and a highly competent tactician. The Americans were as much impressed with his courage and skill as they were angered by his willingness to burn out or kill his opponents. As one officer ruefully admitted, "That fellow Cailles is something of a man. He has only about 300 rifles, but he can give a deal of trouble with them."[30] Neighboring Cavite was the home of Aguinaldo and many of the revolutionary leaders, but the resistance movement there was comparatively weak. Five years of warfare, banditry, and disease had left fields and towns ruined, the economy disrupted, and the population exhausted. Many of the most committed revolutionaries had either been killed or, like Cailles and Belarmino, been assigned to other provinces. Somewhat to their surprise, some garrison officers concluded Cavite's countryside was "as free from criminals as any part of the United States."[31] The guerrillas in Tayabas were so disorganized and factious that, at Trias's request, Malvar took over the province in January 1901 and dispatched his brother-in-law, Eustacio Maloles, to sort things out. Maloles proved unable to coordinate the province's feuding movements, and for most of the war the province's main contribution was as a sanctuary and source of supplies.

Despite its diversity, the resistance in southwestern Luzon did share a number of characteristics. For the first eighteen months it was supported and led by the upper classes, who either cajoled or coerced the peasantry into aiding the guerrillas. This unusually high level of elite support in turn allowed the guerrillas to maintain strong contacts within the occupied towns and develop a sophisticated infrastructure that provided food, shelter, and recruits. A second characteristic was that in each province there were semipermanent military units, or columns, that were responsible for operations in a specific area. Membership shifted depending on the level of fighting: troops were obtained either from the estates of officers or by recruiting parties that conscripted single men, usually unwilling. Except when concentrated for a major operation, the columns were broken into small bands, perhaps one or two officers and thirty men. When under attack, they would disperse, take shelter in the barrios and towns, and regroup later at a designated rendezvous. Colonel James Lockett's description of the military resistance at Naic, Cavite, might be applied to many areas: the guerrillas "are scattered through all the barrios of the country. The rifles are kept concealed in bunches at various places known to the Captains and to a few trusted men. When it is desired to mobilize a command the Captains are notified and they through their officers and sergeants get the men together and issue arms."[32] A third, and eventually disabling, characteristic was that the resistance, even in Batangas and Laguna, was never able to achieve the unity of purpose necessary to overcome the Americans' military and logistical superiority. The guerrilla units were scattered in barrios or camps, often miles apart. When not in his headquarters on the Tayabas-Batangas border, Malvar had to travel long distances to locate his scattered commands and pass on instructions, which often were ignored. Here was a crucial weakness. The troops remained loyal to their local chiefs, who were haughty, factionalized, and insubordinate. Glenn May concluded that "Malvar's command was nothing more than a loose collection of local units, each of them functioning as the private force of a local magnate."[33] Cailles faced similar problems: an American investigation into one area's military forces concluded they were "not kept well in hand and many of the arms were in the hands of a kind of local militia which . . . was without organization."[34]

Having learned the folly of fighting conventional operations, southwestern Luzon's military leaders adopted a strategy of attrition. They rarely challenged the occupiers openly, preferring to harass towns, supply trains, or small patrols. With the exception of the victory at Mabitac, the few times Cailles and Malvar concentrated their forces to launch large-scale operations were failures. Even given this commitment to low-level guerrilla war, the pace of combat was far less than the revolutionary leadership wished: over a six-month period one of Malvar's columns had but one engagement and killed only one American (a civilian). The revolutionary leadership emphasized the necessity of preserving the limited supply of weapons, ordering they be taken out of hiding only for military operations. Hampered by poor ammunition, the *insurrectos* learned to fire a few shots and flee; if pursued, they would become "amigos." The rebels were much more active in discouraging cooperation with the invaders. Cailles in particular struck at *americanistas* through arson, kidnapping, and assassination, publicizing their fate as a deterrence to others. He justified such tactics on the grounds that if the guerrillas were not ruthless "the blood of our brothers, who have chosen to shed their blood rather [than] to be slaves of our enemies, will cry out to heaven."[35]

Both the guerrilla tactics and the depth of the resistance surprised the Americans. The relative ease with which the Wheaton-Schwan expedition had taken the main towns and scattered the opposition had led some to believe the area would soon be pacified. This opinion was encouraged by the relatively low level of combat in the first months of 1900. Throughout the department, officers reported that beyond sniping at patrols or into occupied towns, the enemy refused to fight. From Batangas, Lt. Col. R. W. Leonard interpreted all disturbances as efforts to extort money, and, as for Malvar, "more weight is given to this brigand than he is entitled to."[36] The diary of Schuyler, whose 46th Infantry occupied northern Cavite, indicates he had few problems with what he termed *ladrones*. Rather, his regiment devoted its time to establishing new schools (one of Schuyler's passions), cleaning up towns, developing close relations with the civil officials, and constructing roads.[37] Other post commanders similarly focused on civil government, on road building, on sanitation projects, on schools, and on other civic action programs. The most vocal advocate of such benevolent assimilation was Col. Cornelius Gardener, whose 30th Infantry occupied Tayabas, and who proclaimed that "no spirit of revenge is contemplated by the military commander, but good will towards all peaceable people."[38] Gardener believed "mere pills will be more effective than bullets," and he boasted that within six months of its arrival, the 30th had opened schools in every town it occupied.[39] He insisted his garrison commanders set up civil governments, recruit police, and cooperate with the local authorities. In the face of much evidence to the contrary from his own officers, Gardener steadfastly insisted that Tayabas was peaceful and that any disturbances were due to intruders from other provinces.

For all but optimists such as Gardener, by mid-1900 the situation in southwestern Luzon had grown far more ominous. Although officers reported their towns' inhabitants had returned from the countryside and that markets were bustling, other signs were disconcerting. After a brief flurry of surrenders and arms discoveries, it was increasingly hard to obtain weapons or information. Unwilling to trust the Tagalogs, few commanders recruited police or auxiliaries, and those who did faced great opposition from their superiors. Municipal government was seldom successful. Few Filipinos would serve as officials, even in Tayabas, and the insurgents, however little they challenged the soldiers, appeared able to murder individuals or destroy property with relative impunity. A growing number of officers concluded that the guerrilla bands were being supported by clandestine rebel organizations within the occupied towns. Despite army benevolence, the inhabitants remained, in the words of one post commander, "surly and intensely hostile, and I believe it is only lack of arms that compels them to limit their operations to cutting telegraph wires and attacking small parties."[40]

After a hiatus between February and May, fighting resumed with such intensity as to approach the conventional warfare of 1899. Patrols and supply wagons were ambushed, towns attacked and burned, and soldiers picked off by snipers and bolomen. This resurgence occurred just when soldiers were most vulnerable, for the summer rainy season sent sick rates soaring and reduced regiments by as much as a third of their strength. Colonel Benjamin Cheatham reported his 37th Infantry was "worked to the limit, our sick report is large, and the continued marching has so weakened the men that even those fit for duty have very little endurance left."[41] In Cavite, Schuyler's 46th Infantry, which had had almost no fighting since the invasion, suffered two bad reverses. On 30 May its band was ambushed and three men were killed, several wounded, and the rest "stampeded," leaving the dead and wagons for the enemy.[42] In July, guerrillas attacked an engineering party that "first lost its head, and then its manhood, and closed the performance by a disgraceful flight."[43] Conditions were even worse elsewhere; Birkhimer dramatically proclaimed that, in Batangas, "we control within the line of our bayonets, but no further."[44] The worst defeat occurred on 17 September at Mabitac, Laguna, when a newly arrived officer launched an unsupported frontal attack on Cailles's entrenched forces. Struggling through waist-deep mud, the soldiers were pinned down for eighty minutes, losing twenty-one killed and another twenty-three wounded. Despite MacArthur's effort to convince Washington that 33 percent casualties were "a profoundly impressive loss and indicates [the] stubbornness of the fight, the fearless leadership of the officers, and [the] splendid response of the men," the debacle of Mabitac shocked soldiers and contributed to the growing feeling that harsher measures were necessary.[45]

The army's response to the guerrilla revival was hampered by both terrain and weather. Schuyler's diary account of a patrol gives some idea of the difficulties. Learning that three insurgent leaders were in a neighboring barrio, the colonel set out with seven mounted soldiers and twenty infantry from Silang, Cavite, at ten at night on 11 July. The men moved through a soaked countryside, along a narrow trail through dense brush. Stumbling onto a small barrio, they rounded up all the males and arrested eight who came from another barrio and claimed to be buying rice. The patrol then set out again and "marched over most awful trail of mud and water frequently in dense shrubbery which required constant dodging." Schuyler impressed a civilian guide, and the man led them "sometimes on the mud track, sometimes through fields at the sides. In one place we traveled down a water sluice about a foot wide for a long distance." Once the moon set, the patrol's difficulties increased: "We made very slow progress floundering along what was supposed to be a road through rice fields." Only when daylight finally broke

Patrol with two prisoners and loot

could they locate the village; then, as Schuyler bitterly noted, "Of course we were too late," and the insurgents had fled. The exhausted patrol then returned; "the road was simply indescribable, the horses continually having to flounder through pools belly deep," having accomplished little more than the capture of one rifle and eight "amigos" at the cost of the complete exhaustion of the command.[46]

On balance, however, the resurgence of fighting in the summer and fall worked to the army's advantage. A series of sustained operations that continued throughout the summer destroyed several of Cailles's camps, captured his papers, and forced him to scatter. The Mabitac defeat only increased the pressure on Laguna's jefe. When the Americans could force the guerrillas to stand and fight, as when the 37th Infantry's mounted detachment found a wire-cutting party, the results were one-sided: the 37th killed twenty-one guerrillas and captured twenty-four rifles. On 17 July, Birkhimer's 28th avenged an attack on Taal that had wounded six of its soldiers: in a skillfully executed maneuver, the infantry drove the guerrillas straight into the cannon and machine guns of a gunboat, killing thirty-eight. As the rainy season drew to a close in September, soldiers could move into the countryside and maintain a more intense pace of operations. Through the hard months of service, post and battalion commanders had developed tactics that were increasingly effective. Captured papers—including most of Trias's correspondence in December—informants, and interrogations provided vital information on the local guerrillas and their agents. By February 1901, local officers had extensive lists of guerrilla leaders and photographs of many of them. Success built on success. With each storehouse or barracks destroyed, each tax collector or spy arrested, each rifle captured or surrendered, not only the guerrillas' military power but their popular support diminished.[47]

Although local assistance remained much weaker than in most other areas of the Islands, by the end of 1900 a surprising number of Filipinos had either accommodated themselves to colonial rule or decided that the alternative was much worse. Revolutionary terrorism, personal antipathy, or mercenary motives led some to assist the Americans; most important, as Glenn May has demonstrated, the guerrillas' strongest supporters—the elite or *principales*—were deserting them. Whether for selfish or humane reasons, many had concluded that independence was impossible and that the war must end.[48] Some joined the Federal Party and, at considerable risk to their lives and property, sought to organize civil governments and negotiate guerrilla surrenders. Others simply stopped providing food, shelter, and taxes. A growing number of post commanders reported their *presidentes,* police, and citizens' posses were actively cooperating in hunting down guerrillas and *ladrones,* capturing rifles, and supplying information. Gradually, the army was pacifying the region.

Sadly, much of the army's success in southwestern Luzon was achieved by substituting coercion for conciliation. Convinced they faced both a recalcitrant population and an enemy who was daily violating the laws of war, Birkhimer spoke for many when he urged Manila to issue G.O. 100 and proclaimed: "We must take firm hold of this bandit and *ladrone* question: the bullet and prison labor, under the lash, are the only instrumentalities in my sight to work our beneficent purposes of reform."[49] Field operations increasingly reflected Birkhimer's punitive views, but, because the guerrillas often refused to fight, the torch proved more common than the bullet. Soldiers burned homes and fields where the telegraph wires were cut or troops were fired on, and in May, under Birkhimer's orders to "leave no shelter for Cailles among his haunts and no hombre to play his and ours as occasion suits," army patrols scoured Laguna's highlands and jungles, burning suspected storehouses and cartels.[50] That month, Cheatham urged the destruction of the property of rich citizens and "burning all the towns where Insurgents are harbored thereby compelling the people to come into the towns during the wet season."[51] On 25 July 1900, departmental headquarters greatly expanded the criteria for destruction: henceforth, any building containing an "unusual quantity" of food suspected "beyond a reasonable doubt" of being used by the guerrillas was to be destroyed.[52] Those who protested found little support from their superiors: when in November an officer complained of the burning of houses and rice near a friendly village, he was told that the 25 July orders covered all such contingencies. No action was taken against the arsonists, but the villagers were forced to move into a garrisoned town—an early example of a growing tendency toward local "concentration."[53] However, the army's attacks on supplies and shelters was by no means the orgy of destruction that some have charged: Schuyler, for example, justified his decision against slaughtering the animals at a guerrilla sanctuary on the grounds that rinderpest had already killed so many livestock that the poor were forced to give up farming and become insurgents.[54]

Perhaps the most successful operations were in Cavite and western Batangas, where Sumner oversaw a series of military operations that clearly turned the tide by early 1901. With the assistance of navy gunboats, soldiers landed at previously inaccessible coastal valleys. Small raiding forces pushed into the interior. One such raid was carried out on 19 December, when the gunboat *Basco* transported a crack force to a remote beach. The troops spread out and surprised eighty guerrillas under Trias, killing thirteen, capturing eleven rifles, and destroying the camp. Another raid in February destroyed a major storehouse containing over twelve tons of rice and several tons of corn, as well as capturing seven rifles. Operations in the hinterland were balanced by sweeps through populated areas in which Americans conducted extensive searches for weapons; they also rounded up all males of military age and paraded them before informants, often former guerrillas, who picked out their former comrades, including members of the infrastructure. Thus on 2 January, Lt. Col. Frank Baldwin spread a combined force of 4th and 46th Infantry in a long line from Imus to San Francisco de Malabon. The navy sent launches to patrol the water and 110 marines under Maj. Littleton W. T. Waller. Over 1,700 men were brought in for questioning, of which 61 were identified as insurgents. The army also benefited from those civilians who, having committed themselves to United States rule, were driven by self-protection to turn on the guerrillas. Thus in January the *presidente* and twenty *principales* of San Francisco de Malabon led a patrol into the surrounding area and turned up ten rifles and a great quantity of ammunition. The Americans also made use of agents such as Macario Bautista, a guerrilla officer who had narrowly escaped hanging by his commander. He led the Americans to his camp and thereafter served as a guide and spy, personally killing at least six guerrillas himself. Perhaps the best indication of the growing effectiveness of army pacification in Cavite is that whereas in September only 32 rifles were seized, in January 228 rifles were captured and another 171 surrendered. Equally telling is that in February only 5 insurgents were killed, but 376 guerrillas and 305 rifles were captured or surrendered.[55]

The entries of Schuyler's diary for January and February details the collapse of resistance in the 1st District. His regiment participated in five major operations. In one, 100 soldiers deployed in a long skirmish line fifteen yards apart and moved across the rice fields, arresting every man as they went along. A total of 700 prisoners were taken, who were then paraded before informants, including a former guerrilla major, who picked out 100 for further investigation. In another operation, navy gunboats ferried troops to two landing points. Wading ashore at 1:00 A.M., they discovered a number of storehouses and had a running fight with a guerrilla band, driving it into range of the gunboat's cannon and inflicting heavy casualties. At the same time, and perhaps more significantly, the 46th's post commanders were conducting intensive operations in their own localities. Thus on 7 January a patrol captured several guerrillas during a "roundup." A search turned up a list of the entire revolutionary organization in the Silang area: the next day, the local jefe began negotiations for surrender. In another town, resistance was all but ended when a guerrilla leader was persuaded by his brother, the town priest, to surrender to Schuyler. The colonel treated his former opponent to lunch and returned him his pistol; the guerrilla returned the favor by advising that the quickest way to pacify the area was to bring all the food into the town and starve the remaining guerrillas out. He also provided the useful information that Trias was waiting for Aguinaldo's permission to surrender but had not heard from him in six months. Noting in late February that "guns seem to be coming our way," Schuyler was also pleased at the shift in popular attitudes—everywhere people were displaying American flags, *presidentes* were furnishing useful information, and conditions were peaceful.[56]

On 15 March 1901, after long negotiations, Trias, his staff, and 200 soldiers surrendered. He had been under constant pressure for months, his storehouses burned, his arms caches destroyed, and his military forces depleted as more and more of them reached an accommodation with the Americans. Out of touch not only with Aguinaldo but also with his subordinates in neighboring provinces, he had grown increasingly disenchanted with the war. A humane man who had denounced the murder of Spanish captives and warned that any who mistreated either Filipinos or Americans would be shot, he may have been influenced by Col. Buenaventura Dimaguila's 30 November letter, which warned that terrorism and assassination were alienating the Filipino people.[57] Almost immediately he issued a proclamation saying he had surrendered because he was convinced that further fighting could only continue the destruction and suffering and because "the people were demanding peace and seeking some means of securing that tranquillity lost on account of the war."[58] But since his surrender, he had become convinced that United States rule would secure for the Filipinos the revolutionaries' goals of internal improvements, removal of friar oppression, and good government. In another letter to Malvar, he warned that all the benefits they had gained in their struggle against the Spanish were in danger of being lost. In John Gates's judgment, Trias's surrender was a turning point in the war, more important than the capture of Aguinaldo a month later, for it marked an open acknowledgment by one of the most prominent revolutionaries that popular sentiment had shifted decisively away from the guerrillas. Indeed, to MacArthur, the surrender was a "most auspicious event" and "indicates [the] final stage [of] armed insurrection."[59]

With Cavite's resistance in tatters, the army turned to Laguna and Batangas Provinces. There conditions had shown little sign of improvement, and field officers were becoming increasingly disenchanted. Along with skirmishes and raids on towns and convoys, there was continuing evidence of tax collectors operating with impunity in occupied towns, of civil officials acting as clandestine agents, and of guerrillas living openly in the barrios, sheltered by the population. Early in 1901, Maj. William L. Pitcher concluded:

"Only the severest measures will bring the Filipinos to terms. There is no gratitude in the hearts of these people. I believe it would be a wise plan to deport all captured natives, or keep them permanently in prison."[60] Captain E. T. Jones agreed: "I am convinced that little headway will be made against the insurrectos here until the natives are forced to assist the U.S. troops with information from motives of policy: in other words, the Americans must convince the people, men, women and children that the troops are more powerful than the insurrectos and that they (the troops) will if necessary inflict upon the natives more punishment than the insurrectos can." This could be done by stopping all trade between towns and sending out columns to destroy houses and fields and shoot every adult male found outside the towns. Such "extreme measures" were justified because the entire population was hostile. Indeed, Jones concluded, "It looks to me as if it will be necessary to annihilate the Tagalogs."[61] These sentiments were not shared by Manila or by Sumner, but they do indicate the frustration of some field officers.

For Cailles and Malvar, the situation was desperate. Not only were they facing increasing military pressure, but their source of legitimacy had disappeared as first Trias and then, in April, Aguinaldo accepted United States authority and urged them to surrender. Most of their comrades had capitulated; resistance north of Manila had all but ceased. In their own provinces, there were clear indications that much of the population wanted peace. Despite threats and the execution of some of its members, the pro-American Federal Party was growing in power and now included Mariano Lopez, Batangas's most prominent sugar planter and the leader of a family with several officers in the guerrilla ranks. Even formally loyal towns were no longer secure. Cailles's deputy, Pedro Caballes, wrote him that Pagsanjan had gone over entirely to the Americans and its *presidente* and police were hunting down guerrillas. He urged that he either be allowed to kill the *americanistas* or burn the town; otherwise there was a danger that all of Laguna might be lost. Another column chief warned Cailles that "public order" in his district was very bad and "will force us to adopt measures of terror" as "every means of attraction used by the commander . . . has been in vain."[62]

After meeting with Cailles in early April, Malvar assumed Trias's title as jefe of Southern Luzon. In a more significant gesture, he broke with the policies of Aguinaldo and the Malolos government and declared that from now on those who contributed to the revolution would be rewarded, irrespective of their socioeconomic status. In short, Malvar belatedly tried to make the Philippine Revolution a social struggle as well as a political one.[63] In addition to broadening the revolutionaries' appeal, Malvar took practical steps to revitalize the resistance. He reorganized the military forces in Southern

Luzon, at least on paper, and sent Eustacio Maloles to resurrect Tayabas. He circulated new instructions for the guerrillas which emphasized that they must avoid combat on any but the most favorable terms and preserve their weapons above everything else. If necessary they must be willing to fight for ten years. He both exhorted citizens to remember their dreams of independence and warned members of the Federal Party and other *americanistas* they would be summarily punished. Malvar also intensified his propaganda campaign, spreading false reports of his own strength and bountiful supply of arms, of imminent European intervention, and of the growth of anti-imperialist sentiment in the United States. How many of these proclamations reflected his effort to impose policy and how many were intended purely for public support is difficult to determine. Nevertheless, by appealing for mass support and reorganizing his forces to fight a prolonged war, he succeeded briefly in reigniting resistance in eastern Batangas.[64]

Despite Malvar's efforts, the revolutionaries' position continued to crumble. Instead of rekindling the resistance, within a month Maloles had surrendered and Tayabas remained quiet.[65] On 27 April a detachment of the 21st Infantry located Cailles's main camp. In the ensuing fight, he managed to escape, but his entire staff was captured with all his correspondence, which revealed a complete picture of the guerrilla movement in Laguna. A round of arrests and raids followed, destroying much of the guerrilla infrastructure. Despite Cailles's declaration that he would execute members of the Federal Party, or any Filipino who negotiated with them, he probably opened talks in April. In May, some newspapers reported that Cailles wanted to surrender and was only waiting to be cleared of any war crimes. Whether true or not, this news must have compromised him with his comrades. After extensive negotiations, during which the army suspended operations, Cailles agreed to come in. On 24 June, in one of the most impressive ceremonies of the war, Cailles led some 600 officers and men into Santa Cruz and surrendered. He not only received the enormous sum of $5,000 for his weapons but was soon appointed governor of Laguna and became among the most ruthlessly efficient of *americanistas*.[66]

Despite MacArthur's optimistic prediction that with Cailles's surrender "it is most probable pacification of all southern Luzon will follow quickly," the war in the southwest continued.[67] In Cavite, Manuel Noriel rejected Trias's appeals and announced he would continue the resistance; and in Laguna, Caballes assumed Cailles's mantle. In Batangas, Malvar proclaimed his willingness to continue fighting for another decade. Even in Tayabas, Lt. Col. Emilio Zurbano maintained a somewhat shaky leadership of the insurgent forces. The persistence of guerrilla warfare barely a day's ride from Manila was a growing embarrassment to both civil and military authorities. Even more embarrassing was the fact that these provinces were officially pacified, for, in a move that was either obtuse or vengeful, MacArthur had insisted that the Philippine Commission extend civil government to Laguna and Batangas. Indeed, a civil government in Batangas had been sworn in on 2 May, at virtually the same time as Malvar informed his chief officers of his decision to continue the war.[68] Not surprisingly, Batangas's brief experiment in civil government was a fiasco, and two months later, on 20 July, the commission had to transfer partial control of the province back to the military. The army, in turn, declared a "state of insurrection" in Batangas, put civil officials under military officers, suspended habeas corpus, and replaced most civil judicial functions with military courts and commissions.[69] Both Taft and MacArthur's successor, Chaffee, wanted this interminable war ended, and they were increasingly willing to sanction drastic measures to ensure this.

The person charged with stamping out these embers of resistance was the newly promoted Brig. Gen. Samuel S. Sumner, who took over the combined 1st and 2nd Districts—Cavite, Batangas, Laguna, and Tayabas—in April 1901. Born into a military family, a Civil War veteran, and a cavalry officer with active service against the Indians and Spanish, Sumner had proved himself in the Cavite campaign, where he had driven Trias to capitulate. He took up his new command with similar vigor, and at first he appeared capable of similar results, forcing first Maloles and then Cailles to surrender. Yet despite these achievements, his superiors displayed little confidence in him and failed to provide him the necessary resources. The new commander of the Department of Southern Luzon, Maj. Gen. James F. Wade, continued his predecessor's passivity and interference. Thus when Sumner requested more troops, Wade dallied. When Sumner urged that Manila fill a long-standing need and create a division of military intelligence, nothing was done. When Sumner pressed for harsher measures, they were rejected. Even more serious, Chaffee appears to have been predisposed to distrust Sumner—both having served for decades in the cavalry, they may well have clashed—and did little to assist him. Indeed, by September Chaffee was writing Washington that Sumner "has not the vigor that the situation requires."[70]

Sumner was a victim of other factors as well. About one of these, the arrival of the monsoon a few months after he took command, he could do little. Roads washed out, bridges collapsed, rural garrisons were all but marooned for weeks, and sick rates soared, incapacitating between one-third and one-half of his soldiers. But other problems were more clearly Sumner's responsibility. In June he advocated that his troops be authorized to occupy any barrio in Batangas and to destroy any that furnished shelter or information to the insurgents. He also wanted to "arrest all the men and bring them to the several posts, force them to surrender arms or give information, and if necessary send all prominent men out of the country and let it be known that they will be held till the active Insurrectos come in and surrender their arms." These were, he explained, "harsh and stringent measure[s] and will entail hardships and suffering on the inhabitants," but they were the "only practicable means" of bringing the recalcitrant Batanguenos to heel.[71] But by the end of the summer Sumner had concluded that there was no solution to the guerrilla war in southwestern Luzon and that "the amount of country actually controlled by us is about as much as can be covered by the fire of our guns."[72] Malvar's guerrillas no longer traveled in organized units; they had dispersed, hidden their weapons, and taken refuge among the population. They could inflict little damage on the Americans, but they were quite able to collect taxes and impose their authority on the population. The army could not offer any inducement that would overcome the fear of assassination, nor could it escalate the level of violence against the guerrillas or pressure on the population without adopting methods that were "inhumane and unwise" and contrary to the policies enunciated by its government.[73] Among the methods Sumner rejected was the forced removal of the population into protected zones, for he maintained that Batangas's rugged terrain and the size of its population "preclude[d] the possibility of inaugurating any system of concentration or any thorough control of the food supply."[74]

Sumner's assessment was overly pessimistic, for he and his soldiers accomplished a great deal. Building on previous efforts, he had implemented a number of measures to restrict the food supply in southwestern Luzon. Under orders to cut off illegal trade in Laguna de Bay, post officers rigorously monitored their towns' supplies; one boasted that no one could leave his area "with so much as one fish or one package of cigarettes."[75] The widespread destruction of crops and storehouses forced many local guerrilla bands to disperse and prompted Malvar to order all inhabitants to grow food. But despite these accomplishments, Sumner's military operations did not finish off Malvar's guerrillas. Badly wounded and seldom capable of striking back, the insurgents continued to absorb punishment and wait for the Americans to tire.

By the fall of 1901, there was a growing demand both from Manila and from field officers for still harsher measures in Batangas. Writing to his close friend Adj. Gen. Henry C. Corbin in late October, Chaffee complained, "Sumner in Wade's Department has accomplished nothing with Malvar of consequence. Unless he does something soon I shall put some one else in command of his Brigade."[76] Taft had also turned against Sumner and wrote Secretary of War Root, "General Wade is incompetent and General Sumner under him is not very much better."[77] Colonel William W. Dougherty gave vent to the frustration of field officers:

> Divers attempts have been made during the past summer and this fall to bring the enemy to an engagement when he came into the province in force, but without avail, it being impossible to make a movement of troops from any of the stations before information of it would be supplied to the raiders by the people who inhabit the outside barrios along the foot of the mountain, thus enabling them to escape into hiding before the arrival of the troops. . . . It is apparent to me, and must be to anyone familiar with the conditions here, that a policy of moderation and forbearance towards those not under arms, but nevertheless actively engaged in supporting the insurrection, is untimely now and can end only in disaster. Accordingly, unless I am prohibited or enjoined by superior authority, I will hereafter invade and destroy all barrios that afford refuge to the enemy and that provide supplies and money for the maintenance of the insurrection in this neighborhood, and compel the people to move into the towns with their means of subsistence and remain there until the enemy leaves the field and surrenders his arm, which can not be long deferred when deprived of the necessary means to keep the field.[78]

Clearly, the officer who was charged with pacification in Batangas would need to be sufficiently ruthless to satisfy both superiors and subordinates and yet respected enough to check officers such as Dougherty from engaging in indiscriminate counterterrorism.

The choice of both Chaffee and Taft—and probably the vast majority of soldiers if consulted—was Brig. Gen. J. Franklin Bell. Bell had already proved himself in a variety of tasks—brigade staff officer, intelligence officer, commander of everything from an elite reconnaissance unit to a crack infantry regiment, provost marshal of Manila, and successful director of the pacification of northwestern Luzon. In the process, he had won a variety of admirers, ranging from the junior officers and their families whom he and his wife graciously entertained, to the virulently antimilitary correspondent Albert Robinson, to the most powerful military and civil officials in Manila. Indeed, one of the few things that both MacArthur and Taft agreed on was that Bell was the most outstanding general in the archipelago. Like virtually all army officers, Bell viewed the Filipinos at best as wayward and violent children who needed to be coerced into behaving properly. But, like many others, his ethnocentrism often led him in the direction of humanitarian action: thus as district commander he refused to prosecute *presidentes* caught aiding the guerrillas, sought to buy carabao to relieve the effects of rinderpest, and maintained, "I believe it the better policy to let some guilty persons escape punishment rather than take the risk of punishing an innocent man, denounced because of assistance to or friendship for Americans."[79] Yet he was also an advocate of "hard war," and if Taft's deputy was correct in asserting that Bell "has no patience with any acts of oppression or cruelty," it was also true that he tended to turn a blind eye to the methods of successful subordinates.[80] Significantly, as commander in northwestern Luzon, Bell had approved the forced relocation of several villages and the systematic devastation of Abra Province.

On 19 November, Chaffee ordered Bell to replace Sumner as commander of the newly organized 3rd Separate Brigade, encompassing the military forces in Batangas, Cavite, Laguna, Marinduque, Morong, and Mindoro. After two weeks to assess the situation, Bell formally took charge on the thirtieth. Unlike Sumner, he was given adequate forces for the task, some 7,600 soldiers and Filipino scouts. In a series of field and telegraphic orders and in a 1 December speech to his top subordinates, Bell outlined the most coherent and well-organized pacification campaign of the war. In designing a strategy, Bell—mistakenly, in the view of Glenn May—maintained that the war continued because the Batangas elite still supported the resistance.[81] In order to achieve victory, the 3rd Separate Brigade must not just separate the guerrillas from the population, it must force the population to help. Contrary to his earlier views, Bell determined that neutrality would no longer suffice; all who did not openly demonstrate their opposition to Malvar would be considered hostile. The test for loyalty would no longer be public protestations but practical deeds such as weapons collected, spies and agents denounced, guerrillas identified or brought in to surrender, and participation in counterinsurgency operations. For those whom post officers, military commissions, or provost marshals judged to be lacking in sufficient zeal, there was a host of penalties ranging from fines through the destruction of property, deportation, imprisonment, and even, Bell suggested, death.

The 3rd Brigade's commander used a great many methods that had been successfully developed both in his own campaigns and in other regional conflicts, the sum total of which was to put unbearable pressure on the guerrillas and their civilian supporters. Recognizing that fast and reliable information is one of the most precious commodities in counterinsurgency, Bell ensured that data passed smoothly from post officers to brigade and down again. A post intelligence officer in each station was charged with making a complete report of the area and its inhabitants; and lists of known and suspected revolutionaries were circulated, often accompanied by descriptions or photographs. Guerrillas who surrendered were forced to name their contacts, identify their comrades, and turn in weapons. Bell's provost marshals, drawn from some of the most experienced counterinsurgency experts in the army, conducted whirlwind investigations. Empowered to make mass arrests and assess large fines and up to two years' imprisonment, they systematically broke open the guerrillas' clandestine infrastructure. Should a confession or captured document reveal the location of a guerrilla band or supply center, Bell had fast-moving cavalry patrols, often accompanied by native scouts or local paramilitary forces, ready to strike immediately.

Bell also escalated the already intense efforts at food deprivation and destruction. The Loboo Mountains of southeastern Batangas had long been suspected as a guerrilla sanctuary and storehouse. In December, Col. Almond B. Wells led a punitive raid into the area designed "to kill or capture all able bodied men in the mountains and to remove or destroy virtually every vestige of food supply found therein."[82] Impressing dozens of civilians from the surrounding area, troops burned or carried away hundreds of tons of rice and over 1,000 livestock. These large devastation campaigns were supplemented by countless raids and forays from individual posts. Typical was the garrison at Cavinti, Laguna, which in January captured nine rifles, confiscated five tons of rice, and destroyed the storehouse of a local guerrilla band.[83] Bell ordered that food should, whenever possible, be brought into towns to feed the population, but until late in the campaign officers tended to plead military necessity and use the torch. The general became more and more concerned about this devastation and issued increasingly strict orders that food be preserved and that Filipinos be allowed to forage.[84] Despite his efforts, the cumulative effect of this devastation was enormous and would contribute to the appalling cholera and fever epidemics that killed thousands of Batanguenos.

Although Bell developed or adapted a variety of measures, both critics and supporters seized on one—the concentration or "reconcentration" of much of Batangas's civilian population. The tactic of forcibly moving people out of hostile areas to separate them from the guerrillas was not novel, within the U.S. Army or other Western powers: indeed, a key factor in turning American public opinion against Spain had been the reconcentration campaign waged by Gen. Valeriano Weyler in Cuba. Concentration had been openly discussed by many officers in the Philippines and practiced by a few; even the humanitarian Gardener, who would become a hero to anti-imperialists for his denunciation of Bell's methods, imposed a form of it in parts of Tayabas in May 1900.[85] But rarely had forced resettlement been applied on the scale or with the vigor that Bell imposed it on eastern Batangas. On 6 December he ordered that post commanders establish a protected zone and in the next twenty days bring in all rural inhabitants, their food, and their possessions. The day after Christmas, the area outside the zones was to be considered enemy territory, and all property could be confiscated or destroyed; all males were to be arrested and, if they attempted to escape, shot.[86]

Concentration was not enforced throughout the 3rd Separate Brigade, nor was it imposed with the same rigor in each place. Some towns that were known to be friendly or were already at war with Malvar's guerrillas were left alone; in other towns, reconcentration became a tool to prod the population into overt action. Of the towns in which it was tried, Capt. Henry C. Hale's plan for Tanauan, Batangas, may have been typical. Hale wished to "secure reasonable control" over the population and also to "reduce to a minimum the hardships of the common people."[87] The protected zone was laid out between the river and a "dead line" marked by flags and outposts manned by barrio residents. Each barrio's inhabitants brought in their property and then took apart, moved, and rebuilt their nipa-and-bamboo houses along a designated street. They were then assigned such tasks as grading streets and digging latrines, and each morning between 500 and 2,000 would go out to the countryside under army guard and collect rice and food, keeping half for themselves and half for the general reserve. According to Col. Arthur Wagner, who inspected Tanauan, conditions were quite good: there was great sickness among the population, especially the children, but he believed (almost certainly incorrectly) that the death rate was unchanged.[88]

Both at the time and later, concentration aroused enormous debate. To some field officers, such as cavalry officer turned provost marshal Capt. Charles D. Rhodes, it was simply a matter of "separating the sheep from the goats."[89] But Chaffee considered the issue so explosive he requested that the letter notifying the secretary of war of Bell's tactics be destroyed; remembering the public outcry against "Weylerism" he wanted no evidence of "what may be considered in the United States as harsh measures or treatment of the people."[90] Chaffee's worries were well founded, for then as now critics have pointed to the hypocrisy of the United States in adopting the same tactics against colonial populations it had vociferously condemned in Spain. Jacob G. Schurman, the head of the first Philippine Commission, editorialized that Bell's resort to Weyler's methods showed the "degeneration" of the American military effort.[91] But to one participant, this accusation ignored a key distinction: "We executed a 'Weyler' campaign, but did it strictly according to military law."[92]

The results of Bell's efforts became apparent almost immediately. In December, Malvar attempted an offensive against a few towns, which was beaten back easily. Thereafter, the army maintained the initiative, and the guerrillas and their supporters were driven ruthlessly. Increasingly, army sweeps and patrols were joined by Filipinos, acting either voluntarily or under coercion, who identified guerrillas and pointed out hideouts. As in Cavite a year earlier, by February the signs of demoralization were apparent: some guerrilla bands killed their officers and then surrendered, others abandoned their rifles, leaving them where patrols could easily find them. By March armed resistance was all but over, and all that remained was to persuade Malvar to surrender. Isolated, alone, beleaguered by American and Filipino patrols, beseeched by his former soldiers and friends to give up, he still fought on. However admirable his courage and devotion to independence might have been in the past, it was now subjecting his fellow citizens to intolerable misery and hardship. Finally, on 4 April, with his wife dangerously ill, Malvar made the only conscionable choice and sent a letter asking for a suspension of hostilities in order to discuss terms. After Bell promised him fair treatment, he surrendered on 16 April. He was followed by all his remaining subordinates, so that by early May the campaign was over.

In explaining his surrender, and no doubt seeking to placate his captors, Malvar gave them full credit: Bell's campaign had "kept me constantly on the move from the month of February down to the last moment" and caused the desertion of most of his officers, until by the time he surrendered "I found myself without a single gun or clerk . . . [as] all my staff officers had already fallen into the hands of the Americans."[93] He cited humanitarian reasons as well: if the farmers were not allowed to plant rice in May, there would be famine. His subordinates, under similar pressure, were unanimous in acknowledging the army's effectiveness. One maintained that without reconcentration the war would have lasted another three years, and Malvar's brother-in law, the former commander of Tayabas, testified, "The means used in reconcentrating the people, I think, were the only ones by which war could be stopped and peace brought about in the province."[94] Although these testimonies should be seen as what they were, confessions made under psychological, if not physical, duress, there is no reason to doubt their essential truth. Neither Malvar nor any prominent revolutionary officer ever repudiated his belief that, however destructive in lives and property, Bell's methods had worked.

The campaign in the Department of Southern Luzon, which began so promisingly with the invasion of January 1900, ended in appalling devastation and controversy seventeen months later. Although the war had consisted of three semiautonomous regional conflicts, they followed a similar pattern. Soldiers had occupied the main towns and attempted, in varying degrees, to win over the population through civic action. However, this alone proved unsuccessful in ending armed resistance, and throughout 1900 commanders continued the policy of attraction but steadily increased the military aspects of pacification—particularly food and property destruction. In 1901 coercive measures escalated even further to encompass the concentration of the population in Marinduque and Batangas and the devastation of both those provinces. Such harsh warfare, directed as much against Filipino civilians as against guerrillas, understandably outraged many Americans and contributed greatly to public disenchantment with the war in the Philippines.

FOURTEEN

SAMAR

The final campaign, in Samar, is probably the best known of the entire war.[1] It featured not only the war's most famous incident—the "Balangiga Massacre"—but also Jacob H. Smith's infamous, if perhaps apocryphal, directives to kill everyone over ten and turn the interior of the island into a "howling wilderness." Samar has also become symbolic within the U.S. Marine Corps for sacrifice and heroism: for years after the campaign, veterans would be saluted in mess halls with the toast "Stand, Gentlemen, he served on Samar!" Controversial at the time, Samar, along with Batangas, became lodged in both the popular and the academic mind as a microcosm of the entire war: indeed, many textbooks view the entire war through the prism of these final regional conflicts. But even at the time the two campaigns were recognized as atypical, and all evidence since then, by both American and Philippine scholars, has further demonstrated their uniqueness. That they continue to be portrayed in both academic and popular accounts as representative of both U.S. Army pacification and Filipino resistance is one of the great historical fallacies of the war.

Samar had remained a backwater since its transfer to the resource-starved 4th District, Department of Southern Luzon, in July 1900. Barring a few expeditions which demonstrated that their ability to inflict punishment on the population was equal to that of the guerrillas, the small occupation force barely held the hemp ports of Calbayog and Catbalogan. This changed in May 1901 when Leyte was turned over to the Philippine Commission. The conflict across the narrow San Juanico Strait in Samar could no longer be ignored: Samar's ferocious rebels threatened to undermine the pacification of Leyte, which in turn provided them a sanctuary and a supply base. On 13 May, MacArthur transferred Samar back to Hughes and the Department of the Visayas, with instructions to take "drastic measures" against Lukban and to "make this an emergency measure and clean up [Samar] as soon as possible."[2] A brief visit soon convinced Hughes that the situation was bad indeed and that the occupation forces "know nothing beyond gun shot range of their stations."[3]

As he had on Panay, Hughes combined active military operations with extensive food and property destruction. On 13 June 1901, he extended the

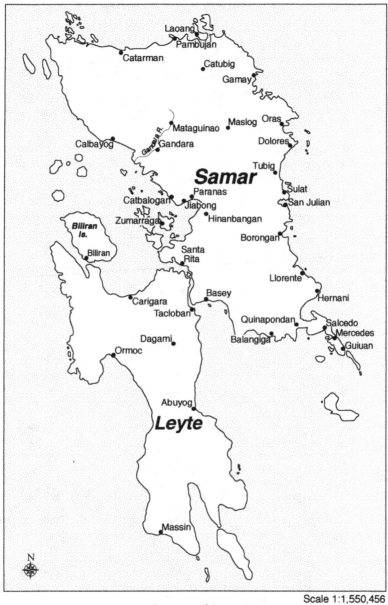

Scale 1:1,550,456

Samar and Leyte

naval blockade to all of the island's ports and instructed garrison officers stationed in coastal towns to seize all civilian boats except those necessary for fishing. He built supply camps in the main river valleys and ordered post commanders to send patrols to congregate upon them, in the process sweeping the interior, destroying crops, and driving the guerrillas out of the mountains. To stop smuggling from Leyte, he extended the line of garrisons south, placing a battalion of the 9th Infantry in the heretofore peaceful southern coastal towns of Balangiga, Lanang, Santa Rita, and Basey. Reinforced by more gunboats, navy skippers extended their patrols of Samar's waters and landed troops along the coast and rivers to search for guerrillas and storehouses. One such joint patrol, commanded by Capt. Mark L. Hersey, was ferried by navy gunboat up the Oras River, then landed and "burned houses by the hundreds for the next twenty miles."[4] In one month the garrison at Laguan destroyed 145 houses and 5,025 bushels of rice. Trekking through Samar's mountains, grasslands, and swamps, Hughes's soldiers performed impressive feats of marching and fighting, but none surpassed the 1st Infantry's Capt. Henry Jackson, who hiked his company completely across the northern

An amphibious landing on Samar: marines going ashore at Balangiga, 1901

half of the island and on 13 August badly wounded Lukban, capturing his family and most of his papers.[5]

Hughes may have been convinced of the success of his policies by the very real evidence of its effects on the civilian population. There could be little distinction between civilian and guerrilla property by troops under orders such as these: "Clear the country of all insurgents, capture the necessary guides and compel them to do such service and generally speaking make the region untenable by the insurgents."[6] As soldiers burned out crops in the interior, the Samarenos soon lost all means of supporting themselves. Their plight was exacerbated by Hughes's establishment of protected zones or "colonies" where "those wishing to escape from Lukban's villains" would be segregated from the guerrillas.[7] Too often this population resettlement meant that several thousand people were confined within areas devastated by two years of warfare. Calbayog, which had been almost deserted in May 1901, grew to 5,000 inhabitants by June; in another area the population soared from 6,000 to 20,000 in three months. The army's destruction of crops and the navy's blocking of coastal trade and fishing created widespread deprivation. Typical was the southern town of Guiuan, where by July the situation was so bad that the post commander, Maj. John J. O'Connell, predicted mass starvation unless he could obtain rice. As protests from the garrisons mounted, Hughes moderated his encouragement of destruction and established conditions under which food could be imported from Leyte. On 24 July he ordered that "the extravagant killing of carabao should not be permitted. These animals are not good beef but they are good for draft and the loss of them would be severely felt when these people wish to take up agricultural pursuits again. You might collect them in some district and hold them as war captives."[8] By September these grudging, haphazard relief efforts were clearly inadequate, and, faced with the specter of famine, Hughes authorized post commanders to appoint agents to purchase rice for each of the occupied towns.

Although the army achieved a number of military successes, the attack upon a twenty-six-man patrol of the 1st Infantry under Lt. Edward E. Downes offered graphic proof of the fragility of its hold in the interior. The patrol left Guiuan on the southeastern tip of Samar on 19 June, ostensibly seeking an overland trail up the narrow peninsula, but it quickly reverted to little more than a marauding expedition, burning houses and rice and slaughtering livestock. On the twenty-second there was a short skirmish in which two soldiers were wounded. The next day, with food and water getting dangerously low and the patrol quite lost, the noncoms urged a return to the coast, but Downes persisted. Marching in single file, carrying the wounded on litters, the patrol pressed on through the dense undergrowth, an easy target for ambush. In the early afternoon, a horde of bolomen suddenly emerged from the undergrowth and charged through the column. For five minutes there was absolute chaos. One soldier reported shooting a boloman at point-blank range; the man staggered, then continued to attack; the desperate soldier knocked his assailant down several times with his rifle before he was finally able to kill him. Two soldiers were killed and another two wounded. Among the fatalities was Downes. He had been about fifteen yards ahead of the patrol and was stabbed in the groin; as he collapsed, his head was forced back and a knife driven into his heart. He sat down, turned to a soldier and said, "Well, I guess I am killed," and died.[9] The survivors—"evidently badly shaken," in the words of the investigating officer—abandoned their dead and scattered.[10] After a three-day ordeal without food and water, they made it back to Guiuan. The Downes attack contributed both to Samar's fearsome reputation and to Hughes's conviction to "do some cleaning up down there."[11]

Ironically, although the population suffered terribly, the widespread crop destruction in Samar may have increased the ferocity and desperation of the resistance. Forced out of their mountain retreats and cut off from their normal sources of supply, the guerrillas soon found that Hughes had spread his forces too thin and that garrisons and expeditions were often undermanned and vulnerable. In September and October, they launched sporadic but effective raids, mauling supply trains, besieging towns, and ambushing isolated detachments. The pattern of the Downes attack was repeated: a patrol would be threading its way through Samar's head-high grasslands or trying to ford one of the innumerable mountain streams and become suddenly overrun by dozens of bolomen. Despite this resurgence, on 11 September Hughes notified Manila that the "enemy has been in hiding for two months, and are liable to stay so," and departed for Cebu.[12]

Less than two weeks later, on 28 September, townspeople and guerrillas virtually annihilated the seventy-four-man garrison of Company C, 9th U.S. Infantry, at Balangiga. The attack, a combined effort by villagers and guerrillas under Lt. Col. Eugenio Daza, was one of the most brilliant tactical operations of the war. In a misguided project to clean up the town, Capt. Thomas W. Connell had crammed dozens of people into tents, some of them Daza's *insurrectos*. Other guerrillas infiltrated the town as laborers, as members of a wedding party, or even dressed as women. As the soldiers began their Sunday breakfast, the police chief approached a sentry, then suddenly pulled a bolo and cut him down. A mob of bolomen charged out of the church and the tents, cutting and slashing the stunned soldiers. Connell and his subordinate, Lt. Edward A. Bumpus, were struck down; desperate soldiers fought off their attackers with Krags, kitchen implements, and even cans of food. A handful of men under veteran noncoms retained their composure and managed to fight their way through to the beach, where they set out on a desperate voyage by *banca* to the closest garrison at Basey. But forty-eight officers and men died in the attack or during the escape. The rebels captured 100 rifles, 25,000 rounds of ammunition, and a large quantity of medicines, food, and equipment.[13]

The "Balangiga Massacre" generated enormous controversy and an equally vast mythology that continues to this day, as the recent furor over the so-called Bells of Balangiga demonstrates.[14] The mythmaking began at once. Hughes and Chaffee blamed the attack directly on Connell and indirectly on all those who pursued conciliatory policies. Balangiga's commander had had a "straightforward, honest nature," which blinded him to "proof of the wiles and duplicity of the people about him": he had treated the Filipinos with compassion, and they responded with treachery.[15] The behavior of the people at Balangiga was duplicitous and barbaric. They had planned the attack for months, writing to Lukban that they intended to follow a "deceptive policy" until they could rise up and slaughter the Americans; then, in a final act, they had mutilated the corpses and dishonored the dead.[16]

Later writers accepted this moral fable but added to it Joseph Schott's reconstruction of the battle compiled from survivors' accounts, which graphically showed that even in the face of overwhelming odds (and Connell's misjudgment) the troops had fought heroically, killing 250 of the enemy. This makes stirring reading, but as an accurate account of events it fails most of the tests for historical evidence. Schott combined survivors' accounts taken down immediately by Capt. Edwin V. Bookmiller with others written as many as five decades later, by which time the veterans had ample time to read, and be influenced by, other accounts of the fight. Moreover, he picked and chose stories with a less than critical judgment; in the process he ignored contrary testimony and accepted dubious evidence at face value. Thus, for example, he disregarded the accounts of every other participant and, relying solely on testimony taken decades after the event from a veteran with a history of mental disorder, asserted that Bookmiller turned several Filipino civilians over to the survivors of Company C for execution. As with so much Balangiga apocrypha, later writers ignore the vast bulk of contrary evidence and repeat this prevarication.[17]

In fact, what little is certain about the massacre is that it was caused by a combination of Connell's overconfidence, carelessness by the garrison, and luck and skill by Daza's guerrillas and the villagers. That Connell was an exceptionally foolish and arrogant officer who bears primary responsibility for his command's destruction is certainly correct; that his errors were based on his humanitarianism is just as certainly not. Indeed, he had confined between 80 and 100 men in two tents designed to hold 16 men each and forced them to work without pay. It also appears that Company C needlessly antagonized the villagers by stealing, brutality, and at least one rape. Contrary to the assertions of many American writers, Lukban himself took no part in the attack and did not know about it until later. Filipino sources, including Daza's own testimony, make it clear that the attack was organized and carried out by local forces and that the primary motive was to avenge soldiers' misconduct. Daza recalled that the soldiers' resistance was confused and ineffectual, and that, far from losing 250 men, the attackers suffered but 28 killed and another 22 wounded. He strongly denied that his partisans had mutilated the dead; not only was this a cultural taboo, but "there was no time to lose for such acts."[18]

Myth and reality, Balangiga profoundly shocked Americans and touched off an immediate outcry for vengeance. According to Taft—hardly a neutral witness—the army high command was completely stampeded by the massacre and expected the imminent outbreak of a full-fledged insurrection.[19] In Samar, navy gunboats and army patrols, under orders to "make a desert of Balangiga," soon did such a thorough job that "with the exception of the stone walls of the church and a few large upright poles of some of the houses, there is today not a vestage [*sic*] of the town of Balangiga left."[20] The navy rushed gunboats and a 300-man marine battalion under Maj. Littleton W. T. Waller to the island, and the army built up its forces to some 4,000 soldiers in the newly created 6th Separate Brigade.[21]

Chaffee's selection of Brig. Gen. Jacob H. Smith to command the 6th Separate Brigade must go down as one of the gravest blunders of the entire war. Smith's career had given ample evidence of his muddy ethics, his limited military skills, and his intemperate character. After a dubious record in the Civil War, Smith wangled a Regular captaincy in 1867; he remained at this rank for almost three decades, during which his temper tantrums and lack of judgment led to his being court-martialed twice for insubordination and once for operating an illegal saloon. After a somewhat shaky performance in Cuba, he had served capably as both regimental and district commander in the Philippines. More important, he had ingratiated himself with both his military and his civil superiors. MacArthur liked him because he was a Civil War veteran; Taft appreciated his enthusiastic cooperation in organizing civil government and thoroughly approved of Smith's willingness to use the noose on guerrillas and brigands. What they overlooked was Smith's propensity for violent extralegal action—as when he attempted the summary execution of prisoners—and his oft-voiced conviction that a major obstacle to pacification was the tendency of officers to treat the Filipinos too leniently.[22]

When Chaffee sought brigadier generals for his new separate brigades in early September, Smith was one of the few available, and his appointment to command the 6th was reasonable. But after Balangiga, it was clearly Chaffee's military and moral responsibility to emphasize exactly what would be tolerated, and to caution Samar's new commander against letting either his own emotions or his troops' behavior get out of hand. Instead, when Smith stopped at his office, he simply told him to recapture the arms and ammunition lost at Balangiga. Whether Smith was correct in his allegation that Chaffee ordered him to "make the interior of Samar a howling wilderness," it is almost certainly true that he urged Smith to employ the harshest methods.[23]

Chaffee also erred in not clarifying the command relationship between Smith and Hughes. The Department of the Visayas' commander believed the creation of the 6th Brigade proved Manila's unhappiness with his failure to pacify Samar and responded by undermining Smith's authority. He overruled Smith's tactical deployments, denied him manpower, and challenged his decisions. Like Chaffee, Hughes pushed Smith to exact vengeance for Balangiga, ordering him to send more troops into southern Samar and "give them a fair opportunity to kill off the bands of utter savages who have hibernated in the brush in that vicinity. . . . Simple burning appears to be no good, they want to be stayed with and either killed or domesticated."[24]

Whether because of Hughes's interference or his own judgment, Smith intensified the destructive policies Hughes had initiated. His first official orders on 21 October urged "both army and navy officers . . . to take all possible precautions to stop illicit trade in rice, hemp, and other contraband of war."[25] To assist the naval blockade, he required all boat owners to obtain passes and to paint their boats red; he limited civilians at each garrisoned town to six fishing vessels and restricted those to nearby waters; and he gave officers freedom to destroy or confiscate any vessel that violated these orders. Successive directives closed the ports of Leyte, circumscribed the hemp and rice trade, limited the number of passes garrison commanders could issue, and required that native boats always be guarded by one or more soldiers. Both gunboats and soldiers were authorized to demolish any village suspected of signaling to the *insurrectos*. To demonstrate his policies in action, in November Smith coordinated an army sweep of northern Samar with naval gunboat patrols, thereby preventing the guerrillas from fleeing by water.[26]

Directly or indirectly, Smith's efforts further escalated the level of violence. By 6th Brigade estimates, between 10 October and 31 December 1901, soldiers and sailors killed or captured 759 *insurrectos* and 587 carabao, and destroyed tons of rice, 1,662 houses, and 226 boats. Gunboats and launches pushed farther up Samar's rivers than ever before; by November the Gandara River was filled with navy vessels assisting army operations. Captain Hugh D. Wise, commander of the launch *Rafaelito,* drove away snipers hiding along the high banks of Samar's rivers by building a seven-foot turret with a Gatling gun on top of his bridge. Waller's marines also obtained vital naval support for their patrols of the Basey-Balangiga area and in their successful assault on a guerrilla camp several miles up the Sojoton River. Yet another instance of cooperation was the support given by the navy to Maj. Edwin F. Glenn's investigations of the *insurrectos'* logistical system. With the assistance of the *Villalobos* and the *Frolic,* Glenn landed at several towns on Samar and Leyte, interrogating suspects and raiding suspected guerrilla storehouses.[27]

Efficient though it appeared, the joint-service effort suffered from an inherent weakness at its very source. Unable to break the habits of decades as a company commander, Smith wandered off to participate in patrols and expeditions, leaving brigade headquarters unclear of his wishes, or even his location. When he was exercising command, the consequences were even worse, as, for example, when he told Capt. A. P. Buffington, "I want this war carried on with more severity. In fact, it is more killing that I want."[28] Despite his ostensible determination to eliminate all sources of the guerrillas' food supply, Smith vitiated his restrictions with a number of exemptions under which post commanders could import food or allow their post's inhabitants to fish outside the area outlined in his general orders. He also failed to clarify the command structure, with the result that post commanders continued to exercise the dispensation granted them by Hughes to allow civilians to transport food. Navy officers, who believed that all passes were bound by the narrow restrictions established under the army's early directives, soon complained: "It was impossible for the officers who issued the passes to exercise any supervision over them and consequently the pass became a most convenient cloak under which to pursue contraband traffic."[29] On 14 January, Adm. Frederick Rodgers summed up the navy's frustration in a blast at Smith's lax direction: "It may safely be said that if the military operations on shore were conducted by the Army with the same unflagging zeal, energy and unity of purpose that characterized the movements afloat, that the termination of hostilities on Samar would be a matter of weeks instead of months."[30]

Rodgers's criticism ignored the problems faced by ground forces on the island. In contrast to their navy compatriots, who seldom witnessed the effects of the blockade at first hand, soldiers on Samar were literally face-to-face with the starvation, disease, and suffering caused by the food deprivation policy. With their towns filled with hungry civilians, many of them only too eager to cooperate, post commanders were caught in an intolerable dilemma. For many of them, humanitarian concern for their charges and a sense of professionalism superseded Smith's directions to let the population suffer. In the face of their demands, Smith allowed post officers special permission to bring in food, but he failed to notify navy captains of these exceptions. Not surprisingly, gunboats disregarded the special passes and continued to sink or confiscate civilian vessels, leading post officers to accuse the navy of destroying any hope of winning over the population. There were also several complaints about gunboats turning their considerable firepower on the wrong targets. When the *Arayat* shelled a pro-American rally of over 1,000 Filipinos, Lt. Harry H. Tebbetts bitterly noted, "The effect was to cause the utmost confusion and alarm among the natives along this part of the coast, to whom but that very day I had guaranteed all the protection that the U.S. could afford."[31]

Smith's leadership failed in civilian relations as well. Leyte had been under civil government since May 1901, but Smith quickly concluded the island was a "seething cauldron of discontent" and required "the same heroic treatment which is being applied to Samar."[32] Clearly exceeding his authority, Smith forbade any interisland commerce and restricted Leyte's rice and hemp trade. Further exacerbating the situation, he abruptly withdrew troops from Leyte, informing its governor, Joseph H. Grant, that if the island was truly pacified there was no need for army forces. Even worse, he allowed his subordinates, including the brutal brigade provost marshal, Major Glenn, to raid up and down Leyte's coast, kidnapping civilians and dragging them off to Samar.[33] Smith's actions infuriated Henry T. Allen, chief of the Philippine Constabulary, Governor Taft's newly created arm for law enforcement, who concluded that Smith was insane and began an active correspondence to discredit him.[34]

Given the chaotic command situation on Samar, the position of Waller's marine battalion was so unclear, and its behavior so disreputable, that it would eventually require a ruling by the U.S. Army's judge advocate general to clarify its status.[35] Smith ordered it to garrison Basey and Balangiga, but Waller soon claimed to command his own subdistrict—though he wisely chose not to issue orders to the neighboring army post commanders.[36] More controversially, Smith allegedly gave verbal instructions to Waller to "kill and burn," take no prisoners, make the interior of Samar a "howling wilderness," and regard every male over ten as a combatant.[37]

An ambitious and ruthless officer with a fondness for the bottle, Waller set out to comply. Between 31 October and 10 November, his marines burned

255 houses and destroyed one ton of hemp, a half ton of rice, thirteen carabao, and thirty boats while killing thirty-nine men and capturing eighteen.
On 17 November the battalion stormed a guerrilla stronghold on the Sojoton
River near Balangiga, killing thirty guerrillas and scattering the rest.[38] Flushed
with success, Waller failed to recognize that navy support alone had permitted his troops to survive in the interior and that the ten-day campaign had
exhausted his men. Instead, he set out on a series of patrols and expeditions
that further weakened his command. To extend his patrols' range, he reduced
their rations. Drenched by continuous showers and savaged by leeches and
ants, the half-starved marines scoured the grasslands, mountains, and swamps
in vain.[39]

Frustrated by the lack of tangible opposition, Waller decided to expand
his area of operations. On 19 November he notified Smith of his intention
to march from Lanang to Basey, "belting the southern end of Samar."[40] The
rationale is still a mystery. Waller's reason—that Smith had suggested explor-
ing a telegraph route—is clearly implausible: as a direct telephone line ran
from Waller's headquarters at Basey to Smith's headquarters at Tacloban,
there was no pressing need for a telegraph line, nor does 6th Brigade correspondence make any reference to it. Numerous army expeditions had already
determined that no likely route existed, and the fate of the Downes patrol
was ample warning of what might go wrong to a lost column. No wonder
that the local army officers, far more experienced with the treacherous interior, urged Waller not to undertake the operation without establishing a secure
supply line and depots. Indeed, shortly before he left, an army officer came
back from a patrol into the very area Waller intended to enter; he not only
confirmed there was no route but "spoke of the hardships of mountain climbing, even when he had a supply camp and shelters for his men."[41] Whether
because of service parochialism, inexperience, or mulish stupidity, Waller disregarded this advice, ignored his logistics, and plunged into the interior without even telling the army officers where he intended to go.

The ensuing march of 6 officers, 50 marines, 2 Filipino scouts, and 33
native porters from Lanang to Basey between 28 December 1901 and 19
January 1902 was one of the great American disasters of the war. As army
officers had warned, the trail quickly disappeared, and the expedition soon
slowed to a crawl as each foot of the way had to be cut through the sodden
and steaming jungle. Although the survivors' recollections of the march are
vague and contradictory, it is clear that after only five days supplies had run
dangerously low and the men were exhausted. On about 2 January, Waller
and his officers decided to abandon their objective and head back, but the
rafts they built sank in the river. In a decision that was either pragmatic or

panicked, Waller took two officers and thirteen of his strongest men and made his way through the jungle to a base camp. His second in command, copying Waller, hacked his way back to Lanang with seven marines and six porters. The remainder, under Lt. Alexander Williams, were left on the trail. Starving and suffering from prolonged exposure, Williams and several marines became convinced that the porters were hoarding food and were plotting against them. The lieutenant claimed he was attacked by three of the porters, although his recollection of the event—that he lacked the strength to fire his pistol but still fought off his armed assailants—is contradictory and confused. Waller, trying desperately to redeem his error without informing his superiors, scraped together a relief force and blundered back into the mountains, accomplishing little except his own physical collapse. In the meantime, the army, at last alerted to the situation, rescued Williams on 18 January. By that time ten marines had either died or disappeared and an eleventh was to die shortly afterward. Starving, barefoot, their clothes in rags, some crazed by their exertions, the marines were literally helpless, their rifles and ammunition carried by their porters.[42]

The ability of military institutions to mythologize their failures is well known, but rarely has such an absolute fiasco as Waller's march been so covered with glory. Even Waller admitted, "As a military movement it was of no other value than to show that the mountains are not impenetrable to us."[43] But very soon the marines transformed this botched patrol into an epic of courage and leadership, and later historians all too willingly accepted the myth. Yet even a cursory glance at the map will show that Waller's march should have been, by the standards of Philippine War service, a comparatively average "hike." In terms of distance, hardship, and enemy opposition, it certainly will not stand up to comparison to such epic marches as that of Young's Cavalry Brigade, or Batchelor's trek into the Cagayan, or Hare and Howze's rescue of Gillmore—all of which had the added virtue of being successful. Indeed, only a few months before the disaster, Jackson's company had marched across Samar with nothing worse than sore feet, and in Waller's own area soldiers had operated for months without getting lost or having their officers abandon them. In retrospect, the affair showed such palpably unprofessional conduct that Waller should have been relieved, if not court-martialed: instead, he was, and is, lauded as a hero and Young, Batchelor, Howze, Hare, and Jackson have long been forgotten.

Waller compounded his shabby record by ordering the execution of twelve civilians without benefit of trial or even the rudiments of an impartial investigation. The first killing, on 19 January, was of a man who was denounced as a spy by the *presidente* of Basey. Because Waller was running a temperature as high as 105 degrees and was pronounced by the camp surgeon to be incompetent to command, authority in Basey fell to Waller's adjutant, Lt. John H. A. Day. Day subjected the suspect to "a real third degree" and claimed to have secured a confession, of which he was later unable to remember any relevant details. Acting "on the spur of the moment," he decided on summary execution and in a few minutes organized a firing squad, personally shot the suspect, and left him unburied in the street as a warning.[44]

The following day saw an even bloodier incident. Williams and many of the survivors were in the hospital on Leyte, and no one at Basey was sure what had happened. Some believed that not ten but twenty marines had died, and nearly everyone accepted the rumor that the porters had been treacherous. Although Basey was connected by telephone with 6th Brigade headquarters, Waller neither asked for information, requested an investigation, nor brought charges against the suspects. Instead, hovering between delirium and lucidity, he ordered that the surviving porters be brought over from Leyte and executed. He then collapsed, so that it fell to a marine private, George Davis, to pick out those who had been guilty of specific crimes. Davis identified three whom he recalled had hidden potatoes, stolen salt, failed to gather wood, and disobeyed orders. He then selected another seven on the grounds that, as he later claimed, "They were all thieves . . . and they were all worth hanging, if I had anything to do with it."[45] Accordingly, the ten men were lined up and shot by Day's firing squad. At Waller's insistence, a final victim was executed later that afternoon—providing through his grim arithmetic a total of eleven victims in exchange for the eleven marines he had lost on the march.

In a report written three months after the incident, Waller gave a variety of reasons for the executions: the hostility of the townspeople of Basey; "reports of the attempted murder of the men and other treachery by the natives"; his own weakened physical condition; and his power of life and death as a (self-appointed) district commander. His conclusion—"It seemed, to the best of my judgment, the thing to do at that time. I have not had reason to change my mind"—suggests a mind unhinged.[46] Clearly, Waller engaged in no procedure, nor made any effort to engage in a procedure, that either a civil or a military court would recognize as an inquiry. Neither then nor since has any evidence emerged to prove that any of his victims were guilty of "attempted treachery" or any other action that warranted the death penalty under the laws of war. Chaffee, believing that Waller's actions were those of a man suffering from "mental anguish," noted: "Those sent to their death continued to the last to carry the arms and ammunition after [the marines] were no longer able to bear them, and to render in their impassive way, such service as deepens the conviction that without their assistance many of the marines who now survive would also have perished." Further, in executing the porters, Waller had violated the laws of war and assumed powers that only a commanding general in the field was allowed. What made his crime even more heinous was that at any minute he could have phoned his commanding officer "but deliberately chose not to consult him regarding his contemplated action."[47]

The subsequent court-martial of Waller and Day for murder is almost as controversial today as it was nearly a century ago. Amid the last death throes of the Philippine War, the trials seem to embody the brutality, ambiguity, and frustration of our first Asian guerrilla conflict. Day claimed he was following Waller's orders when he executed the alleged spy. Waller swore Day had acted without his permission. The court accepted Day's version, thus suggesting Waller had committed perjury. At his own trial, Waller adopted a similar defense and claimed that Smith had ordered him to make the interior of Samar a "howling wilderness." These charges provoked national outrage. Opponents of Philippine annexation, recovering from Bryan's crushing defeat, focused on the issue of atrocities to discredit the army.[48] Waller's acquittal by an army court did little to resolve the controversy, for both the military authorities who examined the trial transcript and President Roosevelt concluded it was a miscarriage of justice. Indeed, the commander in chief was so incensed he issued an army general order that Waller's actions "had sullied the American name."[49] Nevertheless, Waller has been acclaimed as one of the heroes of the war: Stuart Miller praises him as an "honorable warrior" and a "sacrificial victim," and Stanley Karnow calls him "a scrupulous professional" and a "scapegoat."[50] Such sentiments imply a moral viewpoint that would do credit to Waller himself.

Unfortunately, Waller was not the only officer who disgraced himself on Samar. Surrounded by a hostile population and rattled by an escape attempt, Capt. William Wallace shot seven prisoners on 4 December 1901. Far more reprehensible were the actions of Major Glenn, who between October 1901 and January 1902 kidnapped civilians from both Leyte and Samar, tortured suspects—including three priests—and conspired in the murder of at least ten Filipinos. As his court-martial transcript shows, Glenn's conduct not only demonstrated a "reckless disregard for human life" but also contributed greatly to the growing impasse between the army and the civil government.[51] In fairness, army operational records demonstrate that many commanders ignored Smith's directives and did their best to protect the population. However, the actions of Waller, Smith, Glenn, and others tainted the reputation of soldiers not only on Samar but throughout the archipelago.[52]

By the end of 1901 there was almost total frustration with the campaign on Samar. The monsoon flooded the countryside and typhoons lashed the seas, all but ending joint army-navy operations. But the weather did nothing to stop the endemic warfare in the countryside, with soldiers, guerrillas, rebels, bandits, and refugees all making a violent passage through the interior. Some Americans encouraged this social conflict: after watching residents of one town attack guerrilla supporters in another, an officer noted with some satisfaction, "It is said a feud has been inaugurated between the people of Guiuan and Salcedo that will last a hundred years."[53] The very success of post commanders in pacifying their areas hampered further efforts, for the cumulative effects of their devastation meant that troops now had to take virtually all their food with them. Even tough, highly competent field commanders complained that "most of our men seem to have reached the limit of their endurance for long hikes. There being no enemy in the immediate vicinity, all hikes are long now [from] 10 to 15 days."[54]

In January the gathering storm between Smith and the civil government of Leyte finally broke. Sixth Brigade headquarters and individual officers had repeatedly encroached on Leyte's civil government, closing ports, attempting to place all civil officials under military authority, interfering in the island's commercial trade, and kidnapping citizens for interrogation, and often for physical abuse. Disregarded were protests from Governor Grant, from Leyte's inhabitants, from numerous merchants, and from Manila. Taft's deputy, Luke Wright, pointedly reminded Chaffee of "the importance of having a man in charge of that section who is less extreme and violent" and complained to Taft of Smith's "insane idea that Leyte is full of insurrectos and that arbitrary and drastic measures are the remedy for the situation there."[55] Mindful of MacArthur's fate, Chaffee hurried down to Samar to resolve the impasse. Privately concluding that "Smith has worked very hard on Samar, but I cannot say that he has worked with good judgment," Chaffee pressured Smith to modify his policies, to accept civil government authority, and to adopt pacification techniques that distinguished between friends and enemies.[56] Chaffee also took steps to restore discipline and control the random devastation of the island.

Chaffee's reforms were never fully implemented because by the time he departed on 28 January, the weather had changed and it was clear that the insurgency on Samar was on its last legs. The guerrillas, whose success had always owed more to terrain and the weakness of the occupying forces than to their own military strength or popular support, were now desperate. With the interior devastated, with the army and navy controlling the rivers and coasts, with the population segregated in protected zones, and with the naval blockade still firm, the *insurrectos'* traditional sources of food had disappeared. They were now dispersed into scattered bands of ragged fugitives who spent more time searching for food than fighting. On 18 February Filipino scouts led by Lt. Alphonse Strebler captured Lukban, sick, malnourished, and disgusted with the war. Although Lukban's chief subordinate, Claro Guevarra, immediately assumed command and declared he would continue to fight, he could not stem the mass defections. After prolonged negotiations, on 27 April Brigadier General Grant accepted the surrender of the last of Samar's guerrillas; on 16 June military rule was formally concluded and civil government begun. The longest and most brutal pacification campaign in the Philippine War had ended.[57]

The aftermath of the Samar campaign was painful. Chaffee's investigation of Smith's abuses prompted a spate of courts-martial, including those of Waller, Smith, Glenn, and several lower ranking officers. These trials were covered extensively by the press, and even supporters of Philippine annexation were shocked at the revelations of destruction, torture, and murder. To some, it appeared that the civilians back home cared more about Filipinos than their own countrymen. An embittered Glenn wrote a brother officer: "I have but one regret through it all which is that our responsible commanders who were in a position to do so did not protect us in doing that which they sent us to do and which in fact they showed great anxiety that we should do in order that credit might come to them."[58] Like Batangas, Samar cast a pall on the army's achievement and, for generations, has been associated in the public mind as typifying the Philippine War.

FIFTEEN

CONCLUSION

In February 1899, the very month that fighting broke out between Filipino and American forces in Manila, *McClure's Magazine* published a poem by Rudyard Kipling entitled "The White Man's Burden." Kipling urged the United States to "have done with childish ways" and assume the responsibilities of imperial overlordship. The poet was grimly realistic about the costs of empire: he predicted the nation would bind its sons to exile, disease, and death, see many of its accomplishments vitiated, and, ultimately, receive little but blame for its efforts—all rather prescient observations. Kipling also warned of "the savage wars of peace," a phrase that later authors have borrowed freely to describe the American occupation of the Philippines.[1] Indeed, opponents of annexation accepted Kipling's terminology while mocking his ideals; they maintained the savagery of the conquest was due to a xenophobic and brutal American soldiery "civilizing" the Filipinos with their Krag rifles.[2] This interpretation of the war has been readily accepted by nonspecialists, so that for the past fifty years college texts have summarized the war in much the same way: "American soldiers tended to dismiss Filipinos as nearly subhuman. Their armed resistance to American occupation often transformed the frustrations of ordinary troops into brutality and torture. To avenge a rebel attack, one American officer swore he would turn the countryside into a 'howling wilderness.' Before long the American force was resorting to a garrison strategy of herding Filipinos into concentration camps, while destroying villages and crops."[3] Ask students what they know about the war, and they will respond with a few clichés: the howling wilderness; the water cure; civilize 'em with a Krag.

The resilience of this myth is impressive, for it continues despite the fact that it has been challenged by virtually every scholar who has undertaken detailed research in the primary sources. One of the more thoughtful critics is Philippine scholar Glenn A. May. In a 1983 article, he argued that "from a purely military perspective, the U.S. victory in the Philippines was due more to the mistakes of the enemy than the cleverness of the U.S. command."[4] Among the causes for Filipino defeat, May singled out "Aguinaldo's inept leadership" and, most controversial, that the narrow *principale* base of the revolution ensured that "Aguinaldo and his army received lukewarm support from the Filipino masses."[5]

American military historians have also posted a strong challenge to the prevailing dogma. In 1973 John M. Gates drew attention to the vital role played by army social reform, or what the guerrillas termed the "policy of attraction." Through extensive mining of the primary sources, he demonstrated the army's commitment to schools, roads, municipal government, health care, sanitation, and other civic projects. The United States won the Philippine War, according to Gates, because it was able to structure a coherent pacification policy that balanced conciliation with repression, winning over the Filipino population and punishing those who resisted.[6] Gates's interpretation has been criticized for overemphasizing the effectiveness of benevolent policies, but its central argument—that the success of the army was dependent on a judicious mixture of carrot and stick—is generally accepted. Even authors such as Andrew Birtle, who maintains that "ultimately military and security measures proved to be the sine qua non of Philippine pacification," acknowledge the importance of civic action.[7]

Thus a century after the end of the conflict, there is a consensus among scholars that rejects the popular mythology of "civilize 'em with a Krag" and instead maintains the war was won by a combination of Filipino mistakes and American military effectiveness. So accepted is this view that specialists now argue over levels of degree: Was this, as May implies, a war that the Filipinos lost? Or, as Gates and Birtle maintain, a war that the United States won?

Certainly, the revolutionary leadership deserves much blame. Contrary to the claims of nationalist authors, neither Aguinaldo's various governments nor the assembly that proclaimed the Philippine Republic in January 1899 was ever more than a small *principale* oligarchy whose base of support rested on the Tagalog-speaking regions of south and Central Luzon. These "nationalists" sought to create a centralized state to govern the entire archipelago, but many Filipinos, particularly outside of Luzon, appear to have favored a federal government with considerable provincial autonomy. Both the nationalists' narrow geographic base and their elitist policies weakened their authority in the countryside and created considerable opposition—opposition that might well have turned to armed resistance had the invasion not subsumed regional and ethnic animosities in the general struggle against the Americans.

The revolutionaries also committed a number of grievous military errors. Many of these were made by Aguinaldo, who was unable to place national interests above personal gain. Focused on imposing personal control on the rest of the archipelago, he consistently underestimated the danger posed by the invaders. The litany of blunders—the failure to attack Manila on 13

August 1898; the insufficient preparations for the Manila uprising; the confusion in the first weeks of February 1899; the decision to fight a conventional war; the delay in switching to guerrilla warfare—all were ultimately Aguinaldo's responsibility. These mistakes cost the revolutionaries irreplaceable trained soldiers, weapons, ammunition, and equipment, and also intangible factors such as discipline and morale. Aguinaldo also bears much of the blame for the strategic mistake of tying Filipino independence to the election of Bryan. However greatly this contributed to guerrilla morale in 1900, it was a major factor in the general collapse of 1901. Rarely has any independence movement been so poorly served by its titular leader.

Beyond Aguinaldo, there were serious internal weaknesses within the resistance movement. Although some excellent regional guerrilla commanders arose, such as Malvar, Lukban, and Cailles, there was no one equivalent to the American Revolution's Nathanael Greene, a general who could effectively combine partisans with regulars to achieve campaign or strategic goals. The guerrillas always remained localized, unable to move out of their home areas or to coordinate their attacks. They never mounted a successful prolonged defense of an area, nor recovered an area once it had been occupied. As a result, they could never establish a "free" territory that might serve as a basis for a new government. Indeed, after 1899 the revolutionaries were essentially fighting a holding action; the best they could hope for was that their opponents would tire.

Although some guerrillas showed an impressive command of small-unit tactics and an even more impressive ability to mobilize popular support, they could not sustain their successes. The decision by some jefes to adopt terrorist tactics to discourage cooperation was, like the attempt to influence the 1900 elections, a shortsighted policy. In virtually every province, terrorism ultimately alienated the population and encouraged collaboration with the occupiers. This was not simply a matter of morality—soldiers employed counterterrorism that was perhaps even more punitive—but also common sense. Beyond the ever diminishing hope of independence, the guerrillas could offer little positive inducement to avoid cooperating with the invaders. Indeed, they could return very little for their demands, which at a minimum included high taxes, impressed labor, and forced service in the militia. In contrast, the Americans could offer both the threat of punishment and a number of rewards, including civil office and business opportunities for the *principales,* and peace and personal security for the peasantry. Over the course of 1900, more and more people made what seemed the more sensible choice.

But if the Filipinos suffered from severe, even insurmountable, internal problems, this did not necessarily guarantee a United States victory. The

American military forces in the islands faced problems equally daunting—terrain, lack of information, unfamiliarity with the population, lack of resources, disease, poor communications, and, of course, armed resistance—any or all or which might have dragged the war on until their fellow citizens decided enough was enough.

One of the first and greatest problems was simply having insufficient forces for the job. By the U.S. Army's estimates, troop strength averaged 40,000 and peaked at 70,000 in December 1900. Even these figures are misleading, for they include soldiers in transit or on detached duty, and they fail to take into account the steady deterioration of troops in the field. The actual number of combat troops available—what the army termed "firing line" strength—was usually no more than 60 percent of the total troop strength in the archipelago: or an average of 24,000 and a peak strength of 42,000. This is, most would agree, an infinitesimal number of men to overcome an enemy force that May estimated as between 80,000 and 100,000 regulars and "tens of thousands more in local organizations."[8]

What gave the edge to American military forces was not their numbers but their effectiveness. Part of this had to do with weapons. The Filipinos had nothing that could stand up to their opponents' field artillery or to the heavily armed gunboats that plied the rivers and seas. In the brush warfare that typified conflict in the boondocks after 1899, the Americans had in the Krag an excellent rifle for tropical service—rugged, reliable, accurate, and powerful—as well as a limitless supply of reliable ammunition. To their superiority in weapons, the Americans added superior skills in their use. The open-order tactics developed by the army in 1891 proved themselves in the paddies and jungles of the Philippines, but, equally important, soldiers quickly adapted to the conditions they faced in the locality. Although Mabitac, Catubig, Marinduque, and Balangiga are dramatic examples of what could go wrong, for the most part soldiers could be confident that they could defend themselves against, if not defeat, any force they faced.

The U.S. Navy also played a crucial role. Indeed, without the navy, the army could not have conducted military operations in the Visayas or southern Philippines. The blockade not only prevented foreign arms shipments but also effectively ended interisland trade. One of the reasons Aguinaldo was unable to centralize his authority is that he could not send large numbers of troops outside Luzon. Navy gunboats shut down coastal traffic—absolutely essential in an archipelago lacking roads—and disrupted the revolutionaries' efforts to raise and transport funds. The navy also played an important role in military operations, allowing the Americans an amphibious capability their opponents lacked. This capability proved vital in such military operations as the occupation of Iloilo, Wheaton's landing at Lingayen Gulf, and Kobbé's hemp expedition. But equally important, gunboat patrols protected and resupplied dozens of coastal troop stations and thus allowed the army to stretch out its scarce manpower. After the Balangiga disaster, for example, it was navy gunboats that alerted the garrisons in southern Samar, and their artillery and machine guns that prevented a repetition of the attack. Although joint army-navy operations were initially characterized by parochialism and bickering, they improved over the course of the war, particularly after Dewey left. Most company officers and gunboat commanders were quite willing to put aside service rivalry and cooperate. The result was a highly effective amphibious capability that was crucial to pacifying coastal regions.

On the army side, the United States soldiers did extraordinarily well. The government fought the war with three different military organizations—State Volunteers, Regulars, and U.S. Volunteers—and all three proved quite successful. The State Volunteers bore the brunt of the conventional war in 1899, the U.S. Volunteers the guerrilla war. The Regulars suffered from a number of problems in 1899, but by mid-1901 they were capable of assuming the full responsibility for pacifying the archipelago. The members of all three organizations showed formidable fighting skill, high morale, and an ability to adapt to local conditions. The U.S. Volunteers in particular seem to have been outstanding soldiers, if the number of testimonials to them by Regulars is any indication. Far from being the bloody-handed butcher of fable, the average soldier in the Philippines was probably as good as or better than any in this nation's history.[9]

At the highest levels, American military leadership was superior to that of its opponents, and far better than critics have given it credit for. While none but the most fervent biographer could find much to like in the personalities of either Otis or MacArthur, their contribution to the victory was considerable. To Otis, more than anyone, is due the successful departure of the first Philippine expeditions and the defeat of the Army of Liberation in 1899. Equally important, he was the key figure in the development of American pacification policy in the islands. He was an advocate of McKinley's "benevolent assimilation," and from the beginning he emphasized that the army's role was as much to restore order and protect the population as it was to suppress armed resistance. MacArthur deserves credit for recognizing that Otis's program placed too much emphasis on civic action and not enough on coercion, and for ultimately establishing a successful, if far harsher, balance. Although he certainly overrated the impact of his December 1900 shift in policy, his adoption of G.O. 100 and his orders to go after the guerrilla infrastructure provided valuable direction. Moreover, as his directives during the Marinduque campaign show, after McKinley's reelection MacArthur turned increasingly to counterterrorism, thus offering a clear and very unpleasant alternative to those who continued armed resistance.

The Americans also produced a remarkably competent cohort of field commanders and post officers. Much of the credit belongs to the army's officer corps—Regular and Volunteer. With the exception of Funston and Bell, these men are all but forgotten now, even within their own service, but a glance at the combat achievements of John G. Ballance, William Kobbé, Arthur Murray, Robert L. Howze, and dozens of others confirms the strength and all-around excellence of army leadership. Equally important were the hundreds of officers assigned to garrison duties in the archipelago's towns, who, more than anyone else came to serve as representatives of United States authority. Their conduct often determined whether the population would accept or reject colonial rule. It is a sad example of history's unfairness that Jacob H. Smith, Edwin F. Glenn, Littleton W. T. Waller, and their ilk have come to typify the American officer in the Philippines.

A crucial component of the American victory was civic action or social reform. Even while engaged in combat operations, soldiers built schools and sanitation systems, roads and bridges, and brought to many a village the first law and the first peace it had known in years. One veteran Regular officer recalled the army's task in the islands: "The formation of local governments including the establishment of educational, sanitary, fiscal and welfare systems. . . . Reversing the policy [of] extermination applied to our American Indians, we were determined to preserve the Filipino [by] raising his standards and cultivating his friendship."[10] The U.S. Army's enemies, if not its own citizens, clearly recognized both the scope and the effectiveness of this "policy of attraction" and devoted a great deal of effort to counter it.

As many acknowledged from the beginning, benevolence and civic action were not enough to overcome Filipino resistance. Despite garrisoning hundreds of posts throughout the archipelago, soldiers found they could neither offer sufficient rewards to win over their opponents nor sufficient protection to save their friends from guerrilla retaliation. In an effort to separate the guerrillas from the population, the army increasingly turned to what Birtle has termed "the policy of chastisement."[11] As Kipling predicted, the Philippine War proved to be a "savage war of peace," far more savage than many Americans were willing to tolerate. Sanctions ranged from fines and arrest through burning to the concentration of the population and the widespread devastation of the countryside. Because the army increasingly relied on punitive measures—and because the degree of punishment escalated over the course of the war—the last campaigns in Samar and Batangas were marked by very harsh warfare indeed. Unfortunately for the historical record, these last campaigns are now perceived as typifying the entire war. Even more distressing, many Americans, particularly in academia, interpret the Philippine War through an ideological perspective developed during the 1960s. At its extreme, this leads to such anachronisms as Stuart Miller's claim that the Philippine War was "our Mylai of 1900."[12] Moral outrage over the American suppression of Philippine independence may be commended, but it has contributed to some very bad history.

After a century of portrayal largely in the context of current sensibilities, a reevaluation of military operations during the Philippine War is long overdue. The imperialist myth of selfless Americans saving their "little brown brothers" from the violent tyranny of Aguinaldo and the Tagalogs has long been discredited. The current view of a brutal and racist soldiery slaughtering defenseless natives has been unchallenged for far too long. The actual war was a far more complex and challenging phenomenon than either of these superficial interpretations acknowledge. When stripped of ideological blinders, the study of the Philippine War can offer great insight into the complexities of localized guerrilla war and indigenous resistance to foreign control. As the most successful counterinsurgency campaign in U.S. history, it is the logical starting point for the systematic examination of military interventions, civic action, and pacification operations. Given the recent interventions into internecine regional struggles, the history of the Philippine War has much to offer both civilian and military readers.

NOTES

Abbreviations

AAAG	Acting Assistant Adjutant General
AAG	Assistant Adjutant General
Adj	Adjutant
AG	Adjutant General
AGO	Adjutant General's Office Document Number
ANJ	*Army and Navy Journal*
B	Book
BG	Brigadier General
Btln	Battalion
Brig	Brigade
BGCVMD	Brig. Gen. Commanding Visayan Military District
Cav	Cavalry
CINC	Commander in Chief, U.S. Naval Forces, Asiatic Station
CG	Commanding General
CO	Commanding Officer
Co	Company
CM	Court(s) Martial
C/S	Chief of Staff
D	District (1D is 1st District, 3D is 3rd District, etc.)
Div	Division
DP	Division of the Philippines
DP8AC	Department of the Pacific and 8th Army Corps
DMI	Department or Division of Military Information
DMJ	Department of Mindanao and Jolo
DNL	Department of Northern Luzon
DSL	Department of Southern Luzon
DV	Department of Visayas
8AC	8th Army Corps
E	Entry or Series Number
EB	Expeditionary Brigade
end	Endorsement
Ex	Exhibit
F	File number
FO	Field Order
GO	General Orders
GCM	General Court Martial

HQ   Headquarters
IB   Independent Brigade
Inf   Infantry
JMSI   *Journal of the Military Service Institute*
LS   Letter Sent Number
LSB   Letters Sent Book
LR   Letter Received Number
LRB   Letters Received Book
MDAC   Military District of Albay and Catanduanes
MDLC   Manuscripts Division, Library of Congress
MHI   Military History Institute, U.S. Army War College, Carlisle, Pa.
MID   Military Information Division
MS   Military Secretary
MSD   Military Sub-District
NA   National Archives, Washington, D.C.
OC   Officer in Charge
OMG   Office of the Military Governor in the Philippine Islands
PIR   Philippine Insurgent Records, National Archives
PB   Provisional Brigade
R   Microfilm Roll
Regt   Regiment
RG   Record Group
RLS   Regiment Letters Sent
RLSB   Regimental Letters Sent Book
RLSCMB   Regimental Letters Sent and Courts Martial Book
RSM   *Report of the Secretary of the Navy*
RWD   *Report of the War Department*
SAWS   Spanish-American War Survey, MHI
SB   Separate Brigade (3SB is 3rd Separate Brigade, etc.)
SD   Select Document
SecN   Secretary of the Navy
SecWar   Secretary of War
SMG   Secretary of the Military Governor
SO   Special Orders
T   Telegram Number
USMA   Special Collections, U.S. Military Academy Library, West Point, N.Y.
USV   U.S. Volunteer(s)
VMD   Visayan Military District

1. The Americans Arrive

1. Nelson A. Miles to SecWar, 3 May 1898, U.S. Army Adjutant General's Office, *Correspondence Relating to the War with Spain ... April 15, 1898 to July 30, 1902* [hereafter *CWS*] (1902; reprint, Washington, D.C.: Center of Military History, 1993), 2:635.

2. Graham Cosmas, *An Army for Empire: The United States Army and the Spanish-American War* (Columbia: University of Missouri Press, 1971), 121.

3. James A. Field Jr., "American Imperialism: The 'Worst Chapter' in Almost Any Book," with comments by Robert L. Beisner and Walter LaFeber, *American Historical Review* 83 (June 1978): 644–83; Ephriam K. Smith, "William McKinley's Enduring Legacy: The Historiographical Debate on the Taking of the Philippine Islands," in *Crucible of Empire: The Spanish-American War and Its Aftermath,* ed. James Bradford (Annapolis, Md.: Naval Institute Press, 1993), 205–50.

4. Francis V. Greene, "Memorandum in Report to Felipe Agoncillo," 3 February 1900, Box 4, Francis Vinton Greene Papers, New York Public Library, New York, N.Y.

5. Wesley Merritt to William McKinley, 12 May 1898, CWS 2:645–46. David F. Trask, *The War with Spain in 1898* (New York: Macmillan, 1981), 370.

6. William McKinley to Wesley Merritt, 19 May 1898, CWS 2:676.

7. Nelson A. Miles to SecWar, 3, 16, and 18 May 1898, CWS 2:635, 647–49.

8. William McKinley to Wesley Merritt, 19 May 1898, CWS 2:676–78.

9. Nelson A. Miles to SecWar, 3 May 1898, CWS 2:635. For a thorough study of the formation and transport of the expeditionary force to the Philippines, see Stephen D. Coats, "Gathering at the Golden Gate: The U.S. Army and San Francisco, 1898" (Ph.D. diss., University of Kansas, 1998).

10. Wesley Merritt to AG, 17 May 1898, CWS 2:648. The term "national guard" will be used interchangeably with "militia," although, strictly speaking, in 1898 only thirty-eight states applied this term to their militias.

11. Henry C. Corbin to Elwell S. Otis, 11 May 1898, 2:636; Henry C. Corbin to Henry C. Merriam, 13 May 1898, 2:639; Wesley Merritt to William McKinley, 13 May 1898, 2:643–44, all in CWS.

12. William R. Braisted, *The U.S. Navy in the Pacific, 1897–1909* (Austin: University of Texas Press, 1958), 14–16.

13. Trask, *War with Spain,* 72–78; Braisted, *U.S. Navy,* 21–22.

14. Trask, *War with Spain,* 95–107.

15. Perry D. Jamieson, *Crossing the Deadly Ground: United States Army Tactics, 1865–1899* (Tuscaloosa: University of Alabama Press, 1994).

16. U.S. War Department, General Orders 100, Instructions for the Government of Armies of the United States in the Field, 24 April 1863, in U.S. Congress, Senate, *Affairs in the Philippine Islands: Hearings Before the Committee on the Philippines of the United States Senate,* 57th Cong., 1st sess., Doc. No. 331, April 1902, 971–82; Mark Grimsley, *The Hard Hand of War: Union Military Policy Towards Southern Civilians, 1861–1865* (New York: Cambridge University Press, 1995), 149–51; Richard S. Hartigan, *Lieber's Code and the Law of War* (Chicago: Precedent Press, 1983). On U.S. Army pacification doctrine, see Andrew J. Birtle, *U.S. Army Counterinsurgency and Contingency Operations Doctrine, 1860–1941* (Washington, D.C.: Center of Military History, 1998).

17. Jerry Cooper, *The Rise of the National Guard: The Evolution of the American Militia, 1865–1920* (Lincoln: University of Nebraska Press, 1997), 1–107; Cosmas, *Army for Empire,* 10–13; John K. Mahon, *History of the Militia and the National Guard* (New York: Macmillan, 1982), 108–24; Geoffrey R. Hunt, "The First Colorado Regiment in the Philippine Wars" (Ph.D. diss., University of Colorado, 1997), 23–42.

18. Cosmas, *Army for Empire,* 97–102.

19. Ibid., 107–10.

20. Edward C. Little to Mrs. Hulbert, 5 June 1898, LS 30, 20th Kansas Inf LSB, E 116, RG 94. Since all State Volunteer regiments that served in the Philippines were infantry, they will be identified in future by their number and state alone.

21. Emory S. West to My Darling Bessie, 30 May 1900, Emory S. West Papers, MHI. "Memoir," 1:2, Kenyon A. Joyce Papers, MHI; Ernest W. Hewson Questionnaire, 1st California Inf, SAWS. On popular enthusiasm for the war and comparisons with the Civil War, see Gerald Linderman, *The Mirror of War: American Society and the Spanish-American War* (Ann Arbor: University of Michigan Press, 1974).

22. Thomas W. Crouch, *A Leader of Volunteers: Frederick Funston and the 20th Kansas in the Philippines, 1898–1899* (Lawrence, Kans.: Coronado Press, 1984), 5–16. On the debate within states over who would receive commissions, see W. E. B. Dodson, *Official History of the Operations of the Second Oregon Infantry, U.S.V. in the Campaign in the Philippine Islands* (n.p., n.d.), 1–4; Jerry Cooper and Glenn Smith, *Citizens as Soldiers: A History of the North Dakota National Guard* (Fargo: North Dakota Historical Society, 1986), 38–41; Hunt, "First Colorado," 53–56.

23. William Shortill Questionnaire, 1st Wyoming Inf, SAWS; Marion Wilcox, ed., *Harpers' History of the War in the Philippines* (New York: Harper Brothers, 1900), 61; Cooper and Smith, *Citizens as Soldiers*, 38–43; John Bowe, *With the Thirteenth Minnesota* (Minneapolis, Minn.: A. B. Farnham, 1905), 8–9; Crouch, "Gathering," 38–42.

24. Margaret I. Reilly, "Andrew Wadsworth: A Nebraska Soldier in the Philippines, 1898–1899," *Nebraska History* 68 (Winter 1987):186–87. Crouch, "Gathering," 80–93.

25. HQ, 1st Div, 8AC to CO, 1st Washington Inf, 3 January 1899, LS 13, E 768, RG 395; HQ, 1st Div, 8AC to CO, 1st Wyoming Inf, 9 December 1898, LS 122, E 768, RG 395; HQ, 1st Div, 8AC to CO, 14th Inf, 29 December 1898, LS 161, E 768, RG 395; Oscar King Davis, *Our Conquests in the Pacific* (New York: Frederick A. Stokes, 1899), 9; Richard R. Poplin, ed., "The Letters of W. Thomas Osborne, a Spanish-American Soldier of Buford County," *Tennessee Historical Quarterly* 22 (June 1963): 156; Joseph I. Markey, *From Iowa to the Philippines: A History of Company M, Fifty-first Iowa Volunteers* (Red Oak, Iowa: Thomas D. Murphy, 1900), 93; William F. Stowbridge, ed., "Now Here I Am in the Army: An 1898 Letter of a Nebraska Volunteer in the Spanish-American War," *Nebraska History* 53 (Fall 1972): 331–38; Crouch, "Gathering," 137–53.

26. Military Information Division, *Military Notes on the Philippines* (Washington, D.C.: War Department, 1898). Oscar T. Williams to Thomas W. Cridler, 22 February, 19 and 22 March 1898, CWS 2:650–52; Henry C. Corbin, "Spanish Troops in the Philippines," 25 May 1898, CWS 2:654–56; T. Bentley Mott, "The Organization and Functions of a Bureau of Military Intelligence," *JMSI* 32 (March–April 1902): 185–86; Trask, *War with Spain*, 105; Jeffrey M. Dowart, *The Office of Naval Intelligence: The Birth of America's First Intelligence Agency, 1881–1918* (Annapolis, Md.: Naval Institute Press, 1979), 67–68; Marc B. Powe, *The Emergence of the War Department Intelligence Agency: 1885–1918* (Manhattan, Kans.: Military Affairs Press, 1985), 30–32.

27. 2462 ACP-1880 (Elwell Stephen Otis), RG 94; "Our Officers in the Philippines," *ANJ*, 18 February 1899, 585; Crouch, "Gathering," 132–37.

28. Henry C. Corbin to Elwell S. Otis, 23 May 1898, *CWS* 2:668–69. 6121 ACP 1872 (Thomas McArthur Anderson), RG 94; Thomas M. Anderson Papers, Manuscripts and University Archives Division, Allen Library, University of Washington, Seattle, Wash.

29. Karl Irving Faust, *Campaigning in the Philippines* (1899; reprint, New York: Arno Press, 1970), 56.

30. Davis, *Our Conquests*, 2. For troop strength, see Elwell S. Otis to AG, 29 June 1898, *CWS* 2:716; Trask, *War with Spain*, 385; E 194, RG 94.

31. *Leslie's Official History of the Spanish-American War* (Washington, D.C.: War Records Office, 1899), 531–32.

32. "Adventures in the Philippines," 13, Ed E. Dunbar Papers, 1st California Inf, SAWS. "Only a Volunteer," 7–21, Ernest W. Hewson Papers, 1st California Inf, SAWS; Dodson, *Official History*, 9–14; Crouch, "Gathering," 329–45.

33. Dodson, *Official History*, 16.

34. *Harpers' History*, 61–62. Hunt, "First Colorado," 83–107. Manpower figures from E 194, RG 94.

35. Frederick L. Wernstedt and J. E. Spencer, *The Philippine Island World: A Physical, Cultural, and Regional Geography* (Berkeley: University of California Press, 1967), 149. In 1900 the population in the Philippines was 7 to 8 million, with 3.7 million on Luzon and 2.5 million in the Visayas. Population and area estimates vary widely in the 1898–1903 period and are the subject of some controversy. These figures are taken from *A Pronouncing Gazetteer ... with a Complete Index* (Washington, D.C.: Government Printing Office, 1902), 155–56.

36. "Philippines: A Family Affair," *The Economist* 347 (16 May 1998): 44. For American views, see "Opinions of Filipinos...," [1900], William C. Brown Papers, MHI; Edward D. Taussig to My Dear Family, 1 October 1900, Edward D. Taussig Papers, MDLC. On families, factions, and local politics, see Alfred W. McCoy, ed., *An Anarchy of Families: State and Family in the Philippines* (Manila: Ateneo de Manila Press, 1994).

37. Glenn A. May, *Battle for Batangas: A Philippine Province at War* (Quezon City: New Day Press, 1993), 25–27; Ken De Bevoise, *Agents of Apocalypse: Epidemic Disease in the Colonial Philippines* (Princeton, N.J.: Princeton University Press, 1975).

38. Ricardo T. Jose, *The Philippine Army, 1935–1942* (Quezon City: Ateneo de Manila University Press, 1992), 7–9; John R. M. Taylor, *The Philippine Insurrection Against the United States, 1898–1903: A Compilation of Documents and Introduction*, 5 vols. (1906; reprint, Pasay City, P.I.: Eugenio Lopez Foundation, 1971), 1:62–63.

39. Glenn A. May, *Inventing a Hero: The Posthumous Re-creation of Andres Bonifacio* (Madison: University of Wisconsin Center for Southeast Asian Studies, 1996); Teodoro A. Agoncillo, *The Revolt of the Masses: The Story of Bonifacio and the Katipunan* (Manila: University of the Philippines Press, 1956). For background on the Philippine Revolution, see Jose S. Arcilla, *An Introduction to Philippine History*, 4th ed. (Manila: Ateneo de Manila University Press, 1971); O. D. Corpuz, *The Roots of the Filipino Nation*, 2 vols. (Quezon City: Aklahi Foundation, 1989); Teodoro M. Kalaw, *The Philippine Revolution* (Manila: Manila Book Co., 1925); Maximo

Kalaw, *The Development of Philippine Politics* (Manila: Escolta Publishers, 1927); John N. Schumacher, *Revolutionary Clergy: The Filipino Clergy and the Nationalist Movement, 1850–1903* (Manila: Ateneo de Manila University Press, 1981); John N. Schumacher, *The Propaganda Movement, 1880–1895* (Manila: Solidaridad Press, 1973).

40. *Harpers' History,* 27–28.

41. "Decree—Regulations for the Organization of the Sandahatan Forces," 11 November 1897, Ex 50, Taylor, *Philippine Insurrection,* 1:384–89.

42. Jose S. Arcilla, "The Philippine Revolution and the Jesuit Missions in Mindanao, 1896–1901," *Journal of History* 24 (January–December 1989): 46–56; Demy P. Sonza, *Visayan Fighters for Freedom* (Iloilo: Augustin Sonza and Sons, 1962), 5–9; Jose R. Quisumbing, "The Katipunan and the Philippine Revolution in Cebu," *Kinaadman* 16 (1994): 39–50; *Harpers' History,* 24–28.

43. Alfredo B. Saulo, *The Truth About Aguinaldo and Other Heroes* (Quezon City: Phoenix Publishing, 1987); David H. Bain, *Sitting in Darkness: Americans in the Philippines* (Boston: Houghton Mifflin, 1984).

44. *Harpers' History,* 71. William H. Taft to Elihu Root, 5 July 1902, Box 2, Clarence R. Edwards Papers, Massachusetts Historical Society, Boston, Mass.; Charles B. Elliott, *The Philippines: To the End of the Military Regime* (Indianapolis: Bobbs-Merrill, 1917), 383–83; *Leslie's Official History,* 555–57; Glenn A. May, *A Past Recovered* (Manila: New Day Publishers, 1987), 156–58; Trask, *War with Spain,* 399; Donald Chaput, "Antonio Narisco Luna de St. Pedro," in *The War of 1898 and U.S. Interventions, 1898–1934,* ed. Benjamin R. Beede (New York: Garland Press, 1994), 265–67.

45. For example, the first draft of the 23 September 1899 proclamation, "Emilio Aguinaldo to all civilized nations, and especially to the great North American Republic," was written by Felipe Buencamino, see Ex 71, Taylor, *Philippine Insurrection,* 1:443–48, 3:4–27. Later printed as a pamphlet, "Authentic Review of the Philippine Revolution by Don Emilio Aguinaldo y Famy, President of the Philippine Republic," it was widely circulated among anti-imperialists. A copy can be found in Box 179, George Frisbie Hoar Papers, Massachusetts Historical Society, Boston, Mass. For two contradictory "autobiographies," see Emilio Aguinaldo and Victor A. Pacis, *A Second Look at America* (New York: Robert Speller and Sons, 1957); Emilio Aguinaldo, *My Memoirs* (Manila: n.p., 1967).

46. Jose M. Alejandrino, *The Price of Freedom* (1949; reprint, Manila: Solar Publishing, 1987); Apolinario Mabini, *The Philippine Revolution,* trans. Leon M. Guerrero (1931; reprint, Manila: National Historical Commission, 1969).

47. "Authentic Review," 8. For discussion of Aguinaldo's negotiations with the Americans, see Trask, *War with Spain,* 398–99; Richard E. Welch, *Response to Imperialism: The United States and the Philippine-American War, 1899–1902* (Chapel Hill: University of North Carolina Press, 1979), 12–14; Taylor, *Philippine Insurrection,* 1:97–103.

48. E. Spencer Pratt to Emilio Aguinaldo, 10 and 11 June 1898, SD 7.9, PIR. Bray's work as Aguinaldo's agent is extensively detailed in Taylor, *Philippine Insurrection,* 2:497–99.

49. Alejandrino, *Price of Freedom,* 93–94; *Harpers' History,* 12.

50. Dewey to SecN, 21 May 1898, RSN 1898, 100. Taylor, *Philippine Insurrec-*

tion, 2:38–39; Nathan Sargent, "Admiral Dewey and the Manila Campaign," 94–95, 99–202, 10 November 1904, Box 475, Subject File OO, RG 45.

51. Receipt from Rounsevelle Wildman, 6 June 1898, SD 141, PIR; *Harpers' History*, 83.

52. Emilio Aguinaldo, "To My Beloved Fellow Countrymen," 24 May 1898, in Dewey to SecN, *RSN 1898*, 104.

53. Felix Unson to Emilio Aguinaldo, 8 July 1898 (my translation), SD 936.5, PIR. Emilio Aguinaldo, "To the People of the Philippines," 18 June 1898, in Dewey to SecN, 17 July 1898, *RSN 1898*, 111–13.

54. Emilio Aguinaldo, [Decree], 20 June 1898, Ex 37, Taylor, *Philippine Insurrection*, 3:125–27.

55. Emilio Aguinaldo, Untitled Memo, 1898, SD 133, PIR. Leandro H. Fernandez, *The Philippine Republic* (New York: Columbia University Press, 1926), 70–71; Sonza, *Visayan Fighters*, 18–28; Arcilla, "Philippine Revolution."

56. Taylor, *Philippine Insurrection*, 2:13–26.

57. *RWD 1898*, 54–60; Taylor, *Philippine Insurrection*, 26–27; *Harpers' History*, 85–90; Trask, *War with Spain*, 409–10.

58. Cosmas, *Army for Empire*, 238–39.

59. Trask, *War with Spain*, 411. An overview of the Spanish defenses can be found in Faust, *Campaigning*, 71–75.

60. *Harpers' History*, 79–80.

61. Dewey to SecN, 1 August 1898, *RSN 1898*, 118; *RWD 1898*, 66–72; Trask, *War with Spain*, 412–14. Owing to the U.S. Army's confusing accounting procedures, the Adjutant General's Office gives 8th Corps' strength at 309 officers, 6,466 men; see E 194, RG 94.

62. Dewey to SecN, 27 August 1898, *RSN 1898*, 125–26.

63. *Harpers' History*, 54.

64. Thomas M. Anderson to AG, 24 December 1898, LS 150, E 768, RG 395; Cosmas, *Army for Empire*, 240–42; Trask, *War with Spain*, 413–20; *Harpers' History*, 52–55; Faust, *Campaigning*, 96–102; Hunt, "First Colorado," 127–39, 154–56. MacArthur's biographer inexplicably has Greene's brigade attacking Manila from the north; see Kenneth Ray Young, *The General's General: The Life and Times of Arthur MacArthur* (Boulder, Colo.: Westview, 1994), 188, 198–200.

65. *Harpers' History*, 55. The term "sham battle" appears in Faust, *Campaigning*, 96.

66. *Leslie's Official History*, 552.

67. *Harpers' History*, 5. John T. McCutcheon, *Drawn from Memory* (Indianapolis: Bobbs-Merrill, 1950), 122.

68. *Harpers' History*, 55.

69. "Memorandum of Verbal Instructions Given the General Officers at Camp Dewey by General Babcock, Chief of Staff," [12 August 1898], *RWD 1898*, 83.

70. Thomas M. Anderson to AG, 24 December 1898, LS 150, E 768, RG 395.

71. Irving Hale to AAG, 2nd Brig, 18 August 1898, in *RWD 1898*, 78; Adam S. Mischel, "Young and Adventurous: The Journal of a North Dakota Volunteer in the Spanish-American War, 1898–1899," *North Dakota History* 60 (Winter 1993): 9; J. R. Johnson, "The Saga of the First Nebraska in the Philippines," *Nebraska History* 30 (June 1949): 148–49; Hunt, "First Colorado," 155–56.

2. A Difficult Situation

1. Wesley Merritt and George Dewey to AG, 13 August 1898, CWS 2:754.
2. Henry C. Corbin to Wesley Merritt, 17 August 1898, CWS 2:754.
3. *Harpers' History*, 65.
4. Harold F. Taggart, ed., "California Soldiers in the Philippines: From the Correspondence of Howard Middleton, 1898–1899," *California Historical Society Quarterly* 30 (December 1951): 296. 10 October 1898, Diary, Henry J. Tunis Papers, 1st South Dakota Inf, SAWS; MS, 158, Francis J. Kernan Papers, USMA; "Record of Service . . . to Outbreak of Filipino Insurrection," 3, Frederick A. Podas Papers, 13th Minnesota Inf, SAWS; Dodson, *Official History*, 23–24.
5. Wesley Merritt, "To the People of the Philippines," 14 August 1898, in RWD 1898 1:3:49–50. "The Third Manila Expedition," ANJ, 2 July 1898, 884.
6. HQ, DP8AC, GO 3, 9 August 1898, in RWD 1898 1:3:50.
7. J. D. Babcock to Thomas M. Anderson, 15 August 1898, CWS 2:815. The Aguinaldo-Anderson negotiations are in CWS 2:813–20.
8. Wesley Merritt to Emilio Aguinaldo, 24 August 1898, CWS 2:819–20.
9. MS, 160, Kernan Papers.
10. 29–31 August 1898, Diary, Robert P. Hughes Papers, MDLC.
11. Frederick Palmer, *With My Own Eyes: A Personal Study of Battle Years* (Indianapolis: Bobbs-Merrill, 1932), 142, 145. On Otis, see 2462 ACP 1880 (Elwell Stephen Otis), RG 94.
12. Quote "tedious lawyer" from Leon Wolff, *Little Brown Brother: How the United States Purchased and Pacified the Philippine Islands at the Century's Turn* (Garden City, N.Y.: Doubleday, 1961), 140; quote "the Philippine war's" from H. W. Brands, *Bound to Empire: The United States and the Philippines* (New York: Oxford University Press, 1992), 50.
13. Stuart C. Miller, *"Benevolent Assimilation": The American Conquest of the Philippines, 1899–1903* (New Haven, Conn.: Yale University Press, 1983), 66. Stuart C. Miller, "Elwell Stephen Otis," in Beede, *War of 1898*, 290–93.
14. Albert G. Robinson, *The Philippines: The War and the People* (New York: McClure, Phillips, 1901), 354.
15. Elwell S. Otis to AG, 7 September 1898, CWS 2:788. Among the more grisly atrocities was the butchery of over 100 Spanish prisoners in the Camarines; see Statement of Ambrosia Escalante, 1 April 1900, SD 2011.2, PIR; Senate, *Affairs*, 1278–80.
16. 15 September 1898, Diary, Tunis Papers.
17. Elwell S. Otis to AG, 16 September 1898, CWS 2:790.
18. William McKinley to SecWar, 21 December 1898, in Henry C. Corbin to Elwell S. Otis, 21 December 1898, CWS 2:858–59.
19. William McKinley to Elwell S. Otis and George Dewey, 8 January 1899, CWS 2:873.
20. HQ, 1st Div, 8AC to CO, 1st Washington Inf, 3 January 1899, LS 13, E 768, RG 395.
21. John M. Stotsenburg to AAG, 16 and 24 October 1898, LS 164 and 188; John M. Stotsenburg to AG, 2nd Div, 24 December 1898, LS 252, in 1st Nebraska Inf RLSCMB; John M. Stotsenburg to F. A. Snyder, 21 October 1898, LR 357; AAAG to CO, 1st Nebraska, 4 January 1899, LR 454, Nebraska Inf LRB, all in E 116, RG 94.

22. 10 October 1898, Diary, Hughes Papers.

23. *American Soldier* (8 August 1898). HQ, 2nd Brig, Circular No. 10, 28 August 1898, E 890, RG 395. For a thorough study of the prewar occupation and reform of Manila, see *RWD* 1901 1:7:77–274; John M. Gates, *Schoolbooks and Krags: The United States Army in the Philippines, 1899–1902* (Westport, Conn.: Greenwood Press, 1975), 57–63.

24. The new regiments included the 20th Kansas Infantry, 51st Iowa Infantry, 1st Tennessee Infantry, 13th Minnesota Infantry, 1st Washington Infantry, 18th Infantry, and 23rd Infantry. On personnel issues, see Arthur MacArthur to AG, 9 November 1898, 4th end to LR 376, 1st Nebraska Inf LRB, E 116, RG 94; "Adventures in the Philippines," 27, Dunbar Papers; Thomas D. Thiessen, "The Fighting First Nebraska: Nebraska's Imperial Adventure in the Philippines, 1898–1899," *Nebraska History* 70 (Fall 1989): 231.

25. Taggart, "California Soldiers," 301. "Moral Conditions in Manila," *Outlook* 68 (31 August 1901): 142; Senate, *Affairs*, 1736–50.

26. "Adventures in the Philippines," 36, Dunbar Papers.

27. William E. Birkhimer to AG, 1st Div, 28 December 1898, LR 423, E 815, RG 395. John B. Mallory to AG, 6 December 1898, LR 458, 1st Nebraska Inf LRB, E 116, RG 94; "Autobiographical Selections," 65, Frank Merrill Papers, 13th Minnesota Inf, SAWS; 25 August 1898, Diary, William Cuffe Papers, Allen Library, University of Washington, Seattle, Wash.; Bowe, *With the Thirteenth*, 26; Markey, *From Iowa*, 91–93.

28. 8 November 1898, Diary, Cuffe Papers. J. R. Johnson, "Colonel John Miller Stotsenburg: Man of Valor," *Nebraska History* 50 (Winter 1969): 348–50.

29. "Only a Volunteer," 44, Hewson Papers. Victor Duboce to AG, 16 December 1898, LS 86, 1st California Inf LSB, E 116, RG 94; HQ, 1st Div, 8AC to CO, 1st California Inf, 15 December 1898, LS 128, E 768, RG 395; Fred W. Dohrman to James F. Smith, 15 May 1900 and Tom O'Neil to James F. Smith, 25 September 1899, both in Correspondence-1899 File, Box 1, James F. Smith Papers, Washington State Historical Society, Tacoma, Wash.

30. "Adventures in the Philippines," 54, 74–75, Dunbar Papers.

31. "Only a Volunteer," 43–44, Hewson Papers.

32. A. Prentiss, ed., *The History of the Utah Volunteers in the Spanish-American War and in the Philippine Islands* (Salt Lake City, Utah: W. F. Ford, 1900), 113.

33. 4 December 1898, Diary, Cuffe Papers.

34. May, *Battle*, 69–71; Jose R. Quisumbing, "The American Occupation of Cebu, 1899–1917," *Kinaadman* 17 (1995): 186. For somewhat partisan accounts of the Philippine Republic, see Teodoro A. Agoncillo, *Malolos: The Crisis of the Republic* (Quezon City: University of the Philippines Press, 1960); Fernandez, *Philippine Republic*.

35. Fernandez, *Philippine Republic*, 103–8.

36. J. Franklin Bell to Wesley Merritt, 29 August 1898, Box 4, Greene Papers.

37. *Harpers' History*, 67; May, *Battle*, 76–79, 116–17.

38. Pedro S. Achútegui and Miguel A. Berbad, *Aguinaldo and the Revolution of 1896: A Documentary History* (Manila: Ateneo de Manila University Press, 1972), 58. Emilio Aguinaldo, "Proclamation," 30 July 1898, Ex 133, Taylor, *Philippine Insurrection*, 3:229–35; May, *Battle*, 76–79; Jose, *Philippine Army*, 10–12. Other

terms for the conventional forces of the Philippine Republic include: the Revolutionary Army; the Republican Army; the Liberating or Liberation Army; and the Philippine Army.

39. Butler D. Price to AG, 26 November 1899, LR 1087, E 816, RG 395; Samuel B. M. Young to AG, DP8AC, 6 January 1900, LS 577, E 836, RG 395. The number of firearms in the hands of Filipino nationalists is the subject of much debate; see Taylor, *Philippine Insurrection,* 2:430–31, 496; *Leslie's Official History,* 598; Alejandrino, *Price of Freedom,* 114.

40. Cormandel to CINC, 11 March 1899, R 367, M 625.

41. Alejandrino, *Price of Freedom,* 18–44. *Harpers' History,* 67; Jose, *Philippine Army,* 12.

42. There is much disagreement on Luna's rank. The term "General in Chief of Operations" is from a captured document; see Harrison G. Otis to AG, 2 April 1899, Box 2, E 764, RG 395. For an admiring biography, see Vicencio R. Jose, *The Rise and Fall of Antonio Luna* (1972; reprint, Manila: Solar Publishing, 1991).

43. Minutes of 14 Jan. 1899 Meeting, and Apolinario Mabini, "Additional Note to the Instructions," 13 January 1899, both in Aguinaldo-Otis Peace Negotiations File, Box 2, James F. Smith Papers.

44. 15 January 1899, Diary, Hughes Papers.

45. 4 February 1899, Diary, Hughes Papers.

46. *Harpers' History,* 56. For a detailed study of how attitudes changed in one state regiment, see Hunt, "First Colorado," 143–78.

47. Thiessen, "Fighting First Nebraska," 234. "Only a Volunteer," 44, Hewson Papers; Taggart, "California Soldiers," 296.

48. "Adventures in the Philippines," 28.

49. Taggart, "California Soldiers," 296. For a sample of other incidents, see Emilio Aguinaldo to Wesley Merritt, 25 August 1898, CWS 2:820; M. Herpolshimer, Letter Report, 27 August 1898, LR 140, 1st Nebraska Inf LRB, E 116, RG 94; 10 January 1899, Diary, Daniel W. Doyle Papers, 13th Minnesota, SAWS; Mischel, "Young and Adventurous," 10.

50. "Diary of Field Service in the Philippines, 1898 to 1901," 4, William A. Kobbé Papers, MHI. "Only a Volunteer," 65–71, Hewson Papers; "Adventures in the Philippines," 4–49; Taggart, "California Soldiers," 297.

51. Elwell S. Otis to AG, 1 January 1899, CWS 2:865–66. Elwell S. Otis to AG, 4 January 1899, CWS 2:867–68; *Leslie's Official History,* 598.

52. James Ovenshine to AG, 1st Div, 29 January 1899, LS 8, E 812, RG 395; 13 January 1899, Diary, Hughes Papers; 12 January 1899, Diary, Doyle Papers; Harry L. Wells, *The War in the Philippines* (San Francisco: Sunset, 1899), 5.

53. *Pronouncing Gazetteer,* 156. Iloilo, with 2,102 square miles and 462,444 people, had roughly half the island's area and population. Capiz Province in the north, with 1,661 square miles and 224,000 people, and the narrow western province of Antique, with 1,340 square miles and 115,434 people, were distinctly secondary theaters.

54. Sonza, *Visayan Fighters,* 18–19; Schumacher, *Revolutionary Clergy,* 176–77; *Harpers' History,* 72–73; McCutcheon, *Drawn from Memory,* 125. Both the inhabitants of Iloilo Province and Iloilo City are referred to as Ilongos.

55. Robert P. Hughes to AAG, DP8AC, 5 August 1899, LS 6, August 1899 LSB, E2464, RG 395.

56. Charles J. Crane, "Who Burned Iloilo, Panay, and Why Were Conditions in Negros More Favorable to Us?" *JMSI* 30 (March 1902): 232–39.

57. Schumacher, *Revolutionary Clergy*, 177–80.

58. [Marcus M. Miller] to AG, DP, 30 December 1898, LS 7, E 2463, RG 395; Henry du R. Phelan, "Report on the Situation in the Island of Panay," 8 April 1899, E 4808, RG 395; Sonza, *Visayan Fighters*, 33–36. There is much confusion over the number and organization of military forces on Panay when the Americans arrived and no figures are better than rough estimates.

59. [Marcus P. Miller] to CO . . . and the people of Iloilo and the Island of Panay, 28 December 1898, LS 5, E 2463, RG 395.

60. [Marcus P. Miller] to AG, DP, 31 December 1898, LS 2, E 2463, RG 395. "The Situation at Iloilo," *ANJ*, 4 March 1899, 636.

61. [Marcus P. Miller] to AG, DP, 30 December 1898, LS 7, E 2463, RG 395.

62. Henry C. Corbin to Elwell S. Otis, 1 January 1899, *CWS* 2:866. *Harpers' History*, 73–75.

63. [Marcus P. Miller] to CO, USS *Baltimore*, 31 December 1898, LS 1; [Marcus P. Miller] to AG, DP, 5 January 1899, LS 9, both in E 2463, RG 395.

64. Otis to AG, 8 January 1899, *CWS* 2:872. [Marcus P. Miller] to AG, DP8AC, 20 January 1899, LS 25, E 2463, RG 395.

65. [Marcus P. Miller] to Roque Lopez, 1 January 1899, LS 8, E 2463, RG 395.

66. "Report of an Interview between Lieut. Henry Du R. Phelan . . . with the Government of the Federal State of Bisayas," 11 January 1899, in Robert P. Hughes to AAG, DP8AC, 5 August 1899, LS 6, August 1899 LSB, E 2464, RG 395. [Marcus P. Miller] to AG, DP8AC, 13 January 1899, LS 13, E 2463, RG 395.

67. [Marcus P. Miller] to AG to HQ, DP8AC, 5 and 20 January 1899, LS 5 and 26, E 2463, RG 395.

68. 19 January 1899, Diary, Charles Julian Papers, MDLC. *Harpers' History*, 75–77, 81–82.

69. HQ, GO 4, 27 January 1899, 51st Iowa Inf LRB, E 116, RG 94. [Marcus P. Miller] to AG, DP, 8 January 1899, LS 14, E 2463, RG 395; *Harpers' History*, 75–77, 81–82.

70. Elwell S. Otis to My dear General [Marcus P. Miller], 15 January 1899, in Robert P. Hughes to AAG, DP8AC, 5 August 1899, LS 6, August LSB, E 2464, RG 395.

3. *The Battle of Manila*

1. *Harpers' History*, 15–16, 72, 104, 137. AAG to CG, 2nd Brig, 1st Div, 14 January 1899, LR 86, E 815, RG 395. Nelson Miles interviewed several Filipino generals who did not know the size of their own units in front of Manila; see "Memorandum of Conversation," 6 November 1902, Inspection tour of P.I. file, Nelson A. Miles Papers, MHI.

2. Thomas M. Anderson to AG, DP8AC, 18 February 1899, LS 130, E 768, RG 395; Faust, *Campaigning*, 126–27; William T. Sexton, *Soldiers in the Sun: An Adventure in Imperialism* (Harrisburg, Pa.: Military Service Publishing Co., 1939), 88–89.

3. John M. Stotsenburg to AG, 2nd Div; John M. Stotsenburg to Luciano San Miguel, 28 January 1899, LS 269–71; FO 6, 2 February 1899, all in 1st Nebraska Inf RLSCMB, E 116, RG 94.

4. Senate, *Affairs*, 1389. As is often the case, it is more than likely that the Americans may have misidentified the village in question. It is usually termed Santol or San Tol, but it is also referred to, most accurately, as "the village in front of blockhouse No. 7"; see Senate, *Affairs*, 1389.

5. John M. Stotsenburg to F. B. Naracong, 3 February 1899, LS 272, 1st Nebraska Inf RLSCMB, E 116, RG 94; emphasis in original.

6. John M. Stotsenburg to AG, 2nd Brig, 4 February 1899, LS 305 and 307, 1st Nebraska Inf RLSCMB, E 116, RG 94.

7. John M. Stotsenburg to Officer in Charge of Outpost, 4 February 1899, LS 306, 1st Nebraska Inf RLSCMB, E 116, RG 94. John M. Stotsenburg to K. A. Storch, 4 February 1899, LS 270, 1st Nebraska Inf RLSCMB, E 116, RG 94; *Harpers' History*, 110.

8. Serapio to General Commanding the Second Zone, 5 February 1899, Ex 813, Taylor, *Philippine Insurrection*, 4:54–41.

9. John M. Stotsenburg to AG, 2nd Div, 6 February 1899; Burt D. Whedon to Adj, 1st Nebraska, 10 February 1899, both in Box 2, E 764, RG 395; Thiessen, "Fighting First Nebraska," 234–37; Donald Chaput, "Private William W. Grayson's War in the Philippines, 1899," *Nebraska History* 61 (Fall 1980): 360. Stuart Miller claims that the Filipinos Grayson fired on are "now believed to have been drunk and unarmed" (Miller, *Benevolent Assimilation*, 61), but neither American nor Filipino sources support this allegation.

10. John M. Stotsenburg to AG, 2nd Div, 6 February 1899, Box 2, E 764, RG 395; John Hall, ed., "The Philippine War: The Diary of Robert Bruce Payne, 1899," *Nebraska History* 69 (Winter 1988): 195–96; Thiessen, "Fighting First Nebraska," 235.

11. 4 February 1899, Diary, Tunis Papers; A. S. Frost to AAG, 2nd Brig, 2nd Div, 8AC, 7 February 1899, Box 2, E 764, RG 395; Henry B. McCoy to AAG, 2nd Brig, 2nd Div, 8AC, 14 February 1899, Box 2, E 764, RG 395; Faust, *Campaigning*, 15; Hunt, "First Colorado," 195–201.

12. Victor D. Duboce to Adj, 1st California, 9 February 1899, Box 2, E 764, RG 395; Thomas M. Anderson to AG, DP8AC, 18 February 1899, LS 130, E 768, RG 395; Don Russell, *Campaigning with King: Charles King, Chronicler of the Old Army*, ed. Paul L. Hedren (Lincoln: University of Nebraska Press, 1991), 122.

13. 5 February 1899, Diary, Hughes Papers. Taylor, *Philippine Insurrection*, 2:194.

14. *Harpers' History*, 109–10; "Fight at Manila with Filipinos," *New York Times*, 6 February 1899.

15. 5 February 1899, Diary, Tunis Papers; A. S. Frost to AAG, 2nd Brig, 2nd Div, 8AC, 7 February 1899, Box 2, E 764, RG 395.

16. John M. Stotsenburg to AG, 2nd Div, 6 February 1899, Box 2, E 764, RG 395; Henry B. McCoy to AAG, 2nd Brig, 2nd Div, 8AC, 14 February 1899, Box 2, E 764, RG 395; *Harpers' History*, 112; Faust, *Campaigning*, 131–32; Hunt, "First Colorado," 205–19.

17. King to Cabell, Dispatch 9:50 A.M., 5 February 1899, Box 2, E 764, RG 395; Thomas M. Anderson to AG, DP8AC, 18 February 1899, LS 130, E 768, RG 395; Samuel Ovenshine to AG, 1st Div, 13 February 1899, LS 19, E 812, RG 395; Frederick W. Grant to AG, 3 July 1899, LS 47, E 812, RG 395; February 1899, Diary, Thomas E. Zeiber Papers, 1st Washington Inf, SAWS; *Harpers' History*, 115–16; Sexton, *Soldiers*, 94.

18. Thomas M. Anderson to AG, DP8AC, 18 February 1899, LS 130, E 768, RG 395. James F. Smith to AG, 7 February 1899, Box 2, E 764, RG 395; Russell, *Campaigning with King,* 122–25.

19. Memorandum, William H. Winders File, 1st Washington Inf, SAWS; Victor D. Duboce to Adj, 1st California, 9 February 1899, Box 2, E 764, RG 395. One Volunteer managed to save the vestments from the flame and almost sixty years later returned them to the church.

20. *Harpers' History,* 125.

21. L. S. Sorley, *History of the Fourteenth United States Infantry, from January, 1890 to December, 1908* (Chicago: n.p., 1908), 36–37.

22. AAG to Ovenshine, Dispatch: 10:30 AM, LS 53, E 768, RG 395. Thomas M. Anderson to AG, DP8AC, 18 February 1899, LS 130, E 768, RG 395.

23. Samuel Ovenshine to AG, 1st Div, 13 February 1899, LS 19, E 812, RG 395. Cooper and Smith, *Citizens as Soldiers,* 75–76.

24. AG to William R. Green, 6 March 1922, Philippine Insurrection File, No. 2159, Legislative and Policy Precedent Files, 1943–1975, RG 407; Thomas M. Anderson to AG, DP8AC, 18 February 1899, LS 130, E 768, RG 395.

25. Mariano Trias, [Report], 15 March 1899, Ex 818, Taylor, *Philippine Insurrection,* 4:553–65.

26. Senate, *Affairs,* 900, see also 1389–98. Much has been made of a telegram from Manila announcing the fighting, which appeared to have been sent before hostilities began. As was immediately noted, the discrepancy is explained by the time-zone difference between Manila and Washington; see James A. LeRoy, *The Americans in the Philippines* (Boston: Houghton Mifflin, 1914), 2:15–19.

27. Carlos Quirino, *Filipinos at War* (Manila: Vera-Reyes, 1981), 146.

28. Miller, *Benevolent Assimilation,* 59; see also 60–63.

29. *RWD* 1899 1:1:5. *RWD* 1900 1:4:200–202; Senate, *Affairs,* 786–77; "The News in Washington," *New York Times,* 6 February 1899.

30. 5 February 1899, Diary of George Dewey, Box 475, Subject File OO, RG 45.

31. *RWD* 1900 1:4:199. Elwell S. Otis to AG, 7 February 1899, *CWS* 2:896; *Harpers' History,* 140.

32. "The Fighting at Manila," *ANJ,* 11 February 1899, 553.

33. Benito Legarda to Emilio Aguinaldo, 7 July 1899, in *RWD* 1900 1:4:203–5. "Filipinos Fleeing Before Americans," *New York Times,* 7 February 1899.

34. Mabini, *Philippine Revolution,* 60; Taylor, *Philippine Insurrection,* 2:198–200. Richard Welch, no supporter of the U.S. Army, concluded Aguinaldo's soldiers and advisers were united in wanting war on 5 February; see Welch, *Response,* 24.

35. Senate, *Affairs,* 900.

36. 5 February 1899, Diary, Hughes Papers; Young, *General's General,* 218–19; Hunt, "First Colorado," 195.

37. "How the Vote Was Taken," *New York Times,* 7 February 1899; Richard E. Welch, *George Frisbie Hoar and the Half-Breed Republicans* (Cambridge, Mass.: Harvard University Press, 1971), 232–47.

38. Thomas M. Anderson to AG, DP8AC, 7 and 9 February 1899, LS 74 and 81, E 768, RG 395. Charles King to AG, 1st Div, 15 February 1899, LS 49, E 800, RG 395; Samuel Ovenshine to AG, 1st Div, 12 February 1899, LS 15, E 812, RG 395;

Frederick W. Grant to AG, 3 July 1899, LS 47, E 812, RG 395; Russell, *Campaigning with King,* 126–27.

39. Victor D. Duboce to Adj, 1st California, 16 February 1899, Box 2, E 764, RG 395; Dispatches: Charles King to Thomas M. Anderson, 15–18 February 1899, LS 65, E 800, RG 395; Russell, *Campaigning with King,* 127; *Harpers' History,* 108.

40. Emory S. West to Miss Price, 20 February 1899, Emory S. West Papers, MHI.

41. Charles King to AG, 1st Div, 21 February 1899, E 764, RG 395. Thomas M. Anderson to AG, DP8AC, 19 and 22 February 1899, LS 131 and 142, E 768, RG 395.

42. John M. Stotsenburg to AG, 2nd Brig, 7 February 1899, Box 2, E 764, RG 395; Henry B. McCoy to AAG, 2nd Brig, 2nd Div, 8AC, 14 February 1899, Box 2, E 764, RG 395; *Harpers' History,* 128–29; Hunt, "First Colorado," 221–24.

43. *RWD* 1899 1:4:103; Crouch, *Leader,* 82–89; *Harpers' History,* 126–27; *Leslie's Official History,* 601–3; Sexton, *Soldiers,* 98.

44. Jose, *Philippine Army,* 13.

45. Emilio Aguinaldo, "Decree," 13 February 1899, SD 866.7, PIR.

46. 18 February 1899, Diary, Hughes Papers; Letter of A. Mabini, President of the Council, to Aguinaldo in Regard to the Advisability of an Attack Upon Manila, February 1899, Ex 603, Taylor, *Philippine Insurrection,* 4:13–15. For an extensive discussion of revolutionary activities in Manila, see Taylor, *Philippine Insurrection,* 2:202–6.

47. "To the Field Officers of the Territorial Militia," 7 February 1899, Ex 816, Taylor, *Philippine Insurrection,* 4:546–48, 548–51. This document is printed in Senate, *Affairs,* 1912–14.

48. 21 February 1899, Diary, Hughes Papers.

49. Henry F. Hoyt, *A Frontier Doctor,* ed. Doyce B. Nunis (1929; reprint, Chicago: Lakeside Press, 1979), 329–30. *Harpers' History,* 137–42; Robert P. Hughes to AAG, 17 March 1899, in *RWD* 1899 1:5:6; Senate, *Affairs,* 510–11; Dodson, *Official History,* 28–30.

50. Antonio Luna to the President of the Republic, 24 February 1899, Ex 611, Taylor, *Philippine Insurrection,* 4:23–24; Donald Chaput, "Antonio Luna de St. Pedro," in Beede, *War of 1898,* 266.

51. *RWD* 1899 1:5:9. Dodson, *Official History,* 29–31; "Record of Service," Podas Papers; *Harpers' History,* 141–42.

52. 22–24 February 1899, Diary, Hughes Papers.

53. Senate, *Affairs,* 1913.

54. *Harpers' History,* 117.

55. Alejandrino, *Price of Freedom,* 116.

56. Emilio Aguinaldo, "Instructions for Generals," 14 February 1899, Ex 605, Taylor, *Philippine Insurrection,* 4:16.

57. Senate, *Affairs,* 895.

58. Apolinario Mabini to Emilio Aguinaldo, 28 February 1899, Ex 615, Taylor, *Philippine Insurrection,* 4:27–28.

59. Thomas M. Anderson to AG, DP8AC, 18 February 1899, LS 130, E 768, RG 395. Walter S. Drysdale, "The Infantry at Caloocan," *Infantry Journal* 28 (April 1926): 425.

60. Hall, "Philippine War," 196.

61. Robert Crosbie to Dear Mother, 24 February 1899, 1st Wyoming Inf, SAWS. 5 February 1899, Diary, Thomas E. Zeiber File, 1st Washington Inf, SAWS.

62. *Harpers' History,* 117.

63. 6 February 1899, Diary, Hughes Papers.

64. 8 February 1899, Diary, Hughes Papers. On looting and burning by one unit, see Hunt, "First Colorado," 209–11, 230–32.

65. Thomas M. Anderson to AG, DP8AC, 9 February 1899, LS 82, E 768, RG 395.

66. Markey, *From Iowa,* 169–70.

67. *Harpers' History,* 128. Russell, *Campaigning with King,* 124; Hunt, "First Colorado," 206–19.

68. "Strength of the Filipinos," *New York Times,* 6 February 1899.

4. The Visayas

1. [Marcus P. Miller] to AG, DP, 31 December 1898, LS 2, E 2463, RG 395.

2. [Apolinario Mabini?] to President of the Federal Council of Iloilo, 24 January 1899, Ex 1222, and "Instructions for the Commission Going to the Visayas," 27 January 1899, Ex 1223, 5:463–67; Anon. to Emilio Aguinaldo, 1 August 1899, Ex 1260, 5:532–39, all in Taylor, *Philippine Insurrection.*

3. Marcus P. Miller to Raymundo Mellissa, 30 January 1900, LS 57, January 1899 LSB, E 2464, RG 395; [Marcus P. Miller] to AG, DP, 7 February 1899, LS 45, E 2463, RG 395.

4. [Marcus P. Miller] to AG, DP, 26 January 1899, LS 31, E 2463, RG 395.

5. [Marcus P. Miller] to AG, DP, 3 February 1899, LS 42, E 2463, RG 395.

6. [Marcus P. Miller] to AG, DP, 8 February 1899, LS 46, E 2463, RG 395.

7. [Marcus P. Miller] to CG, Native Forces, 10 February 1899, LS 49, E 2463, RG 395. Thomas H. Barry to Marcus P. Miller, 8 February 1899, in Robert P. Hughes to AAG, DP8AC, 5 August 1899, LS 6, August 1899 LSB, E 2464, RG 395; Marcus P. Miller to AG, DP8AC, 20 February 1899, LS 47, February 1899 LSB, E 2464, RG 395.

8. Vernon L. Williams, "The U.S. Navy in the Philippine Insurrection and Subsequent Native Unrest, 1898–1906" (Ph.D. diss., Texas A&M University, 1985), 137–41.

9. Louis Ostheim to Victor H. Bridgman, 13 February 1899, LS 29, February 1899 LSB, E 2464, RG 395; [Marcus P. Miller] to AG, DP8AC, 16 February 1899, LS 57, E 2463, RG 395; Faust, *Campaigning,* 242–43.

10. Poplin, "The Letters of W. Thomas Osborne," 162.

11. [Marcus P. Miller] to Senior Naval Officer, 12 February 1899, LS 52, E 2463, RG 395. An Ilongo historian concludes the revolutionaries set fire to at least part of the town; see Sonza, *Visayan Fighters,* 26.

12. Crane, "Who Burned Iloilo?" 235–36, 239.

13. [Albert P. Niblack], "The Capture of Ilo Ilo, Described by an Officer of the United States Navy," in *Harpers' History,* 129–31; "Capture of Iloilo," *ANJ,* 8 April 1899, 746.

14. George Dewey, 6 March 1899, F 7063–104, RG 80. Frank F. Wilde to CINC,

28 February 1899, F 7063–104, RG 80; "Who Captured Iloilo?" *ANJ*, 29 April 1899, 816; Williams, "U.S. Navy," 143–44.

15. C. S. Sperry to My dear Edith, 25 February 1899, Box 3, Sperry Papers. For similar sentiments, see "Memoirs of a Naval Career," 25:30, Bowman H. McCalla Papers, MDLC.

16. Anon. [Marcus P. Miller] to Senior Naval Officer, 12 February 1899, LS 52, E 2463, RG 395. [Marcus P. Miller] to AG, DP8AC, 20 February 1899, LS 47, February 1899 LSB, E 2464, RG 395; Marcus P. Miller to CO, USS *Boston,* 8 March 1899, R 367, M 625.

17. Braisted, *U.S. Navy,* 68–69.

18. HQ, 1st IB, GO 7, 17 February 1899, E 882, RG 395.

19. Marcus P. Miller, "To the Army and People of the Island of Panay," 21 February 1899, LS 52, February 1899 LSB, E 2464, RG 395.

20. [Marcus P. Miller] to Vicente Franco, 18 February 1899, LS 63, E 2463, RG 395.

21. HQ, 1st IB, GO 11, 16 February 1899, E 882, RG 395.

22. Marcus P. Miller to AG, DP8AC, 2 March 1899, LS 76, March 1899 LSB, E 2464, RG 395.

23. [Marcus P. Miller] to AG, DP8AC, 15 February 1899, LS 56, E 2463, RG 395. Louis Ostheim to V. H. Bridgman, 13 February 1899, LS 29, February 1899 LSB, E 2464, RG 395; [Marcus P. Miller] to AG, DP8AC, 17 February 1899, LS 58, E 2463, RG 395; Marcus Miller to AG, DP8AC, 20 and 21 February 1899, LS 45 and 50, February 1899 LSB, E 2464, RG 395.

24. [Marcus P. Miller] to AG, DP8AC, 18 February 1899, LS 40, February 1899 LSB, E 2464, RG 395.

25. Gregory Dean Chapman, "Taking Up the White Man's Burden: Tennesseans in the Philippine Insurrection, 1899," *Tennessee Historical Quarterly* 47 (Spring 1988): 36.

26. Marcus P. Miller to AG, DP8AC, 3 March 1899, LS 76, March 1899 LSB, E 2464, RG 395.

27. Marcus P. Miller to AG, DP8AC, 17 and 18 March 1899, LS 29 and 31, March 1899 LSB, E 2464, RG 395; Faust, *Campaigning,* 244.

28. Leandro Fullon to Timoteo Marella, 13 April 1899, Ex 1243, Taylor, *Philippine Insurrection,* 5:501.

29. Timoteo Marella to Martin Delgado, 9 April 1899, Ex 1243, Taylor, *Philippine Insurrection,* 5:500.

30. [Marcus P. Miller] to AG, DP8AC, 15 February 1899, LS 56, E 2463, RG 395; Untitled Statement by Mariana Aquilar, [April 1899], April 1899 LSB, E 2464, RG 395; Leandro Fullon to Timoteo Marella, 13 April 1899, Ex 1243, 5:501; Leandro Fullon to Martin Delgado, 13 April 1899, Ex 1243, 5:502; Santos Capadocia to Leandro Fullon, 10 April 1899, Ex 1244, 5:502–8; ["Petition to Emilio Aguinaldo"], 1 August 1899, Ex 1260, 5:532–39; Ananias Diocno to Secretary of the Interior, 25 August 1899, 5:543–44, all in Taylor, *Philippine Insurrection.*

31. Thomas Barry to Thomas R. Hamer, 21 May 1899, E 2064, RG 395. Marcus P. Miller to AG, DP8AC, 21 March 1899, LS 19, March 1899 LSB, E 2464, RG 395.

32. Senate, *Affairs,* 562–63. William W. Wotherspoon, "Major General R. P.

Hughes, U.S. Army, 1839–1909," Biographical Material File, Hughes Papers; [Robert P. Hughes] to My Dear Governor [Elwell S. Otis], 22 December 1899, LS 19, December 1899 LSB, E 2464, RG 395; H. V. Bronson, "Visayan Campaigns I: The Insurrection of the Sugar Planters of Panay," *Military Historian and Economist* 2 (1917): 301. Hughes did not arrive in Iloilo until early June.

33. Henry du R. Phelan, "Report on the Situation in the Island of Panay," 8 April 1899, E 4808, RG 395.

34. Martin Delgado, [Decree], 25 May 1899, Ex 1253, Taylor, *Philippine Insurrection,* 5:518–19.

35. [Robert P. Hughes] to AAG, DP8AC, 13 August 1899, LS 34, August 1899 LSB. BGCVMD to AAG, DP8AC, 26 July 1899, LS 84, July 1899 LSB; Instructions for Tennessee Outpost, June 1899, LS 28, June 1899 LSB; BGCVMD to AAG, 10 June 1899, LS 53, June 1899 LSB, all in E 2464, RG 395; *RWD* 1900 1:5:231–34.

36. 24th June 1899, Diary, Hughes Papers.

37. [Proclamation], 27 November 1898, Ex 1313, Taylor, *Philippine Insurrection,* 5:622. On the revolution in Negros, see Maria F. H. Romero, *Negros Occidental Between Two Foreign Powers (1898–1909)* (Manila: Enterprise Publications, 1974), 69–133; Caridad Aldecoa-Rodrigues, *Negros Oriental and the Philippine Revolution* (Dumaguete, P.I.: Provincial Government of Negros Oriental, 1983), 81–134. I am very grateful to Dr. Filomeno Aguilar for providing background in Negros history.

38. Violeta L. Gonzanga, "The Negrense Betrayal of the Revolution: Capitulation and American Expansion in Negros Island" (paper delivered at the International Conference on the Centennial of the Philippine Revolution, 22 August 1996, Manila, P.I.).

39. LeRoy, *Americans,* 2:87–88.

40. Cited in Romero, *Negros Occidental,* 106–7.

41. Elwell S. Otis to AG, 25 February 1899, *CWS* 2:916. [Marcus P. Miller] to AG, DP8AC, 18 February 1899, LS 59, E 2463, RG 395; Marcus Miller to AG, DP8AC, 19 February 1899, LS 42, February 1899 LSB, E 2464, RG 395; *Harpers' History,* 231; Aldecoa-Rodrigues, *Negros Oriental,* 135–39.

42. "Adventures in the Philippines," 74–75, Dunbar Papers; Questionnaire, Hewson Papers; William H. Taft to Elihu Root, 5 July 1902, Box 2, Clarence R. Edwards Papers, Massachusetts Historical Society, Boston, Mass.

43. James F. Smith to AAG, DV, 25 July 1900, LS 1124, E 2616, RG 395. Gates, *Schoolbooks,* 90–91.

44. HQ MSD Negros, GO 1, 11 March 1899; GO 5, 10 August 1899, both in E 2621, RG 395; James F. Smith to Hugh T. Sime, 31 August and 9 September 1899, LS 328 and 340, E 2616, RG 395.

45. Circular, 1st California, 28 March 1899, E 2937, RG 395.

46. James F. Smith to AAG, VMD, 8 August 1899, LS 290, LSB 1, E 2616, RG 395; Aldecoa-Rodrigues, *Negros Oriental,* 157.

47. CG, VMD to C. S. Sperry, 5 May 1899, LS 3, April 1899 LSB, E 2464, RG 395. LeRoy, *Americans,* 2: 106–8.

48. Crane, "Who Burned Iloilo?" 232–39; Bronson, "Visayan Campaigns," 304–5; Aldecoa-Rodrigues, *Negros Oriental,* 141–50.

49. James F. Smith to the People of Negros, 9 October 1899, LS 377; Telegram:

Smith to Mann, 20 August 1899, LS 299; James F. Smith to AG, VMD, 30 August 1899, LS 325, all in LSB 1, E 2616, RG 395.

50. Dionisio Papa, "Ultima Republica Federal Filipina—Canton de Isla de Negros," 29 March 1899, E 2940, RG 395. Evelyn Tan Cullamar, *Babaylanism in Negros, 1896–1907* (Manila: New Day Publishers, 1986).

51. Romero, *Negros Occidental,* 173.

52. Translation of letter from Dionisio Papa, General in Chief and Political and Military Governor, Philippine Republic of Negros to Presidentes of Bayauan and Tolon, 21 September 1901, E 2940, RG 395.

53. BGCVMD to AAG, DP8AC, 1 July 1899, LS 1, July 1899 LSB, E 2464, RG 395. 28th June 1899, Diary, Hughes Papers; James F. Smith to AAG, VMD, 31 July 1899, LS 266, E 2616, RG 395.

54. Senate, *Affairs,* 536.

55. James F. Smith to Victor Duboce, 1 July 1899, LS 150, E 2616, RG 395.

56. James F. Smith to John A. Miller, 8 July 1899, LS 192, E 2616, RG 395. James F. Smith to CO, Carlota, 3 July 1899, LS 155 and 158, E 2616, RG 395.

57. James F. Smith to AAG, VMD, 31 July 1899, LS 266, E 2616, RG 395.

58. *RWD* 1899 1:5:353–60. Telegram: Smith to Mann, 22 July 1899, E 2616, RG 395; James F. Smith to CO, 6th Inf, 20 July 1899, LS 250, E 2616, RG 395; James F. Smith to AAG, VMD, 31 July 1899, LS 266, E 2616, RG 395; BGCVMD to AAG, DP8AC, 26 July 1899, LS 84, July 1899 LSB, E 2464, RG 395; *Harpers' History,* 234; Elkanah Babcock, *A War History of the Sixth U.S. Infantry* (Kansas City: Hudson-Kimberly Publishing, 1903), 61–62.

59. Telegrams: Smith to Mann, 2 September, 2 and 9 October 1899, LS 332, 364, and 374, E 2616, RG 395; Romero, *Negros Occidental,* 185–87; Babcock, *War History,* 63–65.

60. James F. Smith to AAG, VMD, 28 September 1899, LS 359, E 2616, RG 395.

61. Charles W. Mann to CO, MSD Negros, 29 October 1899, in Z. W. Torrey to [HQ, VMD], 9 October 1899, No. 467, E 2511, RG 395; "Danao River Expedition," Harry C. Logan Papers, MHI; "Only a Volunteer," 124–25, Hewson Papers.

62. James F. Smith to CO, Carlota, 4 July 1899, LS 160, E 2616, RG 395; Porfirio Erescamilla to James F. Smith, 17 July 1899, E 2631, RG 395; Charles W. Miner to Secretary of U.S. Military Governor, 4 March 1901, LS 299, E 2616, RG 395.

63. "Only a Volunteer," 114–15, Hewson Papers. Victor Duboce to James F. Smith, 7 April 1899, LS 177, 1st California Inf RLSCMB, E 116, RG 94.

64. [Robert P. Hughes] to My dear General [Elwell S. Otis], 22 August 1899, LS 57, August 1899 LSB, E 2464, RG 395.

65. Juan Araneta to James F. Smith, 7 August 1899, No. 1175, E 2631, RG 395.

66. Victor Duboce to James F. Smith, 10 April 1899, LS 178, 1st California Inf RLSCMB, E 116, RG 94.

67. James F. Smith, Proclamation, 13 August 1899, LS 320, E 2616, RG 395.

68. [Robert P. Hughes] to My dear General [Elwell S. Otis], 22 August 1899, LS 57, August 1899 LSB, E 2464, RG 395. James F. Smith, Declaration, 13 August 1899, LS 320, E 2616, RG 395; [Robert P. Hughes] to AAG, DP8AC, 19 August 1899, LS 51, August 1899 LSB, E 2464, RG 395; James F. Smith to Hugh T. Sime, 31 August 1899, LS 328, E 2616, RG 395.

69. James F. Smith to the Civil Governor and Advisory Council, Island of Negros, 6 November 1899, LS 504, E 2616, RG 395. James F. Smith to AAG, DV, 25 July 1900, LS 1124, E 2616, RG 395; *Harpers' History,* 235–36.

70. Quisumbing, "American Occupation," 186. Anon. to Emilio Aguinaldo, 19 February 1899, Ex 1388, 5:761–62; [Emilio Aguinaldo] to Marchial Velez, [December 1898?], Ex 1385, 5:754; [Emilio Aguinaldo?] to President of the Provincial Council of Cebu, 24 January 1899, Ex 1387, 5:760–61; Anon., 22 February 1899, Ex 1386, 5:755–59, all in Taylor, *Philippine Insurrection.*

71. Braisted, *U.S. Navy,* 69; Faust, *Campaigning,* 245; *Harpers' History,* 142–44; LeRoy, *Americans,* 2:112–14; Quisumbing, "American Occupation," 187.

72. [Thomas R. Hamer] to AAAG, 1st IB, 6 April 1899, LS 6, E 2601, RG 395. [Thomas R. Hamer] to AAAG, 11 April 1899, LS 9, E 2601, RG 395; Thomas R. Hamer to AAG, VMD, 28 July 1899, E 2601, RG 395.

73. Thomas R. Hamer to AG, VMD, 1 May 1899, LS 16. [Thomas R. Hamer] to AAAG, VMD, 13 May 1899, LS 21; Thomas R. Hamer to AAG, VMD, 28 July 1899, all in E 2601, RG 395; Faust, *Campaigning,* 246.

74. Thomas R. Hamer to AG, DP8AC, 4 May 1899, LS 16, E 2601, RG 395.

75. Thomas Barry to Thomas R. Hamer, 21 May 1899, E 2064, RG 395.

76. Thomas R. Hamer to AAG, VMD, 28 July 1899, E 2601, RG 395.

77. Thomas R. Hamer to SMG, 29 May 1899, LS 37, E 2601, RG 395.

78. Arcadio Maxilom to Apolinario Mabini, 15 May 1899, Ex 1393, Taylor, *Philippine Insurrection,* 5:775–78.

79. Thomas R. Hamer to AAG, VMD, 28 July 1899, E 2601, RG 395; Juan Climaco to Superior Military Commander, 29 March 1899, Ex 1390, Taylor, *Philippine Insurrection,* 5:767–69; Schumacher, *Revolutionary Clergy,* 136–37; Quisumbing, "Katipunan," 39–50; Quisumbing, "American Occupation," 186.

80. Arcadio Maxilom, Circular No. 63, 7 August 1899, Ex 1399, 5:785–86. Antonio Luna to Arcadio Maxilom, 2 June 1899, Ex 1395, 5:799–80; Apolinario Mabini to Arcadio Maxilom, 11 April 1899, Ex 1391, 5:770; 2:421–23, all in Taylor, *Philippine Insurrection.*

81. Faust, *Campaigning,* 246. Thomas R. Hamer to AG, VMD, 1 May 1899, LS 16, E 2601, RG 395.

82. [Thomas R. Hamer] to AG, VMD, 1 May 1899, LS 16, E 2601, RG 395.

83. 29 June and 26 July 1899, Diary, Hughes Papers. BGCVMD to AAG, DP8AC, 15 June 1899, LS 71, June 1899 LSB, E 2464, RG 395; 17 June 1899, Diary, Hughes Papers; BGCVMD to CO, MSD Cebu, 7 July 1899, LS 20, July 1899 LSB, E 2464, RG 395; Thomas R. Hamer to AG, VMD, 28 June 1899, LS 41; Thomas R. Hamer to Robert P. Hughes, 27 June 1899, LS 54, Thomas R. Hamer to AAAG, VMD, 21 July 1899, LS 75, all in E 2601, RG 395.

84. [Robert P. Hughes] to My dear General [Otis], 22 August 1899, LS 57, August 1899 LSB, E 2464, RG 395.

85. [Robert P. Hughes] to AAG, DP8AC, 19 August 1899, LS 51, August 1899 LSB, E 2464, RG 395.

86. BGCVMD to AAG, DP8AC, 23 June 1899, LS 95, June 1899 LSB, E 2464, RG 395. [Robert P. Hughes] to CO, MSD Cebu, 4 September 1899, LS 9, September 1899 LSB, E 2464, RG 395.

87. 24 August 1899, Diary, Hughes Papers.

88. [Robert P. Hughes] to AG, DP8AC, 1 September 1899, LS 6, September 1899 LSB, E 2464, RG 395; *Harpers' History,* 237; Taylor, *Philippine Insurrection,* 2:421.

89. [Robert P. Hughes] to Thomas R. Hamer, 15 September 1899, LS 38, September 1899 LSB, E 2464, RG 395; Thomas R. Hamer to CO, MSD Cebu, 27 September 1899, E 2601, RG 395; [Robert P. Hughes] to AG, DP8AC, 2 and 9 October 1899, LS 3 and 16, October 1899 LSB, E 2464, RG 395; HQ, MSD Cebu, GO 5, 4 October 1899, E 2612, RG 395.

90. [Robert P. Hughes] to Simon Snyder, 2 October 1899, LS 31, October 1899 LSB, E 2464, RG 395.

5. The Spring Campaign

1. *Harpers' History,* 148.

2. *RWD* 1899 1:4:114; *Harpers' History,* 238.

3. Otis to AG, 27 November 1898, *CWS* 2:840; Otis to AG, 20 February 1899, *CWS* 2:908; Otis to AG, 20 April 1899, *CWS* 2:969; Otis to AG, 1 June 1899, *CWS* 2:999.

4. Corbin to Otis, 20 March 1899, *CWS* 2:939. *RWD* 1899 1:1:6.

5. Thomas R. Hamer to AAAG, VMD, 21 July 1899, LS 75, E 2601, RG 395.

6. 6 March 1899, "Diary of Cpl. Lisle D. Tucker, Co. E, 13th Minn., 1 Jan. 1899 to August 1899," Spear-Tucker Collection, MHS. Carl I. Stone to My Dear Folks, 1 March 1899, Carl I. Stone Papers, MHS; Nelson A. Miles to SecWar, 1 December 1898, *CWS* 2:841; Fred R. Brown, *History of the Ninth U.S. Infantry, 1799–1909* (Chicago: R. R. Donnelley and Sons, 1909), 186, 226–28, 230; Bradford G. Chynoweth, *Bellamy Park* (Hicksville, N.Y.: Exposition Press, 1975), 25; John Scott Reed, "Burden and Honor: The United States Volunteers in the Southern Philippines, 1899–1901" (Ph.D. diss., University of Southern California, 1994), 48–49.

7. Samuel B. M. Young to AG, 1st Div, 14 August 1899, LS 389, E 824, RG 395.

8. H. Roger Grant, "Letters from the Philippines: The 51st Iowa Volunteers at War, 1898–1899," *Palimpsest* 29 (November–December 1974): 172. *RWD* 1899 1:4:175; Markey, *From Iowa,* 210.

9. Henry C. Corbin to Elwell S. Otis, 6 March 1899, *CWS* 2:924.

10. Theodore Roosevelt to John Hay, 1 July 1899, Box 2, Greene Papers. *Harpers' History,* 181–82; Gates, *Schoolbooks,* 108.

11. 17 May 1899, Diary, Cuffe Papers; L. Beckurts to AG, 10 September 1899, E 184, RG 94; Cooper and Smith, *Citizens as Soldiers,* 92–93; Young, *General's General,* 238.

12. William G. Haan to AG, 1st Div, 8AC, 12 May 1899, Box 1, Edwards Papers; *RWD* 1899 1:1:20; *RWD* 1899 1:4:178; *RWD* 1900 1:2:296.

13. Stanley Karnow, *In Our Image: America's Empire in the Philippines* (New York: Random House, 1989), 150–53; LeRoy, *Americans,* 2:82–83; Taylor, *Philippine Insurrection,* 2:209.

14. Emilio Aguinaldo to Mariano Trias, 18 February 1899, Ex 607, Taylor, *Philippine Insurrection,* 2:200–201.

15. Apolinario Mabini to Emilio Aguinaldo, 6 March 1899, Ex 618, Taylor, *Philippine Insurrection,* 4:32–33, also 2:213–17; Alejandrino, *Price of Freedom,* 131–39; Kalaw, *Philippine Revolution,* 187–91; Saulo, *Truth About Aguinaldo,* 15; Chaput, "Antonio Luna," 265–67.

16. *RWD* 1899 1:4:110; Frederick Funston, *Memories of Two Wars* (London: Constable and Co, 1912), 220–21.

17. R. B. Wallace to AG, 6 September 1899, LS 10, 37th Inf LSB, E 117, RG 94. HQ, 2nd Brig, 1st Div, Circular No. 3, 15 February 1899, and GO 6, 20 September 1899, E 820, RG 395; HQ, 1st Brig, 1st Div, GO 22, 7 November 1899, E 805, RG 395; "Daily Register of Men, Women, and Children going in and out of various Manila posts and estimated food products, 14 November 1899 to 5 February 1900," E 808, RG 395; *RWD* 1900 1:4:207.

18. Palmer, *With My Own Eyes,* 151.

19. "Efficiency Report in Case of Captain Loyd Wheaton, 20th Inf—1890," 5249 ACP 1889 (Loyd Wheaton), RG 94; see also "Report of the services in the Philippine Islands of Brigadier and brevet Major General Loyd Wheaton, U.S. Vols." On Wheaton, see Robinson, *Philippines,* 359–60; Sexton, *Soldiers,* 105–6; C. David Rice, "Loyd Wheaton," in Beede, *War of 1898,* 593–95.

20. *RWD* 1899 1:4:111, 1:5:364–71; *Harpers' History,* 148–51; Sexton, *Soldiers,* 106.

21. *Leslie's Official History,* 610.

22. *Harpers' History,* 151.

23. Miller, *"Benevolent Assimilation,"* 69. Sexton, *Soldiers,* 107.

24. *RWD* 1899 1:5:366.

25. "The Story of the First Washington—The Pasig Delta Campaign," F 26–6, Joseph Smith Papers, Allen Library, University of Washington, Seattle, Wash.

26. *RWD* 1899 1:4:111–12, 1:5:377–78. The organization of the 2nd Division was: 1st Brigade—two battalions of the 3rd Artillery, 20th Kansas, and 1st Montana; Hale's 2nd Brigade—1st Nebraska, 1st South Dakota, and 10th Pennsylvania; 3rd Brigade—13th Minnesota, 1st Wyoming, 4th Infantry, and one battalion of the 17th Infantry; Wheaton's provisional brigade—22nd Infantry, 2nd Oregon, and one battalion 3rd Infantry; Division Reserve—one squadron of the 4th Cavalry and Utah Battery.

27. *RWD* 1899 1:5:382.

28. *Harpers' History,* 164.

29. *RWD* 1899 1:5:381.

30. Harrison Gray Otis to AG, 2 April 1899, Box 2, E 764, RG 395.

31. *RWD* 1899 1:5:379.

32. John M. Stotsenburg to AG, 2nd Brig, 2 April 1899, LS 309, 1st Nebraska Inf RLSCMB, E 116, RG 94; Thiessen, "Fighting First Nebraska," 249.

33. Funston, *Memories,* 244–50; *RWD* 1899 1:5:387.

34. H. C. Thompson, "War Without Medals," *Oregon Historical Quarterly* 59 (December 1958): 314–15.

35. C. U. Ganterbein, *The Official Records of the Oregon Volunteers in the Spanish War and Philippine Insurrection* (Salem, Oreg.: J. R. Whitney, 1903), 71.

36. Leopold Parker to John G. Ballance, 19 November 1901, 3137 ACP 1891 (John Green Ballance), RG 94.

37. *Harpers' History,* 165. On the Malolos campaign, see Harrison G. Otis to

AG, 2 April 1899, Box 2, E 764, RG 395; John M. Stotsenburg to AG, 2nd Brig, 2 April 1899, LS 309, 1st Nebraska Inf RLSCMB, E 116, RG 94; *Harpers' History,* 161–65; McCutcheon, *Drawn from Memory,* 136; Faust, *Campaigning,* 158–73.

38. Funston, *Memories,* 226.

39. Sexton, *Soldiers,* 115. Hoyt, *Frontier Doctor,* 349.

40. *Harpers' History,* 162.

41. MacArthur to Otis, 31 March 1899, in *RWD* 1899 1:5:395.

42. Otis to MacArthur, 31 March 1899, in *RWD* 1899 1:5:395. John M. Stotsenburg to AG, 2nd Brig, 2 April 1899, LS 309, 1st Nebraska Inf RLSCMB, E 116, RG 94; Sexton, *Soldiers,* 118.

43. Harrison Gray Otis to AG, 2 April 1899, Box 2, E 764, RG 395. Faust, *Campaigning,* 159, 163–64.

44. William H. Barrett Questionnaire, 2nd Oregon Inf, SAWS. William Shortill Questionaire, 1st Wyoming Inf, SAWS; Harrison G. Otis to AG, 2 April 1899, Box 2, E 764, RG 395; John J. Weisenburger to J. B. McCoy, 28 April 1899, Box 2, E 764, RG 395; *RWD* 1899 1:4:175; "The Story of the First Washington—March and Money," F 26–7, Joseph Smith Papers; Cooper and Smith, *Citizens as Soldiers,* 81; Markey, *From Iowa,* 211; Philip M. Shockley, *The Krag-Jorgensen Rifle in Service* (Aledo, Ill.: World Wide Gun Report, 1960), 35; Hunt, "First Colorado," 249–52.

45. Otis to SecWar, 16 and 19 May, *CWS* 2:990–93. Russell W. Alger to Otis, 19 May 1890, *CWS* 2:993.

46. Harold F. Taggart, ed., "California Soldiers in the Philippines: From the Correspondence of Howard Middleton, 1898–1899," *California Historical Society Quarterly* 31 (June 1952): 168–69.

57. HQ, 1st Div, GO 19, 6 April 1899, in "Orders Issued Relative to Burning of Private Property," AAG, 1st Div to H. J. McGrath, 11 July 1899, LS 346, E 769, RG 395. The expedition comprised three dismounted troops of the 4th Cavalry, eight companies of the 14th Infantry, four companies each of the 1st Idaho and 1st North Dakota Infantry, and two light artillery pieces.

48. LeRoy, *Americans,* 2:160; see also 2:67–68, 83, 159–60. Stuart C. Miller, "Henry Ware Lawton," in Beede, *War of 1898,* 253–54.

49. Henry W. Lawton to Henry C. Corbin, 8 November 1898, Box 1, Corbin Papers. On Lawton, see Karnow, *In Our Image,* 148–49; Graham Cosmas, "San Juan and El Caney, 1–2 July 1898," in *America's First Battles, 1776–1965,* ed. Charles A. Heller and William A. Stofft (Lawrence: University Press of Kansas, 1986), 127–28, 142–45; Jack C. Lane, *Armed Progressive: General Leonard Wood* (San Rafael, Calif.: Presidio Press, 1978), 64–65; Trask, *War with Spain,* 235–37.

50. Otis to AG, 11 April 1899, *CWS* 2:962; Frank W. Carpenter, "Journal of the Sta. Cruz Expedition," April 1899, E 789, RG 395; John J. Weisenberger to AG, 1st Div, 25 April 1899, E 764, RG 395; Henry W. Lawton to AG, DP8AC, 10 April 1899, LS 229, E 768, RG 395; Russell, *Campaigning with King,* 129; *Harpers' History,* 168–69; Sexton, *Soldiers,* 125.

51. Cooper and Smith, *Citizens as Soldiers,* 91–92; Faust, *Campaigning,* 204–6.

52. "The Story of the First Washington—Battles and Expeditions," F 26–9, Joseph Smith Papers; 11–12 April 1899, Diary, Cuffe Papers.

53. Telegrams: Otis to Lawton, 15 April 1899, and Barry to Lawton, 12 April 1899, both in E 764, RG 395; Faust, *Campaigning,* 206.

54. Quote "piratical raid" from *Harpers' History*, 170–71; quote "strategic vague-ness" from Cooper and Smith, *Citizens as Soldiers*, 90.

55. Faust, *Campaigning*, 206.

56. May, *Battle*, 80. Juan Cailles to Lt. Gen. SecWar, 13 April 1899, SD 1195.3, PIR.

57. Otis to Lawton, 15 April 1899, E 764, RG 395.

58. Wheaton's 1st Brigade consisted of the 20th Kansas; 1st Montana; a battal-ion of the 51st Iowa; and a squadron of the 4th Cavalry. Hale's 2nd Brigade had the 1st Nebraska; 1st South Dakota; and two battalions of the 51st Iowa.

59. *RWD* 1899 1:4:113–14; 1:5:75, 400; *Harpers' History*, 179, 181.

60. HQ, 2nd Div, FO 26, 22 April 1899, in *RWD* 1899 1:5:401.

61. HQ, 1st Div, GO 20, 19 April 1899, E 788, RG 395.

62. Alejandrino, *Price of Freedom*, 130–31; Quirino, *Filipinos at War*, 154–55; Sexton, *Soldiers*, 141.

63. Taylor, *Philippine Insurrection*, 2:213–16.

64. MacArthur to Ames, 11 April 1899, E 764, RG 395.

65. 11 April 1899, "Diary of Cpl. Lisle D. Tucker." *RWD* 1899 1:5:396–97.

66. Faust, *Campaigning*, 175–77. MacArthur to AG, 11 April, E 764, RG 395.

67. Henry B. Mulford to AG, 2nd Brig, 25 April 1899, LS 327, 1st Nebraska Inf RLSCMB, E116, RG 94; J. R. Johnson, "Colonel John Miller Stotsenburg," 352–53; Palmer, *With My Own Eyes*, 148; Faust, *Campaigning*, 178–79.

68. *RWD* 1899 1:5:402–3.

69. *RWD* 1899 1:5:403–5. Faust, *Campaigning*, 184.

70. *RWD* 1899 1:5:405; Sexton, *Soldiers*, 144; *Harpers' History*, 194–98.

71. *RWD* 1899 1:5:406. McCutcheon, *Drawn from Memory*, 139.

72. 2nd Division losses for April were 26 dead and 143 wounded; see *RWD* 1899 1:5:406. Luna's claim is repeated in Kalaw, *Philippine Revolution*, 187.

73. Otis to AG, 28 and 29 April 1899, 3 May 1899, CWS 2:978–79, 281; *RWD* 1899 1:5:209; *Harpers' History*, 198; LeRoy, *Americans*, 2:80–82; Taylor, *Philippine Insurrection*, 2:221–28.

74. Markey, *From Iowa*, 234. McCutcheon, *Drawn from Memory*, 139; Faust, *Campaigning*, 189–90.

75. Markey, *From Iowa*, 235.

76. Ibid., 237.

77. *Harpers' History*, 190–91.

78. Young, *General's General*, 237.

79. MacArthur to Lawton, 9 May 1899, in *RWD* 1899 1:5:192. Barry to Lawton, 10 May 1899, in *RWD* 1899 1:5:193, 89.

80. Henry B. Mulford to AG, 8AC, 8 May 1899, LS 329, 1st Nebraska Inf RLSCMB, E 116, RG 94. *RWD* 1899 1:5:409; Faust, *Campaigning*, 191. Casual-ties among the 1st Nebraska's officers were even higher—one colonel was killed, another invalided home, all three majors were wounded; seven of the original twelve captains and four of the replacement captains were wounded or on sick report, as were half the lieutenants.

81. *RWD* 1899 1:5:411–12.

82. Owen Summers to AAG, 1st Div, 10 June 1899, Box 2, E 788, RG 395; *Harpers' History*, 179–80. Lawton's provisional division consisted of the 22nd Infantry,

eight companies of the 3rd Infantry, the 1st North Dakota, a four-troop squadron of the 4th Cavalry (one troop mounted), and a composite battery of 1.65-inch Hotchkiss mountain guns and 3.2-inch field guns.

83. Lawton to AG, DP8AC, 26 April 1899, in Faust, *Campaigning*, 212–13. For criticism of Otis, see William Dinwiddie, "Lawton's Advance on San Isidro," in *Harpers' History*, 181–83; LeRoy, *Americans*, 2:37; Sexton, *Soldiers*, 130.

84. Otis to Lawton, 27 April 199, *RWD* 1899 1:5:134–35.

85. On the Taguig fights, see John J. Weisenberger to AG, 1st Div, 20 April 1899; John J. Weisenburger to J. B. McCoy, 28 April 1899, both in E 764, RG 395.

86. Barry to Lawton, 29 April 1899, in *RWD* 1899 1:5:147.

87. The telegraphic correspondence is in Lawton to AG, 29 April 1899, *RWD* 1899 1:5:147; see also 81–83; Cooper and Smith, *Citizens as Soldiers*, 95–96; *Harpers' History*, 181–82.

88. Lawton to AG, 8AC, 1 May 1899, in *RWD* 1899 1:5:157. For operations, see John G. Ballance to Adj, 22nd Inf, 5 May 1899, E 788, RG 395; Leopold Parker to John G. Ballance, 19 November 1901, in 3137 ACP 1891 (John Green Ballance), RG 94; *RWD* 1899 1:5:85, 150–55; *Harpers' History*, 183.

89. Lawton to AG, DP, 3 May 1899, in *RWD* 1899 1:5:164.

90. Lawton to MacArthur, 9 May 1899, in *RWD* 1899 1:5:192. Barry to Lawton, 3 May 1899; Clarence R. Edwards to W. H. Young, 4 May 1899; Barry to Lawton, 5 May, all in *RWD* 1899 1:5:164–69. On civil government, see *RWD* 1899 1:5:88.

91. Otis to AG, 11 May 1899, CWS 2:986.

92. Barry to Lawton, 6 May 1899, in *RWD* 1899 1:5:178; Taylor, *Philippine Insurrection*, 2:218–19.

93. James F. Case to AG, 1 June 1899, E 764, RG 395; Faust, *Campaigning*, 223.

94. William E. Birkhimer to AAG, 1st Div, 15 May 1899, Box 1, E 788, RG 395; Deposition of Frank W. Summerfield, 2 June 1899, LS 308, E 769, RG 395; Henry W. Lawton to AG, 19 June 1899, LS 308, E 769, RG 395; Cooper and Smith, *Citizens as Soldiers*, 99.

95. Report of Private J. H. Killian, [June 1899?], E 754, RG 395; Cooper and Smith, *Citizens as Soldiers*, 100.

96. *Harpers' History*, 189. Owen Summers to AAG, 1st Div, 10 June 1899, E 788, RG 395; *RWD* 1899 1:5:97; Cooper and Smith, *Citizens as Soldiers*, 100–101.

97. *RWD* 1899 1:5:100.

98. The worst sickness rates were in the 17th and 9th Infantry, two Regular regiments that took part in the campaign for only a few days and had virtually no combat, see *RWD* 1899 1:5:114–17.

99. Jonathan W. Hannay to AAG, 1st Div, 3 June 1899; L. M. Cooke to Adj, 3rd Inf, 20 May 1899; W. C. Butler to CO, 3rd Inf, 29 May 1899, all in E 764, RG 395; *RWD* 1899 1:5:98–102.

100. Brown, *Ninth Infantry*, 253.

6. *Summer Stalemate*

1. *RWD* 1899 1:4:162–65.

2. 22 August 1899, Diary, William Pierce Evans Papers, USMA. J. Franklin Bell and George F. Becker to Albert J. Beveridge, 1 August 1899, Series 1, R 3, Roosevelt Papers.

3. Lewis P. Burlingham to Parents, 1 June 1899, Lewis P. Burlingham Papers, MHS. Hunt, "First Colorado," 278–79.

4. Reilly, "Andrew Wadsworth," 192. Emory S. West to Miss Price, 11 May 1899, West Papers; Hall, "Philippine War," 198.

5. Brown, *Ninth Infantry,* 254. Robert H. Hall to AG, 9 June 1899, E 764, RG 395. Hall's provisional brigade consisted of the 2nd Oregon, six companies of the 1st Colorado, four troops of the 4th Cavalry (all but one dismounted), two battalions of the 4th Infantry, a battalion of the 9th Infantry, and four guns.

6. *Harpers' History,* 211–12; Faust, *Campaigning,* 194–96; Cooper and Smith, *Citizens as Soldiers,* 102–4.

7. E. D. Scott to Chief of Artillery, 2 July 1899, E 764, RG 395. Hunt, "First Colorado," 267–68. Ovenshine's brigade was nine companies of the 13th Infantry, eight companies of the 14th Infantry, two companies of the 12th Infantry, and four field guns. Wheaton's 1st Brigade was two battalions each of the 9th and 21st Infantry, six companies of the 1st Colorado, and six field guns.

8. AAAG, 2nd Brig to AG, 1st Div, 2 August 1899, LS 48, E 812, RG 395; *Harpers' History,* 214. Based on an anonymous account that has since been lost, two historians claim that a large American force was decisively defeated on 10 June; see Gregorio F. Zaide, *The Philippine Revolution* (Manila: Modern Book Co., 1954), 324–25; Quirino, *Filipinos at War,* 159–60.

9. AG, 1st Div to R. A. Brown, 28 June 1899, E 769, RG 395. Henry W. Lawton to Thomas Franklin, 9 June 1899, LS 300, E 769, RG 395; Samuel Seay to George H. Patten, 18 June 1899; W. L. Kenly to H. M. Andrews, 25 June 1899; George H. Penrose to Chief Surgeon, 26 June 1899; H. M. Andrews to AG, 1st Div, 29 June 1899, all in E 764, RG 395; AAAG, 2nd Brig to AG, 1st Div, 2 August 1899, LS 48, E 812, RG 395; Brown, *Ninth Infantry,* 262–65; *Harpers' History,* 213–14; Faust, *Campaigning,* 237–40.

10. Otis to AG, 20 June 1899, CWS 2:1016. *RWD* 1899 1:4:140–41.

11. HQ, 2nd Brig, 1 Div to AG, 23 July 1899, LS 41, E 812, RG 395.

12. *RWD* 1899 1:4:138.

13. *RWD* 1899 1:4:142.

14. James Parker to AG, 14 August 1899, LR 835, E 826, RG 395; Samuel B. M. Young to AG, 1st Div, 14 August 1899, LS 389, E 824, RG 395; Samuel B. M. Young to AG, DP, 6 January 1900, LS 577, E 836, RG 395.

15. [Jacob H. Smith] to AG, DNL, 28 September 1900, LS 1018, LSB 2, E 2206, RG 395; *RWD* 1900 1:4:208; Brown, *Ninth Infantry,* 276–77, 82–96; *Harpers' History,* 222–23; Markey, *From Iowa,* 258–62; A. B. Feur, *Combat Diary: Episodes from the History of the Twenty-second Regiment* (New York: Praeger, 1991), 130.

16. Peter Gowing, "Mandate in Moroland: The American Government of Muslim Filipinos, 1899–1920" (Ph.D. diss., Syracuse University, 1968), 219–28, 235–47; George W. Jornacion, "The Time of Eagles: United States Army Officers and the Pacification of the Philippine Moros, 1899–1913" (Ph.D. diss., University of Maine at Orono, 1973), 47–50; Arcilla, "Philippine Revolution," 46–56.

17. 4 July 1899, Diary, Spear-Tucker Collection; Markey, *From Iowa,* 270; Cooper and Smith, *Citizens as Soldiers,* 108.

18. Bowe, *With the Thirteenth,* 168.

19. Thompson, "War Without Medals," 322–24.

20. *The Medal of Honor of the United States Army* (Washington, D.C.: Govern-

ment Printing Office, 1948), 242–44. This trend continued throughout the Philippine War; of the thirty-eight Medals of Honor awarded to soldiers after the departure of the State Volunteers, twenty-five went to U.S. Volunteers.

21. [Robert P. Hughes] to AAG, 19 August 1899, LS 51, August 1899 LSB, E 2464, RG 395.

22. Robinson, *Philippines,* 58–60.

23. Miller, *Benevolent Assimilation,* 195.

24. 8 February 1899, Diary, Hughes Papers.

25. *RWD* 1899 1:4:175.

26. "The Story of the First Washington—March and Money," F 26-7, Joseph Smith Papers. Hunt, "First Colorado," 230–32.

27. "The Story of the First Washington—The Battle of Santa Anna," F 26-3, Joseph Smith Papers.

28. Crouch, *Leader,* 219–25. The investigation and testimony can be found in U.S. Senate, *Affairs,* 1420–84. Edward C. Little to Herbert Welsh, 7 January 1903, 1903 File, Moorefield Storey Papers, Massachusetts Historical Society. Little missed most of his regiment's fighting, and therefore a chance of glory, by wounding himself with his own pistol.

29. Todd L. Wagoner, "Fighting Aguinaldo's Insurgents in the Philippines," *Kansas Historical Quarterly* 18 (May 1951): 157.

30. *RWD* 1899 1:4:182–83. If the 3rd Artillery (694) and 14th Infantry (616) are added, then four Regular regiments accounted for 25 percent of the summary courts-martial.

31. On the U.S. Volunteers, see Edward E. Hardin to AG, 23 August 1899, LS 450, 29th Inf LSB, E 117, RG 94; AG to C. P. Cabot, 3 February 1922, Philippine Insurrection File, No. 2159, Legislative and Policy Precedent Files, 1943–1975, RG 407; Allan R. Millett, *The General: Robert L. Bullard and Officership in the United States Army, 1881–1925* (Westport, Conn.: Greenwood Press, 1975), 112–17. The best single account is Reed, "Burden and Honor."

32. Brian M. Linn, "The Thirty-third Infantry, United States Volunteers: An American Regiment in the Philippine Insurrection" (M.A. thesis, Ohio State University, 1981), 18–20; *ANJ,* 8 July 1899; Lawrence Benton Questionnaire, 33rd Inf, SAWS. On other units, see Millett, *General,* 115–19; Reed, "Burden and Honor," 1–57.

33. Walter S. Schuyler to AG, [14 October 1899], 46th Inf LSB, E 117, RG 94; 27 October to 14 November 1899, 1899 Diary, Walter S. Schuyler Papers, Huntington Library, San Marino, Calif.; "History of the 41st Infantry, U.S.V.," 30 June 1901, E 187, RG 94; "History of the 26th Infantry, U.S.V.," [July 1901], E 187, RG 94.

34. *RWD* 1899 1:4:226.

35. AAAG, 2nd Brig to AG, 1st Div, 2 August 1899, LS 48, E 812, RG 395; J. Franklin Bell to Chief Quartermaster, 20 August 1899, LS 31, 36th Inf LSB, E 117, RG 94; *RWD* 1899 1:5:413; Brown, *Ninth Infantry,* 261.

36. Senate, *Affairs,* 2850.

37. Robert H. Noble, "Preface," *A Compilation of Insurgent Documents . . . and Samar,* PIR. John R. M. Taylor, "Translations of Documents Showing Relations Between the Insurgents of the Philippines and Japan. 1899–1900. Introductory Note," SD 430, PIR.

38. John T. Farrell, "An Abandoned Approach to Philippine History: John R. M. Taylor and the Philippine Insurrection Records," *Catholic Historical Review* 39 (January 1954): 391; History of the Intelligence Section: Philippine Department, F 10560-152-187, Army War College Records, RG 165.

39. James F. Smith to AG, DP8AC, 5 April 1899, LS 10, August 1899 LSB, E 2464, RG 395. For references to hiring local spies, see Thomas M. Anderson to AG, DP8AC, 22 February 1899, LS 141, E 768, RG 395; HQ, 2nd Brig, 1st Div, SO 39, 4 November 1899, SO 44, 17 November, SO 52, 8 December, all in E 830, RG 395.

40. *RWD* 1900 1:5:190–94.

41. Jose Banuelo and Cadido Hizon to Emilio Aguinaldo, 12 and 25 June 1898, SD 7.3, PIR; Otis to AG, 3 June 1899, *CWS* 2:1001; Henry W. Lawton to Theodore Schwan, 20 September 1899, LS 411, E 769, RG 395; Matthew A. Batson to Chief Ordnance Officer, 22 September 1899, E 5804, RG 395; ACP 49261891 (Matthew A. Batson), RG 94; 1332 ACP1891 (Percival G. Lowe), RG 94; 4945 ACP1891 (Joseph C. Castner), RG 94; Clarence R. Edwards to Joseph C. Castner, 15 December 1900, Box 1, Edwards Papers; Matthew A. Batson to AG, 15 July 1901, in Request for Brochure on Philippine Scouts, 21 September 1953, Philippines File, No. 388, Legislative and Policy Precedent Files, 1943–1975, RG 407; *RWD* 1900 1:4:209, 1:7:123–37; Edward M. Coffman, "Batson of the Philippine Scouts," *Parameters* 7 (1977): 68–72; James R. Woolard, "The Philippine Scouts: The Development of America's Colonial Army" (Ph.D. diss., Ohio State University, 1975), 5–18.

42. "Instructions to the Mayor (Captain Municipal) Appointed Under General Field Orders No. _____, Dated Headquarters First Division, Eighth Army Corps, July _____, 1899," E 769, RG 395. For an excellent account of the creation of civil government, see Gates, *Schoolbooks and Krags,* 87–90.

43. Palmer, *With My Own Eyes,* 145. For Dewey's lack of interest in the war, see 1899 Entries, Diary of George Dewey, Box 475, Subject File OO, RG 45. Interestingly, Dewey's diary never mentions disagreements with Otis but rather suggests cordial social relations. Like the alleged Lawton-Otis feud, the Dewey-Otis feud may be largely a journalistic invention.

44. *RSN* 1899, 3.

45. Harry Knox, Memorandum, 20 May 1900, R 377, M 625.

46. The cities of Iloilo and Cebu were opened on 22 February and 14 March, respectively. The "friendly ports"—meaning those that had U.S. garrisons—on Negros and Cebu were also opened for trade, but because they had very shallow harbors they were restricted to small coastal vessels. On 26 December, Zamboanga, Jolo, and Siassi were opened for trade.

47. W. H. Whiting to CINC, 4 March 1899, R 367, M 625; D. W. Wurtbaugh to CINC, 4 December 1899, R 374, M 625.

48. John C. Bates to Commander, Asiatic Squadron, 21 December 1899, R 374, M 625. BGCVMD to AAG, DP8AC, 15 June 1899, LS 71, June 1899 LSB, E 2464, RG 395; Vicente Lukban to Antonio Luna, 8 July 1899, Ex 1321, Taylor, *Philippine Insurrection,* 5:632–35; Cormandel to CINC, 11 March 1899, R 367, M 625.

49. Thomas R. Hamer to SMG, 29 May 1899, and C. H. Murray to CO, MSD Cebu, 5 June 1899, both in Box 1, E 2604, RG 395; Otis to AG, 26 June 1899, *CWS* 2:1019.

50. E. S. Sperry to John C. Watson, 28 November 1899, R 373, M 625.

51. Edward D. Taussig to My Dear Family, 1 October 1900, Taussig Papers. See the personal reminisces in "Sons of Gunboats" file, Operations of Gunboats in the Philippines, 1900–1902, Subject File OO, Box 469, RG 45. For instructions on joint service cooperation, see "Memorandum prepared by CO, U.S. Naval Forces in the Philippine Islands expressing his views on working of gunboats in P.I.," in AAAG to William G. Haan, 5 June 1899, LS 19 and 21, June 1899 LSB, E 2464, RG 395. An extensive discussion of gunboats and naval technology can be found in Williams, "U.S. Navy," 65–89.

52. Thomas Barry, AG to Thomas R. Hamer, Cmdg-Sub District of Cebu, 21 May 1899, E 2064, RG 395; H. W. Standley, "Sons of Gunboats" (1945), Operations of Gunboats in the Philippines, 1900–1902, Subject File OO, Box 469, RG 45; Palmer, *With My Own Eyes,* 145.

53. George S. Simonds to AG, DSL, 16 November 1900, LS 122, E 5770, RG 395; S. S. Eberle to Sunderland, 11 March 1938, F 6761, E 310, RG 165; John F. Bass, "A Night on the Gunboat Laguna De Bay," in *Harpers' History,* 145–48.

54. AAAG to William G. Haan, 5 June 1899, LS 19 and 21, June 1899 LSB, E 2464, RG 395.

55. John Bass, "The Situation in the Philippines," in *Harpers' History,* 218–22.

56. Thomas M. Anderson to AG, DP8AC, 21 February 1899, LS 134, E 768, RG 395.

57. Edwin Segerstrom to Dear Mother and Sisters, 25 April 1899, in Frank Harper, ed, *Just Outside Manila: Letters from Members of the 1st Colorado Regiment in the Spanish-American War and Philippine-American Wars* (Denver: Colorado Historical Society, 1991), 90; John L. Jordan to Mother, 28 April 1900, John L. Jordan Papers, SAWS; James Parker, *The Old Army: Memories, 1872–1918* (Philadelphia: Dorrance and Co., 1929), 385; Russell, *Campaigning with King,* 130; Linderman, *Mirror of War,* 72–74.

58. Frederick Jackson to My Dear Parents, 3 September 1900, Frederick Jackson Papers, Box 1, Bishop Museum, Honolulu, Hawaii.

59. Funston, *Memories,* 208–9; Crouch, *Leader,* 215–25.

60. McCutcheon, *Drawn from Memory,* 165. One conspicuous exception to the pro-annexationists was correspondent Albert G. Robinson, who later wrote the widely cited book *The Philippines: The War and the People.* Unfortunately for his credibility, Robinson did not arrive in the archipelago until several months after many of the incidents he claimed as "personal observations and experiences," and during his brief stay he seldom left Manila; see Palmer, *With My Own Eyes,* 152.

61. McCutcheon, *Drawn from Memory,* 133. For correspondents in Cuba, see Charles H. Brown, *The Correspondents' War: Journalists in the Spanish-American War* (New York: Charles Scribner's Sons, 1967).

62. Palmer, *With My Own Eyes,* 157.

63. Ibid, 151.

64. Karnow, *In Our Image,* 150. For other, equally unsubstantiated accounts of the Otis-Lawton feud, see Miller, *Benevolent Assimilation,* 70, 97; Bain, *Sitting in Darkness,* 83; Frank E. Vandiver, *Black Jack: The Life and Times of John J. Pershing,* 2 vols. (College Station: Texas A&M University Press, 1977), 1:243–44; Young, *General's General,* 228–30.

65. Elwell S. Otis to My Dear General [Lawton], 2 November 1899, Box 1, Edwards Papers; *Harpers' History,* 214. When news of Lawton's arrival reached Otis, he and Hughes agreed: "That will put some noses out of joint, but it will put us in a very much better situation"; see 2 January 1899, Hughes Diary. The noses referred to were probably Anderson's and MacArthur's.

66. Otis to AG, 17 January 1899, *CWS* 2:881. Corbin to Otis, 13 January 1899, *CWS* 2:878.

67. H. A. Greene to Editor, *Manila American,* 8 April 1900, in L. I. Cooke and Charles T. Spear Collection, MHS.

68. "The Army and the Correspondents," *ANJ,* 22 July 1899, 1121. Otis to AG, 1 July 1899, *CWS,* 2:1025; Gates, *Schoolbooks,* 106–8; McCutcheon, *Drawn from Memory,* 141. This account follows the version of McCutcheon, who was the only participant. Although Palmer was not present, historians have accepted his implausible claim that Otis threatened to shoot the recalcitrant correspondents; see Palmer, *With My Own Eyes,* 145–46. Even more improbable is the assertion by the recently arrived and much-disliked Robinson that he led the correspondents; see Robinson, *Philippines,* 80–90.

69. Corbin to Schwan, 13 September 1899, *CWS* 2:1068. Charles G. Starr to Officers Serving on the Personal and Official Staff of Maj. Gen. H. W. Lawton, 2 August 1899, Box 1, Edwards Papers.

70. AAG, 1st Div to John G Ballance, 9 December 1899, LS 527, E 769, RG 395. Schwan to Corbin, 11 and 15 September 1899, *CWS* 2:1067, 1069.

71. Corpuz, *Roots,* 2:429–33; Welch, *Response,* 29–30.

72. Kalaw, *Philippine Revolution,* 173, 188–89; Alejandrino, *Price of Freedom,* 121–49.

73. Senate, *Affairs,* 69. On the assassination, see Luke Wright to Elihu Root, 20 July 1902, Box 2, Edwards Papers; C. N. Murphy, "The Death of Antonio Luna," n.d., SD 861.3, PIR; Taylor, *Philippine Insurrection,* 2:229–31.

74. Jose, *Rise and Fall of Antonio Luna,* preface. On the debate over Aguinaldo's culpability, see Mabini, *Philippine Revolution,* 61–63; Alejandrino, *Price of Freedom,* 149–59; Kalaw, *Development of Philippine Politics,* 215–16; Corpuz, *Roots,* 2:415–17. One Aguinaldo partisan postulates that Luna was the victim of an army deception; see Saulo, *Truth About Aguinaldo,* 26–28.

75. J. Franklin Bell and George F. Becker to Albert J. Beveridge, 1 August 1899, Series 1, R 3, Roosevelt Papers.

76. Victor D. Duboce to Adj, 1st California, 16 February 1899, E 764, RG 395; Samuel B. M. Young to AG, 1st Div, 14 August 1899, LS 389, E 824, RG 395; May, *Battle,* 69–88. One sympathetic source claims Aguinaldo began to consider guerrilla war during the summer, but it presents no evidence; see Corpuz, *Roots,* 2:418, 433. Others believe that until quite late he failed to appreciate the possibilities inherent in guerrilla resistance; see May, *Past Recovered,* 157; Gates, *Schoolbooks,* 97–98.

7. *The Northern Offensive*

1. *RWD* 1899 1:4:162–65.
2. Otis to AG, 14 August 1899, *CWS* 2:1053.

3. Otis to AG, 17 September 1899; Corbin to Otis, 18 September 1899, *CWS* 2:1070–71; *RWD* 1900 1:4:211–12.

4. HQ, 1st Div, FO 48, 28 October 1899, 35th Inf Orders, E 117, RG 94.

5. *RWD* 1900 1:4:207–12.

6. [Samuel B. M. Young] to AAG, 1st Div, 26 September 1899, LS 27. [Samuel B. M. Young] to AAG, 1st Div, 22 September 1899, LS 5; Young to C/S, 8AC, 27 September 1899, LS 44; Young to AG, 1 October 1899, LS 98, all in E 836, RG 395.

7. *RWD* 1899 1:4:213.

8. *RWD* 199 1:4:214; also see 212–15. Benjamin F. Cheatham to AG, 15 October 1899, LS 13, 1st Btln, 37th Inf LSB, E 117, RG 94; *Harpers' History,* 297–98.

9. Otis to AG, 14 August and 7 October 1899, *CWS* 2:1053, 1082; HQ, Cav Brig, FO 1, 11 October 1899, E 840, RG 395. The shortage of cavalry was Otis's doing: in August he told the War Department to stop purchases of transportation animals; see Otis to AG, 17 August 1899, *CWS* 2:1054.

10. Feur, *Combat Diary,* 132. On the military operations of Young and the Cavalry Brigade, see Records of the Cavalry Brigade, E 835–40, RG 395; Samuel B. M. Young, "Our Soldiers in the Philippines," 13 November 1902, Box B, Young Papers; LeRoy, *Americans,* 2:126–31, 140–45; Sexton, *Soldiers,* 176–88, 206–15. Young's final report is in Samuel B. M. Young to AG, DP8AC, 6 January 1900, E 836, RG 395.

11. "Wearing the Khaki: The Diary of a High Private," 36–38, Walter I. Cutter Papers, MHI; *RWD* 1900 1:4:218.

12. Lawton to Schwan, 28 October 1899, *RWD* 1899 1:4:222, 219–20.

13. 17 October 1899, Diary, Box 1, Harold P. Howard Papers, MacArthur Memorial. Lawton's dispatches make up much of his report in *RWD* 1900 1:6:39–261. For a defense of Lawton, see LeRoy, *Americans,* 2:127.

14. Young's forces at this time were Ballance's four companies of the 22nd Infantry, the Lowe Scouts, a two-company mountain battery of the 37th Infantry, three troops of cavalry, and a supply train with eight days' rations.

15. Elwell S. Otis to My Dear General [Lawton], 2 November 1899, Box 1, Edwards Papers. LeRoy, *Americans,* 2:129.

16. Samuel B. M. Young to AG, DP8AC, 6 January 1900, E 836, RG 395.

17. Woolard, "Philippine Scouts," 32–33.

18. Samuel B. M. Young to AG, DP8AC, 6 January 1900, E 836, RG 395. Feuer, *Combat Diary,* 136–37; HQ, Cav Brig, Memorandum Instructions, 7 November 1899, E 840, RG 395.

19. 12 November 1899, Diary, Howard Papers; *RWD* 1899 1:4:264.

20. Simeon A. Villa, "The Flight and Wanderings of Emilio Aguinaldo, from His Abandonment of Bayambang Until His Capture in Palanan," 23 March 1901, Taylor, *Philippine Insurrection,* 5:2–3; Orlino A. Ochosa, *The Tinio Brigade: Anti-American Resistance in the Ilocos Provinces, 1899–1901* (Quezon City: New Day Publishers, 1989), 72–74; LeRoy, *Americans,* 2:135. Both contemporaries and later authors have been confused by the similarity between the northwestern town of Bayambang, Pangasinan (where Aguinaldo departed from), and the northern town of Bayombong, Nueva Vizcaya (his final destination).

21. Young to Otis, 17 November 1899, in *RWD* 1899 1:4:264; LeRoy, *Americans,* 2:129–31.

22. Harry Knox to CINC, 7 November 1899, R 373, M 625. Wheaton's report is in *RWD* 1900 1:6:528–32. The U.S. Navy had thoroughly reconnoitered the gulf, landing armed parties and identifying and shelling enemy defenses; see 27 March to 8 May 1899, Diary, Charles Julian Papers, MDLC; Asa Walker to CINC, 3 March 1899, R 367, M 625.

23. Sexton, *Soldiers*, 188. For other critical views of Wheaton, see LeRoy, *Americans*, 2:138–39; Beede, *War of 1898*, 594.

24. *RWD* 1899 1:4:268.

25. Henry W. Lawton to C/S, 19 November 1899, Box 1, Edwards Papers; *CWS* 2:1100–1108; J Franklin Bell to AG, 2nd Div, 5 December 1899, LS 97, 36th Inf LSB, E 117, RG 94; *RWD* 1899 1:4:266–68.

26. Elwell S. Otis to My Dear General [Lawton], 2 November 1899; Henry W. Lawton to C/S, 19 November 1899, both in Box 1, Edwards Papers.

27. *RWD* 1900 1:6:529.

28. "Report of the services in the Philippine Islands of Brigadier and brevet Major General Loyd Wheaton, U.S. Vols.," [1901?], 5249 ACP 1889 (Loyd Wheaton), RG 94.

29. *RWD* 1900 1:6:536–43; Carl Musgrove, "Brief History of the 33rd US.V.I.," 9–12, Texas State Archives, Austin, Tex.; Ochosa, *Tinio Brigade*, 18–73, passim.

30. *RWD* 1900 1:6:558–59.

31. *RWD* 1899 1:4:243; Brown, *Ninth Infantry*, 318–19. For a critical view of MacArthur, see LeRoy, *Americans*, 2:133, also 134–37. For a different view, see Young, *General's General*, 245–48.

32. MacArthur to AG, 8 November 1899, in *RWD* 1899 1:4:245.

33. Schwan to MacArthur, 8 November 1899, in *RWD* 1899 1:4:245.

34. Brown, *Ninth Infantry*, 325 Palmer, *With My Own Eyes*, 154; Sexton, *Soldiers*, 194–95, 197.

35. Otis to AG, 2 December 1899, *CWS* 2:1112. J. Franklin Bell to AG, 2nd Div, 21 January 1900, LSB 1, E 2206, RG 395.

36. "Memoirs," 25:33, 34–40, McCalla Papers. Batchelor's report is in *RWD* 1900 1:6:373–80. It is likely that Lawton authorized Batchelor's march and recalled it only after receiving orders from Otis; see *RWD* 1899 1:4:272–73.

37. Villa, "Flight," Taylor, *Philippine Insurrection*, 5:4–5.

38. Alexander McCrackin to CO, *USS Oregon*, 29 November, R 373, M 625; "Memoirs," 25:19–21, McCalla Papers.

39. Little's account is quoted verbatim in Moorfield Storey and Marcial P. Lichauco, *The Conquest of the Philippines by the United States, 1898–1925* (New York: G. P. Putnam's Sons, 1926), 106–10; Wolff, *Little Brown Brother*, 286–88; Bain, *Sitting in Darkness*, 196–97. The story that del Pilar's body was stripped appears in James H. Blount, *The American Occupation of the Philippines, 1898–1912* (New York: G. P. Putnam's Sons, 1912), 249; Miller, *Benevolent Assimilation*, 96.

40. Telesforo Carrasco, *A Spaniard in Aguinaldo's Army: The Military Journal of Telesforo Carrasco y Perez*, trans. Nick Joaquin (Manila: Solar Publishing, 1986), 45–46. Corpuz, *Roots*, 2:440–41.

41. March's report is in *RWD* 1900 1:6:331–34. James McCutcheon wrote two accounts of the battle: "Aguinaldo's Rear Guard," in *Harpers' History*, 317–21, and *Drawn from Memory*, 161–65. For veterans' accounts, see "Letters and Reminis-

cences," 30–31, Milton Nixon Papers, 33rd Inf, SAWS; Musgrove, "Brief History," 15–16. Gregorio del Pilar's life is covered in Teodoro M. Kalaw, *An Acceptable Holocaust: Life and Death of a Boy-General*, trans. M. A. Foronda (Manila: National Historical Commission, 1974).

42. MS, Oliver Trafton Papers, 33rd Inf, SAWS.

43. *RWD* 1:7:138–51; Ochosa, *Tinio Brigade,* 86–87; "Memoirs," 25:21–22, McCalla Papers.

44. *RWD* 1900 1:6:322, 283–84; Ochosa, *Tinio Brigade,* 88–90.

45. *RWD* 1900 1:6:322–28; Sexton, *Soldiers,* 211–14.

46. *RWD* 1900 1:7:69; see also 70–71, 76; Louis A. Craig to AG, 19 April 1901, LS 131, 32nd Inf LSB, E 117, RG 94.

47. Otis to AG, 24 November 1899, *CWS* 2:1107.

48. Henry W. Lawton to C/S, 19 November 1899, Box 1, Edwards Papers.

49. MacArthur to Schwan, 20 November 1899, in *RWD* 1899 1:4:258.

8. The Occupation of the Archipelago

1. Otis to AG, 24 November 1899, *CWS* 2:1107.

2. LeRoy, *Americans,* 2:158. [James Lockett] to AG, 3 January 1900, LS 64, 11th Cav LSB, E 117, RG 94; *RWD* 1900 1:7:194–201; William Dinwiddie, "General Lawton's Last Fight," in *Harpers' History,* 325–31; H. H. Sargent, "The Action of San Mateo: The Death of Major General Lawton, U.S. Volunteers," *JMSI* 30 (January 1902): 42–61. Sargent's account was disputed by Lawton's aides; see Edward L. King to H. H. Sargent, August 1900, Box 1, Edwards Papers.

3. "In Memorium: Funeral Oration at Obsequies of Major General Henry W. Lawton, U.S. Volunteers, by Professor M. Woolsey Stryker," 812 ACP1881 (Henry W. Lawton), RG 94.

4. "Memories," 65, John H. Parker Papers, USMA. For accounts of Lawton's close brushes with death, see Palmer, *With My Own Eyes,* 149–50; *Harpers' History,* 168–69.

5. LeRoy, *Americans,* 2:160; Dean Worcester, *The Philippines Past and Present* (New York: Macmillan, 1930). Worcester was a close friend of Mrs. Lawton; his correspondence with her appears in the Henry W. Lawton Papers, MDLC.

6. Samuel S. O'Connor to Adj, 13 February 1900, LS 10, Co I, 46th Inf LSB, E 117, RG 94. James Lockett to AG, 30 December 1899, LS 64, 11th Cav LSB, E 117, RG 94.

7. "I Was There! 1899–1902. Diary of a Volunteer in the Spanish-American War," 10, William Dillon Papers, Huntington Library.

8. 14 January 1900, 1900 Diary, Schuyler Papers. Gerald W. McFarland, "John Coalter Bates," in Beede, *War of 1898,* 41–42.

9. "Memories," 70, John H. Parker Papers, USMA. Schwan's Brigade consisted of the 30th and 46th Infantry, a mixed force of nine companies of 11th and 4th Cavalry, two companies of Macabebes, and some artillery.

10. Frederick D. Grant to AG, DP8AC, 17 August 1899, LS 59, E 812, RG 395.

11. Bates's report is in *RWD* 1900 1:6:640–59; Wheaton's is in *RWD* 1900 1:7:625–28. For the southern campaign, see LeRoy, *Americans,* 2:163–169; May, *Battle,* 95–127; Sexton, *Soldiers,* 224–31.

12. "Memories," 66–69, Parker Papers. John H. Parker to Theodore Roosevelt, 11 March 1900, Series 1, Roll 4, Roosevelt Papers; 1 and 2 January 1900, Diary, Robert L. Bullard Papers, MDLC; May, *Battle,* 107; Millett, *General,* 125–27.

13. "Memories," 70, Parker Papers; Millett, *General,* 125–26.

14. "Memories," 69, Parker Papers.

15. Mariano Trias to Emilio Aguinaldo, 2 January 1900, Ex 1033, Taylor, *Philippine Insurrection,* 5:165–67; May, *Battle,* 96–100.

16. 5 January 1900, Diary, Schuyler Papers. Charles A. Baker, *A History of the 30th Infantry, U.S. Volunteers in the Philippine Insurrection, 1899–1901* (n.p., n.d.), 63, MHI.

17. 6–10 January 1900, 1900 Diary, Schuyler Papers.

18. 7 January 1900, "Diary of Jack Brennen, Scout and Interpreter, Co C., 28th U.S. Volunteer Infantry, Philippine Islands," Washington Historical Society, Tacoma, Wash.

19. William E. Birkhimer to AAG, 9 January 1900, LS 253, 28th Inf LSB, E 117, RG 94.

20. 7 January 1900, "Diary of Jack Brennen."

21. "History of the 38th Infantry, U.S.V.," [1901], E 187, RG 94.

22. "Autobiography," 38–41, Bullard Papers; "History of the 38th"; "History of the 39th Infantry, U.S.V.," [1901], E 187, RG 94; May, *Battle,* 108–20; Millett, *General,* 127–29; Sexton, *Soldiers,* 227–28.

23. "Memories," 71, Parker Papers; Millett, *General,* 129–30.

24. "History of the 45th Infantry, U.S.V.," [1901], E 187, RG 94; Parker, *Old Army,* 299–303. One participant claimed there were thirty enemy killed at Nasugbu; see Austin Camersford to Glen N. Ranck, 21 January 1900, Manuscripts and University Archives Division, Allen Library, University of Washington, Seattle, Wash.

25. William H. Johnston to AG, 27 January 1900, LS 3, 2nd Btln, 46th Inf LSB, E 117, RG 94; May, *Battle,* 124–26.

26. Sand 30, "Trench, Parapet, or the Open," *JMSI* 30 (July 1902): 481–82; LeRoy, *Americans,* 2:166. For a Filipino perspective, see "Diario de Operaciones realizades por las fuerzas de Battalon Banahao," n.d., SD 942.3, PIR.

27. E. B. Barry, "Diary of Service in the Philippines," 11, George B. Hunt Papers, MHS.

28. Theodore Schwan to Henry C. Corbin, 16 February 1900, Box 1, Corbin Papers. LeRoy, *Americans,* 2:167–68. Schwan's column lost eleven killed and fifty-two wounded.

29. 1 February 1900, "Diary of Jack Brennen." Benjamin F. Cheatham to AG, Schwan's Expeditionary Brigade, 7 February 1900, AGO 31886, RG 94; *ANJ,* 10 March 1900; Baker, *History of the 30th,* 59. For reports of the prevalent skirmishing, see 38th, 39th, and 45th Infantry histories, E 187, RG 94.

30. [Robert P. Hughes] to My dear General [Otis], 22 August 1899, LS 57, August 1899 LSB, E 2464, RG 395.

31. Poplin, "Letters of W. Thomas Osborn," 167. AAG to W. J. Whitthorne, 12 August 1899, LS 27; [Robert P. Hughes] to AAG, DP8AC, 13 August 1899, LS 34, both in August 1899 LSB, E 2464, RG 395; HQ, VMD, GO 35, 6 September 1899, E 882, RG 395; 24 September 1899, Diary 33, Francis Henry French Diaries, used by permission of the Vinton Trust; [Robert P. Hughes] to AG, DP8AC, 26 and 29 September 1899, LS 65 and 66, September 1899 LSB, E 2464, RG 395; August–September 1899, Hughes Diary.

32. 14 December 1899, Diary, Hughes Papers. For reports on the campaign, see [Robert P. Hughes] to My Dear Governor [Otis], 22 December 1899, LS 19, December 1899 LSB, E 2464, RG 395; November–December 1899, Diary 33, French Diaries; S. M. Ackley to CINC, 4 December 1899, "Military-Naval Operations in the Philippines," Box 410, Subject File OJ, RG 45; Bronson, "Visayan Campaigns," 299–308.

33. Babcock, *War History*, 74.

34. Smith to Schwan, 18 December 1899, LS 511, LSB 1, E 2616, RG 395.

35. James F. Smith to AAG, VMD, 3 January 1900, LS 540, LSB 1, E 2616, RG 395. HQ, MSD Negros, Circular, 15 December 1899, E 2937, RG 395; Smith to Cole, 11 December 1899, LS 7, December 1899 LSB, E 2464, RG 395.

36. James F. Smith to AAG, VMD, 3 January 1900, LS 540, LSB 1, E 2616, RG 395. James F. Smith to C. H. Murray, 13 February 1900, LS 691, E 2616, RG 395; Babcock, *War History*, 77.

37. Hughes to Schwan, 20 December, TS 413, E 2466, RG 395. [Robert P. Hughes] to My Dear Governor [Otis], 22 December 1899, LS 19, December 1899 LSB, E 2464, RG 395.

38. Smith to Schwan, 18 December 1899, TS 511, E 2616, RG 395.

39. HQ, MSD Negros to CO, 6th Inf, 20 January 1900. Charles W. Miner to CO, MSD Negros, 19 January 1900, both in Box 1, James F. Smith Papers.

40. HQ, MSD Negros, GO 1, 20 January 1900, E 2621, RG 395. H. S. Dalton to Bernard A. Byrne, 20 January 1900, LS 601, LSB 1, E 2616, RG 395.

41. Cormandel to CINC, 11 March 1899, R 367, M 625; Corbin to Otis, 9 January 1900; Otis to AG, 10 January 1900, *CWS* 2:1130–31; Norman G. Owen, "Winding down the War in Albay, 1900–1903," *Pacific Historical Review* 48 (November 1979): 557–58.

42. Vito Belarmino to Emilio Aguinaldo, 5 May 1899, SD 769.1, PIR; Vicente Lukban to Secretary of Treasury, 8 July 1899, SD 1242.3, PIR.

43. William H. Taft to Elihu Root, 12 August 1900, Series 21, Roll 640, Taft Papers.

44. Vicente Lukban, "Compoblanos Samarenos and Leytenos," 1 January 1899, SD 928.1, PIR; Vicente Lukban to Local Chief of Cabilian, 3 January 1899, SD 928.8, PIR; Donald Chaput, "Leyte Leadership in the Revolution: The Moxica-Lukban Issue," *Leyte-Samar Studies* 9 (1975): 3–12; Schumacher, *Revolutionary Clergy*, 138, 141–43.

45. Cormandel to CINC, 11 March 1899, R 367, M 625.

46. "History of the 47th Infantry, U.S.V.," [1901], E 187, RG 94; Harry Knox to CINC, 5 November 1899, R 373, M 625.

47. William A. Kobbé to AG, DP, 24 January 1900, No. 6, E 893, RG 395; *RWD* 1900 1:7:8–43; Raymond P. Rodgers to CINC, 25 January 1900, "Military-Naval Operations in the Philippines" File, Box 410, Subject File OJ, RG 45.

48. "History of the 47th Inf."

49. *RWD* 1900 1:7:11.

50. Henry T. Allen to AG, PB, 10 February 1900, LS 2, 3rd Btln, 43rd Inf LSB, E 117, RG 94. John C. Gilmore to AAG, PB, 27 January 1900, 43rd Inf LSB, E 117, RG 94; Raymond P. Rodgers to CINC, 29 January 1900, "Military-Naval Operations in the Philippines" File, Box 410, Subject File OJ, RG 45; William H. Wilson to "My dear ones at home," 29 January 1900, 43rd Inf Box, SAWS; *RWD* 1900 1:7:12–13.

51. James M. Bell to AAG, 3 March 1900, E 2418, RG 395; Walter Howe to AAG, 12 February 1900, LS 43, 47th Inf LSB 1, E 117, RG 94; Edward A. Goodwin to AAAG, 25 February 1900, E 2427, RG 395; E. H. Gheen to CINC, 1 March 1900, R 376, M 677; James M. Bell to CO, Libmanan, 14 April 1900, E 2418, RG 395; "Diary of Service in the Philippines," 14–17, Hunt Papers.

52. HQ, MGAC, FO 1, 19 February 1900; Henry T. Allen to AG, 1D, DV, 30 April 1900, both in Box 32, Allen Papers; James M. Bell to AAG, DP8AC, 24 March 1900, E 2418, RG 395; Samuel P. Lyon to Mary Lyon, 18 March 1900, Samuel Lyon Papers, MHI; McCutcheon, *Drawn from Memory,* 153–61.

53. Palmer, *With My Own Eyes,* 159. Harvey Hale, "Report of a trip made to the Island of Leyte," 27 January 1900, F 811, Box 2, E 2511, RG 395.

54. *RWD* 1900 1:7:257–58.

55. *RWD* 1900 1:4:448.

56. Theodore Schwan to Henry C. Corbin, 16 February 1900, Box 1, Corbin Papers.

57. AAG, 2nd Division to CG, 2nd Brig, 30 January 1900, LR 3, E 4330, RG 395.

58. *ANJ,* 14 April 1900.

9. The Guerrilla War

1. Memoranda Showing Provinces . . . from reports of the Military Governor, 24 May 1902, F 4865–6, RG 350.

2. 7 February 1901, Journal, Schuyler Papers; Carrasco, *A Spaniard,* 71; Villa, "Flight and Wanderings," Taylor, *Philippine Insurrection,* 5:1–95, also 2:408. Aguinaldo's order book is reprinted as Ex 1002, Taylor, *Philippine Insurrection,* 5:111–16. On Aguinaldo's importance, see Gates, *Schoolbooks,* 157–58; LeRoy, *Americans,* 2:205–6; Taylor, *Philippine Insurrection,* 2:308–14, 408.

3. Albino Dizon to CG of Central Luzon, August 1900, Ex 1121, Taylor, *Philippine Insurrection,* 5:275–76; John H. Beacom to AG, 31 October 1901, LS 29, E 3726, RG 395; J. Franklin Bell to Adna R. Chaffee, in Adna R. Chaffee to Henry C. Corbin, 17 March 1902, Corbin Papers. For an excellent look at the guerrilla command structure in one province, see May, *Battle,* 165–78.

4. Robinson, *Philippines,* 72. Matthew A. Batson to AG, 1st Div, 18 September 1899, E 5804, RG 395; Samuel B. M. Young to AG, 1st Div, 14 August 1899, LS 389, E 824, RG 395; *Harpers' History,* 142.

5. May, *Battle,* 100.

6. Francisco M[acabulos], "Orders to Detachments," 16 November 1899, Ex 1019, Taylor, *Philippine Insurrection,* 5:142–43. Aguinaldo ordered specific units to wage guerrilla war prior to his 13 November general order; see Emilio Aguinaldo to Casimiro Tinio, 18 October 1899, SD 1198.1, PIR.

7. Tomas Mascardo to My Dear Soldiers and Dear Compatriots, August 1900, Ex 1082, Taylor, *Philippine Insurrection,* 5:224–26. See also Manuel Tinio to Presidente, Santa Cruz; Manuel Tinio to Presidente, Candon, [September 1900], both in SD 576.9, PIR; Emilio Aguinaldo to Artemo Ricarte, 27 June 1900, Ex 996, 5:102–3; Emilio Aguinaldo to Filipinos, August 1900, Ex 1003, 5:117–18; Juan Cailles to Pablo Estilla, 6 August 1900, Ex 1084, 5:227, all in Taylor, *Philippine Insurrection.*

8. Gates, *Schoolbooks,* 161–63.

9. For an overview of guerrilla forces, see Birtle, *U.S. Army,* 110–12; Brian M. Linn, *The U.S. Army and Counterinsurgency in the Philippine War, 1899–1902* (Chapel Hill: University of North Carolina Press, 1989), 17, 37–41; May, *Battle,* 163–84; Taylor, *Philippine Insurrection,* 2:408; Reed, "Burden and Honor," 81. On militia and regulars and the guerrrilla war, see Emilio Aguinaldo, "Decree," 13 February 1899, SD 866.7, PIR; Manuel Tinio to Joaquin Alejandrino, 8 September 1900, SD 576.1, PIR; "Ano de 1900: Ejercito Republicano de Filipinas," 19 November 1900, SD 1014.4, PIR; Edward D. Taussig to My Dear Family, 22 November 1900, Taussig Papers; Arcadio Maxilom, [Orders], 16 January 1900, in "Translation of order, captured . . . January 27, 1900," E 2511, RG 395; Ananias Diocno to Roque Lopez and Pedro Darroca, 28 October 1899, Ex 1276, 4:565–67; Luciano San Miguel to the Politico-Military Commander of this Province of Zambales, 19 December 1899, Ex 1023, 5:151–52; Ramon F. Santos to Engracio Orense, 11 December 1900, Ex 1131, 5:292–93; Vito Belarmino, "Instructions for Attack on American Troops Quartered in the Town of Ligao, Albay Province," [16 December 1900], Ex 1137, 5:298–99, all in Taylor, *Philippine Insurrection.*

10. Pantaleon Garcia, "Instructions for Guerrillas and Flying Columns," 25 November 1899, Ex 1020, Taylor, *Philippine Insurrection,* 5:143–45.

11. "K.K." to Vicente Lukban, 10 January [1900], Ex 1319, 5:630–31. For guerrilla tactics, see Garcia, "Instructions for Guerrillas and Flying Columns"; Francisco M[acabulos], "Orders to Detachments," 16 November 1899, Ex 1019, 5:142–43; [Anon.], "Plan of Combat," January 1900, Ex 1030, 5:160–61; "General Order of the General Staff," 12 February 1900, Ex 1282, 5:573–75; Paulo Pardo to Ambrosio Moxica, 2 March 1900, Ex 1373, 5:727–38; Francisco Jalandoni, "Guerrilla Warfare," 1 June 1900, Ex 1290, 5:584–91; Maria del Rosario to Junta Amigos de Manila, 2 August 1900, Ex 1121, 5:276–77, all in Taylor, *Philippine Insurrection.*

12. Samuel B. M. Young to William McKinley, 4 July 1900, Box 3, Young Papers.

13. "16 Months in the Philippines," 93, John D. LaWall Papers, 27th Inf Box, SAWS. For similar incidents, see Delphy T. E. Casteel to "My Darling One," 29 July to 4 August 1900, Delphy T. E. Casteel Papers, 27th Inf Box, SAWS; J. Milton Thompson to AG, 24 August 1900, LS 839, E 2312, RG 395.

14. James L. Anderson to HQ, 2D, DV, 26 December 1900, LS 616, 44th Inf LSB, E 117, RG 94.

15. Carrasco, *A Spaniard,* 80–129.

16. John L. Jordan to Mother, 10 January 1900, Jordan Papers.

17. William E. Birkhimer to AG, 2D, DSL, 15 July 1900, LS 516, 28th Inf LSB, E 117, RG 94.

18. Leonicio Alarilla to Casmirio Tinio, 4 February 1900, Ex 1043, Taylor, *Philippine Insurrection,* 5:177–78.

19. George C. Lewis to Adj, 2nd Btln, 3rd Inf, 26 November 1899, LR 810, E 4330, RG 395. William R. Staff to Adj, 3 January 1901, LS 2, Co B, 49th Inf LSB, E 117, RG 94; Edward L. King to Clarence R. Edwards, 1 August 1900, Box 1, Edwards Papers; Taylor, *Philippine Insurrection,* 2:430–31. A test of gunpowder made from matches revealed it was accurate and powerful at close range, but at 200

yards the bullet dropped almost three feet; see C. J. Sterett to AAG, 2D, DSL, 15 December 1900, LS 8, LSB 1, E 3284, RG 395.

20. Luciano San Miguel to N. Cosmopolita, 8 December 1899, Ex 1023, Taylor, *Philippine Insurrection,* 5:148.

21. [Robert P. Hughes] to CO, 1D, 12 November 1900, November 1900 LSB, E 2465, RG 395. The bolo did have a considerable psychological effect; see Peter Konrad Questionnaire, 5th Inf, SAWS.

22. Estimates of the number of firearms in revolutionary hands vary from 20,000 to 40,000 and represent little more than guesses; see Alejandrino, *Price of Freedom,* 114; Jose, *Philippine Army,* 12; Taylor, *Philippine Insurrection,* 2:496. On soldiers' views of the importance of rifles, see John L. Jordan to Mother, 11 July 1900, Jordan Papers; "Memories," 66–69, Parker Papers. On poison, see Leonicio Alarilla to Casmirio Tinio, 4 February 1900, Ex 1043, 5:177–78; Ramon Santos to Eleuteria Reveta, 14 October 1900, Ex 1104, 5:252–54, both in Taylor, *Philippine Insurrection.*

23. John H. Page to AG, 2nd Div, 31 October 1899, LS 57, E 4923, RG 395; Walter Howe to AG, 15th April 1900, LS 539, 47th Inf LSB; C. P. Lee to Adj, 18 April 1900, E 2428, RG 395; "Projecto de un Codigo deseñales de dia y noche para las guerrillas de Abra," [1900?] SD 628.1, PIR; Benjamin F. Cheatham to AG, DSL, 8 August 1900, 37th Inf LSB 2, E 117, RG 94; "K.K." to Vicente Lukban, 10 January [1900], Ex 1319, Taylor, *Philippine Insurrection,* 5:630–31.

24. Pablo Tecson to Isidro Torres, 29 August 1900, SD 545.2, PIR; Luciano San Miguel to E. R. Magpuci, 3 January 1900, Ex 1023, 5:152–54; "Brigadier General" to Anon., 16 September 1900, Ex 1093, 5:237–39; Buenaventura Dimaguila to Mariano Trias, 30 November 1900, Ex 1125, 5:281–88, all in Taylor, *Philippine Insurrection;* Carrasco, *A Spaniard,* 83, 88–89; William H. Scott, *Ilocano Responses to American Aggression, 1900–1901* (Quezon City: New Day Publishers, 1986), 41–42.

25. *RWD* 1900 1:5:61.

26. [Anon. Articles], 1 January 1900, Ex 1032, 5:162–65; Jose Cavestany to the Presidente, 15 May 1900, Ex 1059, 5:195–97; Teodoro Sandico, "Organization of Committees," 15 July 1900, Ex 1078, 5:216–21, all in Taylor, *Philippine Insurrection.*

27. Buenaventura Dimaguila to Mariano Trias, 30 November 1900, Ex 1125, 5:281–88. Julio Herrera to Presidentes of Nagcalran et al., 6 May 1900, Ex 1058, 5:194; Jose Alejandrino, General Order, July 1900, Ex 1074, 5:210–11; Pantaleon Garcia to Isidro Torres, 10 February 1900, Ex 1044, 5:178–79, all in Taylor, *Philippine Insurrection;* Vito Belamino to Patricio Alcala, 13 October 1900, SD 341.9, PIR.

28. Leandro Fullon to Local Chiefs, 20 February 1900, Ex 1283, 5:575–76; Ramon F. Santos to Commander of National Militia, 27 September 1900, Ex 1099, 5:247; Praxedes Magalona, [Memorandum], 3 October 1900, Ex 1302, 5:605–8; Barotoc Viejo, "Minute," 1 November 1900, Ex 1412, 5:803–4; Ramon F. Santos to Torino Poblete, 12 December 1900, Ex 1132, 5:293–94; Pedro Caballes, "Resumé of the Provisions and Instructions Issued or Given by These Headquarters from the 13th of August to the Present Date," 19 December 1901, Ex 1171, 5:357–58, all in Taylor, *Philippine Insurrection.* For an account of how an exceptionally efficient tax and supply system worked, see "Proceedings of a Board of Officers to Inquire into Allegations Made by Maj. Cornelius Gardener, 13th U.S. Infantry in His Report of December 16, 1901," AGO 431607, RG 94; May, *Battle,* 168–69.

29. Walter Howe to AG, IB, 15 April 1900, LS 5399, 47th Inf LSB 2, E 117, RG 94; Bronson, "Visayan Campaigns," 306–7; 25 October 1900, Diary, Box 1, Howard Papers; William E. Birkhimer to AG, DMJ, 5 January 1901, LS 1528, 28th Inf LSB, E 117, RG 94; Jose Cavestany to Presidente of _____, 15 May 1900, Ex 1059, 5:195–97; Pablo Astilla et al., [Declaration], 30 June 1900, Ex 1073, 5:208–9; Jose Alejandrino to Francisco Dizon, 8 October 1900, Ex 1109, 5:249; Buenaventura Dimaguila to Mariano Trias, 30 November 1900, Ex 1125, 5:281–88, all in Taylor, *Philippine Insurrection;* see also 2:483–85.

30. Julio Infante, [Directive], December 1900, Ex 1126, 5:288; Vito Belarmino to Jose Natera, 17 June 1900, Ex 1068, 5:203–5; Mariano Noriel, [Declaration], 1 October 1900, Ex 1100, 5:249–50; E. Paro to General in Chief, 22 November 1900, Ex 1305, 5:610; Buenaventura Dimaguila to Mariano Trias, 30 November 1900, Ex 1125, 5:281–88; "Emilio Zurbano, Military Governor of Tayabas, to His Fellow Citizens," 23 April 1901, Ex 1154, 5:324–26, all in Taylor, *Philippine Insurrection;* "Report of an interview with a woman, resident of Ligao, Albay Prov., November 13, 1901," E 2424, RG 395; Judge Advocate to Provost Marshal General, 11 December 1900, LS 144, E 5371, RG 395.

31. J. Milton Thompson to AG, DNL, 24 September 1900, LS 1196, E 2312, RG 395. May, *Battle,* 170.

32. Carrasco, *A Spaniard,* 77, 111–13; Mariano Noriel, [Orders], 1 October 1900, Ex 1100, 5:248–49; Raymundo C. Jerciel, [Order], 30 November 1900, Ex 1108, 5:260–62; Vito Belarmino, [Order], 7 November 1900, 5:265–66, all in Taylor, *Philippine Insurrection;* Linn, *U.S. Army,* 19.

33. Pantaleon Garcia to Isidro Torres, 10 February 1900, Ex 1044, Taylor, *Philippine Insurrection,* 5:178–79.

34. Jose Alejandrino, General Order, July 1900, Ex 1074, Taylor, *Philippine Insurrection,* 5:210–11; Vicente Lukban, "People to Be Killed," 1 February 1901, SD 824.1, PIR; Lukban, "To the People of Leyte," 20 November 1900, SD 502.5, PIR; Manuel Tinio to Pantaleon Gonzales and Saturnio Singson, 15 June 1900; Manuel Tinio to Pedro Legaspi, 10 March 1900; Manuel Tinio, "Proclamation," 20 March 1900, all in SD 353, PIR; "Translation of Juan Villamor's Proclamation," [1900], LS 629, E 2157, RG 395; Casmirio Tinio to Jefe Local of Toro and Santa Rita, 17 March 1900, SD 51.9, PIR; Jose Alejandrino, General Order, July 1900, Ex 1074, 5:210–11; Julio Infante, [Manifesto], September 1900, 5:230–31; Francisco S. Dizon, [Proclamation], 20 September 1900, Ex 1094, 5:239–41, all in Taylor, *Philippine Insurrection.*

35. Senate, *Affairs,* 1006–376.

36. May, *Battle,* 181.

37. Quote "cruelty deliberately" from William H. Taft to Henry M. Hoyt, 8 September 1900, Box 1, Edwards Papers; quote "without that system" from Senate, *Affairs,* 70. John C. Gilmore to AG, 1D, DV, 13 June 1900, 43rd Inf LSB, E 117, RG 94; GCM 34401, Edwin F. Glenn, RG 153; "List of Men Executed or Ordered to be Executed by Order of General Juan Cailles as shown by his letter and order book 24 August 1900 to 25 April 1901," SD 716.2, PIR; William Newman to CO, Calbayog, 14 October 1901, LR 570, E 3503, RG 395; Francisco Rafael to Vicente Lukban, 13 January 1901, SD 891.7, PIR; Rafael to Jorge Langara, 2 October 1901, SD 830.1, PIR; Z. Acerill to Vicente Lukban, 1 November 1901, SD 891.10, PIR.

38. Emilio Aguinaldo, "Notice of Justice," 3 August 1900, Ex 1006, 5:122–23; Emilio Aguinaldo, "Proclamation," 20 November 1900, Ex 1015, 5:135–36; Emilio Aguinaldo, "In Self Defense—Sensational Proclamation," 17 January 1901, Ex 1016, 5:136–38, all in Taylor, *Philippine Insurrection*.

39. Jose Alejandrino to "Simo," 12 February 1900, SD 323.5, PIR; Miguel Malvar, "Proclamation," 4 February 1901, SD 692.1, PIR; Funston, *Memories*, 375–76; "An account of the attack on Borongan, flight, capture, imprisonment, and release of Cpl. Fred Allen, Co. I, 43rd Infantry, U.S.V.," in Arthur Murray to AG, DV, Report No. 15, Box 32, Allen Papers.

40. Bernard Lichtig Questionnaire, 30th Inf Box, SAWS.

41. Frank L. Rose Questionnaire, 30th Inf Box, SAWS. *ANJ*, 22 September 1900.

42. Joseph Dickman to Isaac Bridgeman and George Cortelyou, 24 April 1901, LS 274, 26th Inf LSB, E 117, RG 94; Roman I. Torres to A. Tecson, 18 January 1900, Ex 1040, Taylor, *Philippine Insurrection*, 5:174; Lyman W. V. Kennon to AG, 1D, DNL, 9 February 1901, LS 412, LSB 3, E 4043, RG 395; Louis A. Craig to AG, 19 April 1901, LS 131, 32nd Inf LSB, E 117, RG 94; Charles F. Anderson Questionnaire; Jesse A. Jackson Questionnaire, both in 45th Inf Box, SAWS; John H. Nankivell, *History of the Twenty-fifth Regiment United States Infantry, 1869–1926* (n.p., 1927), 90, 103–5; Hoyt, *Frontier Doctor*, 362–63.

43. May, *Battle*, 286. For the debate on popular support, see Scott, *Ilocano Responses*; Reynaldo C. Ileto, *Payson and Revolution: Popular Movements in the Philippines, 1840–1900* (Manila: Ateneo de Manila University Press, 1979); May, *Past Recovered*, 3–24; John N. Schumacher, "Recent Perspectives on the Revolution," *Philippine Studies* 30 (1982): 445–92. On women, see Raymundo C. Jeciel [Isabela Province], 1 January 1901, Ex 1139, Taylor, *Philippine Insurrection*, 5:301–2.

44. William H. Wilson to Parents, 17 February 1900, 43rd Inf, SAWS; Robert L. Bullard, "Why Has the Philippine War Lasted So Long," 1901, Box 9, Bullard Papers; R. D. Walsh to "My Dear Sep" [Clarence R. Edwards], 4 November 1900, Box 1, Edwards Papers; Florencio Trinidad to Juan Cailles, 23 March 1901, SD 712.1, PIR; "Statement of Cecilio Rosal," 25 January 1901, E 3092, RG 395.

45. Taylor, *Philippine Insurrection*, 2:372–74.

46. Isidro Torres to Bonifacio Morales, 20 September 1900, Ex 1095, Taylor, *Philippine Insurrection*, 5:241–42.

47. James M. Bell to CO, Montalban, 18 January 1900, LS 66, 27th Inf LSB, E 117, RG 94. For similar sentiments, see Robert Gage to George W. Kirkman, 18 January 1900, LS 15, 49th Inf LSB, E 117, RG 94; William E. Birkhimer to AAG, Wheaton's Expeditionary Brigade, 15 March 1900, LS 364, 28 Inf LSB, E 117 RG 94.

48. Otis to AG, 16 July 1899, 2:1033; Corbin to Otis, 18 September 1899, 2:1070–71; Otis to AG, 29 September 1899, 2:1077, all in *CWS*; HQ, DP, GO, 17 April 1900, in *RWD* 1900 1:1:5; see also 1:4:442–45; Gates, *Schoolbooks*, 283–85; Birtle, *U.S. Army*, 4–5, 119–34.

49. AG, DP to [CG, VMD], 16 May 1900, LS 286, 44th Inf LSB, E 117, RG 94.

50. Senate, *Affairs*, 558.

51. J. Franklin Bell to AG, DNL, 26 April 1900, E 2209, RG 395. C. P. Johnson to AAG, 13 August 1900, 49th Inf LSB, E 117, RG 94.

52. Frederick D. Grant to AG, DNL, 15 April 1901, in *RWD* 1901 1:5:136.

53. *RWD* 1901 1:4:97; Birtle, *U.S. Army,* 113; Taylor, *Philippine Insurrection,* 285.

54. J. Franklin Bell to AG, 2nd Div, 26 March 1900, LS 61, LSB 1, E 2206, RG 395.

55. Gates, *Schoolbooks,* 128–40. [Robert P. Hughes] to CO, 2D, DV, 26 July 1900, LS 106, July 1900 LSB, E 2465, RG 395; AAG to CO, 2D, DV, 5 August 1900, LS 17, August 1900 LSB, E 2465, RG 395.

56. Robert E. Spence to [Archie] Miller, 1 January 1900, LS 29, 2nd Btln, 32nd Inf LSB, E 117, RG 94.

57. Robert E. Spence to Louis A. Craig, 11 February 1900, LS 143, 2nd Btln, 32nd Inf LSB, E 117, RG 94; Delphy Casteel to "My Darling One," 7 January 1900, Casteel Papers; Proceedings of a council . . . , 1 June 1900, LR 16, E 4330, RG 395; J. Franklin Bell to OMG, 2 June 1900, E 2209, RG 395.

58. James M. Bell, GO 7, 27 April 1900, E 5379, RG 395; Benjamin F. Cheatham to AG, 2D, DSL, 9 May 1900, LS 115, 37th Inf LSB, E 117, RG 94; Testimony of Matthew F. Steele, 762–66, in AGO 421607, RG 94; Buenaventura Dimaguila to Mariano Trias, 30 November 1900, Ex 1125, Taylor, *Philippine Insurrection,* 5:281–88.

59. J. Franklin Bell to Emerson Liscum, 22 May 1900, E 2209, RG 395.

60. E. H. Plummer to Dear Murray, 8 January 1900, LS 1405, 35th Inf LSB, E 117, RG 94.

61. William H. Johnston to AG, 1 April 1900, LS 46, and 27 June 1900, LS 143, 2nd Btln, 46th Inf LSB, E 117, RG 94.

62. *RWD* 1900 1:4:10.

63. Parker, "Random Notes," 317–19. Samuel B. M. Young, "Our Soldiers in the Philippines," Address before Men's Club of Church of Epiphany, 13 November 1902, Box B, Young Papers.

64. Robert L. Howze to Chief Engineer, 9 July 1900, LSB 1, E 4043, RG 395.

65. Edward D. Taussig to My Dear Family, 22 November 1900, Taussig Papers; J. Franklin Bell to AG, 2nd Div, 18 March 1900, LS 43, LSB 1, E 2206, RG 395; *RWD* 1900 1:5:197.

66. *RWD* 1901 1:2:928–30.

67. AAG to CG, 2nd Brig, 2nd Div, 5 February 1900, E 4330, RG 395; Vito Belarmino to Francisco Lucban, 12 October 1900, Ex 1103, Taylor, *Philippine Insurrection,* 5:251–52; Arthur Murray to AG, DV, Report No. 15, 21 November 1900, Box 32, Allen Papers; A. W. Greely, "Lines of Information. Their Development and Their Value to Strategy and Tactics," *JMSI* 36 (March–April 1905): 233–34; *RWD* 1900 1:2:948, 976; *RWD* 1901 1:2:929.

68. HQ to Presidente, Orani, 12 January 1900, LS 23, 2nd Btln, 32nd Inf LSB, E 117, RG 94. For a sample of reports on Filipino support for schools, E. H. Brown to Adj, 4th Inf, 19 June 1900, E 5668, RG 395; C. P. Johnson to CO, 2D, DNL, 16 May 1900, 49th Inf LSB, E 117, RG 94; J. Milton Thompson to AG, 27 June 1900, LS 973, 42nd Inf LSB, E 117, RG 94; Arthur Murray to AG, DV, Report No. 10, 1 September 1900, Box 32, Allen Papers.

69. "*Memories,*" 76, Parker Papers.

70. Ibid., 79.

71. [Robert P. Hughes] to AG, DP, 11 October 1900. [Robert P. Hughes] to CO, 2D, DV, 3 October 1900; [Robert P. Hughes] to E. J. McClernand, 11 October 1900, all in October 1900 LSB, E 2465, RG 395.

72. James F. Smith to AG, DV, 26 May 1900, LS 946, LSB 2, E 2616, RG 395; Charles W. Miner to Fred W. Atkinson, 30 October 1900, LS 221, LSB 3, E 2616, RG 395.

73. Thomas W. Darrah to CO, San Miguel, 7 December 1900, LS 4396, 35th Inf LSB, E 117, RG 94.

74. E. E. Carr to AG, 1D, DNL, 1 February 1901, E 4690, RG 395. E. H. Plummer to AG, DNL, 4 January 1901, LS 445, 35th Inf LSB, E 117, RG 94.

75. OMG, GO 87, 18 June 1900, E 2353, RG 395. Otis to AG, 3 June 1899, *CWS* 2:1001; Enoch H. Crowder to CG, DNL, 20 June 1900, E 2809, RG 395; *RWD* 1900 1:4:10.

76. AAG, VMD to Alvin A. Barker, 20 February 1900, LS 118, February 1900 LSB, E 2465, RG 395; Requisition for Ordinance Stores for 3rd District, Department of Southern Luzon, 27 May 1900; James Parker to AAG, 3D, 22 January 1901, LS 197, E 3929, RG 395; Reports from all posts 1st District . . . relative to arming native police, [1900], E 2353, RG 395; James Lockett to AG, DSL, 31 July 1900, E 2418, RG 395; Joseph Dorst to AG, Nueva Caceres, 15 and 22 September 1900, LS 465 and 541, E 3929, RG 395; F. T. Arnold to Adj, 18 December 1900, E 2353, RG 395; James Parker to AAG, 3D, 22 January 1901, LS 197, E 3929, RG 395; Linn, *U.S. Army*, 50–51, 109–10.

77. Thomas H. Barry to CG, DNL, 22 December 1900, E 2809, RG 395.

78. William H. Johnston to AG, 26 March 1900, LS 37, 2nd Btln, 46th Inf LSB, E 117, RG 94. AAG, 3D, DNL to CO, 36th Inf, 14 September 1900, LS 662, LSB 2, E 2206, RG 395.

79. William H. Johnston to AG, 1D, DSL, 27 June 1900, LS 143, 2nd Btln, 46th Inf LSB, E 117, RG 94. AAG, VMD to R. H. Sillman, 26 February 1900, LS 137, February 1900 LSB, E 2465, RG 395; AAG, VMD to CO, Sara, Panay, 10 March 1900, E 5249, RG 395; Adj to CO, Caloocan, 22 March 1900, LS 49, E 4923, RG 395; AAG to CO, 4D, DV, 13 November 1900, E 3081, RG 395. For statistics on assassinations and assaults, including civic officials, see Senate, *Affairs*, 1000–1005.

80. Otis to SecWar, 10 April 1900, *CWS* 2:1159.

81. "General Otis Reviews His Work," *Harpers' History,* 375–79. Otis to AG, 3 April 1900, *CWS* 2:1156.

82. "Memoirs of a Naval Career," 25:45, McCalla Papers.

83. Ibid., 25:47–48; "U.S. Naval Vessels in the Philippines," 5 January 1900, R375, M 625; *RSN* 1900, 544–48; Braisted, *U.S. Navy in the Pacific,* 70–114; Williams, "U.S. Navy in the Philippine Insurrection," 191–227.

84. On U.S. Marine Corps activities, see *RSN* 1900. For reports on operations, see H. L. Draper to CINC, 1 January 1900, R 375; Bowman McCalla to CINC, 21 March 1900, R 376; Arthur P. Nazro to CINC, 12 May 1900, R 377, all in M 625.

85. On MacArthur, see Young, *General's General,* 160–63; Karnow, *In Our Image,* 171; *Harpers' History,* 164–65; McCutcheon, *Drawn from Memory,* 135.

86. Gates, *Schoolbooks,* 140–49.

87. John G. Ballance to Samuel B. M. Young, 17 April 1900, LR 258, Box 6, Young Papers. Gates, *Schoolbooks,* 192–99.

88. William H. Taft to Elihu Root, 12 August 1900, Series 21, R 640, Taft Papers. On the election, see Manuel Tinio to Presidente Santa Cruz and Manuel Tinio to Presidente, Candon, [September 1900], SD 576.9, PIR; Juan Cailles to Pablo Estilla, 6 August 1900, Ex 1084, Taylor, *Philippine Insurrection*, 5:227; John L. Jordan to Mother, 18 May 1900, Jordan Papers; Frank W. Carpenter to Clarence R. Edwards, 31 July 1900, Box 1, Edwards Papers.

89. AAG, 2nd Div to CO, 1st Brig, 30 January 1900, LR 3, E 4330, RG 395. MacArthur to Schwan, 23 and 26 November 1899, in *RWD* 1900 1:7:59–60.

90. *RWD* 1900 1:5:61–62. Johnston's report is in *RWD* 1900 1:7:557–59. "To Whom It May Concern," ACP 417696 (William T. Johnston), RG 94; Linn, *U.S. Army*, 42–44.

91. The reference to MacArthur's sickness appears in Dean C. Worcester to Mrs. Henry W. Lawton, 10 October 1900, Box 2, Lawton Papers.

92. MacArthur to AG, 28 May 1900, CWS 2:1172–73. Citing their untrustworthiness, MacArthur opposed expanding the existing Filipino military forces until 1901; see MacArthur to AG, 7 August 1900, CWS 2:1197.

93. MacArthur to AG, 31 August 1900, CWS 2:1203–4.

94. Ibid.

95. MacArthur to AG, 19 September 1899, CWS 2:1211; *RWD* 1901 1:5:287–89, 455–57; Linn, *U.S. Army*, 23; Andrew J. Birtle, "The U.S. Army's Pacification of Marinduque, Philippine Islands, April 1900–April 1901," *Journal of Military History* 61 (April 1997): 261–62.

96. MacArthur to AG, 19 September 1900, CWS 2:1211.

97. [Clarence R. Edwards] to John T. Knight, 27 September 1900, Box 1, Edwards Papers. Taft to Root, 21 September and 10 October 1900, Series 21, Taft Papers; William R. Shafter to Henry C. Corbin, 21 November 1900, Box 1, Corbin Papers.

98. *ANJ*, 10 November 1900.

99. John L. Jordan to My dear mother, 29 October 1900, Jordan Papers. Delphy T. E. Casteel to My Darling One, 14–20 October 1900, Casteel Papers, 27th Inf, SAWS.

100. Samuel B. M. Young to Theodore Roosevelt, LS 190, Box 6, Young Papers. Young to AG, DNL, 12 November 1900, LS 3066, LSB 3, E 2150, RG 395.

101. John H. Parker to Theodore Roosevelt, 18 November 1900, Series 1, R 7, Roosevelt Papers.

102. AAG, DNL to CO, 3rd Inf, 2 May 1900, LR 245, RG 395. For instances of G.O. 100 restricting military actions, see HQ, 1st Brig, U.S. Expeditionary Forces, GO 4, 5 July 1898, E 890, RG 395; Beck to AAG, Aparri, 6 June 1900, LS 395, 49th Inf LSB, E 117, RG 94; Thomas W. Darrah to CO, San Miguel, 7 December 1900, LS 4396, 35th Inf LSB, E 117, RG 94. For support of issuing G.O. 100, see Samuel B. M. Young to George M. Sternberg, 7 April 1900, LS 123, Box 6, Young Papers; Robert L. Bullard to AG, 2D, DSL, 8 October 1899, LS 864, 39th Inf LSB, E 117, RG 94; Gates, *Schoolbooks*, 190–91.

103. Enoch Crowder to CG, DV, 30 June 1900, LS 29, July 1900 LSB, E 2465, RG 395.

104. Samuel B. M. Young to Richard Comba, 19 November 1900, LS 2653, LSB 3, E 2150, RG 395. On G.O. 100's being authorized, see AAG, VMD to CO, SD of Cebu, 12 February 1900, LS 61, E 2465, RG 395; William A. Mann to CO, Post of

———, 12 February 1900, LS 79, February 1900 LSB, E 2465, RG 395; AAG, VMD to Alexander Greig, 12 March 1900, LS 56, March 1900 LSB, E 2465, RG 395; HQ, 1D, DNL, Office of Chief Assistant, "Orders," 15 June 1900, E 5583, RG 395; Thomas N. Darrah to All Officers, 21 June 1900, LS 1571, 35th Inf LSB, E 117, RG 94.

105. [Jacob H. Smith] to AG, DNL, 30 October 1900, LSB 3, E 2206, RG 395. Frederick Funston to AG, 2nd Div, 27 March 1900, E 2263, RG 395.

106. Proceedings of a Board of Officers . . . , 21 December 1900, LR 4496, E 4047, RG 395; Kennon to AG, 1D, DNL, 3 December 1900, T 609, LSB 2, E 4043, RG 395.

107. CO, Laoag, to AG, 1D, DNL, 30 September 1900, LR 3856, LSB 4, Box 5, Young Papers.

108. AAG to CO, 35th Inf, in E. H. Plummer to CO, San Idelfonso and San Miguel, 1 November 1900, LS 3804, 35th Inf LSB, E 117, RG 94.

109. AAG, DNL to CO, Vigan, 30 September 1900, LS 1745, LSB 3, E 2150, RG 395. Young to AG, DNL, 30 September 1900, LS 1748, LSB 3, E 2150, RG 395.

110. Dean C. Worcester to Mrs. Henry W. Lawton, 5 December 1900, Box 2, Lawton Papers. Gates, *Schoolbooks,* 174–78.

111. *RWD* 1900 1:5:60.

112. Edward D. Taussig to My Dear Family, 1 October 1900, Taussig Papers. MacArthur to AG, 26 and 28 October, *CWS* 2:1222–23; Birtle, "U.S. Army's Pacification," 263–65. On reactions to the elections, see Hugh A. Drum to My dear Mary, 10 September 1900, Drum Family Letters File, Box 8, Hugh A. Drum Papers, MHI; 6 November 1900, Diary, Bullard Papers; Juan Cailles to Emiliano Riego de Dios, 21 November 1900, SD 653.4, PIR; Buenaventura Dimaguila to Mariano Trias, 22 November 1900, Ex 1125, 5:281–88; Emilio Aguinaldo to Generals and Commanders of Guerrillas, Order No. 397, 8 January 1901, Ex 1002, 5:114, both in Taylor, *Philippine Insurrection.*

113. *RWD* 1901 1:4:93.

114. *RWD* 1901 1:91–92.

115. *RWD* 1901 1:4:93. Gates, *Schoolbooks,* 206; Taylor, *Philippine Insurrection,* 2:279–80.

116. R. C. Day to Theodore Roosevelt, 27 December 1900, R 8, Roosevelt Papers; Loyd Wheaton to AG, DP, 31 May 1901, LS 427, E 2129, RG 395; Charles J. Crane, "The Fighting Tactics of Filipinos," *JMSI* 30 (July 1902): 507. On MacArthur's proclamation confirming existing practices, see May, *Battle;* 149; Birtle, *U.S. Army,* 35–36.

117. Gates, *Schoolbooks,* 225–43.

118. Memoranda: Showing Provinces . . . , 24 May 1902, F 4865–6, RG 350.

119. A list of the most important surrenders appears in *RWD* 1901 1:5:125–31. On the importance of Trias, see MacArthur to AG, 16 March 1901, *CWS* 2:1259; Samuel S. Sumner to AG, DSL, 12 March and 13 April 1901, E 2349, RG 395; May, *Battle,* 182–84.

120. John G. Ballance to AG, DNL, 8 June 1901, LS 903, LSB 5, E 2150, RG 395.

121. William McCaskey to AG, 1D, DNL, 29 May 1901, LR 1766, LRB 4, E 4043, RG 395. Taylor, *Philippine Insurrection,* 2:280–84. Aguinaldo ordered the court-martial and execution of Federal Party members; Emilio Aguinaldo, "In Self

Defense—Sensational Proclamation," 17 January 1901, Ex 1016, Taylor, *Philippine Insurrection,* 5:136–38.

122. Thomas Barry to CG, DSL, 6 January 1901, AGO 369141, RG 94. HQ, DNL, GO 22, 29 December 1900, E 2173, RG 395.

123. *RWD* 1901 1:4:131.

124. Dean C. Worcester to Mrs. Henry W. Lawton, 16 June 1900, Box 2, Lawton Papers; William H. Taft et al. to SecWar, 21 August 1900, Box 1, Edwards Papers; *RWD* 1900 1:4:24–25; Gates, *Schoolbooks,* 141–42. McKinley's instructions to the commission can be found in Senate, *Affairs,* 105–10. In addition to Taft, the commission included Dean C. Worcester, Luke I. Wright, Henry C. Ide, and Bernard Moses.

125. Dean C. Worcester to Mrs. Henry W. Lawton, 10 October 1900, Box 2, Lawton Papers. On the Taft-MacArthur relationship, see [Enoch R. Crowder] to Clarence R. Edwards, 3 February 1901, Edwards Papers; Gates, *Schoolbooks,* 176, 192–93; D. Clayton James, *The Years of MacArthur,* vol. 1, *1880–1941* (Boston: Houghton Mifflin, 1970), 36–42; Ralph E. Minger, *William Howard Taft and United States Foreign Policy: The Apprenticeship Years, 1900–1908* (Urbana: University of Illinois Press, 1975), 42–50; Carol M. Petillo, *Douglas MacArthur: The Philippine Years* (Bloomington: Indiana University Press, 1981), 53–55; Young, *General's General,* 257–90.

126. *RWD* 1900 1:5:62.

127. Senate, *Affairs,* 135–36.

128. William H. Taft to Henry M. Hoyt, 7 January 1901, Box 1, Edwards Papers; William H. Taft to Elihu Root, 10 and 30 November 1900, Series 21, Taft Papers.

129. HQ, DP, GO 179, 20 July 1901, in Senate, *Affairs,* 128–31.

130. Harold Hammond to Mrs. Van Nest, 31 October 1901, Hammond Papers, USMA.

131. Dean C. Worcester to Mrs. Henry W. Lawton, 5 May 1901, Box 2, Lawton Papers. May, *Battle,* 216.

132. MacArthur to AG, 16 March 1901, CWS 2:1259. Elihu Root to Adna R. Chaffee, 26 February 1901, Series 21, Taft Papers.

133. *RWD* 1901 1:4:90–91.

134. Dean C. Worcester to Mrs. Henry W. Lawton, 10 July 1901, Box 2, Lawton Papers. Indicative of MacArthur's conservatism are his recommendations for promotions to general, which, with the exception of J. Franklin Bell, were all Civil War veterans; see MacArthur to AG, 3 February 1901, 3587 ACP 1875 (Luther R. Hare), RG 94.

135. William H. Carter, *The Life of Lt. General Chaffee* (Chicago: University of Chicago Press, 1917). Stuart Miller claims Chaffee so despised civilians that he pronounced the word with an exaggerated sibilant, but he provides no source for the anecdote. In a not untypical series of factual errors on the same page, Miller also asserts that Chaffee and Jacob H. Smith served together in the 6th Cavalry, that Smith was Chaffee's chief of staff, and that Chaffee secured the promotion of J. Franklin Bell; see Miller, *Benevolent Assimilation,* 196.

136. Adna R. Chaffee to Henry C. Corbin, 2 September 1901, Box 1, Corbin Papers. *RWD* 1901 1:7:10–11.

137. Elihu Root to Adna R. Chaffee, 26 February 1901, Series 21, Taft Papers.

138. *RWD* 1901 1:7:8. Corbin to Chaffee, 5 October 1901, and Chaffee to Corbin, 17 October 1901, AGO 401920, RG 94.

139. Adna R. Chaffee to Henry C. Corbin, 30 September 1901, Box 1, Corbin Papers. May, *Battle,* 234–35.

140. Gates, *Schoolbooks,* 248–65. On Balangiga, see Robert P. Hughes to AG, 30 November 1901, LS 7825, E 2483, RG 395; Eugenio Daza y Salazar, "Some Documents on the Philippine-American War in Samar," *Leyte-Samar Studies* 17 (1983): 165–87; Brown, *Ninth Infantry,* 578–96; James O. Taylor, *The Massacre of Balangiga* (Joplin: n.p., 1931); Edward C. Bumpus, *In Memoriam* (Norwood, Mass.: n.p., 1902); Joseph Schott, *The Ordeal of Samar* (Indianapolis: Bobbs-Merrill, 1964), 35–55.

141. Mark D. Van Ells, "Assuming the White Man's Burden: The Seizure of the Philippines," *Philippine Studies* 43 (1994): 617.

142. Richard E. Welch, "American Atrocities in the Philippines: The Challenge and the Response," *Pacific Historical Review* 43 (May 1974): 234. LeRoy, *Americans,* 2:223–28. An earlier version of this section appeared in "Taking Up the White Man's Burden," in *1898: Enfoques y Perspectivas,* ed. Luis E. Gonzales-Vales, Academia Puertorriqueña de la Historia, 1997, 111–42. My thanks to Dr. Gonzales-Vales and the Academia Puertorriqueña de la Historia for permission to reprint it.

143. HQ, 2nd Div, FO 26, 22 April 1899, in Senate, *Affairs,* 986; italics in original.

144. Adna R. Chaffee to Henry C. Corbin, 5 November 1901, Corbin Papers.

145. Birtle, *U.S. Army,* 126–35.

146. "Our Soldiers in the Philippines," Young Papers.

147. Senate, *Affairs,* 558–59. Benjamin Foulois to Dear Mamma, 16 February 1900, Box 4, Benjamin Foulois Papers, MDLC.

148. Charles J. Crane, *The Experiences of a Colonel of Infantry* (New York: Knickerbocker Press, 1923), 340.

149. Arthur Murray to AG, DV, 4 June 1900, Report No. 6, 43rd Inf LSB, E 117, RG 94; Senate, *Affairs,* 988–89.

150. Arthur Murray to Henry T. Allen, 12 May 1901, Box 7, Allen Papers.

151. [Robert E.] Spence to Miller, 3 January 1900, LS 35, 2nd Btln, 32 Inf LSB, E 117, RG 94. Charges and Specifications against Cook Mark C. McCrea, [27 November 1900], Co G, 35th Inf LSB, E 117, RG 94; E. H. Palmer to CO, Santa Maria, 2 December 1900, LS 4324, 35th Inf LSB, E 117, RG 94; William H. Johnston to AG, 27 January 1900, LS 3, 2nd Btln, 46th Inf LSB, E 117, RG 94; Oral History, 16, Clenard McLaughlin Papers, MHI.

152. HQ, 3rd SB, GO 10, 14 March 1902, E 5101, RG 395.

153. Arthur L. Wagner, *The Service of Security and Information* (Washington, D.C.: James J. Chapman, 1893), 100. For international law on the impressment of guides and the right to execute them for misleading troops, see Articles 92–97 in G.O. 100, Senate, *Affairs,* 979. On justifiable force, see William H. Johnston to AG, 11 March and 22 May 1900, 2nd Btln, 46th Inf LSB, E 117, RG 94; Delphy Casteel to "My Darling One," 22 to 28 April 1900, Casteel Papers; John L. Jordan to Mother, 11 July 1900, Jordan Papers.

154. Jonathan Shay, *Achilles in Vietnam: Combat Trauma and the Undoing of Character* (New York: Scribner, 1994) 3–21, passim.

155. Joseph T. Dickman to Isaac Bridgeman and George Cortelyou, 24 April 1901, LS 274, 26th Inf LSB, E 117, RG 94.

156. Testimony of William H. Taft, Senate, *Affairs*, 74–76. William H. Taft to Elihu Root, 18 August 1900, Series 21, Taft Papers. For a sample of guerrilla atrocities, see Carson E. Ellis to Dear Mother and Mabel, March 1899, 1st Washington Inf Box, SAWS; George Gelbach to My Dear Bro, 6 September 1900, 46th Inf Box, SAWS; C. P. Johnson to AAG, 2D, DNL, 18 November 1900, 49th Inf LSB, E 117, RG 94; James H. Parker to Theodore Roosevelt, 18 November 1900, Series 1, R 7, Roosevelt Papers; "Sixteen Months in the Philippines," 91–92, LaWall Papers.

157. Robert A. Brown, "Report of an Investigation of the Killing of a Native Filipino, by First Lieutenant Preston Brown, 2nd U.S. Infantry, at Binangonan, Infanta Province, P.I. on December 22, 1900," Box 16, E 2330, RG 395.

158. William A. Kobbé to AG, DP, 10 September 1900, in *RWD* 1900 1:5:257–58.

159. Nelson Miles to SecWar, 19 February 1902, AGO 389439, RG 94. For a similar incident, see Edwin F. Glenn to AG, DV, 22 June 1901, Box 28, E 2483, RG 395.

160. Frederick K. Ward to AG, 1D, DSL, 22 October 1901, E 2355, RG 395. Adna R. Chaffee to Henry C. Corbin, 30 September 1901, Box 1, Henry C. Corbin Papers, MDLC; William L. Pitcher to AG, 3 January 1901, LS 4, E 4727, RG 395.

161. Senate, *Affairs*, 1527–33; 1727–36, 2776–78.

162. Testimony of Major Matthew F. Steele, "Proceedings of a Board of Officers to Inquire into Allegations made by Maj. Cornelius Gardener, 13th Infantry in his Report of December 16, 1901," AGO 421607, RG 94.

163. MS, Oliver Trafton Papers, 33rd Inf Box, SAWS.

164. 8 October 1901, Diary, Frederick Presher Papers, 1st Cav Box, SAWS. See also Homer Cook Questionnaire, 1st Cav Box, SAWS; 19–20 January 1901, Diary, Charles D. Rhodes Papers, MDLC.

165. Charles M. Foote, "Report of an Investigation of Outrages by American Soldiers in Batangas Province, P.I., February 1902," AGO 476653, RG 94.

166. Edmund Block to H. L. Wilfrey, 18 July 1902, F 2760, RG 350.

167. Henry T. Allen to Dear Sep [Clarence R. Edwards], 8 April 1902, Box 2, Edwards Papers.

168. J. Franklin Bell to "My dear Colonel" [William] Bisbee, 30 March 1900, LS 69, LSB 1, E 2206, RG 395.

10. *Moroland and the Eastern Visayas*

1. William H. Taft to Elihu Root, 12 August 1900, R 640, Taft Papers. In the first six months of 1900, the U.S. Army forces on Samar and Leyte were successively part of Brig. Gen. William Kobbé's Provisional Brigade, then the Office of the Military Governor of Albay and Catanduanes, then of the Visayan Military District, then the Department of the Visayas. Finally, in July, Samar was transferred to the Department of Southern Luzon. Both islands were in the U.S. Navy's Fourth Patrol Area throughout the war.

2. E. S. Sperry to Watson, 28 November 1899, R 373, M 625; Arthur P. Nazro to CINC, 30 March 1900, R 376, M 625.

3. "Diary of Field Service," 190–91, Kobbé Papers. For a typical joint operation, see AAG, DV to M. C. Rayzor, 23 August 1900, and [Robert P. Hughes] to J. F. Huston, 31 August 1900, August 1900 LSB, E 2465, RG 395.

4. *RWD* 1900 1:5:258.

5. Owen J. Sweet to AG, DMJ, 15 January 1900, LS 6. Owen J. Sweet to AG, DP, 7 and 30 June 1900, LS 9 and 16, all in E 2121, RG 395.

6. *RWD* 1900 1:5:257; Gowing, "Mandate in Moroland," 325–27.

7. Owen J. Sweet to AG, DP, 9 May 1900, LS 2, E 2121, RG 395. Palmer, *With My Own Eyes,* 160.

8. Owen J. Sweet to AG, DMJ, 23 January 1901, LS 7, E 2121, RG 395.

9. *RWD* 1900 1:5:266.

10. O. J. Sweet to AG, DMJ, 6, 11, and 13 November 1900, LS 37–39, E 2121, RG 395.

11. "History of the 31st Infantry," 18 June 1901, E 187, RG 94. "Diary of Field Service," 190–91, Kobbé Papers; *RWD* 1900 1:5:259–60; Taylor, *Philippine Insurrection,* 2:451–52; Gowing, "Mandate in Moroland," 337–39; Helmick, "From Reveille to Retreat," 141, Eli and Charles Helmick Papers, MHI.

12. Jose Roa to Emilio Aguinaldo, 26 January 1899, Ex 1427, Taylor, *Philippine Insurrection,* 5:825–27. Felipe Rendon to Emilio Aguinaldo, 2 August 1899, Ex 1429, Taylor, *Philippine Insurrection,* 5:828; [John A. Wagner] to AG, DMJ, [June 1900], Co M, 31st Inf LSB, E 117, RG 94; Arcilla, "Philippine Revolution," 46–56.

13. [James F. Case] to Adj, 40th Inf, 10 April 1900, LS 54, 3rd Btln, 40th Inf LSB, E 117, RG 94.

14. Edward A. Goodwin AG, 27 April 1900, LS 42, 40th Inf LSB, E 117, RG 94. For an overview of the U.S. Volunteers and the Mindanao campaign, see Reed, "Burden and Honor," 109–11.

15. J. F. Case to AAG, 1D, DMJ, 21 December 1900, LS 61, 3rd Btln, 40th Inf LSB, E 117, RG 94.

16. *RWD* 1900 1:5:262. For a more successful operation, see Edward A. Goodwin to AG, 5 May 1900, LS 58, 40th Inf LSB, E 117, RG 94.

17. William E. Birkhimer to S. W. Crawford, 27 December 1900, LS 1507, 28th Inf LSB, E 117, RG 94. William E. Birkhimer to AG, DMJ, 29 December 1900, LS 1501, 28th Inf LSB, E 117, RG 94; "History of the 28th Infantry," [1901], E 187, RG 94; J. F. Case to AAG, 1D, DMJ, 21 December 1900, LS 61, and 1 January 1901, LS 62, 3rd Btln, 40th Inf LSB, E 117, RG 94; Reed, "Burden and Honor," 111–12.

18. *RWD* 1901 1:6:264.

19. *RWD* 1901 1:6:296, 266–71.

20. [John A. Wagner] to AG, DMJ, [June 1900], Co M, 31st Inf LSB, E 117, RG 94.

21. John A. Wagner to Hunter Liggett, [January 1900?]. John A. Wagner to Adj, 3rd Btln, 19 January 1900; [John A. Wagner] to AG, DMJ, [June 1900?], all in Co M, 31st Inf LSB, E 117, RG 94.

22. John A. Wagner to AAG, DMJ, 14 June 1900, Co M, 31st Inf LSB, E 117, RG 94. John A. Wagner to AAG, DMJ, 30 September 1900, Co M, 31st Inf LSB, E 117, RG 94.

23. George L. Brown to Inspector of Schools, 4 July 1901, LS 12, E 2124, RG 395.

24. *RWD* 1900 1:5:269.

25. E. M. Holt, "Resistance on Samar: General Vicente Lukban and the Revolutionary War, 1899–1902," *Kabar Seberang Sulating Maphilindo* 10 (December 1982): 1–14; Donald Chaput, "Vicente Lukban," in Beebe, *War of 1898*, 263–64. For Lukban's communiqués and propaganda, see Taylor, *Philippine Insurrection*, 5:629–709.

26. "An account of the attack on Borongan, flight, capture, imprisonment, and release of Cpl. Fred Allen, Co. I, 43rd Infantry, U.S.V.," and "Narrative of Sgt. George F. Doe, Co. I, 43rd, of captivity from capture at Borongan, Samar, March 14, 1900," both in Arthur Murray to AG, [April 1900?], Box 32, Allen Papers. For graphic descriptions of Filipino atrocities, see the testimony in GCM 30756 (Julien E. Gaujot); GCM 34401 (Edwin F. Glenn); GCM 30757 (Norman E. Cook), RG 153; Z. Acerill to Vicente Lukban, 11 January 1901, SD 891.10, PIR; Ward Dabney to Adj, 25 October 1901, E 2574, RG 395; Elias Chandler to Adj, Calbayog, 21 October 1901, LR 4651, E 3503, RG 395; Thomas M. Bains to Adj, Catbalogan, 14 December 1901, LR 1033, E 3450, RG 395; Ralph L. Bitney to Mother, 23 January 1902, 1st Inf Box, SAWS.

27. John C. Gilmore to AAG, PB, 14 February 1900, 2nd Btln, 43rd Inf LSB, E 117, RG 94. Henry T. Allen to AG, MDAC, 31 March 1900, Box 32, Allen Papers; Henry T. Allen to William A. Kobbé, 20 April 1900, F 1900, Kobbé Papers, MHI; Reed, "Burden and Honor," 89–92; "History of the 43rd Infantry," [June 1901], E 187, RG 94. One 43rd Infantry company was transferred from Samar to Leyte on 23 February, another on 6 June.

28. "Diary of Field Service," 151, Kobbé Papers.

29. Henry T. Allen to Editor, New York *Sun*, 22 February 1900, LS 10, 3rd Btln, 43rd Inf LSB, E 117, RG 94. Allen was no more overoptimistic than his officers; see William S. Conrow to William H. Burt, 27 February 1900, LS 25, 3rd Btln, 43rd Inf LSB, E 117, RG 94; William G. Wilson to Parents, 16 February 1900, 43rd Inf Box, SAWS; John C. Gilmore to AG, DP, 12 May 1900, Box 32, Allen Papers; Frank C. Prescott to Adj, MSD Samar, 26 May 1900, Co L, 43rd Inf LSB, E 117, RG 94.

30. Henry T. Allen to AG, 1D, DV, 30 April 1900, Box 32, Allen Papers. HQ, MSD Samar, "Proclamacion Americano," 23 February 1900, LS 22, 3rd Btln, 43rd Inf LSB, E 117, RG 94; Heath Twichell, *Allen: The Biography of an Army Officer, 1859–1930* (New Brunswick, N.J.: Rutgers University Press, 1974), 106.

31. Henry T. Allen to AG, VMD, 15 April 1900, Box 32, Allen Papers.

32. [Robert P. Hughes] to Henry T. Allen, 28 April 1900, LS 90, April 1900 LSB, E 2465, RG 395; HQ, MSD Samar, SO 51, 16 May 1900, E 5788, RG 395.

33. John S. Fair to Adj, 2nd Btln, 15 April 1900, LS 39, Co E, 43rd Inf LSB, E 117, RG 94. Henry T. Allen to AG, MDAC, 16 March 1900, Box 32, Allen Papers; John C. Gilmore to AAG, PB, 15 March 1900; W. Mills to H. J. Stewart, 28 March 1900; John C. Gilmore to AAG, MDAC, 14 April 1900; John C. Gilmore to AAG, District of Samar and Leyte, 18 May 1900, all in 2nd Btln, 43rd Inf LSB, E 117, RG 94; John Cooke to John C. Gilmore, 10 April 1900, LS 24, Co F, 43rd Inf LSB, E 117, RG 94; Frank C. Prescott to Adj, MSD Samar, 26 May 1900, Co L, 43rd Inf LSB, E 117, RG 94.

34. *RWD* 1900 1:7:231–34; John C. Gilmore to AG, DV, 6 July 1900, 2nd Btln, 43rd Inf LSB, E 117, RG 94.

35. New York *Herald,* 16 May 1900; New York *Evening Star,* 16 May 1900, in AGO 307686, RG 94; Henry T. Allen to AG, 1D, DV, 30 April 1900, Box 32, Allen Papers; [Robert P. Hughes] to Henry T. Allen, 3 September 1900, September 1900 LSB, E 2465, RG 395; John C. Gilmore to AG, 6 July 1900, 2nd Btln, 43rd Inf LSB, E 117, RG 94; *RWD* 1900 1:4:398; "Diary of Field Service," 175–76, Kobbé Papers.

36. Goberno Militar de Samar, "Habitants de Samar," 25 April 1900, in Henry T. Allen to AG, 1D, DV, 30 April 1900, Box 32, Allen Papers; Twichell, *Allen,* 107–8.

37. Henry T. Allen to AG, 1D, DV, 30 April 1900, Box 32, Allen Papers. John S. Fair to Adj, 2nd Btln, 6 May 1900, Co E, 43rd Inf LSB, E 117, RG 94.

38. John C. Gilmore to Arthur Murray, 18 May 1900, Box 32, Allen Papers.

39. Michael J. Spellman to Adj, 2nd Btln, 22 May 1900, LS 9, Co G, 43rd Inf LSB, E 117, RG 94.

40. Henry T. Allen to AAG, 1D, DV, 21 May 1900, Box 32, Allen Papers.

41. Arthur Murray to AG, DV, 31 May 1900, Box 32, Allen Papers.

42. *RWD* 1900 1:4:398; Henry T. Allen to AG, 31 March 1900; Henry T. Allen to AG, 1D, DV, 30 March and 30 April 1900, all in Box 32, Allen Papers; Senate, *Affairs,* 545; LeRoy, *Americans,* 2:188–89.

43. Owen T. Kenan to Adj, Catbalogan, 28 February 1901, LR 177, E 3450, RG 395. R. O. Patterson to Adj, 3 January 1901, LR 49, E 3450, RG 395; L. S. Carson to Adj, 5 January 1901, LR 16, E 3450, RG 395; J. N. Kineborough to Adj, 3 February 1901, LR 70, E 3503, RG 395.

44. Braulio Cruz and 21 signatures to Citizen-Governor of the Province of Leyte, 13 February 1899, Ex 1368, 5:718–20; Emilio Aguinaldo, Instructions to General Mojica [Moxica], 1 January 1899, Ex 1369, 5:720–22; Esteban Aparri, [Proclamation], 14 March 1899, Ex 1370, 5:722–23; Ambrosio Moxica, [Proclamation], 20 May 1900, Ex 1379, 5:741–43, all in Taylor, *Philippine Insurrection;* see also 2:439–40.

45. Arthur Murray to Ambrosio Moxica, 3 May 1900, Box 32, Allen Papers.

46. Report of H. A. Thayer, 4 April 1900, in Arthur Murray, Report No. 3, 20 April 1900, Box 32, Allen Papers. Reed, "Burden and Honor," 97. As a point of comparison, there were forty-three engagements on Samar during this period, but twenty-four Americans were killed in fighting on Samar and only four on Leyte; see "History of the 43rd Infantry."

47. Robert P. Hughes to AG, 8 May 1900, LS 33, May 1900 LSB, E 2465, RG 395. Robert P. Hughes to AG, 17 April 1900, LS 45, April LSB, E 2465, RG 395; Office of Commander of MSD Leyte to AG, MDAC, 16 March 1900; [Arthur Murray], Report of 1 February to 28 March 1900; Arthur Murray, Report No. 2, 4 April 1900, all in Box 32, Allen Papers.

48. Hughes to Barber, [3 June 1900], LS 31, June 1900 LSB, E 3465, RG 395.

49. [Robert P. Hughes] to AG, DP, 20 May 1900, LS 86, May 1900 LSB, E 2465, RG 395; Arthur Murray to AG, DV, Report No. 5, 16 May 1900, and Arthur Murray to AG, DV, 11 July 1900, both in Box 32, Allen Papers; *ANJ,* 23 June 1900; "History of the 43rd Infantry."

50. [Robert P. Hughes] to AG, DV, LS 39, June 1900 LSB, E 2465, RG 395.

51. Arthur Murray, Report No. 4, 30 April 1900, Box 32, Allen Papers.

52. Arthur Murray to AG, DV, 17 August 1900. Arthur Murray, Report No. 4, 30 April 1900, both in Box 32, Allen Papers.

53. Office of Commander, MSD Leyte, Circular No. 2, 17 April 1900, in Arthur Murray, Report No. 4, 30 April 1900, Box 32, Allen Papers.

54. Henry T. Allen to AAG, 1D, DV, 6 September 1900, Box 32, Allen Papers.

55. Arthur Murray to AG, DV, Report No. 10, 1 September 1900. Arthur Murray to AG, MDAC, Report of 1 February to 28 March 1900, both in Box 32, Allen Papers.

56. Harry M. Dey to Adj, 1st MSD, 1D, DV, 31 July 1900. John C. Gilmore to AG, 1D, DV, 31 July 1900; Lincoln G. Andrews, 16 July 1900, in Arthur Murray to AG, DV, 1 August 1900, Box 32, Allen Papers; Linwood Hanson to Adj, 1D, DV, 20 July 1900, in Arthur Murray, Report No. 8, 1 August 1900; Frank C. Prescott to Adj, 2nd MSD, 1D, DV, 1 August 1900, all in Box 32, Allen Papers.

57. Julio Vilag to Ambrosio Moxica, 31 March 1900, Ex 1375, Taylor, *Philippine Insurrection,* 5:738–39. Arthur Murray to AG, District of Albay and Catanduanes, Report of 1 February to 28 March 1900, Box 32, Allen Papers; Leon Rojas to General [Ambrosio Moxica], 21 April 1900, Ex 1377, Taylor, *Philippine Insurrection,* 5:740–41.

58. Arthur Murray to AG, DV, Report No. 16, 3 December 1900, Box 32, Allen Papers.

59. Arthur Murray, Report No. 4, 30 April 1900, Box 32, Allen Papers. For reports on police activity, see Arthur Murray to Robert P. Hughes, 22 May 1900, in Arthur Murray, 4 June 1900, Report No. 6; Michael E. Morris to AG, 1st MSD, Leyte, 30 June 1900; Frank C. Prescott to Adj, 2nd MSD, 1D, DV, 1 August 1900, all in Box 32, Allen Papers.

60. Arthur Murray, Report No. 4, 30 April 1900, Box 32, Allen Papers.

61. Donald Chaput, "Founding of the Leyte Scouts," *Leyte-Samar Studies* 9 (1975): 5–10.

62. Arthur Murray to AG, DV, Report No. 16, 3 December 1900. Arthur Murray to AG, DV, 1 August 1900; Report of Henry T. Allen, 6 August 1900; Henry T. Allen to AAG, 1D, DV, 6 September 1900; Linwood Hanson to Adj, 1st MSD, 17 September 1900; Arthur Murray to AG, DV, Report No. 15, 21 November 1900, all in Box 32, Allen Papers. For accounts of the campaigns against Moxica, see Henry T. Allen, "Scouting in the Mountains of Leyte" and "Big Game Hunting in Leyte," both in Box 40, Allen Papers.

63. Report of Washington L. Goldsborough, 17 and 19 June 1900. Report of Washington Goldsborough, 11 July, both in Arthur Murray to AG, DV, 11 July 1900, Report No. 7, Box 32, Allen Papers.

64. Lincoln Andrews to Adj, 17 March 1900, Box 32, Allen Papers. In mitigation, Cilley may have been delirious from the typhoid fever that killed him shortly afterward.

65. Arthur Murray to AG, DV, Report No. 10, 1 September 1900; emphasis in original. Arthur Murray, Report No. 8, 1 August 1900, both in Box 32, Allen Papers.

66. Arthur Murray to AG, DV, 17 August and 10 October 1900, Box 32, Allen Papers.

67. [Robert P. Hughes] to Arthur Murray, 22 August, August 1900 LSB, E 2465, RG 395. Arthur Murray to AG, DV, Report No. 11, 15 September 1900, Box 32,

Allen Papers; [Robert P. Hughes] to Arthur Murray, 19 October, October 1900 LSB, E 2465, RG 395.

68. Your Old Friend and General [Ambrosio Moxica] to Citizens of Leyte, November 1900, Ex 1383, 5:748–49. Julio Vilag to Ambrosio Moxica, 31 March 1900, Ex 1375, 5:738–39; Ambrosio Moxica, [Proclamation], 20 May 1900, Ex, 1379, 5:741–43; Augustin Banez Bello to BG [Moxica], 21 August 1900, Ex 1381, 5:746–47, all in Taylor, *Philippine Insurrection;* Arthur Murray to AG, DV, 1 August 1900 and 1 September 1900; Henry T. Allen to AAG, 1D, DV, 6 September 1900, all in Box 32, Allen Papers.

69. Hughes to Barry, 29 December 1900, E 2466, RG 395. Arthur Murray to AG, DV, Report No. 17, 2 January 1901, Box 32, Allen Papers.

70. Arthur Murray to AG, DV, Report 16, 12 March 1901, Box 32, Allen Papers.

71. "History of the 43rd Infantry."

11. *Panay*

1. Senate, *Affairs,* 573, 581. *RWD* 1901 1:6:5; *Pronouncing Gazetteer,* 156. After Manila's reorganization of May 1900, the department had four districts: the 1st District being Leyte under Col. Arthur Murray of the 43rd Infantry; the 2nd, Cebu under Col. Edward J. McClernand of the 44th Infantry; the 3rd, Negros governed by Brig. Gen. James F. Smith, with military operations under Col. Charles W. Miner of the 6th Infantry; and the 4th, Panay under Col. Edmund Rice of the 26th Infantry. Samar was briefly part of the Visayan Military District and in June was transferred to join Romblon and Masbate in the 4th District, Department of Southern Luzon.

2. 12–17 February 1900, Diary 34, French Diaries. For an overview of the Panay campaign, see Bronson, "Visayan Campaigns," 305–7; Reed, "Burden and Honor," 104–6.

3. During the war, department headquarters often referred to the northeast section of the island as Concepcion Province, but the civil government included this as part of Iloilo.

4. Robert P. Hughes to C. R. Paul, 5 March 1900, LS 22, March 1900 LSB, E 2465, RG 395.

5. Adj, VMD to J. F. Huston, 8 and 17 February 1900, LS 30 and 95, February 1900 LSB, E 2465, RG 395. Robert P. Hughes to My Dear Governor [Otis], 13 March 1900, LS 61, March 1900 LSB, E 2465, RG 395; 19 and 24 February 1900, Diary 34, French Papers; 26 February 1900, Diary, R. H. McMaster Papers, MHI; "Notes on Gordon Scouts," Gordon-Allen Family Papers, MHI; *RWD* 1900 1:5:243–45.

6. Robert P. Hughes to Walter S. Scott, 5 May 1900, LS 17, May 1900 LSB, E 2465, RG 395. On military operations, see Edward D. Anderson to AG, VMD, 11 February 1900, 26th Inf LSB, E 117, RG 94; AAG, VMD to James T. Dickman, 14 February 1900, LS 73; AAG, VMD to H. C. Hale, 6 March 1900, LS 26; Robert P. Hughes to J. F. Huston, 24 April 1900, LS 79; AAG to Walter S. Scott, 24 April 1900, LS 80; Robert P. Hughes to CO, Calivao, 2 May 1900, LS 1; Robert P. Hughes to J. F. Huston, 6 May 1900, LS 24, all in February–May LSB, E 2465, RG 395.

7. Robert P. Hughes to AG, DP, 20 May 1900, LS 86, May 1900 LSB, E 2465, RG 395; Leandro Fullon to Field and Line Officers, 2 June 1900, Ex 1291, Taylor, *Philippine Insurrection,* 5:591–92.

8. AAG, VMD to James T. Dickman, 17 March 1900, LS 74, March 1900 LSB, E 2465, RG 395.

9. C. R. Paul to AG, 1SB, 12 and 23 February 1900, No. 872 and 1001, E 2511, RG 395; Leandro Fullon to Field and Line Officers, 2 June 1900, Ex 1291, Taylor, *Philippine Insurrection,* 5:591–92; *RWD* 1900 1:5:252.

10. "Guerrilla Warfare," 1 June 1900, Ex 1290, 5:584–91. "General Order of the General Staff," 12 February 1900, Ex 1282, 573–75, both in Taylor, *Philippine Insurrection.*

11. Walter H. Gordon to AG, 4D, VMD, 15 May 1900, in 3927 ACP 1886 (Walter Henry Gordon), RG 94; William Tutherly to AG, DV, 1 March 1901, LS 212, Co's A–F, 26th Inf LSB, E 117, RG 94; *RWD* 1900 1:5:252; Taylor, *Philippine Insurrection,* 2:408; Bronson, "Visayan Campaigns," 303–4; Reed, "Burden and Honor," 135–38.

12. Praxedes Magalona, Memorandum . . . , 3 October 1900, Ex 1302, Taylor, *Philippine Insurrection,* 5:605–8.

13. *RWD* 1900 1:5:252. Leandro Fullon, General Order for the Day, 11 May 1900, Ex 1288, Taylor, *Philippine Insurrection,* 5:581–83.

14. Walter H. Gordon to AG, 4D, VMD, 15 May 1900, in 3927 ACP 1886 (Walter Henry Gordon), RG 94.

15. D. Gellada to Presidente of Tigbauan, 29 September 1900, Ex 1298, Taylor, *Philippine Insurrection,* 5:599–601. Gabriel Sinoy, Presidente of Dingle and Major of Macheteros, [Confession], 25 November 1900, November 1900 LSB, E 2465, RG 395; Francisco Jalandoni to the Delegation of Northern Iloilo, 30 September 1900, Ex 1299, 5:601–2; Leandro Fullon, [Decree], 25 January 1900, Ex 1280, 5:571–72; 2:403–8, all in Taylor, *Philippine Insurrection.*

16. Severino Cabives, [Proclamation], 10 March 1900, Ex 1286, Taylor, *Philippine Insurrection,* 5:579–80.

17. Leandro Fullon to Local Chiefs, 20 February 1900, Ex 1283, Taylor, *Philippine Insurrection,* 5:575–76.

18. Severino Cabives, [Proclamation], 10 March 1900, Ex 1286, Taylor, *Philippine Insurrection,* 5:579–80; E. Paro to General in Chief, 22 November 1900, Ex 1305, Taylor, *Philippine Insurrection,* 5:610; Bronson, "Visayan Campaigns," 306–7.

19. Mercedes Manio et al., [Declaration], 5 March 1900, Ex 1285, Taylor, *Philippine Insurrection,* 5:577–78.

20. Praxedes Magalona, Memorandum . . . , 3 October 1900, Ex 1302, Taylor, *Philippine Insurrection,* 5:605–8.

21. National Army of Operations, Iloilo, [Proclamation], 1 October 1900, Ex 1301, 5:603–5. Francisco Jalandoni to Nicolas Roses, 1 June 1900, Ex 1289, 5:583–84, both in Taylor, *Philippine Insurrection.*

22. S. M. Ackley to CINC, 6 February 1900, "Military-Naval Operations in the Philippines," Box 410, Subject File OJ, RG 45.

23. Robert P. Hughes to Inspector General, 8 March 1900, LS 42, March 1900 LSB, E 2465, RG 395. On Delgado's efforts to ensure good treatment, see "General Order of the General Staff," 12 February 1900, Ex 1282, 5:573–75. On retaliation

against towns that cooperated, see Leandro Fullon to Local Chiefs, 3 April 1900, Ex 1287, 5:580; Francisco Jalandoni to Nicolas Roses, 1 June 1900, Ex 1289, 5:583–84; D. Gellada to Presidente of Tigbauan, 29 September 1900, Ex 1298, 5:599–601; National Army of Operations, Iloilo, [Proclamation], 1 October 1900, Ex 1301, 5:603–5; [Anon.] to Jose Talcon, 31 October 1900, Ex 1303, 5:608–9; Martin Delgado, My Dear Compatriots, 2 December 1900, Ex 1307, 5:612–13, all in Taylor, *Philippine Insurrection*.

24. AAG to CO, 4D, 15 June 1900, LS 41, June 1900 LSB, E 2465, RG 395.

25. Adj, HQ, VMD to Alvin A. Barker, 5 January 1900, LS 16, January 1900 LSB, E 2465, RG 395.

26. Robert P. Hughes to My Dear Governor [Otis], 13 March 1900, LS 61, March 1900 LSB, E 2465, RG 395.

27. AAG to J. F. Huston, 8 August 1900, LS 26, August 1900 LSB, E 2465, RG 395.

28. AAG, DV to AG, DP, 5 November 1900. Robert P. Hughes to Walter S. Scott, 11 August 1900, LS 36; AAG, DV to AG, DP, 5 November 1900, all in August–November 1900 LSB, E 2465, RG 395.

29. [Ralph Van Deman] to Chief Engineer Officer, 4 February 1900, LS 11, February 1900 LSB. Adj, VMD to COs, 20 January 1900, LS 78, January 1901 LSB, both in E 2465, RG 395.

30. 30 January 1900, Diary 34, French Papers. [Edward D. Anderson] to Adj, 11 February, 13 March, and 26 June 1900, 26th Inf LSB, E 117, RG 94; William B. Baker to My own darling, 1 July 1900, William B. Baker Papers, 26th Inf Box, SAWS.

31. Alvin A. Barker to Adj, 29 December 1899, No. 694. Alvin A. Barker to AAG, 17 February 1900, No. 59, both in E 2511, RG 395.

32. Fred McDonald to Adj, 2 January 1900, No. 694; Alvin A. Barker to Adj, 2 January 1900, No. 694, both in E 2511, RG 395.

33. AAG, VMD to COs, 10 March 1900, LS 55, March 1900 LSB, LS 2465, RG 395.

34. Pedro Mondejar to Local Presidente of Pavia, 5 December 1900, Ex 1308, 5:613–14. Pedro Mondejar to Juan Somociera, 30 November 1900, Ex 1306, 5:611; Praxedes Magalona, Memorandum . . . , 3 October 1900, Ex 1302, 5:605–8; [Anon.] to Jose Talcon, 31 October 1900, Ex 1303, 5:608–9; Martin Delgado to My Dear Compatriots, 2 December 1900, 5:612–13, all in Taylor, *Philippine Insurrection*; Hughes to Barry, 9 January 1909, E 2466, RG 395.

35. Reed, "Burden and Honor," 86, 107.

36. Edward D. Anderson to AAG, DV, 7 June 1900, in Robert H. Sillman to Edward D. Anderson, 4 June 1900, No. 177, E 2511, RG 395.

37. De Bevoise, *Agents of Apocalypse*, 64–65. On property destruction, see [Edward D. Anderson] to AG, DV, 25 April 1900, 26th Inf LSB, E117, RG 94; Walter H. Gordon to AG, 4D, VMD, 15 May 1900, in 3927 ACP 1886 (Walter Henry Gordon), RG 94; Robert P. Hughes to AG, DP, 20 May 1900, LS 86, May 1900 LSB, E 2465, RG 395; Mann to Barber, 9 June 1900, E 2466, RG 395; Robert H. Sillman to T. Ryan, 24 June 1900, LS 261–62, Co's K–M, 26th Inf LSB, E 117, RG 94; F. H. Peck to James T. Dickman, 10 June 1900, LS 74, Co's A–F, 26 Inf LSB, E 117, RG 94; William B. Baker to My own darling Pete (?), 13 July 1900, William B. Baker Papers, SAWS; "Notes on Gordon Scouts."

38. Clarence H. Bowers, "Builders of an Island Empire," *Bulletin of the American Historical Collection* 33 (July–September 1995): 7–16.

39. AAG, VMD to CO, Baratoc Nuevo, 13 February 1900, LS 68, February 1900 LSB, E 2465, RG 395.

40. F. H. Peck to James T. Dickman, 10 June 1900, LS 74, Co's. A–F, 26th Inf LSB, E 117, RG 94. Mann to Barber, 9 June 1900, E 2466, RG 395; Hughes to Barber, 10 June 1900, LS 24 and Robert P. Hughes to AG, DV, 15 June 1900, LS 39, both in June 1900 LSB, E 2465, RG 395; *RWD* 1900 1:5:250; Taylor, *Philippine Insurrection,* 2:407; Bronson, "Visayan Campaigns," 305.

41. Joseph T. Dickman to AG, DV, 12 June 1900, 26th Inf LSB, E 117, RG 94.

42. "Notes on Gordon Scouts."

43. John Hickey to AG, DV, 5 July 1900, LS 46, Co's A–F, 26th Inf LSB, E 117, RG 94; Robert P. Hughes to AG, DP, 10 July 1900, LS 28, July 1900 LSB, E 2465, RG 395.

44. Robert P. Hughes to AG, DP, 18 October, October 1900 LSB, E 2465, RG 395; R. S. Golderman to AAG, 4D, DV, 3 July 1900, LS 268, Co's K–M, 26th Inf LSB, E 117, RG 94.

45. Robert H. Sillman to Edward D. Anderson, 4 June 1900, No. 177, E 2511, RG 395.

46. *RWD* 1901 1:6:8. Guy V. Henry to Adj, 38th Inf, 6 January 1901, 26th Inf LSB, E 117, RG 94; "Notes on Gordon Scouts."

47. William Tutherly to AG, DV, 1 March 1901, LS 212, Co's A–F, 26th Inf LSB, E 117, RG 94.

48. Hughes to CO, Janiuay, 22 December 1900, E 2466, RG 395. Noble to CO, Janiuay, 31 December 1900, E 2466, RG 395; *RWD* 1901 1:6:9.

49. Noble to Boardman, 31 December 1900, E 2466, RG 395. Hughes to Praxedes Magalona, 31 December 1900, E 2466, RG 395; Hughes to Anderson, 31 December, E 2466, RG 395.

50. William Tutherly to AG, DV, 1 March 1901, LS 212, Co F, 26th Inf LSB, E 117, RG 94; Bronson, "Visayan Campaigns," 307.

51. Senate, *Affairs,* 1527–47, 2767.

52. Noble to CO, Baratoc Nuevo, 23 January 1901, E 2466, RG 395; Simons to Henry [Pototan], 23 January 1901, E 2466, RG 395; Noble to Henry, 24 January 1901, E 2466, RG 395; Reed, "Burden and Honor," 105–7.

53. On the surrender of Delgado and his lieutenants, see the telegraphic correspondence January–March 1901 in E 2466, RG 395; Sonza, *Visayan Fighters,* 28.

54. Noble to Shanks, 24 February 1901, E 2466, RG 395. Hughes to Shanks, 11 February 1901, E 2466, RG 395.

55. *RWD* 1901 1:6:10; Sonza, *Visayan Fighters,* 13–15, 40.

12. Northern Luzon

1. Arthur Murray to AG, DV, 31 May 1900, Box 32, Allen Papers. On manpower figures, see *RWD* 1900 1:5:45–51.

2. MacArthur to Schwan, 23 and 28 November 1899, in *RWD* 1900 1:7:59–60. AAG to CG, 2nd Brigade, 30 January 1900, LR 3, E 4330, RG 395.

3. *RWD* 1901 1:5:5.

4. Palmer, *With My Own Eyes,* 151. 5249 ACP 1889 (Loyd Wheaton), RG 94; *RWD* 1900 1:5:45.

5. *RWD* 1900 1:5:197.

6. Figures from RWD 1900 1:5:206; AAG, DNL, "Chronological list of actions . . . ," 15 May 1901, LR 8073, E 2133, RG 395. These figures are difficult to interpret, since one or two particularly sanguinary engagements (such as occurred in February 1901) may account for nearly all the casualties in any month.

7. AAG, DNL to CG, 1D, DNL, 30 December 1900, LS 955, E 2130, RG 395. Wheaton to Young, 25 September 1900, LR 3709, LRB 4, Box 5, Young Papers; AAG, DNL to CO, Vigan, 30 September 1900, LS 1745, LSB 3, E 2150, RG 395; Wheaton to AG, "Diary of Events. January 12, 1901 to January 30, 1901," AGO 338335, RG 94.

8. AAG, DNL, "Chronological list of actions . . . ," 15 May 1901, LR 8073, E 2133, RG 395.

9. *RWD* 1901 1:5:6.

10. J. Franklin Bell to AG, 2nd Div, 18 March 1900, LS 45, LSB 1, E 2206, RG 395; William R. Grove to Quartermaster, 6 June 1900, LS 265, 36th Inf LSB, E 117, RG 94.

11. Emerson H. Liscum to AG, 20 January 1900, LS 167, E 872, RG 395. Noble to CO, Caloocan, 22 February 1900, E 4330, RG 395; *RWD* 1900 1:5:197.

12. Lyman W. V. Kennon to AG, 4D, DNL, 13 May 1900, E 3248, RG 395. C. P. Johnson to CO, 2D, DNL, 11 and 16 May 1900, 49th Inf LSB, E 117, RG 94; Ewing E. Booth to AG, 3D, DNL, 11 August 1900, LS 466, 36th Inf LSB, E 117, RG 94; J. Milton Thompson to AG, 27 June 1900, LS 973, 42nd Inf LSB, E 117, RG 94; Linn, *U.S. Army,* 35.

13. J. Milton Thompson to AG, DNL, 14 January 1901, LS 187, E 2312, RG 395.

14. J. Franklin Bell to AG, 2nd Div, [March 1900], LS 71, LSB 1, E 2206, RG 395.

15. *RWD* 1901 1:5:109–10. Luther R. Hare to AG, DSL, 13 July 1900, LS 933, E 2348, RG 395; J. Franklin Bell to MS, 2 June 1900, E 2209, RG 395; Linn, *U.S. Army,* 34–36, 83–84.

16. J. Milton Thompson to AG, DNL, 1 August 1900, LS 608, E 2312, RG 395. Enoch H. Crowder to CG, DNL, 20 June 1900, E 2809, RG 395; [Jacob H. Smith] to AG, DNL, 9 August 1900, LS 110, LSB 1, E 2206, RG 395; "Reports from all posts 1st District . . . relative to arming native police," [July 1900?], E 2353, RG 395; Benjamin Alvord to CG, 5D, DNL, 15 August 1900, E 2809, RG 395; HQ, 5D, DNL, Special Orders 66, 11 October 1900, E 2809, RG 395; Thomas H. Barry to CG, DNL, 22 December 1900, E 2809, RG 395; Linn, *U.S. Army,* 50–51, 84.

17. Frederick D. Grant to AG, DNL, 15 April 1900, in *RWD* 1900 1:7:78.

18. Benjamin Alvord to Frederick Funston, 2 January 1901, cited in Linn, *U.S. Army,* 83. E. H. Plummer to AG, DNL, 26 June 1900, LS 1606, 35th Inf LSB, E 117, RG 94; R. D. Walsh to "My Dear Sep" [Clarence R. Edwards], 4 November 1900, Box 1, Edwards Papers.

19. E. H. Plummer to CO, San Miguel, 13 July 1900, LS 1840, 35th Inf LSB, E 117, RG 94.

20. Matthew Batson to AG, 31 December 1900, LS 167, E 5805, RG 395.

21. James I. Hixon to Adj, 32nd Inf, 15 January 1900, E 2816, RG 395; J. Milton Thompson to AG, Provost Marshal, 23 August 1900, LS 821, E 2312, RG 395; Request for Brochure on Philippine Scouts, 21 September 1953, No. 388, Legislative and Policy Precedent Files, 1943–1975, RG 407; Linn, *U.S. Army*, 43, 81–83.

22. On the 1st District, see Linn, *U.S. Army*, 29–61; Brian M. Linn, "Provincial Pacification in the Philippines, 1900–1901: The First District, Department of Northern Luzon," *Military Affairs* 51 (April 1987): 62–66; Scott, *Ilocano Responses;* Ochosa, *Tinio Brigade.*

23. Samuel B. M. Young to AG, DP8AC, 9 January 1900, in *RWD* 1900 1:6:285; Luther R. Hare to AG, 15 February 1900, LS 139, E 5578, RG 395; Otis to SecWar 10 April 1900, *CWS* 2:1159; Samuel B. M. Young to AG, DNL, 7 May 1900, LS 181, E 2150, RG 395; "History of the 48th Infantry, U.S.V.," 24 June 1901, E 187, RG 94.

24. *RWD* 1900 1:7:257–64; ACP 417696 (Crispulo Patajo), RG 94; William T. Johnston, "A Brief Record of Services Since 1898," ACP 4625 (William T. Johnston), RG 94.

25. Linn, *U.S. Army*, 41–49; Scott, *Ilocano Responses*, 70–71, 75, 101–3.

26. Samuel B. M. Young to AG, DNL, 7 September 1900, LS 167, Box 6, Young Papers; S. B. M. Young to AG, DNL, 17 January, LS 83, LSB 4, E 2150, RG 395.

27. William H. Beck to AG, DP, 2 May 1900, LS 242, 49th Inf LSB, E 117, RG 94.

28. William B. Cochran to AG, 2D, DNL, 5 June 1900, LS 1, E 2851, RG 395. Carter P. Johnson to CO, 2D, DNL, 15 May 1900; Robert Gage to AAG, Aparri, 26 May 1900, LS 331; William H. Beck to AAAG, DNL, 3 June 1900, LS 377; Beck to AG, Aparri, 12 June 1900, LS 403; Robert Gage to George Weber, 14 June 1900, LS 416, all in 49th Inf LSB, E 117, RG 94.

29. William H. Beck to AAG, 2D, DNL, 3 June 1900, LS 378, 49th Inf LSB, E 117, RG 94.

30. Carter P. Johnson to AAG, 30 April 1900, Btln LSB, 49th Inf, E 117, RG 94.

31. Robert Gage to AAG, 2D, DNL, 21 May 1900, LS 309, 49th Inf LSB, E 117, RG 94.

32. Carrasco, *A Spaniard*, 80–129; William M. Hawkins to AAG, 2D, DNL, 9 May 1900, LS 44, Co M LSB, 49th Inf, E 117, RG 94; Bowman McCalla to CINC, 7 March 1900; E. K. Moore to CINC, 24 March 1900, both in R 376, M 625.

33. Emilio Aguinaldo to Francisco Macabulos, 27 June 1900, Ex 998, Taylor, *Philippine Insurrection*, 5:105–6; S. B. M. Young to Henry C. Corbin, 26 October 1901, in 3587 ACP 1875 (Luther R. Hare), RG 94; Villa, "Flight and Wanderings," Taylor, *Philippine Insurrection*, 5:46–75; Adj to William H. Hawkins, 14 April 1900, LS 214; William H. Beck to CO, Piat, 10 May 1900, LS 273; Beck to AG, 10 and 11 May 1900, LS 275 and 281; Robert Gage to CO, US Troops in Field, 22 May 1900, LS 315; William H. Beck to AAG, 2D, DNL, 3 June 1900, LS 378, all in 49th Inf LSB, E 117, RG 94.

34. Carter P. Johnson to AAG, 2D, DNL, 29 October 1900, 49th Inf LSB, E 117, RG 94. *RWD* 1901 1:5:103–5.

35. Carter P. Johnson to AAG, 2D, DNL, 18 November 1900, 49th Inf LSB, E 117, RG 94.

36. Carrasco, *A Spaniard,* 117–33; *RWD* 1901 1:5:103–5.

37. Luciano San Miguel to Emilio Aguinaldo, 8 December 1899, Ex 1023, Taylor, *Philippine Insurrection,* 5:147–48. Lewis E. Gleeck, *Nueva Ecija in American Times: Homesteaders, Hacenderos, and Politicos* (Manila: Historical Conservation Society, 1981); John A. Larkin, "Philippine History Reconsidered: A Socioeconomic Perspective," *American Historical Review* 87 (June 1982): 613–24; John A. Larkin, *The Pampangans: Colonial Society in a Philippine Province* (Berkeley: University of California Press, 1972); Rosario M. Cortes, "The Politico-Social Milieu in Pangasinan on the Eve of the Revolution" (paper presented at the International Conference on the Centennial of the 1996 Philippine Revolution, 1996, Manila). The deep antipathy toward the friar orders can be seen in the surveys in Box 20, E 2133, RG 395.

38. Frederick Funston to AG, DNL, 27 October 1900, E 2263, RG 395; Frederick Funston to John J. Crittenden, 1 January 1901, E 2262, RG 395; Benjamin Alvord AAG to CG, 4D, 10 January 1901 E 2270, RG 395; 28 January 1901, 1901 Diary, Brown Papers. On the dispute with Aguinaldo, see Emilio Aguinaldo to Baldomero Aguinaldo, 10 November 1900 and 9 January 1901, Nos. 313 and 386, SD 849, PIR. Alejandrino's autobiography is curiously silent on this affair; see Alejandrino, *Price of Freedom,* 194.

39. Guy H. Preston to Provost Marshal, 14 June 1900, LS 220, 41st Inf LSB, E 117, RG 94; Robert D. Walsh to CO, 1 July 1900, in E. H. Plummer to Arthur MacArthur, 1 July 1900, LS 1689, 35th Inf LSB, E 117, RG 94; Tomas Mascardo to Jose Alejandrino, 1 November 1900, SD 625.1, PIR; Brown, *Ninth Infantry,* 389–90; Albino Dizon to the CG of Central Luzon, August 1900, and Mario del Rosario, [Commission], 21 August 1900, Ex 1121, Taylor, *Philippine Insurrection,* 5:275–77.

40. Pablo Tecson to Isidro Torres, 29 August 1900, SD 545.1, PIR. Pedro Padilla to Casmirio Tinio, 31 January 1900, SD 51.8, PIR.

41. Francisco M[acabulos] y Soliman, "Orders to Detachments," 16 November 1899, Ex 1019, 5:142–43; Pantaleon Garcia, "Instructions for Guerrillas and Flying Columns," 25 November 1899, Ex 1020, 5:143–45; Leonicio Alarilla to Casmirio Tinio, 4 February 1900, Ex 1043, 5:177–78; Urbano Lacuna to Tomas Tagunton, 29 November 1900, Ex 1124, 5:280, all in Taylor, *Philippine Insurrection.*

42. Pantaleon Garcia to Isidro Torres, 10 February 1900, Ex 1044, 5:178–79; Jose Alejandrino, General Order, July 1900, Ex 1074, 5:210–11; Tomas Mascardo to My Dear Soldiers and Dear Compatriots, August 1900, Ex 1082, 5:224–26; Jose Alejandrino, General Order, September 1900, Ex 1088, 5:231–32, all in Taylor, *Philippine Insurrection.* On the Katipunan, see Luciano San Miguel to Emilio Aguinaldo, 8 December 1899, Ex 1023, 5:147–48; [Memorandum], January 1900, Ex 1031, 5:161–62, both in Taylor, *Philippine Insurrection.*

43. Teodoro Sandico, "Organization of the Committees," 15 July 1900, Ex 1078, Taylor, *Philippine Insurrection,* 5:216–19.

44. David R. Sturtevant, *Popular Uprisings in the Philippines, 1840–1940* (Ithaca, N.Y.: Cornell University Press, 1976), 103–9; Larkin, *Pampangans,* 118–28.

45. Pantaleon Garcia to Isidro Torres, 1 February 1900, Ex 1042, Taylor, *Philippine Insurrection,* 5:175–76.

46. Isidro Torres to Bonifacio Morales, 20 September 1900, Ex 1095, Taylor, *Philippine Insurrection,* 5:241–42; Pablo Padilla to Marcelino Garcia, 13 January 1900, SD 498.1, PIR.

47. C. Gonzales to Teodoro Sandico, 3 August 1900, Ex 1083, Taylor, *Philippine Insurrection*, 5:226–27.

48. Senate, *Affairs*, 1002–4. The breakdown by district was 3rd District: 106 assassinated (11 municipal officers) and 131 assaulted (15 municipal officials); 4th District: 7 assassinated and 16 assaulted (4 municipal officials); 5th District: 77 assassinated (including 17 municipal officers) and 17 assaulted (6 municipal officials); 6th District: 14 assassinated (1 municipal officer) and 3 assaulted. Since many assassinations were not reported and many in the assaulted category had been kidnapped and never returned, it is likely the death toll was much higher. For reports from individual towns, see Box 20, E 2133, RG 395.

49. Quote "insurrection" from Loyd Wheaton to AG, DP, 31 May 1901, LS 427, E 2129, RG 395; quote "coercion" from LeRoy, *Americans*, 2:231.

50. Emerson H. Liscum to AG, 16 January 1899, LS 129, E 872, RG 395; E. T. C. Richmond to AG, 5D, DNL, 18 December 1900, LS 323, 41st Inf LSB, E 117, RG 94; E. H. Plummer to AG, DNL, 4 January 1901, LS 445, 35th Inf LSB, E 117, RG 94; Linn, *U.S. Army*, 74–75.

51. E. T. C. Richmond, "History of the 41st Infantry, U.S.V.," 30 June 1901, E 187, RG 94.

52. Ibid.

53. J. Franklin Bell to AG, 2nd Div, 21 January 1900, LS 5, LSB 1, E 2206, RG 395. J. Milton Thompson to AG, 27 June 1900, LS 973, 42nd Inf LSB, E 117, RG 94; E. H. Plummer, "History of the 35th Infantry, U.S.V.," 3 May 1901, E 187, RG 94; Richmond, "History of the 41st Infantry."

54. Nankivell, *History of the Twenty-fifth*, 101–3. Schenck was killed in action three weeks later. On the shooting of the prisoners, see Nick Joaquin, *The Aquinos of Tarlac: An Essay on History as Three Generations*, 3rd ed. (Manila: Solar Publishing, 1986), 65; Brown, *Ninth Infantry*, 341, 348–51; Senate, *Affairs*, 1205–6. A military court sentenced Aquino to life in prison, but Taft's civil administration freed him.

55. Erneste V. Smith to AG, DNL, 21 March 1900, E 2264, RG 395; Frederick Funston to AG, 2nd Div, 28 March 1900, E 2262, RG 395; Joseph E. Wheeler, "Report of Expedition and Engagement," 7 April 1900, LR 4516, E 2133, RG 395.

56. Adj to CO, Malolos, 23 March 1900, LR 76, E 4330, RG 395. AAG to CO, Caloocan, 22 March 1900, LR 76, E 4330, RG 395; Richmond, "History of the 41st Infantry."

57. Clarence S. Nettles to CO, Guagua, 23 March 1900, Co L, 41st Inf LSB, E 117, RG 94.

58. [William E. Wilder] to AG, 4 April 1900, LS 47; William E. Wilder to Benjamin Alvord, 5 April 1900, LS 50, both in E 5805, RG 395; Frederick D. Grant to AG, DNL, 15 April 1900, in *RWD* 1900 1:7:78.

59. Brown, *Ninth Infantry*, 371–75.

60. E. H. Plummer to W. C. Short, 31 May 1900, LS 1300; E. H. Plummer to AG, 5D, DNL, 31 May–5 June 1900, LS 1303–89 passim, all in 35th Inf LSB, E 117, RG 94.

61. Brown, *Ninth Infantry*, 377–90; Linn, *U.S. Army*, 73–74.

62. E. H. Plummer to Arthur MacArthur, 13 July 1900, LS 1842, 35th Inf LSB, E 117, RG 94. *RWD* 1901 1:5:110.

63. E. H. Plummer to AG, 5D DNL, 16 and 30 October 1900, LS 3543 and 3781, 35th Inf LSB, E 117, RG 94.

64. AAG to CO, 25th Inf, 21 November 1900, LS 2571, E 2206, RG 395. E. T. C. Richmond to AG, 5D, DNL, 16 October 1900, LS 3487, 41st Inf LSB, E 117, RG 94; AAG, 5D to CO, 35th Inf, in E. H. Plummer to CO San Idelfonso and San Miguel, 1 November 1900, LS 3804, 35th Inf LSB, E 117, RG 94; [Jacob H. Smith] to AG, DNL, 26 October 1900, LS 1787, LSB 3, E 2206, RG 395.

65. [AAG, 3D] to CO, 12th Inf, 13 November 1900, LS 2319, E 2206, RG 395. Smith to AG, DNL, 14 November 1900, LS 2387, E 2206, RG 395.

66. AAG to COs, 1 October 1900, LS 1063. AAG to CO, Cabaruan, 2 October 1900, LS 1096, both in LSB 2, E 2206, RG 395.

67. J. Milton Thompson to AG, DNL, 14, 19, 23 November–8 December 1900, LS 1758–993 passim, E 2312, RG 395; "History of the 42nd Infantry, U.S.V.," 28 May 1901, E 187, RG 94; *RWD* 1901 1:5:174–76.

68. AAAG to CO, Pasig, 26 December 1900, LS 2221, E 2312, RG 395; J. Milton Thompson to COs, 28 December 1900, LS 2271, E 2312, RG 395.

69. E. H. Plummer to AG, DNL, 5 February 1901, LS 447, 35th Inf LSB, E 117, RG 94.

70. Morton J. Henry to [Adj], 14 December 1900, LR 641, 32 Inf LSB, E 117, RG 94. E. H. Plummer to AG, DNL, 4 and 5 January 1901, LS 445 and 447, 35th Inf LSB, E 117, RG 94.

71. James Clark to AG, DNL, 3 May 1901, LS 24, Co G, 41st Inf LSB, E 117, RG 94; E. H. Plummer to COs, 11 February 1901, LS 714, E. H. Plummer to Walter C. Short, 11 February 1901, LS 745, both in 35th Inf LSB, E 117, RG 94; Louis A. Craig to AG, 19 April 1901, LS 131, 32nd Inf LSB, E 117, RG 94.

72. E. H. Plummer to AG, DNL, 4 January 1901, LS 445, 35th Inf LSB, E 117, RG 94.

73. Benjamin Alvord to CG, 4D, 10 January 1901, E 2270, RG 395; 29 January 1901, 1901 Diary, Brown Papers.

74. MacArthur to AG, 12 February 1901, *CWS* 2:1253; E. H. Plummer to AG, 5D, DNL, 11 February 1901, LS 337, 35th Inf LSB, E 117, RG 94; Frederick Funston to AG, DNL, 25 May 1901, LS 2759, E 2262, RG 395; Richmond, "History of the 41st"; Linn, *U.S. Army*, 75.

75. MacArthur to AG, 28 March 1901, *CWS* 2:1262–63; James D. Taylor to Adj, 24th Inf, 8 April 1901, LR 10677, Box 34, E 2133, RG 395; Frederick Funston to AG, DNL, 12 February 1901, E 2262, RG 395; *RWD* 1901 1:5:122–30; MS, 175–76, Kernan Papers; Funston, *Memories*, 384–426; Sexton, *Soldiers*, 259–66; Welch, *Response*, 36–37, 124–25. For largely negative portrayals of Funston's actions, see Bain, *Sitting in Darkness*; Karnow, *In Our Image*, 182–84; Miller, *Benevolent Assimilation*, 167–70.

76. *RWD* 1901 1:1:32.

77. *CWS* 2:1261–64. The best discussion of the importance of Aguinaldo's capture is in Gates, *Schoolbooks*, 233–36.

13. Southern Luzon

1. *RWD* 1900 1:5:47–48. The 1st and 2nd Districts were combined on 10 April 1901.

2. William H. Taft to Elihu Root, 23 October 1900, Series 21, Taft Papers.

3. Walter S. Schuyler to AG, 1D, 13 May 1900, LS 928, 46th Inf LSB, E 117, RG 94; William A. Birkhimer to AG, DSL, 30 May 1900, E 2353, RG 395; Mariano Trias, "Proclamation," 24 November 1900, Ex 1122, Taylor, *Philippine Insurrection*, 5:186–87.

4. William J. Faulkner to Adj, 9 April 1901, LS 33, Co F, 29th Inf LSB. Edward E. Hardin to AG, 10 May 1900, LS 891, 29th Inf LSB; Edward E. Hardin to AG, 12 October 1900, LS 46, 29th Inf LSB 2, all in E 117, RG 94; Reed, "Burden and Honor," 53–54.

5. On the Marinduque campaign, see M. H. Wilson to CO, Boac, 26 September 1900, LS 162, Co F, 29th Inf LSB, E 117, RG 94; John L. Jordan to My dear Mother, 29 October 1900, Jordan Papers; Devereaux Shields to AG, DSL, 31 October 1900, in *RWD* 1900 1:5:455–57. This account is based on Birtle, "U.S. Army's Pacification."

6. William Howe to AG, 3D, DSL, 29 July 1900, 47th Inf LSB 2, E 117, RG 94; Joseph Dorst to AAG, DSL, 8 September 1900, LR 1129, E 2330, RG 395; Joseph Dorst to AG, Nueva Caceres, 21 October 1900, LS 740, E 3929, RG 395.

7. Vito Belarmino to Mariano Trias, 28 February 1900, Ex 1045, Taylor, *Philippine Insurrection*, 5:180–81. This account of the war in the 3rd District is based on Elias Ataviado, *The Philippine Revolution in the Bicol Region*, vol. 1, *From August 1896 to January 1899*, trans. Juan T. Ataviado (Manila: Encal Press, 1953); Elias Ataviado, *Lucha y Libertad (Conmonitorio de la Revolucion Filipina en las Tierras Albayanas)*, vol. 2, *De febrero de 1899 a abril de 1900* (Manila: Commonwealth Press, 1941); Linn, *U.S. Army*, 95–118; and Owen, "Winding Down the War in Albay," 557–89. In 1902, Albay Province encompassed 1,711 square miles and a population of 228,139; Ambos Camarines had an area of 3,161 and a population of 194,022; Sorsogon had an area of 675 square miles and a population of 98,650, see *Pronouncing Gazetteer*, 155.

8. Engracio Orense to CO, 2nd Zone, 30 January 1900, Ex 1041, Taylor, *Philippine Insurrection*, 5:174–75.

9. Charles G. Starr to AG, 3D, DSL, 17 September 1900, LS 76, E 4380, RG 395. Vito Belarmino to Jose Natera, 17 June 1900, Ex 1068, 5:203–5; Ramon F. Santos to Military Central and Zone Commanders, Circular 21, 24 August 1900, Ex 1086, 5:228–29; Ramon Santos to Esteban Nieves, 4 December 1900, Ex 1129, 5:290–91; Vito Belarmino to Ramon F. Santos, 15 March 1901, Ex 1149, 5:318; all in Taylor, *Philippine Insurrection*.

10. Vito Belarmino to Francisco Lucban, 12 October 1900, Ex 1103, Taylor, *Philippine Insurrection*, 5:251–52.

11. Ranaisco Roldan, "Orden de la Plaza," 27 June 1900, SD 1198.4, PIR; "Ano de 1900: Ejercito Republicano de Filipinas," 19 November 1900, SD 1014.4, PIR; Ramon F. Santos, Circular, 10 February 1901, Ex 1143, Taylor, *Philippine Insurrection*, 5:305–6.

12. William Howe to AAG, 3D, DSL, 19 June 1900, LS 749, 47th Inf LSB 2, E 117, RG 94; Hugh J. Sime to AG, 3D, DSL, 12 May 1900, LR 7, E 2490, RG 395; Ramon F. Santos to Eleuterio Reveta, 14 October 1900, Ex 1104, 5:252–53; Vito Belarmino, "Instructions for Attack on American Troops Quartered in the Town of Ligao, Albay Province," [16 December 1900], Ex 1137, 5:298–99, both in Taylor, *Philippine Insurrection*.

13. Hugh Wise to Adj, 47th Inf, 12 February 1900, LS 57, E 2668, RG 395.

14. Hugh Wise to Adj, 47th Inf, 23 January 1900, LS 19, E 2668, RG 395.

15. Joseph Dorst to AG, Nueva Caceres, 4 July 1900, LS 1064, LSB 3, E 117, RG 94; William L. Bliss to Aunt, 30 April 1900, Harry L. Bliss File, 45th Inf, USV; Claude Harris Questionnaire, 11th Cavalry, USV; Purl A. Mulkey Questionnaire, 45th Inf, USV; Charles E. Brossman Questionnaire, 47th Inf, USV, all in SAWS.

16. Thomas MacGregor to AG, DSL, 12 October 1900, E 2420, RG 395. James M. Bell to AAG, DSL, 8 June 1900, E 2418, RG 395; Hugh Wise to Adj, 47th Inf, 1 July 1900, LS 129, E 3668, RG 395; Esteban Delgado to Ramon Santos, 4 July 1900, SD 1014.3, PIR; Thomas MacGregor to CO, Ligao, 7 October 1900, LR 90, E 4085, RG 395; William Howe to AAG, 3D, DSL, 22 October 1900, LS 1111, 47th Inf LSB 3, E 117, RG 94; James Parker to AAG, 3D, 22 January 1901, LS 197, E 3929, RG 395; E. Villareal to Ramon Santos, 13 February 1901, SD 1014.7, PIR; Antonio Guerrera to My Dear General [Belarmino], 15 March 1901, Ex 1149, Taylor, *Philippine Insurrection,* 5:318–20.

17. Charles G. Starr in George M. Wray to AG, DSL, 1 October 1900, LS A1916, E 2033, RG 395. James Parker to AAG, DP, 18 May 1900, LS 43, E 4577, RG 395; Joseph Dorst to AG, Nueva Caceres, 3 August 1900, LS 195, E 3929, RG 395; George V. H. Moseley to CO, San Jose, 18 February 1901, LS 2000, E 2418, RG 395; Clarence Linninger, *The Best War at the Time* (New York: Robert Speller and Sons), 1964), 189.

18. James Lockett to AG, DSL, 31 July 1900, E 2418, RG 395.

19. James M. Bell to AAG, DSL, 27 May 1900, E 2418, RG 395; "Requisition for Ordinance Stores for 3rd District, DSL," 27 May 1900, E 2420, RG 395; James Lockett to AG, DSL, 31 July 1900, E 2418 RG 395; Joseph Dorst to AG, Nueva Caceres, 15 September 1900, LS 465, E 3929, RG 395; William H. Johnson to AG, 3D, DSL, 25 November 1900, LR 20, E 2420, RG 395; James Parker to AAG, 3D, DSL, 8 November 1900, LS 104, E 5032, RG 395; James Lockett to AG, 3D, DSL, 30 December 1900, LS 117, E 5032, RG 395. Although firearms were requested in June, the shotguns did not arrive until January; see James Parker to COs, 4 January 1901, LS 30, E 3929, RG 395.

20. Edwin T. Cole to AG, 3D, DSL, 24 May 1900, E 2420, RG 395.

21. James M. Bell to AG, DP, 29 May 1900, E 2418, RG 395; James M. Bell to AG, DSL, 3 July 1900, E 2418, RG 395; Charles G. Starr to AG, 3D, DSL, 8 October 1900, LS 114, E 4830, RG 395; Thomas MacGregor to AG, DSL, 31 October 1900, LS 1162, E 2418, RG 395; James M. Bell to MS, 3 March 1901, LS 55, E 2440, RG 395.

22. George M. Wray, Record of Troop D 11th Cavalry, USV for the month of May 1900, LR 37, E 4085, RG 395; Charles G. Starr to William Howe, 18 June 1900, LS 3, E 4082, RG 395; Charles G. Starr to AG, DSL, 4 September and 12 October 1900, LS 56 and 123, E 4830, RG 395. For similar tactics, see William Howe to AG, 20 April 1900, LS 549, 47th Inf LSB, E 117, RG 94.

23. Joseph Dorst to AG, Nueva Caceres, 23 August 1900, LS 344, E 3929, RG 395. HQ, SD Iriga, GO 2, 3 July 1900, E 2420, RG 395; William Howe to AG, DSL, 5 August 1900, LS 870, 47th Inf LSB 2, E 117, RG 94; AG, 3D, DSL to CO, Legaspi, 10 August 1900, E 4833, RG 395; Charles G. Starr to AAG, 3D, DSL, 25 August 1900, LS 42, E 4830, RG 395; Joseph Dorst to AG, Nueva Caceres,

27 August and 9 October 1900, LS 358 and 644, E 3929, RG 395; HQ, 3D to CO, Libmanan, 30 October 1900, E 4077, RG 395; Adj, 45th Inf to COs, 23 November 1900, LS 1082, E 3929, RG 395.

24. William C. Forbush to AG, 3D, DSL, 1 December 1900, LS 19, E 2835, RG 395; George Curry to AAG, 3D, DSL, 26 December 1900, in *RWD* 1:5:396; Sterling Adams to AG, 3D, DSL, 28 January 1901, LS 92, E 4082, RG 395; William C. Forbush to Adj, SD Albay, February 1901, LS 8, E 3835, RG 395; Partido Federal to Military Commander, 2 May 1901, LR 338, E 5376, RG 395.

25. "Autobiography," Box 9, Bullard Papers. Charles J. Crane to AG, 2D, DSL, 14 November 1900, LS 1084, E 4134, RG 395; May, *Battle,* 5–8. This overview of the guerrilla resistance in southwestern Luzon is drawn from May, *Battle;* Linn, *U.S. Army,* 119–61.

26. Samuel S. Sumner to AG, DSL, 28 September 1901, E 2349, RG 395.

27. *RWD* 1901 1:7:389.

28. Matthew F. Steele to Stella, 30 April 1900, Box 7, Matthew F. Steele Papers, MHI.

29. Samuel B. M. Young to Henry C. Corbin, 26 October 1901, 3587 ACP 1875 (Luther R. Hare), RG 94. Frank W. Carpenter to Clarence R. Edwards, 28 September 1900, Box 1, Edwards Papers.

30. Matthew F. Steele to Stella, 26 August 1900, Box 7, Steele Papers. Robert H. Hall to AG, DSL, 16 January 1901, LR 493, E 2408, RG 395; HQ, DSL to CO, Bauan, 11 March 1901, LR 122B, E 3092, RG 395; Taylor, *Philippine Insurrection,* 2:339; Worcester, *Philippines,* 235–36.

31. William H. Johnston to AG, 1D, DSL, 22 May 1900, LS 104, 2nd Btln, 46th Inf LSB, E 117, RG 94. James Lockett to AG, 1D, DSL, 11 May 1900, E 2353, RG 395; Walter S. Schuyler to AG, 1D, 13 May 1900, LS 928, 46th Inf LSB, E 117, RG 94.

32. James Lockett to AG, 1D, DSL, 11 May 1900, E 2353, RG 395. George B. Duncan to AG, 1D, DSL, 5 January and 5 February 1901, E 2353, RG 395; Statement of Cecilio Rosal, 25 January 1901, E 3092, RG 395; C. W. Mason to AG, 1D, DSL, 29 April 1901, E 5668, RG 395; "List of Officers Serving with Insurgent Forces in the Vicinity of Tanauan, in the Province of Batangas," in Clarence S. Nettles to OC, DMI, 7 November 1901, LR 4968, E 2354, RG 395.

33. May, *Battle,* 174. Miguel Malvar, "Guerrilla Warfare. Instructions," 27 October 1900, SD 1132.4, PIR.

34. Charles Crawford to AG, 3SB, 30 January 1902, E 4638, RG 395.

35. Juan Cailles to Vicente Sotomayor, 24 April 1900, Ex 1056, 5:191–92. [Juan Cailles] to Local Chiefs and Commanders, 3 September 1900, Ex 1056, 5:192–93; Julio Herrera to Presidentes of Nagcarlan, et al., 6 May 1900, Ex 1058, 5:194; Julio Infante to Juan Cailles, 18 November 1900, Ex 1118, 5:271–73, all in Taylor, *Philippine Insurrection;* Linn, *U.S. Army,* 133–35; May, *Battle,* 181.

36. Robert W. Leonard to AAG, 26 May 1900, LS 503, 28th Inf LSB, E 117, RG 94. George M. Anderson to AG, 1D, 21 February 1900, LS 442, 38th Inf LSB, E 117, RG 94.

37. 1 January to 28 April 1900, Journal, Schuyler Papers. William H. Johnston to Adj, 6 March 1900, LS 21, 2nd Btln, 46th Inf LSB, E 117, RG 94.

38. Cornelius Gardener, "To the Inhabitants of the Province of Tayabas," February 1900, E 5473, RG 395.

39. Cornelius Gardener to CO, Tayabas, [1901?], E 5477, RG 395. On Tayabas, see Cornelius Gardener to Adj, 21 June 1900, LS 1190, 30th Inf LSB 2, E 117, RG 94; "People of Lucena," in Cornelius Gardener to AG, DSL, 8 February 1901, E 2760, RG 395; Linn, *U.S. Army,* 124–27.

40. Thomas G. Carson to Adj, 11th Cav, 26 July 1900, LS 21, 11th Cav LSB, E 117, RG 94. Benjamin F. Cheatham to AG, 2 March 1900, LS 27, 1st Btln, 37th Inf LSB, E 117, RG 94; Benjamin F. Cheatham to AG, 2D, DSL, 9 May 1900, LS 115, 37th Inf LSB, E 117, RG 94; William C. Brown to AG, 2D, DSL, 9 May 1900, E 2408, RG 395; George M. Anderson to AG, 2D, DSL, 5 June 1900, LS 278, E 2408, RG 395; Charles J. Crane to Presidente, Lipa, 19 July 1900, LS 609, 38th Inf LSB 2, E 117, RG 94; A. L. Parmeter to CO, Lake District, 29 September 1900, SD 1303.3, PIR.

41. Benjamin F. Cheatham to AG, 2D, DSL, 8 August 1900, LS 45, 37th Inf LSB 2, E 117, RG 94. On sickness, see "Report of Chief Surgeon on Sanitary Conditions at San Pablo and San Tomas," 14 May 1900, E 2408, RG 395; William C. Brown to AG, 2D, DSL, 22 May 1900, E 2408, RG 395; Cornelius Gardener to AAG, DSL, 21 June and 28 July 1900, LS 1190 and 1499, 30th Inf LSB 2, E 117, RG 94; E. H. Fitzgerald to CO, 30th Inf, 24 July 1900, E 5486, RG 395; John H. Baker to Adj, 25 July 1900, LS 67, Co F, 46th Inf LSB, E 117, RG 94; Matthew F. Steele to Stella, 9 August 1900, Box 7, Steele Papers.

42. 30 May 1900, Journal, Schuyler Papers.

43. Luther R. Hare to AG, DSL, 6 August 1900, LS 1157, E 2348, RG 395.

44. William E. Birkhimer to AG, 2D, DSL, 15 July 1900, LS 516, 28th Inf LSB, E 117, RG 94.

45. MacArthur to AG, 19 September 1900, CWS 2:1211. Descriptions of the battle appear in Benjamin F. Cheatham to AG, DSL, 17 September 1900, 37th Inf LSB 2, E 117, RG 94; Horace M. Reeves to James C. Bates, 20 September 1900, LR B2436, E 2033, RG 395. For American reactions, see William H. Taft to Elihu Root, 18 September 1900, Series 21, Taft Papers; Hugh A. Drum to My dear John, 23 September 1900, Drum Family Letters File, Box 8, Drum Papers; *ANJ,* 17 and 22 September 1900. For a Filipino perspective, see Faustino Pautua to Miguel Estrada, 21 September 1900, SD 631, PIR.

46. 12 July 1900, Journal, Schuyler Papers.

47. Robert W. Leonard to AAG, 2D, DSL, 6 July 1900, LS 513, 28th Inf LSB, E 117, RG 94; William E. Birkhimer to AG, 2D, DSL, 15 July 1900, LS 516, 28th Inf LSB, E 117, RG 94; Thomas G. Carson to Adj, 11 Cav, 26 July 1900, LS 21, 11th Cav LSB, E 117, RG 94; Benjamin F. Cheatham to AG, DSL, 8 August 1900, LS 452, 37th Inf LSB 2, E 117, RG 94; Linn, *U.S. Army,* 145; May, *Battle,* 151–52. For intelligence files, see E 2117 and E 3118, RG 395.

48. May, *Battle,* 198–205.

49. William E. Birkhimer to CG, 1D, DSL, 18 April 1900, E 2353, RG 395. William E. Birkhimer to AG, 2D, DSL, 15 July 1900, LS 516, 28th Inf LSB, E 117, RG 94; John H. Parker to Theodore Roosevelt, 18 November 1900, R 7, Roosevelt Papers.

50. 31 May 1900, Diary, Brown Papers.

51. Benjamin F. Cheatham to AG, 2D, DSL, 29 May 1900, LS 191, 37th Inf LSB, E 117, RG 94.

52. AAG, DSL to CG, 1D, DSL, 25 July 1900, E 2353, RG 395.

53. See endorsements on Austin H. Brown to Adj, 11 November 1900, E 2353, RG 395. For other accounts of burning, see Miguel Malvar, "Provisions and Instructions Issued by the Superior Commander of Southern Luzon for Observation in this Department," 28 April 1901, 5:329–32; Sixto Reyes to General and Politico-military Commander [Juan Cailles?], 2 June 1900, Ex 1064, 5:200–201, both in Taylor, *Philippine Insurrection;* Benjamin F. Cheatham to AG, 2D, DSL, 29 June 1900, LS 281, 37th Inf LSB 1, E117, RG 94; William E. Birkhimer to AG, 2D, DSL, 18 July 1900, LS 517, 28th Inf LSB, E 117, RG 94; Willard A. Holbrook to Adj, 38th Inf, 23 September 1900, LS 44, E 5052, RG 395.

54. Walter S. Schuyler to AG, 30 May 1901, in *RWD* 1:5:260–62.

55. *RWD* 1901 1:5:241–44; George B. Duncan to AG, 1D, DSL, 5 January 1901, E 2353, RG 395; George B. Duncan to Adj, 4th Inf, 5 February 1901, E 5668, RG 395; Samuel S. Sumner to AG, DSL, 12 March 1901, E 2349, RG 395; Arthur A. Wagner to AG, DNP, 26 January 1902, LR 10, E 3913, RG 395.

56. 22 February 1901, Journal, Schuyler Papers; see also 7 January to 25 February 1901. Schuyler's views are confirmed by a sergeant in his regiment; see Manuscript, George Gelbach Papers, 46th Inf Box, SAWS.

57. Mariano Trias to Military Chief of Mindoro, 29 March 1900, Ex 1052, 5:186–87; Mariano Trias, "Proclamation," 24 November 1900, Ex 1122, 5:276–78; Buenaventura Dimaguila to Mariano Trias, 30 November 1900, Ex 1125, 5:281–88, all in Taylor, *Philippine Insurrection.*

58. Mariano Trias to My Dear Companions, March 1901, Ex 1148, 5:315–18. Mariano Trias to My Dear Comrade, 13 April 1901, Ex 1155, 5:315–18, both in Taylor, *Philippine Insurrection.*

59. MacArthur to AG, 16 March 1901, CWS 2:1259. Gates, *Schoolbooks,* 230–35.

60. William L. Pitcher to AG, 2D, DSL, 3 January 1901, LS 4, E 4727, RG 395.

61. E. T. Jones to AG, 2D, DSL, 27 February 1901, LR 1028, E 2408, RG 395.

62. Manuel Quiogue to Juan Cailles, 31 March 1901, Ex 1152, 5:323. Pedro Caballes to Juan Cailles, March 1901, Ex 1147, 5:314–15; Pedro Caballes to My General [Cailles], 29 March 1901, Ex 1151, 5:322, all in Taylor, *Philippine Insurrection.*

63. May, *Battle,* 212–16; Miguel Malvar, "Copy of a Reply to General Trias," 19 April 1901, Ex 1155, Taylor, *Philippine Insurrection,* 5:328–29.

64. Miguel Malvar, "Provisions and Instructions Issued by the Superior Commander of Southern Luzon for Observation in this Department," 28 April 1901, Ex 1156, 5:329–33. Miguel Malvar to Vicente Lukban, 14 May 1901, Ex 1161, 5:339–40; Miguel Malvar, "General Instructions and Dispositions Issued by these Superior Headquarters Since the 26th of last June to the Present Date," 28 August 1901, Ex 1168, all in Taylor, *Philippine Insurrection;* Miguel Malvar to Juan Cailles, 4 April 191, SD 692.3, PIR; S. R. Gleaves OC, DMI, 1D, DSL, 25 October 1901, E 2353, RG 395; "Abridgment to General Resolutions and Instructions . . . ," 25 June 1901, in Ralph Van Deman, "Appendix H," 5 December 1901, LS 256, E 2635, RG 395; Ralph Van Deman, "Report," 12 December 1901, SD 796.1, PIR.

65. "Proclamation of Lieutenant Colonel Emilio Zurbano, Military Governor of Tayabas, to His Fellow Citizens," 23 April 1901, Ex 1154, Taylor, *Philippine Insurrection,* 5:324–26.

66. Juan Cailles to Countrymen, 15 April 1901, SD 706.2, PIR; AAG to CO, Santa Cruz, 17 April 1901, E 2349, RG 395; *RWD* 1901 1:5:248; *ANJ,* 25 May 1901. For the papers captured at Cailles's headquarters, see SD 716 and 719, PIR.

67. MacArthur to AG, 24 June 1901, *CWS* 2:1288.

68. May, *Battle,* 217–19.

69. HQ, DP, GO 179, 20 July 1901, in Senate, *Affairs,* 128–31.

70. Adna R. Chaffee to Henry C. Corbin, 30 September 1901, Box 1, Corbin Papers. Samuel S. Sumner to AG, DSL, 4, 28, and 29 September 1901, E 2349, RG 395; Senate, *Affairs,* 2854. On Sumner's problems, see May, *Battle,* 224–31.

71. Samuel S. Sumner to AG, DSL, 18 June 1901, E 2349, RG 395. Samuel S. Sumner to AG, DSL, 28 September 1901, E 2349, RG 395.

72. Samuel S. Sumner to AG, DSL, 2 August 1901, E 5101, RG 395.

73. Samuel S. Sumner to AG, DSL, 28 September 1901, E 2349, RG 395. Samuel S. Sumner to William S. McCaskey, 19 July 1901, E 2349, RG 395.

74. Samuel S. Sumner to AG, DSL, 4 September 1901, E 2349, RG 395.

75. E. N. Jones to AG, 1D, DSL, 18 August 1901, LS 15, E 3105, RG 395. HQ, DSL to CO, Calamba, 2 August 1901, LR 331, E 3287, RG 395; Charles H. Hunter to AG, 1D, DSL, 29 August 1901, E 2355, RG 395; Daniel Cornman to AG, 1D, DSL, 6 September 1901, E 2355, RG 395. On revolutionary food-growing programs, see "Provisions and Instructions Issued by the Superior Commander of Southern Luzon for Observation in this Department," 28 April 1901, Ex 1156, 5:329–33; Office of Lt. Col., Zone of Batangas, [Orders], October 1901, Ex 1170, 5:356–57, both in Taylor, *Philippine Insurrection.*

76. Adna R. Chaffee to Henry C. Corbin, 5 November 1901, Corbin Papers.

77. William H. Taft to Elihu Root, 14 October 1901, Box 164, Root Papers.

78. William W. Dougherty to AG, 3rd SB, 1 November 1901, E 2354, RG 395. For a sample of other calls for harsh measures, see William L. Pitcher to AG, 2D, DSL, 3 January 1901, LS 4, E 4727, RG 395; William Hase to AG, Batangas, 23 November 1901, E 5052, RG 395.

79. J. Franklin Bell to J. A. Lockwood, [1900], E 2209, RG 395. Robinson, *Philippines,* 360–61; MacArthur to AG, 3 February 1901, in 3587 ACP 1875 (Luther R. Hare), RG 94; J. Franklin Bell to Emerson Liscum, 22 May 1900, E 2209, RG 395; J. Franklin Bell to AG, 27 May 1900, E 2209, RG 395; J. Franklin Bell to AG, 27 May 1900, E 2209, RG 395; Emma Elnora Sloan to My Dear Sisters, 29 November 1900, Carl Stone Papers, MHS. On Bell's ethnocentrism, see George F. Becker to Henry C. Lodge, 7 December 1900, AGO 354897, RG 94; J. Franklin Bell to Henry C. Corbin, 17 May 1901, Corbin Papers. For a good description of Bell, see May, *Battle,* 244–48.

80. Luke Wright to Elihu Root, 20 July 1902, Box 2, Edwards Papers. Another civilian ordered to investigate troop abuses was also impressed with Bell, see J. W. Jenks to William C. Sanger, 10 July 1902, Box 2, Edwards Papers.

81. May, *Battle,* 252. Bell's belief that the upper class supported the guerrillas was shared by many, see William H. Taft to Elihu Root, 14 July 1900, Series 21, Taft Papers; Henry T. Allen to Adna R. Chaffee, 2 February 1902, Box 7, Allen Papers.

82. M. F. Davis to George V. H. Moseley, 26 December 1901, Box 38, George V. H. Moseley Papers, MDLC. Linn, *U.S. Army,* 157; May, *Battle,* 256.

83. "Report of Operations—Cavinti, Laguna," January 1901, E 3490, RG 395.

84. J. Franklin Bell to CO, San Juan, 21 March 1902, E 5055, RG 395.
85. Cornelius Gardener to CO, Lucban, 9 May 1900, LR 95, E 4163, RG 395.
For references to concentration, either advocated or in practice, see AAG, VMD to
CO, Barotoc Nueva, 13 February 1900, LS 68, February 1900 LSB, E 2465, RG
395; R. W. Leonard to AAG, 1 July 1900, LS 511, 28th Inf LSB, E 117, RG 94;
Edward D. Taussig to My Dear Family, 1 October 1900, Edward D. Taussig Papers; Eusebio San Jose to Gregorio Mascate, 19 December 1900, SD 1198.8, PIR;
E. H. Plummer to AG, DNL, 4 January 1901, LS 445, 35th Inf LSB, E 117, RG 94.
86. J. Franklin Bell to CO, Gunboat *Napindan,* 16 December 1901, E 2349, RG
395; J. Franklin Bell to All Station Commanders, 16 January 1902, E 3287, RG 395;
John W. Furlong to George W. Kirkpatrick, 27 January 1902, LS 7, E 5096, RG 395.
87. Henry C. Hale to Adj, Tanauan, 15 January 1902, Henry Clay Hale Papers,
USMA. [Charles Crawford] to AG, 3rd SB, 30 January 1902, E 4638, RG 395;
Charles Miller to Presidente, Lucban, 9 February 1902, LS 39, LSB 4, E 4162, RG
395; J. Franklin Bell to William E. Dougherty 25 February 1902, E 2354, RG 395.
88. Arthur L. Wagner to Loyd Wheaton, 22 March 1901, LS 7788, E 2635, RG
395. For reports on other towns, see Patrick A. Connoly to AG, 3S, 20 December
1901, LS 253, E 5007, RG 395; "Report of Operations—Calauan" and "Report of
Operations—Bay," January 1901, in E 3121, RG 395. On conditions in the zones,
see May, *Battle,* 262–67.
89. 11 December 1901, Diary, Rhodes Papers.
90. Adna R. Chaffee to Henry C. Corbin, 10 January 1902, Corbin Papers.
91. Jacob G. Schurman, "The Philippines Again," *Independent* 54 (8 May 1902):
1104–7.
92. "One Soldier's Journey," 1:77, Moseley Papers.
93. Miguel Malvar, "The Reason for My Change in Attitude," 15 April 1902, Ex
1172, Taylor, *Philippine Insurrection,* 5:358–59. Milton F. Davis to AG, DNP,
25 February 1902, LS 4811, E 2635, RG 395; George C. Barnhardt, "Arms Secured
at Paete, Sinaloan, and Neighboring Towns Between August 1st, 1901 and February 28th, 1902," [March 1902], E 2349, RG 395; Adna R. Chaffee to Henry C.
Corbin, 17 March 1902, Corbin Papers; Oscar J. Brown to Theodore Wint, 4 April
1902, LS 241, E 4134, RG 395.
94. "Testimony of Eustacio Maloles," AGO 421607, RG 94, see also testimony
of Miguel Malvar, Noberto Mayo, Bernardo Marques, Ladislao Magcansay, and
Genero Brillante.

14. Samar

1. An earlier version of this chapter appeared in two articles: "We Will Go Heavily
Armed: The Marines' Small War on Samar, 1901–1902," in *New Interpretations in
Naval History: Selected Papers from the Ninth Naval History Symposium,* ed. William R. Roberts and Jack Sweetman (Annapolis, Md.: Naval Institute Press, 1991),
273–92; and "The Struggle for Samar," in *Crucible of Empire: The Spanish-American War and Its Aftermath,* ed. James C. Bradford (Annapolis, Md.: Naval Institute
Press, 1993), 158–82. I am grateful to the U.S. Naval Institute Press for its kind
permission to reprint this material.

2. Barry to Hughes, 6 and 13 March 1901, Box 28, E 2483, RG 395.

3. Robert P. Hughes to AG, 14 May 1901, Box 28, E 2483, RG 395. Robert P. Hughes to Robert Noble, 13 June 1901, E 2552, RG 395.

4. Mark L. Hersey to AG, DV, 7 July 1901, Box 49, E 2483, RG 395. Robert P. Hughes to Robert H. Noble, 13 June 1901, E 2552, RG 395; A. B. Buffington to Leslie F. Cornish, 14 June 1901, E 3447, RG 395; Brown, *Ninth Infantry,* 555–65. Hughes believed southern Samar was peaceful; see Senate, *Affairs,* 570, also 553–54.

5. Robert P. Hughes to AG, 3 June 1901, Box 1, E 2550, RG 395; "Report of Operations for the Garrison of Laguan, Samar, P.I., for the month of June 1901," Box 34, E 2483, RG 395.

6. Charles J. Crane to Guy Carleton, 27 May 1901, E 2550, RG 395.

7. Robert P. Hughes to CO, Laguan, 8 July 1901, E 2550, RG 395. The term "colonies" appears in Arthur L. Conger to CO, Borongan, 23 July 1901, E 2550, RG 395. Robert P. Hughes to AG, 1 June 1901, E 2552, RG 395; Robert Noble to CO, Guiuan, 31 August 1901, LR 257, E 3817, RG 395; Testimony of Waldo E. Ayer, GCM 30739 (Jacob H. Smith), RG 153; Senate, *Affairs,* 554–69.

8. Robert P. Hughes to Francis E. Lacey, 24 July 1901, E 2550, RG 395. John J. O'Connell to AG, July 1901, LS 75, E 3815, RG 395; Robert H. Noble to "My dear O'Connell," 5 August 1901, LR 235, E 3818, RG 395; John H. O'Connell to CO, Tacloban, 22 July 1901, E 2574, RG 395; Robert H. Noble to all COs, 10 September 1901, LR 310, E 2503, RG 395.

9. "Statement of Sergeant C. Denning, Company H, 1st Infantry, June 30, 1901," in John J. O'Connell to CG, 30 June 1901, Box 36, E 2483, RG 395. For other accounts, see "Statement of Private Luther Jessup" in same letter; Surgeon, Co H, 1st Inf to Anon., 25 June 1901, LR 181, E 3817, RG 395.

10. Robert Noble to AG, 10 September 1901, E 2551, RG 395.

11. Robert H. Noble to Charles J. Crane, 20 June 1901, E 2550, RG 395. Robert P. Hughes to J. E. Downes, 28 September 1901, Box 36, E 2483, RG 395.

12. Robert P. Hughes to AG, DP, 11 September 1901, in *RWD* 1902 1:9:623. Robert P. Hughes to AG, 3 June 1901, E 2550, RG 395; J. R. Selfridge to Chief of the Bureau of Navigation, 9 October 1901, E 390, RG 45.

13. The number of American casualties at Balangiga is somewhat controversial, in part because some accounts do not include the two medical personnel or the missing. The most complete listing concluded that thirty-six Americans were killed in the massacre, eight died as a result of wounds, twenty-two were wounded, and four missing and presumed dead; see "Return of Casualties: Company C, 9th U.S. Infantry, Action at Balangiga, Samar, 28 September 1901," E 2076, RG 395; James O. Taylor, *The Massacre of Balangiga* (Joplin, Mo.: n.p., 1931), 66–67. For accounts of the "Balangiga Massacre," see Edwin V. Bookmiller to AG, DV, 1 October 1901, in *RWD* 1902 1:9:625–27; Robert P. Hughes to AG, 30 November 1901, LS 7825, Box 39, E 2483, RG 395; Daza y Salazar "Some Documents," 165–87; Brown, *Ninth Infantry,* 578–96; Edward C. Bumpus, *In Memoriam* (Norwood, Mass.: n.p., 1902); Schott, *Ordeal of Samar,* 35–55; Elam L. Stewart, "The Massacre of Balangiga," *Infantry Journal* 30 (April 1927): 407–14.

14. "The Bells of Balangiga Have a Different Ring in Manila, Cheyenne," *Wall Street Journal,* 19 November 1997; "U.S. and Philippines Split over Bells of Balangiga,"

International Herald Tribune, 2 December 1997; "Battle's Heavy Toll Resounds in Conflict over Church Bells," Washington Post, 8 April 1998.

15. Robert P. Hughes to AG, DP, 30 November 1901, LR 7825, Box 39, E 2493, RG 395. Senate, Affairs, 569–70; Adna R. Chaffee to Henry C. Corbin, 25 October 1901, Corbin Papers.

16. P[edro] Abayan to General in Chief of this Province of Samar, 30 May 1901, Ex 1350, Taylor, Philippine Insurrection, 5:689. Balangiga was occupied as part of Hughes's efforts to stop smuggling from Leyte; see Senate, Affairs, 554.

17. Schott, Ordeal, 55. This story is repeated in Karnow, In Our Image, 191; Miller, Benevolent Assimilation, 204. Where the figure of twenty executed came from is something of a mystery, since the apparent source, Arnold Irish, wrote only that "we shot all the natives in the town except those whom we took prisoners and helped bury our dead"; see Taylor, Massacre, 17. After returning from the Philippines, Irish suffered nightmares and "a nervous breakdown and brain fever combined" (ibid., 18). His account of the summary execution is contradicted not only by Bookmiller's own report but also by three other survivors' accounts; see Taylor, Massacre, 27, 32, 37. Two other eyewitnesses make no mention of any execution; see "Notes made by Ensign Hellweg on Villalobos on massacre at Balangiga," October 1901, Area File 10, RG 45; R. M. Blackford to AG, 1D, DV, 17 October 1901, LR 164, E 2571, RG 395.

18. Daza, "Some Documents," 174–77. Gates, Schoolbooks, 248–49; Holt, "Resistance on Samar," 9. The report of 250 dead appears in Taylor, Massacre, 37; Karnow, In Our Image, 191; Schott, Ordeal, 55. Interestingly, Bookmiller, the first person on the scene, gave a relatively accurate estimation of fifty Filipino casualties; see Edwin V. Bookmiller to AG, DV, 1 October 1901, in RWD 1902 1:9: 625–27.

19. William H. Taft to Elihu Root, 14 October 1900, Box 164, Root Papers.

20. Quote "make a desert" from Robert P. Hughes to Issac DeRussy, 29 September 1901, E 2551, RG 395. Quote "with the exception" from R. M. Blackford to AG, 8 October 1901, LS 164, E 2571, RG 395.

21. On 1 November 1901 there were elements of the 1st, 7th, 9th, 11th, 12th, and 26th Infantry regiments and seven companies of Philippine Scouts assigned to the 6th Separate Brigade; see HQ, DV, GO 66, 1 November 1901, E 2505, RG 395.

22. [Jacob H. Smith] to AG, DNL, 30 October 1900, LSB 3, E 2206, RG 395; AAG to COs, 1 October 1900, LS 1063, LSB 2, E 2206, RG 395; Dean C. Worcester to Mrs. Henry W. Lawton, 14 December 1900, Box 2, Lawton Papers; William H. Taft to Elihu Root, 23 February 1901, in Jacob Hurd Smith Personnel File, R 371, M 1064; Tel.: MacArthur to AG, 3 February 1901, 3587 ACP 1875 (Luther R. Hare), RG 94; David L. Fritz, "Before the 'Howling Wilderness': The Military Career of Jacob Hurd Smith, 1862–1902," Military Affairs 43 (December 1979): 186–90. Smith was a popular commander whom the troops called "Our Jakey"; see "Wearing the Khaki," 44, Cutter Papers.

23. H. O. Heistand to Adna R. Chaffee, 26 December 1902, E 2065, RG 395. The phrase "howling wilderness" is usually ascribed to Smith, but Heistand suggests Chaffee was its author. For Chaffee's orders to Smith, see Adna R. Chaffee to Henry C. Corbin, 5 November 1901, Box 1, Corbin Papers; RWD 1902 1:9:188; Blount, American Occupation, 378–79.

24. Robert P. Hughes to Jacob H. Smith, 15 October 1901, Box 49, E 2483, RG 395. On Hughes's unhappiness, see Adna R. Chaffee to Henry C. Corbin, 28 November and 9 December 1901, Box 1, Corbin Papers. For examples of Hughes's interference, see Hughes to Hall, 19 and 22 October 1901, E 2551, RG 395; Hughes to Smith, 11 October 1901, T 3, E 3451, RG 395; Hughes to Smith, 19 October 1901, E 2521, RG 395; Robert P. Hughes to Adna R. Chaffee, 28 November 1901, Box 1, Corbin Papers.

25. HQ in the Field, 1D, DV, FO 1, 21 October 1901, *RWD* 1902 1:9:206. Complete texts of most of Smith's field orders can be found in *RWD* 1902 1:9:206–15.

26. HQ, 6SB, Circular No. 7, 27 December 1901, in *RWD* 1902 1:9:211. A. B. Buffington to CO, Calbiga, 10 October 1901, LS 183, E 3447, RG 395; George H. Shields to COs on Gandara River, 1 November 1901, LS 5, E 2496, RG 395.

27. William Swift to CINC, 8 January 1902, E 391, RG 45. Edwin F. Glenn to J. T. Helm, 18 October 1901, E 390, RG 45; Campbell King to AG, 6SB, 12 November 1901, LS 122, E 2815, RG 395; Dana T. Merrill to AG, 6SB, 14 November 1901, E 2574, RG 395; W. R. Shoemaker to CINC, 30 November 1901, E 390, RG 45; J. K. Cogswell to Jacob H. Smith, 9 January 1902, LR 169, E 2571, RG 395; Williams to AG, 6SB, 18 February 1902, LS 21, E 2573, RG 395; Hugh D. Wise to George Montgomery, 26 February 1902, LR 2663; Lt. Walter G. Penfield to Chief Engineering Officer, 30 November 1901, LR 885, E 2571, RG 395; Testimony of John H. A. Day, GCM 10196 (John H. A. Day), RG 153; J. M. Helm to William Swift, 6 January 1902, LR 43, E 2571, RG 395; *Manila Times*, 31 January 1902.

28. Testimony of Capt. A. P. Buffington, GCM 30739.

29. William Swift to CINC, 8 January 1902, E 391, RG 395. J. M. Helm to William Swift, 6 January 1902, LR 43, E 2571, RG 395; HQ, 6SB, SO 12 and 21, 16 and 26 November 1902, E 2576, RG 395; HQ, 6SB to CO, Guiuan, 22 November 1901, LR 300, E 2571, RG 395.

30. Frederick Rodgers to CINC, 14 January 1902, E 391, RG 45.

31. Harry H. Tebbetts to Adj, Mao, 21 September 1901, E 2483, RG 395. George H. Shields to CO, Calbayog, 17 October 1901, LS 18, E 2595, RG 395; Charles Robe to Waldo E. Ayer, 21 November 1901, E 3454, RG 395; Waldo E. Ayer to Charles Robe, 21 and 22 November 1901, E 2573, RG 395; Campbell King to AG, 6SB, 19 November and 3 December 1901, LS 128 and 137, E 3815, RG 395; Frank deL. Carrington to CO, USS *Frolic*, 18 December 1901, LS 250, E 3447, RG 395; James H. Grant to Waldo E. Ayer, 2 January 1902, LR 31, E 2571, RG 395.

32. Jacob H. Smith, "Campaign in Samar and Leyte," *Manila Critic*, 1 February 1902, Philippine Island Miscellany 1900–1901, Corbin Papers. Jacob H. Smith to AG, DP, 29 October 1901, in *RWD* 1902 1:9:222–23.

33. Henry C. Corbin to CG, DP, 24 March 1902; Edwin F. Glenn to J. P. Sanger, May 1902; Jacob H. Smith to J. P. Sanger, 31 May 1902, all in AGO 425323, RG 94; James H. Grant to Jacob H. Smith, 30 November 1900, LR 458, E 2571, RG 395.

34. Henry T. Allen to Arthur Murray, 1 February 1902; Henry T. Allen to William H. Taft, 16 January and 7 February 1902, all in Box 7, Allen Papers.

35. George Davis to SecWar, 27 June 1902, GCM 30313 (Littleton W. T. Waller), RG 153.

36. "Report of Maj. Littleton W. T. Waller," [1902], Littleton W. T. Waller Papers, U.S. Marine Corps Historical Center, 8–10 [hereafter Waller Report]. Waller's

defenders have perpetuated the confusion over his authority by claiming he was in charge of all of southern Samar or even the entire island; see Paul Melshen, "He Served on Samar," *U.S. Naval Institute Proceedings* 105 (November 1979): 45; Karnow, *In Our Image,* 191.

37. GCM 30313; GCM 30739; Waller to Smith, 31 October 1901, Waller Report, 10–12; Porter to Waller, 2 November 1901, Waller Report, 15–16; Waller to Anon., 10 November 1900, Waller Report, 21. On the dispute over the origins of the phrase "howling wilderness," see note 23. It should be noted that no copy of Smith's "howling wilderness" order was ever found.

38. Waller Report, 23–31; Waller to AG, 6 November 1901, LR 129, E 2571, RG 395.

39. Waller Report, 26, 43–48; Waller to Rodgers, 17 December 1901, Area File 10, RG 45.

40. Waller to Smith, 19 November 1901, RG 395, 3451, Box 1. For the confusion over Waller's mission, see Waller to Smith, 31 October 1901, and Judge Advocate's Summary, GCM 30313; Waller Report, 42; Smith to Chief Signal Officer, 2 November 1901, E 3451, RG 395; Schott, *Ordeal,* 104–6.

41. Waller to AG, 6SB, 25 January 1901, Waller Report, 49. Brown, *Ninth Infantry,* 561.

42. Waller Report, 58; William Swift to Smith, 20 December 1901, E 2574, RG 395; Kenneth P. Williams to CO, Lanang, 19 January 1902, in *RWD* 1902 1 9:446; Waller Report, 60–68.

43. Waller to AG, 6SB, 25 January 1902, in Waller Report, 58.

44. Testimony of John H. A. Day, RG 153, GCM 10196. For Waller's incapacity for command, see Testimony of Dr. George A. Ling. The identity of the victim was unknown at the time of the killing, but he was later alleged to be an *insurrecto* leader named Captain Victor.

45. Testimony of George Davis, GCM 30313. Despite voluminous correspondence and records, the events of 19–20 January 1902 are still unclear, and the evidence is inconclusive as to how many Filipinos were executed on 20 January. The preceding is based on the correspondence in the Waller Reports and GCMs 30313 and 10196.

46. Waller Report, 76–77.

47. HQ, DP, GO 93, 7 May, 1902, E 2070, RG 395.

48. Allan R. Millett, *Semper Fidelis: The History of the U.S. Marine Corps* (New York: Free Press, 1980), 154; Gates, *Schoolbooks,* 256; Welch, *Response,* 138–41.

49. GO 80, 16 July 1902, F 3490-27, RG 350.

50. Miller, *Benevolent Assimilation,* 227; Karnow, *In Our Image,* 193.

51. George W. Davis, 16 February 1903, in GCM 34401 (Edwin F. Glenn), RG 153. Henry C. Corbin to CG, DP, 24 March 1902, AGO 425353. RG 94; Nelson Miles to SecWar, 19 February 1903, AGO 389439, RG 94; Welch, *Response,* 138–41; Schumacher, *Revolutionary Clergy,* 144–46.

52. HQ of the Army, GO 80, 16 July 1902, F 3490-27, RG 395. For evidence that many soldiers refused to sanction atrocities, see William M. Swaine testimony, GCM 34401; Elihu Root to Theodore Roosevelt, 12 June 1902, GCM 30739; "Investigation regarding the character of the recent War on the Island of Samar, P.I., conducted by Colonel Francis Moore, 11th U.S. Cavalry, (Special Investigator) in obedience to instructions contained in letter of Adjutant General, Division of the Philippines, dated June 20th 1902," AGO 411745, RG 94.

53. W. R. Shoemaker to CINC, 30 November 1901, E 390, RG 45.

54. Mark L. Hersey to AG, 6SB, 1 February 1902, LS 27, E 2853, RG 395. J. K. Cogswell to Jacob H. Smith, 9 January 1902, LR 169, Box 4, E 2571, RG 395; Edgar A. Macklin to AG, 6SB, 13 January 1902, E 2399, RG 395.

55. Luke E. Wright to William H. Taft, 13 January 1902, Series 3, R 34, Taft Papers. On the Smith-Leyte controversy, see correspondence in AGO 425323, RG 94; Joseph H. Grant to Jacob H. Smith, 14 November 1902, LR 202, E 2571, RG 395; Henry T. Allen to Arthur Murray, 1 February 1902, Box 7, Allen Papers; Dean Worcester to William H. Taft, 5 April 1902, Box 164, Root Papers; *RWD* 1901 1:9:221–24.

56. Adna R. Chaffee to Henry C. Corbin, 17 March 1902, Corbin Papers; *RWD* 1902 1:9:216–25; James H. Grant to Waldo E. Ayer, 2 January 1902, LR 31, Box 3, E 2571, RG 395; Adna R. Chaffee to Theodore Roosevelt, 25 February 1902, Series 1, R 25, Roosevelt Papers.

57. *RWD* 1902 1:9:416–74; Harry H. Tebbetts to Adj, 23 January 1902, LS 1, E 3378, RG 395; N. V. Ellis to AG, 6SB, 27 February 1902, LS 163, E 3815, RG 395; L. W. Jordan to AG, Laguan, 22 March 1902, E 2574, RG 395; J. H. Comfort to CINC, 27 March 1902, E 391, RG 45; Eugene F. Ganley, "Mountain Chase," *Military Affairs* 24 (February 1961): 203–10.

58. Edwin F. Glenn to Matthew F. Steele, 10 February 1903, Box 17, Steele Papers. Glenn's trial transcript offers graphic testimony on the savagery of the fighting on Samar; see GCM 34401; *Manila Times,* 7 January 1903.

15. Conclusion

1. Rudyard Kipling, "The White Man's Burden," *McClure's Magazine* 12 (February 1899).

2. Storey and Lichauco, *Conquest of the Philippines;* Wolff, *Little Brown Brother;* Schirmer, *Republic or Empire? American Resistance to the Philippine War* (Cambridge, Mass.: Schenkman, 1972); Miller, *Benevolent Assimilation;* Mark D. Van Ells, "Assuming the White Man's Burden: The Seizure of the Philippines," *Philippine Studies* 43 (1994): 607–22. For works that blame the savagery of the war on the Filipino opposition, see Charles B. Elliott, *The Philippines to the End of the Military Regime* (Indianapolis: Bobbs-Merrill, 1917); LeRoy, *Americans;* Forbes, *Philippine Islands.*

3. James W. Davidson, William E. Gienapp, Christine L. Heyerman, Mark H. Lytle, and Michael Stoff, *Nation of Nations* (New York: McGraw-Hill, 1996), 2:588. On the absence of revisionism in textbook treatments, see John M. Gates, "Two American Wars in Asia: Successful Colonial Warfare in the Philippines and Cold War Failure in Vietnam" (paper presented at the Conference on the American Military Experience in Asia, 1898–1998, 24–25 October 1998, Madison, Wisconsin).

4. May, *Past Recovered,* 157.

5. Ibid., 156, 159.

6. Gates, *Schoolbooks.*

7. Birtle, "U.S. Army's Pacification," 282. Birtle explores the relationship between civic action and repression thoroughly in his *U.S. Army,* 108–39.

8. May, *Past Recovered,* 152. Manpower statistics from, *RWD* 1899 1:1:5–6; 1:4:114, 141–42; 1900 1:2:20, 30; 1:4:210; 1901 1:2:63; F 12184, RG 153; AG to

William R. Green, 6 March 1922, and Statistics from Principal Wars and other belligerent incidents, Philippine Insurrection File, No. 2159, Legislative and Policy Precedent Files, 1943–1975, RG 407. On the differences between organizational, effective, and firing-line manpower, see Adj to COs, 17 January 1900, LS 9, 36th Inf LSB, E 117, RG 94. On the effects of climate and disease on manpower, see Johnathan Thompson to AG, 1D, DNL, 27 April and 28 1900, LS 521 and 528, 42 Inf LSB, E 117, RG 94. Beck to AAG, Aparri, 6 June 1900, LS 402, 49th Inf LSB, E 117, RG 94; Cornelius Gardener to CO, Tiaon, 14 August 1900, LS 1689, 30th Inf LSB, E 117, RG 94; William F. de Niedman to Chief Surgeon, 27 September 1900, LS 157, E 2330, RG 395; Grove to AG, DNL, 7 October 1900, LS 672, 36th Inf LSB, E 117, RG 94; Brown, *Ninth Infantry,* 340.

    9. Samuel B. M. Young to AG, 15 October 1900, Box 6, Young Papers; Parker, *Old Army,* 369–71; George T. Fry, "Our Land Forces for National Defense," *Infantry Journal* 11 (January–February 1915): 469.

    10. Hugh Drum, "The Dato of the Malanos," Drum Papers.

    11. Birtle, *U.S. Army,* 126–35.

    12. Stuart C. Miller, "Our Mylai of 1900," *Trans-Action* 7 (September 1970): 19–26. The "Philippines as Vietnam" argument has been discredited by American and Philippine scholars; see John M. Gates, "The Philippines and Vietnam: Another False Analogy," *Asian Studies* 10 (1972): 64–76; May, *Past Recovered,* 150–70; Welch, *Response,* xiv–xv, 153.

BIBLIOGRAPHY

Historical writing is often summarized as explaining what happened and why. Normally the first authors establish the basic chronology and later ones offer new interpretations of why those events occurred. But in the case of the Philippine-American conflict, the "what happened" was quickly subordinated to the "why." Imperialist works such as Charles B. Elliott's *The Philippines to the End of the Military Regime* (1917), W. Cameron Forbes's *The Philippine Islands* (1928), and James A. LeRoy's *The Americans in the Philippines* (1915) portrayed the Americans as benevolent altruists, quelling Aguinaldo's tyranny, suppressing terrorism, and aiding the Filipino people. Anti-imperialist books such as Albert G. Robinson's *The Philippines: The War and the People* (1901) and Moorfield Storey's *The Conquest of the Philippines* (1926) described the Americans as brutal conquerors, ruthlessly crushing a legitimate independence movement. Concerned with attacking or defending contemporary U.S. politics and culture, those writers consulted only the most accessible primary materials and often accepted lurid anecdotes without question. They stereotyped the Filipinos either as primitives desperate for American tutelage or as heroic patriots opposing imperialism. Thanks in part to New Left critiques of American imperialism and an almost perverse insistence on treating the Philippines as an early Vietnam, subsequent accounts have been, if anything, even more partisan. Leon Wolff's *Little Brown Brother* (1961) and Stanley Karnow's *In Our Image: America's Empire in the Philippines* (1989) are both entertaining but unreliable. Even more factually inaccurate is Stuart C. Miller's *"Benevolent Assimilation": The American Conquest of the Philippines, 1899–1903* (1982).

The works of participants are of somewhat limited use. On the Filipino side Emilio Aguinaldo's *A Second Look at America* (1957) and *My Memoirs* (1967), Jose Alejandrino's *The Price of Freedom* (1949), and Apolinario Mabini's memoirs, reprinted as *The Philippine Revolution* (1969), are all hampered by their partisanship and their unwillingness to discuss the war in any detail. Somewhat more useful are the accounts of lower-level personnel, such as Telesforo Carrasco's *A Spaniard in Aguinaldo's Army* (1986) and Juan Villamor's *Inedita Cronica de la Guerra Americano-Filipina en el Norte de Luzon, 1899–1901* (1924). On the American side there are Frederick Funston's *Memories of Two Wars* (1912); Clarence Linninger's *The Best War at the Time* (1964); Joseph I. Markey's *From Iowa to the Philippines* (1900); and James Parker's *The Old Army* (1929). A number of veterans' letters and diaries have been printed in the journals of various state historical associations.

The U.S. Navy has largely ignored its role in the Philippines. William R. Braisted's *The U.S. Navy in the Pacific, 1897–1906* (1958) remains the best overview. Ronald Spector's *Admiral of the New Empire: The Life and Career of George Dewey* (1974) is very good. Frederick Sawyer's *Sons of Gunboats* (1946) is a colorful account of operations by a participant.

On the Philippine side, Teodoro M. Kalaw's *The Philippine Revolution* (1925), Teodoro Agoncillo's *Malolos* (1960), and O. D. Corpuz's *The Roots of the Filipino Nation* (1989) discuss the war in the context of creating a Filipino national identity. Most of the treatments of revolutionary leaders tend to be semihagiographies such as Vicencio R. Jose's *The Rise and Fall of Antonio Luna* (1991); Demy P. Sonza's *Visayan Fighters for Freedom* (1962); and Alfred B. Saulo's *The Truth About Aguinaldo and Other Heroes* (1987). The most interesting scholarship has taken a regional approach. The work of Glenn A. May, and especially his excellent *Battle for Batangas: A Philippine Province at War* (1991), is a marvelous study of the war from both the American and the Filipino sides. Also important are Caridad Aldecoa-Rodrigues's *Negros Oriental and the Philippine Revolution* (1983); John A. Larkin's *The Pampangans* (1972); Orlino A. Ochosa's *The Tinio Brigade: Anti-American Resistance in the Ilocos Provinces, 1899–1901* (1989); John Schumacher's *Revolutionary Clergy* (1981); and William Henry Scott's *Ilocano Responses to American Aggression, 1900–1901* (1986). Ken De Bevoise's *Agents of Apocalypse* (1995) uses innovative methods to explore the epidemiological catastrophe that took place in the archipelago. Essential to understanding both the war and Philippine historiography is Glenn May's *A Past Recovered* (1987).

Far more than Korea, the Philippine conflict is America's "forgotten war." The army's "official" history, John R. M. Taylor's *The Philippine Insurrection Against the United States,* was suppressed by the government but reprinted in 1971 in the Philippines. Taylor's work suffers from its author's topical rather than narrative approach, but it is invaluable as a source of documentation on the Filipino side. Two of the first, and best, accounts of military operations were written by journalists—Karl Irving Faust's *Campaigning in the Philippines* (1899) and a collection edited by Marion Wilcox as *Harpers' History of the War in the Philippines* (1900). Since then, there have been only two operational studies—William T. Sexton's *Soldiers in the Sun* (1939) and Uldarico Baclagon's *Philippine Campaigns* (1952)—both of which focus on conventional operations and gloss over the guerrilla war. Popular accounts such as Joseph Schott's *The Ordeal of Samar* (1964) and Russell Roth's *Muddy Glory* (1981) are limited by their authors' reluctance to differentiate between colorful anecdotes and actual events. Some of the best works are biographies such as Edward M. Coffman's *The Hilt of the Sword: The Career of Peyton C. March* (1966); Thomas W. Crouch's *A Leader of Volunteers: Frederick Funston and the 20th Kansas in the Philippines, 1898–1899* (1984); Allan R. Millett's *The General: Robert L. Bullard and Officership in the United States Army, 1881–1925* (1975); and Heath Twichell's *Allen: The Biography of an Army Officer, 1859–1930* (1974). Unfortunately, the only treatment of a senior American officer, Kenneth Ray Young's *The General's General: The Life and Times of Arthur MacArthur* (1994), fails to offer a balanced treatment of its subject. Essential for understanding the dispatch of the Philippine expedition and the First Battle of Manila are Graham Cosmas's *An Army for Empire: The United States Army and the Spanish-American War* (1971) and David F. Trask's *The War with Spain in 1898* (1981).

The exploits of individual regiments have garnered a sizable amount of space. Of particular use to me were Elkanah Babcock's *A War History of the Sixth U.S. Infantry* (1903); Fred R. Brown, *History of the Ninth U.S. Infantry, 1799–1909* (1909); John Bowe, *With the Thirteenth Minnesota* (1905); Jerry Cooper's *Citizens* as *Soldiers* (1986); A. B. Feur's *Combat Diary: Episodes from the History of the Twenty-second Regiment* (1991); and John H. Nankivell's *History of the Twenty-fifth Regiment United States Infantry, 1869–1926* (1927). The experience of African-American troops is covered in Willard B. Gatewood's *Smoked Yankees and the Struggle for Empire* (1971). John M. Gates's influential *Schoolbooks and Krags* (1973) is an excellent overview of the evolution of U.S. pacification policy and the difficulty of balancing repression and conciliation. Brian M. Linn's *The U.S. Army and Counterinsurgency in the Philippine War* (1979) studies the dynamic of guerrilla war in four districts of Luzon. Andrew Birtle's *U.S. Army Counterinsurgency and Contingency Operations Doctrine, 1860–1941* (1998) is an excellent overview.

Much of the best work on the Philippines is still in dissertation form. For my purposes, of special value was John Scott Reed, "Burden and Honor: The United States Volunteers in the Southern Philippines, 1899–1901" (University of Southern California, 1994). Also very useful were Stephen D. Coats, "Gathering at the Golden Gate: The U.S. Army and San Francisco, 1898" (University of Kansas, 1998); Peter Gowing, "Mandate in Moroland: The American Government of Muslim Filipinos, 1899–1920" (Syracuse University, 1968); Geoffrey R. Hunt, "The First Colorado Regiment in the Philippine Wars" (University of Colorado, 1997); Vernon L. Williams, "The U.S. Navy in the Philippine Insurrection and Subsequent Native Unrest, 1898–1906" (Texas A&M University, 1985); and James R. Woolard, "The Philippine Scouts: The Development of America's Colonial Army" (The Ohio State University, 1975).

Scholars who wish to pursue the war in detail will soon find themselves sifting through primary documents. The *Annual Report of the War Department* from 1899 to 1902 includes not only the reports of the major commanders but also those of dozens of lower-level personnel. The *Annual Report of the Navy Department* during these years is shorter and less helpful. At the National Archives there are thousands of military reports in the Records of the United States Army Overseas Operations and Commands (RG 395) and the army's correspondence—including that of the State and U.S. Volunteer regiments—in Records of the Adjutant General's Office (RG 94). The Spanish-American War Survey at the U.S. Army Military History Institute at Carlisle Barracks gives scholars access to hundreds of veterans' letters, diaries, and personal papers. It is the first place anyone should go for a view of the war in the boondocks. In addition, private and state archives and historical societies often contain diaries, unit histories, and correspondence by veterans.

U.S. Government Record Groups, National Archives, Washington, D.C.

RG 45. Naval Records Collection of the Office of Naval Records and Library
RG 80. General Records of the Department of the Navy, 1798–1947
RG 94. Records of the Adjutant General's Office, 1780–1917
RG 153. Records of the Judge Advocate General's Office
RG 165. Records of the War Department General and Special Staffs
RG 350. Records of the Bureau of Insular Affairs
RG 395. Records of U.S. Army Overseas Operations and Commands, 1898–1942

RG 407. Records of the Adjutant General's Office, 1917–
Microcopy 254. Philippine Insurgent Records, 1896–1901, with Associated Records
   of the U.S. War Department, 1900–1906

Archival Collections

Huntington Library, San Marino, Calif.
   William Dillon Papers
   Charles F. Manahan Papers
   Walter S. Schuyler Papers
MacArthur Memorial, Norfolk, Va.
   Harold P. Howard Papers
Manuscripts and University Archives Division, Allen Library, University of
      Washington, Seattle, Wash.
   Thomas M. Anderson Papers
   William Cuffe Papers
   William Dowe Mercer Papers
   Glenn N. Ranck Papers
   Joseph Smith Papers
Manuscripts Division, Library of Congress, Washington, D.C.
   Henry T. Allen Papers
   Robert L. Bullard Papers
   Henry C. Corbin Papers
   Benjamin Foulois Papers
   Robert P. Hughes Papers
   Charles Julian Papers
   Louis A. Kaiser Papers
   Henry W. Lawton Papers
   Bowman H. McCalla Papers
   George V. H. Moseley Papers
   George Collier Remey Papers
   Charles D. Rhodes Papers
   Theodore Roosevelt Papers
   Elihu Root Papers
   Charles S. Sperry Papers
   William H. Taft Papers
   Edward D. Taussig Papers
Massachusetts Historical Society, Boston, Mass.
   Clarence R. Edwards Papers
Minnesota Historical Society, St. Paul, Minn.
   Lewis Preston Burlingham Papers
   L. I. Cooke and Charles T. Spear Collection
   George B. Hunt Papers
   Spear-Tucker Collection
   Carl I. Stone Papers

Rare Books and Manuscripts Divisions, New York Public Library, New York, N.Y.
  Francis Vinton Greene Papers
Special Collections, Library, U.S. Military Academy, West Point, N.Y.
  William B. Bacon Papers
  Bernard A. Byrne Papers
  William Pierce Evans Papers
  Henry Clay Hale Papers
  Harold Hammond Papers
  Francis J. Kernan Papers
  John H. Parker Papers
U.S. Army Military History Institute, Carlisle Barracks, Pa.
  Matthew A. Batson Papers
  William E. Birkhimer Papers
  William H. C. Bowen Papers
  William C. Brown Papers
  Delphey T. E. Casteel Papers
  William A. Castle Papers
  Walter I. Cutter Papers
  Hugh A. Drum Papers
  Gordon-Allen Family Papers
  Eli and Charles Helmick Papers
  John L. Hines Papers
  Howell-Taylor Family Papers
  Richard Johnson Papers
  John L. Jordan Papers
  Kenyon A. Joyce Papers
  William A. Kobbé Papers
  Michael Joseph Lenihan Papers
  Harry C. Logan Papers
  Samuel Lyon Papers
  Clenard McLaughlin Papers
  Richard H. McMaster Papers
  Nelson A. Miles Papers
  Spanish-American War Survey
  Matthew F. Steele Papers
  Emory S. West Papers
  Samuel B. M. Young Papers
U.S. Marine Corps Historical Center, Washington, D.C.
  Harold Kinman Papers
  Littleton W. T. Waller Papers
Vintron Trust (private collection)
  Francis Henry French Diaries
Washington Historical Society, Tacoma, Wash.
  "Diary of Jack Brennen, Scout and Interpreter, Co. C., 28th U.S. Volunteer
    Infantry, Philippine Islands."
  James F. Smith Papers

Government Publications and Documents

U.S. Army. Adjutant General's Office. *Correspondence Relating to the War with Spain and Conditions Growing out of the Same Including the Insurrection in the Philippine Islands and the China Relief Expedition, Between the Adjutant-General of the Army and Military Commanders in the United States, Cuba, Porto [sic] Rico, China, and the Philippine Islands From April 15, 1898 to July 30, 1902.* Washington, D.C.: Government Printing Office, 1902.

A Pronouncing Gazetteer and Geographical Dictionary of the Philippine Islands, United States of America, with Maps, Charts, and Illustrations. Also the Law of Civil Government in the Philippine Islands Passed by Congress and Approved by the President July 1, 1902, with a Complete Index. Washington, D.C.: Government Printing Office, 1902.

Annual Reports of the Navy Department, 1899–1902.

Annual Reports of the War Department, 1899–1902.

U.S. Congress. Senate. *Affairs in the Philippine Islands. Hearing Before the Committee on the Philippines of the United States Senate.* S. Doc. 331, 57th Cong., 1st sess., 1902.

———. *Charges of Cruelty, Etc. to the Natives of the Philippines.* S. Doc. 205, 57th Cong., 1st sess., 1902.

Newspapers

Army and Navy Journal
Manila American
New York Times

Books

Achútegui, Pedro S., and Miguel A. Berbad. *Aguinaldo and the Revolution of 1896: A Documentary History.* Manila: Ateneo de Manila Press, 1972.

Agoncillo, Teodoro A. *Malolos: The Crisis of the Republic.* Quezon City: University of the Philippines Press, 1960.

———. *The Revolt of the Masses: The Story of Bonifacio and the Katipunan.* Manila: University of the Philippines Press, 1956.

Aguinaldo, Emilio. *My Memoirs.* Manila: N.p., 1967.

Aguinaldo, Emilio, and Victor A. Pacis. *A Second Look at America.* New York: Robert Speller and Sons, 1957.

Aldecoa-Rodrigues, Caridad. *Negros Oriental and the Philippine Revolution.* Dumaguete, P.I.: Provincial Government of Negros Oriental, 1983.

Alejandrino, Jose M. *The Price of Freedom.* 1949. Reprint, Manila: Solar Publishing, 1987.

Alvarez, Santiago V. *The Katipunan of the Revolution: Memoirs of a General.* Translated by Paula Carolina S. Malay. Manila: Ateneo de Manila University Press, 1992.

Arcilla, Jose S. *An Introduction to Philippine History.* 4th ed. Manila: Ateneo de Manila University Press, 1971.

Ataviado, Elias. *Lucha y Libertad (Conmonitorio de la Revolucion Filipina en las Tierras Albayanas.* Vol. 2, *De febrero de 1899 a abril de 1900.* Manila: Commonwealth Press, 1941.

————. *The Philippine Revolution in the Bicol Region.* Vol. 1, *From August 1896 to January 1899.* Translated by Juan T. Ataviado. Manila: Encal Press, 1953.

Babcock, Elkanah. *A War History of the Sixth U.S. Infantry.* Kansas City: Hudson-Kimberly Publishing, 1903.

Baclagon, Uldarico. *Philippine Campaigns.* Manila: Liwavway Publishers, 1952.

Bain, David H. *Sitting in Darkness: Americans in the Philippines.* Boston: Houghton Mifflin, 1984.

Barrows, David P. *History of the Philippines.* New York: World Book Company, 1926.

Beede, Benjamin R., ed. *The War of 1898 and U.S. Interventions, 1898–1934.* New York: Garland Press, 1994.

Birtle, Andrew J. *U.S. Army Counterinsurgency and Contingency Operations Doctrine, 1860–1941.* Washington, D.C.: Center of Military History, 1998.

Bisbee, William H. *Through Four American Wars.* Boston: Meadow Publishing, 1931.

Blount, James H. *The American Occupation of the Philippines, 1898–1912.* New York: G. P. Putnam's Sons, 1912.

Bowe, John. *With the Thirteenth Minnesota.* Minneapolis, Minn.: A. B. Farnham, 1905.

Bradford, James C., ed. *Crucible of Empire: The Spanish-American War and Its Aftermath.* Annapolis, Md.: Naval Institute Press, 1993.

Braisted, William R. *The U.S. Navy in the Pacific, 1897–1909.* Austin: University of Texas Press, 1958.

Brands, H. W. *Bound to Empire: The United States and the Philippines.* New York: Oxford University Press, 1992.

Brown, Charles H. *The Correspondents' War: Journalists in the Spanish-American War.* New York: Charles Scribner's Sons, 1967.

Brown, Fred R. *History of the Ninth U.S. Infantry, 1799–1909.* Chicago: R. R. Donnelley and Sons, 1909.

Buck, Beaumont B. *Memories of Peace and War.* San Antonio: Naylor, 1935.

Carrasco, Telesforo. *A Spaniard in Aguinaldo's Army: The Military Journal of Telesforo Carrasco y Perez.* Translated by Nick Joaquin. Manila: Solar Publishing, 1986.

Carter, William H. *The Life of Lt. General Chaffee.* Chicago: University of Chicago Press, 1917.

Chynoweth, Bradford G. *Bellamy Park.* Hicksville, N.Y.: Exposition Press, 1975.

Coffman, Edward M. *The Hilt of the Sword: The Career of Peyton C. March.* Madison: University of Wisconsin Press, 1966.

Cooper, Jerry. *The Rise of the National Guard: The Evolution of the American Militia, 1865–1920.* Lincoln: University of Nebraska Press, 1997.

Cooper, Jerry, and Glenn Smith. *Citizens as Soldiers: A History of the North Dakota National Guard.* Fargo: North Dakota Historical Society, 1986.

Corpuz, O. D. *The Roots of the Filipino Nation.* 2 vols. Quezon City: Aklahi Foundation, 1989.

Cosmas, Graham. *An Army for Empire: The United States Army and the Spanish-American War.* Columbia, Mo.: University of Missouri Press, 1971.

Crane, Charles J. *The Experiences of a Colonel of Infantry.* New York: Knickerbocker Press, 1923.

Crouch, Thomas W. *A Leader of Volunteers: Frederick Funston and the 20th Kansas in the Philippines, 1898–1899.* Lawrence, Kans.: Coronado Press, 1984.

———. *A Yankee Guerrillero: Frederick Funston and the Cuban Insurrection, 1896–1897.* Memphis: Memphis State University Press, 1975.

Dastrup, Boyd. *King of Battle: A Branch History of the U.S. Army's Field Artillery.* Washington, D.C.: US Army Center of Military History, 1992.

Davis, Oscar King. *Our Conquests in the Pacific.* New York: Frederick A. Stokes, 1899.

De Bevoise, Ken. *Agents of Apocalypse: Epidemic Disease in the Colonial Philippines.* Princeton, N.J.: Princeton University Press, 1995.

Dery, Luis C. *The Army of the First Philippine Republic and Other Historical Essays.* Manila: De la Salle University Press, 1995.

Dodson, W. E. B. *Official History of the Operations of the Second Oregon Infantry, U.S.V. in the Campaign in the Philippine Islands.* N.p., n.d.

Dowart, Jeffrey M. *The Office of Naval Intelligence: The Birth of America's First Intelligence Agency, 1881–1918.* Annapolis, Md.: Naval Institute Press, 1979.

Eager, Frank D. *History of the Operations of the First Nebraska Infantry, U.S.V. in the Campaign in the Philippine Islands.* N.p., n.d.

Elliott, Charles B. *The Philippines: To the End of the Military Regime.* Indianapolis: Bobbs-Merrill, 1917.

Eyot, Canning, ed. *The Story of the Lopez Family: A Page from the History of the War in the Philippines.* Boston: James H. West, 1904.

Faust, Karl Irving. *Campaigning in the Philippines.* 1899. Reprint, New York: Arno Press, 1970.

Fernandez, Leandro H. *The Philippine Republic.* New York: Columbia University Press, 1926.

Feur, A. B. *Combat Diary: Episodes from the History of the Twenty-second Regiment.* New York: Praeger, 1991.

Forbes, W. Cameron. *The Philippine Islands.* Cambridge, Mass.: Riverside Press, 1928.

Funston, Frederick. *Memories of Two Wars.* London: Constable and Co., 1912.

Ganterbein, C. U. *The Official Records of the Oregon Volunteers in the Spanish War and Philippine Insurrection.* Salem, Oreg.: J. R. Whitney, 1903.

Gates, John M. *Schoolbooks and Krags: The United States Army in the Philippines, 1899–1902.* Westport, Conn.: Greenwood Press, 1973.

Gatewood, Willard B., Jr. *Black Americans and the White Man's Burden, 1898–1903.* Urbana: University of Illinois Press, 1975.

———. *Smoked Yankees and the Struggle for Empire: Letters from Negro Soldiers, 1898–1902.* Urbana: University of Illinois Press, 1971.

Gauld, Charles A. *Thomas M. Anderson: First U.S. General Overseas.* Vancouver, Wash.: Fort Vancouver Historical Society, 1973.

Gleeck, Lewis E. *Laguna in American Times: Coconuts and Revolutionarios.* Manila: Historical Conservation Society, 1981.

————. *Nueva Ecija in American Times: Homesteaders, Hacendros, and Politicos.* Manila: Historical Conservation Society, 1981.

Grimsley, Mark. *The Hard Hand of War: Union Military Policy Towards Southern Civilians, 1861–1865.* New York: Cambridge University Press, 1995.

Harper, Frank, ed. *Just Outside Manila: Letters from Members of the 1st Colorado Regiment in the Spanish-American War and Philippine-American Wars.* Denver: Colorado Historical Society, 1991.

Hartigan, Richard S. *Lieber's Code and the Law of War.* Chicago: Precedent Press, 1983.

Holbrook, Franklin F. *Minnesota in the Spanish-American War and the Philippine Insurrection.* Saint Paul: Minnesota War Records Commission, 1923.

Holmes, Richard. *Acts of War: The Behavior of Men in Battle.* New York: Free Press, 1985.

Hoyt, Henry F. *A Frontier Doctor.* Edited by Doyce B. Nunis. 1929. Reprint, Chicago: Lakeside Press, 1979.

Ileto, Reynaldo C. *Pasyon and Revolution: Popular Movements in the Philippines, 1840–1900.* Manila: Ateneo de Manila University Press, 1979.

Jamieson, Perry D. *Crossing the Deadly Ground: United States Army Tactics, 1865–1899.* Tuscaloosa: University of Alabama Press, 1994.

Jessup, Philip C. *Elihu Root.* New York: Dodd, Mead, 1938.

Joaquin, Nick. *The Aquinos of Tarlac: An Essay on History as Three Generations* 3d ed. Manila: Solar Publishing, 1986.

Jose, Ricardo T. *The Philippine Army, 1935–1942.* Quezon City: Ateneo de Manila University Press, 1992.

Jose, Vicencio R. *The Rise and Fall of Antonio Luna.* 1972. Reprint, Manila: Solar Publishing, 1991.

Kalaw, Maximo. *The Development of Philippine Politics.* Manila: Escolta Publishers, 1927.

Kalaw, Teodoro M. *An Acceptable Holocaust: Life and Death of a Boy-General.* Translated by M. A. Foronda. Manila: National Historical Commission, 1974.

————. *The Philippine Revolution.* Manila: Manila Book Co., 1925.

Karnow, Stanley. *In Our Image: America's Empire in the Philippines.* New York: Random House, 1989.

Larkin, John A. *The Pampangans: Colonial Society in a Philippine Province.* Berkeley: University of California Press, 1972.

LeRoy, James A. *The Americans in the Philippines.* 2 vols. Boston: Houghton Mifflin, 1914.

Leslie's Official History of the Spanish-American War. Washington, D.C.: War Records Office, 1899.

Linderman, Gerald. *The Mirror of War: American Society and the Spanish-American War.* Ann Arbor: University of Michigan Press, 1974.

Linn, Brian M. *The U.S. Army and Counterinsurgency in the Philippine War, 1899–1902.* Chapel Hill: University of North Carolina Press, 1989.

Linninger, Clarence. *The Best War at the Time.* New York: Robert Speller and Sons, 1964.

Mabini, Apolinario. *The Philippine Revolution.* Translated by Leon M. Guerrero. 1931. Reprint, Manila: National Historical Commission, 1969.

Mabry, Charles R. *The Utah Batteries: A History.* Salt Lake City: Daily Reporter Printers, 1900.

Mahon, John K. *History of the Militia and the National Guard.* New York: Macmillan, 1982.

Majul, Cesar. *Mabini and the Philippine Revolution.* Quezon City: University of the Philippines Press, 1960.

Manuel, E. Arsenio. *Dictionary of Philippine Biography.* 2 vols. Quezon City: Filipiana Productions, 1970.

Markey, Joseph I. *From Iowa to the Philippines: A History of Company M, Fifty-first Iowa Volunteers.* Red Oak, Iowa: Thomas D. Murphy, 1900.

May, Glenn A. *Battle for Batangas: A Philippine Province at War.* Quezon City: New Day Press, 1993.

———. *Inventing a Hero: The Posthumous Re-creation of Andres Bonifacio.* Madison: University of Wisconsin Center for Southeast Asian Studies, 1996.

———. *A Past Recovered.* Manila: New Day Publishers, 1987.

McCoy, Alfred W., ed. *An Anarchy of Families: State and Family in the Philippines.* Manila: Ateneo de Manila Press, 1994.

McCutcheon, John T. *Drawn from Memory.* Indianapolis: Bobbs-Merrill, 1950.

Meketa, Ray. *Luther Rector Hare: A Texan with Custer.* Bryan, Tex.: J. M. Carroll, 1983.

Miller, Stuart C. *"Benevolent Assimilation": The American Conquest of the Philippines, 1899–1903.* New Haven, Conn.: Yale University Press, 1982.

Millett, Allan R. *The General: Robert L. Bullard and Officership in the United States Army, 1881–1925.* Westport, Conn.: Greenwood Press, 1975.

———. *Semper Fidelis: The History of the U.S. Marine Corps.* New York: Free Press, 1980.

Muller, William G. *The Twenty-fourth Infantry Past and Present.* N.p., n.d.

Nankivell, John H. *History of the Twenty-fifth Regiment United States Infantry, 1869–1926.* N.p., 1927.

Ochosa, Orlino A. *The Tinio Brigade: Anti-American Resistance in the Ilocos Provinces, 1899–1901.* Quezon City: New Day Publishers, 1989.

Palmer, Frederick. *With My Own Eyes: A Personal Study of Battle Years.* Indianapolis: Bobbs-Merrill, 1932.

Parker, James. *The Old Army: Memories, 1872–1918.* Philadelphia: Dorrance and Co., 1929.

Prentiss, A., ed. *The History of the Utah Volunteers in the Spanish-American War and in the Philippine Islands.* Salt Lake City, Utah: W. F. Ford, 1900.

Quirino, Carlos. *Filipinos at War.* Manila: Vera-Reyes, 1981.

Robinson, Albert G. *The Philippines: The War and the People.* New York: McClure, Phillips, 1901.

Rodney, George B. *As a Cavalryman Remembers.* Caldwell, Idaho: Caxton Printers, 1944.

Romero, Maria F. H. *Negros Occidental Between Two Foreign Powers (1898–1909).* Manila: Enterprise Publications, 1974.

Roth, Russell. *Muddy Glory: America's "Indian Wars" in the Philippines.* West Hanover, Mass.: Christopher Publishing House, 1981.

Russell, Don. *Campaigning with King: Charles King, Chronicler of the Old Army.* Edited by Paul L. Hedren. Lincoln: University of Nebraska Press, 1991.

Salamanca, Bonifacio S. *The Filipino Reaction to American Rule, 1901–1913.* Quezon City: New Day Publishers, 1984.

Saulo, Alfredo B. *The Truth About Aguinaldo and Other Heroes.* Quezon City: Phoenix Publishing, 1987.

Sawyer, Frederick. *Sons of Gunboats.* Annapolis, Md.: Naval Institute Press, 1946.

Schott, Joseph. *The Ordeal of Samar.* Indianapolis: Bobbs-Merrill, 1964.

Schumacher, John N. *Revolutionary Clergy: The Filipino Clergy and the Nationalist Movement, 1850–1903.* Manila: Ateneo de Manila University Press, 1981.

Scott, William H. *Ilocano Responses to American Aggression, 1900–1901.* Quezon City: New Day Publishers, 1986.

Sexton, William T. *Soldiers in the Sun: An Adventure in Imperialism.* Harrisburg, Pa.: Military Service Publishing Co., 1939.

Shay, Jonathan. *Achilles in Vietnam: Combat Trauma and the Undoing of Character.* New York: Scribner, 1994.

Shockley, Philip M. *The Krag-Jorgensen Rifle in Service.* Aledo, Ill.: World Wide Gun Report, 1960.

Sonza, Demy P. *Visayan Fighters for Freedom.* Iloilo: Augustin Sonza and Sons, 1962.

Sorley, L. S. *History of the Fourteenth United States Infantry, From January, 1890 to December, 1908.* Chicago, 1908.

Spector, Ronald. *Admiral of the New Empire: The Life and Career of George Dewey.* Baton Rouge: Louisiana State University Press, 1974.

Storey, Moorfield, and Marcial P. Lichauco. *The Conquest of the Philippines by the United States, 1898–1925.* New York: G. P. Putnam's Sons, 1926

Sturtevant, David R. *Popular Uprisings in the Philippines, 1840–1940.* Ithaca, N.Y.: Cornell University Press, 1976.

Taylor, John R. M. *The Philippine Insurrection Against the United States, 1898–1903: A Compilation of Documents and Introduction.* 5 vols. 1906. Reprint, Pasay City, P.I.: Eugenio Lopez Foundation, 1971.

Trask, David F. *The War with Spain in 1898.* New York: Macmillan, 1981.

Twichell, Heath. *Allen: The Biography of an Army Officer, 1859–1930.* New Brunswick, N.J.: Rutgers University Press, 1974.

Villamor, Juan. *Inedita Cronica de la Guerra Americano-Filipina en el Norte de Luzon, 1899–1901.* Manila: Juan Fajardo, 1924.

Wagner, Arthur L. *Organization and Tactics.* New York: B. Westermann and Company, 1895.

———. *The Service of Security and Information.* Washington: James J. Chapman, 1893.

Welch, Richard E. *Response to Imperialism: The United States and the Philippine-American War, 1899–1902.* Chapel Hill: University of North Carolina Press, 1979.

Wells, Harry L. *The War in the Philippines.* San Francisco: Sunset, 1899.

Wernstedt, Frederick L. and J. E. Spencer. *The Philippine Island World: A Physical, Cultural, and Regional Geography.* Berkeley: University of California Press, 1967.

Wilcox, Marion, ed. *Harpers' History of the War in the Philippines*. New York: Harper Brothers, 1900.
Wilcox, Willis B. *Through Luzon on Highways and Byways*. Philadelphia: Franklin Book Co., 1901.
Wolff, Leon. *Little Brown Brother: How the United States Purchased and Pacified the Philippine Islands at the Century's Turn*. Garden City, N.Y.: Doubleday, 1961.
Worcester, Dean. *The Philippines Past and Present*. New York: Macmillan, 1930.
Yap-Diangco. *The Philippine Guerrilla Tradition*. Manila: MCS Enterprises, 1971.
Young, Kenneth Ray. *The General's General: The Life and Times of Arthur MacArthur*. Boulder, Colo.: Westview, 1994.
Zaide, Gregorio F. *The Philippine Revolution*. Manila: Modern Book Co., 1954.

Articles

Anon. "The Soldier Teacher in the Philippines." *Harper's Weekly,* 18 January, 1902, 42.
Arcilla, Jose S. "The Philippine Revolution and the Jesuit Missions in Mindanao, 1896–1901." *Journal of History* 24 (January–December 1989): 46–56.
Arens, Richard. "The Early Pulahan Movement in Samar." *Leyte-Samar Studies* 11 (1977): 57–113.
Birtle, Andrew J. "The U.S. Army's Pacification of Marinduque, Philippine Islands, April 1900–April 1901." *Journal of Military History* 61 (April 1997): 255–82.
Boughton, Donald H. "How Soldiers Have Ruled in the Philippines." *International Quarterly* (December–March 1902): 222–23.
Bowers, Clarence H. "Builders of an Island Empire." *Bulletin of the American Historical Collection* 33 (July–September 1995): 7–28.
Bronson, H. V. "Visayan Campaigns I: The Insurrection of the Sugar Planters of Panay." *Military Historian and Economist* 2 (1917): 299–308.
Burdett, Thomas F. "A New Evaluation of General Otis' Leadership in the Philippines." *Military Review* 55 (January 1975): 79–87.
Chapman, Gregory Dean. "Taking Up the White Man's Burden: Tennesseans in the Philippine Insurrection, 1899." *Tennessee Historical Quarterly* 47 (Spring 1988): 27–40.
Chaput, Donald. "Founding of the Leyte Scouts." *Leyte-Samar Studies* 9 (1975): 5–10.
———. "Leyte Leadership in the Revolution: The Moxica-Lukban Issue." *Leyte-Samar Studies* 9 (1975): 3–12.
———. "Private William W. Grayson's War in the Philippines, 1899." *Nebraska History* 61 (Fall 1980): 355–66.
Coffman, Edward M. "Batson of the Philippine Scouts." *Parameters* 7 (1977): 68–72.
Crane, Charles J. "The Fighting Tactics of Filipinos." *Journal of the Military Service Institution* 30 (July 1902): 499–507.
———. "The Filipinos' War Contribution." *Journal of the Military Service Institution* 22 (September 1901): 270–74.
———. "Paragraphs 93, 97 and 88, of General Orders 100." *Journal of the Military Service Institution* 32 (March–April 1903): 254–56.

———. "Who Burned Iloilo, Panay, and Why Were Conditions in Negros More Favorable to Us?" *Journal of the Military Service Institution* 30 (March 1902): 232–39.

Cullinane, Michael. "Quezon and Harry Bandholtz." *Bulletin of the American Historical Collection* 9 (January–March 1981): 79–90.

Daza y Salazar, Eugenio. "Some Documents on the Philippine-American War in Samar." *Leyte-Samar Studies* 17 (1983): 165–87.

deOcampo, Esteban A. "Gregorio del Pilar: An Appraisal." *Journal of History* 24 (1979): 39–46.

Drysdale, Walter S. "The Infantry at Caloocan." *Infantry Journal* 28 (April 1926): 421–25.

Farrell, John T. "An Abandoned Approach to Philippine History: John R. M. Taylor and the Philippine Insurrection Records." *Catholic Historical Review* 39 (January 1954): 385–407.

Fritz, David L. "Before the 'Howling Wilderness': The Military Career of Jacob Hurd Smith, 1862–1902." *Military Affairs* 43 (December 1979): 186–90.

Ganley, Eugene F. "Mountain Chase." *Military Affairs* 24 (February 1961): 203–21.

Gates, John M. "Indians and Insurrectos: The U.S. Army's Experience with Insurgency." *Parameters* 13 (March 1983): 59–68.

———. "The Philippines and Vietnam: Another False Analogy." *Asian Studies* 10 (1972): 64–76.

———."War-Related Deaths in the Philippines." *Pacific Historical Review* 53 (November 1983): 367–78.

Grant, H. Roger. "Letters from the Philippines: The 51st Iowa Volunteers at War, 1898–1899." *Palimpsest* 29 (November–December 1974): 162–77.

Guerrero, Milagros C. "Understanding Philippine Revolutionary Mentality." *Philippine Studies* 29 (1981): 240–56.

Hall, John, ed. "The Philippine War: The Diary of Robert Bruce Payne, 1899." *Nebraska History* 69 (Winter 1988): 193–98.

Hickman, Edwin A. "Remarks on the Last Days of the Insurrection in Southern Luzon." *Journal of the U.S. Cavalry Association* 14 (October 1903): 297–308.

Holli, Melvin G. "A View of the American Campaign Against the 'Filipino Insurgents': 1900." *Philippine Studies* 17 (1969): 97–111.

Holt, E. M. "Resistance on Samar: General Vicente Lukban and the Revolutionary War, 1899–1902." *Kabar Seberang Sulating Maphilindo* 10 (December 1982): 1–14.

Howard, O. O. "Is Cruelty Inseparable from War?" *Independent,* 15 May 1902, 1161–62.

Hunt, Michael H. "Resistance and Collaboration in the American Empire, 1898–1903: An Overview." *Pacific Historical Review* 48 (November 1979): 467–71.

Ileto, Reynaldo C. "Toward a Local History of the Philippine-American War: The Case of Tiaong, Tayabas (Quezon) Province, 1901–1902." *Journal of History* 27 (1982): 67–79.

Johnson, J. R. "Colonel John Miller Stotsenburg: Man of Valor." *Nebraska History* 50 (Winter 1969): 339–58.

———. "The Saga of the First Nebraska in the Philippines." *Nebraska History* 30 (June 1949): 139–62.

Landor, A. Henry. "The American Solider As He Is." *North American Review* 178 (1904): 897–903.

Langellier, J. Philip. "General Frederick Funston: Kansas Volunteer." *Military History of Texas and the Southwest* 16 (1980): 79–106.

Larkin, John A. "Philippine History Reconsidered: A Socioeconomic Perspective." *American Historical Review* 87 (June 1982): 613–24.

Linn, Brian M. "Guerrilla Fighter: Frederick Funston in the Philippines, 1900–1901." *Kansas History* 10 (Spring 1987): 2–16.

———. "Intelligence and Low-Intensity Conflict in the Philippine War, 1899–1902." *Intelligence and National Security* 6 (January 1991): 90–114.

———. "Pacification in Northwestern Luzon: An American Regiment in the Philippine-American War, 1899–1901." *Pilipinas* 3 (December 1982): 14–25.

———. "Provincial Pacification in the Philippines, 1900–1901: The First District, Department of Northern Luzon." *Military Affairs* 51 (April 1987): 62–66.

———. "The Struggle for Samar." In *Crucible of Empire: The Spanish-American War and Its Aftermath*, edited by James C. Bradford, 158–82. Annapolis, Md.: Naval Institute Press, 1993.

———. "We Will Go Heavily Armed: The Marines' Small War on Samar, 1901–1902." In *New Interpretations in Naval History: Selected Papers from the Ninth Naval History Symposium*, edited by William R. Roberts and Jack Sweetman, 273–92. Annapolis, Md.: Naval Institute Press, 1991.

Mahan, Bruce E. "The 51st Iowa." *Palimpsest* 6 (June 1951): 177–222.

May, Glenn A. "Filipino Resistance to American Occupation: Batangas, 1899–1902." *Pacific Historical Review* 48 (November 1979): 531–56.

———. "Why the United States Won the Philippine-American War, 1899–1902." *Pacific Historical Review* 52 (November 1982): 353–77.

———. "The 'Zones' of Batangas." *Philippine Studies* 29 (1981): 89–103.

Melshen, Paul. "He Served on Samar." *U.S. Naval Institute Proceedings* 105 (November 1979): 43–48.

Mischel, Adam S. "Young and Adventurous: The Journal of a North Dakota Volunteer in the Spanish-American War, 1898–1899." *North Dakota History* 60 (Winter 1993): 2–21.

Mott, T. Bentley. "The Organization and Functions of a Bureau of Military Intelligence." *Journal of the Military Service Institution* 32 (March–April 1902): 184–208.

Owen, Norman G. "Winding Down the War in Albay, 1900–1903." *Pacific Historical Review* 48 (November 1979): 557–89.

Palmer, Frederick. "White Man and Brown Man in the Philippines." *Scribner's Magazine* 27 (January–June 1900): 73–86.

Poplin, Richard R., ed. "The Letters of W. Thomas Osborne, a Spanish-American Soldier of Buford County." *Tennessee Historical Quarterly* 22 (June 1963): 152–69.

Quisumbing, Jose R. "The American Occupation of Cebu, 1899–1917." *Kinaadman* 17 (1995): 185–200.

———. "The Katipunan and the Philippine Revolution in Cebu." *Kinaadman* 16 (1994): 39–50.

Raines, Edgar F. "Major General Franklin Bell, U.S.A.: The Education of a Soldier." *Register of the Kentucky Historical Society* 83 (Autumn 1985): 315–46.

Reilly, Margaret I. "Andrew Wadsworth: A Nebraska Soldier in the Philippines, 1898–1899." *Nebraska History* 68 (Winter 1987): 183–99.

Robinson, Michael C., and Frank N. Schubert. "David Fagen: An Afro-American Rebel in the Philippines." *Pacific Historical Review* 44 (February 1975): 68–83.

Robredillo, Lope C. "The Dolores Resistance Against the Americans, 1899–1906." *Leyte-Samar Studies* 31 (1987): 1–27.

Ryan, James A. "The Defense of Captain J. A. Ryan." *Journal of the U.S. Cavalry Association* 13 (October 1902): 185–92.

Schreurs, Peter. "Surigao, from General Aguinaldo to General Bates, 1898–1900." *Philippine Quarterly of Culture and Society* 11 (1983): 57–68.

Schumacher, John N. "Recent Perspectives on the Revolution." *Philippine Studies* 30 (1982): 445–92.

Sibert, W. L. "Military Occupation of Northern Luzon." *Journal of the Military Service Institution* 30 (May 1902): 404–8.

Smith, Ephriam K. "William McKinley's Enduring Legacy: The Historiographical Debate on the Taking of the Philippine Islands." In *Crucible of Empire: The Spanish-American War and Its Aftermath,* edited by James Bradford, 205–50. Annapolis, Md.: Naval Institute Press, 1993.

Stewart, Elam L. "The Massacre of Balangiga." *Infantry Journal* 30 (April 1927): 407–14.

Stowbridge, William F., ed. "Now Here I Am in the Army: An 1898 Letter of a Nebraska Volunteer in the Spanish-American War." *Nebraska History* 53 (Fall 1972): 331–38.

Taggart, Harold F., ed. "California Soldiers in the Philippines: From the Correspondence of Howard Middleton, 1898–1899." *California Historical Society Quarterly* 30 (December 1951): 289–305.

———. "California Soldiers in the Philippines: From the Correspondence of Howard Middleton, 1898–1899." *California Historical Society Quarterly* 31 (March 1952): 49–67.

———. "California Soldiers in the Philippines: From the Correspondence of Howard Middleton, 1898–1899." *California Historical Society Quarterly* 31 (June 1952): 163–73.

Thiessen, Thomas D. "The Fighting First Nebraska: Nebraska's Imperial Adventure in the Philippines, 1898–1899." *Nebraska History* 70 (Fall 1989): 210–72.

Thompson, H. C. "Oregon Volunteer Reminiscences of the War with Spain." *Oregon Historical Quarterly* 59 (September 1948): 192–204.

———. "War Without Medals." *Oregon Historical Quarterly* 59 (December 1958): 293–325.

Turnbull, Wilfrid. "Reminiscences of an Army Surgeon in Cuba and the Philippines." *Bulletin of the American Historical Collection* 2 (April 1974): 31–49.

Van Ells, Mark D. "Assuming the White Man's Burden: The Seizure of the Philippines." *Philippine Studies* 43 (1994): 607–22.

Wagoner, Todd L. "Fighting Aguinaldo's Insurgents in the Philippines." *Kansas Historical Quarterly* 18 (May 1951): 145–74.

Ward, John A. "The Use of Native Troops in Our New Possessions." *Journal of the Military Service Institution* 31 (November 1902): 793–805.

Welch, Richard E. "American Atrocities in the Philippines: The Challenge and the Response." *Pacific Historical Review* 43 (May 1974): 233–53.
———. "The Philippine Insurrection and the American Press." *Historian* 36 (November 1973): 34–51.
White, Herbert A. "The Pacification of Batangas." *International Quarterly* 7 (June–September 1903): 431–44.

Doctoral Dissertations

Borromeo, Soledad M. "El Cadiz Filipino: Colonial Cavite, 1571–1896." Ph.D. dissertation, University of California at Berkeley, 1973.
Coats, George Y. "The Philippine Constabulary: 1901–1917." Ph.D. dissertation, Ohio State University, 1968.
Coats, Stephen D. "Gathering at the Golden Gate: The U.S. Army and San Francisco, 1898." Ph.D. dissertation, University of Kansas, 1998.
Fritz, David L. "The Philippine Question: American Civil/Military Policy in the Philippines, 1898–1905." Ph.D. dissertation, University of Texas at Austin, 1977.
Gowing, Peter. "Mandate in Moroland: The American Government of Muslim Filipinos." Ph.D. dissertation, Syracuse University, 1968.
Guerrero, Milagros C. "Luzon at War: Contradictions in Philippine Society, 1898–1902." Ph.D. dissertation, University of Michigan, 1977.
Hunt, Geoffrey R. "The First Colorado Regiment in the Philippine Wars." Ph.D. dissertation, University of Colorado, 1997.
Mulrooney, Virgina F. "No Victor, No Vanquished: United States Military Government in the Philippine Islands, 1898–1901." Ph.D. dissertation, University of California at Los Angeles, 1975.
Raines, Edgar F. "Major General J. Franklin Bell and Military Reform: The Chief of Staff Years, 1906–1910." Ph.D. dissertation, University of Wisconsin at Madison, 1977.
Reed, John Scott. "Burden and Honor: The United States Volunteers in the Southern Philippines, 1899–1901." Ph.D. dissertation, University of Southern California, 1994.
Williams, Vernon L. "The U.S. Navy in the Philippine Insurrection and Subsequent Native Unrest, 1898–1906." Ph.D. dissertation, Texas A&M University, 1985.
Woolard, James R. "The Philippine Scouts: The Development of America's Colonial Army." Ph.D. dissertation, Ohio State University, 1975.

INDEX

Abad, Francisco, 278–80
African-Americans, 125, 153–54, 263
Aglipay, Gregorio, 261, 263
Aguinaldo, Baldomero, 266
Aguinaldo, Emilio, x, 18(photo), 19–20, 24, 26, 38, 47, 52, 60, 65, 78, 84, 88, 112, 115, 172, 193, 209, 228, 234, 255, 264, 266, 295, 322, 328
  capture of, 207, 215, 258, 274–76, 295
  escape of, 146, 147, 148, 149–50, 151, 154–56
  as military leader, 17–19, 22, 25, 34–36, 53–54, 55, 57–58, 61, 62–63, 64, 91–92, 103, 136–38, 185–86, 194, 195, 323–24
  as political leader, 17–20, 21–22, 33–34, 65, 71, 75, 109, 136, 296, 323
  prewar relations with Americans, 20–21, 22–23, 25, 26–27, 30, 36
Alarilla, Leonicio, 190
Alejandrino, Jose, 21, 36, 62, 136, 151, 194, 195, 266, 267, 268, 270, 274
Alger, Russell A., 3, 13, 100
Allen, Henry T., 177–78, 223, 232–34, 235, 236, 315
Americanistas, 81–82, 127, 191, 260, 281, 297
  terrorism against, 86, 129, 139, 187, 194–95, 247, 268, 281, 289, 296, 297
  See also Federal Party; Police; Scouts
Anderson, Edward D., 243, 248, 250
Anderson, George S., 166, 167, 252
Anderson, James L., 189
Anderson, Thomas M., 7, 13–15, 22–23, 25, 37, 64, 133

commands division, 44, 49, 50–51, 52, 55, 56, 95
Andrews, Lincoln C., 235
Aquino, Servillano, 137, 195–96, 267, 269–70, 272
Araneta, Juan, 73, 78, 82
Arguelles, Manuel, 109
Army, U.S.
  joint operations with U.S. Navy, 23–25, 48, 57, 60, 67–69, 81, 130, 149, 154–55, 158, 176–80, 207, 225, 236, 275, 293, 299, 312, 313–16, 325–26
  manpower, 6, 15, 32, 42, 88–89, 143, 209, 213, 219, 225, 325
  Regulars, 6–7, 8–9, 10, 12, 32, 52, 63, 89–90, 125, 326
  relations with U.S. Navy, 24–25, 39, 68–69, 84, 130, 131, 132, 170, 177, 207, 225, 239, 314–15, 326
  See also individual regiments; Volunteers
Army of Liberation, 22, 35–36, 42, 52, 57–58, 62–63, 65, 91–92, 105, 109, 110, 111, 112, 114, 115, 136, 137, 143, 146, 147, 149, 150, 152, 187, 265, 269, 326
  military operations of, 48–52, 56, 60, 95–99, 106–9, 122, 145
Atrocities. *See* Misconduct, American; Misconduct, insurgent

Babylanes, 73, 77–78, 79–81, 83, 87, 123, 128, 172
Balangiga, 219, 306, 308, 310–12, 313, 315, 325, 326
Baldwin, Frank, 294

417